*the devils'
glossary*

ANTI-BRAINWASHING
FIELD GUIDE

the devils' glossary

First published by Alexander Coppen 2025 in the United States Of America.

Copyright © 2025 by Alexander Coppen

All rights reserved. No part of this publication may be reproduced, stored or transmitted in any form or by any means, electronic, mechanical, photocopying, recording, scanning, or otherwise without written permission from the publisher. It is illegal to copy this book, post it to a website, or distribute it by any other means without permission.

Alexander Coppen asserts the moral right to be identified as the author of this work.

Citation(s):

Coppen, A. (2025). the devils' glossary. ISBN 979-8-99-165532-3.
Coppen, Alexander. The Devils' Glossary. 2025. ISBN 979-8-99-165532-3.

The author may be contacted via email at ac@devilslane.com for enquiries or corrections. If you are an ordained minster involved in Christian apologetics for an established church, you may request an electronic copy of this book for free.

first edition

ISBN: 979-8-99-165532-3 (print)
ISBN: 979-8-99-165533-0 (electronic)

Library of Congress Control Number: 2024927358

For my dearest of friends, John & Hope, without whose integrity and support, this book would have seemed futile; for James, who suggested teaching; and for Gene, who gave me the D.C. night sky.

Do not trust humanity without collateral security; it will play you some scurvy trick. Remember it hurts no one to be treated as an enemy entitled to respect until he shall prove himself a friend worthy of affection. Cultivate a taste for distasteful truths. Most important of all, endeavor to see things as they are, not as they ought to be.

— Ambrose Bierce

Contents

Preface — v
Acknowledgments — vi
Prologue — 1
Introduction — 3

I The Poisoned Well

What Is Idea Laundering? — 11
Patterns Of Folly & Deceit — 13
The Social Science Story Template — 18
The River Of Stupidity — 44
The Poisonous Core of Narcissism — 54
Preoccupation With Sexual Depravity — 61
Intellectuals Against Common Sense — 75
The Testimonial of Criminals — 94
The Gnostic Philosophical Pathway — 109
The Shroud of Syncretic Animism — 127
The Mind Virus — 137
Deconstructing Transhuman Theology — 143

II The A-Z of Jargon & Doublespeak

A B C — 167
D E F — 214
G H I — 248
J K L — 282

M N O	293
P Q R	319
S T U	347
V W	392
X Y Z	402

III The Basics of Broken Thinking

How Do You Know What Is True?	407
How Do We Know What We Know?	409
What Is Liberty?	412
What Are Rights?	414
What Are Fallacies?	423
What Are Sophistry & Casuistry?	431
What Is Reification?	434
What Is Magical Thinking?	436
What Are In/Out-Groups?	438
What Is Falsification?	442
What Is Paralogic?	444
What Are Cognitive Biases?	446
What Is Superstimulus?	453
Is It Caused, Or Correlated?	457
What Is Hegelian Dialectic?	460
Do Fish Understand Water?	464

IV Dark Arts & Dirty Tricks

What Is A Black Legend?	471
What Are Luxury Beliefs?	475
What Are Hermeticism & Gnosticism?	477
What Is Millenarianism?	480
What Is Scientism?	482
Did It Originate In The Soviet Bloc?	484

What Is Third Way Eurocommunism?	501
What Is The Paradox Of Tolerance?	510
How Do Cults Recruit And Control?	516
What Is The Behavioural Sink?	520
Are Women The Fairer Sex?	525
Should Quacks Make Up Pathologies?	546
What Is Brain Jamming?	552
What Is Malicious Conflation?	556
What Is Loaded Language?	559
What Is Semantic Overloading?	563
What Is The Science Of Homosexuality?	567
What Are Active Measures?	604
What Is Evil?	609

V   Deprogramming Alternative Theology

Anti-Corruption & Counter-Extremism (ACCE)	617
Module 1: Destroying Traditions	620
Module 2: Social Engineering	623
Module 3: Ideological Subversion	625
Module 4: Franco-American Scripture	627
Module 5: The Communist Dragon	630
Module 6: Deprogramming	632
Reloaded Language	635
Anger, Bad Faith, Treachery	641
Condemn, Accuse, Rebuke	643
Disgust, Revulsion, Ugliness	645
Depravity, Degeneracy, Rotten	647
Evil, Malicious, Wicked	649
Frauds, Charlatans, Phoneys	651
Incompetence, Boring, Laziness	653
Nonsense, Absurd, Worthless	655

Partisan, Favouritism, Partiality	658
Stupidity, Foolishness, Self-Love	659
Further Reading List	661

Preface

This book started as a list and became a five-year rabbit hole of research. The house of cards it revealed was so fragile, it was barely believable. It became immediately clear why activists are so defensive and vociferous when their precious notions are criticised.

Einstein was once asked to explain general relativity. He replied with a wonderfully simply analogy: when one is with a pretty girl, an hour feels like a minute; when one sits on a hot stove, a minute feels like an hour[1].

This book is written in plain and *simple* language for people who did not go to university. The kind of ordinary working people who have more to do with their time than sit in faculty lounges dreaming up multi-syllable terminology for flummoxing and intimidating others.

One should not need a degree, or two decades of dry academic reading, to understand things they are accused of daily. There are times for long words and heavy rhetoric, and there are times for curt shortcuts.

You might understand many of these concepts, such as Hegel's theories, already. You might even consider your interpretation to be far superior to these summaries. However, this book is not for you. It is for those who haven't yet engaged with these complex notions. This is a beginning; a starting list of bookmarks.

Hopefully, it is an entertaining read. Funny, in part; alarming in others. Deeply offensive, one can only pray.

---

[1] Calaprice, Alice, *The Expanded Quotable Einstein* (Princeton University Press, 2000)

Acknowledgments

I am, first, deeply indebted to the overwhelmingly large population of self-righteous frauds, firebrands, charlatans, pseuds, imposters, quacks, and crooks in academia for the belly laughs. The endless attempts at trying to rehabilitate paedophilia; the apocalyptic eschatology; the absurdity of the data collection. Just when you think it can't get worse, it always does. You are a truly terrible class of people society has little use of.

I am profoundly grateful to the intellectuals who have informed me in person, and on the page. The Scrutonites; the debating societies; the amateur researchers; the rebellious pastors.

However, I must acknowledge one group above all: the professors who threw me out of psychology at the end of my higher education for pointing out what an utter crock of **** all this humanities nonsense was.

Your lies about the communist authorship of *"The Authoritarian Personality"*[2], and deliberate attempts to obfuscate the Nazi camp origins of course material[3], set me out on this amusing journey. Your design of a course which set out to inculcate students with a specific worldview, unknowingly against their will, encouraged me to be even more determined to utterly wreck yours.

What delightful fun it has been.

---

[2] Adorno, Theodor W., Else Frenkel-Brunswik, Daniel J. Levinson, and Nevitt Sanford, *The Authoritarian Personality* (Harper, 1950)

[3] Lifton, Robert J., *The Nazi Doctors* (Basic Books, 1986)

Prologue

In 1906, journalist Ambrose Bierce first assembled his *"Cynic's Word Book"* of satirical mis-definitions[4]. Five years later, in 1911, it was re-published as *"The Devil's Dictionary"*[5]. Seventy years later, The *Franklin Library* named it one of *"The 100 Greatest Masterpieces of American Literature."*[6] His work was in response to his times: a broadside to the moral posturing and the sanctimonious hypocrisy of observance to Victorian-style etiquette[7]. In today's sanctimonious world of secular Christianity, whiners would have banned, censored, and "cancelled" him in minutes.

Bierce's definitions show his fierce wit; these definitions are still relevant today.

> DISCRIMINATE, v.i. *To note the particulars in which one person or thing is, if possible, more objectionable than another.*
>
> RADICAL, n. *A miscreant who would forestall the future by discrediting the past and abolishing the present.*
>
> SELF-ESTEEM, n. *An erroneous appraisement.*

Our bookshelves have always suffered an ever-expanding litany of nonsense, particularly in sections like Gnostic philosophy, "self-help", "mind/body/spirit" and the *"New Age"*. Flights of fancy are nothing new

---

[4] Bierce, Ambrose, *The Cynic's Word Book* (Doubleday, 1906)

[5] Bierce, Ambrose, *The Devil's Dictionary* (Doubleday, 1911)

[6] Bierce, Ambrose, *The Devil's Dictionary* (The Franklin Library, 1980)

[7] O'Conner, Richard, *Ambrose Bierce* (Little, Brown, 1951)

in literature[8].

For at least thirty years, one area of the Academy which has been largely ignored for its transparent illegitimacy appears to be the "engine" of the staggeringly poor scholarly material, which appears at *astonishing* speed and volume from authors who are clearly ideological and keen to disguise the true origins of their memes : the *neo-humanities* and *social sciences*. Its force-multiplication is due to one factor: social media and the Internet.

These "disciplines" include the *"ologies"* (psychology, sociology, "sexology" etc) the grievance-based *"studies"* (women's studies, gender studies, etc), and *education* itself. Their "journals" have published a corpus of such stunning, incomprehensible, and subjective idiocy and radicalism it is barely conceivable.

Their contents are *indistinguishable from fiction.*

Most of these papers and theories are the intellectual equivalent of the manuscript for *"Harry Potter"* or a *Guide To Astrology*. Disingenuous proselytisers offer these papers and theories to ordinary people as the basis of a "correct" worldview.

The result is a corruption and derangement of our mechanisms for making sense of the world and the demoralisation of our own soul as it copes with having to say and believe what we know not to be true objectively, or from our own experience.

This glossary is an attempt at an homage to Bierce's work, for our own times; one hundred years later. Its tone might be somewhat more contemptuous. The pluralisation of "Devils" reflects the collective, multi-disciplinary guilt in crimes against language and philosophy. It attempts to shine an antiseptic daylight on the origins of these neologisms and axioms apparent whose adherents are desperate to embed in our culture as "accepted truths", when they are anything else but such things.

---

[8] Izod, John, *Myth, Mind and the Screen* (Cambridge University Press, 2001)

Introduction

Imagine, for a moment, you had guests over for dinner. During the evening, one guest - otherwise perfectly polite - , asserts they have special knowledge of the world, and embarks on a zealous evangelical quest to explain to the others everything they know and believe is entirely wrong.

They assert their companions' perception of reality is manufactured in an invisible magic compartment of one's own mind one cannot see or know; programmed exclusively by "society" and the words we use. Humans are born indistinguishably from one another without traits or nature, and there is actually is no male, nor female. One's sexual behaviours are unrelated to reproduction; changeable, yet fixed from birth; and in every one of us, there is a magic spirit entity which varies how we dress.

They go on to explain, with religious passion, the world is unjustly organised for the benefit of an intrinsically malevolent, card-carrying oligarchy who has historically invaded other countries to enslave the peoples physically and psychologically. They have engineered institutions, practices, and language to maintain the prison of this shared illusion, so it behaves in a self-reinforcing manner.

Not only are they under an invisible tyranny one cannot see, but their inability to perceive or believe it indicates they suffer multiple pathologies deserving of insults and slurs, even if they object to adults having sexual contact with a child or the surgical removal of their genitals.

As a result, they assert the only way to create Heaven on earth is to defile everything which holds life together, then start again through radically destroying our economy, culture, relationships, and nations. Women should behave as men, who are simultaneously disposed to rape and subjugate from birth. Personally, each guest should voluntarily submit themselves to public shaming, which could help them renounce their own worldview, upon such a time they will find moral clarity and purpose.

You would rightly ask such a guest to leave and suggest they consult a psychiatrist at their earliest convenience, for obvious reasons. It sounds mad; they are mad; and it is mad.

Now imagine it is your twenty-year-old daughter, who, until that point, was a rather ordinary, yet pleasant girl. In addition, she believes your description of this insanity is a symptom of the invisible cosmic tyranny; merely a fictional "label" confirming her previous diagnosis, supported by a century of important-looking scientific papers.

Further still, imagine you had scraped and saved every penny for the previous two decades to pay for her to train in a profession, so the better start in life you sacrificed to provide her meant she wouldn't suffer the hardships you did on the way up.

No, this is not *"scientology"* or a mystical Gnostic cult hidden far in the mountains. It is exactly what is being taught to impressionable students at schools and universities near you today, by radical sociology professors with serious sexual problems and a lapsed attendance record at church, who grieve the loss of the USSR.

The Faustian arrangement is simple: universities charge fees for fake courses; professors give out top grades for the opportunity to brainwash; and the student gets an easy route for obtaining letters after their name, which helps them climb the ladder to a cosy non-job in HR. Everyone makes bank: the university cashes in; the professor priest cash in; and the student cashes in. The lowest level of effort, for the most profitable outcome, for each party.

On October 7, 1955, key Beat poets, including Allen Ginsberg, Jack Kerouac, and Neal Cassady, held an event, the *"Six Gallery Reading,"* in San Francisco. Ginsberg ranted a chilling, prophetic warning at writer William S. Burroughs in response to the idea older generations were critical of the emerging movement and its provocative, boundary-

INTRODUCTION

pushing ideas.

We'll get you through your children.[9]

Your children need degrees for the high-paying jobs so they can afford an ordinary home. The easiest way to get one is a fake sociology program which hands out a doctorate for any insanity they submit. The price they have to pay for it is silently enduring life in a cult, away from the protection of their family; amid cowardly, spiteful intellectual predators, and virulent radical peers, for three or four years in their early lives.

The thesis of this work is blunt: social science has devolved over the last century into a secular Gnostic theology supplanting puritan Christianity, yet refuses to identify its own dogma as religious. It is most notably opposed by Christians, Muslims, Hindus, and other faiths who recognise its nature.

It is rightly described as a virus, but wrongly as one targeting the mind. The malicious intent of many priest professors is even laid out in their own scripture:

> *This paper theorizes that one future pedagogical priority of women's studies is to train students not only to master a body of knowledge but also to serve as symbolic "viruses" that infect, unsettle, and disrupt traditional and entrenched fields. In this essay, we first posit how the metaphor of the virus in part exemplifies an ideal feminist pedagogy, and we then investigate how both women's studies* and *the spread of actual viruses (e.g., Ebola, HIV) produce similar kinds of emotional responses in others.*
>
> *In doing so, we frame two new priorities for women's studies: training male students as viruses and embracing "negative" stereotypes of feminist professors as important future directions for the*

---

[9] Jonah Raskin, *American Scream: Allen Ginsberg's "Howl" and the Making of the Beat Generation* (Berkeley: University of California Press, 2004), pp. 78-79.

potentially liberatory aspects of the field.[10]

It was born in the early twentieth century via the fracture of socialist totalitarianism; took root in the fertile soil of the Civil Rights era thanks to the permissive weaknesses of liberalism; finally catalysed by the simultaneous fashionable assaults of *"New Atheism"* and Californian technology gurus' utopian idealism during the Internet's printing-press-style revolution.

It targets the imagination of young women afraid of being socially excluded in a world where they are left to fend for themselves, and weak men possessing a latent, unfulfilled religious impulse.

It is the official dogma of gullible civil servants, legislators, teachers, corporations, and bureaucrats managing almost all of the major public institutions. It is enforced almost exclusively by women (out of a perceived fear of exclusion) and predominantly opposed by men. It correlates exactly with the increasing numbers of women in the education system and workforce, and both sexes overwhelmingly claim their lives are made miserable by it[11].

However, influence and subjugation have shown themselves to be insufficient for those intoxicated with this political tendency. Inevitably, the goal for this humanist religion of zealots and radicals, as always, is ultimately a *theocracy*.

Federal bill *C-4* in Canada, *"An Act to amend the Criminal Code (conversion therapy)"*, was unanimously passed as this book was being prepared. It declares normal sexuality a "myth" and makes parents guilty of an indictable crime, punishable by five years' imprisonment, if they refuse to accept their own child's claims about a magic gender-soul.

The foul smell of its *staggeringly* execrable preamble reads:

---

[10] Breanne Fahs and Michael Karger, 'Women's Studies as Virus: Institutional Feminism, Affect, and the Projection of Danger', *Generos: Multidisciplinary Journal of Gender Studies*, 5.1 (2016), 71–89

[11] Callie Patteson, 'How Single, Woke Females Are Reshaping the US', *New York Post*, 17 January 2023

INTRODUCTION

> *Whereas conversion therapy causes harm to society because, among other things, it is based on and propagates myths and stereotypes about sexual orientation, gender identity and gender expression, including the myth that heterosexuality, cisgender gender identity, and gender expression that conforms to the sex assigned to a person at birth are to be preferred over other sexual orientations, gender identities and gender expressions;*[12]

Although this work takes a somewhat empirical approach to evidence and data, it makes no claim to impartiality. The swindlers purveying this fictional slop deserve none. Nor do they deserve pity, quarter, or aid.

It is specifically written as an indictment and prosecution of the social sciences; a post-mortem archaeology of the misuse, abuse, and blatant corruption in this group of subjects for political gain.

---

[12] Parliament of Canada, *Bill C-4: An Act to amend the Criminal Code (Conversion Therapy)*, 44th Parliament, 1st Session, Royal Assent, 8 December 2021

I

The Poisoned Well

How did we get here? Where do you start when trying to understand the mind virus plague infecting Western intellectual life? One must examine the landscape and perceive the scale of the problem. Its source is the humanities departments of the US university system, and its tentacles spread across the Anglosphere: the Gnostic confluence of French postmodern philosophy with American sociology.

What Is Idea Laundering?

Money laundering is legitimising funds which are illegitimate. It takes place in three distinct phases: *placement* (smuggling, disguising, or misrepresentation), *layering* (obscuring to avoid detection), and *integration* (mixing it into normal systems)[13].

Idea laundering is its intellectual analogue: using "front groups" and academic institutions to give legitimacy to invalid, ideological, or illegitimate notions, so they can be smuggled and integrated into our wider *sense-making* systems, such as journalism, arts, politics, and popular culture. In most incidences, as with banks, journal editors are not only complicit, but are instigators[14].

Put simply, it's the circular process of a) writing nonsense, b) getting it published in a fringe journal, and c) attempting to make it appear authentic by citing other nonsense in the references. Then, repeating the same thing over and over until the layers of nonsense are built up so deeply, the original idea seems like something we've known forever[15].

At the lighter end of the scale, it may be simply for reasons of academic ego; in darker portraits, it is a deliberate process conducted for nakedly political aims; in some circumstances, authors even state in

---

[13] Levi, Michael, and Peter Reuter, 'Money Laundering', *Crime and Justice*, 34 (2006)

[14] Boghossian, Peter, '"Idea Laundering" in Academia: How Nonsensical Jargon like "Intersectionality" and "Cisgender" Is Imbued with an Air of False Authority', *The Wall Street Journal* (24 November 2019)

[15] Lindsay, James, 'Idea Laundering in Peer-Reviewed Journals', *New Discourses* (5 October 2020)

their "literature" pernicious goals of sedition and derangement.

Once a bad idea has been published as scholarly work, the next paper references the previous one as an authoritative primary source; a false epistemology is constructed for gullible blogger-journalists and activists to reference axiomatically as "truth". It is astounding how many sources of information on the Internet have been deliberately "edited" to give the impression these "ideas" are older or more credible than they are.

The Hirschfield/Kinsey process typically works as follows:

1. A partisan organisation or lobbyist "think-tank" (a social science department, *Media Matters, American Civil Liberties Union, Anti-Defamation League, Southern Poverty Law Center, Hope Not Hate, Center for Countering Digital Hate,* etc.) conducts a fraudulent questionnaire survey of some kind (typically portrayed as a *"qualitative"* study);
2. The doctored results of these "studies" are falsely cited as authoritative "research" in low-tier publications with favourable audiences such as *Vox, Pink News, Slate, The Atlantic,* etc;
3. Researchers subsequently layer these multiple circular references as citations in further "research" (journal papers) and encyclopaedic resources (Wikipedia, etc.) to enhance their authoritative credibility.
4. Eventually, gullible reporters at authoritative mainstream publications (*New York Times, Time,* etc.) cite their conclusions as common axioms established in the public mind.

Patterns Of Folly & Deceit

Creativity and mental illness often overlap. Artists recreate what they have imagined whilst in a state of play, in physical form: the painter on his canvas; the musician within his sheet notation; and the novelist on his page. Images, sound, smell are retrieved from memory and materialised into reality.

A schizophrenic also sees and hears much in his imagination. As does a superstitious maverick or a religious fundamentalist. When this *pathos* (passion) crosses a line, the person is referred to as paranoid, disordered, or delusional in his or her perception[16].

Rather than what they perceive, traditional academics employ methodology for removing their own influence as they attempt to explain what they *observe;* not in the internal world, but in the natural external one[17].

Social science has devolved into a bizarre position straddling these worlds - science, artistry, psychiatry, religion - from its early nineteenth-century roots[18]. What started as an earnest positivist search to examine the human mind and our broader social structures for intelligibility began collapsing into farce with Marx, Adler, and Freud. As Karl Popper observed when discussing his notion of *Falsification*[19]:

---

[16] Carson, Shelley H., 'Creativity and Psychopathology: A Shared Vulnerability Model',*Revue canadienne de psychiatrie, 56(2)* (2011), 144–153

[17] Daston, Lorraine, and Peter Galison, *Objectivity* (Zone Books, 2007)

[18] Snow, Charles Percy, 'The Two Cultures' (*The Rede Lecture,* 1959)

[19] Popper, Karl, *Logik der Forschung* (Hutchinson, 1959)

I found that those of my friends who were admirers of Marx, Freud, and Adler, were impressed by a number of points common to these theories, and especially by their apparent explanatory power. These theories appear to be able to explain practically everything that happened within the fields to which they referred. The study of any of them seemed to have the effect of an intellectual conversion or revelation, open your eyes to a new truth hidden from those not yet initiated. Once your eyes were thus opened you saw confirmed instances everywhere: the world was full of verifications of the theory. Whatever happened always confirmed it. Thus its truth appeared manifest; and unbelievers were clearly people who did not want to see the manifest truth; who refuse to see it, either because it was against their class interest, or because of their repressions which were still "un-analyzed" and crying aloud for treatment.[20]

It starts with our preoccupation: our *Pathos*[21] of some kind towards some kind of *Phenomena*[22], which we try to explain in a low-resolution way as a *Heuristic*[23]. Often we mis-attribute it to the supernatural, which is *Magical Thinking*[24]. Our brains can easily be fooled, meaning our broken reasoning is contaminated by *Fallacies*[25], such as mistaking correlation for causation[26].

When we refer to an imaginary phenomenon as if it were unquestion-

---

[20] Popper, Karl, *Conjectures and Refutations* (Routledge, 1963)

[21] Aristotle, *Rhetoric*, (Cosimo Classics, 2007)

[22] Kant, Immanuel, *Critique of Pure Reason*, (Cambridge Press, 1998; first publ. 1781)

[23] Tversky, Amos, and Daniel Kahneman, 'Judgment Under Uncertainty: Heuristics and Biases', *Science*, 185.4157 (1974), 1124–31

[24] Frazer, James George, *The Golden Bough* (Oxford Press, 1998; first publ. 1890)

[25] Walton, Douglas N., *A Pragmatic Theory of Fallacy* (University of Alabama Press, 1995)

[26] Freedman, David A., Robert Pisani, and Roger Purves, *Statistics*, 4th edn (W. W. Norton & Company, 2007)

able fact, or physically real, we are engaging in *Reification*[27].

If we have been indoctrinated into some form of *Ideology*[28], we start with an answer and look backwards from the self-serving conclusion for tendentious evidence to satisfy our *Confirmation Bias*[29].

If we believe it is mystical knowledge available only to an enlightened elect as part of a titanic battle between good and evil, it is *Gnosticism*.[30]

We try to suggest an explanation for a testable hypothesis, which usually isn't *Falsifiable*[31] and wrongly referred to a *Theory*.[32] Often others might have a superficial answer from the back of a postcard, because they are repeating *Sophistry*[33]. When they misappropriate one set of circumstances for arguing a completely different one, it's *Casuistry*[34].

When this breaks under questioning or lack of evidence during our *Zealotry*[35], it becomes quackery or *Pseudoscience.*[36] When we use thick prose to conceal how vapid it is or invent jargon to sound important, that is *Obscurantism*[37].

Humanities' scholars, meanwhile, are professional and industrial-grade fraudsters. The products of their imaginations are typically involved in *Debasing* one thing from another[38]: socialisation from human nature;

---

[27] Lukács, Georg, *History and Class Consciousness*, (MIT Press, 1971; first publ. 1923)

[28] Marx, Karl, and Friedrich Engels, *The German Ideology*, (International Publishers, 1970; first publ. 1846)

[29] Nickerson, Raymond S., 'Confirmation Bias: A Ubiquitous Phenomenon in Many Guises', *Review of General Psychology*, 2.2 (1998), 175–220

[30] Jonas, Hans, *The Gnostic Religion* (Beacon Press, 1963)

[31] Popper, Karl, *The Logic of Scientific Discovery* (Huntingdon, 1959)

[32] Kuhn, Thomas S., *The Structure of Scientific Revolutions* (U. of Chicago Press, 1962)

[33] Plato, *Sophist*, (Hackett Publishing, 1997; ca. 360 BCE)

[34] Jonsen, Albert, Toulmin, Stephen, *The Abuse of Casuistry* (U. of CA Press, 1988)

[35] Hoffer, Eric, *The True Believer* (Harper & Row, 1951)

[36] Bunge, Mario, 'What Is Pseudoscience?', *The Skeptical Inquirer*, 9.1 (1984), 36–46

[37] Habermas, Jürgen, *The Theory of Communicative Action* (Beacon Press, 1984)

[38] Orwell, George, *Nineteen Eighty-Four* (Secker & Warburg, 1949)

gender from sex; language from culture, and so on. They *Misappropriate Science* to describe phenomena to self-prescribe gravitas[39].

Then, of course, there is the *Plagiarism*[40]: endless re-packaging of older manifestos with new names, often deliberately mangling *Doublespeak* language[41] to hide their malevolent intent.[42]

Layer upon layer of frivolous journal papers engage in mutual *Circular Citation*[43] until their notions are eventually codified as *Axioms*[44], or wrongly presented in HR meetings and magazine articles as established fact. When that fails, they often edit the *Primary Sources*[45] of dictionaries for *False Historicisation*[46][47] to give the impression a notion is older than it is.[48]

There is no conclusion or verifiable result, only *Insight* requiring further study. When adherents attempt to standardise it as doctrinal orthodoxy, the accumulated *Theology*[49] is defended as *Scripture*[50].

Moreover, the single greatest consumers of this "research" are those

---

[39] Sokal, Alan, and Jean Bricmont, *Fashionable Nonsense* (Picador, 1999)

[40] Mallon, Thomas, *Stolen Words* (Mariner Books, 2001)

[41] Orwell, George, 'Politics and the English Language', *Horizon*, April 1946

[42] McCabe, Donald L., and Linda Klebe Treviño, 'Academic Dishonesty: Honor Codes and Other Contextual Influences', *The Journal of Higher Education*, 64.5 (1993), 522–38

[43] Goodhart, Charles A. E., 'Problems of Monetary Management: The UK Experience', *Papers in Monetary Economics, Reserve Bank of Australia*, 2 (1975), 5–17

[44] Euclid, *The Thirteen Books of Euclid's Elements*, (Dover Publications, 1956; ca. 300 BCE)

[45] Howell, Martha, and Walter Prevenier, *From Reliable Sources* (Cornell Press, 2001)

[46] Juderías, Julián, *La Leyenda Negra y la Verdad Histórica* (Tip. de la "Revista de archivos, bibliotecas y museos", 1914)

[47] White, Hayden, *Metahistory* (Johns Hopkins University Press, 1973)

[48] Greenberg, Steven A., 'How Citation Distortions Create Unfounded Authority: Analysis of a Citation Network', *BMJ*, 339 (2009), b2680

[49] Comte, Auguste, *The Positive Philosophy of Auguste Comte*, trans. by Harriet Martineau (Cambridge University Press, 2009; first publ. 1830)

[50] Latour, Bruno, and Steve Woolgar, *Laboratory Life* (Princeton University Press, 1986)

who use it for manipulation and abuse: conditioning[51], propaganda[52][53], licentiousness[54], advertising[55], and inflicting trauma[56].

There is no such thing as the *"unconscious mind"*[57]. There is no such thing as *"empathy"*[58]. There is no such thing as *"homophobia"*[59]. There is no such thing as *"gender identity"*[60]. These are not scientific facts. They are all made up, laundered in this corpus of deceit, and have no hope of ever being proved true or false.

They may be heuristics of observable phenomena, but to form legitimate academic topics, they must be distinguishable from schizophrenic delusion, fiction, or ephemera. Giving a feeling or perception a name does not reify it as reality, if it does not correspond to the natural world via evidence. it simply means you can imagine it.

There is a place for creative fiction writing: *literature*. There is a place for supernatural curiosity and dogmatic orthodoxy policing: *religion*. There is a place for resolving psychiatric problems: *medicine*. There is even a place for ideology: *political parties*.

If you believe words have some transformational effect on the fabric of material reality, you are not a scholar. You are someone who believes in witchcraft and *magic spells*.

---

[51] Chomsky, Noam, Edward S. Herman, *Manufacturing Consent* (Pantheon Books, 1988)

[52] Bernays, Edward L., *Propaganda* (Horace Liveright, 1928)

[53] Ellul, Jacques, *Propaganda* (Vintage Books, 1965)

[54] Packard, Vance, *The Hidden Persuaders* (Pocket Books, 1957)

[55] Sherif, Muzafer, and S. Stansfeld Sargent, "Ego-Involvement and the Mass Media," *Journal of Social Issues*, 3.3 (1947), 8–16

[56] McCoy, Alfred W., *A Question of Torture* (Henry Holt and Co., 2006)

[57] Grünbaum, Adolf, *The Foundations of Psychoanalysis* (U. of California Press, 1984)

[58] Bloom, Paul, *Against Empathy* (Ecco, 2016)

[59] Weinberg, George, *Society and the Healthy Homosexual* (St. Martin's Press, 1972)

[60] Soh, Debra, *The End of Gender* (Simon & Schuster, 2020)

The Social Science Story Template

Marxism tells a story which has captured the world for more than one hundred and fifty years. It's a religious story[61][62][63]; a false tale about the world[64] which has led to the murder of a million people for every year it's been in print[65]. The story's been constantly reworked and repeated, with universities charging hundreds of thousands of dollars per student for courses covering its different interpretations. It is the basis of almost all contemporary "rights" movements.

Marx's monomyth is a theological template from *Genesis 3*[66]. All one needs for the recipe is ingredients to substitute, and one can create one's own justice movement with religious theology for political activism.

- Something you envy and/or resent in others (e.g. being *normal*)
- A dominant group who has it (e.g. the *normal*)
- A victim group who doesn't have it (e.g. the *abnormal*)
- A fictional pathology ending with "ism" (e.g. *normalism*)

---

[61] Kolakowski, Leszek, *Main Currents of Marxism* (W. W. Norton & Co. 2005)

[62] Gray, John, *Black Mass* (Farrar, Straus and Giroux, 2007)

[63] Voegelin, Eric, *Science, Politics, and Gnosticism* (Regnery Gateway, 1968)

[64] Scruton, Roger, *Fools, Frauds and Firebrands* (Bloomsbury Publishing, 2015)

[65] Courtois, Stéphane, Nicolas Werth, Jean-Louis Panné, Andrzej Paczkowski, Karel Bartošek, Jean-Louis Margolin, *The Black Book of Communism* (Harvard Press, 1999)

[66] *The Bible*, Genesis 3:1 (New International Version), n.d.: 'Now the serpent was more crafty than any of the wild animals the Lord God had made. He said to the woman, "Did God *really* say, 'You must not eat from any tree in the garden'?"'

- A "structural" illness which results (e.g. *abnormative stigmatisation*)
- The "consciousness" of your cause to raise (e.g. *abnormness*)
- A prefix for the "studies" degree (e.g. *Normativity Studies*)

This hypothesis is simple and always explains *everything*. A country club conspiracy of elites can explain all the natural distribution phenomena occurring in nature, aiming to deprive others of what they have reserved for themselves.

Thomas Sowell describes the personal allure of this perennial ideology he felt, in his scathing and brutal 1985 book on the matter:

> *[Marx] took the overwhelming complexity of the real world and made the parts fall into place, in a way that was intellectually exhilarating*[67].

Anyone offering a *"studies"* degree can vomit out a sociology curriculum based on this ancient tale of woe, which appears as an intellectual discipline with enormous explanatory power. Merely accompanying the *interdisciplinary toolkit* with a bunch of mindless jargon no-one can understand is enough to make it sound extremely academic.

It works for almost *any* subject: fast food, antiques, construction, dentistry. One can just make it up as one goes along, then charge thousands in consultancy fees or tuition loans.

Remember: it's not trivial bull****, this is a unique, subjective analytical *lens* through which we can critique the *power dynamics* and *social relations* which have led to the *structural inequity* we find today in the *fast food delivery industry*, and the means to *justice* and *emancipation*.

> There is a special type of property which has been constructed in society called [_____].
>
> One group, a superstructure called [_____], have given

---

[67] Sowell, Thomas, *Marxism: Philosophy and Economics* (William Morrow, 1985)

themselves exclusive access to it which others, an infrastructure of everyone else, [_____], don't have.

They have created an ideology called [_____] to justify why they should control access to it, which imposes the situation and allows it to continue.

The system exists to exclude those below from the power and privilege that access to [_____] provides.

This creates a dialectical conflict of social relations between those who have access to [_____] and those who don't, where a person's identity is defined by which group they belong to.

The goal of [_____] is to reveal this [_____] to people by bringing those on the margins to the centre of society to create awareness of how society is structured unfairly against them.

Most people participate in this [_____] because they possess a false consciousness. They need to be enlightened so they can achieve a [_____] consciousness, which will lead to a revolutionary consciousness driving them to flip the system over.

There are those who want to preserve the injustice of this social structure because of the benefits they receive for participating in it. They are called [_____].

When [_____] become aware, they will seize the means of producing [_____] to overturn it and enforce a situation of equality.

Eventually, acts of equalisation will become spontaneous, which will produce [_____] justice.

One can do this all day, endlessly. It's trivial. Any university can trot out two-year remote essay-writing classes where every student gets first-class marks to credential themselves into an HR career.

Class: Classical Marxism

Marx was always desperate to have been a French revolutionary. His ideas were formulated after spending time with anarchists in Paris, and in the context of conditions during the *Industrial Revolution* in England compared to the agrarian past[68]. Classical Marxism was a response to Adam Smith's ideas on the division of labour and its effects[69].

> There is a special type of property which has been constructed in society called *capital*. One group, a superstructure of *the upper and upper-middle class*, has given themselves exclusive access to it which others, an infrastructure of everyone else, *the Proletariat*, don't have.
>
> They have created an ideology called *capitalism* to justify why they should control access to it, which imposes the situation and allows it to continue. The system exists to exclude those below from the power and privilege that access to *capital* provides.
>
> This creates a dialectical conflict of social relations between those who have access to *capital* and those who don't, where a person's identity is defined by which group they belong to.
>
> The goal of *class theory (aka dialectical materialism)* is to reveal this *class antagonism* to people by bringing those on the margins to the centre of society to create awareness of how society is structured unfairly against them. Most people participate in this *class structure* because they possess a false consciousness. They need to be enlightened so they can achieve a *class consciousness*, which will lead to a revolutionary consciousness, driving them to flip the system over.
>
> There are those who want to preserve the injustice of this social structure because of the benefits they receive from

---

[68] McLellan, David, *Karl Marx: A Biography* (Palgrave Macmillan, 2006)

[69] Wheen, Francis, *Karl Marx: A Life* (W. W. Norton & Company, 2001)

participating in it. They are called *fascists, reactionaries, Nazis.*

When *the Proletariat* become aware, they will seize the means of producing *capital* to overturn it and enforce a situation of equality. Eventually, acts of equalisation (*socialism*) will become spontaneous, which will produce *class justice*, or *advanced communism*.

In modern terms, old-school Marxism could be known as *Critical Class Theory*.

Academic Marxism: Critical Theory

This *"postmodern meta-bull****"*[70], *"Kritische Theorie"*, was defined in 1937 by German sociologist Max Horkheimer as an explicitly anti-science Marxist project, designed *"not merely to understand society but to change it... to uncover the structures of domination and oppression that exist within society and to provide a means for social transformation."*[71]

> There is a special type of property which has been constructed in society called *academic knowledge*.
>
> One group, a superstructure called academics, has given themselves exclusive access to it which others, an infrastructure of everyone else, *non-academic laypeople*, don't have.
>
> They have created an ideology called *traditional theory* to justify why they should control access to it, which imposes the situation and allows it to continue.
>
> The system exists to exclude those below from the power and privilege that access to *academia* provides.
>
> This creates a dialectical conflict of social relations between those who have access to *academic credentials* and those who

---

[70] Dawkins, Richard, *The God Delusion* (Houghton Mifflin, 2006)

[71] Horkheimer, Max, *Critical Theory: Selected Essays* (Seabury Press, 1972; ca. 1937)

don't, where a person's identity is defined by which group they belong to.

The goal of *Critical Theory* is to reveal this *bias/power-driven system of academic hegemony* to people by bringing those on the margins to the centre of society to create awareness of how society is structured unfairly against them.

Most people participate in this *structural power-bias of academic credentialism* because they possess a false consciousness. They need to be enlightened so they can achieve a *critical* consciousness, which will lead to a revolutionary consciousness, driving them to flip the system over.

There are those who want to preserve the injustice of this social structure because of the benefits they receive for participating in it. They are called *scientific essentialists*.

When *humanities scholars* become aware, they will seize the means of producing *academic knowledge* to overturn it and enforce a situation of equality.

Eventually, acts of equalisation will become spontaneous, which will produce *academic social* justice.

Congratulations, you now have a degree in *"sociology"*.

Homework: *discuss how the power relations of traditional theory promote endemic stereotypical attitudes and contribute toward dominant scientific culture.*

Sex Marxism: Feminism

Feminism's origins lie in English writer Mary Wollstonecraft's noble arguments in 1792 for women being allowed access to education to fulfil their potential[72]. The modern Franco-American radicalism is derived

---

[72] Wollstonecraft, Mary, *A Vindication of the Rights of Woman*, (J. Johnson, 1792)

from the Soviet demands on women in factories[73], and the late-1940s rants of lesbian Marxist Simone de Beauvoir[74].

> There is a special type of property which has been constructed in society called *masculinity*.
>
> One group, a superstructure called *the Patriarchy*, has given themselves exclusive access to it which others, an infrastructure of everyone else, *women*, don't have.
>
> They have created an ideology called *misogyny* to justify why they should control access to it, which imposes the situation and allows it to continue.
>
> The system exists to exclude those below from the power and privilege that access to *maleness* provides.
>
> This creates a dialectical conflict of social relations between those who have access to *maleness* and those who don't, where a person's identity is defined by which group they belong to.
>
> The goal of *feminism* is to reveal this *systemic misogyny* to people by bringing those on the margins to the centre of society to create awareness of how society is structured unfairly against them.
>
> Most people participate in this *structural sexism* because they possess a false consciousness. They need to be enlightened so they can achieve a *feminist* consciousness, which will lead to a revolutionary consciousness driving them to flip the system over.
>
> There are those who want to preserve the injustice of this social structure because of the benefits they receive from participating in it. They are called *sexists and misogynists*.
>
> When *women* become aware, they will seize the means of producing *the Patriarchy* to overturn it and enforce a situation

---

[73] Stites, Richard, *The Women's Liberation Movement in Russia* (Princeton Press, 1978)

[74] De Beauvoir, Simone, *The Second Sex* (Knopf, 1953; first publ. 1949)

of equality.

Eventually, acts of equalisation will become spontaneous, which will produce *gender* justice.

Congratulations, you now have a degree in *"women's studies"*.

Homework: *discuss how the power relations of structural misogyny promote endemic masculinity and contribute toward dominant patriarchy culture.*

Gay Marxism: Gay Liberation

The *Committee for Homosexual Freedom* spawned the modern gay rights movement in 1969, which then became the *Gay Liberation Front* (GLF). It was named regarding the communist movements of the *Algerian National Liberation Front* (FLN) and the *Vietnamese National Liberation Front* ("*Viet Cong*"), and produced a manifesto[75].

> There is a special type of property which has been constructed in society called *morally acceptable sexuality*.
>
> One group, a superstructure called *heterosexuals*, has given themselves exclusive access to it which others, an infrastructure of everyone else, *homosexuals*, don't have.
>
> They have created an ideology called *homophobia* to justify why they should control access to it, which imposes the situation and allows it to continue.
>
> The system exists to exclude those below from the power and privilege that access to *heterosexuality* provides.
>
> This creates a dialectical conflict of social relations between those who have access to *social acceptance* and those who don't, where a person's identity is defined by which group they belong to.

---

[75] Abelove, Henry, *The Lesbian and Gay Studies Reader* (Routledge, 1993)

The goal of *gay liberation* is to reveal this *systemic homophobia* to people by bringing those on the margins to the centre of society to create awareness of how society is structured unfairly against them.

Most people participate in this *structural anti-gay hate* because they possess a false consciousness. They need to be enlightened so they can achieve a *gay rights* consciousness, which will lead to a revolutionary consciousness driving them to flip the system over.

There are those who want to preserve the injustice of this social structure because of the benefits they receive from participating in it. They are called *bigots and homophobes*.

When *homosexuals* become aware, they will seize the means of producing *sexual morality* to overturn it and enforce a situation of equality.

Eventually, acts of equalisation will become spontaneous, which will produce *sexual* justice.

Congratulations, you now have a degree in gay rights activism.

Homework: *discuss how the historical misrepresentation of sexual minorities by homophobic narrators promote systemic discrimination and contribute toward dominant heterosexual culture.*

Race Marxism: Critical Race Theory

The pseudo-subject of *"critical legal studies"* has its origins within the 1976 writings of lawyer Derrick Albert Bell Jr. at *Harvard University*, which drew *"inspiration from Marxist analysis"*[76] and later devolved into the study of *"whiteness"* as a pathology[77].

---

[76] Delgado, Richard, Jean Stefancic, *Critical Race Theory* (NY University Press, 2001)

[77] Roediger, David R., *The Wages of Whiteness* (Verso, 1991)

There is a special type of property which has been constructed in society called *whiteness* through another social construction called *race*.

One group, a superstructure of *white Europeans*, has given themselves exclusive access to it which others, an infrastructure of everyone else, *people of colour*, don't have.

They have created an ideology called *white supremacy* to justify why they should control access to it, which imposes the situation and allows it to continue.

The system exists to exclude those below from the power and privilege that access to *whiteness* provides.

This creates a dialectical conflict of social relations between those who have access to *whiteness* and those who don't, where a person's identity is defined by which group they belong to.

The goal of *Critical Race Theory* is to reveal this *systemic racism* to people by bringing those on the margins to the centre of society to create awareness of how society is structured unfairly against them.

Most people participate in this *structural racism* because they possess a false consciousness. They need to be enlightened so they can achieve a *racial* consciousness, which will lead to a revolutionary consciousness driving them to flip the system over.

There are those who want to preserve the injustice of this social structure because of the benefits they receive from participating in it. They are called *racists and white supremacists*.

When *people of colour* become aware, they will seize the means of producing *whiteness* to overturn it and enforce a situation of equality.

Eventually, acts of equalisation will become spontaneous, which will produce *racial* justice.

Congratulations, you now have a degree in *"whiteness studies"*.

Homework: *discuss how the colonial policies of structural racism promote endemic white supremacy and contribute toward systemic whiteness culture.*

Classroom Marxism: Critical Pedagogy

Brazilian "liberation theology" advocate Paulo Freire introduced Marxism as a theory of teaching in 1968. It was imported to the US by Marxist history professor Henry Giroux in 1983[78] as part of the disastrous *"critical turn in education"*[79].

> There is a special type of property which has been constructed in society called *literacy*.
>
> One group, a superstructure called *the literate*, have given themselves exclusive access to it which others, an infrastructure of everyone else, *the illiterate*, don't have.
>
> They have created an ideology called *classical education* to justify why they should control access to it, which imposes the situation and allows it to continue.
>
> The system exists to exclude those below from the power and privilege that access to *education* provides.
>
> This creates a dialectical conflict of social relations between those who have access to *literacy* and those who don't, where a person's identity is defined by which group they belong to.
>
> The goal of *Critical Pedagogy* is to reveal this *systemic classicism bias* to people by bringing those on the margins to the centre of society to create awareness of how society is structured unfairly against them.
>
> Most people participate in this *structural erudition* because they possess a false consciousness. They need to be enlightened so they can achieve a *critical education theory* consciousness,

---

[78] Giroux, Henry A., *Theory and Resistance in Education* (Bergin & Garvey, 1983)

[79] Porfilio, Brad J., Derek R. Ford, *Leaders in Critical Pedagogy* (Sense Publishers, 2015)

> which will lead to a revolutionary consciousness, driving them to flip the system over.
>
> There are those who want to preserve the injustice of this social structure because of the benefits they receive from participating in it. They are called *colonisers*.
>
> When *teachers* become aware, they will seize the means of producing *literacy* to overturn it and enforce a situation of equality.
>
> Eventually, acts of equalisation will become spontaneous, which will produce *education* justice.

Congratulations, you now have a degree in *"critical pedagogy"*.

Homework: *discuss how the academic relations of structural literacy promote endemic colonial learning and contribute toward indigenous educator oppression.*

Sexual Marxism: Gender Theory & Queer Theory

As possibly the worst of all sociology sub-genres, so-called *"queer theory"* came out of *"queer studies"* around 1990 and birthed modern *"gender theory"*[80]. Its earliest feminist advocates, influenced by Michel Foucault (Gloria Anzaldúa, Teresa de Lauretis, Gayle Rubin, Judith Butler)[81], explicitly confess to being Marxist activists.

> There is a special type of property which has been constructed in society called *the sexual/gender binary*.
>
> One group, a superstructure called *cisgender-heterosexuality*, have given themselves exclusive access to it which others, an infrastructure of everyone else, *the sexually depraved*, don't have.

---

[80] Halperin, David M., 'The Normalization of Queer Theory', *Journal of Homosexuality*, 45.2–4 (2003), 339–43

[81] Foucault, Michel, *The History of Sexuality, Volume 1* (Pantheon Books, 1978)

They have created an ideology called *cisgender-heteronormativity* to justify why they should control access to it, which imposes the situation and allows it to continue.

The system exists to exclude those below from the power and privilege that access to *normal sexuality* provides.

This creates a dialectical conflict of social relations between those who have access to *normality* and those who don't, where a person's identity is defined by which group they belong to.

The goal of *Queer Theory* is to reveal this *systemic homophobia/queerphobia/transphobia* to people by bringing those on the margins to the centre of society to create awareness of how society is structured unfairly against them.

Most people participate in this *structural cisheteronormativity binary* because they possess a false consciousness. They need to be enlightened so they can achieve a *queer* consciousness, which will lead to a revolutionary consciousness, driving them to flip the system over.

There are those who want to preserve the injustice of this social structure because of the benefits they receive from participating in it. They are called *bigots, fascists, transphobes, cishet scum*.

When *sexual deviants* become aware, they will seize the means of producing *sexual and gender norms* to overturn it and enforce a situation of equality.

Eventually, acts of equalisation will become spontaneous, which will produce *sexual/gender* justice.

Congratulations, you now have a joint degree in *"gender studies"* and *"queer studies"*.

Homework: *discuss how the heterosexual relations of structural transphobia influence queer performativity and contribute toward dominant cisheteronormativity in hegemonic masculinised culture.*

Immigration Marxism: Postcolonial Theory & Cultural Theory

The Leninist influence of anti-Imperialism (*"colonialism"*) arrived in the early 1960s via the advocacy of militant Marxist Franz Fanon's books, through militant Marxist black civil rights activists[82]. Socialist professor Edward later expanded it to Asia[83].

> There is a special type of property which has been constructed in society called *Western civilisation*.
>
> One group, a superstructure called *European empires*, has given themselves exclusive access to it which others, an infrastructure of everyone else, *colonised indigenous people*, don't have.
>
> They have created an ideology called *imperialism* to justify why they should control access to it, which imposes the situation and allows it to continue.
>
> The system exists to exclude those below from the power and privilege that access to *imperial power* provides.
>
> This creates a dialectical conflict of social relations between those who have access to *civilisation* and those who don't, where a person's identity is defined by which group they belong to.
>
> The goal of *Postcolonialism* is to reveal this *systemic imperialism* to people by bringing those on the margins to the centre of society to create awareness of how society is structured unfairly against them.
>
> Most people participate in this *structural colonialism* because they possess a false consciousness. They need to be enlightened so they can achieve a *multicultural* consciousness, which will lead to a revolutionary consciousness, driving them to flip the system over.

---

[82] Fanon, Frantz, *The Wretched of the Earth* (Grove Press, 1963; first publ. 1961)

[83] Said, Edward W., *Orientalism* (Pantheon Books, 1978)

> There are those who want to preserve the injustice of this social structure because of the benefits they receive from participating in it. They are called *colonisers*.
>
> When *the colonised* become aware, they will seize the means of producing *demography* to overturn it and enforce a situation of equality.
>
> Eventually, acts of equalisation will become spontaneous, which will produce *multicultural* justice.

Congratulations, you now have a joint degree in *"cultural studies"* and *"postcolonial studies"*.

Body Marxism: Fat Studies

The truly unbelievable, and comically named, silly subject of *"fat acceptance"*, began to be mentioned in 1983[84] and became an academic discipline in 2009[85]. It advocates for *"body diversity"* against *"fatphobia"*.

> There is a special type of property which has been constructed in society called *slimness*.
>
> One group, a superstructure called *healthy and attractive*, has given themselves exclusive access to it which others, an infrastructure of everyone else, *fat people*, don't have.
>
> They have created an ideology called *healthism* to justify why they should control access to it, which imposes the situation and allows it to continue.
>
> The system exists to exclude those below from the power and privilege that access to *healthiness* provides.

---

[84] Schoenfielder, Lucy, Barbara Wieser, *Shadow on a Tightrope* (Aunt Lute Books, 1983)

[85] Rothblum, Esther, and Sondra Solovay (eds.), *The Fat Studies Reader* (New York University Press, 2009)

This creates a dialectical conflict of social relations between those who have access to *athletic physique* and those who don't, where a person's identity is defined by which group they belong to.

The goal of *fat activism* is to reveal this *systemic thin normativity* to people by bringing those on the margins to the centre of society to create awareness of how society is structured unfairly against them.

Most people participate in these *structural body ideals* because they possess a false consciousness. They need to be enlightened so they can achieve a *fat* consciousness, which will lead to a revolutionary consciousness, driving them to flip the system over.

There are those who want to preserve the injustice of this social structure because of the benefits they receive from participating in it. They are called *fatphobes*.

When *people of size* become aware, they will seize the means of producing *body ideals* to overturn it and enforce a situation of equality.

Eventually, acts of equalisation will become spontaneous, which will produce inclusion and *body* justice.

Congratulations, you now have a degree in *"fat studies"*.

Homework: *discuss how the social relations of favoured athletic normativity promote systemic fatphobia and contribute toward establishing a dominant patriarchy of healthism.*

Ability Marxism: Disability Studies

The application of Marxist *"critical theory"* to disability (*"disability studies"* or *"critical disability theory"*) as a "social and cultural identity" appeared in 1982 as the *Society for Disability Studies*[86] and in the university system in 1997[87].

> There is a special type of property which has been constructed in society called *ability*.
>
> One group, a superstructure called the *able-bodied*, have given themselves exclusive access to it which others, an infrastructure of everyone else, the *disabled*, don't have.
>
> They have created an ideology called *ableism* to justify why they should control access to it, which imposes the situation and allows it to continue.
>
> The system exists to exclude those below from the power and privilege that access to *able-bodiedness* provides.
>
> This creates a dialectical conflict of social relations between those who have access to *ability* and those who don't, where a person's identity is defined by which group they belong to.
>
> The goal of *disability studies* is to reveal this *systemic ableism* to people by bringing those on the margins to the centre of society to create awareness of how society is structured unfairly against them.
>
> Most people participate in this *structural ableism* because they possess a false consciousness. They need to be enlightened so they can achieve an *ableist* consciousness, which will lead to a revolutionary consciousness, driving them to flip the system over.
>
> There are those who want to preserve the injustice of this social structure because of the benefits they receive from participating in it. They are called *ableists*.
>
> When the *differently abled* become aware, they will seize the means of producing *ability* to overturn it and enforce a situation

---

[86] Ramirez, Anthony, 'Disability as Field of Study?', *The New York Times*, 21 Dec 1997

[87] Davis, Lennard J. (ed.), *The Disability Studies Reader* (Routledge, 1997)

of equality.

Eventually, acts of equalisation will become spontaneous, which will produce inclusion and *disability* justice.

Congratulations, you now have a degree in *"disability studies"*.

Homework: *discuss how the normative relations of systemic discrimination promote structural able-bodied queer relativism, which contributes toward a hegemony of dialectic of ability.*

Environmental Marxism: Eco-Climate Justice

The modern "eco" movement has its roots in anti-vivisection radicalism and the anarcho-communist *Animal Liberation Front* (ALF) formed in 1974[88]. "Critical environmental justice" groups began their most virulent activity about capitalist climate pollution with the 1982 PCB protests in North Carolina[89].

> There is a special type of property which has been constructed in society called *the right to industrially exploit natural resources*.
>
> One group, a superstructure called in*dustrialists*, has given themselves exclusive access to it which others, an infrastructure of everyone else, *the planet, nature, and animals*, don't have.
>
> They have created an ideology called *industrialisation* to justify why they should control access to it, which imposes the situation and allows it to continue.
>
> The system exists to exclude those below from the power and privilege that access to *resource exploitation* provides.
>
> This creates a dialectical conflict of social relations between those who have access to *exploitation* and those who don't, where identity is defined by which group they belong to.

---

[88] Peters, James M., *Animal Rights* (Peter Lang Publishing, 1999)

[89] Martinez-Alier, Joan, *The Environmentalism of the Poor* (Edward Elgar, 2002)

The goal of *environmentalism* is to reveal this *systemic profit motive* to people by bringing those on the margins to the centre of society to create awareness of how society is structured unfairly against them.

Most people participate in this *structural exploitation of nature* because they possess a false consciousness. They need to be enlightened so they can achieve an *eco* consciousness, which will lead to a revolutionary consciousness driving them to flip the system over.

There are those who want to preserve the injustice of this social structure because of the benefits they receive from participating in it. They are called *exploiters and climate deniers*.

When *consumers* become aware, they will seize the means of producing *eco-husbandry* to overturn it and enforce a situation of equality.

Eventually, acts of equalisation will become spontaneous, which will produce *climate* justice.

Congratulations, you now have a degree in *"climate studies"*.

Homework: *discuss how the power relations of structural climate change denial promote endemic fascism and contribute to a culture of dominant patriarchal capitalism.*

Anti-Jew Marxism: Anti-Zionism

Hatred of Jews is a shape-shifting virus which has existed throughout history. The modern species emerged after the *Six-Day War* in 1967 when the USSR allied with Arabs and condemned *"zionology"* as *"bourgeois nationalism."*[90]

---

[90] Behbehani, Hashim S., *The Soviet Union and Arab Nationalism* (Routledge, 1986)

There is a special type of property which has been constructed in society called the *Holy Land*.

One group, a superstructure called *Jews*, has given themselves exclusive access to it which others, an infrastructure of everyone else, *Palestinians,* don't have.

They have created an ideology called *Zionism* to justify why they should control access to it, which imposes the situation and allows it to continue.

The system exists to exclude those below from the power and privilege that access to the *Holy Land* provides.

This creates a dialectical conflict of social relations between those who have access to the *Holy Land* and those who don't, where a person's identity is defined by which group they belong to.

The goal of *anti-Zionism* is to reveal this *systemic Zionism* to people by bringing those on the margins to the centre of society to create awareness of how society is structured unfairly against them.

Most people participate in this *structural Palestinian apartheid* because they possess a false consciousness. They need to be enlightened so they can achieve a *anti-Zionist* consciousness, which will lead to a revolutionary consciousness driving them to flip the system over.

There are those who want to preserve the injustice of this social structure because of the benefits they receive from participating in it. They are called *Zionists, Benjamins, Jews, Occupiers, Them, etc.*

When *gentiles* become aware, they will seize the means of occupying *Palestine* to overturn it and enforce a situation of equality.

Eventually, acts of equalisation will become spontaneous, which will produce inclusion and *Justice for Palestine*.

Congratulations, you now have a degree in *"middle east studies"*.

Homework: *discuss how Zionist ideological hegemony in cisheteronorative culture reveals the structural racial dominance across domains, or a rationalisation of how and why Jews run the world while keeping all the money and Israel should be destroyed.*

Mental Health Marxism: Autism & Dyslexia

The issues of dyslexia and autism emerged from *"disability studies"* in 1999[91], but were formalised by Thomas Armstrong's and Nick Walker's essays about *"neurodiversity"* in 2010[92].

> There is a special type of property which has been constructed in society called *neurotypicality*.
>
> One group, a superstructure called the *neurotypical*, has given themselves exclusive access to it which others, an infrastructure of everyone else, the *neurodivergent*, don't have.
>
> They have created an ideology called *cognitive conformity* to justify why they should control access to it, which imposes the situation and allows it to continue.
>
> The system exists to exclude those below from the power and privilege that access to *neurotypicality* provides.
>
> This creates a dialectical conflict of relations between those who have access to *neurotypicality* and those who don't, where a person's identity is defined by which group they belong to.
>
> The goal of *neurotypicality studies* is to reveal this *systemic neuroableism* to people by bringing those on the margins to the centre of society to create awareness of how society is

---

[91] Singer, Judy, "'Why Can't You Be Normal for Once in Your Life?': From a "Problem with No Name" to the Emergence of a New Category of Difference', in Mairian Corker and Sally French (eds.), *Disability Discourse* (Open University Press, 1999)

[92] Armstrong, Thomas, *The Power of Neurodiversity* (Da Capo Lifelong Books, 2010)

structured unfairly against them.

Most people participate in thiese unfair standards of *structural cognitive conformity* because they possess a false consciousness. They need to be enlightened so they can achieve a *neurodiverse* consciousness, which will lead to a revolutionary consciousness, driving them to flip the system over.

There are those who want to preserve the injustice of this social structure because of the benefits they receive from participating in it. They are called *neuroableists or conformists*.

When the *neurodivergent* become aware, they will seize the means of producing *ability* to overturn it and enforce a situation of equality.

Eventually, acts of equalisation will become spontaneous, which will produce inclusion and *cognitive neurodiversity* justice.

Congratulations, you now have a degree in *"neurodiversity studies"*.

Homework: *discuss how the normative relations of systemic discrimination promote structural able-bodied queer relativism, which contributes toward a hegemony of dialectic of ability.*

Common Enemy Meta-Identity Marxism: Intersectionality

The DEI movement comes from one place as a cumulative "theory" of mixed oppression: in 1989, via Marxist critical race theory advocate Kimberlé Crenshaw[93].

So what do we get when we metaphysically jam all these complaints together against the *cisgender straight white Christian able-bodied educated athletic male meat-eating non-autistic capitalist Israeli imperialist coloniser?*

---

[93] Crenshaw, Kimberlé, 'Demarginalizing the Intersection of Race and Sex: A Black Feminist Critique of Antidiscrimination Doctrine, Feminist Theory and Antiracist Politics', *University of Chicago Legal Forum*, 1989, 139–67

There is a special type of property which has been constructed in society called *only suffering one oppression at a time*.

One group, a superstructure called *cisgender straight White able-bodied educated athletic capitalist men*, has given themselves exclusive access to it which others, an infrastructure of everyone else, *disabled fat black lesbian feminist transgender immigrants*, don't have.

They have created an ideology called *meritocracy* to justify why they should control access to it, which imposes the situation and allows it to continue.

The system exists to exclude those below from the power and privilege that access to *not suffering any oppression* provides.

This creates a dialectical conflict of social relations between those who have access to *privilege* and those who don't, where a person's identity is defined by which group they belong to.

The goal of *intersectionality* is to reveal these *systemic interlocking types of oppression* to people by bringing those on the margins to the centre of society to create awareness of how society is structured unfairly against them.

Most people participate in this *structural system of inequity* because they possess a false consciousness. They need to be enlightened so they can achieve a *intersectional* consciousness, which will lead to a revolutionary consciousness driving them to flip the system over.

There are those who want to preserve the injustice of this social structure because of the benefits they receive from participating in it. They are called *the privileged*.

When *marginalised groups* become aware, they will seize the means of producing *society and culture* to overturn it and enforce a situation of equality.

Eventually, acts of equalisation will become spontaneous, which will produce *social* justice.

This pattern of endless, splintering minor attribute categorisation continues almost indefinitely.

In November 2021, activist Tessa Watkins published the absurd *"Wheel of Privilege and Power"*[94] (which she claims was *"adapted from Sylvia Duckworth (Instagram post), "anti-oppression" by the Canadian Council for Refugees*[95]*, and Olena Hankivsky, PhD*[96]*)*.

There is an essence to almost all these "identity" charts, which closely resembles an *astrological chart*.

Other than *"fategories"* (the *"fat spectrum"*)[97], Watkins gives us an overview of how Marxian *"intersectionality"* magically explains the *"oppression"* suffered by convicted criminals (e.g. rapists, murderers, etc) through the justice system, using her tiers of *"power"*, *"erasure"*, and *"marginalized"*.

> *Power: no dealings with the justice system or had dealings but never convicted*
>
> *Erased: had dealings but never convicted, convicted and awaiting sentencing, previously served a sentence in jail or prison, and/or had records expunged*
>
> *Marginalized: convicted and currently serving a sentence in jail or prison*

Among the insane list of Marcusian *"erased"* minority vs. visible *"privileged"* categories she lists are:

- *"Neurodiversity"* (*"neurodivergent"* vs. *"neurotypical"*)

---

[94] Watkins, Tessa, 'Wheel of Privilege and Power', *Just1Voice*, 21 November 2021

[95] 'Anti-Oppression', Canadian Council for Refugees, 19 August 2020

[96] Hankivsky, Olena, 'Intersectionality 101', *The Institute for Intersectionality Research & Policy, SFU*, 1 April 2014

[97] Gerhardt, Linda, 'Fategories: Understanding the Fat Spectrum', *Fluffy Kitten Party: Fat Activism, Health at Every Size, Anti-Diet Culture*, 1 June 2021

- *Mental health* (vulnerable vs. stable)
- *Physical ability* (disabled vs. *"able-bodied"*)
- *Religion* (everyone else vs. Christian)
- *Wealth* (poor vs. rich)
- *Age* (minor/sensor vs. adult)
- *Education* (elementary vs. post-secondary)
- *Housing* (homeless vs. homeowner)
- *Transportation* (no access vs. car owner)
- *Political affiliation* (uninvolved vs. partisan)
- *Marriage* (separated/divorced/*"polygamous"* vs. monogamous)
- *Citizenship* (*"undocumented"* vs. citizen)
- *Employment* (student/unemployed vs. salaried)
- *Language* (non-English vs. native speaker)
- *Communication* (monolingual vs. high *"EQ"*)
- *Sexuality* (LGB vs. heterosexual)
- *Gender* (*"trans"* vs. *"cis"*)
- *Body size* (fat vs. slim/muscular)[98]
- *Skin colour* (non-white vs. white)
- *Incarceration* (convicted vs. no record)
- *Number of kids* (parents vs. *"child-free"*)
- *Type of kids* (adopted vs. biological)
- *Left/right-handedness* (left vs. right)
- *HIV status* (positive vs. negative)
- *Dietary preference* (meat vs. vegan)[99]

This ultimately translates into job advertisement statements to avoid lawsuits, typified in the following boilerplate style:

> *[Company Name] provides equal employment opportunities to all employees and applicants without regard to race, color, religion,*

---

[98] Categories hilariously include *"infinitifat", "superfat", "largefat", "midfat"*, and *"smallfat"*.

[99] Watkins, T. (2021, November 21). *Wheel of privilege and power*. Just1Voice.

> *sex, sexual orientation, gender identity or expression, age, national origin, ancestry, disability, medical condition, genetic information, marital status, family status, pregnancy, veteran status, military status, citizenship, or any other characteristic protected by applicable federal, state, or local laws.*

If you follow this path of subdivision and micro-categorisation long enough, ironically, you arrive at... the *Individual*. Which is the basis of English common law from several centuries ago[100].

It is crucial when developing your "studies" template to create your eighty-thousand-dollar sociology course you adhere to a strict code of conduct:

1. Critics might attempt to dismiss your *"analytical lens"* and desire to gain social status for helping your minority group achieve *"liberation"* and *"emancipation"* as facetious, or even vapid. It is important to explain to them they don't understand the profundity of the theory because they have never studied it.
2. It explains *everything* perfectly. If they do not agree, see #1, and discontinue any further conversation because you shouldn't be giving a *"platform"* to a *"bigot"* if they intend to engage in microaggressions.

---

[100] Blackstone, William, *Commentaries on the Laws of England* (Clarendon Press, 1765–69)

The River Of Stupidity

Is it really *that* bad? It's worse. Dozens of social media accounts (for example *"Real Peer Review"*[101] and its library of 1000+ papers) and academic commentators (for example, the *"Sokal Squared"* trio[102]) have lamented what has been referred to as "pathological idiocy" in our institutions being pervasive for several decades.

Lenin wrote in 1913,

> *There can be no "impartial" social science in a society based on class struggle. In one way or another, all official and liberal science defends wage-slavery ... To expect science to be impartial in a wage-slave society is ... foolishly naïve.*[103]

In 1959, British scientist and novelist Charles Snow gave a lecture he called *"The Two Cultures"* in which he argued science and the humanities had become irreversibly separated into different worldviews.

> *A good many times I have been present at gatherings of people who, by the standards of the traditional culture, are thought highly*

---

[101] Real Peer Review, *X Profile*, https://x.com/realpeerreview

[102] Boghossian, Peter, 'Peter Boghossian: Has Academia Been Corrupted by "Woke" Ideology?', *HARDtalk* (Interview), *BBC World Service*, 6 Dec 2023

[103] Lenin, V. I., 'The Three Sources and Three Component Parts of Marxism', in *Lenin's Collected Works*, Vol. 19 (Progress Publishers, 1913)

educated and who have with considerable gusto been expressing their incredulity at the illiteracy of scientists. Once or twice I have been provoked and have asked the company how many of them could describe the Second Law of Thermodynamics. The response was cold: it was also negative. Yet I was asking something which is the scientific equivalent of: Have you read a work of Shakespeare's? I now believe that if I had asked an even simpler question – such as, What do you mean by mass, or acceleration, which is the scientific equivalent of saying, Can you read? – not more than one in ten of the highly educated would have felt that I was speaking the same language. So the great edifice of modern physics goes up, and the majority of the cleverest people in the western world have about as much insight into it as their neolithic ancestors would have had[104].

Thirty years later, the *"Science Wars"* were raging in the United States as fringe faculty lounge activists, such as feminist philosopher Luce Irigaray, were making insane claims such as equations (e.g. $E=mc^2$) were inherently *"sexed"*[105]. Many of their views were attributed to a bad reading of Thomas Kuhn's 1962 book, *"The Structure of Scientific Revolutions"* (in which the term *"paradigm shift"* was coined)[106].

In 1994, Richard Webster pointed out that Margaret Mead's influential anthropological work in Samoa (*"Coming of Age in Samoa"*) was nonsense - her teenage informants admitted to having misled her about their sexual practices.[107]

Senior scientists, such as Norman Levitt, Paul Gross, Jean Bricmont and Alan Sokal) accused many writers (e.g. Jacques Derrida, Gilles Deleuze, Jacques Lacan, Jean-François Lyotard and others) of simply

---

[104] Snow, Charles Percy, *The Two Cultures: And a Second Look: An Expanded Version of The Two Cultures and the Scientific Revolution* (Cambridge University Press, 1964)

[105] Irigaray, Luce, *Sexes and Genealogies* (Columbia University Press, 1987)

[106] Kuhn, Thomas S., *The Structure of Scientific Revolutions* (University of Chicago, 1962)

[107] Freeman, Derek, *Margaret Mead and Samoa* (Harvard University Press, 1983)

either going mad, or printing nonsense which was incomprehensible or meaningless.

Gross and Levitt wrote the seminal book (*"Higher Superstition"*) describing the humanities' descent into idiocy in 1994.

They described a persistent trend.

> *The academic left has developed an extraordinary hostility to science and technology, far beyond the healthy skepticism that is always in order in the sciences themselves.*[108]

They were quickly followed by Sokal's maddeningly brilliant 1996 hoax in the journal *Social Text* (*"Transgressing the Boundaries"*[109]) which preceded his 1997 book *"Fashionable Nonsense"* (aka *"Intellectual Impostures"*)[110].

As the authors noted of this creeping ultracrepidarian tendency:

> *"The problem arises when authors invoke scientific concepts outside their field of expertise, without bothering to understand them, and without regard for their relevance.*

Sokal's infamous quip perhaps sums up the era.

> *Anyone who believes that the laws of physics are mere social conventions is invited to try transgressing those conventions from the windows of my apartment. (I live on the twenty-first floor.)*[111]

By 1998, the humanities - particularly the social "sciences" - were done

---

[108] Gross, Paul, Norman Levitt, *Higher Superstition* (Johns Hopkins University Press, 1994)

[109] Sokal, Alan, 'Transgressing the Boundaries: Towards a Transformative Hermeneutics of Quantum Gravity', *Social Text*, 46/47 (1996), 217–52

[110] Sokal, Alan, and Jean Bricmont, *Fashionable Nonsense* (Picador, 1997)

[111] Sokal, Alan, 'A Physicist Experiments with Cultural Studies', *Lingua Franca*, 1996

for. *Toast. Over.* But it didn't stop them. They simply swelled their numbers with easily obtainable sociology degrees and out-published anyone else.

This virulent pathology persists to the present day.

On September 23 2019, a group of five hundred prominent scientists and professionals, led by the *CLINTEL* co-founder Guus Berkhout, sent a registered letter to the *United Nations Secretary-General*[112] stating that there is no climate emergency and climate policies should benefit the lives of people[113].

The response was staggering. Dozens of NGO *"fact checker"* personnel and social scientists attempted to undermine it as *"misleading"*. Their rationale? They were *unqualified* because they were from the natural sciences.

> *Ten fact-checking organizations, including Climate Feedback, reviewed the credentials of a little over 200 of the signatories but could only confirm that 2 had published research in atmospheric or climate science, which means at least 200 of the 500 are not scientists with relevant expertise.*
>
> *The largest single group of signers—approximately 60 of the 200 we reviewed from the US, Canada, Brazil, Norway, Sweden, Denmark, Belgium, France, and Germany—includes academics in the physical sciences, such as physics, chemistry, or geology. However, we could not confirm that any have published research relevant to climate change, so they are making a point outside their domain of expertise.*[114]

---

[112] Retrieved from clintel.nl/wp-content/uploads/2019/09/ecd-letter-to-un.pdf

[113] Perry, Mark J., 'There Is No Climate Emergency, Say 500 Experts in Letter to the United Nations', *American Enterprise Institute*, 24 September 2019

[114] Science Feedback, 'Letter to UN Was Not Signed by 500 Experts on Climate Science – Breitbart', *Science Feedback*, 3 October 2019

The words of Karl Popper are probably the only appropriate response to behaviour like this.

> *I can only say that when I read either Adorno or Habermas, I feel as if lunatics were speaking.*[115]

Not all garbage from the "ologies" is the same; some is absurd, some is malignant, and the remainder straddles the distance between laughable and baffling. At times, one finds oneself convulsed with ridicule. At others, astounded what one is reading had ever been printed.

1. *Fan Fiction:* Creative writing and wild flights of fancy: my diary; someone else's diary; the poem I wrote at fourteen; fairies and spirit creatures; animal fetishes, cartoon drawings, and fantasy hero creatures (*Examples: "emotional labour", "latinx", "spirit murder"*).

2. *Pseudoscientific Imagineering:* Misappropriated scientific concepts; abstract terminology; unfalsifiable hypotheses; the magical mind and invisible thought processes; quasi-religious imagery and unobservable "systems"; reification of ideas as reality. (*Examples: "addiction", "empathy", "patriarchy", "unconscious bias"*).

3. *Manipulative Intellectualism:* Vapid subject material with mangled language; impenetrable paragraphs of pretentious obscurantism; *ism, ist, icity, ity, ivity, tive* everywhere; circular references to dreadful papers; misrepresented as "theory"; useless data wrongly analysed; political confirmation-searching and ideological possession. (*Examples: "algorithmic fairness", "cisgender", "inclusive language"*).

4. *Tenured Radicalism:* Overtly political themes; obvious resentment;

---

[115] Popper, Karl, 'Letter to Raymond Aron', 13 September 1969, in Stephen Hicks, *Popper to Aron: Letter on Adorno and Habermas* (30 September 2021)

frequent references to revolutionary thought and figures; demands for social restructuring; obvious attempts to re-brand communism or directly advocate for it. (Examples: *"antiracism", "rape culture", "use your platform"*).

5. *Sociopathy:* Apologism for murder and/or infanticide; depraved fetishes; barbarous Mengele-esque procedures; advocacy for or defence of paedophilia. (*Examples: "biopower", "minor attracted person", "TERF"*).

Truly, some of these masterpiece works of literature are extraordinary to behold. Below are merely a *fraction* of the most egregious.

- Improvement of *"human-ice relations"*[116].
- Menstruation being a fictional process[117].
- Men and women as "hostage" to society's "production" of gender[118].
- The scientific method as a mechanism of oppression[119].
- The natural world not being real, merely stereotypes[120].
- Erectile dysfunction being affected by ideas of the penis[121].

---

[116] Carey, Mark, M. Jackson, Alessandro Antonello, and Jaclyn Rushing, 'Glaciers, Gender, and Science: A Feminist Glaciology Framework for Global Environmental Change Research', *Progress in Human Geography*, 40.6 (2016), 770–93

[117] Hasson, Katie Ann, 'Not a "Real" Period?: Social and Material Constructions of Menstruation', *Gender & Society*, 30.6 (2016), 958–83

[118] West, Candace, and Don H. Zimmerman, 'Doing Gender', *Gender & Society*, 1.2 (1987)

[119] Harding, Sandra, 'Significant Differences: The Construction of Knowledge, Objectivity, and Dominance', *Women's Studies International Forum*, 18.2 (1995)

[120] Ramler, Amy, 'Naturalizing Gender Through Childhood Socialization Messages in a Zoo', *Social Psychology Quarterly*, 47.2 (2016), 89–101

[121] Potts, Annie, 'The Essence of the Hard On: Hegemonic Masculinity and the Cultural Construction of Erectile Dysfunction', *Men and Masculinities*, 3.1 (2000)

- Fat men refusing to act like women[122].
- *Wikipedia* as an anti-feminist website[123].
- The wording of STEM courses not being feminine enough [124].
- Blood being a fiction which only exists once it leaves the body[125].
- Pilates as a racial practice derived from social oppression[126].
- Breastfeeding as *"mammalian class' milk supply"*[127].
- Squirrel oppression[128].
- Ejaculating on photos as an expression of fondness[129].
- How pet dogs are *"co-opted for postcolonial racial discourse"*[130].
- *Paw Patrol*'s role in cementing capitalism oppression[131].

---

[122] Monaghan, Lee F., 'Fat Male Sexuality: The Monster in the Maze', *Sexualities*, 19.8 (2016), 965–82

[123] Hutchinson, Kristine, 'Wikipedia's Politics of Exclusion: Gender, Epistemology, and Feminist Rhetorical (In)Action', *Computers and Composition*, 37 (2015)

[124] Parson, Laura, 'Are STEM Syllabi Gendered? A Feminist Critical Discourse Analysis', *The Qualitative Report*, 21.1 (2016), 102–16

[125] Wahlberg, Ayo, 'Beyond the Person: The Construction and Transformation of Blood as a Resource', *Critical Public Health*, 26.4 (2016), 409–20

[126] Pullen, Kirsten, 'The Pilates Pelvis: Racial Implications of the Immobile Hips', *Theatre Research International*, 36.1 (2014), 21–40

[127] Barad, Karen, 'The Lactating Man', in R. B. Earle and D. Slater (eds.), *Making Milk: The Past, Present, and Future of Our Primary Food* (New York: Bloomsbury Academic, 2017), pp. 200–22

[128] Gillespie, Katharine, 'When "Angelino" Squirrels Don't Eat Nuts: A Feminist Posthumanist Politics of Consumption Across Southern California', *Gender, Place & Culture*, 23.2 (2016), 146–61

[129] Nagle, Laura, 'Fluids on Pictures on Screens: Pseudonymous Affect on Reddit's TributeMe', *Social Media + Society*, 6.1 (2020), 1–11

[130] Springer, Carrie, 'Can Dogs Be Racist? The Colonial Legacies of Racialized Dogs in Kenya and Zambia', *History Workshop Journal*, 89.1 (2020), 120–45

[131] Kanayama, Makoto, 'Whenever There's Trouble, Just Yelp for Help: Crime, Conservation, and Corporatization in *Paw Patrol*', *Crime, Media, Culture* (2020), 1–18

- The difficulties of getting up on time during Covid[132].
- Guessing ejaculate volume by watching pornography[133].
- Remembering one's own teenage fascination with witchcraft[134].
- Post-punk goth music as a new approach to biology[135].
- Personally touring gay bathhouses in China[136].
- Witchcraft on university campuses to groom recruits[137].
- The role of ghosts in the uptake of feminism[138].
- Demons as an explanation of infertility[139].
- Imagining oneself as a racialised superhero[140].
- Abnormal sexual behaviour should include normal behaviour[141].

---

[132] Lambert, Katherine, 'Of Late Alarms, Long Queues, and Online Attendances: My Experiences of COVID Time', *Qualitative Inquiry*, 26.8–9 (2020), 935–39

[133] Puts, David A., Bailey, Drew H., 'Duration of Cunnilingus Predicts Estimated Ejaculate Volume in Humans: A Content Analysis of Pornography', *Evolutionary Psychological Science*, 2.4 (2016), 279–85

[134] Gant, Tessa, '"Leaving My Girlhood Behind": Woke Witches and Feminist Liminality in *Chilling Adventures of Sabrina*', *Feminist Media Studies*, 19.6 (2019), 866–78

[135] Macdonald, Briony, 'ALIENATED LIFE: Toward a Goth Theory of Biology', *Journal of the Theoretical Humanities*, 25.4 (2020), 153–74

[136] Zheng, Tingting, '"Good Hard Fuck" Made in China: A Case Study of Chinese Semi-Professionally Produced Gay Porn', *Porn Studies*, 6.4 (2019), 443–55

[137] Maddrell, Avril, 'A Feminist Coven in the University', *Gender, Place & Culture*, 25.8 (2018), 1075–91

[138] Puar, Jasbir K., 'Lesbian Ghosts Feminism: An Introduction', *Feminist Theory*, 20.3 (2019), 293–95

[139] Rasheed, Rafia, 'Infertility Caused by Jinn', *Journal of Reproductive System and Sexual Disorders*, 7.2 (2018), 41–46

[140] Lewis, Patricia, 'Redefining the Black Superwoman: Racial and Gender Microaggressions at Predominantly White Institutions' (unpublished doctoral dissertation, *Illinois State University*, 2019)

[141] Grace, Melissa, 'Fagchild Tools: Softening the Body Politic and Sexualizing Paul Ryan in a Pussy-Grabbing Era', *Cambridge Studies in Sexualities*, 17.4 (2018)

- Diagnosis of fictional disease in HBO *"Game of Thrones"*[142].
- Poetry concerning *"life, death, brevity, and the unknowable"*[143].
- Personal thoughts of having a *"tranimal, hippopotamus alter-ego"*[144].
- Irish mens' drug use deciding whether they feel male or female[145].
- Humans possessing two legs as a form of prejudice[146].
- Female cross-dressing as a means of political rebellion[147].
- Walking tours by homosexuals as political dissent[148].
- The Mariana Islands as *"resistance to colonial cartographic violence"*[149].
- Drone warfare's effects of *"disorientating"* sexual behaviour[150].
- Teeth as a means of determining racial identity[151].
- Biological functioning of the penis being a conspiracy theory[152].

---

[142] Bernstein, David, 'Greyscale—A Mystery Dermatologic Disease on HBO's *Game of Thrones*', *JAMA Dermatology*, 152.11 (2016), 1204–05

[143] Hogan, Anne, 'The Dead Chick', *Qualitative Inquiry*, 25.7 (2019), 719–20

[144] Turnbull, Michael, 'EGO HIPPO: The Subject as Metaphor', *Angelaki: Journal of the Theoretical Humanities*, 22.1 (2017), 21–41

[145] Adams, John, 'A Psychoactive Paradox of Masculinities: Cohesive and Competitive Relations Between Drug-Taking Irish Men', *Gender, Place & Culture*, 25.6 (2018)

[146] Shepard, N. (2015). We swam before we breathed or walked: Able-bodied belonging in popular stories of evolutionary biology. *Disability & Society, 30*(7)

[147] Halberstam, Jack, 'Staging Dissents: Drag Kings, Resistance, and Feminist Masculinities', *Signs: Journal of Women in Culture and Society*, 44.3 (2019)

[148] Kilgore, Daniel, 'Queer Walking Tours and the Affective Contours of Place', *Cultural Geographies*, 26.2 (2019), 239–58

[149] Tuck, Eve, 'Archipelagic Rhetoric: Remapping the Marianas and Challenging Militarization from "A Stirring Place"', *Communication and Critical/C

[150] Daggett, Cara, 'Drone Disorientations: How "Unmanned" Weapons Queer the Experience of Killing in War', *International Feminist Journal of Politics*, 17.3 (2015)

[151] Moya, Paula M. L., 'Straight and White: Talking with My Mouth Full', *Qualitative Inquiry*, 14.7 (2008), 1175–91

[152] Stoltenberg, John, 'Refusing to Be a Man: Essays on Sex and Justice', *Women's Studies International Forum*, 7.6 (1984), 547–49

- Diary reflection on an absent father[153].
- Paedophilia as an invention of the right-wing to oppress society[154].
- Fat people being given different medical advice as a public hazard[155].

These examples will seem unbelievable; preposterous, even. However, they are the rule rather than the exception. Thousands more are churned out each year, often funded by taxpayer cash or university endowment.

At the time of writing, subjects highlighted by *Real Peer Review* include *"rape myth acceptance"*; *"antiracist"* interventions in ecology; *"whiteness"* in physics; complaints about computing *"quantum supremacy"*; the evil spirit of *"wypio-yōkai"*; problems with *"white talk"*; dancing as mathematics; the *"ableist"* use of "fitness" in evolutionary biology; and the *"male gaze"* in *"lesbian relations."*

A rapid, low-resolution method of spotting fraud is the emphasis of credentials in an individual's name; if a person quoting this "research" is keen for an audience to notice "MA" or "PhD" in their title, the likelihood their data is of any value is inversely proportional to the effort put into persuading anyone of it.

---

[153] Harding, Sarah K., 'Reflexive Encounters with Embodied Resistance to Relational Forgiveness', *Reflective Practice*, 18.5 (2017), 674–88

[154] Edelman, Lee, 'The Political Use and Abuse of the "Pedophile"', *Journal of Homosexuality*, 55.3 (2008), 429–41

[155] Cooper, Charlotte, 'Sizeism Is a Health Hazard', *Fat Studies*, 5.2 (2016)

The Poisonous Core of Narcissism

In ancient Greece, they held a superstition it was unlucky, or even fatal, to see one's own reflection[156]. In the mythology of Ovid's *"Metamorphoses"* (Book III), *Narcissus* was the rape-child of the river god *Cephissus* and the nymph *Liriope* who grew into an extraordinarily handsome hunter from *Thespiae, Boeotia*[157]. His mother was told by the blind gender-swapping prophet *Tiresias* he would have a long life, provided he never recognised himself[158].

When he was sixteen, he was spied on by a mute, infatuated mountain nymph (or *Oread*), named *Echo*. Her approach to soliciting him was disastrous, and she died heartbroken. A young man, *Ameinias*, had also fallen in love with him, but had been ignored[159].

Nemesis, the goddess of revenge, cursed *Narcissus* so he could never be loved by the one he fell in love with. As he approached a pond to quench his thirst, which no-one had ever visited, he mistook his own reflection in the water for a beautiful marble statue and fell in love with it as if it were someone else[160].

Eventually, he realised his love could not be reciprocated and could not have his object of desire. He died from starvation and passion, turning

---

[156] Vernant, J.-P. (1991). *Mortals and Immortals* Princeton University

[157] Ovid. (1986). *Metamorphoses*. Oxford University Press

[158] Segal, Charles. (1998). *Orpheus* Johns Hopkins University Press

[159] Ovid, *Metamorphoses,* Oxford University Press, (2004)

[160] Graves, Robert, *The Greek Myths,* Penguin Books, (2017)

into a white and gold flower. What we now call the genus *Daffodil*[161]. The Greeks called it *hubris*[162].

In 1889, psychiatrists Paul Näcke and Havelock Ellis used the term *"narcissism"* (*"Narzissismus"*) to describe an *(auto-)*erotic fascination with oneself, or a *"sexual perversion in which a person is aroused by their own body and not by another person."*[163]

> *Narcissus-like, [the individual] falls in love with himself, and his own image becomes an object of desire.*[164]

In 1911, Austrian psychoanalyst Otto Rank published the first clinical paper about the condition of *"Narcissism"*, which he defined as an extreme form of self-admiration and self-focus.

> *Narcissism designates a condition in which the subject's libido is invested in the ego itself, rather than directed outward toward external objects.*[165]

Three years later, in 1914, Sigmund Freud published his infamous thesis on it describing his notion of *"libidinal energy."*[166]

Fascinatingly, what is seldom mentioned in discussion of this disorder

---

[161] Beaulieu, Marie-Claire. (2016). *The Sea in the Greek Imagination*, University of Pennsylvania Press

[162] Fisher, Nick R. E. (1992). *Hybris*, Aris & Phillips

[163] Näcke, Paul. (1899). "Die sexuellen Perversionen in ihrer Entwicklung dargestellt" (Sexual Perversions in Their Development). *Archiv für Psychiatrie und Nervenkrankheiten*

[164] Ellis, Havelock. (1898–1920). *Studies in the Psychology of Sex*. F.A. Davis

[165] Rank, Otto. (1911). "Der Künstler und andere Beiträge zur Erotik und Psychopathologie" (The Artist and Other Contributions to Eroticism and Psychopathology). F. Deuticke

[166] Freud, Sigmund. (1914). "On Narcissism: An Introduction." In *Standard Edition of the Complete Psychological Works of Sigmund Freud, (1914-1916)*, Hogarth Press

is the long list of modern maladies which are strongly correlated or co-morbid with it.

- Frequent pornography use[167] and lower likelihood of seeing it as problematic[168]
- Increased engagement in casual sex and extramarital affairs[169][170]
- Support for feminist ideals[171]
- Academic cheating and dishonesty[172]
- Over-claiming knowledge in academic or intellectual settings within areas where they lack true competence[173]

---

[167] Carroll, Jason S., Padilla-Walker, Laura M., Nelson, Larry J., Olson, Chad D., Barry, Carolyn M., and Madsen, Stephanie D. (2008). "Generation XXX: Pornography Acceptance and Use Among Emerging Adults." *Journal of Adolescent Research*, 23(1)

[168] Grubbs, Joshua B., Julie J. Exline, Kenneth I. Pargament, Joshua N. Hook, and Robert D. Carlisle, "Transgression as Addiction: Religiosity and Moral Disapproval as Predictors of Perceived Addiction to Pornography," *Archives of Sexual Behavior*, 44.1 (2015), 125–36

[169] Campbell, W. Keith, and Craig A. Foster, "Narcissism and Commitment in Romantic Relationships: An Investment Model Analysis," *Personality and Social Psychology Bulletin*, 28.4 (2002), 484–95

[170] McNulty, James K., and Widman, Laura. (2014). "Sexual Narcissism and Its Implications for Sexual Satisfaction." *Social Psychological and Personality Science*.

[171] Konrath, Sara, Meng-Han Ho, and Sasha Zarins, "The Social Consequences of Narcissism: Aggression, Interpersonal Functioning, and Prosocial Behavior," *Current Directions in Psychological Science*, 25.1 (2016), 32–37

[172] Barger, A. C., & Grandey, A. A. (2006). *Service With a Smile and Encounter Satisfaction*, Academy of Management Journal

[173] Paulhus, Delroy L., Peter D. Harms, Mary N. Bruce, and Debra C. Lysy, "The Over-Claiming Technique: Measuring Self-Enhancement Independent of Ability," *Journal of Personality and Social Psychology*, 84.4 (2003), 890–904

- Optimism bias[174] and overconfidence in personal abilities[175]
- High spending on luxury brands and beauty products[176]
- Higher debt-to-income ratios[177]
- Increased expectation of partner roles and relationship dissatisfaction[178]
- Heavy social media use, with sensitivity to "likes" and positive comments[179]
- Authoritarian values[180] and less sympathy for minorities[181]
- Social manipulation and relational aggression[182]

---

[174] Weinstein, Neil D., "Unrealistic Optimism About Future Life Events," *Journal of Personality and Social Psychology*, 39.5 (1980), 806–20

[175] Campbell, W. Keith, Angelica M. Bonacci, Jeremy Shelton, Julie J. Exline, and Brad J. Bushman, "Narcissism, Confidence, and Risk Attitude," *Journal of Behavioral Decision Making*, 17.4 (2004), 297–311

[176] Rose, Paul, and Daniel J. Segrist, "The Price of Perfectionism: Public Disapproval Mediates the Relationship Between Narcissistic Traits and Spending on Luxury Products," *Journal of Consumer Psychology*, 24.4 (2014), 472–78

[177] Raskin, Robert, and Howard Terry, "A Principal-Components Analysis of the Narcissistic Personality Inventory and Further Evidence of Its Construct Validity," *Journal of Personality and Social Psychology*, 54.5 (1988), 890–902

[178] Wurst, Sarah N., Tobias M. Gerlach, Michael Dufner, and others, "Narcissism and Romantic Relationships: The Differential Impact of Narcissistic Admiration and Rivalry," *Journal of Personality and Social Psychology*, 112.2 (2017), 280–306

[179] Fox, Jesse, and Margaret C. Rooney, "The Dark Triad and Trait Self-Objectification as Predictors of Men's Use and Self-Presentation Behaviors on Social Networking Sites," *Personality and Individual Differences*, 76 (2015), 161–65

[180] Duckitt, John, and Chris G. Sibley, "Authoritarianism and Social Dominance Orientation: Relationships with Various Forms of Prejudice," *European Journal of Personality*, 19.7 (2005), 593–601

[181] Hatemi, Peter K., and others, "The Role of 'Dark Personalities' (Narcissism, Machiavellianism, Psychopathy), Prejudice, and Ideology in Explaining Support for Trump and Populist Leaders," *Personality and Individual Differences*, 151 (2019), 109529

[182] Baughman, Hannah M., Rebecca Dearing, Sarah Giammarco, Carolyn Vernon, "The Narcissistic Personality Inventory as a Predictor of Relational Aggression in Women: Mediating Role of Trait Anger," *Personality and Individual Differences*, 56 (2014)

- Less healthy eating practices[183]
- Dominance-providing video games[184]
- Heavy drinking and recreational drug use[185]
- Dismissal of health warnings and engagement in risky behaviours[186]
- Highly competitive and self-promotional workplace behaviours[187]
- Controlling and manipulative parenting behaviours[188]
- Self-serving choices and dishonesty for financial gain[189]

In 1997, Jonathan Haight proposed *"Moral Foundations Theory"*, popularised in his book *"The Righteous Mind"*. He posted six *"foundations"* of moral reasoning: *care/harm, fairness/cheating, loyalty/betrayal, authority/subversion, sanctity/degradation, liberty/oppression*[190]. They discovered sensitivity to these correlated with political ideology, and left-leaning

---

[183] Whiteside, Stephen P., and Donald R. Lynam, "The Five Factor Model and Impulsivity: Using a Structural Model of Personality to Understand Impulsivity," *Personality and Individual Differences*, 30.4 (2001), 669–89

[184] Sioni, Sean R., James M. Burleson, and Christopher S. Bekerian, "Escaping in Digital Games: The Relationship Between Immersion, Escapism, and Aggression in Online Video Games," *Cyberpsychology, Behavior, and Social Networking*, 16.2 (2013), 127–32

[185] Hill, Patrick L., and Brent W. Roberts, "Narcissism, Well-Being, and Risk," *Journal of Research in Personality*, 46.5 (2012), 556–60

[186] Vazire, Simine, and David C. Funder, "Impulsivity and the Self-Defeating Behavior of Narcissists," *Review of General Psychology*, 10.2 (2006), 154–65

[187] Grijalva, Emily, and Daniel A. Newman, "Narcissism and Counterproductive Work Behavior: Meta-Analysis and Consideration of Collectivist Culture," *Journal of Management*, 41.1 (2015), 208–31

[188] Horton, Robert S., and Tessa Tritch, "Clarifying the Links Between Grandiose Narcissism and Parenting," *Journal of Research in Personality*, 48 (2014)

[189] Campbell, W. Keith, Brian J. Hoffman, Stacy M. Campbell, and Giuseppe Marchisio, "Narcissism in Organizational Contexts," *Human Resource Management Review*, 21.4 (2011), 268–84

[190] Haidt, Jonathan, *The Righteous Mind* (Pantheon Books, 2012)

participants only valued two[191].

> *Liberals consistently showed greater endorsement and use of the Harm/care and Fairness/reciprocity foundations compared to the other three foundations, whereas conservatives endorsed and used the five foundations more equally.*[192]

In 2021, researchers at the *University of Western Ontario* (led by Christopher Marcin Kowalski) conducted a study on the possible links between the so-called *"Dark Triad"* of personality traits (sub-clinical psychopathy, Machiavellianism, and narcissism)[193], and political orientation. The results were published in *Behavioral Sciences,* and deeply alarming: left-wing ideology was *strongly* correlated with them all.

> *A pattern of correlations emerged in Table 1, such that in several instances, high scores on a Dark Triad trait predicted left/liberal political orientations. Specifically, all three dark traits (especially Machiavellianism) were associated with a rejection of socio-religious conservatism, and Narcissism was correlated with an overall left/liberal political outlook. With regard to interest in politics, higher Machiavellianism scores were associated with lower levels of interest in politics.*[194]

---

[191] Haidt, Jonathan, and Jesse Graham, "When Morality Opposes Justice: Conservatives Have Moral Intuitions That Liberals May Not Recognize," *Social Justice Research*, 20.1 (2007), 98–116

[192] Graham, Jesse, Jonathan Haidt, and Brian A. Nosek, "Liberals and Conservatives Rely on Different Sets of Moral Foundations," *Journal of Personality and Social Psychology*, 96.5 (2009), 1029–46

[193] Paulhus, Delroy L., and Kevin M. Williams, "The Dark Triad of Personality: Narcissism, Machiavellianism, and Psychopathy," *Journal of Research in Personality*, 36.6 (2002), 556–63

[194] Kowalski, Colin M., Philip A. Vernon, and Julie A. Schermer, "The Dark Triad and Political Orientation: Links Between Narcissism, Machiavellianism, Psychopathy, and Ideology," *Behavioral Sciences*, 11.1 (2021), Article 1

In 2022, *Emory University* researcher Thomas H. Costello and five colleagues surveyed 7,258 adults to research left-wing authoritarianism, the results of which they published in the *Journal of Personality and Social Psychology*. It went even further, suggesting left-wing ideology was a predictor of personal aggression and political violence.

> *Relative to right-wing authoritarians, left-wing authoritarians were lower in dogmatism and cognitive rigidity, higher in negative emotionality, and expressed stronger support for a political system with substantial centralized state control. Our results also indicate that LWA powerfully predicts behavioral aggression and is strongly correlated with participation in political violence.* [195]

---

[195] Costello, Thomas H., Samuel M. Bowes, Sarah T. Stevens, Ian D. Waldman, Scott O. Lilienfeld, and Robert F. Krueger, "Clarifying the Structure and Nature of Left-Wing Authoritarianism: A Psychometric and Behavioral Analysis," *Journal of Personality and Social Psychology*, 122.6 (2022), 1–23

Preoccupation With Sexual Depravity

Despite their claims to the contrary, social scientists were not the first to investigate or understand sexual behaviour. Their findings are at odds with far more rigorous work preceding *"sexology"* or other dubious areas of study. This corpus of knowledge goes against the strange sexual fetishes and radical political yearnings of many of these so-called "scholars."

In *Romans 1*, around 50 A.D. during the early *Roman Empire* near its height of power, St Paul eerily narrated the fate which accompanied polytheistic worship in *Ancient Greece* to the early Christians based in Rome. He described three stages of imperial collapse.

In the first stage (*v. 22-24*), the civilisation's hubris causes it to forsake religious sentiment for its own scientific marvel, and adorn its walls with symbols of the created natural world. The result is the permissiveness of sexual revolution, or a cultural obsession with physical sexuality.

When the civilisation goes one step further (*v. 25-27*) by substituting religious thought with falsehood, - actually begins to *worship* aspects of the created natural world -, the result is the perversion of a widespread *homosexual* revolution which causes epidemic disease.

In the terminal stage (v. *28-32*), when the civilisation tramples religious sentiment underfoot as throwaway garbage, what's left is a people suffering a profanity of *"depraved mind"* (*"reprobate", adokimos*[196][197]) who can no longer morally reason or function, utterly consumed with wickedness. They know what they are doing is morally abhorrent, but not only do they continue, they actually *approve* of others doing it[198].

This observation was corroborated in 1934, when Oxbridge social anthropologist Joseph Daniel Unwin published *"Sex and Culture"*, studying what he termed cyclical *"sexual entropy."* He was curious about how attitudes to sexuality correlated with the "cultural achievement" of societies.

He examined eighty native cultures and sixteen different historical peoples: Sumerians, Babylonians, Egyptians, Assyrians, Hellenes, Persians, Hindus, Chinese, Japanese, Sassanids, Arabs (Moors), Romans, Teutons, and Anglo-Saxons.

He concluded sexual constraints have always led to human flourishing, because frustration is channelled into aggressive expansion and notable achievement in the arts and sciences. After these nations become prosperous, societies become more sexually permissive and liberal, which leads to an irrevocable loss of cohesion, impetus, and purpose three generations later.

Societies practicing what he termed *"absolute monogamy"* (strict marital fidelity) for at least three generations tended to show the highest levels of social development and cultural achievement. The three societies Unwin identified as achieving this highest *"rationalistic"* level were *Ancient Athens* (during its Golden Age), the *Roman Empire* (during its rise and early period), and the *English*.

Inversely, *"zoistic"* societies practicing complete sexual permissiveness, displaying little energy or cultural achievement, were the *Tannese* (from

---

[196] Thayer, Joseph Henry, *Greek-English Lexicon of the New Testament*, Hendrickson, 1996

[197] The Greek term "adokimos" (*Strong's Concordance* number 96) is translated in various ways in the New Testament, including *"depraved mind," "reprobate mind," "disqualified," "rejected,"* or *"unapproved."* This term appears in passages such as *Romans 1:28, 1 Corinthians 9:27,* and *2 Timothy 3:8.*

[198] Holy Bible, New International Version, 'Romans 1', Zondervan, 2011

the island of *Tanna* in what is now *Vanuatu*), the *Nambikwara* of Brazil, the *Mafulu* of New Guinea, and *Yahgan* of Tierra del Fuego[199].

Two decades later, by which point the United States had become a nuclear and economic superpower, Herbert Marcuse published *"Eros and Civilization"* (1955), which argued sexual repression was a tool of domination used by civilisation to control people, and sexual "liberation" would lead to a better, more creative, and more free society without violence[200].

Unwin observed comparative anthropological data across eighty-six societies. Marcuse imagined philosophical and psychoanalytic reasoning derived from Freud and Marx. The dichotomy could not be any more stark, and the former's earlier thoughts adequately describe the latter:

> *The history of these societies consists of a series of monotonous repetitions; and it is difficult to decide which aspect of the story is the more significant: the lamentable waste of human energy or the pathetic simplicity of the human outlook.*[201]

The first documented attempt to catalogue the extensive list of human sexual depravity was made in an 1886 book by German forensic psychiatrist Richard Freiherr von Krafft-Ebing titled *"Psychopathia Sexualis: eine Klinisch-Forensische Studie"* (*"Psychopathia Sexualis, with Especial Reference to the Antipathetic Sexual Instinct: A Medico-forensic Study"*), which claimed homosexuals had a mental illness caused by degenerate heredity, and coined the terms *"sadism and masochism."*

Krafft-Ebing categorised roughly forty-five disorders (later nearly three hundred) into *paradoxia* (sexual desire at the wrong time in life - too young or too old); *anesthesia* (insufficient sexual desire); *hyperesthesia* (excessive sexual desire); and *paraesthesia* (sexual desire directed at the

---

[199] Unwin, Joseph Daniel, *Sex and Culture*, Oxford University Press, 1934

[200] Marcuse, Herbert, *Eros and Civilization*, Beacon Press, 1955

[201] Unwin, Joseph Daniel, *Sex and Culture*, Oxford University Press, 1934

wrong objects/targets)[202].

However, contemporary ideas about sexuality start at the beginning of the century with the Darwinian study of *eugenics,* popularised by Dawin's cousin, Francis Galton, and his 1883 book, *"Inquiries into Human Faculty and Its Development."*[203] It prompted the formation of the *British Eugenics Education Society* of 1907, the *American Eugenics Society* of 1921, and three subsequent *International Eugenics* conferences[204].

Feminist suffragettes of the time were feverish supporters.

Marie Charlotte Carmichael Stopes founded the first contraceptive clinic in Britain, edited the newsletter *Birth Control News*[205], and wrote the controversial 1918 sex manual *"Married Love: A New Contribution to the Solution of Sex Difficulties."*[206]. Despite being completely opposed to abortion, *Marie Stopes International* is the largest provider of foeticide in the UK and operates in thirty-seven countries[207].

In Canada, Henrietta Muir Edwards, Nellie McClung, Louise McKinney, Emily Murphy, and Irene Parlby - known as the *"Famous Alberta Five"* - campaigned for eugenics legislation in Canadian provinces which resulted in the sterilisation of thousands of children in Alberta[208].

In America, the infamous Margaret Haggins Sanger opened the first birth control clinic in the U.S[209], founded the monthly periodical *Birth Control Review*[210], and was prosecuted for her 1914 book *"Family Limita-*

---

[202] Krafft-Ebing, Richard Freiherr von, *Psychopathia Sexualis, with Especial Reference to the Antipathetic Sexual Instinct: A Medico-Forensic Study*, trans. by Franklin S. Klaf, New York: G.P. Putnam's Sons, 1965

[203] Galton, Francis, *Inquiries into Human Faculty and Its Development*, Macmillan, 1883

[204] Kevles, Daniel J., *In the Name of Eugenics*, Harvard University Press, 1985

[205] Hall, Lesley A., *The Life and Times of Marie Stopes*, Sutton Publishing, 1997

[206] Stopes, Marie, *Married Love*, Fifield & Co., 1918

[207] Marie Stopes International, *Annual Report*, various years

[208] Greene, Vivian, *Eugenics and the Famous Five*, University of Alberta Press, 2002

[209] Chesler, Ellen, *Woman of Valor*, Simon & Schuster, 1992

[210] *Ibid.*

tion."[211] Despite being opposed to abortion, she founded the *American Birth Control League and National Committee on Federal Legislation for Birth Control*. The former became *Planned Parenthood Federation of America*, who disavowed her in 2020 on account of her beliefs about *"race hygiene"*[212].

The scientific climate during the time was equally febrile; supplanted by Franz Mesmer's ideas of *"animal magnetism"*[213] and the American mystical *"New Thought"* about *"forces"*[214]. Much of the scientific search was centred around discovering a biological source of homosexuality[215][216].

In the previous years, Hungarian journalist Karl Maria Kertbeny and German jurist Karl Heinrich Ulrichs - both confessed pederasts - created lengthy correspondence in which they attempted to coin new terms for sexual conditions which could replace "sodomite" and "pederast": *"Monosexual; Homosexual; Heterosexual; und Heterogenit."* Kertbeny suggested *"monosexual"* for masturbators, and named practitioners of anal intercourse *"pygists"*[217]. Ulrich (pseudonym *"Numa Numantius"*) had created his own within his self-published pamphlet *"Forschungen über das Rätsel der mannmännlichen Liebe"*: *Urning* (gay) and *Dioning* (lesbian)[218].

Ulrichs' believed male homosexuals were a *"third sex"*, or possessed a female soul enclosed in a male body (*"anima muliebris in corpore virili inclusa"*), and there was a *"germ"* (*"keim"*) which determined whether

---

[211] Sanger, Margaret, *Family Limitation*, New York, 1914

[212] 'Planned Parenthood Disavows Margaret Sanger', Planned Parenthood, 2020

[213] Darnton, Robert, *Mesmerism and the End of the Enlightenment in France*, Harvard University Press, 1968

[214] Braden, Charles S., *Spirits in Rebellion*, Southern Methodist University Press, 1963

[215] Ellis, Havelock, *Sexual Inversion*, F.A. Davis Company, 1897

[216] Terry, Jennifer, *An American Obsession*, University of Chicago Press, 1999

[217] Katz, Jonathan Ned, *The Invention of Heterosexuality*, Dutton, 1995

[218] Ulrichs, Karl Heinrich, *Forschungen über das Rätsel der Mannmännlichen Liebe*, self-published, 1864–1879

sexual organs would develop male or female[219].

In 1912, endocrinologist Eugene Steinach, Director of Vienna's *Biological Institute of the Academy of Sciences,* developed a *"combination of vasectomy and vasoligature"* which became known as the *"Steinach operation"*, as an attempt to "rejuvenate" men. The testicles of heterosexual men were transplanted into the abdominal cavities of homosexuals[220][221].

Around 1920, Franco-Russian Serge Voronoff was obsessed with transplanting testicle slices from chimpanzees and baboons into the human scrotum. His later work included transplants of monkey ovaries into women. He also tried the reverse, transplanting a human ovary into a female monkey, and then tried to inseminate the monkey with human sperm. He documented these efforts as *"Rejuvenation by Grafting"*[222].

Many of these gruesome operations were performed by German surgeon Richard Mühsam, who received referrals to Steinbach from homosexual cross-dresser Magnus Hirschfield[223], a staunch believer same-sex attraction was "in the glands *(glandula inclusa)*" and fascinated with studying *"the vaginal secretions of lesbians for the presence of spermatozoa, and the urine of gay men for menstrual blood."*[224]

Hirschfield recruited Baron Ferdinand von Reitzenstein, editor of *Geschlecht und Gesellschaft ("Gender and Society"),* as the director of the ethnological-anthropological department of his institute to study the *"anthropology of woman."*[225] von Reitzenstein advocated for a *"benevolent colonialism"* of Africa so they could learn the more sophisticated

---

[219] Crocq, Marc-Antoine, 'How Gender Dysphoria and Incongruence Became Medical Diagnoses: A Historical Review', *Dialogues in Clinical Neuroscience,* 23.1 (2022), 44–51

[220] Sengoopta, Chandak, *The Most Secret Quintessence of Life,* U. of Chicago Press, 2006

[221] Kozminski, Michael A., and David A. Bloom, 'A Brief History of Rejuvenation Operations', *The Journal of Urology,* 187.3 (2012), 1130–34

[222] Voronoff, Serge, *Rejuvenation by Grafting,* Brentano's, 1925

[223] Hirschfeld, Magnus, *Sexual Anomalies and Perversion,* Emerson Books, 1948

[224] LeVay, Simon, *Queer Science,* MIT Press, 1996

[225] Herzer, Manfred, *Magnus Hirschfeld,* Prometheus Books, 1990

European idea of *"gender order"*[226].

Hirschfield advocated the use of patient questionnaires, and a theory of *"sexual intermediaries"*, which he described as types of naturally occurring human sexual variations such as hermaphroditism, homosexuality, and transvestism[227]. He opened his donation-funded clinic in Tiergarten, Berlin, during 1919, jointly with psychotherapist Arthur Kronfeld and dermatologist Friedrich Wertheim in an elegant neoclassical mansion that had once belonged to the great violinist Joseph Joachim[228].

Its various names were the *Institute of Sex Research, Institute of Sexology, Institute for Sexology* or *Institute for the Science of Sexuality*. Its "work" of conducting the first "sex reassignment" surgeries (*genitoplasty*) was published in the German journal *Zeitschrift für Sexualwissenschaft und Sexualpolitik*. The building housed a library of 20,000 depravities viewable as the *"Museum of Sex."*[229]

The Soviet Union legalised sodomy in 1917[230], and abortion on-demand in 1920[231]. In 1919, György Lukács, the Hungarian Marxist philosopher and *Deputy Commissar for Culture* in Hungary's communist government, advocated using *"sex education"* as part of a campaign of *"cultural terrorism"* to weaken family bonds and traditional values holding back the adoption of socialist ideology[232].

In 1923, German immigrant Henry Gerber created the *Society for Human Rights* in Chicago as the US "gay rights" organisation[233].

---

[226] Schrader, Paul, 'Fears and Fantasies: German Sexual Science and Its Research on African Sexualities, 1890–1930', *Sexualities*, 22.7–8 (2019)

[227] Hirschfeld, Magnus, *Sexual Intermediates*, F.A. Davis Company, 1923

[228] Tamagne, Florence, *A History of Homosexuality in Europe*, Algora Publishing, 2006

[229] Oosterhuis, Harry, and Hubert Kennedy, eds., *Homosexuality and Male Bonding in Pre-Nazi Germany*, Haworth Press, 1991

[230] Healey, Dan, *Homosexual Desire in Revolutionary Russia*, U. of Chicago Press, 2001

[231] Goldman, Wendy Z., *Women, the State and Revolution*, Cambridge Press, 1993

[232] Kadarkay, Arpad, *Georg Lukács*, Blackwell, 1991

[233] Katz, Jonathan Ned, *Gay American History*, Penguin Books, 1992

In the background, the inter-war German *Weimar Republic* had collapsed into staggering hyperinflation and mind-boggling sexual depravity after the humiliating *Treaty of Versailles*[234]. Berlin had over nine hundred nightclubs and about 100,000 prostitutes[235]. Five hundred men a month were arrested for sodomy, and at least thirty per cent had been blackmailed for it[236][237].

Despite being illegal until 1927, prostitution was so widespread it devolved into sixteen different specialisations including enormously expensive child prostitutes ordered through phony pharmacies (*"medicine"*) for instant home delivery by taxi, labeled *"Marlene Dietrichs"* or *"Lillian Harveys."*[238]

"Gravelstones" were the physically deformed from north Berlin; *"telephone girls"* were children who could be selected by their attributes to modern film stars and ordered by phone; *"munzis"* were pregnant women; *"tauentzien girls"* were mother-daughter teams; *"sugar-lickers"* were nighttime pederasts; *"breslauers"* were men with large penises; lesbians were ultra-feminised *"madis,"* or tuxedoed *"dodos".* Laces of a boot denoted sexual services: cobalt-blue (pegging), white (dog-collaring), scarlet (cross-dressing), and gold (defecation on the chest).[239][240]

Poet W.H Auden said *"Berlin is the buggers daydream."*[241] American screenwriter Ben Hecht simply described it as a *"prime breeding ground of evil"*[242]. Professor Gregory Woods notes visiting British officers

---

[234] Beachy, Robert, *Gay Berlin*, Alfred A. Knopf, 2014

[235] Merriman, John M., *A History of Modern Europe*, W.W. Norton & Co. 2010

[236] Moreck, Curt, *Führer durch das lasterhafte Berlin*, 1931

[237] Beachy, Robert, *Gay Berlin*, Alfred A. Knopf, 2014

[238] Hewitt, D.G., "17 Reasons Why Germany's Weimar Republic Was a Party-Lovers Paradise," *History Collection*, 18 October 2018

[239] Barzini, Luigi, *The Europeans*, Simon and Schuster, 1983

[240] Gordon, Mel, *Voluptuous Panic*, Feral House, 2000

[241] Auden, W.H., 'Berlin', quoted in *Auden and Modernism* (Palgrave Macmillan, 1990)

[242] Hecht, Ben, *A Child of the Century* (Simon and Schuster, 1954)

recorded they felt *"an almost physical nausea was the open and blatant evidence, which confronted us wherever we went, of the unnatural"* which they said *"flourished like a horrible fungus in the moral decay."*[243]

In 1933, university students from the *National Socialist Student League (Deutsche Studentenschaft)* sacked Hirschfield's "clinic", and the *Sturmabteilung* (SA) followed, publicly burning everything inside. The doctors were scattered from the country[244].

At the end of the *Second World War*, US psychologist Madison Bentley published a paper which declared biological sex was nature, and gender was nurture[245].

The same year, New Zealand-born medical psychology John Money wrote a thesis on hermaphroditism[246], and rebranding "sexual preference" to "sexual orientation." Greek physician Alexander Polycleitos Cawadias had proposed rebranding hermaphroditism to *"Human Intersex"* two years previously[247].

Two years later in 1947, with funding from the *Rockefeller Foundation*, bisexual zoologist Alfred Charles Kinsey founded the *Institute for Sex Research* at *Indiana University* (now the *Kinsey Institute for Research in Sex, Gender, and Reproduction*), and adopted Hirschfield's questionnaire/interview-based methods to solicit responses from 5,300 men and 8,000 women. He also collected a personal museum of depravities from around the world[248].

A year later, he published the first *"Kinsey Report"* (*"Sexual Behavior in the Human Male"*), which claimed ten per cent of men were homosexual,

---

[243] Woods, Gregory, 'The Sodomitic Reputation of Weimar Berlin', *Gragoatá*, 8.14 (2004), 11–20

[244] Herzer, Manfred, *Magnus Hirschfeld: A Biography*, (Prometheus Books, 1990)

[245] Bentley, Madison, 'The Theory of Behavior', *American Psychologist*, 1.9 (1946), 405–16

[246] Money, John, *Hermaphroditism: An Inquiry into the Nature of Sexual Development* (unpublished doctoral thesis, Harvard University, 1946)

[247] Cawadias, Alexander, *Hermaphroditos: The Human Intersex* (Heinemann Medical, 1944)

[248] Gathorne-Hardy, Jonathan, *Sex, the Measure of All Things*, (Indiana Press, 1998)

forty per cent had homosexual sex, and nearly fifty per cent of the male subjects had "reacted" sexually to persons of both sexes in the course of their adult lives[249].

Five years later in 1953, he published the second, (*"Sexual Behavior in the Human Female"*), which claimed roughly seven per cent of women were the same, on top of twenty-five per cent of married women had had abortions, and forty per cent had affairs[250].

These fraudulent, deeply unethical publications became the source of the 0-6 *Kinsey Heterosexual–Homosexual Rating Scale*, used to "measure" a person's overall balance of heterosexuality and homosexuality[251].

In 1955, the aforementioned radical German communist Herbert Marcuse, - who had fled *Weimar* Germany in 1934 to work at the *Frankfurt School*'s new office at *Columbia University* in New York -, published *"Eros and Civilization: A Philosophical Inquiry into Freud"* which attempted to fuse the theories of Karl Marx and Sigmund Freud.

Marcuse's ideas became the intellectual justification for the anti-Vietnam movement and the *Sexual Revolution*. He claimed sexual "repression" wasn't naturally necessary, but a tool of social control; sexual restrictions were arbitrary rather than essential for civilisation, and sexual experimentation (*"free love"*, nudity, gay relationships, etc) was a form of political resistance. His notion of *"polymorphous perversity"* contended human sexuality naturally extends beyond traditional heterosexual, procreative sex, and limiting it to convention was part of capitalism's mechanism for controlling people's lives[252].

Trials of the first contraceptive pill (*"Enovid"*) started the same year. It was approved for medical use in the treatment of menstrual disorders in

---

[249] Kinsey, Alfred C., Wardell B. Pomeroy, Clyde E. Martin, and Paul H. Gebhard, *Sexual Behavior in the Human Male* (W.B. Saunders, 1948)

[250] Kinsey, Alfred C., Wardell B. Pomeroy, Clyde E. Martin, and Paul H. Gebhard, *Sexual Behavior in the Human Female* (W.B. Saunders, 1953)

[251] Weeks, Jeffrey, *Sexuality*, 3rd edn (Routledge, 2010)

[252] Marcuse, Herbert, *Eros and Civilization* (Beacon Press, 1955)

1957[253]. In the UK, the *Obscene Publications Act 1959* became law[254]; in the US, *Roth v. United States* redefined obscenity under the 1st Amendment[255].

John Money was positing six variables from his extended studies into hermaphroditism: so-called *"assigned"* sex, genitals, internal organs, hormonal/secondary, gonads, and chromosomes. He came up with the term *"gender role."*[256]

In 1963, UCLA psychiatrists Robert Stoller and Ralph Greenson published their new idea *"gender identity"* at the 23rd *International Psycho-Analytic Congress* in Stockholm[257].

A decade on in 1965, with funding from transsexual philanthropist Reed Erickson[258], John Money co-founded the *Johns Hopkins Gender Identity Clinic* to perform the first "sex change" operations in the US and chemically castrate paedophiles with *Depo-Provera (medroxyprogesterone acetate)*[259]. In his most notorious 1966 case, where he attempted to end the nature/nurture debate, he persuaded the parents of a twin boy who had lost his penis, David Reimer, to be castrated and raised as a girl with tragic consequences[260].

By the early seventies, the US and UK had both legalised abortion[261][262]

---

[253] Eig, Jonathan, *The Birth of the Pill* (W.W. Norton & Co., 2014)

[254] *Obscene Publications Act 1959*, 7 & 8 Eliz. 2 c. 66

[255] *Roth v. United States*, 354 U.S. 476 (1957)

[256] Money, John, and Anke A. Ehrhardt, *Man and Woman, Boy and Girl* (Johns Hopkins University Press, 1972)

[257] Stoller, Robert J., and Ralph R. Greenson, 'The Development of Gender Identity', presented at the 23rd International Psycho-Analytic Congress, Stockholm, 1963

[258] *Reed Erickson* (Erickson Educational Foundation, 1970s)

[259] Terry, Jennifer, *An American Obsession* (University of Chicago Press, 1999)

[260] Colapinto, John, *As Nature Made Him* (Harper Perennial, 2006)

[261] *Roe v. Wade*, 410 U.S. 113 (1973)

[262] *Abortion Act 1967*, 1967 c. 87

and sodomy[263][264] like the USSR; *"gay liberation"* had emerged from Marcuse's ideas of political *"sexual minorities,"* and twisted the emotion of disgust into the fabricated pathology of *"homophobia"*[265]; Denmark had legalised pornography[266]; Germany was placing vulnerable children with known paedophiles[267]; and the US court system had established the *Miller Test*[268] for obscenity, on top of confirming the legality of private pornography possession in one's home[269].

Inversely, Robert Stoller had concluded sexual perversions expressed latent aggression and revenge fantasy for childhood injury[270]. William Masters and Virginia Johnson mapped out the physiological stages of sexual arousal and orgasm and developed psychotherapy for sexual dysfunction[271].

Across the Atlantic, postmodern French philosopher Michel Foucault, a deeply depraved man, had published five major books which served as an intellectual justification for the absolute worst human behaviours, many of which he engaged in personally[272].

He argued that the modern concept of sexuality emerged in the 19th century, and sexual acts before the Victorian period weren't seen as revealing fundamental truths about who someone was. He

---

[263] *Lawrence v. Texas*, 539 U.S. 558 (2003)

[264] *Sexual Offences Act 1967*, 1967 c. 60

[265] Weinberg, George, *Society and the Healthy Homosexual* (St. Martin's Press, 1972)

[266] Skretting, Kathrine, 'Denmark 1969: Legalizing Visual Pornography', in *Pornography: Film and Culture*, ed. by Peter Lehman (Rutgers University Press, 2006)

[267] Aviv, Rachel, 'The German Experiment That Placed Foster Children with Pedophiles', *The New Yorker*, 19 July 2021

[268] *Miller v. California*, 413 U.S. 15 (1973)

[269] *Stanley v. Georgia*, 394 U.S. 557 (1969)

[270] Stoller, Robert J., *Perversion* (Pantheon Books, 1975)

[271] Masters, William H., and Virginia E. Johnson, *Human Sexual Response* (Little, Brown and Company, 1966)

[272] Kimball, Roger, 'The Perversions of M. Foucault', *The New Criterion*, March 1993.

claimed "power" produces knowledge about sexuality through medicine, psychiatry, criminal justice, and education, and control over sexuality became a way to regulate populations and individual bodies[273].

His ideas inspired the early development of the Marxist pseudo-subject of *"queer theory"* as the AIDS epidemic raged[274], of which he was France's first public victim[275].

While the *North American Man/Boy Love Association* (NAMBLA) was formed in the US and *Vereniging Martijn* in Holland, *Paedophile Action for Liberation* in the UK had developed as a breakaway group from *South London Gay Liberation Front*, with its own magazine, "Palaver."[276] In parallel, the *Paedophile Information Exchange* (PIE) campaigned for the abolition of the age of consent[277], alongside Michel Foucault and seventy French intellectuals[278]. As one would have suspected, all ended in criminal infamy.

John Money continued during the eighties, helping rename "perversions" as *"paraphilias"* in the DSM-III, such as *"chronophilia", "nepiophilia", "infantilism", "juvenilism", "adolescentilism", "gerontilism"*, and more[279]. His work during the decade included the absurd ideas of the *"lovemap"*, the *"bodymind"*, and ultimately popularised the notion of sexual *"orientation"* in his 1988 book "*Gay, Straight and In-Between: The Sexology of Erotic Orientation*"[280].

In 1990, Berkeley sociologist Judith Butler fused the ideas of Jacques Derrida, Jacques Lacan, Simone de Beauvoir, and Michel Foucault, in

---

[273] Foucault, Michel, *The History of Sexuality*, (Pantheon Books, 1978)

[274] Halperin, David M., *Saint Foucault* (Oxford University Press, 1995)

[275] Johnson, Daniel, 'Michel Foucault: The Prophet of Pederasty', *The Critic*, April 2021

[276] Cook, Matt, *Queer Domesticities* (Palgrave Macmillan, 2014)

[277] Lambert M. Surhone, Miriam T. Timpledon, and Susan F. Marseken (eds.), *Paedophile Information Exchange* (VDM Publishing, 2010)

[278] *Le Monde*, 'Open Letter from French Intellectuals on Age of Consent Laws', Jan 1977

[279] Money, John, *Lovemaps* (Irvington Publishers, 1986)

[280] Money, John, *Gay, Straight, and In-Between* (Oxford University Press, 1988)

her book *"Gender Trouble: Feminism and the Subversion of Identity"*. Butler argued *"gender"* is *"culturally constructed"*; not a natural or biological fact, but a series of repeated actions and deconstructible/subvertible *"performances"* which act to know naturalise heterosexuality[281].

At the same time, neuropsychologist Marshall Kirk and advertising executive Hunter Madsen documented their idea for a fresh approach to "gay rights" campaigning because they felt the movement had been unsuccessful in the wake of the AIDS crisis. Their Machiavellian book, *"After the Ball: How America Will Conquer its Fear and Hatred of Gays in the 90s"*[282], laid out a six-point plan for depicting homosexual behaviour in the media which historian Jonathan Kirsch described in the Los Angeles Times as *"propaganda on the highest levels of insight and calculation."*[283]

With the emergence of the Internet, "transgender" and "polyamory" Usenet newsgroups began organising, creating new lexicons of jargon such as the terms *"cis"* and *"transphobia"*[284].

By 2008, social science journals were opening discussing sex change surgeries for children as *"gender-affirming health care"*[285], and sociologists were advocating compassion towards *"minor-attracted persons"*[286].

---

[281] Butler, Judith, *Gender Trouble* (Routledge, 1990)

[282] Kirk, Marshall, and Hunter Madsen, *After the Ball* (Doubleday, 1989)

[283] Kirsch, Jonathan, 'After the Ball: A Machiavellian Gay Manifesto', *Los Angeles Times*, 26 November 1989

[284] Whittle, Stephen, 'The Trans-Cyberian Mail Way', *Social & Legal Studies*, 7.3 (1998)

[285] Levine, Stephen B., et al., 'Reconsidering Informed Consent for Trans-Identified Children, Adolescents, and Young Adults', *Journal of Sex & Marital Therapy*, 47.1 (2021), 1–20

[286] Allyn Walker, *A Long, Dark Shadow* (University of California Press, 2021)

Intellectuals Against Common Sense

In the Wisdom literature of the *Book of Proverbs*, King Solomon makes a desperate appeal to the childlike mind to the *Simple* (those who believe anything), through the character of *Lady Wisdom*, which makes clear appearing "clever" and being wise are two different things:

> *How long will you who are simple love your simple ways? How long will mockers delight in mockery and fools hate knowledge? Repent at my rebuke! Then I will pour out my thoughts to you, I will make known to you my teachings. But since you refuse to listen when I call and no one pays attention when I stretch out my hand, since you disregard all my advice and do not accept my rebuke, I in turn will laugh when disaster strikes you; I will mock when calamity overtakes you— when calamity overtakes you like a storm, when disaster sweeps over you like a whirlwind, when distress and trouble overwhelm you*[287].

The *Simple* are complacent in their lack of knowledge and content with a shallow understanding; overly trusting, unprepared for the dangers of life, taking things at face value without critical thinking; lacking insight, easily tempted and misled; especially when encountering morally dangerous situations[288].

---

[287] Proverbs 1:22-27, *NIV* (Zondervan Publishing House, 2011)

[288] Waltke, Bruce K., *The Book of Proverbs: Chapters 1–15*, (Wm. B. Eerdmans Co., 2004)

As the years of experience mount up, it becomes abundantly obvious many of our youthful presuppositions end up as casualties of their conflicts with reality. There are mimetic axioms we retain, which are remnants of wishful thinking. We grow up. We gain knowledge of the world which disabuses us of our ignorance.

A potent example of critical weakness is the lack of any *Limiting Principle*, or when to stop[289]: for example, crime rose after the Netherlands drug experiment[290]; and Sweden's "progressive" prisons devolved into rioting[291]. Chemical castration drugs for children against their parents' wishes[292], and German experiments housing vulnerable children with known paedophiles[293] equally outraged the public.

Some ideas are plain *wrong*. Not nuanced, relative, or subjective. So categorically and demonstrably wrong, in fact, they place one in a position of catastrophic error. The following is an introductory starter list of wishful sophistry often preached by left-wing ideologues in which each notion is a factual error. There are hundreds more.

Humans don't have a fixed nature

Genetically identical twins display the same behaviours even when raised apart[294]. Infants as young as six months prefer helpful individuals over

---

[289] Schwartz, Bernard, 'The Tension between Free Speech and a Limiting Principle', *The University of Chicago Law Review*, 53.1 (1986), 143–153

[290] MacCoun, Robert, and Peter Reuter, *Drug War Heresies* (Cambridge Press, 2001)

[291] Pratt, John, and Anna Eriksson, *Contrasts in Punishment* (Abingdon: Routledge, 2013)

[292] Priest, Maura, 'Transgender Children and the Right to Transition: Medical Ethics When Parents Mean Well but Cause Harm', *American Journal of Bioethics*, 19.2 (2019)

[293] Aviv, Rachel, 'The German Experiment That Placed Foster Children with Pedophiles: With the Approval of the Government, a Renowned Sexologist Ran a Dangerous Program. How Could This Happen?', *The New Yorker*, 19 July 2021

[294] Plomin, Robert, John C. DeFries, Valerie S. Knopik, and Jenae M. Neiderhiser, 'Top 10 Replicated Findings from Behavioral Genetics', *Perspectives on Psychological Science*, 11.1 (2016), 3–23

harmful ones[295]. Emotions are universally recognised across separated cultures[296], as is cheating in social exchanges[297]. All six-thousand known human languages use the same grammar structure[298]. Every known society has marriage customs and family units[299]. Infants in all cultures show identical responses to faces at three months old[300].

Humans are essentially good

Normal students became cruel guards in three days during the Stanford Prison experiments[301]. Sixty-five per cent of participants in Milgram's study would shock to death on mild authority[302]. *"Lord of the Flies"* happened for real on 'Ata island in 1965, exactly as in the book[303]. Our brain's reward system predisposes us to substance abuse[304], tribalism,

---

[295] Hamlin, J. Kiley, Karen Wynn, and Paul Bloom, 'Social Evaluation by Preverbal Infants', *Nature*, 450.7169 (2007), 557–559

[296] Ekman, Paul, 'An Argument for Basic Emotions', *Cognition and Emotion*, 6.3–4 (1992)

[297] Cosmides, Leda, and John Tooby, 'Cognitive Adaptations for Social Exchange', in *The Adapted Mind: Evolutionary Psychology and the Generation of Culture*, ed. by Jerome H. Barkow, Leda Cosmides, and John Tooby (Oxford University Press, 1992)

[298] Chomsky, Noam, *Aspects of the Theory of Syntax* (MIT Press, 1965)

[299] Murdock, George Peter, *Social Structure* (Macmillan, 1949)

[300] Johnson, Mark H., Stanislaw Dziurawiec, Hadyn Ellis, and John Morton, 'Newborns' Preferential Tracking of Face-Like Stimuli and Its Subsequent Decline', *Cognition*, 40.1–2 (1991), 1–19

[301] Zimbardo, Philip G., 'On the Ethics of Intervention in Human Psychological Research: With Special Reference to the Stanford Prison Experiment', *Cognition*, 3.1 (1973), 243–256

[302] Milgram, Stanley, 'Behavioral Study of Obedience', *The Journal of Abnormal and Social Psychology*, 67.4 (1963), 371–378

[303] Bregman, Rutger, *Humankind* (Bloomsbury Publishing, 2020)

[304] Volkow, Nora D., Gene-Jack Wang, Joanna S. Fowler, and Dardo Tomasi, 'Addiction Circuitry in the Human Brain', *Annual Review of Pharmacology and Toxicology*, 52 (2012), 321–336

and inter-group violence[305]. Our immediate evolutionary siblings murder[306], as an evolutionary strategy[307], like lying and manipulation[308]. We even murder ourselves[309]. We take *pleasure* in morally indefensible practices such as torture[310], cannibalism[311], beastiality[312], paedophilia[313], genocide[314], and necrophilia[315].

---

[305] Cikara, Mina, Matthew M. Botvinick, and Susan T. Fiske, 'Us versus Them: Social Identity Shapes Neural Responses to Intergroup Competition and Harm', *Psychological Science*, 22.3 (2011), 306–313

[306] Wrangham, Richard W., and Dale Peterson, *Demonic Males* (Houghton Mifflin, 1996)

[307] Gómez, José María, Miguel Verdú, and Adrián González-Megías, 'The Phylogenetic Roots of Human Lethal Violence', *Nature*, 538.7624 (2016)

[308] Byrne, Richard, Andrew Whiten, *Machiavellian Intelligence* (Clarendon Press, 1988)

[309] Van Heeringen, Cornelis, and J. John Mann, 'The Neurobiology of Suicide', *The Lancet Psychiatry*, 1.1 (2014), 63–72

[310] Bandura, Albert, 'Moral Disengagement in the Perpetration of Inhumanities', *Personality and Social Psychology Review*, 3.3 (1999), 193–209

[311] Colard, Thibaut, Yann Delannoy, Amélie Becart, Grégory Tournel, and Vincent Hedouin, 'Cannibalism in Prehistory: An Anthropological Approach', *Journal of Forensic Sciences*, 60.1 (2015), 70–76

[312] Aggrawal, Anil, *Forensic and Medico-Legal Aspects of Sexual Crimes and Unusual Sexual Practices* (CRC Press, 2009)

[313] Schiffer, Boris, and Cécile Vonlaufen, 'Sexual Preference in Pedophiles and Hebephiles: A Neurobiological Approach', *Nature Reviews Neuroscience*, 12.9 (2011)

[314] Decety, Jean, K. J. Michalska, and Katherine D. Kinzler, 'The Contribution of Emotion and Cognition to Moral Sensitivity: A Neurodevelopmental Study', *Cerebral Cortex*, 22.1 (2012), 209–220

[315] Rosman, Jay P., and Phillip J. Resnick, 'Sexual Attraction to Corpses: A Psychiatric Review of Necrophilia', *Bulletin of the American Academy of Psychiatry and the Law*, 17.2 (1989), 153–163

  Note: *Male mallards have also been observed to show this behaviour on occasion.*

Humans have a sexual orientation

No "gay gene" or biological marker has ever been found despite genome-wide studies[316]. Identical twins only match sexual behaviour twenty per cent of the time[317]. No animal populations show "orientation", or any evolutionary mechanism for non-reproductive *"orientation"*[318]. Reproductive success (passing on genes) is measured by fitness and selection for fertility markers, not subjective preference[319].

Human sexuality varies across a spectrum

Every successful mammal species has clear male/female role patterns, and no animal shows a *"spectrum"* of mating behaviour[320]. All human populations show ~97% male-female pairing and every society needs above 2.1 children per couple to continue[321]. Genes which don't copy themselves disappear; non-reproductive behaviour can't be inherited; dead ends don't make next generations, and continuation requires offspring[322].

---

[316] Ganna, A., et al., 'Large-Scale GWAS Reveals Insights into the Genetic Architecture of Same-Sex Sexual Behaviour', *Science*, 365.6456 (2019)

[317] Bailey, J. M., and Pillard, R. C., 'A Genetic Study of Male Sexual Orientation', *Archives of General Psychiatry*, 48.12 (1991), 1089–96

[318] Vasey, P. L., and VanderLaan, D. P., 'Avuncular Tendencies and the Evolution of Male Androphilia in Samoan Fa'afafine', *Archives of Sexual Behavior*, 39 (2010),

[319] Dawkins, Richard, *The Selfish Gene* (Oxford University Press, 1976)

[320] Clutton-Brock, T. H., and Vincent, A. C. J., 'Sexual Selection and the Potential Reproductive Rates of Males and Females', *Nature*, 351.6321 (1991), 58–60

[321] Livi-Bacci, Massimo, *A Concise History of World Population* (Wiley-Blackwell, 2012)

[322] Dawkins, Richard, *The Selfish Gene* (Oxford University Press, 1976)

Humans are more cooperative than competitive

Chimps wage war between groups[323]. All two hundred or more human societies have a history of warfare[324]. Sports exist in every known culture[325].

There is no truth, just perception

Gravity works the same everywhere[326]. Water always boils at 100°C at sea level[327]. Babies die without care in all cultures[328]. Maps got more accurate, not just "different"[329]. 2+2=4 in every culture ever found[330].

Morality subjectively varies across cultures

Every human society in history has prohibited murder and incest despite having no contact with each other[331]. Every known group has had property concepts and protected its young[332]. No successful society has endorsed random killing[333].

---

[323] Wrangham, R. W., and Glowacki, L., 'Intergroup Aggression in Chimpanzees and War in Nomadic Hunter-Gatherers', *Human Nature*, 23.1 (2012)

[324] Keeley, Lawrence H., *War Before Civilization* (Oxford University Press, 1996)

[325] Brown, Donald E., *Human Universals* (McGraw-Hill, 1991)

[326] Einstein, Albert, 'The Field Equations of Gravitation', *Sitzungsberichte der Preussischen Akademie der Wissenschaften zu Berlin*, 1915

[327] Jones, Simons, *Fundamentals of Thermodynamics* (McGraw-Hill, 1980)

[328] Bowlby, John, *Attachment and Loss, Volume I* (Basic Books, 1969)

[329] Harley, J. B., and Woodward, D., *The History of Cartography, Volume 1* (University of Chicago Press, 1987)

[330] Dehaene, Stanislas, *The Number Sense* (Oxford University Press, 1997)

[331] Brown, D. E. (1991). *Human Universals*. McGraw-Hill

[332] Murdock, G. P., 'The Common Denominator of Cultures', in *The Science of Man in the World Crisis*, ed. by Ralph Linton (Columbia University Press, 1945)

[333] Keeley, Lawrence H., *War Before Civilization* (Oxford University Press, 1996)

It Happens In Nature So It Must Be OK

Male lions kill the offspring of rival males[334]. Cuckoos abandon theirs[335]. Masked boobys kill their siblings[336]. Male bed bugs forcibly pierce the abdomen of females to inseminate them[337]. Hyenas and frigatebirds steal food from other animals[338]. Mallards engage in copulation with other dead ducks[339].

We will only be free when we reach equality

Unequal merchants created free trade in the *Venice Republic*[340]. The *USSR* enforced equality and lost all freedom[341]. China enforced equality, but Hong Kong was free with inequality[342]. Singapore has rampant inequality but one of the highest freedom index scores[343].

---

[334] Brook Vinnedge and P. Verrell, 'Variance in Male Mating Success and Female Choice for Persuasive Courtship Displays', *Animal Behaviour*, 56.2 (1998), 517–522

[335] L. Ebensperger et al., 'Multiple Mating Is Linked to Social Setting and Benefits the Males in a Communally Rearing Mammal', *Behavioral Ecology*, 30.3 (2019), 675–683

[336] Regina Vega-Trejo et al., 'The Effects of Familiarity and Mating Experience on Mate Choice in Mosquitofish, *Gambusia holbrooki*', *Behavioral Ecology*, 25.5 (2014), 1205–1211

[337] Rolanda Lange et al., 'Female Fitness Optimum at Intermediate Mating Rates under Traumatic Mating', *PLoS ONE*, 7.8 (2012)

[338] Hodder Education, 'Animal Courtship', *Biological Sciences Review*, 25.3 (2022)

[339] S. O'Sullivan, 'Advocating for Animals Equally from within a Liberal Paradigm', *Environmental Politics*, 16.1 (2007), 1–19

[340] Lane, Frederic C., *Venice: A Maritime Republic* (Johns Hopkins University Press, 1973)

[341] Applebaum, Anne, *Gulag* (Doubleday, 2003)

[342] Vogel, Ezra F., *Deng Xiaoping and the Transformation of China* (Harvard University Press, 2011)

[343] Tan, Kenneth Paul, *Singapore* (National University of Singapore, 2008)

Hierarchy is oppression

Every orchestra, army (3x survival rate), and surgery room (50% fewer deaths) needs a director[344]. The single queen bee colony system evolved a hundred million years ago[345]. Wolf packs alpha structure increases pack survival by eighty per cent[346]. Seven hundred studied chimp groups demonstrate them. All birds, primates, and fish have them. Even *bacteria* organise hierarchically[347].

Lack of education causes evil

Nazi leadership IQ averaged 128; including Mengele, who had two PhDs[348]. Ted Kaczynski, the *"Unabomber"*, got a PhD in mathematics from *Harvard University* at 16[349]. Sophisticated financial crimes increase with education level[350].

An exception exists, which means it disproves the rule

A warm day in winter doesn't mean winter isn't cold[351]. Finding one tall Chinese person doesn't change that Chinese people are, on average,

---

[344] Gawande, Atul, *The Checklist Manifesto* (Metropolitan Books, 2009)

[345] Wilson, Edward O., and Hölldobler, Bert, 'Eusociality: Origin and Consequences', *Proceedings of the National Academy of Sciences*, 102.38 (2005), 13367–71

[346] Mech, L. David, and Boitani, Luigi, *Wolves: Behavior, Ecology, and Conservation* (University of Chicago Press, 2003)

[347] Sapolsky, Robert M., *A Primate's Memoir* (Simon & Schuster, 2001)

[348] Gilbert, Gustave M., *Nuremberg Diary* (Farrar, Straus and Company, 1947) (Based on IQ tests conducted during the Nuremberg trials)

[349] Chase, Alston, *Harvard and the Unabomber* (W.W. Norton & Co. 2000)

[350] Weisburd, David, and Waring, Elin J., *White-Collar Crime and Criminal Careers* (Cambridge University Press, 2001)

[351] Kahneman, Daniel, *Thinking, Fast and Slow* (Farrar, Straus and Giroux, 2011)

shorter than Dutch people[352]. Some people survive skydiving without a parachute[353].

Talking is always better than force

Bullies don't stop just because you talk nicely to them[354]. Police cannot talk offenders into handcuffs[355]. Pearl Harbour was attacked during peace negotiations[356]. The Taliban retook Afghanistan despite twenty years of dialogue[357].

Disparities always prove discrimination

Asians earn fifteen per cent more than whites in the US[358]. Jews have twenty per cent of all Nobel prizes despite being 0.2% of the world's population[359]. The NBA is seventy-five per cent black[360].

What happens in your bedroom is no-one else's business

Unless it's someone's spouse committing murder or adultery; a woman being beaten or raped; a child or pet being imprisoned, neglected, beaten,

---

[352] NCD Risk Factor Collaboration (NCD-RisC), 'A Century of Trends in Adult Human Height', *eLife*, 5 (2016), e13410

[353] West, John B., 'Parachute Descent: Can You Survive Without One?', *BMJ*, 328.7451 (2004), 1459–60

[354] Olweus, Dan, *Bullying at School* (Blackwell, 1993)

[355] Bittner, Egon, *The Functions of the Police in Modern Society* (National Institute of Mental Health, 1970)

[356] Wohlstetter, Roberta, *Pearl Harbor* (Stanford Press, 1962)

[357] Coll, Steve, *Ghost Wars*, (Penguin Books, 2004)

[358] U.S. Bureau of Labor Statistics, *Labor Force Characteristics by Race and Ethnicity, 2020*

[359] Feldman, Burton, *The Nobel Prize* (Arcade Publishing, 2000).

[360] Lapchick, Richard, *The 2021 NBA Racial and Gender Report Card* (The Institute for Diversity and Ethics in Sport, 2021)

or raped; storage of toxic chemicals, or child pornography.

OK in private and if you aren't harming anyone else

Unless it's crime, which always requires privacy; or suicide; or self-harm. Japan's "private" decision not to marry caused a population crisis[361]. Iceland's private banking system crashed the entire economy in 2008[362].

Open-mindedness is a virtue

Neville Chamberlain was open to Hitler's promises[363]. Scientists rejected Einstein because they were "too open" to old theories[364]. Rome fell because it was "open" to Germanic tribes[365].

The right side of history

The geocentric universe was 'settled science' for 1500 years[366]. Eugenics was 'scientific consensus' in the 1920s[367]. Lobotomies won a Nobel Prize in 1949[368]. History isn't a moral arc, it is a graveyard of 'inevitable' and 'permanent' systems that all failed[369]: Aztecs thought their gods

---

[361] Kawaguchi, Daiji, and Lee, Sang-Hyop, 'Marriage and Fertility in Post-Industrial Societies: Japan and South Korea in Comparison', *Review of Economics of the Household*, 15.2 (2017), 297–322

[362] Wade, Robert, and Sigurgeirsdottir, Silla, 'Lessons from Iceland', *New Left Review*, 65 (2010), 5–29

[363] Charmley, John, *Chamberlain and the Lost Peace* (Ivan R. Dee, 1989)

[364] Pais, Abraham, *Subtle Is the Lord* (Oxford University Press, 1982)

[365] Heather, Peter, *The Fall of the Roman Empire* (Oxford University Press, 2006)

[366] Lindberg, David C., *The Beginnings of Western Science* (University of Chicago, 1992)

[367] Kevles, Daniel J., *In the Name of Eugenics* (Harvard University Press, 1985)

[368] El-Hai, Jack, *The Lobotomist* (Wiley, 2005)

[369] Hobsbawm, Eric, *The Age of Extremes* (Pantheon Books, 1994)

guaranteed their rule[370]; the Roman Empire was *"eternal"*[371]; the Soviet Union was *"scientific socialism"*[372]; Nazi Germany was the *"thousand-year Reich"*[373].

All cultures are equally valuable

Life expectancy varied 2-3x between cultures pre-contact[374]. Agricultural efficiency varied 10x between systems[375]. Four societies invented writing (Mesopotamia, Egypt, China, Maya)[376]; only Western Europe developed calculus[377]. 51% of all inventions were created in England, and few have ever been produced in Africa[378].

Revolutions produce progress

Liberty became terror in the *French Revolution* and killed more than the monarchy[379]. The Chinese *Cultural Revolution* destroyed three thousand years of art[380]. Cambodia's "Year Zero" killed twenty-five per cent of its population trying by trying the "new society"[381]. Literacy went up

---

[370] Townsend, Camilla, *The Aztecs: The Lost Civilization* (Thames & Hudson, 2009)

[371] Ward-Perkins, Bryan, *The Fall of Rome and the End of Civilization* (Oxford Press, 2006)

[372] Kotkin, Stephen, *Stalin: Volume I*, (Penguin Press, 2014)

[373] Kershaw, Ian, *The Nazi Dictatorship* (Oxford University Press, 2000)

[374] Steckel, Richard H., Rose, Jerome C., *The Backbone of History* (Cambridge Press, 2002)

[375] Diamond, Jared, *Guns, Germs, and Steel* (W.W. Norton, 1997)

[376] Houston, Stephen D., *The First Writing* (Cambridge University Press, 2004)

[377] Boyer, Carl B., and Merzbach, Uta C., *A History of Mathematics* (Wiley, 2011)

[378] Mokyr, Joel, *The Lever of Riches* (Oxford University Press, 1990)

[379] Schama, Simon, *Citizens* (Random House, 1989)

[380] MacFarquhar, Roderick, Schoenhals, Michael, *Mao's Last Revolution* (Harvard University Press, 2006)

[381] Kiernan, Ben, *The Pol Pot Regime* (Yale University Press, 2002)

in Castro's Cuba, but poverty got worse[382]. At least fifteen (sixty per cent) of the twenty-five revolutions in the last two centuries have led to authoritarian or tyrannical regimes[383].

Satiating an appetite controls it

Rome's bread & circuses led to more demands, not less[384]. Sugar cravings develop within six weeks and increase with consumption[385]. Gambling addiction worsens with "controlled" betting[386]. *What you feed and attend grows with reinforcement; what you starve and neglect, dies*[387].

Legislation decreases usage and black markets

The Netherlands' coffee shop model still relies on an illegal supply chain[388]. California's illegal cannabis trade dwarfed its legal market *after* legislation[389]. Canada's euthanasia program (MAiD) grew from 1,018 cases in 2016 to 13,241 in 2022, and expanded from terminal

---

[382] Mesa-Lago, Carmelo, *Market, Socialist, and Mixed Economies* (Johns Hopkins Press, 2000)

[383] Dunn, John, *Modern Revolutions* (Cambridge University Press, 1989)

[384] Juvenal. *The Satires of Juvenal and Persius* (Harvard University Press, 1999).

[385] Avena, Nicole M., Rada, Pedro, and Hoebel, Bartley G., 'Evidence for Sugar Addiction: Behavioral and Neurochemical Effects of Intermittent, Excessive Sugar Intake', *Neuroscience & Biobehavioral Reviews*, 32.1 (2008), 20–39

[386] Shaffer, Howard J., and Korn, David A., 'Gambling and Related Mental Disorders: A Public Health Analysis', *Annual Review of Public Health*, 23 (2002)

[387] James, William, *The Principles of Psychology* (Henry Holt and Company, 1890)

[388] Bewley-Taylor, David R., and Jelsma, Martin, *The Limits of Tolerance* (Brookings Institution Press, 2012)

[389] California Department of Public Health. *Annual Report: Medical Marijuana Identification Card Program.* (California Department of Public Health, 2021)

Crime is caused by poverty

Singapore went from poor to rich by keeping its crime rate the lowest in the developed world[391]. Switzerland was historically poor in the 19th century but had low crime[392]. US crime rates rose during the economic boom of the 1960s[393].

Safety creates strength and resilience

Trees grown in bio-domes snap in storms, whereas bent trees survive[394]. Bone density decreases one per cent per month in zero gravity[395]. Immune systems need early exposure to develop[396]. *Calm seas do not good sailors make.* True strength and resilience arise from adapting to challenges, stressors, and adversity, As muscles grow through resistance, and immune systems develop through exposure to pathogens, resilience emerges from successfully navigating difficulties rather than avoiding them.

---

[390] Government of Canada, Health Canada, *Third Annual Report on Medical Assistance in Dying in Canada, 2022* (Health Canada, 2023)

[391] Barr, Michael D., Skrbiš, Zlatko, *Constructing Singapore* (NIAS Press, 2008)

[392] Head, Randolph, *Early Modern Democracy in the Grisons* (Cambridge Press, 1995)

[393] Blumstein, Alfred, and Wallman, Joel, *The Crime Drop in America* (Cambridge University Press, 2000)

[394] Rees, William E., 'Ecological Footprints and Appropriated Carrying Capacity: What Urban Economics Leaves Out', *Environment and Urbanization*, 4.2 (1992), 121–30

[395] Smith, Scott M., et al., 'Benefits for Bone from Resistance Exercise and Nutrition in Long-Duration Spaceflight: Evidence from Biochemistry and Densitometry', *Journal of Bone and Mineral Research*, 27.9 (2012), 1896–1906

[396] Rook, Graham A., et al., 'Microbial "Old Friends", Immunoregulation, and Socioeconomic Status', *Clinical & Experimental Immunology*, 139.1 (2003), 1–9

Hedonistic pleasure satisfies

Dopamine receptors downregulate with overuse, and increased novelty is required for the same pleasure[397]. Drug tolerance is universal, and sugar tolerance develops in weeks[398]. Addiction cycles prove returns diminish over time[399].

Intent matters more than outcome

The Smallpox vaccine saved millions, but killed a percentage of people it was given to[400]. Sparrow-killing in China caused a famine[401]. *Thalidomide* was intended to help pregnant mothers but mutilated ten thousand babies[402].

Governing by theory is better than practical experience

Rome's practical roads still stand, as opposed to Greece's theoretical "perfect" designs[403]. The *French Revolution* produced a murderous disaster[404]. Mao's *"Great Leap"* theory killed thirty million people[405].

---

[397] Volkow, Nora D., and Fowler, Joanna S., 'Addiction: A Disease of Compulsion and Drive—Involvement of the Orbitofrontal Cortex', *Cerebral Cortex*, 10.3 (2000), 318–25

[398] Koob, George F., and Le Moal, Michel, 'Drug Addiction, Dysregulation of Reward, and Allostasis', *Neuropsychopharmacology*, 24.2 (2001), 97–129

[399] Hyman, Steven E., Malenka, Robert C., and Nestler, Eric J., 'Neural Mechanisms of Addiction: The Role of Reward-Related Learning and Memory', *Annual Review of Neuroscience*, 29 (2006), 565–92

[400] Fenner, Frank, et al., *Smallpox and Its Eradication* (World Health Organization, 1988)

[401] Shapiro, Judith, *Mao's War Against Nature* (Cambridge University Press, 2001)

[402] Stephens, Trent D., and Brynner, Rock, *Dark Remedy* (Basic Books, 2001)

[403] Laurence, Ray, *The Roads of Roman Italy* (Routledge, 1999)

[404] Schama, Simon, *Citizens* (Random House, 1989)

[405] Dikötter, Frank, *Mao's Great Famine* (Walker & Company, 2010)

Religion causes most wars

Only seven per cent of wars have been primarily religious, with most being tribal warfare over resources or territory[406]. World War I, World War II, Vietnam, Iraq, and the *Cold War* were based on secular ideologies[407].

Rehabilitation is more effective than punishment

Low IQ people respond to incentives rather than ideas[408]. Two per cent of criminals still re-offend despite the best conditions in Norway's prison system[409]. Psychopathy has no cure[410]. Crime dropped seventy per cent after Singapore implemented harsh punishments[411].

The state can run things as efficiently as private companies

Wait times at the US *Dept of Veteran Affairs* are twenty-two per cent longer than private clinics[412]. Germany's hybrid health system has a wait time of three weeks, whereas the UK *National Health Service* has a waiting list of 7.4 million[413]. Indian railways improved by three hundred per

---

[406] Parker, Geoffrey, *The Cambridge History of Warfare* (Cambridge Press, 2005)

[407] Taylor, Alan J. P., *The Origins of the Second World War* (Hamish Hamilton, 1961)

[408] Herrnstein, Richard J., and Murray, Charles, *The Bell Curve*, (Free Press, 1994)

[409] Pratt, Travis C., 'The Effects of Norway's Correctional Policies on Recidivism: Evidence from Halden Prison', *Journal of Scandinavian Studies in Criminology and Crime Prevention*, 9.1 (2008), 21–34

[410] Hare, Robert D., *Without Conscience*, (Guilford Press, 1999)

[411] Quah, Jon S. T., *Public Administration Singapore-Style* (Emerald Group, 2007)

[412] *Access and Quality in VA Healthcare, 2020* (U.S. Department of Veterans Affairs, 2020)

[413] OECD Health Statistics, *Health at a Glance: Europe, 2023*

cent after private competition was allowed[414]. The USSR took ten times more labour to make a car than Ford[415].

Moral progress comes with technological progress

IBM machines made the Holocaust more efficient[416]. Nuclear physics produced the atomic bomb[417]. Social media increased youth suicide by seventy per cent[418]. More people were killed in the twentieth century than the previous twenty combined[419].

Population growth always leads to resource shortages

Food production has increased by three hundred per cent, as the population has doubled between 1961 and 2020[420]. Japan's population decline led to economic stagnation[421]. The Netherlands is the most dense European country, but has the highest food exports[422]. *Note: this doesn't apply to welfare.*

---

[414] Kumar, Manoj, and Singh, Suresh K., 'Privatization of Indian Railways: Analyzing the Challenges and Opportunities', *Journal of Transport Economics and Policy*, 45.3 (2020)

[415] Nove, Alec, *An Economic History of the USSR* (Penguin Books, 1969)

[416] Black, Edwin, *IBM and the Holocaust* (Crown Publishers, 2001)

[417] Rhodes, Richard, *The Making of the Atomic Bomb* (Simon & Schuster, 1986)

[418] Twenge, Jean M., Joiner, Thomas E., Rogers, Megan L., and Martin, Gabrielle N., 'Increases in Depressive Symptoms, Suicide-Related Outcomes, and Suicide Rates among U.S. Adolescents After 2010 and Links to Increased New Media Screen Time', *Clinical Psychological Science*, 6.1 (2018), 3–17

[419] White, Matthew, *Atrocities: The 100 Deadliest Episodes in Human History* (Norton, 2011)

[420] FAO of the United Nations (FAO), *FAOSTAT Statistical Database, 2021*

[421] Nishimura, Kiyohiko G., Takáts, Előd, 'Population Aging, Macroeconomic Trends, and Monetary Policy', *Bank for International Settlements Working Papers* (2012)

[422] CBS (Statistics Neth.), *Agricultural Exports Top the EU Rankings, 2021* (CBS, 2021)

Governments can engineer economies through metrics

Soviet grain quotas led to false reporting and actual shortages; the USSR met all timber quotas but produced no nails[423]. Hurricane damage and China's empty cities count as "growth"[424]. Venezuelan price controls under Chavez led to ninety per cent goods shortages[425].

Stigmas and taboos are negative and harmful

Incest taboo prevents genetic disorders, such as *Habsburg jaw*[426]. Orthodox Jewish dietary laws prevented food poisoning before refrigeration was invented[427]. Japanese shame about debt produces four per cent credit card use, whereas the US has eighty per cent[428].

The welfare state is sustainable

Welfare was designed around a onetime demographic anomaly (the *Baby Boom*), and requires endless pyramidal growth of each generation to be larger and richer than the last[429]. *Baby Boomers* were forty per cent of the population, *Gen Z* is just nineteen per cent[430]. Life expectancy has

---

[423] Nove, Alec, *An Economic History of the USSR* (Penguin Books, 1992)

[424] Krugman, Paul, 'The Myth of Asia's Miracle', *Foreign Affairs*, 73.6 (1994)

[425] Hausmann, Ricardo, Rodriguez, Francisco, *Venezuela Before Chávez* (Penn State University Press, 2014)

[426] Alvarez, Gonzalo, et al., 'The Role of Inbreeding in the Extinction of a European Royal Dynasty', *PLoS One*, 4.4 (2009)

[427] Soler, Josep, 'The Semiotics of Food in the Bible', *Food and Foodways*, 1.1 (1979)

[428] Doi, Takeo, *The Anatomy of Dependence* (Kodansha International, 1973)

[429] Kotlikoff, Laurence J., and Burns, Scott, *The Coming Generational Storm: What You Need to Know about America's Economic Future* (MIT Press, 2004)

[430] Fry, Richard, *The Baby Boom Cohort in the United States* (Pew Research Center, 2020)

jumped fifteen years since 1950[431]. Birth rates have plummeted from 3.6 to 1.6[432]. Welfare costs are rising faster than any possible GDP growth[433]. The UK *National Insurance* fund exhausts in 2032[434], and the US *Social Security* trust fund collapses in 2034[435].

Minority groups suffer worse outcomes

The rural poor live longer than the urban wealthy in most regions of the world[436]. Nigerian immigrants outlive white Americans and have the highest education rate[437]. Japanese-Americans have the longest US lifespan[438]. Indians have a median income sixty per cent above the US average[439].

---

[431] UNDESA, Population Division, *World Population Prospects 2019*

[432] World Bank, *World Development Indicators, 2021* (World Bank, 2021)

[433] OECD, *Health at a Glance 2019: OECD Indicators* (OECD Publishing, 2019)

[434] OBR, *Fiscal Risks and Sustainability Report 2023* (HM Treasury, 2023)

[435] Board of Trustees, Federal Old-Age and Survivors Insurance and Federal Disability Insurance Trust Funds, *The 2023 Annual Report of the Board of Trustees of the Federal Old-Age and Survivors Insurance and Federal Disability Insurance Trust Funds* (U.S. Government Publishing Office, 2023)

[436] Murray, Christopher J. L., et al., 'Eight Americas: Investigating Mortality Disparities Across Races, Counties, and Race-County Combinations in the United States', *PLOS Medicine*, 3.9 (2006)

[437] Hamilton, Tod G., 'The Healthy Immigrant Effect: Inverted Trajectories in Health Status Among African Immigrants in the United States', *Demography*, 51.4 (2014)

[438] Hastings, Katherine G., et al., 'Leading Causes of Death Among Asian American Subgroups', *American Journal of Public Health*, 105.4 (2015)

[439] Pew Research Center, *Key Facts About Asian Americans* (Pew Research Center, 2017)

Compassion solves social problems

Food aid crashed local farming in Ethiopia[440]. Mental care for the homeless without enforcement killed two thousand people in New York, and LA's death rate of forty per cent was ten times higher than the intervention rate.[441] Dutch cities have rebelled against social tolerance ("gedoogbeleid") policies and drug tourism[442].

Diversity training reduces prejudice

Studies at *Harvard* concluded mandatory training increased bias by six per cent[443]. Desegregated units in the US Army performed better with no training[444]. Bias "training" was correlated with fewer minorities in management across eight hundred American firms[445].

---

[440] De Waal, Alex, *Famine Crimes* (Indiana University Press, 1997)

[441] Torrey, E. Fuller, *American Psychosis* (Oxford University Press, 2014)

[442] Dutch Ministry of Justice and Security. *Evaluation of the Coffeeshop Policy in the Netherlands*. 2018

[443] Dobbin, Frank, and Kalev, Alexandra, 'Why Diversity Programs Fail', *Harvard Business Review*, 94.7-8 (2016)

[444] Moskos, Charles C., Jr., *The American Enlisted Man* (Russell Sage Foundation, 1970)

[445] Kalev, Alexandra, Dobbin, Frank, and Kelly, Erin, 'Best Practices or Best Guesses? Assessing the Efficacy of Corporate Affirmative Action and Diversity Policies', *American Sociological Review*, 71.4 (2006), 589-617

The Testimonial of Criminals

Throughout this book, you'll notice certain social "scholars" having their names prefixed with some rather unpleasant descriptors. This is, of course, deliberate; these facts are entirely ignored by the academic community as irrelevant because of the so-called "knowledge" they have "contributed" to their fields.

Most of what comes out of social science is academic fraud for the purposes of *"credentialism"*[446], but in many cases, the individuals producing this work went far beyond mere sophistry and were engaged in questionable campaigns or morally depraved criminality.

In *"Beyond Good and Evil,"* Nietzsche posits philosophy is more akin to the arts; rarely an objective discipline, nor a subject which is detached from the author's personal inclinations. Much can be inferred about the private man from what the public persona is most interested in; and what they are arguing for or against.

> *It has gradually become clear to me what every great philosophy up till now has consisted of—namely, the confession of its originator, and a species of involuntary and unconscious autobiography; and moreover that the moral (or immoral) purpose in every philosophy has constituted the true vital germ out of which the entire plant has always grown.*[447]

---

[446] Sokal, Alan, and Bricmont, Jean, *Fashionable Nonsense* (Picador, 1999)

[447] Nietzsche, Friedrich, *Beyond Good and Evil*, (Vintage, 1989).

THE TESTIMONIAL OF CRIMINALS

The list of moral disgrace goes on and on, endlessly, but as a starting point:

- *Jean-Jacques Rousseau* threw his own children into foundling homes (where mortality rates exceeded eighty per cent) while writing about ideal education and child rearing[448];
- *Karl Marx* was a racist, antisemitic adulterer described by his peers as "intolerably dirty"[449], expelled from Brussels, Cologne, and Paris, and obsessed with Satanic themes[450];
- *Friedrich Engels* lived off factory profits and concealed evidence of child labour in his family's facilities[451];
- *Freidrich Nietzsche*'s eventual insanity and death were caused by syphilis caught in a homosexual brothel in Genoa - although this is debated[452];
- *Wilhelm von Gloeden* publicly idealised photography of naked young boys in Sicily[453];
- *Edward Carpenter* regularly pursued relationships with working-class teenage boys[454];
- *Otto Gross* manipulated patients into sexual relationships, abandoned children he fathered, and ran a drug ring in Vienna exploiting addicted patients while posing as their therapist[455];
- *Sigmund Freud* was preoccupied with incestuous child sexuality and saw himself as a Messianic figure[456];

---

[448] Johnson, Paul, *Intellectuals* (Harper Perennial, 2007)

[449] *Ibid.*

[450] Kengor, Paul, *The Devil and Karl Marx* (TAN Books, 2020)

[451] *The Condition of the Working Class in England* (Swan Sonnenschein, 1892).

[452] Lively, Scott, and Abrams, Kevin, *The Pink Swastika* (Founders, 1995)

[453] Von Gloeden, Wilhelm, *Taormina* (Twin Palms Publishers, 1997)

[454] Carpenter, Edward, *The Intermediate Sex* (George Allen & Unwin, 1908)

[455] Jung, Carl G., *Memories, Dreams, Reflections* (Pantheon Books, 1961)

[456] Webster, Richard, *Why Freud Was Wrong* (HarperCollins, 1995)

- *Magnus Hirschfeld* was a cross-dressing communist (aka *"Tante Magnesia"*) who categorised paedophilia and operated a clinic which castrated boys[457];
- *Georg Lukács* organised lectures and literature "to *"instruct"* children about free love, about the nature of sexual intercourse, about the archaic nature of the bourgeois family codes, about the outdatedness of monogamy"[458];
- *John Watson* was thrown out of Johns Hopkins for having an affair with a student and *"unorthodox sex research"*[459];
- *Marie Bonaparte* performed unauthorised genital surgeries on female patients[460];
- *Wilhelm Stekel* fabricated most of his case studies and patient details[461];
- *Wilhelm Fliess* performed unnecessary nasal surgeries on patients[462];
- *André Breton* and several other Surrealists published defences of child sexuality and adult access to children[463];
- *Martin Heidegger* was an enthusiastic member of the Nazi Party[464];
- *Ernst Bloch* abandoned his first wife and young child in dangerous circumstances while fleeing Germany[465];
- *Edmund Wilson* maintained predatory relationships with much younger women seeking literary mentorship[466];

---

[457] Dose, Ralf, *Magnus Hirschfeld* (Monthly Review Press, 2014)

[458] Zitta, Victor, *Georg Lukács' Marxism* (Springer Science & Business Media, 1964)

[459] Harris, Ben, 'Letting Go of Little Albert: Disciplinary Memory, History, and the Uses of Myth', *Journal of the History of the Behavioral Sciences*, 47.1 (2011), 1–17

[460] Roudinesco, Elisabeth, *Jacques Lacan & Co* (University of Chicago Press, 1990)

[461] Sulloway, Frank J., *Freud, Biologist of the Mind* (Harvard University Press, 1992)

[462] Gay, Peter, *Freud* (W.W. Norton & Company, 1988)

[463] Dean, Carolyn J., *The Frail Social Body* (University of California Press, 2000)

[464] Farías, Victor, *Heidegger and Nazism* (Temple University Press, 1989)

[465] Geoghegan, Vincent, *Ernst Bloch* (Routledge, 1996)

[466] Dabney, Lewis, *Edmund Wilson* (Farrar, Straus and Giroux, 2005)

- *Mao Zedong* was a paedophile obsessed with underage girls[467];
- *Bruno Bettelheim* hit and mock disabled children to terrorise them psychologically[468];
- *Paul de Man* wrote antisemitic articles for Belgian newspapers, calling for the deportation of Jews[469];
- *Doris Lessing* abandoned her two young children in Rhodesia to pursue her political and literary career[470];
- *Simone de Beauvoir* collaborated with the Nazis, publicly defended the decriminalisation of paedophilia, exploited her profession as a teacher to seduce female pupils, and lost her teaching licence in 1943 for molesting a seventeen-year-old in 1939[471][472];
- *Sidney and Beatrice Webb* covered up Stalin's famines and wrote propaganda defending the Soviet show trials[473];
- *Paul Robeson* consistently defended Stalinist policies, denied documented atrocities, and defended the execution of Jewish intellectuals[474];
- *Alfred Kinsey* was a bisexual adulterer who circumcised himself, encouraged his research fellows to have orgies, and based his research on a serial Nazi paedophile who described crying infants' "orgasms"[475];
- *Wilhelm Reich* was criminally prosecuted for defrauding patients

---

[467] Zhisui, Li, *The Private Life of Chairman Mao* (Random House, 1996)

[468] Cohen, David, *Bruno Bettelheim* (Basic Books, 1997)

[469] Barish, Evelyn, *The Double Life of Paul de Man* (W.W. Norton & Company, 1991)

[470] Klein, Carole, *Doris Lessing* (Carroll & Graf, 2000)

[471] Johnson, Paul, *Intellectuals* (Harper Perennial, 2007)

[472] Valls-Carol, Rosa, Puigvert, Lidia, Vidu, Ana, and López de Aguileta, Garazi. 'Presenting Beauvoir as a Feminist: Neglecting Her Defense and Accusations of Pedophilia', *Social and Education History*, 11.2 (2022), 106–128

[473] Malia, Martin. 'The Webbs and the Soviet Famine', *The New Criterion*, 10.3 (1991)

[474] Duberman, Martin, *Paul Robeson* (The New Press, 1989)

[475] Jones, James H., *Alfred C. Kinsey* (W. W. Norton & Co., 1997)

with fake cancer cures[476];
- *Franz Fanon* authorised experimental electroshock on Arab patients without consent[477];
- *Richard Hofstadter* physically abused his first wife[478];
- *Eric Fromm* exploited multiple female clients sexually[479];
- *Lucien Goldman* helped suppress evidence of antisemitic purges in Romania[480];
- *W.E.B. Du Bois* wrote extensive defences of Mao's *Great Leap Forward* despite mounting evidence of mass casualties[481];
- *Gregory Bateson* deliberately traumatised schizophrenic patients[482];
- *Che Guevara* was a racist mass murderer who enjoyed torturing animals and sent homosexuals to concentration camps in Guanahacabibes[483];
- *Donald Winnicott* subjected child patients to extreme isolation experiments[484];
- *Ernest Mandel* used party funds for personal luxuries[485];
- *Herbert Marcuse* worked for the forerunner of the CIA, had multiple affairs with graduate students while married, and was denounced

---

[476] United States Court of Appeals for the First Circuit. 'Wilhelm Reich et al., Defendants, Appellants, v. United States of America, Appellee', *Federal Reporter, Second Series*, 239 F.2d (1957), 134–141

[477] Cherki, Alice, *Frantz Fanon* (Cornell University Press, 2006)

[478] Brown, David S., *Richard Hofstadter* (U. of Chicago, 2006)

[479] Funk, Rainer, *Erich Fromm* (Continuum, 2000)

[480] Goldman, Lucien, *Human Sciences and Philosophy*, (Brill, 2018)

[481] Du Bois, W. E. B., 'The People's Republic of China: A Symposium', *The American Monthly* (1959)

[482] Weinstein, Deborah, *The Pathological Family: Postwar America and the Rise of Family Therapy* (Cornell University Press, 2013)

[483] HuffPost, 'Che Guevara: The Man Behind the Myth', *Huffington Post*, 9 Oct 2017

[484] Caldwell, Lesley, and Robinson, Helen T., eds., *The Collected Works of D. W. Winnicott: Volume 8, 1967–1968* (Oxford University Press, 2016)

[485] Fletcher, Ian, ed., *Ernest Mandel* (Pluto Press, 2002)

in 1969 by Pope Paul VI *"for promoting the "disgusting and unbridled" manifestations of eroticism and the "animal, barbarous and subhuman degradations"*[486];

- *Ernest Borneman* wrote extensive defences of child sexuality and adult access while teaching, and had his research seized by police[487];
- *Max Horkheimer* and *Theodor Adorno* were extremely controlling and psychologically abusive to their research assistants and students[488];
- *R.D. Laing* injured patients with experimental "regression therapy"[489];
- *Felix Guattari* covered up the killing of patients with dangerous experimental treatments[490];
- *Karl Menninger* allegedly covered up patient abuse at his clinic[491];
- *John Money* was a bisexual paedophile who forced children to perform sex acts in front of his camera[492];
- *Michel Foucault paid cash* to sodomise boys in Tunis graveyards[493], caught AIDS from frequenting bathhouses, and gave his last words in praise of paedophilia[494];
- *Betty Friedan* publicly acknowledged falsely accusing her husband of domestic abuse[495];
- *Daniel Cohn-Bendit* wrote about sexual encounters with kindergarten

---

[486] 'Refusing Marcuse: 50 Years After One-Dimensional Man', *Dissent Magazine* (2019)

[487] Sonenschein, David, 'On Having One's Research Seized', *The Journal of Sex Research*, 23.3 (1987), 408–414

[488] Wiggershaus, Rolf, *The Frankfurt School* (MIT Press, 1994)

[489] Mullan, Bob, *Mad to Be Normal* (Free Asso. Books, 1995)

[490] Guattari, Félix, *Molecular Revolution* (Penguin Books, 1984)

[491] Friedman, Lawrence J., *Manninger* (Alfred A. Knopf, 1990)

[492] Colapinto, John, *As Nature Made Him* (HarperCollins, 2000)

[493] Campbell, Matthew, 'French Philosopher Michel Foucault "Abused Boys in Tunisia"', *The Sunday Times*, 28 March 2021

[494] Johnson, Daniel, 'Michel Foucault: The Prophet of Pederasty', *The Critic*, April 2021

[495] 'Betty Friedan, Feminist Icon, Dies at 85', *The New York Times*, 7 February 2006

children[496];
- *Guy Hocquenghem* appeared on French television arguing for abolishing the age of consent[497];
- *Shulamith Firestone* argued post-revolution adult-child relations would be acceptable[498];
- *Jules Masserman* sexually assaulted patients under drug-induced states[499];
- *Salvador Minuchin* withheld food from anorexia patients[500];
- *Howard Zinn* was a closet communist who plagiarised Hans Koning's work and believed the USSR merely gave socialism a *"bad name"*[501];
- *René Schérer* published defenses of paedophilia[502];
- *David Thorstad* campaigned against age of consent laws[503];
- *Jacques Derrida, Jean-François Lyotard,* and *Jean-Paul Sartre* defended paedophilia in public and vehemently opposed an age of sexual consent for children[504];
- *Kate Millett* suffered bipolar disorder and schizophrenia, was committed to a mental asylum twice [505], was described by her own sister as a psychopath, and subjected family to *"extreme psychological abuse and manipulation"*[506];

---

[496] Connolly, Kate, 'Sixties Hero Revealed as Kindergarten Sex Author', *The Guardian*, 27 January 2001

[497] Hocquenghem, Guy, *The Screwball Ass* (Semiotext(e), 1978)

[498] Firestone, Shulamith, *The Dialectic of Sex* (William Morrow, 1970)

[499] 'Trust Betrayed', *Chicago Tribune*, 27 September 1992

[500] Minuchin, Salvador, Fishman, Howard C., *Family Therapy Techniques* (Harvard University Press, 2004)

[501] Grabar, Mary, *Debunking Howard Zinn* (Regnery History, 2019)

[502] Schérer, René, *L'Amour interdit* (Éditions Galilée, 1980)

[503] Wald, Alan, *The Early Homosexual Rights Movement, Against the Current*, 8.3 (1992)

[504] *French Parliament*, 'Petition Against the Age of Consent Law', *Le Monde* (1977)

[505] Millett, Kate, *The Loony Bin Trip* (Simon & Schuster, 1990)

[506] Chesler, Phyllis, *Politically Incorrect Feminist* (St. Martin's Press, 2018)

THE TESTIMONIAL OF CRIMINALS

- *Allen Ginsberg* repeatedly defended NAMBLA and promoted adult-child sexual relationships[507];
- *Dennis Altman* defended *"man-boy"* relationships[508];
- *Angela Davis* was a antisemitic communist who encouraged Jim Jones, denounced Aleksandr Solzhenitsyn and other USSR dissidents as "Zionist fascists", and was awarded the *International Lenin Peace Prize* by East Germany in 1979[509];
- *Roger Moody* explicitly advocated for adult-child relations[510];
- *Pat Califia* wrote extensive defences of child-adult sex[511];
- *Pier Paolo Pasolini* wrote essays defending child sex tourism[512];
- *Marshall Sahlins* suppressed evidence of violent practices in his Pacific fieldwork[513];
- *Stephen Jay Gould* manipulated data to support his political views[514];
- *Louis Althusser* strangled his wife Hélène to death in their École Normale Supérieure apartment and avoided prison through an insanity defence[515];
- *Gayle Rubin* argued extensively against age of consent laws and wrote defences of child-adult sex (aka child rape)[516];
- *Gore Vidal* openly defended Roman Polanski, wrote essays promoting relationships between adult men and underage boys and admitted

---

[507] Beatdom. 'Allen Ginsberg and NAMBLA', *Beatdom*, 21 February 2011

[508] Altman, Dennis, *The Homosexualization of America* (St. Martin's Press, 1982)

[509] Britannica, 'Angela Davis', *Britannica* (n.d.)

[510] Moody, Roger, *Indecent Assault* (Pluto Press, 1980)

[511] Califia, Pat, *Public Sex* (Cleis Press, 1994)

[512] Schwarz, Bart, *Pasolini Requiem* (Pantheon Books, 1992)

[513] Obeyesekere, Gananath, *The Apotheosis of Captain Cook* (Princeton Press, 1992)

[514] Gould, Stephen Jay, *The Mismeasure of Man* (W. W. Norton, 1981)

[515] Althusser, Louis, *The Future Lasts Forever: A Memoir* (The New Press, 1993)

[516] Rubin, Gayle, 'Thinking Sex: Notes for a Radical Theory of the Politics of Sexuality', in *Pleasure and Danger: Exploring Female Sexuality*, ed. by Carole Vance (Routledge, 1984), pp. 267–319

to paedophilia in Thailand and the Philippines[517].
- *Maurice Godelier* had an unhealthy interest in incest[518];
- *Noam Chomsky* denied the existence of the *Alic* concentration camp[519], and advocated for the forced isolation of mRNA *"refuseniks"* by the state, without food[520];

This list could continue for many more pages.

Four individuals particularly stand out because of the staggering nature of their depravity. All involved in the same pseudo-discipline (so-called *"sexology"*), and revered with inexplicable heroic gravitas within the social sciences.

All four were undoubtedly paedophiles who were never criminally prosecuted for the horrific things they did under the premise of academic research.

Magnus Hirschfield

Known as the *"Einstein of Sex"*[521], Hirschfeld was a homosexual, cross-dressing, eugenics-obsessed doctor in Weimar Berlin who lived in a "throuple" with his male lover and a young medical student[522], spending his early life campaigning extensively for the decriminalisation of sodomy and abortion[523]. In 1910, he invented the term *"transvestite"*

---

[517] Vidal, Gore, *The Second American Revolution and Other Essays* (Random House, 1981)

[518] Godelier, Maurice, *Forbidden Fruit* (Polity Press, 2021)

[519] Haaretz. 'The West's Leftist Male Intellectuals Who Traffic in Genocide Denial', *Haaretz*, 24 November 2017

[520] The Independent. 'Noam Chomsky Calls for Unvaccinated to Be Isolated from Society', *The Independent*, 20 October 2022

[521] Von Praunheim, Rosa (dir.), *The Einstein of Sex – Life and Work of Dr. M. Hirschfeld* [Film] (Rosa von Praunheim Filmproduktion, 1999)

[522] Mancini, Elena, *Magnus Hirschfeld and the Quest for Sexual Freedom* (Palgrave Macmillan, 2010)

[523] Bullough, Vern L., *Before Stonewall* (Harrington Park Press, 1991)

("*Geschlechtsverirrungen*")[524], and pioneered the use of questionnaires for research into sexual behaviour.

In 1919 he opened the *Institut für Sexualwissenschaft* with psychotherapist Arthur Kronfeld and dermatologist Friedrich Wertheim[525], which housed a library of twenty thousand depravities viewable as the *Museum of Sex*[526], infamously routed by university students from the *National Socialist Student League* who conducted the iconic book-burning incident of 1933[527]. In 1934, he had fled to Nice and wrote his book *"Rassismus (Racism)"*, which provided the modern-day framework of science being cited as the overall cause of racism[528].

His private clinic employed forty doctors who *"conducted around 18,000 consultations for 3,500 people in its first year"*[529][530] and invented the gruesome procedure of "sex change" (genital transplantation; castration, penectomy and vaginoplasty, or *Genitalumwandlung*). Almost all the "patients" were severely mentally ill, and many of them were minors[531].

At least one surgeon, Erwin Gohrbandt, joined the *Luftwaffe* in

---

[524] Hirschfeld, Magnus, *Die Transvestiten: Eine Untersuchung über den erotischen Verkleidungstrieb mit umfangreichen bibliographischen und dokumentarischen Belegen* (Alfred Pulvermacher, 1910)

[525] Herrn, Rainer, *Sexualwissenschaft: Institutionalisierung und Professionalisierung der Sexualwissenschaft durch Max Marcuse und andere Vertreter der ersten Generation* (Männerschwarm Verlag, 2010)

[526] Baumgardt, David, 'The Institut für Sexualwissenschaft 1919–1933: Founding and Early Years', in *Magnus Hirschfeld: Pioneer of Sexology*, ed. by Elena Mancini (Haworth Press, 1995), pp. 62–75

[527] Plant, Richard, *The Pink Triangle* (Holt, Rinehart & Winston, 1986)

[528] Hirschfeld, Magnus, *Rassismus* (Editions de l'Épi, 1934)

[529] Hirschfeld Society, *The Institute for Sexual Science (Institut für Sexualwissenschaft)*

[530] Isherwood, Christopher, *Christopher and His Kind* (Farrar, Straus and Giroux, 1976)

[531] Abraham, Felix, 'Genitalumwandlungen an zwei männlichen Transvestiten', *Zeitschrift für Sexualwissenschaft und Sexualpolitik*, 18 (1931), 223–26

1940[532] and published his results participating in the *Dachau Hypothermia Experiments*[533].

Alfred Kinsey

Known as the *"Father of the Sexual Revolution"*[534], Kinsey was a bisexual zoologist who believed children were "sexual from birth", and founded the *Institute for Sex Research* at *Indiana University* after studying gall wasps[535]. Using questionnaires, he published two "reports" of 5,300 men[536] and 8,000 women[537] which claimed 10-36% of men were homosexual; 95% of men had engaged in homosexuality, incest, rape, paedophilia, and even bestiality; 40% of married women had affairs; and 25% of married women had abortions[538][539]. His fraudulent research data to create a sexuality "scale"[540] was collected from the personal logs of a Nazi paedophile (given under different names) who kept detailed diaries of over eight hundred sexual encounters with children, and even

---

[532] Krieter-Spiro, Monika, 'The Activities of Surgeon Erwin Gohrbandt (1890–1965) on Behalf of the Berlin University, the City's Municipal Council, and the Berlin Surgical Society', *Chirurg*, 61 (1990), 840–45

[533] Berger, Robert L., 'Nazi Science—The Dachau Hypothermia Experiments', *New England Journal of Medicine*, 322 (1990), 1435–40

[534] Toufexis, Anastasia, 'The Father of the Sexual Revolution', *The New York Times*, 31 August 1981

[535] Jones, James H., *Alfred C. Kinsey* (W.W. Norton & Co., 1997)

[536] Kinsey, Alfred C., Wardell B. Pomeroy, and Clyde E. Martin, *Sexual Behavior in the Human Male* (W.B. Saunders, 1948)

[537] Kinsey, Alfred C., Wardell B. Pomeroy, Clyde E. Martin, and Paul H. Gebhard, *Sexual Behavior in the Human Female* (W.B. Saunders, 1953)

[538] Gebhard, P. H., *Kinsey* (Indiana University Press, 1979)

[539] 'Croatian Journalist Exposes Alfred Kinsey Link to Sex-Ed', *The Interim*, 12 Nov 2007

[540] Reisman, J. A., *Kinsey: Crimes and Consequences* (Institute for Media Education, 1998)

THE TESTIMONIAL OF CRIMINALS

with babies as young as two months old[541][542][543].

He idolised Aleister Crowley[544], circumcised himself with a pocket knife minus anaesthesia, stimulated himself with urethral insertion and ropes[545], encouraged his staff to have orgies with each other, and hired a film technician to tape employees for "scientific" porn films in his attic[546]. During his "open marriage", he had sex with multiple men, including a student[547].

In 1949, he testified before the *California General Assembly's Subcommittee on Sex Crimes*, urging them to grant immediate paroles to suspected child molesters on the basis of societal "hysteria" does more harm to children than the actual molestation[548]. He died in 1956 before he could be charged by *US Customs* for trafficking footage of extreme sexual depravity[549].

---

[541] Reisman, J. A., *Kinsey, Sex and Fraud* (Lochinvar-Huntington House, 1990)

[542] Reisman, J. A., and T. McIlhany, prods, *The Kinsey Syndrome* [Documentary] (Jeremiah Films, 2008

[543] Reisman, J. A., prod., M. Schlessinger, dir., *Kinsey's Pedophiles* [Documentary] (American History Films, 1998)

[544] American Family Association, '10 Men Who Destroyed American Culture', *AFA Journal*, March 2010

[545] Scott, A. O., 'Alfred Kinsey: Liberator or Pervert?', *The New York Times*, 3 Oct 2004

[546] Grossman, M., 'A Brief History of Sex Ed: How We Reached Today's Madness', *Public Discourse*, 16 July 2013

[547] Pomeroy, W. B., *Kinsey and the Institute for Sex Research* (Harper & Row, 1972)

[548] Kinsey, A. C., 'Testimony Before the California General Assembly's Subcommittee on Sex Crimes', 3 May 1949, California State Archives, Sacramento, CA

[549] PBS, 'Kinsey Establishes the Institute for Sex Research', *American Experience*

John Money

Known as the *"Father of F***ology"*[550], Money was a New Zealand born bisexual professor of pediatrics and medical psychology who emigrated to the US in 1947, and got his PhD from Harvard University 1952 with a thesis on hermaphroditism[551]. In 1946, he had written of rebranding *"sexual preference"* to *"sexual orientation"* and is regarded as the progenitor of the terms "gender role"[552][553].

In 1965, he co-founded the *Johns Hopkins Gender Identity Clinic*, funded in part by female-to-male philanthropist Reed Erickson[554], which performed the first sex reassignment surgeries and chemical castrations of sex offenders in the United States[555].

In 1966, he convinced the parents of eight-month infant twins to castrate one of their children and raise him as a girl after he suffered a botched circumcision to investigate nature vs nurture. When the twins were six, he began showing them pornography, ordering them to strip for "inspections", and photographing them acting out sexual behaviour. The experiment was a catastrophic failure, and both traumatised twins killed themselves in adult life[556].

In 1985, he testified before Attorney General Edwin Meese's commission, claiming pornography was not detrimental to minors; paedophilia

---

[550] Dreger, A., 'Pervert or Sexual Libertarian? Meet John Money, the Father of "F***ology"', *Salon*, 4 January 2015

[551] *Hermaphroditism: An Inquiry into the Nature of Sexual Development in Humans* [Doctoral dissertation] (Harvard University Library, 1953)

[552] Money, J., and A. A. Ehrhardt, *Man & Woman, Boy & Girl* (Johns Hopkins Press, 1972)

[553] Money, J., J. G. Hampson, and J. L. Hampson, 'An Examination of Some Basic Sexual Concepts: The Evidence of Human Hermaphroditism', *Bulletin of the Johns Hopkins Hospital*, 97.4 (1955), 301–19

[554] Conway, L., 'The Story of Reed Erickson and the Erickson Educational Foundation'

[555] Money, J., and M. Schwartz, 'Sex Reassignment at Birth: Long-Term Review and Clinical Implications', *Johns Hopkins University Press*

[556] Colapinto, J., *As Nature Made Him* (HarperCollins, 2000)

was not always harmful to children; and adolescents should receive explicit instruction about masturbation[557].

In 1986, he defined lists of *"abnormal love"* under the umbrella term *"paraphilias"* to replace *"perversions"*. Two of them were *"chronophilia"* and *"nepiophilia"*, or sexual attraction to toddlers and infants[558].

In 1991 he stated in PAIDIKA: The Journal of Paedophilia a mutual sexual relationship between *"boy aged ten or eleven who's intensely erotically attracted toward a man in his twenties or thirties"* was merely *"a love affair between an age-discrepant couple"* and not *"pathological in any way."*[559]

Michel Foucault

Foucault was a homosexual atheist drunk-driving Frenchman[560] who wrote five influential books during the postmodern period about prisons[561], madness[562], and sexuality[563]. A former communist, he decorated his teenage bedroom with pictures of torture and self-harmed[564].

Along with scores of other French academics, he signed a petition in 1977 to legalise sex with children aged thirteen[565]. In 1968, while he was a visiting professor at the *University of Tunis*, his friend Guy Sorman

---

[557] Simmons, N., 'Sex Researcher's Early Work Continues to Provoke Discussion', *Bay Area Reporter*, 30 March 2006

[558] Money, J., 'Paraphilias: Phenomenology and Classification', *American Journal of Psychotherapy*, 40.2 (1986), 161–73

[559] 'Interview: John Money', *PAIDIKA: The Journal of Paedophilia*, 2.3 (Spring 1991), 5.

[560] Miller, J., *The Passion of Michel Foucault* (Simon & Schuster, 1993)

[561] Foucault, M., *Discipline and Punish* (Pantheon Books, 1977; orig. pub. 1975)

[562] Foucault, M., *Madness and Civilization* (Pantheon Books, 1965; orig. pub. 1961)

[563] Foucault, M., *The History of Sexuality* (Pantheon Books, 1978; orig. pub. 1976)

[564] Eribon, D., *Michel Foucault*, (Harvard University Press, 1991)

[565] 'Petition to Repeal Age-of-Consent Laws', *Le Monde*, 1977

testified publicly French journalists knew[566] Foucault paid eager nine-year-old boys cash to "stretch out" and rape them on gravestones in the local cemetery of Sidi Bou Saïd[567][568]. (It's notable one desperate, catty LGBT writer attempted a "debunking" of the story on the basis reporters from local Arab newspaper *Jeune Afrique* investigated and said it was older teens under some trees[569], i.e. source: *trust me, bro*).

Chomsky debated him in 1971 and was at a loss for words about the depth of his sociopathy[570]. In 1974, his lectures at *Collège de France* concerned *"child masturbators"*[571], before becoming a visiting professor in California in 1980. He was "happily speechless" at the endless number of homosexual bathhouses in San Francisco offering sadomasochistic gay sex who he knowingly infected with sexual disease[572].

Two years after he died in 1984 at fifty-seven proclaiming his *"love of boys"* as last words on his deathbed[573], before his male lover revealed he was the country's first public victim of AIDS.

---

[566] Kishkovsky, S., 'France's Reverence for Intellectuals Shielded Michel Foucault from Scandal', *The Spectator*, 10 April 2021

[567] Sorman, Guy., 'Michel Foucault, the Great Philosopher, Was Also a Pedophile', *The Sunday Times*, 7 March 2021

[568] Chrisafis, A., 'French Philosopher Michel Foucault Abused Boys in Tunisia, Claims Writer', *The Times*, 29 March 2021

[569] 'The Black Masses of Michel Foucault: The Bullshit of Guy Sorman', *Lundi Matin*, 5 April 2021

[570] Chomsky, N., and M. Foucault, *The Chomsky-Foucault Debate* (The New Press, 1971)

[571] Foucault, M., *Abnormal* (Picador, 1974–75)

[572] Gimball, Roger., 'The Perversions of M. Foucault', *The New Criterion*, June 2021

[573] Johnson, Daniel., 'Michel Foucault: The Prophet of Pederasty', *The Critic*, April 2021

The Gnostic Philosophical Pathway

Academic Gnosticism, as a distorted, perverse Franco-Germanic existentialist idealism, is structured in a biblical-style timeline of philosophical revelation. It embeds its own circular logic, with each decade layering on more nonsense and jargon over time, always citing the previous nonsense. It's hard to understand or follow without a timeline to refer to.

Despite every iteration being demonstrably and empirically fallacious as it increasingly disconnects from reality, each possesses a hypnotic, universal, explanatory quality which appeals to our worst desires. They capture human imagination in a way which fortifies them against reason.

Reality and truth become less important as the theology progresses than the extent to which the ideas serve our nature. The ideas themselves also become noticeably worse - which is to say, thinner and less meaningful - over time.

It's easier to understand where all this jargon comes from if one can see the entire picture, just as Marcuse is more comprehensible if you hear the words in Lucifer's voice. Which is, of course, naturally, whom Saul Alinsky's book is dedicated to[574].

It's difficult to pin down a topic as broad as left-wing thought, but it one were to summarise it pithily in one line, one might start with

---

[574] Alinsky, Saul D., *Rules for Radicals* (Random House, 1971)
Lucifer described as *'the first radical known to man who rebelled against the establishment and did it so effectively that he at least won his own kingdom'* (epigraph).

something akin to the *Enlightenment*-era *Tabula Rasa*[575] rejection of *Total Depravity* doctrine[576]:

> *Man is not born with an unchangeable nature.*

However, it is not enough, simply due to the Everest-style height of empirical evidence mounted in one direction to make it as absurd a claim as it is. One needs to become more metaphysical. An improved version might be:

> *Man's own misconception he has an unchangeable nature is at the heart of his inability to transcend his condition.*

British journalist Malcolm Muggeridge summed up this conflict well in 1976:

> *The depravity of man is at once the most empirically verifiable reality but at the same time the most intellectually resisted fact*[577].

One doesn't need a three-year university degree with a hundred thousand dollars in tuition debt to understand left-wing incoherent thought. For the simple reason, most of it is about an inch deep and a well of catastrophic and continuous error. It does, however, require a significant cognitive effort to untangle the mass of philosophical spaghetti it creates.

By the outbreak of World War II, the entire dogma is stooped in farce consisting of cultural relativism; sexual depravity; quasi-religious invisible ideas; Marxian offshoots; the idealistic or the mystical. None of which are the good kind, or even *interesting*. It's a deluge of unreadable mediocrity which descends into utter madness around the seventies.

---

[575] Locke, John, *An Essay Concerning Human Understanding* (Thomas Basset, 1690)

[576] Calvin, John, *Institutes of the Christian Religion* (Jean Girard, 1536)

[577] Muggeridge, Malcolm, *A Third Testament* (Little, Brown, 1976)

Error compounds error. One fraud is built upon another. The succeeding era combines the error with the fraud. Eventually, there is a chain of fallacy and sophistry so thick it appears as legitimate, authoritative knowledge discovered about the world on an evolutionary basis.

This is by no means a comprehensive list of every aspect of the doctrine (or a genealogical history of *empiricism* and *rationalism*), but it is a simplistic overview tour of the significant "thinkers" whom tenured radical professors tout as their ideological "stack", which allows for easy tracking of how this school of thought devolves into the mess we know it as today.

18th Century

Most roads lead back to Swiss philosopher *Jean-Jacques Rousseau* (1712–1778), the *"Father of the French Revolution"*, which delineated left and right as a battle between radical reform (republic) vs continuity of the traditional *Ancien Regime* (monarchy).

> *Paraphrased: Mankind is fundamentally good until he encounters society. Instead of monarchy, we can express what we want collectively and package it into the State as a type of contract*[578].

Across the channel, English economist *Thomas Robert Malthus* (1766 - 1834), the *"Father of Modern Demography"*, argued population grows geometrically (exponentially), and food production only grows arithmetically (linearly), which leads to a "trap" where resources cannot sustain the population, causing inevitable cycles of famine, disease, and mortality.

---

[578] Rousseau, Jean-Jacques, *The Social Contract* (Penguin Classics, 2006; orig. pub. 1762)

Paraphrased: Unchecked population growth will surpass agricultural production[579].

The other major arch-villain in the bookshelf is former alchemist and German philosopher *Georg Wilhelm Friedrich Hegel* (1770–1831), the *"Father of Modern Historicism and Totalitarianism,"* whose dense writing is almost impenetrable to anyone not using prescription amphetamines to get through it.

> *Paraphrased: Greek reason is not enough. As in alchemy, ideas and society evolve through clashes between contradictory forces to create something new, because things are bad and need to be changed. After enough cycles, perfection is reached. The State, the culture and the Spirit of the Age are man's version of the Holy Trinity.*

18th Century

There's no doubt who the absolute monarch of left-wing thought is.

German sociologist *Karl Marx* (1818–1883), the *"Father of Communism"*, a former Young Hegelian, rewrote *Genesis 3* into a revolutionary political monomyth about how rebellion provoked by the *Industrial Revolution* in England would inevitably establish man's own *Kingdom of Heaven*.

> *Paraphrased: Mankind's history can be thought of scientifically as a sequence of stages, defined by conflicts between rich and poor about how we produce the things we need. The spoils of the industrialised world are so unequal the working class will inevitably revolt and push us to the next stage where they are distributed equally. At the*

---

[579] Malthus, Thomas Robert, *An Essay on the Principle of Population* (J. Johnson, 1798)

end of these stages is Advanced Communism[580].

Less well-known at the time was German lawyer *Karl Heinrich Ulrichs* (1825 - 1895), who established the nascent "gay rights" movement, while establishing new terminology for sodomy.

> *Paraphrased: Pederasty should be recognised as a separate sexual "orientation" known as "homosexuality" with legal rights*[581].

20th Century

Pre-WW2 Modernity

Without doubt, the key cornerstone of the social sciences was the work of Austrian neurologist, *Sigmund Freud* (1856 - 1939), known as the *"Father of Psychoanalysis"*, who believed the problems of the present can be solved by interrogating the past, and provided a scientific-sounding substitute for the *Soul*.

> *Paraphrased: Humans cannot control a set of basic feral instincts which play out in an invisible unconscious mind*[582].

Violent political revolution emerged via exiled Russian politician *Vladimir Lenin* (1870-1924), who formalised Marx's ideas into a political force to organise the working class and establish the world's first

---

[580] Marx, Karl, and Friedrich Engels, *The Communist Manifesto*, (ca. 1848)

[581] Kennedy, Hubert, *Karl Heinrich Ulrichs* (Routledge, 2010)

[582] Freud, Sigmund, 'The Unconscious', in *The Standard Edition of the Complete Psychological Works of Sigmund Freud*, vol. 14, (Hogarth Press, 1915)

communist state.

> *Paraphrased: The oppressed working class will not rise up to fulfil their destiny by themselves. They need to be organised into a political party who will lead them as a Vanguard and understand their religion is outdated*[583].

Parallel to the *Bolshevik Revolution* and Russian civil war, Hungarian philosopher *György Lukács* (1885 – 1971) advocated violent *"cultural terrorism"* to break the hold of traditional Christianity over families resisting socialism.

> *Paraphrased: Western culture should be seen through Marxist eyes, because capitalism turns people into objects and Christianity is an impediment to socialism. Sex education can be used to detach children from their parents' traditions*[584].

In *Weimar* Germany, the field of eugenic *"sexology"* was established by German doctor *Magnus Hirschfield* (1868 – 1935), whose clinic (the *Institute for Sexual Research*) operated as a museum of sexual depravity and published the first *"sex change"* surgeries.

> *Paraphrased: Medical surgery can be used to be used to achieve a eugenic change of biological sex*[585].

In America, German physicist *Franz Uri Boas* (1858 – 1942), the *"Father*

---

[583] Lenin, Vladimir Ilyich, *The State and Revolution* (Penguin Classics, 1992)

[584] Lukács, Georg, *History and Class Consciousness* (MIT Press, 1971)

[585] Dose, Ralf, *Magnus Hirschfeld* (Monthly Review Press, 2014)

of American Anthropology" pioneered activism in science by opposing *"scientific racism"* and claiming the morality of human cultures is relative.

> *Paraphrased: All humans see their world through their own cultural bias, therefore no culture is better or worse than any other*[586].

In a similar vein to Lukács, Mussolini imprisoned Italian communist Antonio Gramsci (1891-1937) and wrote thirty notebooks documenting the *"hegemony"* of social keystones protecting societies against the onslaught of socialism.

> *Paraphrased: Resistance to man's transformation is held together by cultural institutions such as schools, universities, churches, and the media. They must be infiltrated from within and Socialism must replace religion*[587].

After he became director of Carl Grünberg's *Institute for Socialist Research*[588] in Frankfurt, German sociologist *Max Horkheimer* (1895 – 1973) established a Hegelian communist "antithesis" to the *Scientific Method* which became known as *"critical theory"*.

> *Paraphrased: Universities must look at academic subjects in Marxist terms and ruthlessly criticise the individual political beliefs of scientists*[589].

---

[586] Boas, Franz, 'The Methods of Ethnology', *American Anthropologist*, 22.4 (1920)

[587] Gramsci, Antonio, *Selections from the Prison Notebooks*, (International Publishers, 1971). Note: Gramsci did not write this. He announced it at a conference.

[588] Grünberg specifically founded IFS as a Marxist research centre. It later became known as the *Institute for Social Research* (or *Institut für Sozialforschung*).

At the same time, Swiss psychologist *Jean Piaget* (1896 - 1980) documented his quasi-religious notions of education being the only means of saving humanity, positing knowledge isn't learned, but rather self-manufactured in the brains of children.

> *Paraphrased: knowledge and reality are constructed in an individual's mind based on their interactions with the world*[590].

Across the world in East Asia, Chinese politician *Mao Zedong* (1893 - 1976) followed Lenin's lead and marched the *Chinese Communist Party* against the *Kuomintang* (KMT) in the *Chinese Civil War*.

> *Paraphrased: Children and students must be radicalised against the preceding generations to violently purge old ideas, culture, habits, and customs*[591].

Post-1945 Postmodernity

Quietly, in the journals being read within the faculty lounge, fringe psychologist *Madison Bentley* (1870 - 1955) recategorised sex and gender as a distinction between biological accident and social "conditioning".

Crystallising what obscure cranks had believed for some time, he quietly declared it was a matter of scientific fact gender is the *"socialised obverse of sex."*

---

[589] Horkheimer, Max, 'Traditional and Critical Theory', in *Critical Theory: Selected Essays* (Continuum, 1937), pp. 188–243

[590] Piaget, J. (1954). *The construction of reality in the child*. Basic Books.

[591] Mao Zedong, *Quotations from Chairman Mao Tse-tung* (Foreign Languages Press, 1967)

THE GNOSTIC PHILOSOPHICAL PATHWAY

Paraphrased: Genitals are nature. Wearing dresses is nurture[592].

At the *University of Indiana*, American biologist *Alfred Kinsey* (1894–1956), the *"Father of the Sexual Revolution"*, published two studies into human sexual behaviour which claimed to show it varied naturally, and existed on an elastic continuum.

Paraphrased: Human sexuality naturally varies between heterosexual and homosexual, even in infants[593].

In post-WWI France, French writer *Simone de Beauvoir* (1908 – 1986) rekindled militant radical feminism as a sociological *resentimente* rather than activism aiming to achieve suffrage.

Paraphrased: Men are the default primary human beings, leaving women subordinated as the "Other" by reproductive slavery[594].

In the bowels of *Johns Hopkins University*, New Zealand psychologist *John Money* (1921 –2006), embarked on gruesome gender-swap experiments with twins, and reinventing terminology for disturbing sexual fetishes.

Paraphrased: Male and female are not fixed biological categories, but social ones. Obscure sexual behaviours should be known as "orientations" or "paraphilias"[595].

---

[592] Bentley, Madison, 'Sanity and Hazard in Childhood', *The American Journal of Psychology*, 58.2 (1945), 212–46

[593] Kinsey, Alfred C., Wardell B. Pomeroy, and Clyde E. Martin, *Sexual Behavior in the Human Male* (W. B. Saunders, 1948)

[594] Beauvoir, Simone de, *The Second Sex*, (Vintage Books, 1989)

As the humanities immersed themselves in the depression of the atomic bomb, French philosopher *Jacques Derrida* (1930-2004) pioneered *"deconstruction"* of the French language for political aims.

> *Paraphrased: Words only refer to other words, and have no meaning of their own*[596].

In California, German sociologist *Herbert Marcuse* (1898-1979), the *"Father of the New Left"*, became a "rock star" among anti-Vietnam students by "synthesising" Marx and Freud together in an attempt to explain "one-dimensional" consumer culture.

> *Paraphrased: The working class chose Nazism because capitalism pacifies them psychologically. They need to be replaced by unemployed blacks, immigrants, and student intelligentsia. Right-wing ideas must be suppressed because the threat of fascism is ever-present*[597].

As anti-war sentiment started to spread, German philosopher *Jürgen Habermas* (1929 -) began attacking modernity and the success of American capitalism, laying the blame on crafty elites, manipulating the *"public sphere"* for their own interests.

> *Paraphrased: Cultural myths are created by state and corporate powers to shape public perception and maintain social order*[598].

---

[595] Money, John, *Venuses, Penises, and Hormones* (Johns Hopkins University Press, 1988)

[596] Derrida, Jacques, *Of Grammatology* (Johns Hopkins University Press, 1967)

[597] Marcuse, Herbert, *One-Dimensional Man* (Beacon Press, 1964)

The next wave of feminism was targeted at disaffected housewives by American psychologist *Betty Friedan* (1921 - 2006), the *"Mother of the Modern Women's Movement"*, who agitated frustration over "traditional roles".

> *Paraphrased: Women are psychologically trapped in domestic life and should pursue their own existence outside of marriage and motherhood[599].*

At the sexual psychopath genius end of the spectrum, French philosopher *Michel Foucault* (1926-1984), the *"Prophet of Pederasty"*, became France's own "rock star" academic by publishing edgy tracts on the subjects of prison, sex, and mental health.

> *Paraphrased: Everything humans make up is about exercising power over others, particularly their physical bodies. What we know and believe is policed by the powerful[600].*

The era of *Postmodernity* was accurately described by French sociologist *Jean-François Lyotard* (1924 – 1998) as a cynical distrust of narrated political mythology discounting minority views, an embrace of relative truth, and the "unknowable" virtue of ugly art.

> *Paraphrased: There is no way of finding objective truth. We only narrate grand stories we tell ourselves[601].*

---

[598] Habermas, Jürgen, *The Structural Transformation of the Public Sphere* (MIT Press, 1962)

[599] Friedan, Betty, *The Feminine Mystique* (Norton, 1963)

[600] Foucault, Michel, *Discipline and Punish* (Vintage, 1975)

As the British Empire voluntarily self-dissolved, French psychiatrist *Frantz Fanon* (1925 - 1981) and his intellectual rants against *"colonialism"* became the favourite text of radical black activists in the West.

> *Paraphrased: People in mercantile colonies are justified in using violence against colonial governments. Mentally ill people get better in their community*[602].

At *Stanford University*, American biologist *Paul R. Ehrlich* (1932 -) wrongly predicted the post-WWII overpopulation of the *Baby Boom* would inevitably result in worldwide famines worse than the effects of the atomic bomb.

> *Paraphrased: Earth is overpopulated and humans must stop reproducing to avoid mass starvation and societal collapse*[603].

Not being fans of *"liberation theology"* as it emerged in South America, the *Junta* expelled Brazilian educator *Paulo Freire* (1921 – 1997) before he published a Marxian interpretation of teaching theory and child literacy which emphasised "different ways of knowing".

> *Paraphrased: Education should be seen as a joint political enterprise between teachers and students to escape oppression*[604].

---

[601] Lyotard, Jean-François, *The Postmodern Condition* (U. of Minn. Press; 1979)

[602] Fanon, Frantz, *The Wretched of the Earth* (Grove Press, 2004; orig. pub. 1961)

[603] Ehrlich, Paul R., *The Population Bomb* (Ballantine Books, 1968)

[604] Freire, Paulo, *Pedagogy of the Oppressed* (Continuum, 1970)

To demonstrate the spirit of *"community organising"*, American activist *Saul Alinsky* (1909 – 1972) responded to the increasingly desperate *New Left* with highly effective methods of political agitation.

> *Paraphrased: Cynical means are justifiable if they achieve the right political ends*[605].

Not to be outdone by Fanon, Palestinian literary critic *Edward Said* (1935 - 2003) decried "imperialist" (*Occident*) depictions of Asia while preaching at *Columbia University*.

> *Paraphrased: Western thought demeans the East through terminology and caricatures*[606].

In the burgeoning period of broadcast TV, French sociologist *Jean Baudrillard* (1929 – 2007) claimed media and consumer culture lead us to live in a world of simulations, where we engage more with images and signs than with any "authentic" reality.

> *Paraphrased: The things we make up become more real than what it's in daily life*[607].

The first generation of *Affirmative Action* graduates emerged from universities,: American professor *Derrick Bell* (1930 – 2011) used his tenure at *Harvard University* to introduce communist race theory for segregation-era historical policy-making in American jurisprudence.

---

[605] Alinsky, Saul D., *Rules for Radicals* (Random House, 1971)

[606] Said, Edward, *Orientalism* (Pantheon, 1978)

[607] Baudrillard, Jean, *Simulacra and Simulation* (University of Michigan Press, 1994)

Paraphrased: The Civil Rights movement of the 1960s was a mirage. Racism must be seen in Marxist terms as the fundamental way society works[608].

In the middle of the civil rights battle, American academic *Howard Zinn* (1922 – 2010) produced an alternative *Black Legend* of the United States to challenge the national mythology taught in schools.

Paraphrased: The true dark legend of the United States as a corrupt villain has been hidden[609].

After the 1968 invasion of Prague, the communist parties of the ex-Soviet bloc in Europe, and their sympathisers in the West, were urged by Spanish communist leader *Santiago Carrillo* (1915 - 2012) to adopt a new strategy of "democratic socialism".

Paraphrased: The failure of the Stalinist USSR means communist parties should adopt democratic norms as a means of establishing socialism in Europe[610].

Under the cover of the booming neoliberal eighties, feminist writer *Gayle Rubin* (1949 -) advocated interpreting the sexual depraved as a Marxist underclass in a battle against people who were normal, which became known as *Queer Theory*.

---

[608] Bell, Derrick, *Faces at the Bottom of the Well* (Basic Books, 1992)

[609] Zinn, Howard, *A People's History of the United States* (Harper & Row, 1980)

[610] Carrillo, Santiago, *Eurocommunism and the State* (Lawrence and Wishart, 1977)

Paraphrased: Heterosexuality is only normal because society organises sex into a moral hierarchy[611].

While the rest of the world weren't interested, member of the black feminist *Combahee River Collective*, and American legal professor, *Kimberlé Crenshaw* (1959 -), devised a method of divining intersecting feminist "oppressions", with straight white Christian males as their common hierarchical enemy.

Paraphrased: Prejudice against individuals is compounded by multiple characteristics at once, like being black and lesbian, but all are in opposition to society's best-off[612].

At *Columbia University*, renowned American geochemist *Wallace Broecker* (1931 – 2019) linked his research into the planet's carbon cycle with the idea the globe's temperature may be cumulatively warming.

Paraphrased: Unrestrained industrialised capitalism has done so much damage to the planet, atmospheric changes are leading to man's extinction unless we embrace collectivism[613].

Stanford's reputation for radicalism remained unchallenged, with En-

---

[611] Rubin, Gayle, 'Thinking Sex: Notes for a Radical Theory of the Politics of Sexuality', in Carol S. Vance (ed.), *Pleasure and Danger: Exploring Female Sexuality* (Routledge & Kegan Paul, 1984), pp. 267–319

[612] Crenshaw, Kimberlé, 'Demarginalizing the Intersection of Race and Sex: A Black Feminist Critique of Antidiscrimination Doctrine, Feminist Theory, and Antiracist Politics', *University of Chicago Legal Forum*, 1989.1 (1989), 139–67

[613] Broecker, Wallace S., 'Climate Change: Are We on the Brink of a Pronounced Global Warming?', *Science*, 189.4201 (1975), 460–63

glish professor *Shelley Fisher Fishkin* (1950 -) attempting to explain the evils of the world as a result of white people suffering a terminally fatal pathology.

> *Paraphrased: White-skinned people from Europe suffer from a pathology of "whiteness", an imaginary belief in their own superiority from which all their literature is derived[614].*

In the wake of the AIDS epidemic, the PR for gay "liberation" needed a desperate boost . Neuropsychologist *Marshall Kirk* (1957 –2005) & advertising executive *Hunter Madsen* strongly urged a move away from what they termed "fascist" gay community behaviour to brainwashing the public.

> *Paraphrased: Gay and lesbian activist groups should deliberately propagandise media audiences[615].*

The fall of the USSR and its defeat in the Cold War convinced Hegelian political commentator *Francis Fukuyama* (1952 -) that Western liberal democracy was humanity's final form.

> *Paraphrased: Humanity has synthesised the end of history, as ideological differences have been resolved by liberalism[616].*

While the nihilistic tones of *Grunge* rock and *"Cool Britannia"* dominated

---

[614] Fishkin, Shelley Fisher, *Was Huck Black? Mark Twain and African-American Voices* (Oxford University Press, 1993)

[615] Kirk, Marshall, and Hunter Madsen, *After the Ball*, (Doubleday, 1989)

[616] Fukuyama, Francis, *The End of History and the Last Man* (Free Press, 1992)

the *Windows 95* computer age, American feminist *Judith Butler* (1956 -) married Bentley and Foucault's ideas as means of establishing "civil rights" for cross-dressers.

> *Paraphrased: Gender is a something women "perform" socially with make-up and clothes*[617].

After China's millennial ascent to the WTO as the post-industrial world's warehouse floor, English sociologist *Anthony Giddens* (1938 -), penned the founding text expounded by Bill Clinton and Tony Blair of a Nordic compromise between communism and capitalism, (a.k.a Deng's *"Socialism with Chinese characteristics"*[618]).

> *Paraphrased: Governments and markets can become "partners"*[619].

21st Century

As the leader of a global networking event in Davos, Switzerland, German mechanical engineer *Klaus Schwab* (1938 -) was convinced the *"Fourth Industrial Revolution"* would emerge between the internationalist blocs of the US, China, EU, and India.

---

[617] Butler, Judith, *Gender Trouble* (Routledge, 1990)

[618] Deng Xiaoping, *Selected Works of Deng Xiaoping* (Foreign Languages Press, 1984)

[619] Giddens, Anthony, *The Third Way* (Polity Press, 1998)

Paraphrased: The world is evolving into a global fascio-communistic transhuman fusion of man and machine, and should be led by a vanguard of stake-holding technocrats following China's example[620].

In the aftermath of globalisation, English philosopher *Nick Land* (1962 -), the *"Godfather of Accelerationism"* gathered essays from Internet-era as *"Dark Enlightenment"* neo-reactionary thinking, advocating a return to hierarchical absolute governance to escape the *Cathedral*[621].

Paraphrased: Neoliberal democracy and freedom are incompatible[622].

The revolt against internationalism, codified by Britain's vote to leave the EU, Donald Trump's disruptive *"alt-right"* victory in the US election, and the shared revulsion towards communist China's cover-up of their fourth lab leak of a deadly virus - was characterised by American historian *Timothy Snyder* (1969 -) as the *"post-truth"* era being a prototypical fascism.

The rise of populist leaders advocating for nationalism and localism is evidence of fascism re-emerging[623].

---

[620] Schwab, Klaus, *The Fourth Industrial Revolution* (Crown Business, 2016)

[621] Moldbug, Mencius, 'A Gentle Introduction to Unqualified Reservations' [Blog post], *Unqualified Reservations* (2008)

[622] Land, Nick, *The Dark Enlightenment* (2012–2013)

[623] Snyder, Timothy, 'The American Abyss', *The New York Times*, 9 Jan 2021

The Shroud of Syncretic Animism

The term "animism" comes from the Latin word *"anima,"* meaning soul or life. It was first coined and introduced to anthropological discussion by the British anthropologist Sir Edward Burnett Tylor in his 1871 book *"Primitive Culture."* Tylor used the term to describe what he considered to be the most primitive form of religious belief, viewing it as the beginning stage in an evolutionary development of religion which would eventually progress to monotheism[624].

Animism is a worldview or religious perspective which attributes a soul, consciousness, or spiritual essence to natural phenomena, including plants, animals, geographic features, and even inanimate objects like stones or weather patterns. At its core, animism holds that there is no fundamental separation between the physical and spiritual worlds, and that all things possess an animating force or spirit worthy of respect and consideration. This perspective stands in contrast to more dualistic worldviews that separate matter from spirit[625].

Animistic worldviews can be found across virtually every continent and throughout human history. They are particularly prominent in indigenous traditions of the Americas, Africa, Asia, and Oceania. For example, many Native American traditions view animals as kin and mountains as living beings[626]. In Japan, Shinto traditions recognise *kami*

---

[624] Edward B. Tylor, *Primitive Culture* (John Murray, 1871)

[625] James G. Frazer, *The Golden Bough* (Macmillan, 1890).

[626] *Black Elk Speaks*, as told to John G. Neihardt (Doubleday, 1932)

(spirits) in natural features like waterfalls and old trees[627]. Throughout Southeast Asia, spirits known as *nats*, *phi*, or similar terms are believed to inhabit the landscape[628]. African traditional religions often include reverence for ancestor spirits that remain active in the community and natural world[629].

Primitive Magical Thinking

Animism crosses cultures and eras, making it difficult to pin down. However, several core themes appear consistently across most animistic worldviews, though their specific expressions vary considerably by culture and context. It typically emphasises knowledge comes from direct engagement with specific landscapes ("ways of knowing") and their inhabitants ("lived experience") rather than from abstract principles.

The most fundamental shared principle is the recognition non-human entities possess a personhood, consciousness, or spiritual essence. This extends beyond animals to include plants, geographic features, weather phenomena, and even manufactured objects. These entities are understood not as passive resources but as active agents with their own volition, perspectives, and purposes[630].

Another common thread is the belief in a relational universe where humans exist within a network of reciprocal relationships with these other-than-human persons. This creates ethical obligations toward non-human entities which go beyond mere resource management to include respect, reciprocity, and proper conduct. Many traditions emphasise that maintaining good relationships with these other beings is essential for human wellbeing and cosmic balance[631].

---

[627] *Kojiki*, trans. Basil Hall Chamberlain (Asiatic Society of Japan, 1919)

[628] Maung Htin Aung, *Burmese Supernatural* (Myanmar Book Centre, 1955)

[629] E. E. Evans-Pritchard, *The Nuer* (Oxford University Press, 1940).

[630] *Nihongi*, trans. W.G. Aston (Tuttle Publishing, 1972)

[631] Franz Boas, *The Mind of Primitive Man* (Macmillan, 1911).

Most animistic systems share a non-dualistic worldview that does not sharply separate material and spiritual realms. The physical and spiritual are seen as interwoven aspects of a single reality rather than separate domains. This contrasts with dualistic worldviews which separate mind from matter or sacred from profane.

Communication or interaction with non-human entities is generally considered possible and may take various forms, including dreams, visions, ritual contexts, or through specially trained individuals like shamans who serve as intermediaries.

West African Spirits In The American South

Animistic traditions from West Africa played a significant role in shaping American religious and cultural landscapes during and after the years of transatlantic slavery. These spiritual ideas, originating from regions such as Nigeria, Benin, Ghana, and Senegal, recognised spirits in natural elements and emphasised ancestral connections[632].

The West African religious traditions which most influenced American spiritual practices included *Yoruba, Fon, Ewe,* and *Akan,* sharing common animistic features: veneration of nature spirits, ancestral reverence, divination practices, and belief in a supreme creator alongside numerous intermediary spirits. Central to many was the understanding spirits inhabited natural features and could be communicated with through ritual specialists[633].

Slaveowners frequently banned African religious practices, viewing them as potential sources of resistance and cultural cohesion, forcing the practice of these traditions in secret or to adaptation of them by blending them with Christianity, creating syncretic traditions that preserved animistic elements while outwardly conforming to European religious

---

[632] Hugh Clapperton, *Travels in Africa* (John Murray, 1820).

[633] Mungo Park, *Travels in the Interior of Africa* (James Ballantyne and Co, 1799)

expectations[634].

Following the *Haitian Revolution* (1791-1804), *Vodou* emerged as a distinct religion blending West African animistic traditions primarily from Dahomey (modern Benin) with Catholic elements. In Louisiana, the religious complex known as *Voodoo* (distinguished from Haitian *Vodou*) incorporated West African animistic beliefs with Catholic, Native American, and European esoteric traditions[635]. Central figures like Marie Laveau in 19th century New Orleans helped establish it as a distinctive American tradition which maintained animistic elements while adapting to the specific social contexts of the American South[636]. Similar syncretic traditions developed in other regions, including *Hoodoo* in the broader American South and *Conjure* practices, which spread throughout black communities.

The belief spirits inhabit natural objects led to the creation of *gris-gris* (protective amulets) and *mojo bags* containing natural elements like roots, herbs, and stones believed to house spiritual power. Ancestor veneration remained central, though often expressed through Catholic saint imagery as a protective disguise. Divination practices persisted, as did the belief in specialist practitioners who could communicate with and influence spirits[637]. The *Great Migration* of the early to mid-20th century dispersed these traditions beyond the South, bringing them to northern urban centres where they continued to evolve[638].

Systems, Structures, Privilege, Isms, Gender Souls

While proponents don't claim the invisible universal animating spirits of "racism", "privilege", "hate", "diversity", "gender", and so on have

---

[634] Code Noir (Imprimerie Royale, 1685).

[635] Thomas Madiou, *Histoire d'Haïti* (J. Courtois, 1847)

[636] *New Orleans Picayune*, 22 August 1839, New Orleans.

[637] Zora Neale Hurston, *Mules and Men* (J. B. Lippincott, 1935).

[638] *Chicago Defender*, 10 February 1945, Chicago.

consciousness, volition, or personhood independent of human society, they share an enormous amount in common with primitive animistic thinking.

They are invisible forces which permeate reality, cannot be directly observed but are said to influence all aspects of society, resist empirical verification or falsification, require specialised knowledge to detect, and demand specific rituals of acknowledgment and propitiation. They become autonomous and act upon the world regardless of individual belief or awareness.

A canonical example of this religious thinking is given in an article in a 2022 paper published in *Health Affairs*, Vol. 41, No. 2:

> *Systemic and structural racism are forms of racism that are pervasively and deeply embedded in and throughout systems, laws, written or unwritten policies, entrenched practices, and established beliefs and attitudes that produce, condone, and perpetuate widespread unfair treatment of people of color. They reflect both ongoing and historical injustices. Although systemic racism and structural racism are often used interchangeably, they have somewhat different emphases. Systemicracism emphasizes the involvement of whole systems, and often all systems—for example, political, legal, economic, health care, school, and criminal justice systems—including the structures that uphold the systems.*[639]

This "force" has an invisible nature with causal agency; a pervasive, all-encompassing quality only recognisable by specialised knowledge; and it must be disposed of by ritual acknowledgment. These spirits actively "produce, condone, and perpetuate" unfair treatment, suggesting an almost autonomous capacity to influence events. The definition

---

[639] Braveman, Paula A., Elaine Arkin, Dwayne Proctor, Tina Kauh and Nicole Holm, 'Systemic and Structural Racism: Definitions, Examples, Health Damages, and Approaches to Dismantling' (2021), 41(2) *Health Affairs*

positions these forces as operating across time ("ongoing and historical") and across all major social systems simultaneously. It is an invisible entity exerting influence throughout the material world while remaining largely imperceptible except for those with magical awareness.

In traditional animism, spirits or animating forces exist within natural elements, affecting human experience while remaining largely invisible. Similarly, concepts like systemic racism or unconscious bias are described as pervasive forces operating beneath visible social interactions, influencing outcomes while often evading direct observation. While the former attributes agency to spirits within objects or places and conducts ceremonies, the latter attributes transformative power to magical "systemic forces" which operate through institutional structures and cultural patterns as a "universal spirit" or "consciousness" — then maps it onto Christian puritanism for public confession and sanctification rituals.

The language used around these concepts takes on quasi-religious characteristics: there are "testimonials" of awakening to these "forces", confessional practices of acknowledging one's complicity, rituals of "affirmation", and authorities who can properly interpret signs of these invisible influences. The emphasis on "lived experience" as special knowledge parallels how traditional animistic systems value experiential understanding of spiritual forces.

Like traditional spirit beliefs that cannot be empirically verified or disproven (falsified), concepts like "unconscious bias" or "systemic racism" are presented in ways which make them impossible to test through conventional empirical methods. When contrary evidence is presented, it is interpreted as further evidence of "system" power rather than as a challenge to the thinking itself.

Professors And Pagan Fetishism

This insanity permeates academic campuses more than they admit. For example, the *US Department of Education* proudly hosts among its "ways of knowing" a 2021 paper by Anita Tijerina Revilla published in the

Journal of Educational Foundations titled *"Attempted Spirit Murder: Who Are Your Spirit Protectors and Your Spirit Restorers?"* for which the abstract is comical:

> *This essay examines Patricia William's concept of spirit murder (1991) as she details the ways that racism and other forms of discrimination have devastating spiritual and emotional long-term impacts on the individual and collective psyche of Black people and other marginalized people in the U.S. I connect William's concept of spirit murder to two other concepts I refer to as spirit protectors and spirit restorers. I argue that people who have been targeted by attempted spirit murder in the academy have either internalized the practice of spirit murder and become spirit murderers themselves, or they have resisted and survived attempted spirit murder in the academy by banding together, protecting each other, and creating spirit restorative teams. Peers, mentors, family, and/or community members have often transformed themselves into spirit protectors and spirit restorers. I pay respects particularly to women, queer people, muxeristas, jotería, and Black Indigenous People of Color, activists, and/or scholars who have been my spirit protectors and restorers*[640].

This stupidity drones on for at least eleven pages, referencing dozens of other female authors writing about the same superstitious nonsense. What's particularly notable is how the paper moves from metaphor to a *literal* application of these spiritual terms, treating them as *operational* categories for analysing academia. The language shifts from using spiritual terminology as illustrative to employing it as an explanatory *framework*, conjecturing these "spirit" concepts has become more than just rhetorical devices in this academic world.

---

[640] Revilla, Anita Tijerina, 'Attempted Spirit Murder: Who Are Your Spirit Protectors and Your Spirit Restorers?' (2021) 34(1) Journal of Educational Foundations 31–46

The *American Psychological Association* hosts a 2023 article from the *Journal of Business Ethics* which advocates drawing on the *"Eastern spiritual traditions of diversity, equity, and inclusion"* to find incoherent "unity in diversity":

> *The areas of review included Buddhist psychology, with some of its foundational concepts such as the Four Noble Truths and the Noble Eightfold Path, the concept of ahimsa (non-harming), and the understanding of the impermanence of everything as inclusive managerial practices; Daoist philosophy, with its observations of oneness and equality, and holistic self-alignment with virtue through practicing tranquility; and Hinduism, which focuses on the absence of distinction between ourselves and others around us, thus forming the foundation for morality and ethical behavior with its emphasis on unity in diversity*[641].

"Diversity" is a universal animating spirit which counteracts the evil spirits of "privilege" and "hate" everywhere on university campuses. As a spiritual practice, Duquesne University (Pittsburgh) even hosts an annual *"Spirit of Diversity"* awards ceremony[642].

Reparations For Injured Ancestors

Animistic perspectives on ancestors vary considerably across different cultures, but they typically share a fundamental understanding: deceased family members or community members remain active participants in the world of the living. Unlike some religious traditions that place the dead in separate realms like heaven or hell, animistic worldviews

---

[641] Marques, Joan, Payal Kumar and Tom Culham, 'Drawing on Eastern Spiritual Traditions of Diversity, Equity, and Inclusion as Guideposts in an Increasingly Unpredictable World' (2024), *Journal of Business Ethics* 611–626

[642] 'Spirit of Diversity Celebration Honors Students', DU Times, 3 May 2024

maintain ancestors continue to exist within the same cosmos as the living, though in a different state of being[643].

Ancestors are not merely remembered or honoured as historical figures but are understood to have ongoing agency and influence in the world. They may protect family members, offer guidance through dreams or divination, influence natural events, cause illness when offended, or bestow blessings when properly venerated. This relationship is typically conceived as reciprocal rather than one-directional – the living have obligations to honour and feed their ancestors through offerings and rituals, while ancestors have responsibilities to protect their descendants and community. They serve as intermediaries between the living and other spiritual entities or forces.

Recently-deceased family members gradually transition into ancestral status through proper funeral rites and ongoing remembrance practices. Some traditions distinguish between different categories of ancestors – those who died recently and still maintain close personal connections to the living, and more distant ancestors who may have transformed into more generalised spiritual forces[644].

Reparations are a form of punishment: when significant harm has been inflicted on a group of people, there exists a moral obligation to acknowledge that harm and provide meaningful compensation. The nation of Germany was punished with reparations for the carnage and destruction of World War I[645].

Just as animistic traditions view ancestors as continuing to exert agency in the present world, reparations frameworks often describe historical traumas as living forces that remain active in contemporary society, requiring specific rituals of acknowledgment and restitution to resolve. The belief economic disparities cannot be addressed without first addressing historical injustices parallels animistic understanding

---

[643] Graham Harvey, *Animism* (New York University Press, 2005)

[644] John S. Mbiti, *African Religions and Philosophy* (Heinemann, 1969).

[645] Treaty of Versailles, 1919, Article 231 (1919).

material prosperity depends on maintaining proper relationships with ancestral spirits.

The concept of "intergenerational trauma" in reparations discussion parallels animistic beliefs about how spiritual harms can travel through bloodlines: spiritual injuries or curses affect descendants; an injury to ancestors manifests as concrete harm to living descendants without requiring direct physical causation.

The language of "healing" and "reconciliation" so often observed often involves ritual elements which parallel traditional spiritual practices: public apologies, ceremonial payments, and formal acknowledgments function similarly to animistic rituals designed to appease offended spirits[646].

Reparations invoke a form of collective responsibility which transcends individual identity, suggesting that racial or ethnic groups function as continuous spiritual entities across time. When contemporary people who never personally owned slaves are called to make restitution to those who were never personally enslaved, it implies a spiritual-like continuity of identity that exists beyond individual lifespans, similar to how animistic traditions view tribal or clan spirits as continuous entities.

---

[646] W.E.B. Du Bois, *The Souls of Black Folk* (A.C. McClurg & Co, 1903).

The Mind Virus

"That's just a social construct."

"Everything is constructed by the way people are socialised."

"*Constructivism*" is an educational theory of learning which asserts students *"construct"* knowledge rather than passively taking in information[647]. *"Social constructionism"* (c. 1966, not to be confused with *"social constructivism"*, 1978) argues knowledge is constructed through social interactions and *reality* itself is shaped by human relationships and institutions[648].

"Critical constructivism" is the insanity which has defiled the Western university system[649]. It adds in *"critical theory"*[650], and argues knowledge is not objective, but shaped by cultural, social, historical, and political factors. When something is "constructed" - like, say, *capitalism* -, it can be *"deconstructed"* by postmodernist language games[651].

Or perhaps more accurately, if you want to "deconstruct" something, you need to explain how it is illegitimate because it was artificially

---

[647] Piaget, Jean, *The Psychology of the Child* (Basic Books, 1972)

[648] Berger, Peter, Thomas Luckmann, *The Social Construction of Reality* (Anchor Books, 1966)

[649] Kincheloe, Joe L., *Critical Constructivism Primer* (Peter Lang Publishing, 2005)

[650] Horkheimer, Max, Theodor W. Adorno, *Dialectic of Enlightenment*, Herder and Herder, 1947)

[651] Taylor, Paul, 'Mythmaking and Mythbreaking in the Mathematics Classroom', in *Theories of Mathematical Learning*, ed. by Leslie P. Steffe and Pearla Nesher (Lawrence Erlbaum Associates, 1996), pp. 127–43

"constructed", and harms people.

As scientific philosopher Larry Laudan wrote in 1990:

> *The displacement of the idea that facts and evidence matter by the idea that everything boils down to subjective interests and perspectives is — second only to American political campaigns — the most prominent and pernicious manifestation of anti-intellectualism in our time.*[652]

"Critical constructivism" emerged in the late 20th century as a response to traditional notions of objective knowledge, and draws from various intellectual currents, including *postmodernism, postcolonialism,* etc[653][654]. Nihilistic "philosophers" like Lyotard[655] and Foucault[656] laid the groundwork by questioning established accounts and challenging the idea of universal truth.

However, its origination lies mostly with German philosopher Jurgen Habermas and his ideas about *"disempowering cultural myths"*[657]. Karl Popper summarised Habermas in brutal terms:

> *I have translated some of their German sentences into simple German. It turns out to be either trivial or tautological or sheer pretentious nonsense. I completely fail to see why Habermas is reputed to have "talent". I do not think that he was born less intelligent than other people; but he certainly did not have the good sense to resist the influence of a pretentious, lying, and intelligence*

---

[652] Laudan, Larry, *Science and Relativism* (University of Chicago Press, 1990)

[653] Habermas, Jürgen, *The Structural Transformation of the Public Sphere* (MIT Press, 1961)

[654] Freire, Paulo, *Pedagogy of the Oppressed* (Herder and Herder, 1970)

[655] Lyotard, Jean-François, *The Postmodern Condition* (U. of Minnesota Press, 1979)

[656] Foucault, Michel, *Power/Knowledge* (Pantheon Books, 1980)

[657] Habermas, Jürgen, *The Structural Transformation of the Public Sphere* (MIT Press, 1961)

destroying University education.[658]

This perspective claims there is no such thing as a completely unbiased point of view. It asserts our understanding of the world is shaped by the people around us and the "context" we're in[659]. In other words, what we know and how we see things are influenced by our culture, history, and the society we live in.

"Critical constructivists" (American sociologists obsessed with French postmodern philosophy) argue that knowledge is not fixed but changes over time and is different in various cultures[660]. They say that our views on the world, ourselves, and others are shaped by factors like history, society, culture, economy, and politics.

After understanding all that, let's hear it in their own mad words.

Based on the understanding that knowledge of the world is an interpretation between people that is crafted in a contextualised space, critical constructivists argue that knowledge is temporally and culturally situated, therefore knowledge and phenomena are socially constructed in a dialogue between culture, institutions, and historical contexts. Critical constructivism maintains that historical, social, cultural, economic, and political contexts construct our perspectives on the world, self, and other.

Critical constructivism theorises the connection between power and knowledge, maintaining that in societies only certain groups and institutions can gain prominence and become sanctioned as proprietors of knowledge, and powerful groups maintain their

---

[658] Popper, Karl, 'Letter to Raymond Aron', 13 September 1969, in Stephen Hicks, *Popper to Aron: Letter on Adorno and Habermas* (2021, September 30)

[659] Spivak, Gayatri Chakravorty, 'Can the Subaltern Speak?', in *Marxism and the Interpretation of Culture*, ed. by Cary Nelson and Lawrence Grossberg (Macmillan Education, 1988), pp. 271–313

[660] Giroux, Henry A., 'Cultural Studies, Public Pedagogy, and the Responsibility of Intellectuals', *Communication and Critical/Cultural Studies*, 3.1 (2002)

knowledge construction legitimacy by continuously undermining alternative knowledges.

This approach works to dismantle mainstream teaching and research practices that, perhaps unknowingly, are implicit in the reproduction of systems of class, race, cultural, and gender oppression, aiming to encourage reflexivity and the opening of questions through conversation and critical self-reflection.

Following Freire, critical constructivists reiterate the notion that knowledge is not a substance that can be deposited like money in a bank and taken out when time for use arrives. Knowledge is constructed in the minds of all people – minds that are formed by the society around them. However, knowledge from some societies is privileged over that of others. Critical constructivism is the practice of searching out alternative discourses and new ways of thinking, while also exposing subjugated knowledge. As such, this practice works to expose elitist assumptions embedded in existing knowledge, questions dominant forms of knowledge production and seeks out non-Western epistemologies so as to include previously excluded and marginalised knowledge in mainstream discourse [661].

The aforementioned Friere was expelled from Brazil, and his imported ideas irrevocably changed the South American education system for the worse, as they did to the America's[662].

This is obviously the kind of self-congratulating idiocy only academics would defend, and none of the constructivists' own criticisms ever apply to themselves or any need to *"deconstruct"* their own employment.

Unsurprisingly, the "alternative discourses" and "new ways of thinking"- other than being a fetish of American academics for the exotic or mystical, and a strawman of their own disillusionment - when given enough time, always lead to the same inevitable conclusion:why

---

[661] *Global Social Theory*. globalsocialtheory.org/concepts/critical-constructivism/

[662] Gadotti, Moacir, *Reading Paulo Freire* (State University of New York Press, 1994)

everything is terrible, and needs to be torn down; then replaced with Marxism, socialism, and communism.

What we now know as *"woke"* is Piaget's *"constructivism"*, fused with the *"critical theory"* of the *Frankfurt School*. During the sixties, it was merged with *"social constructionism"* and Frantz Fanon's ideas of *"colonialism"*. In the radical seventies, it was fused with *"social constructivism"*, *"critical pedagogy"*, and Michel Foucault's cynical insanity.

In the final loop, it was fused again with *"critical race theory"* and *"intersectionality"* during the eighties to create the alternative Gnostic worldview of *"critical constructivism."* One converts to this religion by absorbing these layers of scripture taught by professor priests, and developing a *"critical consciousness"* of the modern world to masquerade and posture as a fake intellectual.

Like Marx, Freud, or Adler, it explains anything and everything.

Particularly if you are impressed by polysyllabic words; narcissistically yearn to be recognised; abandoned churchgoing some years ago; and have a grudge against your father.

In this religion, everything we know is invisibly *"constructed"* within our *"unconscious mind"* by the society we live in, and the corrupt *"power relations"* between the privileged classes and institutions which underpin our materialistic Western existence. It forms an invisible, multi-layered system of oppression only the enlightened can see. Awareness of this magical evil world can be illuminated to the fascist working class by puritanically cleansing the words they use, personal involvement in unusual sexual behaviour, suppressing the hateful speech of critics, and enforcing prejudicial quotas in the workplace.

It explains *everything*.

Or, as Malcolm Muggeridge put it more gracefully:

> *So the final conclusion would surely be that whereas other civilisations have been brought down by attacks of barbarians from without, ours had the unique distinction of training its own destroyers at its own educational institutions, and then providing them with facilities*

for propagating their destructive ideology far and wide, all at the public expense.

Thus did Western Man decide to abolish himself, creating his own boredom out of his own affluence, his own vulnerability out of his own strength, his own impotence out of his own erotomania, himself blowing the trumpet that brought the walls of his own city tumbling down, and having convinced himself that he was too numerous, labored with pill and scalpel and syringe to make himself fewer.

Until at last, having educated himself into imbecility, and polluted and drugged himself into stupefaction, he keeled over—a weary, battered old brontosaurus—and became extinct.[663]

---

[663] Muggeridge, Malcolm, *Vintage Muggeridge* (Collins, 1985)

Deconstructing Transhuman Theology

"critical theory" & "constructivism"
(Max Horkheimer, 1937) & (Jean Piaget, 1937)
↓
"decolonisation"
(Frantz Fanon, 1961)
↓
"social constructionism"
(Peter L. Berger and Thomas Luckmann, 1966)
↓
"deconstruction"
(Jacques Derrida, 1967)
↓
"critical pedagogy"
(Paulo Freire, 1968)
↓
Michel Foucault
(1961 - 1976)
↓
"critical race theory" & "intersectionality"
(Derrick Bell, 1976 - Kimberlé Crenshaw, 1989)
↓
"critical constructivism," aka *"Woke"*
(2000 -)

Anatomy Of The Religion

From psychology (Piaget) comes the fundamental notion knowledge is *"constructed"* in the mind - we don't simply perceive reality directly, but actively *build* our understanding of it. Simultaneously, from the *Frankfurt School* (particularly Horkheimer), comes *"critical theory"* - the idea we must examine how power shapes society and knowledge itself. When these ideas merge, they suggest what we "know" is constructed under conditions of power.

The congregation believe things are *"constructed"* in the mind, and that our understanding of reality is shaped by *"social forces"* rather than reflecting any objective truth. This constructivist foundation leads them to see everything - from gender to race to economic systems - as *"socially constructed"* rather than natural or given. They argue what we think of as "common sense" or "natural" is actually created through *"power relationships"* in society.

Fanon's writing after *World War II* suggests colonial power wasn't about physical or economic control, but created deep psychological and cultural domination. Colonised people *"internalised"* the coloniser's worldview, seeing themselves through the coloniser's eyes. Liberation requires not mere political independence, but a complete hygienic *"decolonisation"* of the mind. This connected perfectly with the constructivist idea knowledge is built in the mind and the critical theorists' focus on hidden power structures.

Building on this, *"social constructionism"* then argues entire social realities - not just individual knowledge - are constructed through collective processes. This posits things we take as "natural" or "given" are actually created through social interactions and institutions. Around the same time, Derrida introduces *"deconstruction"*, a method of taking apart texts and ideas to reveal hidden assumptions and *"power dynamics"*.

Foucault then provides crucial input about how *"power"* operates. He introduces the idea of *"discourse"* - the way language and knowledge work together to create what we accept as truth. He suggests *"power"* isn't just top-down force, but operates through institutions, knowledge systems, and ways of thinking which shape how we understand ourselves and the world.

These *"power relationships"* are seen as *"systemic,"* meaning they're built into the very structure of society rather than just being individual acts of discrimination. Including Gramsci, they use the term *"hegemony"* to describe how dominant groups maintain their power not just through force, but through controlling what people think is normal or possible. In their view, this control operates through this *"discourse"* - the way we talk about things, the stories we tell, and the assumptions we make.

From education theory, *"social constructivism"* emphasises learning and development happen through social interaction, while Freire's *"critical pedagogy"* argues education either serves to maintain *"oppressive"* systems or can be used for liberation through *"consciousness-raising."*

They reject what they call *"positivism"* - the idea that we can objectively study society as we study nature. Instead, they believe all knowledge is *"situated"* within *"power relationships"*. Any claim to objectivity or universal truth is seen as suspicious, potentially masking them.

These strands come together in *"critical race theory"* (from Bell and others) and *"intersectionality"* (from Crenshaw). They apply the earlier ideas specifically to race and other forms of *"oppression"*, claiming different forms of *"domination"* interact and reinforce each other. They emphasise *"oppression"* isn't merely about individual acts but is *"systemic"* - built into society's basic structures.

They believe different forms of *"oppression"* (like *"racism,"* *"sexism,"* or class exploitation) interact and overlap in complex ways. Someone might be *"privileged"* in some ways and *"oppressed"* in others. They emphasise *"lived experience"* as a source of knowledge, arguing people who experience *"oppression"* understand it in ways that others can't.

Central to their academic priesthood's thinking is the concept of *"critical consciousness"* - or becoming aware of these magical invisible hidden *"power structures."* They believe most people operate under *"false consciousness,"* accepting their place in the *"power structure"* without questioning it. They see *"decolonisation"* as necessary - not just politically, but mentally, freeing people's minds from dominant ways of thinking.

The result is a comprehensive worldview where:

- Knowledge and reality are seen as *"constructed"* under conditions of *"power"* (from *"constructivism"* and *"critical theory"*)
- These *"constructions"* serve to maintain dominant groups' power (from Foucault)
- *"Oppression"* operates through multiple, *"intersecting"* systems (from *"critical race theory"*)
- *"Liberation"* requires *"deconstructing"* these *"systems"* (from Derrida) and developing *"critical consciousness"* (from Freire)
- Personal experience of *"oppressed"* groups provides special insight (*"standpoint theory"*)
- Claims of objectivity or universal truth are seen as masks for *"power"* (from *postmodernism*)

This creates in the puritan followers of this religion what we call *"woke"* - seeing these magic hidden power structures which shape everything. Each theoretical contribution reinforces the others, creating a self-supporting system of interpretation where every aspect of society can be seen in terms of *"power"* and *"oppression."*

A Day In The Life Of A Believer

Imagine you're looking at the world through their eyes: They believe beneath the surface of everything - our laws, our customs, our everyday interactions - there's a hidden magic system of *"power"* and *"oppression."* This magical *"system"* isn't obvious at first glance; it's woven into the fabric of society. It's in our language, our institutions, even in the way we think. They believe most people are blind to this *"system,"* just like fish might not notice the water they swim in.

According to this view, society is divided into groups - some who have *"power"* and *"privilege,"* and others who are *"oppressed."* But it's not simple or obvious; these *"power dynamics"* apparently *"intersect"* and overlap in complex ways. Someone might have *"privilege"* in one area of their life but face *"oppression"* in another. The really important thing is that these aren't just random inequalities - they believe they're part of a *"system"* which maintains itself through institutions, culture, and ways of thinking that most people take for granted.

They believe that becoming *"aware"* of this system is like taking a special pill that lets you see the truth. Once you become *"conscious"* of these *"power dynamics"*, you start seeing them everywhere - in movies, in jokes, in the way people talk, in who gets hired for jobs, in how children are taught in school. This awakening is seen as a profound, almost spiritual experience. The *enlightened* who've become *"aware"* feel a deep responsibility to help others see these hidden structures and to fight against them.

The ultimate goal is *"liberation"* - freeing society from these *"oppressive systems."* But here's the catch: they believe resistance to their ideas actually proves them right. If you disagree with their analysis, they see this as evidence that you're either benefiting from the system of *"oppression"* (and thus blind to it) or so dominated by it that you can't see your own *"oppression."* Every challenge to their worldview is interpreted as evidence supporting it.

In their daily lives, followers of this belief system spend a lot of time *"analysing power dynamics"*, *"checking their privilege"*, and trying to *"educate"* others. They see themselves as fighting for *"justice"* against a *"system"* so deeply embedded that most people can't even see it. They believe *"dismantling"* this *"system"* requires questioning everything - our traditions, our institutions, even basic concepts like merit or objectivity.

It's worth noting that for many believers, this worldview provides a powerful sense of purpose and meaning. It explains injustice, provides a clear moral framework, and offers a path to making the world better. It creates a strong sense of community among those who share these beliefs, united in what they see as a crucial struggle for *"justice."*

New Puritan Moral Hygiene

At its core, the *"mind virus"* manifests striking parallels with puritan theology. Like religious doctrine, it posits an original corruption - *"systemic oppression"* - which taints all social behaviour and institutions, functioning much like the concept of *Original Sin*.

It is a *secular humanist theology* which offers a complete worldview with built-in defenses against criticism, much like traditional religious systems, while suffering from fundamental logical and empirical weaknesses obscured by its own structure.

The path to salvation is clearly defined through *"consciousness-raising"* and the *"deconstruction"* of *"power structures."* A priesthood emerges in the form of enlightened academic theorists and activists who possess special insight to "see" and interpret these *"power structures"*. Those who question or reject core tenets face moral condemnation, effectively becoming *heretics*. The system even includes ritual elements, particularly in the form of *confession* - the acknowledgment of *"privilege"* and *"complicity"* in systems of oppression.

The intrinsically persuasive nature of this virus stems from several key characteristics. First, it demonstrates remarkable *internal coherence*. Second, it is *self-reinforcing*, allowing any criticism to be explained away as *"resistance to liberation"*. Third, it provides a complete worldview that explains both personal and societal phenomena, while offering both a diagnosis (*"oppression"*) and cure (*"consciousness-raising"* and activism).

The psychological appeal of this system cannot be understated. It provides *moral clarity and purpose* in an often confusing world. It offers *community and identity* to its adherents, while creating a way to understand suffering and injustice. Perhaps most powerfully, it appeals simultaneously to intellectual sophistication and moral righteousness, satisfying both the mind and conscience of its followers.

Criticism from outside can be readily dismissed as emerging from *"privilege"* or *"false consciousness."* Evidence which contradicts the *"theory"* can be explained as manifestations of *"systemic oppression"*. Even the theory's own contradictions are reframed as evidence of complexity rather than weakness.

However, the falsity of this virus emerges from several crucial flaws. The system resists empirical testing by design, making it fundamentally *unfalsifiable*. It employs circular logic, where *"power structures"* explain everything, and everything in turn proves the existence of them. The selective emphasis on *"power"* and *"oppression"* obscures other important factors and reduces complex social phenomena to *"power relations"*. Finally, it contains significant internal contradictions, particularly in the tension between epistemological relativism and moral absolutism.

The Fatal Paradox: Knowledge, Power, and Self-Contradiction

At the heart of this belief system lies a devastating logical paradox which undermines its entire foundation. The framework asserts that all knowledge is *"socially constructed"* and fundamentally shaped by *"power relations"*. Knowledge, in this view, isn't a reflection of reality but rather a tool that dominant groups use to maintain their position. There is no "objective truth" - only perspectives shaped by power.

But this creates an immediate and inescapable problem: *What about this claim itself?* If all knowledge claims are merely expressions of *"power relations"*, then *this very assertion must also be just another expression of power*. The theory literally devours itself. It's like claiming "there is no truth" - a statement that, if true, makes itself *false*.

Consider the implications: When adherents of this worldview claim to have special insight into power structures, they're making a truth claim about reality.

They're saying, *"This is how the world actually works."* But according to their *own* theory, such claims can't be about truth - they can only be about power.

They're trapped in a logical impossibility of their own making.

This creates two equally fatal options:

1. If they maintain that all knowledge claims are expressions of power, then their own framework has no special claim to truth. It's just another power play, no more valid than the systems it criticises. In this case, why should anyone accept it?
2. If they claim their analysis reveals genuine truth about power structures, then they're admitting that objective knowledge independent of power relations is possible. But this contradicts their fundamental premise and collapses their entire theoretical foundation.

This isn't just an abstract philosophical problem. It manifests in practical contradictions throughout their thinking. They claim all perspectives are shaped by social position, yet insist their analysis of power structures is universally valid. They reject claims to objective knowledge while presenting their own critiques as objective insights into social reality.

The adherents might respond acknowledging this paradox is itself part of their religion - they're being more honest by recognising how power shapes their own claims. But this is simply pushing the contradiction back one level. It doesn't resolve the fundamental problem: either their claims about power and knowledge are true (in which case not all knowledge is merely about power), or they're just another expression of power (in which case they can be dismissed).

Historical Blindness: Beyond Power and Oppression

The religion's insistence *"power relations"* explains all historical developments represents a fundamental misunderstanding of human civilisation. While *"power dynamics"* certainly play a role in history, reducing everything to *"oppression"* and *"domination"* creates a myopic view, which fails to account for humanity's most significant developments.

Consider the *Agricultural Revolution*. This transformative period wasn't primarily driven by *"power relations"* but by human innovation in response to environmental challenges[664]. Early humans didn't develop farming as a tool of *"oppression"* - they developed it to survive and thrive[665]. The complex irrigation systems of ancient civilisations, the development of crop rotation, the domestication of animals - these weren't about *"power"* but about human ingenuity and cooperation in the face of natural challenges[666].

The *Scientific Revolution* presents an even more dramatic counter-example. The religion cannot explain why the *Scientific Method* emerged and proved so successful. If all knowledge is merely about *"power"*, why, then, does the scientific method work consistently across cultures? Why can people from entirely different power positions arrive at the same scientific conclusions?[667] The development of germ theory, calculus, or the laws of thermodynamics cannot be reduced to *"power relations."* These discoveries represent genuine insights into how the physical world actually operates[668].

Constitutional democracy poses another problem. While *"power struggles"* certainly played a role, the development of democratic systems also reflected evolving philosophical ideas about human dignity, rights, and governance. The concept of individual rights, the separation of powers, the idea of consent of the governed[669] - these weren't simply tools of *"oppression"* but represented genuine intellectual and moral progress in how humans organised their societies[670].

Technological advancement further exposes this worldview's limitations. The development of the printing press, electricity, antibiotics,

---

[664] Diamond, Jared. *Guns, Germs, and Steel* (W.W. Norton & Co., 1997).

[665] Tainter, Joseph. *The Collapse of Complex Societies* (Cambridge University Press, 1988).

[666] Childe, V. Gordon. *Man Makes Himself* (Watts & Co., 1936).

[667] Kuhn, Thomas S. *The Structure of Scientific Revolutions* (U. of Chicago Press, 1962).

[668] Popper, Karl. *The Logic of Scientific Discovery* (Hutchinson, 1959)

[669] Locke, John. *Two Treatises of Government* (Awnsham Churchill, 1689).

[670] Montesquieu, Charles de Secondat. *The Spirit of the Laws*, (J. Nourse P. Vaillant, 1750).

or computers can't be explained primarily through the *"lens"* of *"power relations"*[671]. While these innovations certainly affected *"power dynamics,"* their development and spread were driven by human curiosity, problem-solving, and the desire to improve life conditions[672].

Even more telling are the great collaborative achievements of human civilisation. The spread of mathematical knowledge from India through the Arab world to Europe, the *Silk Road*'s exchange of goods and ideas, or modern international scientific cooperation[673] - these examples show how human progress often depends on cooperation and mutual benefit, not merely *"power"* and *"domination."*[674]

This historical blindness matters because it distorts our understanding of both past and present. By seeing everything through as *"power"* and *"oppression,"* the academic priesthood misses the complex interplay of factors which *actually* drive human development: innovation, cooperation, adaptation to environmental challenges, the pursuit of knowledge, and the gradual refinement of moral ideas.

Reality Check: When Theory Meets Practice

Perhaps the most damning critique of this belief system comes from examining its real-world effects. While claiming to promote *"liberation"* and *"justice,"* the practical implementation of these ideas often produces exactly the *opposite*: increased division, decreased cooperation, and a kind of societal paralysis that makes actual progress nearly impossible.

Consider what happens when institutions fully embrace this religion. Universities which have most thoroughly adopted these ideas haven't become more open and *"inclusive"* - they've often become ideological monocultures where genuine debate becomes impossible. Any dis-

---

[671] Shapin, Steven. *The Scientific Revolution* (University of Chicago Press, 1996).

[672] Eisenstein, Elizabeth. *The Printing Press as an Agent of Change* (Cambridge Press, 1979).

[673] Needham, Joseph. *Science and Civilisation in China* (Cambridge Press, 1954).

[674] Abu-Lughod, Janet L. *Before European Hegemony* (Oxford University Press, 1989).

agreement is labelled as *"harmful"* or evidence of *"privilege,"* creating an intellectual environment more reminiscent of religious orthodoxy than academic inquiry.

The workplace provides another stark example. When organisations implement these ideas, they often find:

- Decreased collaboration as people become hesitant to interact
- Reduced meritocracy as performance metrics are viewed with suspicion
- Increased tension as every interaction is scrutinised for *"power dynamics"*
- Lower productivity as energy is diverted to constant analysis of *"privilege"*
- Rising conflict as people are encouraged to view colleagues as *"oppressor"* and *"oppressed"*

In education, the results are particularly troubling. Schools which fully embrace this worldview often see:

- Declining academic standards as objective measures are questioned
- Increased racial consciousness and division among students
- Reduced emphasis on individual achievement
- Growing hostility between different student groups
- Parents and teachers afraid to address problems directly

The religion's emphasis on *"lived experience"* and rejection of objective standards creates practical impossibilities in problem-solving. How do you build a bridge if you believe mathematics is a *"tool of oppression"*? How do you develop medical treatments if you reject the scientific method as *"Western dominance"*? How do you run a complex organisation if every decision must be analysed through multiple *"intersecting"* layers of *"power dynamics"*?

By insisting that everything is interconnected through *"systems of oppression,"* the religion's sacred scripture creates a kind of paralysis where no problem can be addressed without simultaneously addressing *all* problems. This "everything is everything" approach makes practical improvements nearly impossible.

Most ironically, societies which most embrace these ideas often become *more*, not less, obsessed with power and privilege. Rather than reducing division, they *amplify* it. Rather than promoting harmony, they *foster* conflict. Rather than solving practical problems, they become trapped in endless cycles of accusation and self-examination.

Moral Maze: The Ethics of Having No Ethics

The religion's treatment of morality represents perhaps its most glaring philosophical contradiction. It simultaneously maintains two incompatible positions: a) all moral claims are *"socially constructed"* products of *"power relations,"* and b) certain moral claims (about *"justice," "oppression,"* and *"liberation"*) are absolutely true and binding. This isn't just a minor inconsistency - it's a *fundamental* contradiction which undermines the *entire* ethical foundation of the worldview.

Consider their central claim: *oppression is wrong and fighting it is a moral imperative.* But if all morality is merely a *"social construct"* shaped by *"power relations,"* then this claim itself has no special moral status. It's just another *"construct,"* another expression of *"power."* They can't claim fighting oppression is objectively right, while simultaneously denying the existence of objective moral truth.

This creates an unsolvable dilemma: If moral relativism is true (all morality is *"constructed"*), then their moral claims about *"justice"* and *"oppression"* are merely *opinions*, no more valid than the systems they oppose. A slave owner's morality would be just as *"constructed"* as an abolitionist's. Their framework provides no basis for saying one is better than the other.

If, however, some moral truths are objective (like "oppression is wrong"), then their fundamental premise about all truth being *"socially constructed"* collapses. They would have to admit that some truths exist independently of *"power relations"* - but this admission would undermine their entire theological foundation.

Believers attempt to escape this contradiction through various sophisticated philosophical manoeuvres. They might argue that they're operating within a particular moral tradition, while acknowledging its constructed nature.

Or they might claim recognising the *"constructed"* nature of morality somehow makes their moral claims more valid. But these are intellectual sleights of hand which don't resolve the basic contradiction.

This moral incoherence has practical consequences. It leads to selective moral relativism - relativistic about traditional moral claims but absolutely certain about their own moral positions. They'll question universal human rights as a *"Western construct"* while asserting their *own* moral frameworks as universal truths. They'll deconstruct traditional moral systems while treating their *own* moral claims as beyond questioning.

Most troublingly, this contradiction undermines their ability to make compelling moral arguments. If you claim all morality is *"constructed"* by *"power relations,"* you can't then make moral appeals which are supposed to transcend *"power relations."* You can't say "this is wrong" - you can only say "this conflicts with our constructed moral framework."

Power Paralysis: When Everything Becomes Oppression

One of the most damaging practical effects of this religion is how it makes actual problem-solving nearly impossible. By insisting on viewing every situation through the *"lens"* of *"power"* and *"oppression,"* it creates a kind of analytical paralysis which prevents practical action and positive change.

Consider what happens when this framework encounters a real-world problem. Take educational achievement gaps. A pragmatic approach might examine multiple factors: teaching methods, family structures, resource allocation, cultural attitudes toward education, study habits, peer influences. But in this religion, *all* these factors must be analysed primarily as manifestations of *"systemic oppression."*

This inevitably creates several paralysing effects:

- Simple solutions become impossible because every problem must be treated as a manifestation of entire systems
- Practical improvements are rejected unless they address the entire system
- Individual agency disappears as everything is attributed to *"systemic forces"*
- Aptitude becomes suspect because all standards are viewed as *"tools of oppression"*
- Cooperation becomes difficult because every interaction is scrutinised for *"power dynamics"*

Woke theology creates a kind of "oppression of the gaps" - wherever there's a problem or disparity, *"oppression"* must be the explanation. This leads to *absurd* conclusions: if a bridge collapses, it must somehow reflect *"systemic oppression."* If a medical treatment fails, *"power dynamics"* must be to blame. If a business struggles, it must be due to *"structural inequities."*

Most destructively, this mindset creates what we might call "the paralysis of purity." Since no solution can be perfect (as all solutions exist within *"systems of oppression"*), *no* solution is acceptable. The perfect becomes the enemy of the good, and practical progress becomes impossible.

Not to mention perverse incentives: rather than encouraging people to solve problems, it rewards them for finding *new* forms of *"oppression"* to report and *"analyse."* Success becomes measured not by positive change, but by one's ability to identify and articulate ever more subtle forms of *"systemic power."*

The Pseudoscience Problem: Unfalsifiability and Circular Logic

The religion's relationship with science represents a particularly revealing contradiction, which reflects the humanities' increasingly hostile behaviour towards the sciences. While claiming to offer insights about *"social reality,"* it violates fundamental principles of scientific inquiry in ways which show it up as pseudoscience.

Karl Popper's criterion of falsifiability is crucial here: for any theory to be scientific, it must be possible to *prove it wrong*. Real scientific theories make *specific* predictions that can be tested and potentially disproven[675]. Einstein's theories, for instance, made precise predictions about light bending around stars - predictions which could have been proven false[676].

But this belief system is constructed to be immune to disproof. Consider how it handles contrary evidence:

- If you find no evidence of *"systemic oppression,"* it just shows how *deeply hidden* it is
- If data contradicts theory, the data itself is dismissed as a product of *"oppressive systems"*
- If someone disagrees, this is taken as evidence of their *"privilege"* or *"false consciousness"*
- If a member of an *"oppressed group"* disagrees, they're labelled as exhibiting *"internalised oppression"*

This creates a closed logical system where everything confirms the theory, and nothing can disprove it. Found oppression? The theory is right. Found no oppression? The theory is still right - you just don't see how deep the oppression goes. This is exactly how pseudoscientific theories operate.

---

[675] Popper, Karl. *Conjectures and Refutations* (Routledge & Kegan Paul, 1963).

[676] Einstein, Albert. 'Zur Elektrodynamik bewegter Körper', *Annalen der Physik*, (1905)

The religion's approach to evidence is particularly telling. Real science carefully gathers evidence and adjusts theories based on findings. This belief system does the opposite - it starts with conclusions and interprets all evidence to fit those conclusions. It's more akin to conspiracy thinking than scientific inquiry: once you "see" the *"system of oppression,"* everything becomes evidence of its existence.

Even more fundamentally, the priesthood's rejection of objectivity undermines the very possibility of scientific inquiry. If all knowledge claims are merely expressions of *"power,"* how can we trust any scientific findings? If objective truth is impossible, why should we believe in any empirical research? The religion cuts off the branch it's sitting on.

The damage this does to thinking is severe. Instead of careful empirical research into social problems, we get predetermined conclusions wrapped in academic language. Instead of testing hypotheses, we get endless restatements of the same theoretical assumptions. Instead of building knowledge, we get ideological reinforcement.

Occam's Razor: When Simple Explanations Are Better

The religion systematically ignores or dismisses simpler explanations for social phenomena. *Occam's Razor* suggests that among competing explanations, we should prefer the one requiring the fewest assumptions. Yet this belief system consistently chooses complex explanations involving *"systemic oppression"* over more straightforward alternatives[677].

Some examples:

- Different educational outcomes might be better explained by varying *cultural attitudes* toward education, family structures, or study habits
- Economic disparities might reflect differences in *cultural values* around saving, investment, and delayed gratification
- Gender representation in certain fields might relate to different

---

[677] William of Ockham. *Summa Logicae* (1323).

average *preferences and choices* rather than *"systemic barriers"*
- Achievement gaps might connect to *specific, addressable factors* like homework completion rates or parent involvement

Instead, the priests of wokery insist on explaining everything through an intricate web of *"systemic oppression,"* requiring gullible students to believe in:

- Vast, coordinated *"systems of power"* that somehow operate without explicit coordination
- Hidden *"biases"* so subtle they can only be detected by specialised theory
- Forms of *"oppression"* so deeply internalised even the oppressed don't recognise them
- *"Power structures"* so pervasive they shape every aspect of reality yet remain invisible to most people

This violates both *Occam's Razor* and common sense. It's like insisting that a baseball game's outcome must be explained by complex conspiracy theories rather than simply looking at how well each team played.

Resistance to simpler explanations reveals its ideological nature. Real inquiry follows evidence wherever it leads. This worldview starts with conclusions about *"systemic oppression"* and forces all evidence to fit a storyline, no matter how many additional assumptions and complications this requires.

The Price of Purity: Societal Decay

When societies embrace this secular theology, they experience predictable forms of institutional and cultural decline. Rather than creating the promised utopia of *"justice"* and *"liberation,"* the religion corrodes the fundamental mechanisms which allow complex societies to function.

Consider the institutional impacts:

- Universities become intellectually homogeneous, prioritising ideological conformity over truth-seeking
- Businesses become less efficient as merit-based decisions are viewed with suspicion
- Government agencies prioritise symbolic representation over effective service delivery
- Scientific institutions lose public trust as objectivity is questioned
- Cultural institutions replace excellence with ideology
- Media organisations abandon journalistic standards for storyline enforcement

The social fabric itself begins to fray:

- Relationships between groups become *more* hostile, not less
- Common ground disappears as everything is viewed through *"power dynamics"*
- Social trust declines as people fear being labelled *"oppressors"*
- Productive dialogue becomes impossible as disagreement is seen as *"violence"*
- Achievement is discouraged as success becomes associated with *"privilege"*
- Individual agency is denied in favour of tribal group "identity"

Most devastatingly, it undermines the very qualities needed for flourishing:

- Innovation declines when merit becomes suspect
- Problem-solving capacity diminishes when everything is attributed to *"systemic forces"*
- Social cooperation breaks down when all interactions are viewed through *"power dynamics"*
- Cultural achievement stagnates when excellence is viewed as *"oppressive"*

- Economic productivity suffers when outcome *"equality"* is prioritised over growth
- Scientific advancement slows when objective truth is questioned

The result is a kind of societal autoimmune disorder where institutions attack their own foundations. Just as religious fundamentalism can cripple a society's ability to adapt and progress, this secular fundamentalism produces rigid orthodoxy which prevents healthy national development.

The Doom Loop

When this belief system takes hold of a vulnerable mind, it initiates a devastating feedback loop. Each turn of the cycle makes them less capable of solving real problems, which in turn "proves" the religion's claims about *"systemic"* failure, leading to even stronger adoption of the theology's prescriptions.

The cycle operates in the following manner:

Stage 1: Initial Adoption

- Institutions embrace the theology as a way to address *"inequities"*
- Traditional standards and practices are questioned as *"tools of oppression"*
- Merit-based systems are dismantled in favour of *"equity"*-based approaches
- People begin viewing all interactions through *"power dynamics"*

Stage 2: Institutional Decay

- Performance declines as competence becomes secondary to ideology
- Problems increase as practical solutions are rejected for ideological reasons
- Trust erodes as people fear being labelled *"oppressors"*
- Productive dialogue becomes impossible

Stage 3: Confirmation Effect

- Rising problems are seen as *"proof"* of *"systemic oppression"*
- Declining institutional performance justifies more radical approaches
- Growing social division *"proves"* societal racism/sexism/etc.
- Increased conflict validates claims about *"power struggles"*

Stage 4: Intensification

- More extreme measures are demanded to fight *"systemic oppression"*
- Remaining merit-based systems are attacked more aggressively
- Moderate voices are increasingly labelled as *"complicit"*
- The range of acceptable dialogue narrows further

Stage 5: Acceleration

- Real problems multiply as practical solutions become impossible
- Social trust completely breaks down
- Institutional competence craters
- Society loses ability to perform basic functions

The tragic irony is that this cycle creates exactly what the religion claims to fight against: a society that's *more* divided, *less* functional, and *less* capable of helping its vulnerable population. The worse things get, the more the religion's diagnoses seem correct, leading to even more destructive *"solutions."*

Detoxifying The Brainwashed Mind

One thing the fanatic radicals of this religion never deconstruct is their own constructions. If one is to confront this virus, a simple set of questions is enough to topple the house of cards:

> 1. The Power Paradox: *"If all claims to truth are just expressions of power, why should I believe your claim about power? Isn't that just your power play?"*

If everything is about power, why isn't your theory just about power, too?

> 2. The Oppression Contradiction: *"If Western civilisation is so oppressive, why do the freest and most prosperous societies in human history stem from it?"*

If our system is so oppressive, why do so many people want to live here?

> 3. The Merit Problem: *"If standards of excellence are just tools of oppression, why do the people claiming this still go to the best doctors when they're sick?"*

If merit is racist, why don't you choose your surgeon by their diversity score?

> 4. The Progress Paradox: *"If systemic racism explains everything, how did we ever make progress on civil rights?"*

If the system is designed to prevent change, how did we ever change?

> 5. The Success Dilemma: *"How do you explain successful people from supposedly oppressed groups? Are they participating in their own oppression?"*

Why do some 'oppressed' people succeed while others don't?"

> 6. The Science Question: *"If all knowledge is socially constructed, why do planes fly and phones work regardless of who built them?"*

If everything is socially constructed, why does gravity work the same for everyone?

> 7. The Action Problem: *"If everything is systemic, what can any individual actually do to change things?"*

If the system controls everything, how can anyone ever fight it?"

> 8. The Measurement Challenge: *"How would you know if oppression had ended? What would that look like?"*

What would success look like? How would we know when we've won?

> 9. The Personal Responsibility Question: *"If personal choices don't matter because everything is systemic, why should anyone try to improve their life?"*

If the system controls everything, why bother trying?

> 10. The Historical Progress Question: *"If power explains everything, how did powerless groups ever gain rights in the first place?"*

If power is everything, how did the powerless ever win?

II

The A-Z of Jargon & Doublespeak

All the definitions, historical usage, and frequency of terms contained herein were meticulously checked via the following primary sources:
Oxford English Dictionary. (OED, 2024). Ibid.
Cambridge Dictionary. (2024). Ibid.
Google Scholar. (n.d.). Ibid.
Google Books Ngram Viewer. (n.d.). Ibid.

A B C

Ableism

The foolish belief disabled people are humourless, fragile creatures requiring your pity, who need yet another thing to worry about.

Inspired by Foucault's "challenging" ideas on mental illness merely being a "social label" (i.e. his)[678], the term arose in the midst of feminist in-fighting. First mentioned in the May 1981 (Volume 11) edition of *"Off Our Backs"* magazine[679]. Later formalised by Castañeda & Peters' 2000 paper *"Addressing Classism, Ableism, and Heterosexism in Counselor Education"*[680].

(Women's Studies, 1981)

---

[678] Foucault, Michel, *Madness and Civilization* (Pantheon Books, 1965; orig. 1961).

[679] 'The Violence of Technicism: Ableism as Humiliation and Degrading Treatment', *Off Our Backs*, 11.5 (1981).

[680] Castañeda, Carmelita, and Marcie L. Peters, 'Addressing Classism, Ableism, and Heterosexism in Counselor Education', *Journal of Multicultural Counseling and Development*, 28.1 (2000), 1–10.

Abortion

> *Manual intervention in a natural healthy pregnancy to deliberately kill a growing child.*

A pregnancy stops (aborts) in two ways: a) spontaneous miscarriage due to chromosomal abnormalities, cervical dysfunction etc[681]., b) a doctor is paid to attack ("induce") the foetus with *Mifepristone, Misoprostol*, or surgical tools in an act of legally sanctioned foeticide[682]. The act was described as *"intent to procure miscarriage"* in the *Offences Against the Person Act 1861*[683]. It was first legalised on-demand in the USSR by Lenin[684].

(Theology, 1537)

Addiction

> *Pathological avoidance of responsibility and/or difficult feelings through the habitual use of chemicals which cause disruption of the brain's natural functioning.*

Before Freud's frequent usage of cocaine[685], drunkards and opium-eaters were considered personally responsible for bad habits. The notion of it being a disease was not posited until 1956 by the *AMA* declaring alco-

---

[681] American College of Obstetricians and Gynecologists, *Management of Early Pregnancy Loss*, ACOG Practice Bulletin, Number 200 (2020).

[682] WHO, *Safe Abortion: Technical and Policy Guidance for Health Systems* (2012).

[683] Parliament of the United Kingdom, *Offences Against the Person Act 1861* (1861).

[684] Goldman, Wendy Z., *Women, the State and Revolution* (Cambridge Press, 1993)

[685] Freud, Sigmund, 'Über Coca', in *Yearbook of Neurology* (Vienna, 1884).

holism an illness[686], and is illustrated perfectly by the disagreement today among professionals between the term and "dependence". *Alcoholics Anonymous* was founded in 1935 by Robert Smith and Bill Wilson[687], and the term was popularised from "habituation" in 1951 by Arthur Grollman in *Pharmacology and Therapeutics*[688].

(Pharmacology, 1951).

ADHD

> *Boredom. A disorder which magically disappears when your child plays video games.*

In 1963, psychologist Keith Conners published a study on the effects of Ritalin *(methylphenidate)* in *"emotionally disturbed children"* and their impulsivity[689]. After fifty-plus years of pharmaceutical profiteering, he publicly confessed he felt *"the over-diagnosis of ADHD was an epidemic of tragic proportions"*[690]. In 1971, R. A. Dykman et al published *"Progress in Learning Disabilities"*[691].

(Psychology, 1963)

---

[686] American Medical Association, 'Proceedings of the House of Delegates', *American Medical Association Proceedings*, 305–306 (1956).

[687] Alcoholics Anonymous World Services, *Pass It On: The Story of Bill Wilson and How the A.A. Message Reached the World* (AA World Services, Inc., 1984).

[688] Grollman, Arthur, *Pharmacology and Therapeutics* (U. of Pennsylvania Press, 1951).

[689] Conners, C. Keith, 'Drug Therapy of Behavioral Disorders', *Journal of Nervous and Mental Disease*, 136.5 (1963), 381–85.

[690] Frances, Allen, 'Keith Conners, Father of ADHD, Regrets Its Current Misuse', *HuffPost* (28 March 2016).

[691] Dykman, Roscoe A., Patricia T. Ackerman, and Doris M. Oglesby, 'Progress in Learning Disabilities', *Journal of Learning Disabilities*, 4.5 (1971)

Adjacent

> *A word people who want to sound intellectual use to mean "guilty by association".*

Get your science right: geometric areas sharing a touching boundary.

Adulting

> *Being a grown up like everyone else.*

In what will assuredly be her only major contribution to human life on Earth, this staggering cringe was popularised by Gabriella Ross ("She/Hers", "BFA/Dance & BS/Kinesiology"), or "TinyDancerA11", on Twitter in 2018[692].

(Internet, 2018)

Affirmative Consent

> *Cunning way to sabotage the date of a woman far more attractive than yourself.*

Feminist writer Lois Pineau's 1989 article *"Date Rape: A Feminist Analysis"* in *Law and Philosophy* is generally regarded as the source of the idea "no means no" or "yes means yes" is not enough[693]. A decade later, it was

---

[692] @TinyDancerA11. (2018, September 17). *Bills are paid. I vacuumed the hall... I think that's enough adulting for today. And tomorrow. And the day after that.*

[693] Pineau, Lois, 'Date Rape: A Feminist Analysis', *Law and Philosophy*, 8.2 (1989)

followed by *"Consent for Sexual Behavior in a College Student Population"*[694] and the hilariously bad *"By the Semi-mystical Appearance of a Condom: How Young Women and Men Communicate Sexual Consent in Heterosexual Situations"* in 1999 by nursing professor Susan Hickman and psychologist Charlene Muehlenhard in *The Journal of Sex Research*[695].

(Feminist Literature, 1989)

Affirming

> *Forcing doctors into agreeing with the patient they can also hear the voices. Killing with kindness.*

"Affirmative care" can be said to have its linguistic origins in *"affirmative action"* (John F Kennedy in the *New York Times*, 1961[696]).Following the WHO's utterly useless *Commission on Social Determinants of Health to Address Gender Identity*[697], the canonical paper referenced most regularly is *"Integrated and gender-affirming transgender clinical care and research"* in the highly credible *Journal of AIDS*[698].

(Medicine, 2016)

---

[694] Hall, D. S. (1998). Consent for Sexual Behavior in a College Student Population. *Electronic Journal of Human Sexuality, 1.*

[695] Hickman, Susan E., and Charlene L. Muehlenhard, 'By the Semi-Mystical Appearance of a Condom: How Young Women and Men Communicate Sexual Consent in Heterosexual Situations', *The Journal of Sex Research*, 36.3 (1999), 258–72.

[696] Kennedy, John F., *Executive Order 10925* (Federal Register Vol. 26, 6 March 1961).

[697] Commission on Social Determinants of Health. (2008). *Closing the gap in a generation: Health equity through action on the social determinants of health* (Final Report). Geneva: World Health Organization.

[698] Reisner, Sari L., Tonia Poteat, and Asa Radix, 'Integrated and Gender-Affirming Transgender Clinical Care and Research', *Journal of Acquired Immune Deficiency Syndromes*, 72.3 (2016), e58–e68

African American

> *Black.*

Apparently traceable as far back as 1782 in a Philadelphia newspaper[699], the phrase was popularised by Jesse Jackson in 1989 at a meeting of seventy-five black groups[700]. Doesn't seem to include white South Africans or North African Arabs.

(Politics, 1989).

Algorithmic Bias/Fairness

> *Lobotomising AI models and deliberately corrupting search engine results so they emphasise left-wing ideology.*

In 2016, *Microsoft* naively put an AI chatbot (*"Tay"*) out into the wild which was to act like a nineteen-year-old girl and "learn" from *Twitter*. After sixteen hours and 96,000 tweets interacting with pranksters, Tay proclaimed feminism "cancer" and *"Hitler was right"*[701]. A year later, Google Images' "racist" machine learning was wrongly labelling black people as *"gorillas"*[702], YouTube was "radicalising" young men away from

---

[699] Schuessler, Jennifer, 'The Term "African-American" Appears Earlier Than Thought: Reporter's Notebook', *The New York Times* (21 April 2015).

[700] Wilkerson, Isabel, '"African-American" Favored by Many of America's Blacks', *The New York Times* (31 January 1989).

[701] Vincent, James, 'Twitter Taught Microsoft's AI Chatbot to Be a Racist Asshole in Less Than a Day', *The Verge* (24 March 2016).

[702] Hern, Alex, 'Google "Fixed" Its Racist Algorithm by Removing Gorillas from Its Image-Labeling Tech', *The Guardian* (12 January 2018).

social justice, and *Word2Vec* apparently contained "sexist bias"[703].

The result being a) bias in the opposite direction, and b) the thousands of university activists/entryists at *Google* attempting to psychologically engineer people by showing you what it thinks what you should look at rather than what you asked for. The attention of outraged activists obsessed with power and the means of knowledge production, of course, on the extraordinary, planet-breaking power and influence of Internet search is entirely coincidental.

(Computer Science, 2018)

Aligned with Our Values

> *A generic weasel statement offered as a reason for firing an employee or partner who has incurred the wrath of a Maoist mob of Red Guards on social media, many of whom work as political commissars in HR departments.*

The vomit-inducing sanctimony of business "values" is yet another jobs scheme for sociology graduates with its origins in a flurry of papers around 1990, such as *"Corporations, culture and commitment: Motivation and social control in organizations"* (C.A. O'Reilly, *California Management Review*[704]) and *"Corporate Culture and Economic Theory"* (David Kreps)[705].

(Business, 1990)

---

[703] Bolukbasi, Tolga, et al., 'Man Is to Computer Programmer as Woman Is to Homemaker? Debiasing Word Embeddings', *Proceedings of the 30th International Conference on Neural Information Processing Systems* (2016), 4349–57.

[704] O'Reilly, Charles A., 'Corporations, Culture, and Commitment: Motivation and Social Control in Organizations', *California Management Review*, 32.4 (1990), 9–25.

[705] Kreps, David M., 'Corporate Culture and Economic Theory', in *Perspectives on Positive Political Economy*, ed. by James E. Alt and Kenneth A. Shepsle (Cambridge University Press, 1990), pp. 90–143.

Ally(ship)

> *A word people who want to sound intellectual™ use for "supporter" when they are embarrassed by "apologist" or "sympathiser".*

The concept of an ally is as old as humanity, but typically refers to situations involving conflict (predominantly in relation to nation states). However, the pulpit-rivalling, self-aggrandising and ego-stroking modern version has its roots in the concept of "privilege" and the theories of "oppression". Although a flood of dreadful papers start to appear around 2000, the most likely source is *"Beyond Tolerance: Gays, Lesbians, and Bisexuals on Campus"* (Nancy J. Evans, Vernon A. Wall, 1991)[706].

(Education, 1991)

Antifascist

> *Morally pure vigilante superhero—ironically dressed as a masked fascist black bloc thug—ready to protect innocent ordinary people from difficult ideas with gang vandalism, sabotage, and violence.*

Communists have called themselves "antifascists" for a century. The first to coin the term was Mussolini himself, who described his own secret police as an organisation which hunted down "anti-fascists"[707].

Conventionally, the starting point of socialist and communist resistance to fascism in Europe is dated to the 1930s in the context of the establishment of the *Third Reich* in 1933 and the outbreak of the Spanish

---

[706] Evans, N. J., & Wall, V. A. *Beyond Tolerance*. ACPA (1991)

[707] Payne, Stanley G., *A History of Fascism, 1914–1945* (U. of Wisconsin Press, 1995).

Civil War in 1936[708] (in which Orwell fought[709]).

The fragments of German socialist and communist parties who resisted the Nazis — 15,000 or so — allied from within housing estates and were called *"Antifaschistische Ausschüsse"*, *"Antifaschistische Kommittees"*, or the now famous *"Antifaschistische Aktion"* (*"Antifa"*)[710][711].

(Political Science, 1932)

Antiracism

> *A clever way to make $20,000/hr in consulting fees, by telling people you despise because of their skin colour, and who reject racism, that they're all intractably racist because of invisible "systems".*

Buried deep within Foucault's "ways of knowing", this doublethink phrase was popularised by *"African American Studies"* professor Henry Rogers, aka *"Ibram X Kendi"*, in his 2018 book *"How To Be An Antiracist"*[712].

It describes absolute devotion to a Gnostic religious belief where the mystical spirit of racism organises all living things. This evil spirit can only be overcome with communist theory, and being more racist.

The notion was supposedly first uttered by radical communist Angela Davis, who allegedly declared, *"In a racist society, it is not enough to be non-racist, we must be anti-racist"* [713].

(Sociology, 2018)

---

[708] Beevor, Antony, *The Battle for Spain* (Penguin, 2006).

[709] Orwell, George, *Homage to Catalonia* (Secker & Warburg, 1938).

[710] Kühnl, Reinhard, *Fascism and Anti-Fascism* (Routledge, 1990).

[711] Copsey, Nigel, *Anti-Fascism in Britain* (Macmillan, 2000).

[712] Kendi, Ibram X., *How to Be an Antiracist* (One World, 2018).

[713] While the exact phrase is widely attributed to Angela Davis, it may not appear verbatim in her published works. However, her writings and speeches, including *"Women, Race, & Class"*, convey similar sentiments, emphasising the importance of *"active resistance"* against racism rather than mere neutrality.

Anti-vaxx(er)

> *Science-denying, ignorant, selfish, insurrectionist who spurns society's collective will for a government to mandate they submit to an experimental, ineffective medical treatment known to cause serious harm, produced by manufacturers given legal immunity despite being punished for serious criminality in the past.*

Formerly a phrase attributed to homeopathic enthusiasts who are suspicious of pathogen cultures being injected into their body (and/or those who followed the storyline of *"The X-Files"*)[714], *Merriam Webster* helpfully updated the definition to include those against authoritarian laws and/or regulations requiring government-mandated experimental medical procedures in 2018[715]. The phrase was originally conceived as a slur on the *misc.health.alternative* Usenet group in 2001[716].

(Internet, 2001)

Anxiety

> *Debilitating, unstoppable, and heartbreaking medical disability special people suffer from when facing the obstacle of needing to something everyone has to, which requires character.*

Feeling anxious is normal; it is one of the twenty-seven human emo-

---

[714] Lowry, Benjamin, *The Truth Is Out There* (Harper Prism, 1995).

[715] Merriam-Webster, 'Anti-Vaxxer', *Merriam-Webster Dictionary* (2018).

[716] *Google Groups* Archive (2001).

tions[717]. When it is persistent at a pathological level, it can become a disorder. The idea children need treatment *without* a diagnosis of a disorder - outside of cult grooming practices of deliberate sensitisation - is traceable back to articles in the *Journal of Adolescent Psychiatry*, such as *"How can epidemiology improve mental health services for children and adolescents?"*[718].

(Psychology, 1993)

Assault Rifle/Weapon

The thing you use to defend yourself when you are 5ft 2in 100lbs, as a 6ft 250lbs meth-starved rapist is following you to your car.

The *Washington Post* claims this phrase riginated in a 1988 paper, *"Assault Weapons and Accessories in America"*, written by gun-control activist Josh Sugarmann, founder of the *Violence Policy Center*[719].

(Activism, 1988)

Asexual

The condition your doctor explains to your spouse you suffer with, after the third weekend you've been "away on business."

---

[717] Cowen, Alan S., and Dacher Keltner, 'Self-Report Captures 27 Distinct Categories of Emotion Bridged by Continuous Gradients', *Proceedings of the National Academy of Sciences*, 114.38 (2017), E7900–E7909.

[718] Costello, Elizabeth J., Barbara J. Burns, Adrian Angold, and Peter J. Leaf, 'How Can Epidemiology Improve Mental Health Services for Children and Adolescents?', *Journal of the American Academy of Child & Adolescent Psychiatry*, 32.7 (1993), 525–533.

[719] Sugarmann, Josh, 'Assault Weapons and Accessories in America', *Violence Policy Center* (1988)

The process of asexual reproduction (*mitosis*) in plants and single-celled organisms was documented around 1665 by Robert Hooke[720]. The fanciful notion humans are magically born with no will to reproduce emerged at the turn of the 20th century within *"The Semi-Insane and the Semi-Responsible"* by French neurologist and parapsychological investigator Smith Ely Jelliffe[721].

(Psychology, 1907)

Assigned At Birth

> *The cruel, ignorant, and misguided actions of biological essentialists from 1811, observing which of the two human forms 99.994% of non-hermaphroditic infants arrived as.*

Despite it not being possible for neonatal children to have experienced any form of socialisation[722], whilst simultaneously displaying gender-specific traits (e.g, face/object attraction)[723], the humanities began assuming medical scientists knew less than they did around 2010, citing John Money's theory of *"Gender Neutrality at Birth"* after the idea of "reassignment" surgery[724].

In the *Columbia Law Review*, Jessica A. Clarke notes[725] usage dramatically increased after U.S. case law on discrimination against transgender people exploded, based on *Title VII* of the *Civil Rights Act*, and the term

---

[720] Hooke, Robert, *Micrographia* (John Martyn and James Allestry, 1665).

[721] Grasset, Joseph, *The Semi-Insane and the Semi-Responsible* (Funk & Wagnalls Co., 1907).

[722] Harris, Judith R., *The Nurture Assumption* (Free Press, 1998).

[723] Connellan, Jennifer, Simon Baron-Cohen, Sally Wheelwright, Alexandra Batki, and Jagjit Ahluwalia, 'Sex Differences in Human Neonatal Social Perception', *Infant Behavior and Development*, 23.1 (2000), 113–20.

[724] Money, John, 'Hermaphroditism, Gender, and Precocity in Hyperadrenocorticism: Psychological Findings', *Bulletin of the Johns Hopkins Hospital*, 96.4 (1952), 253–64.

[725] Clarke, Jessica A., 'Sex Assigned at Birth', *Columbia Law Review*, 122.7 (2022), 1823–92.

notoriously appeared in the Obama-era *2016 Affordable Care Act*[726].

(*Psychology, 2014*)

Assisted Dying

A compassionate way for the state to save on palliative hospice care.
Suicide is progressive.

An upgrade to what we used to call *euthanasia* (Greek: "an easy or happy death"), or *"mercy killing"*. The Swiss legalised *"assisted suicide"* in 1976[727], followed by Holland in 2001[728], which Canada renamed *"Medical Assistance in Dying"* (MAiD) during 2016[729]. Its current euphemism derives from the 1993 book *"Lawful exit : the limits of freedom for help in dying"* by journalist Derek Humphry[730].

The body of the first user of a *Sarco* "assisted suicide pod" at the *Last Resort* clinic in Switzerland was found with unexplained strangulation marks[731].

(*Law, 1976*)

---

[726] Nondiscrimination in Health Programs and Activities, 81 *Federal Register* 31,376, 31,467 (18 May 2016).

[727] Hurst, Samia A., and André Mauron, 'Assisted Suicide and Euthanasia in Switzerland: Allowing a Role for Non-Physicians', *BMJ*, 326.7383 (2003), 271–73.

[728] Griffiths, John, Heleen Weyers, and Maurice Adams, *Euthanasia and Law in Europe* (Oxford University Press, 2008).

[729] Downie, Jocelyn, and Angela Lloyd-Smith, 'Medical Assistance in Dying: Reflections on the Carter Decision', *Health Law Journal*, 23 (2015), 1–26.

[730] Humphry, Derek, *Lawful Exit* (Hemlock Society, 1993).

[731] Marsden, Emma. 'Woman Using Suicide Pod Reportedly Found with "Strangulation" Marks Inside', *Newsweek*, 30 October 2024

Authentic

> *Not being a fraud, imposter, charlatan, pseud, or pretentious social-climber.*

Get your science right: something with an undisputed origin.

Autoethanography

> *My diary.*

First described by Walter Goldschmidt in *"Anthropology and the Coming Crisis: An Autoethnographic Appraisal"*[732], diary entries as "academic research" was expanded by Stanley Brandes in 1979 within *"Ethnographic autobiographies in American anthropology"*[733].

(Anthropology, 1977)

BAME

> *Non-white (British).*

In the late seventies, the *Anti-Nazi League* (founded by the *Socialist Workers Party*) coined the term *"Black, Asian, and Minority Ethnic"* as a super-category for those who were *"politically black"*[734]. The term became

---

[732] Goldschmidt, Walter, 'Anthropology and the Coming Crisis: An Autoethnographic Appraisal', *Anthropologist*, 79.2 (1977).

[733] Brandes, Stanley, 'Ethnographic Autobiographies in American Anthropology', *American Anthropologist*, 81.2 (1979), 311–32.

[734] Holborow, Peter, 'The Anti-Nazi League and Its Lessons for Today', *International Socialism*, 163 (2019).

orthodoxy in the UK *Civil Service*[735] and appeared on the census. By 1990, it was clear everyone under the label hated it[736].

(Government, 1979)

Bigot

> *Unperson who stubbornly refuses to accept behaviour should not be subject to morality at all, even after threats, mobbing, vilification, and the condemnation of intellectual™ professors.*

Although it's traditionally been with us for four centuries as a French-pejorative term for overly-religious Normans who were obsessively tied to their beliefs, the contemporary meaning of the word as someone prejudiced against identity groups re-emerged in the seventies and nineties, in magazines such as *Face*[737].

(Activism, late-60s)

Binary

> *It's fashionable to talk about them. It sounds intellectual™. They're not supposed to exist and only humans created them in their foolish chimp-like minds to oppress others.*

Although "fashionable" discussion started around 1953, the term resonates to Jacques Derrida. He was *profound*, despite not being able to understand *"signs"*. With his dislike of Western *"logocentrism"*[738] and his

---

[735] Bunglawala, Z., 'Please, Don't Call Me BAME or BME!', *Civil Service Blog*, 8 July 2019.

[736] Modood, Tariq, 'Political Blackness and British Asians', *Sociology*, 28.4 (1994)

[737] *Face Magazine* (Various Issues, Late 1990s).

[738] Derrida, Jacques, *Of Grammatology* (Johns Hopkins University Press, 1976).

self-admitted "Marxist" concept of *"deconstruction"*[739], his broader thesis was text could only be understood at all in the concept of competing opposites (which he also misunderstood from the original definition of a binary of *being one of two*).

(Literature, 1967)

Biological Essentialism

> *Science. The "Nature" bit in Nature vs Nurture, or "Hardware" bit in Hardware vs Software. The arch-enemy global supervillain trying to destroy the Brave Movement to define everything you've ever heard of as something society, (whomever that is) just made up with words. What Joseph Mengele and the Nazis did.*

Darwin's theses introduced the idea of populations and *polymorphism*[740], which updated the classical Greek theories of *Forms*[741]. Since the 1930s, essentialism has been seen as outdated. Children can grasp it, professors can't. Sociology's sharpest anti-positivist slur in the fight to prove it's all really nurture. The term emerged from nowhere, back from the grave, in the nineties.

(Sociology, mid-90s)

---

[739] Derrida, Jacques, *Specters of Marx* (Routledge, 1994).

[740] Darwin, Charles, *On the Origin of Species by Means of Natural Selection, or the Preservation of Favoured Races in the Struggle for Life* (John Murray, 1859).

[741] Plato, *The Republic*, (Hackett Publishing Company, 1992).

Biopower

> *One French child rapist's bizarre attempt to explain everything in terms of sadomasochist sex.*

Michel Foucault's thought in his 1978 *"History of Sexuality"* theorising governments and those with "power" use biological notions to enslave "*bodies*"[742].

(Sociology, 1978)

BIPOC

> *Non-white (American).*

An upgrade to PoC (*"People of Color"*) and *"women of color"* (inscribed at the 1977 *National Women's Conference* in Houston[743]), BIPOC's first appearance was traced back by the *New York Times* to a random 2013 Tweet by a sex party organizer named *GRIND*[744].

(Internet, 2013)

Biphobia

> *Being a little suspicious of female university students who kiss each other at a bar for male attention, or tick the "bisexual" survey form box to get special accommodations.*

---

[742] Foucault, Michel, *The History of Sexuality*, (Pantheon Books, 1978).

[743] National Women's Conference, *Proceedings* (1977).

[744] Garcia, Sandra, 'Where Did BIPOC Come From?', *The New York Times*, 17 Jun 2020

Made-up in a July–August 1982 edition of the bimonthly bisexual magazine *Bi-monthly*, published in San Francisco[745]. Redefined in 1992 by researcher Kathleen Bennett as the *"denigration of bisexuality as a valid life choice"* in Elizabeth Weise's book *"Closer to Home: Bisexuality and Feminism."*[746]

(Literature, 1982)

Birthing Person

Mother.

Where does one begin with an abstraction so reductive? Truly one of the worst possible protologisms in recent memory, the linguistic relegation of mothers to broodmare laboratory apes emerged - as it always does - on the university campus, where it then floated downstream to public officials.

In this case, around 2020 at *Harvard Medical School*[747], where it was parroted by *Vogue* magazine; then by Cori Bush as *"maternal justice"* in the *US Congress* through the encouragement of the pro-abortion lobby organisation, *NARAL*[748].

(Education, 2020)

---

[745] *Bi-Monthly*, 'I Have Put Up with Innumerable Arguments about "When Will Bisexuals Make Up Their Minds"', July–August 1982.

[746] Weise, Elizabeth Reba (ed.), *Closer to Home* (Seal Press, 1992).

[747] Harvard Medical School, *Advancing Equity and Diversity in Reproductive Health* (2020).

[748] Bush, Cori, 'Cori Bush's Testimony on Black Maternal Health before the U.S. House Committee on Oversight and Reform', *Congressional Record*, 13 April 2021.

Black Lives Matter

> *Communist agitation group organised on social media for racketeering and embezzlement, derived as modern reincarnation of the Black Liberation Army. Buying Large Mansions.*

Although described as a spontaneous *Twitter* "movement" (i.e. hashtag[749]), the three "community organisers" of BLM - Patrisse Cullors, Alicia Garza, and Opal Tometi - were radicalised much earlier than reported.

Cullors in 2001 at the *Labor Community Strategy Center* (LCSC), Garza in 2002 at the *School of Unity and Liberation* (SOUL), and Tometiin in 2009 at the activist group *Witness*[750].

The trip confessed to being *"trained Marxists"*, who adopted a communist fist as their logo[751] with the mentoring of ex-*Weather Underground* members[752] after their study of Lenin and Mao.

> *Its leaders hobnob with militant leftists such as Angela Davis and former Weather Underground members Eric Mann and Susan Rosenberg. Mann, who mentored BLM Global Network co-founder Patrisse Cullors, maintains that whether the issue is race, sex, gender, immigration, or the environment, the revolutionary goal remains the same.*[753]

---

[749] Garza, Alicia, 'A Herstory of the #BlackLivesMatter Movement', *The Feminist Wire*, 7 October 2014.

[750] Cullors, Patrisse, Alicia Garza, and Opal Tometi, 'Black Lives Matter Founders Reflect on the Movement', *The New Yorker* (2020).

[751] Jensen, Carsten, 'Raised Fists: Origins of a Symbol of Resistance', *Jacobin* (2019)

[752] Mann, Eric, *Playbook for Progressives* (Beacon Press, 2011).

[753] 'Americans Deserve to Know Who Funded BLM Riots', *Newsweek*, 16 March 2023.

It was their public ceremonies of Nigerian *Odu Ifa* witchcraft[754][755][756] which apparently netted them an entire series of multi-million dollar California mansions[757] - and the country several billions in repairs.

(*Internet, 2013*)

Bodied

Where your magic identity soul lives.

Not people. Lumps of flesh put in prison; enslaved on trading ships; or too fat to be attractive. An overly-literal neologism derived from Michel Foucault's bizarre ideas about the government "subjugating" bodies (*"biopower"*)[758] which was popularised in *"Scripting the Black Masculine Body"* (2006), by sociologist Ronald Jackson[759].

(*Sociology, 2006*)

Bodily Autonomy

Not something the policeman arresting you is going to see as a persuasive argument.

---

[754] Cullors, Patrisse, *When They Call You a Terrorist* (St. Martin's Press, 2018).

[755] 'BLM Co-Founder, LA Chapter Leader Discuss Group's Occultic Practices of Invoking Spirits, African Ancestral Worship', *Christian News Network*, 28 August 2020.

[756] Berkley Center for Religion, Peace, and World Affairs, 'The Fight for Black Lives Is a Spiritual Movement' (2020).

[757] Charter, David, 'BLM Co-Founder Admits Using Mansion Bought with Donations', *The Times*, 10 May 2022.

[758] Foucault, Michel, *The History of Sexuality* (Pantheon Books, 1978).

[759] Jackson II, Ronald L., *Scripting the Black Masculine Body* (State University of New York Press, 2006).

In the history of our species, no human society on planet Earth has agreed with the idea people have absolute physical "autonomy" over their body, let alone it being a "fundamental right". Law enforcement is empowered to make arrests and detain the infectious or mentally ill; courts imprison or execute those found guilty of a crime; employers can demand drug testing, as border officers may perform searches; vaccinations are mandatory[760].

Both Martha C. Nussbaum's *Sex and Social Justice* (1999)[761], and Diana Tietjens Meyers' *Gender in the Mirror: Cultural Imagery and Women's Agency* (2002)[762], also draw upon Michel Foucault's idiotic concept of *"biopower"*[763], which hypothesises institutions "oppress" people through control of their bodies. Not unlike what Foucault apparently did to little boys in Tunis graveyards[764].

(Womens' Studies, 1999)

Body/Fat Positivity

> *Having a totally reasonable belief that no-one should dare shame you - by finding you unattractive - if you refuse to moderate your diet or exercise regularly.*

Despite obesity becoming endemic in Western culture, the "body acceptance" movement can trace itself back to Lew Louderback's 1967 essay *"More People Should be Fat!"*[765] and the establishment of the *National*

---

[760] Gostin, Lawrence O., *Public Health Law* (University of California Press, 2008).

[761] Nussbaum, Martha C., *Sex and Social Justice* (Oxford University Press, 1999).

[762] Meyers, Diana T., *Gender in the Mirror* (Oxford University Press, 2002).

[763] Foucault, Michel, *The History of Sexuality* (Pantheon Books, 1978).

[764] Sorman, Guy, 'Michel Foucault, the Great Philosopher, Was Also a Pedophile', *The Sunday Times*, 7 March 2021.

[765] Louderback, Lew, 'More People Should Be Fat!', *Saturday Evening Post*, 240.19 (1967).

Association to Advance Fat Acceptance (NAAFA) in 1969[766]. Multiple "scholars" in 1983 claimed that fat hatred is formed or influenced by other forces of "oppression", but popularisation of the term is attributed to Kathleen LeBesco and her 2004 contribution to one of the world's stupidest publication resumes[767], *"Revolting Bodies?: The Struggle to Redefine Fat Identity"*[768].

(Literature, 1969)

Born In The Wrong Body

Thinking like a girl when you're a boy. Doing boy stuff if you're a girl. Being upset about it because... society.

The rationalist concept of the mind and body being separate has been with us since Greek times as *Mind-Body Dualism*[769]. It's also the concept in the philosophy of *Soma* (body)[770] and *Psyche* (mind)[771]. The expression finds its modern routes in German psychiatrist Richard von Krafft-Ebing's theory of *"Sexual Inversion"* which was included on his large list of seriously disturbing sexual behaviour[772].

(Psychology, 1928)

---

[766] National Association to Advance Fat Acceptance, *Founding Documents* (1969).

[767] LeBesco, Kathleen, *Scientific Contributions of Kathleen LeBesco*, ResearchGate

[768] LeBesco, Kathleen, *Revolting Bodies?* (University of Massachusetts Press, 2004).

[769] Descartes, René, *Meditations on First Philosophy*, (Cambridge Press, 1996).

[770] Plato, *Phaedo*, (Hackett Publishing Company, 1997).

[771] Aristotle, *De Anima (On the Soul)*, (Penguin Classics, 1986).

[772] Krafft-Ebing, Richard von, *Psychopathia Sexualis* (Enke, 1886).

Born This Way

> *Supernatural personal understanding of one's own biological state minutes after birth.*

Although the spirit behind the term goes back decades into the nature/nurture debate around homosexuality, the contemporary phrase is associated with the single and album of the same name released by dancer *"Lady Gaga"* (Stefani Joanne Angelina Germanotta) in 2010, which arch-Queen *Elton John* declared the *"New Gay Anthem"*[773]. A precedent was released in 1975[774]. "Gaga" so insightfully commented,

> *It's almost like a sermon. I heard this song, and I just said, 'Man, does that answer every question.'*[775]

Yes, Stefani, it does. *Wow.* Thank you.

The *LA Times* made reference to Robert Alan Brookey's *"Reinventing the Male Homosexual: The Rhetoric and Power of the Gay Gene"* with its key quote *"this belief in a predetermined sexual orientation is most visible in the emerging conservatism in the gay rights movement"*[776].

(Music, 1975)

---

[773] Gaga, Lady, *Born This Way*, Interscope Records, 2010.

[774] Valentino (Performer), Jones, Bunny (Songwriter), and Spierer, Charles (Composer), *I Was Born This Way* [Song], Gaiee Records, Distributed by Motown, 1975.

[775] Lady Gaga, interview with Howard Stern, *The Howard Stern Show*, quoted in 'LGBT Anthem: Lady Gaga's "Born This Way"', *NPR*, 20 May 2019

[776] Brookey, R. A., *Reinventing the Male Homosexual*, Indiana University Press, 2002.

BRIDGE

A textbook exercise in rebranding bad ideas with silly acronyms.

The *"Breakthrough Recruitment for Inclusive Diversity Growth and Excellence"* initiative originated at *NASA* around 2019 under its *Office of Diversity and Equal Opportunity* (ODEO), aiming to identify, attract, and retain talented individuals from "historically underrepresented groups" in STEM[777]. "Bridge" is also the name for a 2022 Californian DEI trade group in the marketing industry which claims it is *"an acronym for Belonging, Representation, Inclusion, Diversity, the G is the Gap and E is for Equity."*[778]

(Technology, 2019)

Cancel Culture

Right-wing nickname for the emergence of radical Maoist Red Guard behaviour encouraged across Western university campuses[779]*, involving mock assassinations, struggle sessions, desecration of monuments, and mob harassment of employers on social media.*

During Joseph Stalin's regime, the Soviet government systematically altered photographs to erase and "unperson" them from historical records. The most infamous example was Nikolai Yezhov, the *People's*

---

[777] Office of Diversity and Equal Opportunity, 'Breakthrough Recruitment for Inclusive Diversity Growth and Excellence (BRIDGE)', 2019 https://www.nasa.gov/offices/odeo

[778] BRIDGE (wearebridge), 'About Us', 2022 http://www.wearebridge.com

[779] Svrluga, Susan, and Joe Heim, 'Threat Shuts Down College Embroiled in Racial Dispute', *The Washington Post*, 1 June 2017.

Commissar for Internal Affairs, who oversaw the *Great Purge*. After his arrest and execution in 1940, he was meticulously edited out of official photographs[780].

As an American euphemism for boycotting products and shaming employers into firing workers, "cancellation" ultimately originates in pre-modern execution and book-burning. Its contemporary equivalent is the Chinese *Cultural Revolution* of 1967-1976, where the student *Red Guard* of the Communist Party terrorised the older generations by violently destroying anything which existed before communism[781]. Modern usage of the term arose around 2016, as a colloquialism used by "*Black Twitter*"[782].

(Internet, 2018)

Centric

> *A word people who want to sound intellectual™ use for "centered". Even more impressive if you add "icity" at the end.*

Get your science right: central or focal; located in or at a centre.

Change Agent

> *Management consultant who produces two PowerPoint presentations a year in exchange for a six-figure salary.*

---

[780] King, David, *The Commissar Vanishes*, Metropolitan Books, 1997.

[781] MacFarquhar, Roderick, and Michael Schoenhals, *Mao's Last Revolution*, Harvard University Press, 2006.

[782] Clark, Meredith D., 'To Tweet Our Own Cause: A Mixed-Methods Study of the Online Phenomenon "Black Twitter"', *Journal of Black Studies*, 46.4 (2015), 343–370.

This vulgarity was widely adopted in management and business contexts to describe leaders, consultants, or employees who drive change within organisations, influenced by the post-WWII ideas of German psychologist Kurt Lewin about *"unfreezing, changing, and refreezing"*[783]. It was reborn within a 1971 issue of *Modern Law Review*[784].

(Psychology, 1947)

Charlatan

> *A person falsely claiming to have a special knowledge or skill; a fraud.*

From the 17th century: *"An empiric who pretends to possess wonderful secrets, esp. in the healing art; an empiric or impostor in medicine, a quack."*

Check Your Privilege

> *An intellectual™-sounding insult used by rich white kids, who want to look cool to their Maoist professor and other lesser-enlightened types.*

The concept of "privilege" is, of course, something which originated with Lenin and the communist revolution in Russia. In 1998, Peggy McIntosh followed up her previous disaster journal entry[785] with a

---

[783] Lewin, Kurt., 'Frontiers in Group Dynamics: Concept, Method and Reality in Social Science; Social Equilibria and Social Change', *Human Relations*, 1.1 (1947), 5–41.

[784] *The Modern Law Review*, 34 (1971), 644.

[785] McIntosh, Peggy, 'White Privilege and Male Privilege: A Personal Account of Coming to See Correspondences Through Work in Women's Studies', Wellesley College, Center for Research on Women, 1988.

sequel: *"White Privilege: Unpacking the Invisible Knapsack"*[786]. But this one had checklists. After word spread on the *Women's Studies Email List (WMST-L)*[787], feminist blogs all over the internet began parroting the trendy new checklist idea.

(Internet, 2007)

Children Are Socialised Into...

> Girls only like dolls because, society. According to people who have never had children.

The first attempt to codify nurture-essentialism definitively as a basis for social engineering was made by dating-failure and psychologist Sandra Bern in 1981 with her proposed *"Gender Schema Theory"* on sex-typing[788]. Of course, it sounds like "stereo-typing," and appears to be something to do with pink and blue.

Unfortunately, Bern based the entire thing on the memorisation of words and ignored the basic scientific fact infants unexposed to social influence display gendered behaviour[789].

(Psychology, 1981)

---

[786] McIntosh, Peggy, 'White Privilege: Unpacking the Invisible Knapsack', *Peace and Freedom Magazine*, July/August 1998.

[787] Korenman, Joan, *The WMST-L File Collection: A Resource for Women's Studies Teaching and Research*, 1991.

[788] Bern, Sandra L., 'Gender Schema Theory: A Cognitive Account of Sex Typing', *Psychological Review*, 88.4 (1981), 354–364.

[789] Connellan, Jennifer, et al., 'Sex Differences in Human Neonatal Social Perception', *Infant Behavior and Development*, 23.1 (2000), 113–118.

Cis/Trans

> Term blatantly misappropriated from science, for promotion to activists lacking the academic ability to understand the subject it was stolen from.

In organic chemistry, when a compound exists in "mirror"-like stereo forms (*isomers*, or possessing *chirality*), the functional groups are referred to in Latin as being on "this side of" and "the other side of" their carbon chain (*cis* and *trans*); often giving them different properties[790]. This loaded language was designed to falsely imply ordinary people and cross-dressers are "natural" or "stereo" equivalents.

"Julia" Serano, prolific wordsmith at the centre of most "trans" literature, has a Ph.D. in biochemistry and molecular biophysics[791]. The term has absolutely no relation to sex or gender whatsoever.

(Chemistry, 1827)

Cisgender

> The 99.999% of humans who experience no difference between their biology and what they think they are, i.e. have a sense of their gender from where the pee comes out and whether they have the thing which they put in, or the receiving bit where it goes in, when making a baby. Latin is legal and intellectual™.

Supposedly first coined on the Usenet group *alt.transgendered* around 1995 by Carl Buijs (or *"Donna Lynn Matthews"*), or biologist Dana Leland

---

[790] Eliel, Ernest L., *Stereochemistry of Carbon Compounds*, McGraw-Hill, 1962.

[791] Serano, Julia M., *Whipping Girl*, Seal Press, 2007.

Defosse[792], or German sexologist Volkmar Sigusch in his research work[793].

It was popularised through a 2007 book titled *"Whipping Girl: A Transsexual Woman on Sexism and the Scapegoating of Femininity"* by biochemist Julia Serano[794], who borrowed it from a 2002 post to the *Women's Studies Email List (WMST-L)* by legendary scholar Emi Koyama[795].

(Feminist Literature, 1995)

Citizens' Assembly

> *Democracy-like early-stage bridge to communist revolution, without the need for voting in those pesky elections.*

As opposed to representative (electing officials) or direct democracy (referendum), this assembly is a form of *deliberative* democracy (as named by Joseph M. Bessette in *"Deliberative Democracy : the majority principle in republican government"*[796]), where politicians who have catastrophically lost the public's trust appease them, by letting them hold a council of randomly chosen individuals, who will never agree, aiming to produce results they can ignore. Their history is reputed to extend back to Athens, however in an unsurprising twist, they were conceived in the seventies by political theorist Robert Dahl as *"mini-publics"* (mini-populaces), and

---

[792] Various, *Usenet Group Alt.Transgendered*, Google Groups Archives, 1995.

[793] Sigusch, Volkmar, 'The Neosexual Revolution', *Archives of Sexual Behavior*, 27.4 (1998)

[794] Serano, Julia M., *Whipping Girl*, Seal Press, 2007.

[795] Koyama, Emi, 'Re: Thoughts on Cisgender', WMST-L Listserv, 19 May 2002.
    (bio: *"multi-issue social justice activist and writer synthesizing feminist, Asian, survivor, dyke, queer, sex worker, intersex, genderqueer, and crip politics, as these factors"*)

[796] Bessette, Joseph M., 'Deliberative Democracy: The Majority Principle in Republican Government', *How Democratic is the Constitution?*, 1980, pp. 102–16.

formalised in his 1989 book *"Democracy and Its Critics"*[797].

(*Political Science, 1989*)

Civil/Domestic Partnership

Having all the characteristics of being married, but not being married.

Unsurprisingly, it was the French who led the way in 1968 with article 515-81 of the *Code Civil* defining a domestic partnership or concubinage (*"concubinage or concubinage notoire"*)[798] for straight or same-sex couples. In 1979, Californian gay rights activist Tom Brougham proposed it as a "new" idea in the US[799].

(*Law, 1968*)

Climate Change

Apocalyptic teen drama episode caused by capitalism, where left-wing extremists save the world by forcing the world to finally realise the promise of communism.

The Earth has *five* different climates *(tropical, dry, temperate, continental, and polar)*[800].

Canadian physicist Gilbert Plass first documented the issue of carbon dioxide (photosynthetic plant food) accumulating in Earth's atmosphere

---

[797] Dahl, Robert A., *Democracy and Its Critics*, Yale University Press, 1989

[798] *Code Civil*, Article 515-81, 1968

[799] Brougham, Tim, 'Proposal for Domestic Partnership in Berkeley, California', 1979.

[800] Peel, Murray C., Brian L. Finlayson, and Thomas A. McMahon, 'Updated World Map of the Köppen-Geiger Climate Classification', *Hydrology and Earth System Sciences*, 11.5 (2007), 1633–1644

due to human industrial activity and rapid population growth. His 1956 paper *"The Carbon Dioxide Theory of Climatic Change"*[801] preceded geochemist Wallace Broecker's 1975 article in *Science* magazine titled *"Climatic Change: Are We on the Brink of a Pronounced Global Warming?"*[802].

Recent government technology programs now focus on "carbon capture", or as we have traditionally called it - *trees*.

(Geochemistry, 1956)

(Come Out Of) The Closet

Announce your narcissism.

In 1965, cross-dresser magazine *Transvestia* featured a plea over *"the struggle to let 'her' out of the closet."*[803] By 1968, *East Bay Gay Discussion Group Fridays* were inviting participants to *"come out of the closet long enuf to attend."*[804]

In November 1969, the *Gay Liberation Front* (GLF) in New York City began publishing its newspaper *"Come Out!"* which included the rallying cry, *"Come out for freedom! Come out now! Power to the people! Gay power to gay people! Come out of the closet before the door is nailed shut!"* [805]

(Literature, 1965)

---

[801] Plass, Gilbert N., 'The Carbon Dioxide Theory of Climatic Change', *Tellus*, 8.2 (1956)

[802] Broecker, Wallace S., 'Climatic Change: Are We on the Brink of a Pronounced Global Warming?', *Science*, 189.4201 (1975), 460–63

[803] Prince, Virginia, 'Transvestia', 6.36 (1965), 86

[804] *Berkeley Barb*, 15 March 1968, 12.1

[805] Gay Liberation Front, 'Come Out for Freedom! Come Out Now!', *Come Out!*, 1.1 (14 November 1969)

Coded

A stupider way of saying "associated with" most people won't notice as a stereotype.

A sequence of DNA encodes traits. Fashionable slang describing symbolic customs and behaviours as socially "encoded" were cited as *"repertoires of coded behavior"* in a 1967 edition of *American Behavioral Scientist*[806], and later popularised by feminist writers lamenting *"feminine-coded"* toys[807].

(*Psychology, 1967*)

Code-Switching

Addressing people with different slang according to their resentments and prejudices.

Although the concept of changing one's dialect was noted in 1953 at the *Conference of Anthropologists and Linguists*[808], the term was politicised in a 1970 edition of the *Council on Anthropology and Education Newsletter* which claimed *"Success in white society rests largely on a Black child's ability to 'code switch' between Black American English and Standard English."*[809]

(*Linguistics, 1953*)

---

[806] 'In Human Communication People in Social Organization Perform and Interpret Repertoires of Coded Behavior', *American Behavioral Scientist*, 8.1 (1964)

[807] 'Children Tend to Avoid Cross-Sex Toys, with Boys' Avoidance of Feminine-Coded Toys Appearing to Be Stronger Than Girls' Avoidance of Masculine-Coded Toys', *Gender & Society*, 14.6 (2000), 778

[808] Lévi-Strauss, Claude, et al., *Results of the Conference of Anthropologists and Linguists*, University of Chicago Press, 1953

[809] *Council on Anthropology and Education Newsletter*, 1 (1970), 23.

Code Of Conduct

> *Arbitrary rules intended to create and enforce a socially engineered political orthodoxy within an organisation resembling professional ethics.*

The hated scourge of the tech world, along with the endless ideological "statements" included on website footers and the so-called *"contributor covenant"*. Ethics are nothing new (nurses[810] and psychologists[811] were publishing codes of practice in the fifties), but the current social justice wrecking ball document style of defining "good behaviour" to replace actual law emerged in the late-eighties.

In 1991, Levi Strauss adopted a "code" derived from the *International Labour Organization* and the *Universal Declaration of Human Rights*[812].

(Public Relations, 1991)

Codependency

> *Indulging your own narcissism by staying married to a drunk and claiming to be a martyr.*

An imaginary pathology suffered by middle-class Western boomer women everywhere, the notion of the *"co-alcoholic"* partner arrived in a 1984 paper by Robert Subby and John Friel titled *"Co-dependency: An*

---

[810] American Nurses Association, *A Code for Professional Nurses*, American Nurses Association, 1950

[811] American Psychological Association, *Ethical Standards of Psychologists*, American Psychological Association, 1953

[812] Baron, David, and J. Adams, 'Levi Strauss & Co. Global Sourcing Guidelines', Stanford Graduate School of Business Case No. P12, 1994.

emerging issue"[813]. It was popularised by ex-alcoholic Melody Beattie in *"Codependent No More: How to Stop Controlling Others and Start Caring for Yourself."*, two years later[814]. Eight years later in 1994, a study in the feminist journal *Sex Roles* " discovered" the condition didn't really have any basis in science at all as anything medical, and overlaps with *"negative feminine traits devalued in both women and men"*[815] (i.e. self-denying, self-sacrificing, or displaying low self-esteem).

Five years later in 1999, Israeli psychology professor Sam Vaknin - convicted fraudster diagnosed with three co-morbid personality disorders - published *"Malignant Self Love: Narcissism Revisited "*, in which he hypothesised the condition of *"inverted narcissism"*:

> *A subtype of narcissism in which an individual derives self-worth by supporting or mirroring the needs of a narcissist, often to the detriment of their own identity and well-being.*[816]

(Psychology, 1984)

Collusion

The way your political enemies unfairly defeated your bad ideas. Obviously.

Despite not being a legal term, "collusion" (Latin *colludere*) has always meant illicit cooperation, or a secret agreement for purposes of trickery

---

[813] Subby, Robert, and John Friel, 'Co-dependency: An Emerging Issue', *Health Communications*, 1984.

[814] Beattie, Melody, *Codependent No More*, Center City, MN: Hazelden, 1986.

[815] Cowan, Gloria, and Lynda W. Warren, 'Codependency and Gender-Stereotyped Traits', *Sex Roles*, 30.9-10 (1994), 631-645.

[816] Vaknin, Sam, *Malignant Self Love*, Narcissus Publications, 1999

or fraud. The contemporary neologism *"Russian collusion"* undoubtedly comes from an industry-scale partisan fraud aiming to sabotage the 2016 U.S election victory of Donald Trump[817]. The accusations were first made by *Yahoo News* during September 2016[818].

(Politics, 2016)

Colonialism

> *An evil conspiracy carried out by centuries of White European men to travel to other places and convert them into prisons for the people they met, while stealing everything they had.*

Hopelessly confused with "colonising", the term has been around since the days of European mercantilism in the 16th century[819]. Usage as a British Empire version of the "slavery" dark legend originated with Frank Fanon's 1961 book *"The Wretched of the Earth"*[820], before being compounded by Edward Said's *"Orientalism"* (1978)[821]. It was somewhat formalised in *"Post-Colonial Drama: Theory, Practice, Politics"* (1996)[822].

Fun fact: only 7% of England's income came from its empire, which cost more to maintain than it produced[823].

(Psychiatry, 1961)

---

[817] Durham, John H., *Report on Matters Related to Intelligence Activities and Investigations Arising Out of the 2016 Presidential Campaigns*, U.S. Department of Justice, 2023.

[818] Isikoff, Michael, 'U.S. Intel Officials Probe Ties Between Trump Adviser and Kremlin', *Yahoo News*, 23 September 2016.

[819] Heckscher, Eli F., *Mercantilism* (Mendel Shapiro), George Allen & Unwin, 1935.

[820] Said, Edward W., *Orientalism*, Pantheon Books, 1978.

[821] Ibid.

[822] Gilbert, Helen, and Joanne Tompkins, *Post-Colonial Drama*, Routledge, 1996.

[823] Offer, Avner, 'The British Empire, 1870–1914: A Waste of Money?', *The Economic History Review*, 43.3 (1990), 501–24.

Community

> *Any group of two or more people, regardless of whether they display any traits which would define a community. Such as the "Latino stamp-collecting transgender pansexual facebook-boycotting community".*

A commune, which is *communitarian* or communist. The term has been most misused, obviously, by fashionable "thinkers" in Silicon Valley social media companies who like to combine Edward Bernays' Freudian ideas[824] with evolutionary biology into *"brain hacking"*[825][826]. The rot started, however, with Albert Muniz and Thomas O' Guinn's 1995 consumer research article *"Brand Community and the Sociology of Brands"*[827].

(Sociology, 1995)

Community Standards

> *Partisan left-wing moral standards. Which you will obey, or be compassionately 'disappeared' for the good of the collective.*

Similar to the behavioural "guidelines" of a housing association, *MySpace* implemented basic content guidelines in 2003 to address issues like

---

[824] Tye, Larry, *The Father of Spin*, Crown Publishers, 1998.

[825] Lewis, Paul, "'Our Minds Can Be Hijacked': The Tech Insiders Who Fear a Smartphone Dystopia', *The Guardian*, 6 October 2017.

[826] Harris, Tristan, *How Technology is Hijacking Your Mind*, 2016.

[827] Muniz, Albert M., and Thomas C. O'Guinn, 'Brand Community and the Sociology of Brands', *Research in Consumer Behavior*, 8 (1995), 323–341.

harassment and explicit material[828]. *Facebook* explicitly published its rules document in 2010[829].

In unrelated history, Lenin originally articulated the ideological foundation of *partiinost ("partisanship"* or *"party-mindedness"*). It referred to the unwavering loyalty to ideology and rejection of any *"bourgeois"* or *"non-socialist"* perspectives in all aspects of society, including art, science, culture, education, and journalism, so everything was subjugated to the policies, principles, and objectives of the *Communist Party of the Soviet Union* (CPSU).

(Internet, 2010)

Compassion

What you will get if you comply. Also, what you won't, if you don't.

Get your philosophy right: pity for the sufferings of others.

Consciousness

An all-consuming focus or obsession, seen in everything, at all times.

Making people hyperaware or extremely sensitive to something, aka "raising consciousness", is, of course, central to Marx's theses of revolution[830] and Mao's ideas of *"agitation"*[831]. The adoption of it as a cultural term can be found in the *Women's Liberation* movement of 1968, printed

---

[828] Boyd, Danah M., 'Friendster and Publicly Articulated Social Networks', *Conference on Human Factors in Computing Systems*, ACM, 2004

[829] Gillespie, Tarleton, *Custodians of the Internet*, Yale University Press, 2018

[830] Marx, Karl, and Friedrich Engels, *The Communist Manifesto*, 1848.

[831] Mao Tse-Tung, *Selected Works of Mao Tse-Tung*, 1967.

in their infamous *"Notes from the First Year"*[832].

(Feminist Literature, 1968)

Conspiracy Theorist

A crank. Fantasist. Someone who figured out what you questionably believed wasn't remotely true, about six months before you did and couldn't continue to deny it anymore.

Although it goes back to 1868[833], modern JFK-era usage of this ever-useful way of discrediting someone as a crank or something as imaginary go back to Karl Popper's *"The Open Society and Its Enemies"*[834], Richard Hofstadter's 1964 essay in *Harper's Magazine*[835] and left-wing rag the *New Statesman* use of the term as a dismissive slur in 1964[836].

(Philosophy, 1952)

Construct

A word people who want to sound intellectual™ use for... "made-up".

This pretentious term is derived from Swiss psychologist Jean Piaget's theory of *constructivism*, published as *"La Naissance de l'intelligence chez l'enfant"* (*"The Origins of Intelligence in Children"*) in 1936. His thesis

---

[832] New York Radical Women, *Notes from the First Year*, 1968.

[833] Boston Post, 'The Testimony of Gen. Sherman Has Blown the Conspiracy Theory of Gen. Butler to the Winds', *Boston Post*, 16 April 1868.

[834] Popper, Karl R., *The Open Society and Its Enemies*, Routledge, 1952

[835] Hofstadter, Richard, 'The Paranoid Style in American Politics', *Harper's Magazine*, October 1964.

[836] *New Statesman*, 'Conspiracy Theorists Will Be Disappointed by the Absence of a Dogmatic Introduction', 1 May 1964

was children progress through four stages of cognitive development and actively *"construct"* knowledge through their experiences and interactions with the world[837].

Conversely, French philosopher Jacques Derrida published his rather silly idea of *"deconstruction"* three decades later in *"De la grammatologie"* (*"Of Grammatology"*), which aimed to *"uncover the assumptions, binaries, and hierarchies"* embedded in literature[838].

In the following decade, Piaget's ideas were adapted into *"social constructionism"* within Peter L. Berger and Thomas Luckmann's 1966 book *"The Social Construction of Reality: A Treatise in the Sociology of Knowledge,"*[839] and *"social constructivism"* by Lev Vygotsky's 1978 book, *"Mind in Society: The Development of Higher Psychological Processes"*[840].

This idiocy reached its zenith when communist *"critical theory"* and *"critical pedagogy"* were fused with them during the early 2000s to *"incorporate critiques of power, inequality, and societal structures"*, which formed the insanity of *"critical constructivism"*, what we now know as *"woke"*[841].

(*Psychology, 1936*)

---

[837] Piaget, Jean, *The Origins of Intelligence in Children*, International Universities Press, 1952. (Original work in French: *La Naissance de l'intelligence chez l'enfant*, 1936.)

[838] Derrida, Jacques, *Of Grammatology* (Gayatri Chakravorty Spivak, Trans.), Johns Hopkins University Press, 1976. (Original work published in French as *De la grammatologie*, Les Éditions de Minuit, 1967.)

[839] Berger, Peter, Thomas Luckmann, *The Social Construction of Reality*, Anchor Books, 1966.

[840] Vygotsky, Lev S., *Mind in Society: The Development of Higher Psychological Processes*, 1978. (Original Russian manuscripts written in the 1930s, published posthumously.)

[841] Kincheloe, Joe L., *Critical Constructivism Primer*, Peter Lang, 2005

Critical Theory

> Communist Theory. An attempt to apply Marxism to basically everything taught in a university and criticise it to death.

First defined by sociologist Max Horkheimer at the *Frankfurt School (Institute of Social (nee. Socialist) Research)*[842] in his 1937 essay *"Traditional and Critical Theory"* as a modernist attempt to do for sociology against positivism what Marx had done against capitalism[843].

Things took a turn for the worse when it just wasn't cool enough for Foucault and his ilk to conform, which resulted in Boje, Fitzgibbons, and Steingard's 1996 manifestos creating the *Journal of Critical Postmodern Organization Science*[844]. By 1981, alternative law programs had spun off *"critical race theory"*[845]. Even in 1997, judges in the US were labeling *"critical race theorists and postmodernists the 'lunatic core' of 'radical legal egalitarianism"*[846].

(*Sociology*, 1937)

---

[842] Jay, Martin, *The Dialectical Imagination*, Little, Brown and Company, 1973

[843] Horkheimer, Max. *Traditional and Critical Theory*. In *Critical Theory: Selected Essays*, translated by Matthew J. O'Connell and others, 188–243.

[844] Boje, David M., David E. Fitzgibbons, and David Steingard, 'Manifesto for Postmodern Organization Science', *Journal of Critical Postmodern Organization Science*, 1.1 (1996), 1–16

[845] Crenshaw, Kimberlé, Neil Gotanda, Gary Peller, and Kendall Thomas, *Critical Race Theory*, The New Press, 1995.

[846] Williams, Patricia J., *Seeing a Color-Blind Future*, Farrar, Straus and Giroux, 1997.

ABC

Critical Pedagogy

> *A way of teaching which absolutely guarantees your education system only turns out communist activists who are almost entirely illiterate.*

"Critical education theory" originates in Brazilian socialist Paolo Friere's disastrous attempt to Marxify the process of learning (literacy), documented in *"Pedagogy of the Oppressed"* (1968), which is the highest-cited work in its field[847].

Developed in the US by the prolific Henry Giroux in the eighties[848], it was responsible for the near-complete destruction of Brazil's public education system[849], and led to Friere's expulsion from the country[850][851]. Its horrific consequences can be seen in American literacy statistics[852].

(Education, 1968)

Critical Race Theory

> *A copy n' paste plagiarism of the Communist Manifesto with the notion of "class" substituted for race. And/or, calling everything racist until you control it.*

Although law professor Roy L. Brooks formally defined *Communist*

---

[847] Freire, Paulo, *Pedagogy of the Oppressed*, Herder and Herder, 1968.

[848] Giroux, Henry A., *Theory and Resistance in Education*, Bergin & Garvey, 1983.

[849] Torres, Carlos A., 'Education and the Reproduction of Class, Gender, and Race Inequalities in Brazil', in *Critical Pedagogy and Predatory Culture: Oppositional Politics in a Postmodern Era*, Routledge, 1994, pp. 85–96.

[850] Mayo, Peter, *Gramsci, Freire, and Adult Education*, Zed Books, 1999.

[851] Gadotti, Moacir, *Reading Paulo Freire*, State University of New York Press, 1994.

[852] McLaren, Peter, *Life in Schools*, Longman, 1994.

Race Marxism in 1994 (*"Critical Race Theory: A Proposed Structure and Application to Federal Pleading"*)[853], the label was already being used five years earlier in the *Florida Law Review*[854] as it grew out of sociology, or *"critical legal studies"*[855].

Formulated by a *"bunch of Marxists"* (Richard Delgado, St. Benedict Center, 1989: *"Richard Delgado & Jean Stefancic, Living History Interview with Richard Delgado & Jean Stefancic"*)[856] - it follows typical communist methodology by opposing liberalism and agitating for revolution, whilst claiming it does not exist, is not there, and/or is something else.

As the austere priesthood put it themselves, gathered religiously in a Catholic building discussing their new dogma:

> *So we gathered at that convent for two and a half days, around a table in an austere room with stained glass windows and crucifixes here and there - an odd place for a bunch of Marxists - and worked out a set of principles. Then we went our separate ways. Most of us who were there have gone on to become prominent critical race theorists, including Kim Crenshaw, who spoke at the Iowa conference, as well as Mani Matsuda and Charles Lawrence, who both are here in spirit. Derrick Bell, who was doing critical race theory long before it had a name, was at the Madison workshop and*

---

[853] Brooks, Roy L., 'Critical Race Theory: A Proposed Structure and Application to Federal Pleading', *Harvard Law Review*, 97.8 (1994), 2004–2029.

[854] Matsuda, Mari J., Charles R. Lawrence, Richard Delgado, and Kimberlé W. Crenshaw, *Words That Wound: Critical Race Theory, Assaultive Speech, and the First Amendment*, Florida Law Review, 47.2 (1993), 509–540.

[855] Unger, Roberto Mangabeira, 'The Critical Legal Studies Movement', *Harvard Law Review*, 96.3 (1983), 561–675.

[856] Delgado, Richard, and Jean Stefancic, 'Living History Interview with Richard Delgado & Jean Stefancic', *St. Benedict Center*, 1989.

has been something of an intellectual godfather for the movement.[857]

(*Sociology, 1989*)

Critique

A word seriously insane people who want to sound intellectual™ use for "criticism". Sounds a bit French, like Derrida, de Beauvoir, Lacan, and Foucault. Even better if you mention Kant and claim to have read his tedious book.

Do not trust anyone whose vanity leads them to embark on a "critique."

Crypto-(ist)

Secret evil villain who is always unmasked at the end of every Scooby Doo episode; or your psychotic ex-boyfriend/girlfriend's pathological delusions you are hiding your "true nature".

Closely related to the indefensible slur of *"implicit bias"*, also used by Churchill in Parliament around 1947 to denounce pacifists[858], and from the Greek root *kruptos*, (meaning "hidden" or "not evident or obvious"), crypto-fascist/crypto-communist became a neologism after Gore Vidal name-called William F. Buckley Jr as a *"crypto-Nazi"* at the 1968 DNC

---

[857] Delgado, Richard, and Jean Stefancic. "Living History Interview with Richard Delgado & Jean Stefancic." *Transnational Law & Contemporary Problems* 19, no. 2 (2010): 221–224.

[858] Hansard, HC, vol. 435, cc. 1688–9 (31 March 1947)
    "*on all occasions when they are challenged by the crypto-communists and pacifists and other trends of left-wing opinion, which they have exploited to the full in bygone days, and which they now very naturally and healthily resent.*"

debate[859]. However, it is claimed critical theory sociologist Theodor Adorno (*Frankfurt School*) coined the term in his 1963 book *"Der getreue Korrepetitor"*[860].

(Sociology, 1947)

Culture

> *The thing you're sick of hearing about.*

From the 1933 nationalist play *"Schlageter"* by Nazi dramatist Hanns Johst, lionising German military officer Albert Leo Schlageter, who was court-martialled and shot by the French in 1923 for sabotaging a section of railroad track in the *Ruhr valley*.
Act 1, *Scene 1*, Friedrich Thiemann:

> *Whenever I hear the word culture... I release the safety-catch of my Browning.*[861]

Get your philosophy right: can you even *define* culture?

Cuck

> *Being weak, ineffectual, and effeminate by allowing yourself to be dominated.*

"Cuckold" is a c. 1250 medieval term for the husband of an unfaithful

---

[859] *Buckley vs. Vidal* (2015), Magnolia Pictures.

[860] Adorno, Theodor W., *Der Getreue Korrepetitor*, Suhrkamp Verlag, 1963

[861] Johst, Hanns, *Schlageter*, Eher Verlag, 1933. Act 1, Scene 1.

wife[862]. During the *"Gamergate"* scandal over 2014, the boyfriend of journalist Zoe Quinn was referred to with the shorthand[863], before political operative Steven Bannon and *Breitbart News* popularized the term as a slur (*"cuckservative"*) by the *"alt-right"*[864].

(Internet, 2014)

Cultural Appropriation

Misrepresenting the normal human behaviour of exchanging and celebrating cultural symbols and motifs as theft. Like iPhones, planes, electricity, cars, and computers.

Derived from the Marxist idea of *"class appropriation"*[865], the popularisation of this abjectly absurd phrase comes from an entry by British painter Kenneth Coutts-Smith in a 1976 book entitled *"The Myth of Primitivism"*, chapter *"Some General Observations on the Concept of Cultural Colonialism"*[866]. Originally referred to in *"Rebellion or Revolution?"* (1968) by a professor of *"African American studies"*, Harold Cruse[867].

(African American Studies, 1968)

---

[862] Skeat, Walter W., *A Concise Etymological Dictionary of the English Language*, Oxford University Press, 1910

[863] Mortensen, Torill Elvira, 'Anger, Fear, and Games: The Long Event of #Gamergate', *Games and Culture*, 13.8 (2016), 787–806.

[864] Breitbart News, 'Explaining "Cuckservative" – The New Conservative Slur Redefining 2016', *Breitbart*, 30 July 2015.

[865] Marx, Karl, *Capital: A Critique of Political Economy, Volume 1*, 1867
　　Appropriation of working class labour (surplus value) for profit by the capitalist class can be considered a form of "class appropriation" in economic terms.

[866] Coutts-Smith, Kenneth, 'Some General Observations on the Concept of Cultural Colonialism', in *The Myth of Primitivism: Perspectives on Art*, Routledge, 1976, pp. 14–25

[867] Cruse, Harold, *Rebellion or Revolution?*, Morrow, 1968.

Cultural Competence

> Not calling the police when your store is being burgled in broad daylight because it's a form of "sharing" in other cultures. NB: Is not required by those doing the integrating.

As a well-meaning initiative for helping minority children with special needs, the terminology was coined in 1989 by Terry Cross at *Georgetown University Child Development Center* in his paper *"Towards A Culturally Competent System of Care"*[868]. It has been expanded into *"3C"* development and *"cultural intelligence"*[869].

(Healthcare, 1989)

Culture War

> The resistance encountered when attempting to demolish the beliefs, traditions, values, and practices of a population who don't agree with you or like you.

As a derivative of the German *"kulturkampf,"* which described a struggle between the government and Catholic church for control of education[870], our modern usage of the term was popularised by James Davison Hunter in his 1991 book[871] of the same name.

---

[868] Cross, Terry L., Barbara J. Bazron, Karl W. Dennis, and Mareasa R. Isaacs, *Towards A Culturally Competent System of Care: A Monograph on Effective Services for Minority Children Who Are Severely Emotionally Disturbed*, Georgetown University Child Development Center, CASSP Technical Assistance Center, 1989.

[869] Earley, P. Christopher, Soon Ang, *Cultural Intelligence*, Stanford University Press, 2003

[870] Blackbourn, David, *Class, Religion, and Local Politics in Wilhelmine Germany*, Yale University Press, 1977

[871] Hunter, James Davison, *Culture Wars*, Basic Books, 1991

An earlier usage in the American context can be traced back to a 1987 *New York Times* article describing partisan party conflict in the US[872].

(Newspapers, 1987)

---

[872] 'A New Cultural War Rages', *The New York Times*, 25 October 1987

D E F

Deadname-(ing)

> *The hurtful practice of referring to a person by the name their parents will bury them with.*

On September 16th, 2014, a user named *"Canola Yogurt"* posted the protological definition on well-known scholarly journal *UrbanDictionary*[873], which was picked up by (now-defunct) crazyperson rag *The Establishment* magazine[874] and syndicated in the *Huffington Post*[875]. On August 13th 2018, actress Laverne Cox tweeted it was *"an act of violence"*[876]. On September 25th 2018, *Twitter* updated their rules and "policies" to include it[877], giving the term wider coverage.

(Internet, 2014)

---

[873] Urban Dictionary, 'Deadname', 16 September 2014

[874] Riedel, Samantha, 'The Pain of Being Deadnamed', *The Establishment* (2016)

[875] The Establishment (contributor, synd'cated), 'Deadnaming a Trans Person Is Violence — So Why Does the Media Do It Anyway?', *HuffPost*, 17 March 2017

[876] Laverne Cox, 'Tweet Stating That Deadnaming Is "an Act of Violence"', *Twitter*, 13 August 2018

[877] Twitter, 'Updating Our Rules Against Hateful Conduct', 25 September 2018

Decenter(ing)

> That's my place, bigot.

JFK was famously *"decentered"* from the US presidency in 1963, as France was during the *Haitian Revolution* of 1791, and Tsar Nicholas II in February 1917. If Marxist protégé Kimberlé Crenshaw was to define the *"marginalised"*, the natural accompaniment of the *"centered"* must surely follow. In Jean Piaget's 1954 theory of cognitive development, *"decentering"* refers to a child's ability to move beyond a singular focus and consider multiple aspects of a situation simultaneously[878]. It was used by Michel Foucault in *"The Order of Things: An Archaeology of the Human Sciences"* (1966)[879].

(Psychology, 1954)

Deconstruction

> One French pervert's attempt to bring Marxism into literature and convince the bottom 2% of students nothing can actually be true.

Deconstruction is a nicer word than its counterpart, *destruction*. Anyone can take some apart. It takes talent to put something together.

Jacques Derrida — who was so, *omg*, profound — published *"Of Grammatology"* in 1967 with its *"spirit of Marx"*[880] after a disastrous study of linguist Ferdinand de Saussure's work on *signifier/signified* (*Semiotics*)[881].

---

[878] Piaget, Jean, *The Construction of Reality in the Child* (Basic Books, 1954).

[879] Foucault, Michel, *The Order of Things* (Pantheon Books, 1970).

[880] Derrida, Jacques, *Of Grammatology* (Johns Hopkins University Press, 1967).

[881] Saussure, Ferdinand de, *Course in General Linguistics*, ed. by Charles Bally and Albert Sechehaye, trans. by Wade Baskin (Philosophical Library, 1959; first publ. 1916).

His idea was simple: demonstrate language and meaning are separate (cough, gender) and always biased from subjectivity, i.e. ergo there is no objective truth which can be known[882]. His intellectual diarrhoea proved quite useful for "scholars" who wanted to attack institutions and claim their critics' points' could not be true. Derrida's work has contributed virtually nothing workable to the human race. But he was so *profound*.

(Literature. 1967)

Decolonise

> *Be intimidated into submitting to a Maoist purge of artworks, objects, and cultural artifacts representing one's culture and traditions under the threat of mob violence or vindictive public disparagement.*

This synonym for "purge" obviously has similarities with Mao's "*Cultural Revolution*" in communist China, but was used extensively in the mid-sixties when describing the process of a British Empire territory realising independence as a republic[883]. A call to politically weaponise the concept is noted around 1971 in *"Three Styles in Study of Kinship"* by John. A. Barnes[884].

(Sociology, 1963)

Defund The Police

> *The smartest idea and most successful political campaign of all time.*

Although this madness has its origins with communist lunatic Angela

---

[882] Caputo, John D., *Deconstruction in a Nutshell* (Fordham University Press, 1997).

[883] Young, Robert J. C., *Postcolonialism* (Wiley-Blackwell, 2001).

[884] Barnes, John A., *Three Styles in the Study of Kinship* (Tavistock Publications, 1971).

Davis and abolitionist organisations like *"Critical Resistance"*[885], the call for Marxist revolution was made by the *"Movement for Black Lives"* (M4BL) after the death of George Floyd in Minneapolis[886].

(Activism, 2020)

Dehumanise-(ing)

> *Refusing to accept an absurd idea merely on the basis a human said it or believes it.*

Law professor Gregory Stanton presented the *"8 Stages of Genocide"* to the US *State Department* in 1996[887] after his work on the *Khmer Rouge*'s horrific crimes in Cambodia[888] and the Rwandan genocide[889]. Stage 3 (*"Dehumanisation"*) describes the process in which the target group is referred to as rodents or insects on government-owned media. In 2012 it was updated to include "discrimination" and "persecution"[890]: we all know where that's going: to another twenty stages.

(Law, 1996)

---

[885] Davis, Angela Y., *Are Prisons Obsolete?* (Seven Stories Press, 2003).

[886] Gilmore, Ruth Wilson, *Golden Gulag* (University of California Press, 2007).

[887] Stanton, Gregory H., 'The 8 Stages of Genocide', presented at the United States Department of State (1996).

[888] Kiernan, Ben, *The Pol Pot Regime* (Yale University Press, 2008).

[889] Dallaire, Roméo, *Shake Hands with the Devil* (Carroll & Graf, 2005).

[890] Stanton, Gregory H., 'The Ten Stages of Genocide', *Genocide Watch* (2013).

Democracy

> *A system of consensus which requires the losers' consent to function. An unnecessary and problematic social construct communism will eventually perfect, but is "ours", "sacred" and must be protected at all costs.*

Athens was the home of ancient democracy[891], but the first representative assembly was held in England during the *2nd Barons' War* in 1265 by rebel leader Simon de Montfort[892], after he seized power from Henry III[893]. It is the worst form of government (apart from all the others), and essentially involving fifty-one people in a room overruling the other forty-nine; or two wolves and a sheep voting on what to have for dinner.

(Political Science, 1265)

Democracy Is An Illusion

> *Voting is pointless. The world is controlled by an elite.*

In 2000, Colin Couch published *"Coping with Post-Democracy"* for the socialist *Fabian Society*[894]. He describes it as a system which *"continues to have and to use all the institutions of democracy, but in which they increasingly become a formal shell."*

(Political Science, 2000)

---

[891] Hansen, Mogens Herman, *The Athenian Democracy in the Age of Demosthenes* (University of Oklahoma Press, 1999).

[892] Maddicott, John Robert, *Simon de Montfort* (Cambridge University Press, 1994).

[893] Prestwich, Michael, *Plantagenet England 1225-1360* (Oxford University Press, 2005).

[894] Crouch, Colin, *Post-Democracy* (Polity Press, 2004).

Denier

> *Skeptic. Someone who is cynical of extremists' claims something is "well-established theory, law, fact or evidence", whilst appearing exaggerated, politicised, or misrepresented.*

Denial implies existence, and is a concept from psychoanalysis originating with Sigmund Freud's daughter, Anna[895]. The attempt to pathologise it as a behaviour, or "denialism" (as opposed to "revisionism") - *useful for smearing one's political enemies* - is undoubtedly derived from the legitimate concerns around anti-Semites inexplicably contesting the observed genocide of six million people, exemplified by books such as Deborah Lipstick's *"Denying the Holocaust – The Growing Assault on Truth and Memory"*[896].

(Political Rhetoric, 1993)

Deny My Existence

> *Absurdly non-seqitur appeal of a person who denies biological reality, accusing a person who disagrees with them of denying "their" reality, in a way which implies it is akin to murder; even though they are alive and exist.*

It's impossible to say when the term first originated, but most contemporary theories associate it with *"transgenderism"* and the *Glomar response* often parroted by military institutions[897]. Denial pre-supposes the thing

---

[895] Freud, Anna, *The Ego and the Mechanisms of Defence* (Hogarth Press, 1936).

[896] Lipstadt, Deborah E., *Denying the Holocaust* (Free Press, 1993).

[897] Aftergood, Steven, 'The Glomar Explorer and the Glomar Response', *Federation of American Scientists* (2001)

exists, as opposed to *rejection* which implies it doesn't.
(*Social Media, 2011*)

Deplatform

> *The use of intimidation, sabotage, or violence to prevent a person from being heard by others. Always justified morally against anyone not fully persuaded of extremist left-wing ideas.*

"*No-Platform*" was a form of "*direct action*" ("*prior restraint*"[898]) devised in 1974 by the *International Marxist Group* (IMG) and *International Socialists* (IS) as an extreme tactic against the hard-right *National Front*'s recruitment activities on university campuses, and was formally adopted by the *National Union of Students* (NUS)[899]. It was so extreme, even the most left-wing newspapers denounced it[900].
(*Political Rhetoric (Extremism), 1974*)

Dialectic

> *A word people who want to sound intellectual™ use for "a way of discerning the truth".*

Get your philosophy right: investigation of metaphysical contradictions.

The phrase "neither confirm nor deny" (Glomar response) is often used to avoid revealing classified information or sensitive activities.

[898] Barendt, Eric, *Freedom of Speech* (Oxford University Press, 2005)

[899] Renton, David, *When We Touched the Sky* (New Clarion Press, 2011)

[900] 'Students and Free Speech', *The Guardian*, 6 May 1974

Direct Action

> *Violence, sabotage, intimidation, rioting, and vandalism which sounds less like any of those and can be cited to sound intellectual™.*

Extremists on both sides rarely describe their holy and righteous vigilante crusades in ways which are likely to lead to their arrest. Frequently attributed to female anarchist Voltairine de Cleyre from her same-titled essay in 1912[901], although more commonly associated with founding member of the *British communist party* William Mellor in his same-titled 1920 book[902], and/or MacDonald's 1911 essay on *Syndicalism*[903] (trade unionism, or the precursor to *Fascism*).

(Literature, 1912)

Discourse

> *A word people who want to sound intellectual™ use for "discussion".*

Get your philosophy right: authoritative written debate between scholars.

Discriminate

> *Unfairly deny access to something to which someone is entitled on account of one or more shared group characteristics.*

---

[901] De Cleyre, Voltairine, 'Direct Action', various anarchist archives (1912).

[902] Mellor, William, *Direct Action* (Leonard Parsons, 1920).

[903] MacDonald, James Ramsay, *Syndicalism* (Williams & Norgate, 1911).

To discriminate in British English is to differentiate, to discern, or to perceive things as distinct *from* one another. In American English, it means unjust treatment *against* one another. This distinction arose in 1819 in America's first lithograph, *Analectic Magazine*, which claimed it was behaviour designed to *"keep the negroes out of the pale of white society."*[904]

(*Literature, 1819*)

Disinformation

> *Damaging stories of your behaviour publicised by your political enemies, which, left unsmeared, will lead to a loss of partisan support.*

Disinformation is a military term and used almost exclusively as a war tactic involving the deceit of a foreign enemy via false information. The USSR created the first department for it in 1959[905], and the term was first mentioned as a communist tactic in a 1967 article published in *The Observer*.

(*Newspapers, 1967*)

Disinvite(d)

> *Method of avoiding bad PR by pandering to vigilante demands, after receiving threats of public mobbing, vilification, and/or of future violence.*

Asking a dinner guest not to come isn't a new phenomenon. The *Foundation for Individual Rights in Education* (*FIRE*) has catalogued over

---

[904] *The Analectic Magazine and Naval Chronicle*, 'April Issue', 6 (1816), 291.

[905] Andrew, Christopher, Vasili Mitrokhin, *The Sword and the Shield* (Basic Books, 1999).

200 *"heckler's vetoes"* from 2000 to 2015, with a noticeable spike in the graph appearing around 2012[906]. Speaker bans have been in place in California against communists since *World War II*[907].

(Political Rhetoric (Extremism), 1940s)

Disparate Impact

A handy way of morally justifying almost anything at all, on the basis someone else alive somewhere might suffer.

Buried deep in the 1964 *Civil Rights Act* is *Title VII* (*"Disparate Impact Liability"*)[908], or the *Skeleton Key* of all "rights" movements derived from the sixties counter-culture. As Professor Gail Heriot (*University of San Diego*) notes[909], there is nothing you can define in law which will not create a disparate impact on another group when it benefits another: laws against murder disproportionately and disparately affect those who kill people, for example. Which makes almost everything *"presumptively illegal"*[910]. Not exactly the legal profession's finest hour.

(Law, 1964)

---

[906] Foundation for Individual Rights in Education (FIRE), *Catalog of Heckler's Vetoes (2000–2015)* (2015)

[907] Schrecker, Ellen, *No Ivory Tower* (Oxford University Press, 1986).

[908] Selmi, Michael, 'Was the Disparate Impact Theory a Mistake?', *UCLA Law Review*, 53 (2006), 701–781.

[909] Heriot, Gail, 'The Sad Irony of Affirmative Action', *University of San Diego* (2010)

[910] *Griggs v. Duke Power Co.*, 401 U.S. 424 (1971).

Diverse

> *When you step off the plane in Africa as the only white, asian, arab, or hispanic person.*

Get your science right: displaying variance.

Diversity

> *Secular version of the Holy Spirit. Achieved by grouping/categorizing people by skin colour, then enforcing differing access to things. Oh, wait...*

We all *value* it. We're all *committed* to it. It's our *strength*.

The multi-billion industry has its roots in the 1961 political demand for *"affirmative action"*[911], but took an aggressive turn around 1987 - as *"critical race theory"* was becoming established[912] - with the *Hudson Institute* publishing *Workforce 2000*[913], and the *Harvard Business Review* following it three years later with R. Roosevelt Thomas' *"From affirmative action to affirming diversity"* in 1990[914]. By 1998, sociologist Milton Bennett had created his scale, or the *"Developmental Model of Intercultural Sensitivity (DMIS)"*[915].

(Activism, 1987)

---

[911] Kennedy, John F., 'Executive Order 10925', *Federal Register*, 6 March 1961.

[912] Crenshaw, Kimberlé, Neil Gotanda, Gary Peller, and Kendall Thomas, eds., *Critical Race Theory: The Key Writings That Formed the Movement* (The New Press, 1995)

[913] Johnston, William B., and Arnold H. Packer, *Workforce 2000* (Hudson Institute, 1987)

[914] Thomas, Roosevelt R., 'From Affirmative Action to Affirming Diversity', *Harvard Business Review* (1990).

[915] Bennett, Milton, *Basic Concepts of Intercultural Communication* (Intercultural, 1998).

Diversity Training

> *Ineffectual and often counter-productive Soviet/Maoist-style psychological re-programming of employees by political social science majors employed in HR departments, centered on the Gnostic concept of the non-existent "unconscious mind", and used by CEOs as a means to placate pathological colleagues.*

Closely aligned with "corporate culture", the pseudoscientific Freudian idea of reprogramming and re-education by social science majors from the HR department was first discussed in the *Peabody Journal of Education* in 1988[916]. Can we brainwash them in the way as *"denazification"* worked in West Germany?[917]

Five years later, the *Wall St Journal* was discussing the *National Skill Standards Board* being subject to a *"Clinton diversity quota"*[918].

Not only has the vast quantity of study literature shown this agitation "training" to be utterly useless[919], but the data shows it is so counterproductive it actually increases the behaviour it aims to prevent[920].

(Education, 1988)

---

[916] Crosby, Faye J., and Susan Clayton, 'Affirmative Action and the Diversity Dilemma', *Peabody Journal of Education*, 65 (1988), 151–67

[917] Schulz, Michael C., 'An Army of Academics', in *Everyday Denazification in Postwar Germany*, ed. by Rebecca Wittmann (Cambridge University Press, 2023)

[918] *The Wall Street Journal*, 'Discussion on the National Skill Standards Board's Diversity Policies' (1998).

[919] al-Gharbi, Musa, 'Research Shows Diversity Training is Typically Ineffective', *RealClearScience*, 5 December 2020

[920] Haskell, David Millard, 'What DEI Research Concludes About Diversity Training: It Is Divisive, Counter-Productive, and Unnecessary', *Aristotle Foundation for Public Policy*, 12 February 202

Diversity, Equity, & Inclusion

> *Didn't Earn It. Division, Entryism, & Indoctrination. A clever way to fool a company into operating as a socialist government on the pretense of avoiding bad PR by being nice.*

Also known as D.I.E, and the opposite of *Unity, Opportunity & Qualification*, few can define it, but everyone is committed to it and it's awesome. When "wellness" fell out of fashion — because it was too costly — the next round of corporate programs appeared. Diversity meant more people with melanin (racism); equity meant the *"gender pay gap"* (feminism), and inclusion meant disabled people (*"ableism"*). Between 1998 and 2013, *Merrill Lynch* had paid half a billion dollars to settle discrimination lawsuits[921]. Around 2007, the *Diversity in Philanthropy Project* (DPP) began a 3-year campaign[922] to start championing the *Green Lining Insititute*'s ideas on *"racial and economic justice"*[923].

(Business, 2007)

Do The Work

> *Demand made of a subjugated disciple to undertake religious-style purification in political orthodoxy.*

"The Work" is a religious term derived from performing religious "works" in order to sanctify oneself. It's also the title of Steven Pressfield's

---

[921] McGeehan, Patrick, 'Merrill Lynch Settles Racial Bias Suit for $160 Million', *The New York Times*, 27 August 2013.

[922] Diversity in Philanthropy Project, *Initiatives for Racial and Economic Justice in Philanthropy* (2007).

[923] The Greenlining Institute, *Equity in Philanthropy Initiative* (2007)

2011 book about overcoming *"resistance"* in completing art[924], with the profound insight that achieving things takes time and effort. Most notably, this neologism has been circulated in *"antiracism"* literature as a struggle of perpetual sanctification for the original sin of one's skin colour at birth.

(Religion, N/A)

Doctors & Engineers

Your rapist's profession before they were a helpless, military-age asylum seeker.

Despite how tricky it is to pinpoint the exact first example of when good-hearted British columnists flattered third world migrants to England as more skilled than their first world counterparts, its association with Pakistani migrants taking jobs in the *National Health Service* during the sixties is well-established[925].

In completely unrelated developments, more than 18,700 suspected victims of child sexual exploitation were identified by local authorities in England by 2019[926], which the Pakistani *Home Office* minister Sajid Javid attributed to a *"high proportion of men of Pakistani heritage"* for *"cultural reasons"*.[927]

(Newspapers, 1958)

---

[924] Pressfield, Steven, *Do the Work* (The Domino Project, 2011)

[925] Simpson, Julian M., *Migrant Architects of the NHS* (Manchester University Press, 2018).

[926] *Characteristics of Children in Need: 2018 to 2019* (Department for Education, 2020).

[927] Sommers, Jack, 'More than 18,700 Children in England Identified as Suspected Victims of Sexual Exploitation Last Year', *The Independent*, 24 November 2019.

Dog Whistle

> *Secret Hitler signal—only given by people who are not left-wing—to assemble and bring on the apocalypse to fight Progress towards the utopia. You couldn't hear it, but it was there.*

Supposedly an analogy for an ultrasonic tone of which is heard by dogs (yet is inaudible to humans), Richard Morin, director of polling for *The Washington Post*, notes in 1988[928] an invisible and untestable polling term the *"Dog Whistle Effect"*: politicians using subjective *"coded language"* to appeal to voters which only politically opposed journalists seem to be able to detect.

If you hear the dog whistle, *you're the dog*.

(Journalism, 1988)

Dogpile

> *An outraged mob of people on the internet who appear in numbers to prove the Appeal to Majority fallacy correct and protect helpless victims by making more.*

Originally a term for pigs rioting, then a sports metaphor, then a search engine, the contemporary meaning is internet commenters attacking someone guilty of *wrongthink*.

(Literature, 1921)

---

[928] Morin, Richard, 'Invisible and Untestable Polling Terms: The "Dog Whistle Effect"', *The Washington Post*, 1988.

Domesticity As Prison

> Women feel unfulfilled as housewives. Because, society.

The battle-cry of bathroom fiction for middle-class women everywhere was humanist Betty Friedan's 1964 bestseller *"The Feminine Mystique"*[929], which claimed women led lives of misery because of the way "society" expected them to reach peak happiness as housewives and mothers. Betty said she was beaten, then that she wasn't[930]. Nobody knows. She was married with kids.

(Feminist Literature, 1964)

Dynamics

> A word a wannabe intellectual™ erroneously uses for "comparative differences", "variations", or "differential".

Social dynamics. Power dynamics. Dynamic has a specific scientific meaning from physics related to motion produced by force; the opposite of static. In music, it refers to a variation in loudness between notes or phrases[931]. The dynamic range of an instrument indicates the difference between its softest and loudest sounds, i.e. its dynamic range[932]. The idea human psychology is *"psychodynamic"* originates with the intellectual

---

[929] Friedan, Betty, *The Feminine Mystique* (W. W. Norton & Co., 1963).

[930] Martin, Douglas, 'Betty Friedan, Who Ignited Cause in *The Feminine Mystique*, Dies at 85', *The New York Times*, 5 February 2006.

[931] Everest, F. Alton, and Ken C. Pohlmann, *Master Handbook of Acoustics*, 6th edn (McGraw Hill Education, 2014).

[932] Cook, Nicholas, *Music* (Oxford University Press, 2000).

bankruptcy of Austrian psychotherapist Alfred Adler[933].

(Psychology, 1956)

Empathy

The invisible, magical, non-religious remedy to all of humanity's behavioural woes, like evil, suffering, war, genocide, murder, psychopathy, rape, etc.

Despite it sounding like a long-established scientific truth, the word *"empathy"* was a synonym for "sympathy" until the fifties. The Greek prefix "em" means "in" or "within"; the prefix "sym" (from "syn") means "together with" or "along with". It is not a magical superpower intuition only possessed by women, and there is no evidence for its existence at all.

"Empathy" was simply made up in 1909 by English psychologist Edward B. Titchener in his book *"Lectures on the experimental psychology of the thought-processes",*[934] as an English translation of a notion in German philosopher Robert Vischer's 1873 Ph.D. dissertation on aesthetics he named *Einfühlung* (*"esthetic sympathy", "feeling into",* or the way people project themselves into works of art)[935]. Which apparently has something to do with the mind's "muscles" and *"social neuroscience".* By 1932, *"empathy"* had become a widely accepted term amongst psychologists.

---

[933] Ansbacher, Heinz L, Rowena R. Ansbacher, *The Individual Psychology of Alfred Adler* (Basic Books, 1956)

[934] Titchener, Edward B., *Lectures on the Experimental Psychology of the Thought-Processes* (The Macmillan Company, 1909).

[935] Visher, Robert, et al., 'On the Optical Sense of Form: A Contribution to Aesthetics', in *Empathy, Form, and Space: Problems in German Aesthetics, 1873–1893*, trans. by [translator's name, if available] (Getty Center for the History of Art, 1993), pp. 89–123. (Originally published in German).

The concept was popularised by psychotherapist Carl Rogers in his books *"Counseling and Psychotherapy"* (1942)[936], *"Client-centered Therapy"* (1951)[937], and *"On Becoming A Person"* (1961)[938].

(Aesthetics, 1909)

Emotional Intelligence (EI/EQ)

A handy way to calm your wife down when she insists the energy crystals told her you were definitely smiling at the receptionist.

First mentioned in *Mensa*'s magazine in 1987[939], this esoteric idea descends from several social science papers (*"Sensitivity to expression of emotional meaning in three modes of communication"* by Michael Beldoch[940], *"Emotional intelligence and emancipation"* by Barbara Leuner[941], *"Frames of Mind: The Theory of Multiple Intelligences"* by Howard Gardner[942]) in the mid-sixties claiming emotion is a form of reasoning.

It was variously defined between 1989-1990 by Stanley Greenspan[943], Peter Salovey and John Mayer[944], but ultimately popularised by Daniel

---

[936] Rogers, Carl, *Counseling and Psychotherapy* (Houghton Mifflin, 1942)

[937] Ibid.

[938] Rogers, Carl, *On Becoming a Person* (Houghton Mifflin, 1961).

[939] Beasley, Keith, 'The Emotional Quotient', *Mensa*, May 1987, p. 25.

[940] Beldoch, Michael, 'Sensitivity to Expression of Emotional Meaning in Three Modes of Communication', in *The Communication of Emotional Meaning*, ed. by J. R. Davitz (McGraw-Hill, 1964), pp. 31–42.

[941] Leuner, Barbara, 'Emotional Intelligence and Emancipation', *Praxis der Kinderpsychologie und Kinderpsychiatrie*, 15.6 (1966), 193–203.

[942] Gardner, Howard, *Frames of Mind* (Basic Books, 1983).

[943] Greenspan, Stanley I., *Emotional Intelligence and the Process of Development* (International Universities Press, 1989).

[944] Salovey, Peter, and John D. Mayer, 'Emotional Intelligence', *Imagination, Cognition and Personality*, 9.3 (1990), 185–211.

Goleman's 1995 book, *"Emotional Intelligence: Why It Can Matter More Than IQ"*[945]. None of which were able to provide any proof of its actual existence or its differentiation from a skill, a behaviour, social conformity. Or why most CEOs display psychopathic traits[946].

(Psychology, 1989)

Emotional Labour

> *It's not whining. It's "work". The mental effort required to deal with other people.*

It's hard to be a waitress or a flight attendant. Or take a call from a friend. Not the physical lifting, but emotionally.

In 1983, sociologist Arlie Hochschild, from *Berkeley* (*where else?*), penned *"The managed heart: commercialization of human feeling"*[947] for the university's journal.

Which was, presumably, *exhausting*.

(Sociology, 1983)

Emotional Support Animal

> *A legal way to take your pet to places like grocery stores and government offices without being asked to tie them up outside.*

Originally designated the noble, legitimate purpose of helping trauma-

---

[945] Goleman, Daniel, *Emotional Intelligence* (Bantam Books, 1995).

[946] Babiak, Paul, Craig S. Neumann, and Robert D. Hare, 'Corporate Psychopathy: Talking the Walk', *Behavioral Sciences & the Law*, 28.2 (2010), 174–93.

[947] Hochschild, Arlie Russell, *The Managed Heart* (University of California Press, 1983)

tised veterans as service/assistance animals[948], any fragile millennial who "gets anxiety" can now register their *Instagram*-friendly pooch as a medical "support" to avoid fees on planes and mean landlords.

"*Assistance animals*" were recognised under the 1988 US federal *Fair Housing Act*[949], after the 1986 *Air Carrier Access Act* (ACAA)[950], on the basis it would be "discrimination" against someone with a "disability". Back in academia around 2009, the stupidity was being advanced with papers like *"Advocating Change within the ADA: The Struggle to Recognize Emotional- Support Animals as Service Animals"*[951].

(Law, 1968)

Empowerment

The soft mental version of the Marxist revolution. POWER! SO MUCH POWER!!!

Historically-speaking, the endowment or bestowal of power was legal terminology (like, for example, *"enumeration"*), and became entwined with the *Civil Rights* era of the early-sixties. Interest seems to have increase around the time of Foucault's death, with publications by Julian Rappaport such as *"In praise of paradox: A social policy of empowerment over prevention"* (1981)[952] and *"Studies in empowerment: Introduction to the*

---

[948] Yount, Rebecca A., Mary D. Olmert, and Mary R. Lee, 'Service Dog Training Program for Treatment of Posttraumatic Stress in Service Members', *US Army Medical Department Journal*, 4–5 (2012), 63–69.

[949] *Fair Housing Amendments Act of 1988*, Pub. L. No. 100-430, 102 Stat. 1619 (1988).

[950] *Air Carrier Access Act of 1986*, Pub. L. No. 99-435, 100 Stat. 1080 (1986).

[951] Bourland, Kristen M., 'Advocating Change within the ADA: The Struggle to Recognize Emotional-Support Animals as Service Animals', *University of Louisville Law Review*, 48.2 (2009), 197–222.

[952] Rappaport, Julian, 'In Praise of Paradox: A Social Policy of Empowerment over Prevention', *American Journal of Community Psychology*, 9.1 (1981), 1–25

issue. Prevention in Human Services" (1984)[953], followed others such as *"Women and the Politics of Empowerment (Women in the Political Economy)"* (Ann Bookman, Sandra Morgen, 1988)[954].

To illustrate just how extreme things have really become, in *"Teaching for Diversity and Social Justice: A Sourcebook"* (1997, an absolutely epic read in itself), the editors give this extraordinary definition Lenin would have endorsed:

> *When target group members refuse to accept the dominant ideology and their subordinate status and take actions to redistribute social power more equitably.*[955]

(Psychology, 1981)

Energy

> *Believing you are a prophet or higher being because your crystals sense someone's mood.*

Energy has a specific scientific meaning from physics[956]: the *quantifiable capacity or potential of a body or system to perform work and produce an effect* (i.e. measurable *work* capability)[957]. The *Gnostic* or *New Age* belief

---

[953] Rappaport, Julian, 'Studies in Empowerment: Introduction to the Issue', *Prevention in Human Services*, 3.2–3 (1984), 1–7.

[954] Bookman, Ann, and Sandra Morgen, eds., *Women and the Politics of Empowerment* (Temple University Press, 1988).

[955] Adams, Maurianne, Lee Anne Bell, and Pat Griffin, eds., *Teaching for Diversity and Social Justice* (Routledge, 1997).

[956] Feynman, Richard P., Robert B. Leighton, and Matthew Sands, *The Feynman Lectures on Physics* (Addison-Wesley, 1963).

[957] Joule, James Prescott, 'On the Mechanical Equivalent of Heat', *Philosophical Transactions of the Royal Society of London*, 140 (1847), 61–82.

inanimate objects possess a spiritual form of it, or it can be "felt" in people or places, or it can be used for "healing", derive from *Magnetism* in the 19th century[958].

The ludicrous term *"energy medicine"* was coined in 1989 with the emergence of the *International Society for the Study of Subtle Energies and Energy Medicine (ISSSEEM)*[959].

(Quackery, 1989)

Enlightened

> *Left-wing intellectualv. Educated themselves. Stands with the Current Thing. University-educated. Middle class. Vegan. Twitterer. Guardian/NYT commenter. Virtuous. Of a "purer" moral condition than others, solely on the basis of one's ideology.*

From *UrbanDictionary*:

> *Baizuo (pronounced "bye-tswaw") is a Chinese epithet meaning naive western educated person who advocates for peace and equality only to satisfy their own feeling of moral superiority: ignorant and arrogant westerners who pity the rest of the world and think they are saviours.*[960]

---

[958] Maxwell, James Clerk, 'A Dynamical Theory of the Electromagnetic Field', *Philosophical Transactions of the Royal Society of London*, 155 (1865), 459–512.

[959] ISSSEEM, *Subtle Energies & Energy Medicine Journal* (1989)

[960] 'Baizuo', *Urban Dictionary*, n.d.,

Equality

> *Ultimate goal of Homo sapiens if he can just be engineered properly by intellectualᵥ people who have already attained said moral condition.*

No matter how insane the level of wishful thinking becomes, no matter how stupid and rabid the *"social science"* commentators are free to be, humans are born unequal due to natural biodiversity and evolutionary adaptation.

We arrive at birth with fixed immutable properties of heredity, outside of our ability to change sans artificial intervention, including IQ, height, skin colour, blood type, genetics, fingerprints, eye colour, aptitude, talent, and more. Nature has no concept of "equality," nor does she value or desire it[961].

(Sociology, 1840)

Equity

> *A clever way to promote socialist equality of outcome as a synonym for fairness and impartiality.*

"Equity" means a share which is equally divided, as defined in jurisprudence[962]. Although economically defined by shareholders in a company[963], in philosophical circles, the phrase refers to Marx's concept of ownership of the means of production by workers (i.e. through the division of labour and its inherent moral value). It was given in his 1875

---

[961] Murray, Charles, *Human Diversity* (Twelve, 2020).

[962] Spence, George, *Equitable Jurisdiction of the Court of Chancery* (Stevens and Norton, 1846).

[963] Brigham, E. F., & Ehrhardt, M. C. (2021). *Financial Management,* Cengage Learning.

"*Critique of the Gotha Program,*" citing *"From each according to his ability, to each according to his needs" (Section 1)*[964]. The trouble being, needs grow exponentially, and abilities are finite[965]. See: Dekulakisation.

(Political Science, 1875)

Erasure

> Being ignored. Usually on account of being insufferable, morally depraved, or histrionic.

Although she doesn't use the word, the concept of being rubbed off the board like chalk comes from high priestess Kimberlé Crenshaw, in her infamous 1989 article, *"Demarginalizing the Intersection of Race and Sex: A Black Feminist Critique of Antidiscrimination Doctrine, Feminist Theory and Antiracist Politics"*[966], and its even worse 1991 sequel, *"Mapping the Margins: Intersectionality, Identity Politics, and Violence Against Women of Color"*[967]. The term exploded in popularity around 2006, culminating in highly scholastic endeavours such as *"Exclusion and Erasure: Two Types of Ontological Oppression"* (2022)[968].

(Sociology, 2006)

---

[964] Marx, Karl, 'Critique of the Gotha Program', in *Karl Marx: Political Writings*, trans. by David Fernbach (Penguin Books, 1975).

[965] Hayek, Friedrich August, *The Road to Serfdom* (University of Chicago Press, 1944).

[966] Crenshaw, Kimberlé, 'Demarginalizing the Intersection of Race and Sex: A Black Feminist Critique of Antidiscrimination Doctrine, Feminist Theory, and Antiracist Politics', *University of Chicago Legal Forum*, 1989.1 (1989), 139–67

[967] Crenshaw, Kimberlé, 'Mapping the Margins: Intersectionality, Identity Politics, and Violence Against Women of Color', *Stanford Law Review*, 43.6 (1991), 1241–99

[968] Richardson, Kevin, 'Exclusion and Erasure: Two Types of Ontological Oppression', *Ergo: An Open Access Journal of Philosophy*, 9.0 (2022)

Environmental, Social, and Governance (ESG)

> *A devilishly clever way of enslaving companies into a Chinese-style plutocracy, by providing access to capital based on how dogmatically one obeys socialist ideology.*

A terrifyingly Orwellian attempt at a *"social credit"* scoring system[969], for ensuring companies wanting investment comply with political ideology. *"Environment, social, and governance"* emerged from a 2004 UN paper titled *"Who Cares Wins Connecting Financial Markets to a Changing World"*[970]. The impetus was derived from UN Secretary General Kofi Annan writing to CEOs to *"participate in a joint initiative under the auspices of the UN Global Compact and with the support of the International Finance Corporation (IFC) and the Swiss Government"* a year earlier[971].

(Politics, 2004)

Essentialism

> *A word you can add to something which exists, in reality, which you don't like to make it look really bad and discriminatory. It sounds intellectual.*

Essentialism has been around since Plato's day[972]. It means something is required and necessary for something to function (*essence* is prior to

---

[969] Ahmed, Nabeel, and Shenglin Chen, 'From Datafication to Data State: Making Sense of China's Social Credit System and Its Implications', *Law & Social Inquiry*, 46.2 (2021), 596–624.

[970] UN Global Compact, *Who Cares Wins* (United Nations, 2004).

[971] United Nations, 'Secretary-General's Initiative on Financial Markets and Sustainability', (2003).

[972] Plato, *The Republic*, (Hackett Publishing, 1992; ca. 380 BCE).

existence). Repudiated by the moronic Jean Paul Sartre in favour of nihilistic *"existentialism"*[973]. Now a synonym for not being *"progressive"*.

(Philosophy, 1939)

Ethic(s)

A word psychopathic people who want to sound intellectual use for morality, to escape being stigmatised as "religious".

Get your philosophy right: moral principles in conduct.

Ethnocentrism

When white students refuse to agree to banana + tree = spirit energy in physics class, and need to eat Asian food they don't like to fix it.

What began as a more polite slur than "xenophobia" by sociologist William Graham Sumner in his 1906 book *"Folkways: A Study of the Sociological Importance of Usages, Manners, Customs, Mores, and Morals"*[974], morphed into a political notion when Sir Edward Evan Evans-Pritchard declared in 1951 the *"ethnocentric attitude has to be abandoned if we are to appreciate the rich variety of human culture and social life."*[975] No, Edward, it doesn't. But thanks anyway.

(Anthropology, 1951)

---

[973] Sartre, Jean-Paul, *Existentialism Is a Humanism* (Yale University Press, 2007; ca. 1946).

[974] Sumner, William Graham, *Folkways: A Study of the Sociological Importance of Usages, Manners, Customs, Mores, and Morals* (Boston: Ginn and Co., 1906).

[975] Evans-Pritchard, Edward Evan, *Social Anthropology* (Cohen & West, 1951).

Ethnomathematics

Something which won't ever hold bridges up or build spaceships.

Yet another risible example of Paulo Freire-esque different *"ways of knowing"*, this fanciful area of study was conceived by Brazilian "educator" Ubiratan D'Ambrosio in 1977 during a presentation for the *American Association for the Advancement of Science*. He compounded this monstrosity in *"Ethnomathematics and its place in the history and pedagogy of mathematics. For the Learning of Mathematics"* (1985)[976].

(*Education, 1977*)

Everything Is About Power

The diary of a paedophile psychopath, written from a BSDM dungeon.
The king of intellectuals everywhere.

The disturbing idea power is the only thing in the world comes directly from the writings of French "philosopher" Michel Foucault, who is worshiped like a god by a whole generation of *Women's Studies* and *Queer Studies'* "professors". Which should tell one all one needs to know, if one perceives most ordinary people wake up in the morning to embark on a feverish search for power.

Beginning with *"Madness and Civilisation"* (1960)[977], descending

---

[976] D'Ambrosio, Ubiratan, 'Ethnomathematics and Its Place in the History and Pedagogy of Mathematics', *For the Learning of Mathematics*, 5.1 (1985), 44–48.

[977] Foucault, Michel, *Folie et déraison* (Gallimard, 1961)

through *"The Order of Things"* (1966)[978], *"Discipline and Punish"* (1975)[979], down to *"A History of Sexuality"* (1976)[980], Foucault's insanity can be summed up with Chomsky's observation *"He struck me as completely amoral, I'd never met anyone who was so totally amoral."*[981]

(Philosophy, 1975)

Experience

> *Anything that happens between you and any company, ever. For example, having a "charlatanism experience" when reading books by pseuds.*

The next bad idea by the useless cynics who came up with selling abstract *"solutions"* instead of products (*Hello, Microsoft!*), has been *"Experiential Marketing"*. The phenomenon can be traced directly back to a 1998 dotcom-madness article by Joseph Pine and James Gilmore in the *Harvard Business Review* titled *"The Experience Economy"*[982]. Next up? The *"Attention Economy"*[983].

(Literature, 1998)

---

[978] Foucault, Michel, *Les mots et les choses* (Gallimard, 1966)

[979] Foucault, Michel, *Surveiller et punir* (Gallimard, 1975)

[980] Foucault, Michel, *Histoire de la sexualité* (Gallimard, 1976)

[981] Chomsky, Noam, Michel Foucault, *The Chomsky-Foucault Debate* (New Press, 2006).

[982] Pine, B. Joseph, and James H. Gilmore, 'Welcome to the Experience Economy', *Harvard Business Review*, 76.4 (1998), 97–105.

[983] Davenport, Thomas H., John C. Beck, *The Attention Economy* (Harvard Business Review Press, 2001).

Fascist

> *Anyone opposed to Communism. You, probably. The author, probably. Daddy. Generic right-wing or conservative person pulled towards authoritarian behaviour out of desperation and frustration with left-wing rhetoric.*

The traditional enemy of left-wing extremists advocating communism after the *Russian Revolution*.

Derived from *fascismo* (Italian) from *fascio* (*"a bundle of sticks"*) with its root in *fasces* (Latin). The *Fascist Revolutionary Party* was founded in 1915 by Italy's youngest prime minister (and former socialist), Benito Mussolini. In 1921 it became the *National Fascist Party*, which used the ancient Roman symbol of a magistrate's bundle of rods tied around an axe, symbolising the ability to order capital punishment upon demand[984].

Mussolini won in 1924 and established a dictatorship[985]. Eight years later in England Oswald Mosley founded the *British Union of Fascists*, which became infamous during the highly propagandised 1936 *Battle of Cable Street*[986].

George Orwell noted in 1944:

> *It will be seen that, as used, the word 'Fascism' is almost entirely meaningless. In conversation, of course, it is used even more wildly than in print. I have heard it applied to farmers, shopkeepers, Social Credit, corporal punishment, fox-hunting, bull-fighting, the 1922 Committee, the 1941 Committee, Kipling, Gandhi, Chiang Kai-Shek, homosexuality, Priestley's broadcasts, Youth Hostels, astrology,*

---

[984] Payne, Stanley G., *A History of Fascism, 1914–1945* (U. of Wisconsin Press, 1995).

[985] Bosworth, Richard J. B., *Mussolini* (Oxford University Press, 2002).

[986] Dorril, Stephen, *Blackshirt: Sir Oswald Mosley and British Fascism* (Viking, 2006)

> *women, dogs and I do not know what else.*[987]

(Political Science, 1915)

Fashionable Nonsense

> *The term Alan Sokal gave to words in stupid glossaries like these.*

The *Sokal Affair* was an amusing prank by physicists[988] during the nineties' *"Science Wars"* between actual scholars and humanities' graduates[989] which was deeply humiliating to advocates of the social sciences. The book it prompted was named *"Fashionable Nonsense: Postmodern Intellectuals' Abuse of Science"*[990].

(Literature, 1997)

Feminism

> *French Marxism for American ladies. A trendy "I like women" label your boyfriend should adopt because Beyonce made it cool in 2014. Formerly a type of man-hating left-wing extremism derided by academia, business, entertainment, and ordinary people.*

Officially, — if you don't count bonobos or mud huts — feminism began in 1792 during the *French Revolution*, with Mary Wollstonecraft's "A

---

[987] Orwell, George, *Collected Essays, Journalism and Letters of George Orwell*, vol. 3 (Harcourt, Brace & World, 1968)

[988] Sokal, Alan, 'A Physicist Experiments with Cultural Studies', *Lingua Franca*, (1996),

[989] Labinger, Jay A., Harry M. Collins, *The One Culture?* (U. of Chicago Press, 2001).

[990] Sokal, Alan, and Jean Bricmont, *Fashionable Nonsense* (Picador, 1998)

Vindication of the Rights of Woman"[991]. In contemporary times, Simone de Beauvoir's horrific *"Second Sex"* in 1949[992], and Betty Friedan's *"The Feminine Mystique"* in 1963[993] are widely considered signalling the beginning of what we know now as the four waves[994] of blue hair, baby-killing on-demand, & armpit hair freedom.

(Literature, 1792)

Filter Bubble

Your social media news feed.

A term by self-described *"left-wing political and internet activist"*, Eli Pariser, who rebranded the idea of an echo chamber to *"filter bubble"* in a well-circulated TED talk describing the self- evident effects of groupthink and confirmation bias[995]. Sadly, what is lesser known is his day job: as CEO of a company (*"Upworthy"*) which depended on it.

Social media has produced an unprecedented rise in teen suicide.[996]

(Internet, 2010)

---

[991] Wollstonecraft, Mary, *A Vindication of the Rights of Woman* (Joseph Johnson, 1792)

[992] De Beauvoir, Simone, *The Second Sex*, (Vintage Books, 1989).

[993] Friedan, Betty, *The Feminine Mystique* (W. W. Norton & Co., 1963)

[994] Baumgardner, Jennifer, Amy Richards, *Manifesta* (Farrar, Straus and Giroux, 2000)

[995] Pariser, Eli, *The Filter Bubble* (Penguin Press, 2011)

[996] Twenge, Jean M., Thomas E. Joiner, Megan L. Rogers, and Gabrielle N. Martin, 'Increases in Depressive Symptoms, Suicide-Related Outcomes, and Suicide Rates among U.S. Adolescents after 2010 and Links to Increased New Media Screen Time', *Clinical Psychological Science*, 6.1 (2018), 3–17.

Fluid

> *Shape-shifting.*

In physics, a fluid is a phase of matter without a fixed shape- a liquid, gas, or plasma - which continually deforms or flows under external force, and assumes the shape of its container[997].

Fortify

> *Rig.*

An *"informal alliance between left-wing activists and business titans"* formed to "save" the 2020 US Presidential election from democracy itself, published in a *"terse, little-noticed joint statement of the U.S. Chamber of Commerce and AFL-CIO."* The confession, as documented in *Time* magazine under the title *"The Secret History of the Shadow Campaign That Saved the 2020 Election",* described this messianic act of self-sacrifice as:

> *A well-funded cabal of powerful people, ranging across industries and ideologies, working together behind the scenes to influence perceptions, change rules and laws, steer media coverage and control the flow of information. They were not rigging the election; they were fortifying it.*[998]

(Politics, 2021)

---

[997] Young, Hugh D., Roger A. Freedman, and A. Lewis Ford, *University Physics with Modern Physics*, 15th edn (Pearson, 2020).

[998] Ball, Molly, 'The Secret History of the Shadow Campaign That Saved the 2020 Election', *Time*, 4 February 2021.

Framework

> *A word people who want to sound intellectual use for "a collection of bad ideas".*

Get your science right: the supporting structure of an object.

Fraud

> *A person or thing intended to deceive others, typically by unjustifiably claiming or being credited with accomplishments or qualities.*

Fraud: a false representation has been made (1) knowingly, or (2) without belief in its truth, or (3) recklessly, careless whether it be true or false. (As defined in *Derry v Peek (1889) 14 App Cas 337*).

See: academic, journalist, activist.

Freedom From Consequences

> *Intellectual-sounding argument issued as a coded threat you are about to be hounded, attacked, fired, and ruined for saying words.*

The arguments surrounding freedom of speech, which has its roots in 17th century British Parliamentary privilege[999], were most famously articulated by John Stuart Mill in *"On Liberty"* (1859)[1000]. They resounded in the American *1st Amendment* protection against consequences to individuals from the government.

---

[999] May, Thomas Erskine, and Ian Loveland, *Erskine May* (London: LexisNexis, 2021)

[1000] Mill, John Stuart, *On Liberty* (J. W. Parker and Son, 1859).

Almost all laws (at least in Western countries) protect individuals from illegal acts which could be consequences of their speech (e.g. assault or murder)[1001]. The most telling insight into the evolution of the phrase is in how it has morphed from the original "freedom from criticism", indicating a much wider scope than mere speech in response. It is the same type of person who cites it every time, for the same reason.

(Politics, Unknown)

[1001] Schauer, Frederick, *Free Speech* (Cambridge University Press, 1982)

G H I

Gaslighting

> *You're imagining it, babe.*

In his 1938 play *"Gas Light"*, Patrick Hamilton created a psychological horror plot where an abusive husband sneaks out at night to switch the house lighting on after his wife has extinguished it, subsequently to convince her she is imagining it[1002]. First mentioned in Anthony Wallace's 1961 *"Culture & Personality"*[1003], it was followed in 1969 by Stanley Plog, a social scientist, - specialising in, ahem... leisure and tourism -, co-opted it for his book *"Changing Perspectives in Mental Illness"*[1004]. Similarly to *"toxic"* and *"triggered"*, the self-help idea of being *"gaslighted"* skyrocketed around 2012[1005].

(Film, 1938)

[1002] Hamilton, Patrick, *Gas Light* (Constable & Co. Ltd., 1938).

[1003] Wallace, Anthony F. C., *Culture and Personality* (Random House, 1961).

[1004] Plog, Stanley C., *Changing Perspectives in Mental Illness* (Holt, Rinehart and Winston, 1969)

[1005] Google Books Ngram Viewer, *Ngram Viewer Dataset*

Gatekeeping

> *The unfathomably selfish idea of not agreeing to anyone changing anything they want on a whim for their own reasons.*

In-group preference is apparently *"deciding who does or does not have access or rights to a community or identity"*. Derived from psychologist Kurt Lewin's 1943 *"Gatekeeping Theory"*, on the mass media, detailed in *"Forces Behind Food Habits and Methods of Change"* of *"The Problem of Changing Food Habits: Report of the Committee on Food Habits 1941–1943"*[1006].

(Psychology, 1943)

Gay

> *Nonthreatening male member of the sisterhood.*

From the Old French *gai*, meaning "joyful" or "carefree," back to the Late Latin *gaius*[1007]. By the 17th century, it meant hedonistic and "carefree" to the point of being morally lax[1008].

In *"Bringing Up Baby"* (1938), Cary Grant's character, Dr David Huxley (a.k.a *"Mr Bone"*), exclaims, *"I just went gay all of a sudden!"* while dressed in a woman's robe[1009].

In 1941, George Henry used in a same-sex context within his book

---

[1006] Lewin, Kurt, 'Forces Behind Food Habits and Methods of Change', in *The Problem of Changing Food Habits: Report of the Committee on Food Habits 1941–1943*, ed. by National Research Council (Washington, D.C.: National Academy of Sciences, 1943)

[1007] Skeat, Walter W., *An Etymological Dictionary of the English Language* (Clarendon, 1963)

[1008] Partridge, Eric, *A Dictionary of Slang and Unconventional English* (Routledge, 2006)

[1009] Benshoff, Harry M., and Sean Griffin, *Queer Images* (Rowman & Littlefield, 2004)

"*Sex Variants: A Study of Homosexual Patterns* "[1010].

(Film, 1938)

Gay Liberation

> *The original plan for everything you're wondering the social origin of. The Communist Manifesto with the notion of class substituted for sexual orientation.*

The six days of *Stonewall Riots* in New York during 1969[1011] were ignited after nine *New York Police Department* officers from the *Public Morals Division* raided *The Stonewall Inn* on Christopher Street, an unlicensed bar owned and operated by the *Genovese* crime family, at 1:20 a.m. on Saturday, June 28, 1969.

It was notorious for drug dealing, child prostitution, and serving as a nightly home for homeless runaways[1012][1013]. A significant proportion, if not the majority, of the bar's patrons who violently attacked police made their sole living as cross-dressing homosexual prostitutes[1014].

A militant wing of protestors formed the *Gay Liberation Front* (named after the communist *Viet Cong*) and *Street Transvestite Action Revolutionaries*, to ally with *Women's Liberation*. It spread to Montreal and London the next year[1015].

Although it only lasted until 1974, the same people, such as Peter

---

[1010] Henry, George W., *Sex Variants* (Paul B. Hoeber, 1941)

[1011] Carter, David, *Stonewall* (St. Martin's Press, 2004)

[1012] Robert Longley, 'Stonewall Riots: History and Legacy', *ThoughtCo*, 14 November 2019

[1013] Riley, Alexander, 'The Darker Side of the Celebrated Stonewall Riots', *Intellectual Takeout*, 28 June 2021

[1014] Chateauvert, Melinda, *Sex Workers Unite* (Beacon Press, 2014)

[1015] Power, Lisa, *No Bath but Plenty of Bubbles* (Cassell, 1995)

Tatchell (himself the subject of allegations of pederasty[1016]), kept campaigning under the banner of *"OutRage!"*[1017]. In 1971, the *GLF* published its communist manifesto[1018], which is frankly insane and terrifying by any standard — it became the political blueprint of the next forty years.

A year before, *"The Red Butterfly"*, a Marxist cell within the *New York Gay Liberation Front*, published the first draft as *"A Gay Manifesto"*. It's interesting reading.

> *A note on exploitation of children: kids can take care of themselves, and are sexual beings way earlier than we'd like to admit. Those of us who began cruising in early adolescence know this, and we were doing the cruising, not being debauched by dirty old men. Scandals such as the one in Boise, Idaho - blaming a "ring" of homosexuals for perverting their youth - are the fabrications of press and police and politicians.*[1019]

(Political Extremism), 1969)

[1016] Tatchell, Peter, 'Tatchell on Sex with Children', *The Guardian*, 26 June 1997, Letters Section.

  "Several of my friends, gay and straight, male and female, had sex with adults from the ages of nine to 13. None feel they were abused. All say it was their conscious choice and gave them great joy. It is time society acknowledged the truth that not all sex involving children is unwanted, abusive and harmful."

  (in relation to his contribution towards the "courageous" 1997 book *" Dares to Speak: Historical and Contemporary Perspectives on Boy-love"*).

[1017] Tatchell, Peter, *We Don't Want to March Straight* (London: Cassell, 1995)

[1018] Gay Liberation Front, *Manifesto of the Gay Liberation Front* (London: 1971)

[1019] Wittman, Carl, *A Gay Manifesto* (The Red Butterfly, 1970)

Gender

Tertiary sex characteristics. What you can pretend to be with the right hair, makeup, and wardrobe.

Gender was a synonym for biological sex until 1945, when the *American Journal of Psychology* published Madison Bentley's seminal article referring to it as the *"socialized obverse of sex"*[1020].

In barbaric, failed 1966 experiments on twins conceived to prove nurture was entirely responsible, John Money extended this sophistry into the concepts of *"gender role"*[1021].

By 1968, psychiatrist Robert Stoller from the *Gender Identity Clinic* at *UCLA* was writing about a *"gender identity"* in *"Sex and Gender: On the Development of Masculinity and Femininity"*[1022].

Contemporary theorists, such as lesbian Marxist sociologist Judith Butler, later attempted to syncretise the bizarre ideas of Michel Foucault[1023] into a grander thesis gender was a *"performance"* entirely separate from biological sex[1024].

(Psychology, 1945)

[1020] Bentley, Mądison, 'The American Journal of Psychology', *The American Journal of Psychology*, 58.1 (1945), 89–93.

[1021] Colapinto, John, *As Nature Made Him* (New York: HarperCollins, 2000).

[1022] Stoller, Robert J., *Sex and Gender* (Science House, 1968).

[1023] Campbell, Matthew, 'French Philosopher Michel Foucault "Abused Boys in Tunisia"', *The Sunday Times*, 28 March 2021.

[1024] Butler, Judith, *Gender Trouble* (Routledge, 1990).

Genderfluid

> *Unwilling to be classified by science as one of the two forms of homo sapiens because that's just something society says.*

Generally attributed to transexual Scientologist Kate Bornstein in her 1994 paper *"Gender Outlaw: On Men, Women and the Rest of Us"*[1025]. Apparently the subject of a 1993 *Suede* concert.

(Women's Studies, 1994)

Genderqueer

> *Not classifiable by science as one of the two forms of homo sapiens.*

Used by the founder of activist group *GenderPAC*, Riki Wilchins, in the newsletter *In Your Face* and Joan Nestle's 2002 work *"Genderqueer: Voices Beyond the Sexual Binary"*[1026], who describes herself as a *"transexual lesbian feminist"*.

(Women's Studies, 1995)

Gender-Affirming (Care)

> *Chemical castration, castration, double mastectomy, genitoplasty, and cross-dressing. For autistic children. Role-playing as a Nazi doctor with a smile and so much "love".*

Few phrases evoke such grotesque moral horror, or involve such a

---

[1025] Bornstein, Kate, *Gender Outlaw* (Vintage Books, 1994).

[1026] Nestle, Joan, Riki Wilchins, Clare Burke, eds., *Genderqueer* (Alyson Books, 2002)

staggering degree of lying by institutions[1027].

The first *"sex change"* operations, or *Genitalumwandlung ("transformation of genitals"*), were carried out by Erwin Gohrbandt, Felix Abraham, and Ludwig Levy-Lenz at Magnus Hirshfield's non-profit *Institut für Sexualwissenschaft ("Institute for Sexual Science")* in Tiergarten, Berlin in 1922[1028]. The private clinic employed forty doctors, conducted around 18,000 consultations for 3,500 people in its first year, and had a *"Eugenics Department for Mother and Child"* offering *"marital counseling"* services[1029].

The most infamous was a severely mentally ill forty-year-old man named Dora (Rudolph) Richter, who had tried to rip off his penis at six years old with a tourniquet. His castration, along with that of fifty-two year-old German painter Arno Ebel (aka "Toni"), was documented in Felix Abraham's grotesque journal paper *"Genitalumwandlungen an zwei männlichen Transvestiten."* (*"Genital Reassignment on Two Male Transvestites"*, 1931)[1030]. Nine years later, his penis was amputated and replaced with a false vagina by Gohrbandt, who later became the chief medical advisor for aeronautical medicine at the Luftwaffe's *Sanitary Services Division*, and participated in the *Dachau Hypothermia Experiments*[1031][1032][1033].

Danish painter Einar Wegener (aka *"Lili Ilse Elvenes"*) had himself castrated in 1930 before having an ovary implanted, his penis removed,

---

[1027] Caraballo, Alejandra, 'To Protect Gender-Affirming Care, We Must Learn from Trans History', *Harvard Public Health*, 21 June 2023

[1028] Herzer, Manfred, *Magnus Hirschfeld*, (Prometheus Books, 1990)

[1029] Tamagne, Florence, *History of Homosexuality in Europe* (Algora Publishing, 2004)

[1030] Abraham, Felix, 'Genitalumwandlungen an zwei männlichen Transvestiten', *Zeitschrift für Sexualwissenschaft und Sexualpolitik*, 18 (1931), 223–26

[1031] Neumann, Hans, 'The Activities of Surgeon Erwin Gohrbandt (1890–1965) on Behalf of the Berlin University, the City's Municipal Council and the Berlin Surgical Society', *Zeitschrift für Ärztliche Fortbildung*, 84.21 (1990), 1053–56

[1032] Annas, George J., and Michael A. Grodin, *The Nazi Doctors and the Nuremberg Code* (Oxford University Press, 1992)

[1033] Meyerowitz, Joanne J., *How Sex Changed* (Harvard University Press, 2002)

and finally his scrotum removed at *Dresden Municipal Women's Clinic*. Finally, he had a womb transplant and a false vagina. The infection from it killed him[1034].

The invention of the phrase can be traced back a 2008 article in the *Sexuality Research and Social Policy* journal (*"The state we're in: Locations of coercion and resistance in trans policy, part 2"* by Dean Spade and Paisley Currah), which merely on its own should have given any author or reader pause for thought whether it was a good idea:

> *Engaging in sex work so they can pay for gender-affirming health care causes many trans people to fall into the maw of the criminal justice system.*[1035]

Translated: cross-dressers become prostitutes to find the money to have their genitals removed, and end up in jail.

Research consistently shows 96% of individuals who present with gender dysphoric traits at age eleven no longer present with them after full brain development by age twenty-six[1036].

A 1991 study in the *Journal of the American Academy of Child & Adolescent Psychiatry* discovered fifty-three per cent of children being evaluated for *Gender Identity Disorder* (GID) had mothers suffering depression and *Borderline Personality Disorder* (BPD), who *"encouraged symbiosis and discouraged the development of autonomy"*[1037].

[1034] Ibid.

[1035] Spade, Dean, and Paisley Currah, 'The State We're In: Locations of Coercion and Resistance in Trans Policy, Part 2', *Sexuality Research & Social Policy*, 5.1 (2008), 67–78

[1036] Rawee, Pien, et al., 'Development of Gender Non-Contentedness During Adolescence and Early Adulthood', *Archives of Sexual Behavior*, 53 (2024), 1813–25

[1037] Marantz, S., and S. Coates. "Mothers of Boys with Gender Identity Disorder: A Comparison of Matched Controls." *Journal of the American Academy of Child & Adolescent Psychiatry*, vol. 30, no. 2, 1991, pp. 310–315

After it was closed in 2023 due to the findings of the UK *Cass Review*[1038], it was revealed the *Tavistock and Portman NHS Foundation Trust* clinic ignored evidence demonstrating 97.5 per cent of children seeking sex changes had autism or depression[1039].

(Sexology, 2008)

Gender Critical

A militant feminist academic whose entire literary career of attacking men has been ruined by men demanding to be recognised as women.

As a reactionary movement to gender ideology, feminist opposition to "genderists" redefining of women emerged in the early seventies and adopted the kinder term "critical" to replace the pejorative "TERF". The first mainstream usage was in a 2018 article published in *The Australian*[1040].

(Literature, 2018)

Gender Essentialism

The idea of women being born female tending to make them act like women. A sinister conspiracy. Highly intellectual™.

Attributed to Derrida/Foucault-loving Australian Women's Studies Dean Elizabeth Grosz in her 1995 scribble *"Space, time and perversion: essays on*

[1038] Cass, Hilary, *Independent Review of Gender Identity Services for Children and Young People: Final Report* (NHS England, 10 April 2024)

[1039] Barnes, Hannah, *Time to Think* (Swift Press, 2023)

[1040] The Australian, 'TERF Usage in Public Discourse', *The Australian* (2018)

the politics of bodies"[1041]. A genius at work. Competitive analyses suggest Angela Harris' 1990 paper *"Race and essentialism in feminist legal theory"* in the *Stanford Law Review*[1042].

(Women's Studies, 1995)

Gender Identity

The academic notion boys might be different from girls because they are boys or girls, and derive part of their identity from it.

This phrase has been mis-attributed to different people, particularly the execrable John Money and his terminology surrounding *"gender neutrality."* It was, in fact, a previously undiscussed idea promoted by Freud-loving psychiatrist Robert Stoller at the *23rd International Psycho-Analytic Congress* in Stockholm, who worked at the *Gender Identity Clinic* at *UCLA*.

His 1968 book *"Sex and Gender: On the Development of Masculinity and Femininity"*[1043], reinforced Madison Bentley's 1945 differentiation between sex (male and female) and gender (*"the amount of masculinity or femininity found in a person,"* p. 9).

Money himself attributed it to UCLA psychologist Evelyn Hooker[1044].

(Psychiatry, 1968)

[1041] Grosz, Elizabeth, *Space, Time, and Perversion* (Routledge, 1995)

[1042] Harris, Angela P., 'Race and Essentialism in Feminist Legal Theory', *Stanford Law Review*, 42.3 (1990), 581–616

[1043] Stoller, Robert J., *Sex and Gender* (Science House, 1968).

[1044] Money, John, 'Gender: History, Theory and Usage of the Term in Sexology and Its Relationship to Nature/Nurture', *Journal of Sex & Marital Therapy*, 11 (1985), 71–79

Gender Pay Gap

> Not being paid in absentia by your employer for making a new human, as you would in a communist system.

Comparing the cumulative lifetime income of males against females determines an equity (equality of outcome) calculation[1045]. In a communist system, both would be equal regardless of circumstances (not unsurprisingly favoured, given most feminist authors *"identify as"* Marxists).

Although the US *Equal Pay Act* of 1963[1046] and United Kingdom *Equal Pay Act* of 1970[1047] (after the *Dagenham/Ford protests*[1048]) cemented the issue's importance, the dreadful and politicised scholarship of median data currently hijacked by activists began when humanities "scholars" started "interpreting" core data such as Gary Becker's 1957 book *"The Economics of Discrimination"*[1049] and Stanley/Jarrell's 1998 *"Gender wage discrimination bias? A metaregression analysis"* (*Journal of Human Resources*)[1050].

(Political Rhetoric, 1957)

Genocide

> When your political enemies inflict a catastrophic military loss.

[1045] Farrell, Warren, *Why Men Earn More* (New York: AMACOM, 2005)

[1046] United States Equal Pay Act, 1963

[1047] United Kingdom Equal Pay Act, 1970

[1048] Coote, Anna, and Beatrix Campbell, *Women's Rights at Work* (Penguin, 1971)

[1049] Becker, Gary S., *The Economics of Discrimination* (University of Chicago Press, 1957)

[1050] Stanley, T. D., and S. B. Jarrell, 'Gender Wage Discrimination Bias? A Meta-Regression Analysis', *Journal of Human Resources*, 33.4 (1998)

Polish-Jewish lawyer Raphael Lemkin coined the term in 1941, making it quite clear: the act of killing a race, or people (*genos*)[1051] in his subsequent book *"Axis Rule in Occupied Europe: Laws of Occupation, Analysis of Government, Proposals for Redress"* (1944)[1052].

The nation of Israel, the attack whom the word was created for, has been slandered with accusations of it in 1982 (Sabra and Shatila massacre), 2006 (*Operation Cast Lead*), 2014 (*Operation Protective Edge*), 2021 (May conflict), and 2023 (responding to the October 7 *Hamas* attacks), every time it has won the battle[1053].

In presumably unrelated events, the UN's *Office of Internal Oversight Services* (OIOS) revealed employees of the *United Nations Relief and Works Agency for Palestine Refugees in the Near East* (UNRWA) were involved in the attacks carried out by *Hamas*[1054].

The impartial *United Nations General Assembly* (UNGA) has passed fifteen resolutions critical of Israel, surpassing the total number of resolutions against all other countries combined[1055]. By 2013, Israel had been condemned in forty-five resolutions by the impartial *United Nations Human Rights Council* (UNHRC)[1056]. Between 1967 and 1989, the *United Nations Security Council* (UNSC) had adopted one hundred and thirty one resolutions[1057].

(*Law, 1941*)

[1051] Irvin-Erickson, Douglas, 'The History of Raphaël Lemkin and the UN Genocide Convention', in *[Insert Full Title of Edited Volume]*, ed. by Simon & Kahn (2023)

[1052] Lemkin, Raphaël, *Axis Rule in Occupied Europe: Laws of Occupation: Analysis of Government: Proposals for Redress* (Carnegie Endowment for International Peace, Division of International Law, 1944)

[1053] Finkelstein, Norman G., *Gaza* (University of California Press, 2018)

[1054] UNOIOS *Report on Allegations of Staff Misconduct in Gaza* (2023)

[1055] UN Watch, *Annual Review of United Nations General Assembly Resolutions* (2022)

[1056] UNHRC, *Resolutions Adopted by the UNHRC (2006–2013)*

[1057] United Nations Security Council, *Compilation of Resolutions Adopted by the United Nations Security Council (1967–1989)* (United Nations Archives, 1989)

Gig Economy

Hiring out your Airbnb so you don't have to go to the office.

Following the political futurism which preached the development of a "knowledge economy", this term was first used in the *New Yorker* magazine in 2009 by its editor, Tina Brown[1058], to describe millennials being paid for social media product placement to pay their bills, rather than acquiring and/or maintaining employment.

(Literature, 2009)

Glass Ceiling

When your abilities don't match your demands.

In 1978, American HR consultant Marilyn Loden, at the *New York Telephone Company,* had a rant during a "women's advancement" panel discussion (*"Mirror, Mirror on the Wall"*, focused on *"messages of limitation which confront women and the effect on aspirations"*) at the Women's Exposition conference, about being told to *"smile more"*[1059].

It later appeared in a 1984 *AdWeek* profile of Gay Bryant, editor of *Working Women* magazine[1060].

(Business, 1978)

[1058] Brown, Thomas, 'The Gig Economy', *The New Yorker*, 2009

[1059] Treisman, Rachel, 'Remembering Marilyn Loden, Who Gave a Name to the Glass Ceiling', *NPR*, 5 September 2022

[1060] Adweek (U.S.), 'Magazine World Supplement', *Adweek*, 15 March 1984, p. 39

GHI

Global Citizen

> A millennial who went to Vietnam for two weeks.

Citizenship is defined by belonging to a *nation* state, i.e. nationality. There is no such thing as a "global" citizen, as the world, and/or the globe, is not a country. Although the idea originated with Marx and the *Comintern*[1061], the whacky, nebulous concept of a *"global consciousness"* and one's identity transcending geography or political borders from membership of "humanity" can be traced back to a 1984 speech by Carole Hahn, President of the *National Council for the Social Studies*[1062]. Its spread into education was furthered by philosopher Martha Nussbaum around 1996[1063].

(Education, 1984)

Global Majority

> White people are only seven per cent of humans, coloniser. Jews, too, whatever.

This malevolent term, with roots in the notion of the *"Global South"* and *"Majority World"* (popularised by Bangladeshi photojournalist Shahidul

---

[1061] While Marx and the *Comintern* did not explicitly use the term "global citizenship", in *"Critique of the Gotha Program"*, Marx discusses the limitations of national approaches to socialism and the need for international coordination among the working class.

The *Comintern*'s founding manifesto called for the overthrow of the capitalist system on a global scale and emphasised internationalism as a fundamental principle for the establishment of a socialist world order.

[1062] Hahn, Carole L., *Becoming Political* (SUNY Press, 1984)

[1063] Nussbaum, Martha C., *For Love of Country?* (Beacon Press, 1996)

Alam)[1064], was introduced to the British public sector by school inspector Rosemary Campbell-Stephens to replace *"ethnic minority"* and *"visible minority,"* which is detailed in her even worse 2021 book, *"Educational Leadership and the Global Majority: Decolonising Narratives."*[1065] An NGO with the same existed around the same time[1066].

The silliness reached its peak in 2021 when the Church of England's *"Antiracism Taskforce"* attempted to replace *"Black, Asian, and Minority Ethnic"* (BAME) with *"United Kingdom Minority Ethnic/Global Majority Heritage"* (UKME/GMH)[1067].

(*Education, 2003*)

Great Replacement

> *The publicly-stated, official policy of governments with no other idea of how to pay the welfare bill.*

In 1925, Austrian-Japanese politician Richard von Coudenhove-Kalergi, creator of the *Paneuropean Union*, published *"Praktischer Idealismus",* in which he predicted the emrgence of a new *"Eurasian-Negroid"* race[1068]. It was portrayed as a plot (the *"Kalergi Plan"*, or *"Coudenhove-Kalergi Conspiracy"*) to mix and replace white Europeans with other races via immigration[1069].

In 2010, French author Renaud Camsu published *"L'Abécédaire de l'in-*

[1064] Alam, Shahidul, 'Majority World', *Drik*, 19 May 2007

[1065] Campbell-Stephens, Rosemary, *Educational Leadership and the Global Majority: Decolonising Narratives* (Springer Nature, 2021)

[1066] Global Majority, 'About Us', https://www.globalmajority.org/about-us

[1067] *From Lament to Action: Report of the Archbishops' Anti-Racism Taskforce* (Church of England, April 2021)

[1068] Coudenhove-Kalergi, Richard N., *Praktischer Idealismus* (Paneuropa-Verlag, 1925)

[1069] Müller, Harald, 'Richard Coudenhove-Kalergi's Vision of Europe: Fascism, Cosmopolitanism, and European Integration', *Journal of European Studies*, 43.1 (2013)

nocence"[1070] and followed it a year later with *"Le Grand Remplacement"*[1071] which referred to the *Grand Dérangement* of the Arcadians in the eighteenth century[1072], and the history of Nazi-occupied France.

Former British Prime Minister Tony Blair's speechwriter Andrew Neather wrote in 2009 Labour's immigration policy was intended to make the UK more multicultural and *"rub the Right's nose in diversity."*[1073] His colleague Peter Mandelson reportedly stated in 2013, *"we sent out search parties for immigrants"*[1074].

Swedish politician Mona Sahlin stated, *"the Swedes must be integrated into the new Sweden; the old Sweden will not return."*[1075]

Vice President Joe Biden spoke in 2015 at *Harvard University* about how it was *"not a bad thing"* America was becoming a majority-minority nation and that "non-white DNA" would become the majority[1076].

Former Irish President Mary Robinson spoke about how Ireland would become a *"rainbow nation"* through immigration, similar to post-apartheid South Africa[1077].

French President Emmanuel Macron described Africa's demographics as Europe's "destiny"[1078].

"Replacement" is referred to as a *"conspiracy theory"* because the change in demography - where most immigrants coincidentally vote for left-

---

[1070] Camus, Renaud, *L'Abécédaire de l'in-nocence* (Éditions David Reinharc, 2010)

[1071] Camus, Renaud, *Le Grand Remplacement* (David Reinharc, 2011)

[1072] Faragher, John Mack, *A Great and Noble Scheme: The Tragic Story of the Expulsion of the French Acadians from Their American Homeland* (W. W. Norton & Company, 2005)

[1073] Neather, Andrew, 'Don't Listen to the Whingers – London Needs Immigrants', *Evening Standard*, 23 October 2009

[1074] Mandelson, Peter, Interview on *The Daily Politics* (BBC, 13 May 2013)

[1075] Sahlin, Mona, Speech at the Swedish Social Democratic Youth League Congress, 2001

[1076] Biden, Joe, Remarks at the Institute of Politics, Harvard University, 2 October 2015

[1077] Robinson, Mary, Speech at the Irish Centre for Migration Studies, 2000

[1078] Macron, Emmanuel, Speech at the University of Ouagadougou, Burkina Faso, 28 November 2017

wing parties[1079] - is not "deliberate".

In November 2024, British Prime Minister Keir *"Two-Tier"* Starmer finally confessed in public:

> *This happened by design, not accident. Policies were reformed deliberately to liberalise immigration. Brexit was used for that purpose, to turn Britain into a one-nation experiment in open borders.*[1080]

(Literature, 2010)

(The) Great Reset

> *An obscure conspiracy theory published in multiple books, by a Bond Villain, available everywhere, promoted at events attended by politicians who subsequently incorporate it into domestic policy without their electorate's consent.*

Billing itself as a successor to the United Nations, the World Economic Forum's first version of its plan was published as a six hundred page "report" in 2010 from the eighteen-month Global Redesign Initiative (GRI) project titled *"Everybody's Business: Strengthening International Cooperation in a More Interdependent World"*[1081]. The Evil Plan is pretty simple: governments and big companies form public-private partnerships as mutual *"stakeholders"* to create a system of technocratic global governance, and the rest of us rent everything while eating insects.

[1079] Hainmueller, Jens, and Michael J. Hiscox, 'Attitudes Toward Highly Skilled and Low-Skilled Immigration: Evidence from a Survey Experiment', American Political Science Review, 104.1 (2010), 61–84

[1080] National Review, 'British Prime Minister Admits Mass Migration to U.K. Happened by Design', National Review, 2 December 2024

[1081] World Economic Forum, *Everybody's Business* (World Economic Forum, 2010)

Not one to be deterred by outrage or horror, as people were dying, Herr Schwab kept trying with his dystopian 2020 novels *"The Fourth Industrial Revolution"*[1082], *"COVID-19: The Great Reset"*[1083], *"Stakeholder Capitalism"*[1084], and the even worse *"Great Narrative: For A Better Future"*[1085] (*Heil, Herr Schwab!*). Unfortunately, the *"Building Back Better"* of the *Fourth Reich* nobody asked for has been set back by almost the entire political spectrum noticing it omits elections and bears a striking resemblance to *"Tutto nello Stato, niente al di fuori dello Stato, nulla contro lo Stato"*[1086].

(Politics, 2008)

Group Identity

Tribe.

A "theory" formulated by social psychologist Henri Tajfel, starting around 1979 and culminating in a 1986 diatribe *"The social identity theory of intergroup behaviour"* whereby an *"individual's self-concept derived from perceived membership in a relevant social group"*[1087]. Ten years later, in 1989, comes Crenshaw's *"intersectionality"*, or as humans have known it for a few thousand years: stereotyping and *tribalism*.

(Psychology, 1979)

[1082] Schwab, Klaus, *The Fourth Industrial Revolution* (World Economic Forum, 2016)

[1083] Schwab, Klaus, Thierry Malleret, *COVID-19* (World Economic Forum, 2020)

[1084] Schwab, Klaus, *Stakeholder Capitalism* (World Economic Forum, 2021)

[1085] Schwab, Klaus, Thierry Malleret, *The Great Narrative* (Forum Publishing, 2022)

[1086] Mussolini, Benito, *La Dottrina del Fascismo* (1932)

[1087] Tajfel, Henri, 'Social Psychology of Intergroup Relations', *Annual Review of Psychology*, 33.1 (1982), 1–39

Hate Speech

> *An attempt to politically separate some words from other words, by inferring a person's invisible and immeasurable intent. So the State can prosecute them.*

Hitler made "hate speeches"[1088]. The first emergence of the intent behind "hate speech" laws is evident in the negotiation between the UK and USSR while drafting the *Universal Declaration of Human Rights* (UDHR), wherein the Soviets fought to include *"hate speech"* provisions which were resisted on the basis they were intended to be used to silence freedom of expression and ideas like liberal democracy with vague definitions such as *"the bloody dictatorship of the most reactionary section of capitalism and monopolies"* (fascism)[1089]. Modern legal usage was popularised by critical race theorist and self-acclaimed "activist scholar" Mari Matsuda in her 1989 article *"Public Response to Racist Speech: Considering the Victim's Story"*[1090].

(Law, 1948)

Hegemon(y)

> *A synonym people who want to sound intellectual™ use for "biggest" or most influential.*

Originally from Ancient Greek, it was used in the 19th century to denote

---

[1088] Kershaw, Ian, *Hitler* (Penguin, 1998)

[1089] Matsuda, Mari J., 'Public Response to Racist Speech: Considering the Victim's Story', *Michigan Law Review*, 87.8 (1989), 2320–81

[1090] Matsuda, M. J. (1989). *Public Response to Racist Speech: Considering the Victim's Story*. Michigan Law Review, *87*(8), 2320-2381.

the global influence of European colonial powers (e.g. Britain as the *"global hegemon"*)[1091]. Later adopted by Marx to describe the *"cultural hegemony"* of the ruling class, i.e. how it brainwashes people outside university to like capitalism[1092]. The idea was most infamously fleshed out by Stalin's ideological cousin, Antonio Gramsci[1093][1094].

Hesitancy

> *Being absolutely certain the demands being made of you obviously cannot be trusted due to the horrendous behaviour and track record of the person issuing them.*

The term *"vaccine hesitancy"* mysteriously appeared spontaneously and simultaneously across all Western media in 2020, as if by magic. Alhough anecdotally discussed in the early 2000s, the term was popularised by the UK *SAGE Working Group on Vaccine Hesitancy* in 2012[1095].

(Medicine, 2012)
See: *Project Coast (South Africa), Tuskegee Syphilis Study*

[1091] Ferguson, Niall, *Empire* (Basic Books, 2004)

[1092] Marx, Karl, and Friedrich Engels, *The German Ideology* (1845)
While Marx did not explicitly use the term "cultural hegemony," he discussed how the ruling class controls the dominant ideology, which serves to perpetuate its power.

[1093] Gramsci, Antonio, *Selections from the Prison Notebooks*, ed. and trans. by Quintin Hoare and Geoffrey Nowell-Smith (International Publishers, 1971)

[1094] Gramsci didn't work for Stalin directly. He was an active member of the *Italian Communist Party* and participated in socialist politics in Italy during the early 1920s. His imprisonment in Italy by Mussolini limited his direct involvement in international communist activities.

[1095] SAGE Working Group, *Report of the SAGE Working Group on Vaccine Hesitancy* (World Health Organization, 2014)

Hermeneutic

> A word people who want to be intellectual™ use for "a way of interpreting something".

Get your philosophy right: interpretation of the Bible.

Heteronormative

> The idea 97%+ of people across cultures all over the world being attracted to the opposite sex could be considered normal or typical.

Popularised through Sokal's favourite journal *Social Text* in 1991 in Michael Warner's dreadful essay: *"Introduction: Fear of a Queer Planet"*[1096].

(*Sociology, 1991*)

Heterosexual

> *Normal functioning mammal.*

One of four neologisms invented by Austrian-born writer (and pederast) Karl Maria Kertbeny in a letter to German jurist (and pederast) Karl Heinrich Ulrichs[1097] to replace the pejorative terms "sodomite" and "pederast".

(*Correspondence, 1868*)

[1096] Warner, Michael, 'Introduction: Fear of a Queer Planet', *Social Text*, 29 (1991), 3–17

[1097] Kertbeny, Karl Maria, *Letters to Karl Heinrich Ulrichs* (1868)

Heuristic

> *A word intellectuals™ use for "learning it yourself by guessing".*

Get your science right: adapting tests via trial and error.

Homophobia

> *A 3000+-year old religious-inspired belief the practice of homosexuality is immoral, shared by over 60% of the world's human population.*

A term coined in 1969 - in the Soviet spirit of pathologising political enemies - by (straight) psychotherapist George Weinberg in gay porn magazine *Screw* to describe the fear of heterosexual men that they might themselves be gay, after people were mean to his lesbian friend.

Later elaborated on in his 1972 book *"Society and the Healthy Homosexual"* with an unsubstantiated claim it was a "medical phobia" in response to a perceived "contagion" based on *"homosexual panic"*[1098].

(Psychology, 1969)

Homosexual

> *A nicer term than "sodomite" for use at dinner parties.*

One of four neologisms invented by Austrian-born writer (and pederast) Karl Maria Kertbeny in a letter to German jurist (and pederast) Karl Heinrich Ulrichs[1099] to replace the pejorative terms "sodomite" and

---

[1098] Weinberg, George, *Society and the Healthy Homosexual* (St. Martin's Press, 1972)

[1099] Kertbeny, K. M. (1868). Letters to Karl Heinrich Ulrichs.

"pederast" (or *"Urning"* and *"Dioning"* from Plato's *Symposium*[1100]). Later found in C.G. Chaddock's translation of Richard von Krafft-Ebing's *"Psychopathia Sexualis"*[1101].

(Correspondence, 1868)

Human Resources

> *Staffing. Personnel. Personal executioner department of a CEO masquerading as a unit for workers' rights. Soviet-style commissar policing adherence to political orthodoxy.*

Although mentioned in similar ways back to 1915 with the Soviet *OrgBuro* of the Bolshevik *Red Army*, the first use of the term *"Human Resources"* comes from a report for the *Yale Labor and Management Center* titled *"The Human Resources Function"* by sociology professor Edward Bakke[1102].

(Sociology, 1958)

Hypermasculinity

> *Macho. Being a bit too manly and not asking for the vegan soy latte you should have.*

Set on a course to prove masculinity is a disorder which needs a cure, psychologists Donald Mosher and Mark Sirkin "developed" the idiotic *"Hypermasculinity Inventory"* (HMI) in 1984 with their paper *"Measuring a*

[1100] Plato, *Symposium* (ca. 385–370 BCE)

[1101] Krafft-Ebing, Richard von, *Psychopathia Sexualis* (F. A. Davis Co., 1886)

[1102] Bakke, Edward Wight, *The Human Resources Function* (Yale Labor and Management Center, 1958)

macho personality constellation" in the *Journal of Research in Personality*[1103]. It's the new *"toxic masculinity"*.

(Psychology, 1984)

-icity

A suffix people who want to sound intellectual™ add to other words to make them sound more sophisticated.

You can find it everywhere, but most likely, it's almost certainly envy of gnostic Carl Jung's cool word *synchronicity*, which he detailed in *"Synchronicity: An Acausal Connecting Principle"* (1960)[1104].

Idea Laundering

Getting a university to publish your fiction so it appears less absurd than it is.

Analogous to money laundering, the concept of "laundering" radical ideas through academic ecosystems was first described as *"the process of having a front group or industry-funded organization propose your idea as a way of giving it credibility"* (Sourcewatch, 2004)[1105]. It was later popularised through the 2018 *"Grievance Studies"* (*"Sokal Squared"*) hoax, where the social sciences yet again not only accepted a feminist version of *"Mein Kampf"* as one of twenty false journal papers, but refused others for not

---

[1103] Mosher, Donald L., and Mark Sirkin, 'Measuring a Macho Personality Constellation', *Journal of Research in Personality*, 18.2 (1984), 150–63

[1104] Jung, Carl G., *Synchronicity* (Princeton University Press, 1960)

[1105] SourceWatch, 'Idea Laundering', (2004)

being extreme enough[1106]. A detailed discussion of the quasi-religious nature percolating underneath the hoax was given by James Lindsay in the Areo article *"Postmodern Religion and the Faith of Social Justice"*[1107].

(Philosophy, 2017)

Identify As

> *Impressive-sounding and intellectual™ way to say "I am" or describe which caricature, avatar, or social construct you believe you are at that moment.*

Just like superheroes in *Marvel* films or referring to yourself in the third person, social psychologist John Turner formulated a way to avoid the phenomena of complex social negotiations such as recognition, reputation, and self-concept with his 1990 *"self categorisation theory"*[1108].

(Psychology, 1990)

Ideology

> *When the problem and the answer are the same, regardless of the question. An idea, which becomes a form of theology.*

Although descended from Destutt de Tracy's 1796 notion of the *"science of ideas"*[1109], the contemporary definition emerged from socialist and

---

[1106] Lindsay, James, Helen Pluckrose, and Peter Boghossian, 'Academic Grievance Studies and the Corruption of Scholarship', *Areo* (2018)

[1107] Lindsay, James, 'Postmodern Religion and the Faith of Social Justice', *Areo* (2017)

[1108] Turner, John C., Michael A. Hogg, Penelope J. Oakes, Stephen D. Reicher, and Margaret S. Wetherell, *Rediscovering the Social Group* (Basil Blackwell, 1987)

[1109] Destutt de Tracy, Antoine Louis Claude, *Éléments d'idéologie* (1796)

communist literature between 1905-1918 (e.g. Marx's *"The German Ideology"*). An example from the *International Journal of Ethics* in 1896 refers to the *"ideology of the older socialists"*[1110]. The first major publication to address the topic was *"Ideology and Utopia"* by sociologist Karl Mannheim in 1929[1111].

(*Sociology, 1907*)

I Feel Like

> *A "softer" and more feminine way to say "I think", "I believe", "I observed", or other direct phrases which are less frightening to people who rarely do such things.*

This irritating trend can be traced directly back to a 1986 paper *"Sexism in the Classroom"* by Maya Sadker and David Sadker[1112]. They also wrote *"Failing At Fairness: How Our Schools Cheat Girls"* in 1995[1113].

(*Education, 1995*)

Imposter

> *A person who pretends to be someone else in order to deceive others, especially for fraudulent gain.*
> See: auto-Tune, sociology, Kardashian

[1110] *International Journal of Ethics*, (1896)

[1111] Mannheim, Karl, *Ideology and Utopia* (Routledge & Kegan Paul, 1929)

[1112] Sadker, Myra, and David Sadker, 'Sexism in the Classroom', *Phi Delta Kappan* (1986)

[1113] Sadker, Myra, and David Sadker, *Failing at Fairness* (Scribner, 1995)

Incel

Young men who haven't figured out how to communicate with women, and end up murdering them instead.

The term was invented by a Canadian *woman* who ran a blog from 1993 to 2000 titled *"Alana's Involuntary Celibacy Project"*[1114]. Fifteen years later, a psychopathic murderer named Elliot Rodger killed three men and three women on a rampage[1115]. Since then, it's been feminists' favourite symbolic bogeyman for their lives of oppression.

(Internet, 1993)

Inclusive

Excluding, then purging, the views of the 99.9% to avoid being sued by the 0.01%.

The primary school notion of "including" (adulterating) arose in two areas in a complimentary way because of affirmative action and the 1964 *Civil Rights Act*. First, an effort to bring children with special needs into the classroom (e.g. Virginia Wilson, *"Teaching Social Studies"*, 1993)[1116], and as noted in the *Academy of Management Learning & Education* in 2008,[1117] a second wave in the late-90s to the concept of "diversity".

(Education, 1993)

[1114] Romano, Aja, 'What a Woman Who Coined the Term "Incel" Thinks of the Movement Today', *Vox*, 23 April 2018

[1115] Winton, Richard, and Joseph Serna, 'Isla Vista Shooting: Gunman Kills 6, Wounds 13 near UC Santa Barbara Campus', *Los Angeles Times*, 24 May 2014

[1116] Wilson, Virginia A., *Teaching Social Studies* (Greenwood Press, 1993)

[1117] Ely, Robin J., and David A. Thomas, 'Diversity at Work: The Practice of Inclusion', *Academy of Management Learning & Education*, 7.4 (2008), 201–19

Inclusive Language

> Words you must exclude.

Also known as a compelled *Speech Code*, this odious doublespeak phrase indicating magical words needing to be excluded from everyday life in order to placate the perpetually offended arose in the late eighties, but can be traced back to the *National Council of Teachers of English* (NCTE) introducing *"non-sexist"* language guidelines in 1974[1118].

(Education, 1974)

Influencer

> *Narcissist braggart and/or social climber who pays dubious software providers to artificially increase "followers" and "likes" on their social media accounts so they can extort companies for freebies.*

The idea of marketing by influence stems from *Marlboro Man* and *Old Spice*, through multi-level marketing, to celebrity endorsement and film product placement, all the way to the 1990 concept of "thought leadership"[1119].

(Internet, 2004)

[1118] NCTE, *Guidelines for Non-Sexist Use of Language in NCTE Publications* (1975)

[1119] McCrimmon, Mitch, 'Thought Leadership: A Radical Departure from Traditional, Positional Leadership', *Management Decision*, 43.7 (2005), 1064–73

Institutional

> Crime of collective guilt which is impossible to demonstrate or prosecute.

The first usage of the term as a linguistic collectivisation was undoubtedly in Stokely Carmichael's *"Black Power: The Politics of Liberation"* (1967)[1120], around the time of the *Kerner Commission* report addressing the cause of the same year's race riots[1121]. It was compounded by the 1999 UK report into the murder of Stephen Lawrence[1122], aggravated by the development of *"critical race theory"*, and made worse by the hopeless *Institution Theory*[1123]. Amongst its many intrinsic contradictions, there is no accepted definition of "institution", and if everyone is to blame, then no-one is to blame.

(Literature, 1967)

Insurrection-(ist)

> A protest by working-class people the government believes it must characterise as a Nazi uprising in order to prevent the middle class from joining it.

The crime of armed revolt against the government, similar to *sedition*, has been defined for hundreds of years. In US law (*18 U.S.C. § 2383*)[1124] it is

---

[1120] Carmichael, Stokely, and Charles V. Hamilton, *Black Power* (Random House, 1967)

[1121] *Report of the National Advisory Commission on Civil Disorders* (U.S. Government Printing Office, 1968)

[1122] Macpherson, William, *The Stephen Lawrence Inquiry* (Home Office, 1999)

[1123] Scott, W. Richard, *Institutions and Organizations* (Sage, 2008)

[1124] 18 U.S.C. § 2383 (2022), 'Rebellion or Insurrection', *United States Code*

GHI

not specifically defined, but is understood to mean a) organised uprising or violent resistance against the U.S. government or its authority, whilst b) distinct from mere protests or riots due to its focus on undermining governmental authority or the rule of law.

The key differences between violent protest is an intent is not to overthrow or disrupt governmental authority unlawfully[1125]. Which is, of course, how the US became a sovereign entity, and additionally involved giving aid and comfort to French forces opposing British authority[1126].

In unrelated events, the Marxist-Leninist *Weather Underground* bombed the US Capitol (1971), the *Pentagon* (1972) and the NYPD (1970)[1127]; the 1992 Los Angeles *Rodney King* riots caused $1.2 billion in damages[1128]; *Occupy Wall Street* $13 million[1129]; the *Ferguson* riots $2.5 million[1130]; and the "mostly peaceful" *Black Lives Matter* riots cost $2 billion[1131].

(Politics, 2020)

Interdisciplinary

> Unable to master one discipline; having no subject or knowledge of its own to discuss. Useless, or syncretic.

[1125] Linder, Douglas, *The Treason Trials of Aaron Burr* (University of Missouri-Kansas City School of Law, 2006)

[1126] Ferling, J. (2007). *Almost a Miracle*, Oxford University Press.

[1127] Federal Bureau of Investigation,*Weather Underground Bombings*, n.d.,

[1128] Cannon, Lou, *Official Negligence* (Westview Press, 1997)

[1129] Associated Press, 'Occupy Protests Cost Cities at Least $13M', *CBS News*, 18 Nov 2011

[1130] Healy, Jack, and Julie Bosman, 'Protests in Ferguson, Mo., Costing Millions in Police Overtime and Lost Sales', *The New York Times*, 23 August 2014

[1131] Smith, Michael, 'Riots Following George Floyd's Death May Cost Insurance Companies up to $2B', *Axios*, 16 September 2020

A bit like a DJ mixing other people's music together. Chemistry is a discipline. As is medicine, physics, biology, mathematics, literature, or astronomy. The first known usage of the term is from a notice of the availability of fellowships for the *American Council of Learned Societies* reprinted in the *Journal of Educational Sociology* referred to *"training of an interdisciplinary nature"*[1132].

(Sociology, 1937)

Internalised Oppression

> *The intellectual™-sounding reason extremists claiming to represent entire minority groups give for individual members of those groups disagreeing with them: because, as Freud said, they don't know they actually hate themselves.*

The roots of "internalisation" go right back to Georg Hegel's *Master–slave dialectic*[1133], but owe their core to Freud's psychoanalytic theories detailed in his 1930 book *"Civilization and its discontents"*[1134].

French Philosopher Michel Foucault and his fetish for gay sex dungeons[1135] continued the guesswork in his 1961 disaster *"Madness and Civilization"*[1136].

In 1971, William Cross Jr kick-started internalised racism with the *"Negrescence Model of Black Identity"*[1137], which naturally lead to

---

[1132] Klein, Julie T., *Interdisciplinarity* (Wayne State University Press, 1990)

[1133] Hegel, Georg Wilhelm Friedrich, *Phenomenology of Spirit* (1807)

[1134] Freud, Sigmund, *Civilization and Its Discontents* (W. W. Norton & Company, 1930)

[1135] Kimball, Roger, 'The Perversions of M. Foucault', *The New Criterion*, March 1993

[1136] Foucault, Michel, *Madness and Civilization* (Tavistock, 1961)

[1137] Cross, William E., 'The Negro-to-Black Conversion Experience: Toward a Psychology of Black Liberation', *Black World*, 20.9 (1971), 13–27

internalised sexism in 2008 (*"The fabric of internalized sexism"*)[1138], which then became misogyny, and on. And on.

(*Psychology, 1930*)

Intersectionality

> The modern framework for competitive victimhood in identity politics, establishing Straight White Man as the common enemy of everyone, everywhere.

"Inspired" by Turner and Tajfel, black critical race theory feminist and Anita Hill legal counsel[1139] Kimberle Crenshaw published *"Demarginalizing the Intersection of Race and Sex: A Black Feminist Critique of Antidiscrimination Doctrine, Feminist Theory and Antiracist Politics"* in 1988[1140], which argued sexism was worse if you were black and we were in a battle against the white Christian male.

(*Feminist Literature, 1988*)

Intersex

> Hermaphrodite. Also: Marxist identity group.

"Inter" means "between". The simple dimorphism of biological sex is defined by the gametes a mammal's reproductive system is organised to produce. If it produces sperm, it is male; if it produces eggs (ova), it is

---

[1138] Bearman, Sarah, and Mark Amrhein, 'The Fabric of Internalized Sexism', *Women & Therapy*, 31.2–4 (2008), 121–38

[1139] Crenshaw, K. (1992). *Critical Race Theory: The Cutting Edge.* Temple University Press.

[1140] Crenshaw, Kimberlé, 'Whose Story Is It, Anyway? Feminist and Antiracist Appropriations of Anita Hill', in *Critical Race Theory: The Cutting Edge*, ed. by Richard Delgado (Philadelphia: Temple University Press, 1992)

female[1141].

Humanities scholars, and the first female editor of *Nature* magazine, Magdalena Skipper,[1142] cannot comprehend ambiguous genitalia/gonads, or abnormal chromosome patterns (0.018 per cent of all births[1143]), do not define biological sex.

The neologism of *"intersex"* was introduced by theorists attempting to characterise homosexuality as a *"third sex"* (*Urning, Uranian, Uraniad*) in 1910[1144]. The term *"intersexuality"* was coined by Richard Goldschmidt in 1917[1145]. The first suggestion to replace the term "hermaphrodite" with *"intersex"* was made by Greek physician Alexander Polycleitos Cawadias in his 1943 book *"Hermaphoditus the Human Intersex"*[1146].

(*Medicine, 1943*)

Islamophobia

> *The belief a dislike of Islamic values and/or revulsion to Jihadist violence is equivalent to the historical persecution of Jews.*

In 1997- four years before 9/11, as the British government opened the country's borders -, the British Home Secretary, Jack Straw published a report by the *Runnymede Trust's Commission on British Muslims and*

[1141] Parker, Geoffrey A., 'The Sexual Cascade and the Rise of Pre-Ejaculatory (Darwinian) Sexual Selection, Gamete Dynamics, and Sperm Competition', *Biological Journal of the Linnean Society*, 112.2 (2014), 233–49

[1142] 'US Proposal for Defining Gender Has No Basis in Science', *Nature*, 30 Oct 2018

[1143] Sax, Leonard, 'How Common Is Intersex? A Response to Anne Fausto-Sterling', *The Journal of Sex Research*, 39.3 (2002), 174–78

[1144] Mayne, Xavier (Edward Prime-Stevenson), *The Intersexes* (Private Press, 1910)

[1145] Goldschmidt, Richard, 'Intersexuality and the Endocrine Aspect of Sex', *Endocrinology*, 1.4 (1917), 433–56

[1146] Cawadias, Alexander P., *Hermaphoditus the Human Intersex* (Heinemann Medical, 1943)

Islamophobia entitled *"Islamophobia: A Challenge for Us All"*[1147].

A bizarre alternative French etymology claims it was invented in Iran after the Islamic Revolution to "counter" American feminists. The term was first used around 1923 in the *Journal of Theological Studies*.

(Politics, 1997)

Isomorphic

A word people who want to sound intellectual™ use for "the same as".

Get your science right: possessing identical physical form.

-ism/-ist

Clever, important-sounding suffix added to made-up pejorative words by intellectuals™ to make them sound less idiotic.

Get your science right: Latin *"-ismus"* = a distinctive trait.

[1147] Runnymede Trust, *Islamophobia: A Challenge for Us All* (Runnymede Trust, 1997)

J K L

Justice

> Revenge. Activist Boomer/Gen-X professors, indoctrinating Millennial/Gen-Z students, to act as a resentful Internet mob in the style of Mao's Red Guards, demanding safe spaces and communism. For their enemies' sin of denying them the occupation of the top social strata.

"Justice" has been the cry of every communist movement in history.

Social justice is as old as humanity and is addressed at length in the *Talmud*[1148]. The contemporary term - a euphemism for any and every revolutionary communist movement - can be attributed to an entanglement of Marx's ideas[1149] and the work of John Rawls, who published the inimitable *"A Theory of Justice"* in 1971[1150].

The pejorative term *"social justice warrior"* (*"SJW"* or Maoist *Red Guard*) has been used as far back as 1991 (*"Quebec nationalists and Canadian*

[1148] Bleich, J. David, *Judaism and Healing* (KTAV Pub. House, 1981)

[1149] Marx, Karl, *Critique of the Gotha Program* (1875)
  Marx dismissed the idea of "equal rights" under capitalism as inadequate for addressing true social justice, arguing that rights should be based on the needs of individuals rather than formal equality.

[1150] Rawls, John, *A Theory of Justice* (Harvard University Press, 1971)

union activist Michel Chartrand") but became a mainstream insult between 2008–2011 as the *"Gamergate"* scandal emerged[1151].

In 2014, as he was being sentenced for the deaths of up to two million Cambodians between 1975-1979, former *Khmer Rouge* head of state Khieu Samphan, 84, raised his voice to a chamber in Phnom Penh, and said,

> *What I want to say today and what I want my countrymen to hear is that as an intellectual I have never wanted anything other than social justice for my country.*[1152]

(Philosophy, 1971)

Ken/Karen

A stereotype of people you wish would stop stereotyping you.

Similar to *"Mzungu", "Obroni", "Gweilo", "Gaijin", "Gringo", "Chele", "Rubio", "Pākehā", "Gubba", "Khawaja", "Béké", "Ofay", "Cracker"*, and other non-racist terms unracist non-white people don't ever use because they can't be racist, because only white people are racist.

Vox, the Internet's most parsimonious rag, claims its origins lie in a 2017 *Reddit* forum, *r/FuckYouKaren*[1153].

According to Apryl Williams, a black *"professor of communication and media at the University of Michigan,"* these are white people *"surveilling*

[1151] Massanari, Adrienne, '#Gamergate and The Fappening: How Reddit's Algorithm, Governance, and Culture Support Toxic Technocultures', *New Media & Society*, 19.3 (2015), 329–46

[1152] Associated Press, 'Khmer Rouge Leader Defends Fighting for "Social Justice" at UN Court', 20 July 2016

[1153] Schwerdtfeger, Bethany, 'Karen: The Anti-Vaxxer Soccer Mom with Speak-to-the-Manager Hair, Explained', *Vox*, 5 February 2020

and patrolling Black bodies in public spaces and then calling the police on them for random, non-illegal infractions", which is apparently to continue the *"historical practice of regulating Black bodies to maintain White supremacist order."* [1154]

(Internet, 2017)

Kink

A cutesy name for the desire to engage in public displays of sexual depravity, often wearing costume.

Although the use of "kinky" to denote sexually depraved or perverted behaviour can be traced back to 1959[1155], the modern use of "kink" as a term for a subculture of sexual fetishism comes from the 2016 book *"Becoming a kink aware therapist"* by Caroline Shahbaz & Peter Chirino[1156], who penned a 2008 embellish doctoral thesis about the *"BDSM community"*. And obviously, the dreadful writing in *"Fifty Shades of Grey"* (2011) by E. L. James (Erika Mitchell).

(Sexology, 2016)

Knowledge Is Power

One French paedophile whacky dogma that academics and politicians conspire to restrict what people are allowed to investigate, discuss, or teach.

[1154] Rosenberg, Alyssa, 'Karen: The Meme That Somehow Became an Insult Against White Women', *The Guardian*, 27 December 2020

[1155] Partridge, Eric, *A Dictionary of Slang and Unconventional English* (Macmillan, 1961)

[1156] Shahbaz, Christy, and P. Chirinos, *Becoming a Kink Aware Therapist: A Guide for Sex-Positive Therapy* (Routledge, 2016)

The infamous phrase *"scientia potentia est"*, credited to Francis Bacon in *Meditationes Sacrae* (1597)[1157], appeared within Thomas Hobbes' *"Leviathan"* in 1668[1158]. It's more activist meaning was "elaborated" on by Michel Foucault's 1976 book *"The History of Sexuality"*, which claimed his idea *"Power-knowledge"* described how what we believe is knowledge is actually policed and curated by the powerful[1159].

(Sociology, 1976)

Language Constructs Reality

The mystical belief if you change the word for something, you change someone's perception. Therefore the material reality of what it is.

Edward Safir, one of the fathers of linguistics, taught a smart student named Benjamin Whorf[1160]. After Whorf died, interest grew in the unofficial *Sapir-Whorf Hypothesis* of linguistic relativity[1161]: which posited there are certain thoughts of an individual in one language that cannot be understood by those who live in another language. The theory was corrupted in the eighties via *"phenomenology"* to support the ideas of *social constructionism*[1162].

(Linguistics, 1953)

[1157] Bacon, Francis, *Meditationes Sacrae and Human Philosophy* (1597)

[1158] Hobbes, Thomas, *Leviathan*, ed. by Richard Tuck, Cambridge Texts in the History of Political Thought (Cambridge University Press, 1991)

[1159] Foucault, Michel, *The History of Sexuality* (Pantheon Books, 1978)

[1160] Nordquist, Richard, 'The Sapir-Whorf Hypothesis Linguistic Theory', *ThoughtCo.*, 25 June 2024

[1161] APA Dictionary of Psychology, 'Sapir-Whorf Hypothesis' (n.d.)

[1162] 'Sapir-Whorf Hypothesis: Examples, Definition, Criticisms', *HelpfulProfessor* (2024)

Land Acknowledgment

> *A public announcement of one's own illegitimacy and lack of right to exist.*

As a relatively recent religious sacrament to *"recognise the history of colonialism"*, the bizarre idea of *"Territory Acknowledgement"* [1163] originated with the apartheid-inspired *Truth and Reconciliation Commission of Canada* (formed in 2008) around 2015 and its strange claims of *"cultural genocide"* [1164]. However, the practice was established in Australia at the alternative lifestyle *Aquarius Festival* in 1973 by activist Gary Foley as the *"Welcome to Country"* ritual [1165].

(Student Festival, 1973)

Latinx

> *A hilariously futile recruitment attempt by activists to refer to people whose entire language and culture are based on gender, and who do not want to exclude gender, as they celebrate it — in a way which... doesn't specify gender.*

Despite the hilarious claims it has been used for hundreds of years, the term appears to have emerged in 2008 on social media [1166], although

---

[1163] University of Waterloo, 'Reconciliation Response Projects: About Territorial Acknowledgment' (n.d.)

[1164] Truth and Reconciliation Commission of Canada, *Calls to Action* (*The Canadian Encyclopedia*, 2015)

[1165] 1Earth Media, 'The First "Welcome to Country" Ceremony in Australia', 19 Nov 2023

[1166] Salinas, Cinthya, and Alfredo Lozano, 'History and Evolution of the Term Latinx', in *Handbook of Latinos and Education* (2nd edn), ed. by Enrique G. Murillo Jr. (Routledge, 2021), pp. 249–63

having been seen in entertainment circles as a casting abbreviation. The first academic "paper" on it was *"Mapping and recontextualizing the evolution of the term Latinx: An environmental scanning in higher education"* by Adele Lozano Cristobal Salinas, in the highly credible-sounding *Journal of Latinos and Education*[1167].

Latinos and latinas - who realised the binary for "nonbinary" in Spanish are *"no binario"* (masculine) or *"no binaria"* (feminine) - hated it across the board[1168].

(Internet, 2008)

Law Of Attraction

The more you think about something, it will magically appear. And make you a lot of money. Teenage witchcraft.

Popularised by Oprah, advertising Rhonda Byrne's 2006 book *"The Secret"*[1169] (which she repackaged after reading Wallace Wattles' *"The Science of Getting Rich"*)[1170], the (Gnostic) *New Thought* concept of imagining oneself into wealth is derived from Phileas Quimby's *"mental healing"* movement from 1865[1171], which he embarked on creating after being obsessed with *Mesmerism*[1172].

The term was first coined by theosophist Helena Blavatsky in an 1877

[1167] Lozano, Alfredo, Cinthya Salinas, *Mapping and Recontextualizing the Evolution of the Term Latinx: An Environmental Scanning in Higher Education* (Routledge, 2021)

[1168] Acevedo, Nicole, 'Many Latinos Say "Latinx" Offends or Bothers Them. Here's Why', *NBC News*, 9 December 2021

[1169] Byrne, Rhonda, *The Secret* (Beyond Words Publishing, 2006)

[1170] Wattles, Wallace D., *The Science of Getting Rich* (Elizabeth Towne, 1910)

[1171] Quimby, Phineas P., *The Quimby Manuscripts* (Thomas Y. Crowell Company, 1865)

[1172] Mesmer, Franz A., *Mémoire sur la Découverte du Magnétisme Animal* (Paris, 1779)

book claiming all religions come from a single *"Ancient Wisdom."*[1173].

(*Literature, 1877*)

Left Wing

> *The centrist orthodoxy of compassion and inclusion which all reasonable people must accept and believe - or else. A term only ever used by Nazis because everyone is left. The only true conclusion for an intellectual™.*

The concepts of *Left* and *Right* wings originated from the seating arrangement in the French parliament after the "explosion in the brain" of the *French Revolution*. Aristocrats sat on the right of the king (defenders preserving traditional, aristocratic, capitalistic, royal interests of the *Ancien Regime*) and commoners sat on the left (innovators agitating for reform, republicanism, socialism, and civil liberties)[1174]. The extreme or far-left refers to the left of social democracy, such as communism, anarchism, Marxism–Leninism, Trotskyism, and Maoism.

(*History, 1789*)

Lens

> *A word people who want to sound intellectual™ use for... "bias". A perception of a subject distorted by ideology or dogma.*

A lens is a transparent optical device that refracts light rays to converge or diverge (i.e. change direction or to separate), forming an image through

---

[1173] Blavatsky, Helena P., *Isis Unveiled* (J. W. Bouton, 1877)

[1174] Millard, Gabriel, 'Relating Ideologies: The Left-Right Spectrum', in *Political Ideologies and Worldviews: An Introduction* (KPU Press, 2024)

Snell's Law[1175]. It is not a "way of looking at things".

Although associated with Marxist *Critical Theory*, the Marxist *"critical lens"* (or *"socioeconomic lens"*) originates with Marx's writing itself[1176] and involves starting with a pre-determined fallacious or ideological conclusion, then searching for evidence to support it (a brain pattern known as *motivated reasoning*[1177] serving one's *confirmation bias*[1178]). Before describing the results in obscure jargon as an *"analytical tool"* and attempting to falsely claim it was actually derived from Plato.

(*Sociology, 1845*)

Liberation

> *The mystical process of bringing the communist Utopia to fruition through debasing anything which has evolved over thousands of years to provide humans with a sense of meaning, purpose, or belonging.*

Liberationism was at first synonymous with Karl Marx's *"progressivist"* (*"progressism"* or "radical") theories and their supporters in the nineteenth century[1179]. Its contemporary usage emerged in the early sixties via neo-Marxist theorists and their attempts to agitate a different kind Marxist revolutionary coalition to replace the missing working class, leading to Sexual Liberation (*"Eros & Civilisation"*, 1955, Marcuse[1180]), the *Black Liberation Army* (1970), Gay Liberation *Stonewall Riots* and the *GLF*, 1969),

---

[1175] Young, Hugh D., Roger Freedman, *University Physics with Modern Physics* (Pearson, 2012)

[1176] Marx, Karl, *Economic and Philosophic Manuscripts of 1844* (1844)

[1177] Kunda, Ziva, 'The Case for Motivated Reasoning', *Psychological Bulletin*, 108.3 (1990)

[1178] Nickerson, Raymond S., 'Confirmation Bias: A Ubiquitous Phenomenon in Many Guises', *Review of General Psychology*, 2.2 (1998), 175–220

[1179] ThoughtCo., 'Progressivism Defined: Roots and Goals' (2024)

[1180] Marcuse, Herbert, *Eros and Civilization* (Beacon Press, 1955)

and Women's Liberation (*National WLM conference*, 1970).

As described by *"An Essay on Liberation"* (1969) by Herbert Marcuse[1181], the term was a simple coded euphemism for "communist revolution".

(*Sociology, 1955*)

Lifestyle

> *Whether you're single or married.*

In 1929, Austrian psychologist Alfred Adler described a *"life-style"* in *"Problems of neurosis: a book of case-histories"* as *"a person's basic character as established early in childhood"*[1182]. By 1961, it had morphed to meaning a person's mode or style of living[1183] (via usage from the art) and spawned yet another dubious concept in sociology[1184], as well a marketing technique for *JC Penny* in 1977 (*"life style merchandising"*)[1185] and a new magazine topic.

(*Sociology, 1961*)

Lived Experience

> *Experience.*

As opposed to what? *Unlived*? They mean *personal* subjective experience.

Apparently this silly, bizarre circular tautology has something to do

---

[1181] Marcuse, Herbert, *An Essay on Liberation* (Beacon Press, 1969)

[1182] Adler, Alfred, *Problems of Neurosis: A Book of Case-Histories* (Harper, 1929)

[1183] MIT Press Reader, 'A Brief History of Consumer Culture' (2024)

[1184] MDPI Encyclopedia, 'Lifestyle (Sociology)' (2024)

[1185] Chain Store Age, General Merchandising Edition, 'Life Style Merchandising: Teen Buying Clout, Beyond Their Years', 58 (October 1982), 58–87

with the gathering of non-scientific data in the field of *"phenomenology"* (ghosts, or something, presumably), which is indistinguishable from opinion, anecdotes, hearsay, women's intuition, or imagination.

The idea seems to originate with German philosopher Wilhelm Dilthey's musings over *"erfahrung"* (*"scientific experience"*) vs *"erlebnis"* (*"personal experience"*)[1186], and expressed itself in lunatic French feminist Simone de Beauvoir's*"The Second Sex"*[1187], written by a deeply disturbed woman who was obsessed with German philosopher Edmund Husserl[1188].

(Quackery, 1931)

(The) Longhouse

A world which makes women grateful for The Patriarchy.

A long communal hall central to agrarian and sedentary societies worldwide, serving as both a residence and a social hub for extended families or communities, run by a tyrannical "Den Mother". It was designed for collective living by cultures such as the Iroquois, Vikings, and early Germanic tribes which occupied pre-modern Europe[1189].

In 2018, Romanian podcaster Costin Alamariu self-published the 77-chapter book *"Bronze Age Mindset"* under the *Twitter* pseudonym *"Bronze Age Pervert"* ("BAP')[1190], derived from Nietzsche's *"Genealogy of*

[1186] Dilthey, Wilhelm, *Selected Works: Volume I, Introduction to the Human Sciences*, ed. by Rudolf A. Makkreel and Frithjof Rodi (Princeton University Press, 1989)

[1187] De Beauvoir, Simone, *The Second Sex* (Vintage Books, 2011)

[1188] Husserl, Edmund, *Ideas* (Macmillan, 1931)

[1189] Schmidt, Peter R., 'Longhouses and Social Organization', in *Encyclopedia of World History*, ed. by Marcia J. Decker (2nd edn) (Oxford University Press, 2017)

[1190] Alamariu, Costin, *Bronze Age Mindset* (Self-published, 2018)

Morals"[1191]. Its central argument posits modern-day "progressivism" is a form of "slave morality" organised as a feminine *gerontocracy* (previously represented as large-breasted, wide-hipped figures often adorned with symbols of snakes)[1192], similar to premodern matriarchal elders who hectored the life and energy from noble warrior youth (*kóryos*) in order maintain societal control.

> More than anything, the Longhouse refers to the remarkable overcorrection of the last two generations toward social norms centering feminine needs and feminine methods for controlling, directing, and modeling behavior.
>
> Speech norms are enforced through punitive measures typical of female-dominated groups––social isolation, reputational harm, indirect and hidden force. To be "canceled" is to feel the whip of the Longhouse masters.[1193]
>
> (Internet, 2018)

Love Is Love

Meaningless doublespeak slogan repeated by celebrities.

An upgrade from *"we're here, we're queer, get used to it"* and *"some people are gay, get used to it"*[1194]. A (terrible) 1984 song by *Culture Club*[1195].

(Music, 1984)

[1191] Nietzsche, Friedrich, *On the Genealogy of Morals*, (Vintage, 1989)

[1192] Lincoln, Bruce, *The Indo-European Myth of Creation* (Oxford Press, 1986)

[1193] L0m3z, 'What Is the Longhouse?', *First Things*, 16 February 2023

[1194] Bronski, Michael, *The Pleasure Principle* (St. Martin's Press, 2003)

[1195] Culture Club, *Love Is Love* (Virgin Records, 1984)

M N O

Male Gaze

> *Filmmakers making women look sexy.*

A self-confessed attempt by British feminist film critic Laura Mulvey in her 1973 essay *"Visual Pleasure and Narrative Cinema"*[1196] to use French Philosopher and "math genius" Jacques Lacan's idiotic ideas as a political "*weapon*".

(Feminist Literature, 1975)

Manifest(ing)

> *The magical ability of twenty-something women to imagine their desires into reality, when they lack a father to tell them to grow up.*

As Californian slang for "materialise", the idea of magically conjuring thoughts into physical objects and events has its root in the Gnostic *New Thought* movement of the late nineteenth century, which evangelised the imaginary *"Law of Attraction"* (aka the *"Laws of Success"* by Prentice

---

[1196] Mulvey, Laura, *Visual Pleasure and Narrative Cinema* (1973), Screen, 16.3 (1975)

Mulford, 1886[1197]). Although its first usage was in *Harmony* magazine in 1903[1198], it was popularised in modern culture around in 1988 in Californian's therapist Marta Hiatt's book *"Mind Magic"*[1199].

(Literature, 1988)

Marginalised

Excluded.

Similar to the term "discriminate", despite being defined in almost all contexts as a demarcated physical space or form of allowance (e.g. financial deposit, profit margin, margin of error), the concept of a "margin" became pejorative in the 1970s press. "Marginalise" meant to "make notes" on the edge of a book; by 1968, it had been perverted so broadly an article in the *Los Angeles Times* from June 20th of that year reported, *"[T]he Negro was kept aside, marginalized, thus composing in its large majority the chronically poor."*[1200]

(Newspapers, 1968)

Meritocracy

Aptitude. The unjust exclusion of unqualified people from positions of responsibility which require qualification.

[1197] Mulford, Prentice, *The Gift of Spirit: A Selection from the Essays of Prentice Mulford*, originally published in *Thought Forces: Essays Selected from the White Cross Library* (1886), modern edition by Floating Press, 2011

[1198] Harmony, 'Affirm What We Desire to Actualize', March 174

[1199] Hiatt, Marta, *Mind Magic*, Chapter IV, p. 49

[1200] *Los Angeles Times*, 20 June 1968

A term referenced from a 1956 socialist publication (A. Fox in *Socialist Commentary*) by British Labour party activist/sociologist Baron Michael Young of Darlington in his 1950 *satirical* article "The Rise of the Meritocracy" for the socialist *Fabian Society*[1201].

(*Sociology*, 1956)

#MeToo

> *Several leading feminists' method of cloaking their own criminality, and useful Hollywood publicity scheme.*

In October 2017, the *New York Times* published an article accusing Harvey Weinstein of serious sexual offenses[1202], and a *Twitter* hashtag *"#metoo"* went viral after actress Alyssa Milano promoted it[1203]. The French version was more honest: *"rat out your pig"*[1204].

The slogan was coined eleven years earlier in 2006 by feminist political activist Tarana Burke[1205]. Many of the feminist celebrity "leaders" of the keyboard "movement" were opportunists and perpetrators themselves: from Asia Argento raping a male teenager[1206], to Rose McGowan previously taking Weinstein's money[1207], to defamatory anonymous

---

[1201] Young, Michael, *The Rise of the Meritocracy*, Socialist Commentary, 956 (1950)

[1202] Kantor, Jodi, and Megan Twohey, 'Harvey Weinstein Paid Off Sexual Harassment Accusers for Decades', *The New York Times*, 5 October 2017

[1203] Milano, Alyssa (@Alyssa_Milano), 'If You've Been Sexually Harassed or Assaulted Write "Me Too" as a Reply to This Tweet', Twitter, 15 October 2017, 1:21 p.m.

[1204] Boring, Nicolas, 'The Weinstein Scandal Seen from France', *The Atlantic*, 18 Oct 2017

[1205] Burke, Tarana, 'About', *MeToo Movement*, 2006, https://metoomvmt.org/about/

[1206] Severson, Kim, 'Asia Argento, a #MeToo Leader, Made a Deal With Her Own Accuser', *The New York Times*, 19 August 2018

[1207] Guglielmi, Jodi, 'Rose McGowan Speaks Out as Report Reveals Alleged $100,000 Sexual Harassment Settlement With Harvey Weinstein', *People*, 5 October 2017

"Shitty Media Men" spreadsheets[1208], to the French journalist Sandra Muller being convicted of defamation[1209].

According to the same newspaper, 201 lives were ruined without seeing a court[1210], with less than ten people being charged[1211]. Sixty per cent of men subsequently refused to be alone with women at all in the workplace[1212]. The process was so counter-productive it became the subject of studies itself[1213].

(Internet, 2017)

Microaggression

Being patronising or condescending. In a small, irrelevant way.

Coined by black psychiatrist Chester Pierce in regards to the *"little ways"* he saw black people being spoken down to, mentioned in the 1970 section *"Offensive Mechanisms"* from *"The Black Seventies"* edited by Floyd Barbour[1214].

(Literature, 1970)

[1208] Donegan, Moira, 'I Started the Media Men List. My Name Is Moira Donegan', *The Cut*, 10 January 2018

[1209] 'French #MeToo Activist Relieved as Appeals Court Overturns Defamation Conviction', *RFI*, 1 April 2021

[1210] Carlsen, Audrey, Maya Salam, Claire Cain Miller, Denise Lu, Ash Ngu, Jugal K. Patel, and Zach Wichter, '#MeToo Brought Down 201 Powerful Men. Nearly Half of Their Replacements Are Women', *The New York Times*, 23 October 2018

[1211] Kight, Stef W., 'The Global #MeToo Movement: Convictions and Charges', *Axios*, 1 September 2019

[1212] LeanIn.Org and SurveyMonkey, 'Survey: Sexual Harassment at Work and the Backlash Against Women', *LeanIn.Org*, 2019

[1213] Mac Donald, Heather, 'The Negative Impact of the #MeToo Movement', *Imprimis*, 47.5 (May 2018), Hillsdale College

[1214] Pierce, Chester M., 'Offensive Mechanisms', in *The Black Seventies*, ed. by Floyd B. Barbour (Porter Sargent Publisher, 1970), pp. 265–82

Mindfulness

> *A new personal superpower invented by white people who like Yoga, to make them immune from anxiety over First World Problems.*

Buddhist meditation. Often decried as *"McMindfulness"*[1215], the modern Gnostic "movement" of being more considerate as a person without needing all that complex religious stuff, gained influence from intellectual™ people in psychology who liked Jon Kabat-Zinn's *"karmic reassignment"*[1216], the *Mindfulness-Based Stress Reduction* (MBSR) program at the *"Center for Mindfulness"* at *Massachusetts Medical School*, which was founded in 1979[1217].

(Psychology, 1979)

Minor-Attracted Person

> *Paedophile.*

The notion of removing stigma from sexual contact with children has an absolutely, staggeringly prolific precedent in academia. Thousands of journal papers are dedicated to it, under different euphemisms.

The acronym *"MAP"* was publicised by paedophile-apologist organisation *B4U-ACT* on their blog in 2007[1218]. However, it was first used in 1998 by "journalist" Heather Elizabeth Peterson, on her religion-based

---

[1215] Purser, Ronald, *McMindfulness* (Repeater Books, 2019)

[1216] Kabat-Zinn, Jon, 'Changing Karma', *Tricycle: The Buddhist Review* (2008)

[1217] Kabat-Zinn, Jon, *Full Catastrophe Living* (Bantam Books, 1990)

[1218] Melsheimer, Michael, 'The Promotion of Understanding', *B4U-ACT Blog* (2007)

paedophile "support" blogs, *Philia* and *Greenbelt*[1219].

(*Internet, 1998*)

Misandry

> *An imaginary, evil thing which doesn't exist, made up by men to discredit feminist claims men are intrinsically evil.*

Perhaps better described as *"androphobia"*[1220], the term is relatively modern. The first recorded usage can be found in *The Spectator* magazine in an anonymous review of the novel *"Blanche Seymour"*[1221].

(*Literature, 1871*)

Misgender

> *Recognising which of two forms another Homo sapiens is.*

Although originally a term in literature denoting inaccurate grammar, the exact source is difficult to pinpoint (although one can safely say the age pedigree will be wildly exaggerated), however the term appears to have emerged in a *Usenet* post (*alt.support.srs*) in 1999[1222].

(*Internet, 1999*)

[1219] Peterson, Heather Elizabeth, 'Not an Oxymoron: Christian Pedophiles Form Online Support Groups', *Greenbelt Interfaith News* (1998)

[1220] 'Fear of Men (Androphobia): Symptoms and Treatment', *Medical News Today*

[1221] *The Spectator*, 'Review of Blanche Seymour (Anonymous)', 1 April 1871, p. 359

[1222] 'Re. Bar Mitzpha', *alt.support.srs*, 24 June, Usenet newsgroup

Misinformation

> *Contradictory evidence leaked during a coordinated media blackout about your behaviour, cause, or ideology which, if left unsmeared, could prompt those who you currently have under your spell to quickly break out of it.*

Invariably, the spread of deliberate false stories is correlated with the rise of social media, and the contemporary weaponisation of the *doublethink* word can be traced back to political damage control after the 2016 disclosures of *Democrat Party* emails by *Wikileaks*[1223]. Before that, *Article 190-1 "Dissemination of fabrications known to be false, which defame the Soviet political and social system"* of the *RSFSR Criminal Code* in 1966[1224] could be considered its direct precedent.

(Politics, 2016)

Misogynoir

> *A classy French-sounding way of disagreeing with black American women who know best.*

It sounds *sophisticated*. Black feminist writer Moya Bailey made it up to address *"misogyny"* directed toward black *"transgender"* women in her exceptionally silly 2021 book about social media, *"Misogynoir*

[1223] Smith, Allan, 'WikiLeaks Releases More Than 19,000 Emails From DNC Hack', *Business Insider*, 22 July 2016

[1224] 'Article 190-1 of the RSFSR Criminal Code: Dissemination of Fabrications Known to Be False, Which Defame the Soviet Political and Social System', *Criminal Code of the RSFSR*, enacted in 1966, translated in *Soviet Criminal Law and Procedure: The RSFSR Codes*, ed. by Harold J. Berman and Peter B. Maggs (Harvard University Press, 1972), pp. 180–81

Transformed: Black Women's Digital Resistance"[1225].

(Feminist Literature, 2008)

Misogyny

> *Criticising someone born with ovaries who promotes bad ideas or acts stupidly. Capitalist pathology, against women.*

Although the term has existed since the 17th century as a term for the hatred of women, the modern perversion of the word to imply "prejudice" against women emerged with the 1974 publication of radical feminist Andrea Dworkin's book *"Woman Hating: A Radical Look at Sexuality"*[1226], in which she argued for *"the development of a new kind of human being and a new kind of human community free from gender and gender roles."*[1227]

(Feminist Literature, 1974)

Moderation

> *Censorship.*

Moderation has always meant *restraint*. To moderate a discussion is to *restrain* it from becoming unruly. In the context of *Silicon Valley*, it means disappearing and erasing something from view as if it never existed, which is doubly strange considering technology companies have had *Section 230* indemnity regarding what their users post for thirty years[1228].

[1225] Bailey, Moya, *Misogynoir Transformed* (New York University Press, 2021)

[1226] Dworkin, Andrea, *Woman Hating* (E. P. Dutton, 1974)

[1227] Gupta, Shivangi, 'Woman Hating by Andrea Dworkin', *Feminism in India*, 11 Jul 2019

[1228] Communications Decency Act of 1996, Section 230, codified at 47 U.S.C. § 230, as part of the *Communications Act of 1934*

The concept of *"content moderation"* derives from Internet *"forum moderation"* and is first found around 1997 in a book about software features when you running your own, *"Virtual Communities Companion: Everything You Need to Know about Online Communities"* by Karla Shelton and Todd McNeeley[1229].

Demonstrated ability to "moderate" (censor) is *required* to publish an app to either the Apple[1230] or Google[1231] phone stores. During a *Senate Judiciary Committee* hearing on January 31, 2024, Senator Thom Tillis (R-NC) was told *Meta* and *TikTok* both employ 40,000 censors each, while *X* (formerly *Twitter*) and *Snap* employ 2,500 a piece[1232].

(Internet, 1997)

Motivation

A pleasurable feeling of will experienced as a result of exercising self-discipline.

The contemporary concept of motivation as a "feeling" — i.e. motivational posts, courses, speeches, and coaching — can broadly be attributed to the *Esalen Institute*'s promotion of the *"Human Potential Movement"*[1233], the development of 80s-style *televangelism*[1234], and con-artist-founded courses such as *"Dare To Be Great"* by Glenn Turner[1235].

(Literature, 1977)

[1229] Shelton, Darla., and Todd McNeeley, *Virtual Communities Companion* (1997)

[1230] Apple, *App Store Review Guidelines* (n.d.), *Apple Developer*

[1231] Google, *User Generated Content Policy* (n.d.), *Google Play Console Help*

[1232] Robertson, A., 'How Big Is Each Company's Content Moderation Workforce?', *The Verge*, 31 January 2024

[1233] Riessman, Frank, Alan Gartner, *The Human Potential Movement* (Harper & Row, 1970)

[1234] 'Televangelism', *Encyclopedia of Religion and Society* (AltaMira Press, 1998)

[1235] Maxa, Rudy, *Dare to Be Great* (Morrow, 1977)

Motte & Bailey

The sophist imposter's debating playbook.

In his 2005 paper for *Metaphilosophy*, philosopher Nickolas Shackel observes five disingenuous tactics employed by postmodern "scholars" and their apologists when engaging in deceitful trickery during argument.

Troll's Truisms (a mildly ambiguous statement by which an exciting falsehood may trade on a trivial truth), *Motte and Bailey Doctrines* (switching between an easy-to-defend "motte" and a hard-to-defend or controversial "bailey"), *Equivocating Fulcra* (presenting multiple terms as if they are already established), the *Postmodernist Fox Trot* (substitution of vague terminology in place of standard rational terminology), and *Rankly Relativising Fields* (the combined aggregate effect)[1236].

It would have been a brilliant companion to *"Higher Superstition"*[1237].

(Philosophy, 2005)

Movement

Four anonymous Chinese sockpuppet crazypeople on Twitter. Spotted by deskbound writers who don't get travel expenses and have a 3pm deadline and no story.

Derived from the 1960s-era collective term of *"The Movement"* (aka a bowel movement), referring to various left-wing student protests and counter-culture associations: the *Civil Rights movement*, the *Berkeley movement*, the *Antiwar movement*, the *Women's liberation movement*, and

---

[1236] Shackel, Nicholas, 'The Vacuity of Postmodernist Methodology', *Metaphilosophy*, 36.3 (2005), pp. 295–320

[1237] Gross, Paul R., Norman Levitt, *Higher Superstition* (Johns Hopkins Press, 1994)

others. A *Baby Boomer* term for politics without duty.

(Political Rhetoric, 1966)

Ms

Fashionable title for an unmarried woman who may or may not be someone's mistress.

First proposed in 1901 as an alternative abbreviation within the *Springfield Sunday Republican*[1238]. A friend of ex-CIA officer Gloria Steinem[1239] heard a *WBAI* radio interview with Sheila Michaels group, *"The Feminists"*, and suggested it as a title for her new magazine[1240]. The magazine *"Ms."* arrived on newsstands in January 1972[1241].

(Literature, 1966)

MSM

What your gay uncle said it was fine to be when he got you alone in the garage.

This preposterous world salad, *"men who have sex with men"*, was invented in 1994 within a study titled *"Necrotizing Ulcerative Periodontitis: A Marker for Immune Deterioration and a Predictor for the Diagnosis of AIDS"*,

---

[1238] *Springfield Sunday Republican*, 10 November 1901, pp. 4–5

[1239] Wilford, Hugh, *The Mighty Wurlitzer* (Harvard University Press, 2008)

[1240] Saner, Emine, 'Sheila Michaels, the Feminist Who Made "Ms." Mainstream, Has Died at 78', *The Guardian*, 7 July 2017

[1241] Cohen, Lizabeth, 'Ms. Magazine's Inaugural Issue: A Feminist Milestone', *The Yale Review*, Yale University

published in the *Journal of Periodontology*[1242]. NUP is when people with AIDS develop a "punched-out" appearance due to rotting gums and teeth. It is apparently meant to distinguish those who *"engage in sexual activities with other men but do not consider themselves gay or bisexual."*

(Medicine, 1994)

Multicultural-(ism)

A magical sci-fi Marxist paradise where people with entirely different and conflicting religious beliefs, moral values, and social norms live mixed together in the Magic Soil of total utopian harmony.

The concept of multiculturalism originated in Canada after the *Holocaust* and decolonisation as *"biculturalism"*, (*"the Canadian mosaic"* as described by John Murray Gibbon in 1938[1243]) through the struggles for co-existence between English and French language via the *Royal Commission on Bilingualism and Biculturalism (1963–1969)*[1244].

Due to the need for immigration to aid GDP and population growth, it became a national policy in 1971[1245], as it also did in Australia in 1973[1246]. The *EU* followed, due to the results of its "guest worker" program[1247].

[1242] M. Glick, J. E. Muzyka, E. J. Salkin, and H. H. Lurie, 'Necrotizing Ulcerative Periodontitis: A Marker for Immune Deterioration and a Predictor for the Diagnosis of AIDS', *Journal of Periodontology*, 65.5 (1994), 393–397

[1243] Gibbon, John Murray, *Canadian Mosaic* (McClelland & Stewart, 1938)

[1244] Canada, *Royal Commission on Bilingualism and Biculturalism: Report of the Royal Commission on Bilingualism and Biculturalism* (Ottawa, 1967–69)

[1245] Government of Canada, *House of Commons Debates: Prime Minister Pierre Trudeau's Announcement of Multiculturalism as Official Policy*, 8 October 1971, Ottawa

[1246] Australian Government, *Speech by Prime Minister Gough Whitlam Announcing Multicultural Policy* (1973, Canberra)

[1247] Castles, Stephen, and Godula Kosack, *Immigrant Workers and Class Structure in Western Europe* (Oxford University Press, 1973)

It was analogous to the Soviet concept of *"korenizatsiya"* ("indigenisation" or "nativisation"), a pluralistic society made up of people from many backgrounds who assimilate into an overarching culture. It was largely abandoned in the thirties under Stalin after he deemed it a threat to national unity[1248].

The "Godfather" of multiculturalism was Jamaican Marxist, founder of *New Left Review* and Foucault-loving "cultural theorist" Stuart Hall, who also blatantly ripped off Derrida[1249]. Unsurprisingly, in 1990, *Marxism Today* praised the whole idea[1250], despite everyone else writing it off as a total failure.

It failed in Germany:

> *This [multicultural] approach has failed, utterly failed. (Angela Merkel, Oct 2010)*[1251]

It failed in Britain:

> *Under the doctrine of state multiculturalism, we have encouraged different cultures to live separate lives, apart from each other and the mainstream. We have failed to provide a vision of society to which they feel they want to belong. (David Cameron, Feb 2011)*[1252]

It failed in France:

[1248] Martin, Terry, 'An Affirmative Action Empire: The Soviet Union as the Highest Form of Imperialism', in Ronald Grigor Suny and Terry Martin (eds), A State of Nations: Empire and Nation-Making in the Age of Lenin and Stalin (Oxford: Oxford University Press, 2001), pp. 67-90

[1249] Chen, Kuan-Hsing, and David Morley, *Stuart Hall* (Routledge, 1996)

[1250] Hall, Stuart, 'The Multicultural Question', *Marxism Today*, 34.1 (1990)

[1251] Eddy, Melissa, 'Merkel Says German Multicultural Society Has Failed', *The New York Times*, 17 October 2010

[1252] Watt, Nicholas, 'State Multiculturalism Has Failed, Says David Cameron', *The Guardian*, 5 February 2011

If you come to France, you accept to melt into a single community, which is the national community... Multiculturalism has failed. (Nicolas Sarkozy, Feb 2011)[1253]

(Politics, 1963)

Multiple Genders

The novel idea that which dangly bits you have has nothing to do with what your mind thinks you are, and you act it all out anyway. It's just society, duh.

From the anti-Zionist Matriarch of Queer everything: professor of Foucault at *Berkeley*, a previous winner of the award for worst writing[1254], and self-described Marxist lesbian, Judith Butler. In her virtually impenetrable scripture *"Gender Trouble: Feminism and the Subversion of Identity"* (1990)[1255], the high priestess of *Woke* claims gender isn't related to biology and is merely a repetitive *"performance"*, like wearing makeup.

(Women's Studies, 1990)

My Body, My Choice

Supporting one's own political side in their 'autonomy', over their own medical choices, when it's politically advantageous.

Despite the attempts of "scholars" to try to root the slogan deep into history, its presence at protests in 1969 was not spontaneous. The slogan

---

[1253] 'Multiculturalism Has Failed, Says French President Sarkozy', *BBC News*, 10 Feb 2011

[1254] Dutton, Denis, 'The Bad Writing Contest', *Philosophy and Literature* (1998)

[1255] Butler, Judith, *Gender Trouble* (Routledge, 1990)

comes from the October 1928 edition of Margaret Sanger's *Birth Control Review*[1256], *in* which Magnus Hirschfeld advocated for *"sexual rights"*[1257].

Dr Bernard Nathanson, co-founder of the *National Association for the Repeal of Abortion Laws* (NARAL), which later became the *National Abortion Rights Action League* (NARL), is on record in a 2002 interview with *Catholic Exchange* saying:

> *I remember laughing when we made those slogans up. We were looking for some sexy, catchy slogans to capture public opinion. They were very cynical slogans then, just as all of these slogans today are very, very cynical.*[1258]

NB: *does not apply to men, developing fetuses, or other people. Or in the case of illegal drugs, infidelity, face masks, hazmat suits, mandated immunotherapy, suicide, euthanasia, etc.*

(Pharmacology, 1928)

Narrative

An adjective illiterate people who want to sound intellectual™ *erroneously use as an abstract noun for "story".*

As Derrida said, it's told by a subjective "narrator" and therefore can't be trusted. Perverted from its original meaning within Lyotard's 1984 nonsense *"The Postmodern Condition: A Report on Knowledge"*[1259].

[1256] Editor, 'When Women Are in Full Control of Their Own Bodies', *Birth Control Review*, 12.10 (October 1928), pp. 286–87

[1257] Hirschfeld, Magnus, 'The Sexual Rights of Women', *Birth Control Review*, 16.4 (April 1932), pp. 102–3

[1258] Nathanson, Bernard, interview, *Catholic Exchange* (2002)

[1259] Lyotard, Jean-François, *The Postmodern Condition* (1979)

The correct noun is *narration:* if writing has a *narrative* (adjective) tone because it is being *narrated* (verb), then it can be considered a *narration* (noun).

(Literature, 1984)

Neo

A word people who want to sound intellectual™ use for "new-ish" about something whose original format has failed catastrophically multiple times before.

Get your science right: Greek "neos" = young.

(Neo)-Nazi

Any meanie who doesn't like communism or Antifa, feels loyalty to a nation, or believes biology plays a role in human life.

The word *"Nazi"* is English slang for *National Socialist German Workers' Party* (*Nationalsozialistische Deutsche Arbeiterpartei*). In 1926, Joseph Goebbels published *"Der Nazi-Sozi"* (*"The Nazi-Sozi"*) which referred to the abbreviated term *"Sozi"* (socialist) conjoined to a common slur for Bavarian peasants[1260]. The party hated Marxism, Communism, Bolshevism, and Jews[1261]. Popularised by Rush Limbaugh's infamous use of the term *"feminazi"*[1262].

(Political Science, 1926)

[1260] Goebbels, Joseph, *Der Nazi-Sozi* (1926)

[1261] Shirer, William L., *The Rise and Fall of the Third Reich* (Simon and Schuster, 1960)

[1262] Limbaugh, Rush, *The Way Things Ought to Be* (Pocket Books, 1992)

Neoliberal

> *Capitalist. Reagan, Thatcher, and Pinochet. What wasn't supposed to happen because the USSR had achieved communism.*

Most commonly attributed to economist Milton Friedman in his 1951 essay *"Neo-Liberalism and its Prospects"*[1263]. Adapted by Bill Clinton and Tony Blair after the USSR collapsed as part of a *"Third Way"*[1264].

(Economics, 1951)

Neurodiverse

> *What you are when you fail physics and get accepted for a sociology degree in lesbian dance therapy. While all the autistic kids are doing PhD physics.*

Not just "diverse" by skin colour, but by brain. Individuals diagnosed with dyslexia, dyscalculia, dyspraxia, ADHD, and autism were formalised as a new Marxist group by a 1998 art review in the *New York Times* about an autistic artist, Margaret Bodell[1265].

(Art, 1998)

[1263] Friedman, Milton, 'Neo-Liberalism and Its Prospects', *Farmand*, 17 February 1951

[1264] Giddens, Anthony, *The Third Way* (Polity Press, 1998)

[1265] Smith, Roberta, 'Art Review; Who's to Say Where Inside Meets Outside?', *The New York Times*, 29 March 2002

No

> *A harmful word which is deeply hurtful to people's feelings and should never, ever be used because it's an act of oppression.*

Get your philosophy right: a denial or refusal.

Nonbinary

> *Not classifiable by science as one of the two forms of homo sapiens. Like Derrida said.*

Binary means to be "one of two" ("bis" latin meaning "twice"). The origin of the term is unclear, but it is most likely associated with the same Derrida-obsessed "scholars" who came up with *"genderqueer"* in the nineties. Possibly in *Usenet* group *soc.support.transgendered*[1266]. This doublespeak literally means "not one of the two morphological shapes of the species."

(Women's Studies, 1995)

Nonconforming

> *Rebellious sci-fi outlaw who won't do what teachers, parents, or OMG SOCIETY says.*

Conform means to take the shape of, to adapt to fit in with new conditions.

[1266] Richards, Christina, Walter Pierre Bouman, and Meg-John Barker, eds., *Genderqueer and Non-Binary Genders* (Palgrave Macmillan, 2017)

In the 17th century, a "conformist" was an individual who complied with the form of worship of the *Church of England*. One who didn't was known as "non-conform" minister[1267].

(Theology, 17th Century)

Non-Crime Hate Incident

A report made to British police about hurty feelings.

In 2014, the universally hated British *College of Policing* formalised the findings of the *Stephen Lawrence Inquiry Report* in 1999[1268] so incidents *"perceived by the victim or any other person to be motivated by hostility or prejudice"* were officially recorded on a person's criminal record as a part of their *Hate Crime Operational Guidance*[1269].

This grotesquely Orwellian idea led to 1,500 "non-crimes" in two years, such as Home Secretary Amber Rudd's 2016 *Conservative Party* conference speech[1270]; a "rough" haircut, and a woman being labelled a "rottweiler"[1271]; a nine-year-old child calling a classmate a "retard"[1272]; journalist Allison Pearson tweeting about *Hamas* rape attacks[1273]; a

---

[1267] Spurr, John, *English Puritanism, 1603–1689* (Macmillan, 1998)

[1268] Macpherson, William, *The Stephen Lawrence Inquiry* (1999)

[1269] College of Policing, *Hate Crime Operational Guidance* (2014)

[1270] Bird, Steve, 'How Amber Rudd's Speech to Tories Was Labelled a Non-Crime Hate Incident', *The Telegraph*, 13 November 2024

[1271] 'Time-Wasting Cops Probed a "Rough" Haircut and a Woman Being Called a "Rottweiler" in Latest "Hate Crime Incidents"', *The Sun*, 13 November 2024

[1272] Doughty, Ellie, 'Child, 9, Among Kids Investigated by Cops for Hate Incidents After Calling Classmate a "R****d"', *The Sun*, 15 November 2024

[1273] Bird, Steve, 'Essex Police Recorded 1,500 Non-Crime Hate Incidents in Two Years', *The Times*, 13 November 2024

refusal to shake someone's hand[1274]; and misdiagnoses by doctors and vicars[1275]. Who knew an idea so vacuous could possibly be abused by political radicals?

(Law Enforcement, 2014)

Normative

> *A word people who want to sound intellectual™ use for "normal".*

Get your science right: a standard tending to correctness.

Of Colour

> *Alternative for racist term "colored" used by intellectual™-sounding people describing anyone with brown skin as an attempt to appear "reverent" towards those they are being condescending to.*

Aside from how stupid the term actually is when considering the opposite of colour is transparent, the intent of the phrase is ambiguous: from Martin Luther King Jr use of *"citizens of color"*[1276], to the *National Women's Conference*'s declaration of "women of colour" in 1977[1277], to teacher manuals circulated in Academia around 1997 (e.g. *"Teaching for Diversity and Social Justice: A Sourcebook"*)[1278], the term is universally attributed to

---

[1274] 'Police Log Hate Incident for Refusal to Shake Hands in Gender Row', *The Times*, 13 Nov 2024

[1275] 'Doctors and Vicars Accused of Non-Crime Hate Incidents', *The Times*, 13 Nov 2024

[1276] King, Martin Luther, Jr., 'I Have a Dream', *American Rhetoric*, 28 August 1963

[1277] Mattingly, Doreen J., and Jessica L. Nare. "A Rainbow of Women: Diversity and Unity at the 1977 U.S. International Women's Year Conference." *Journal of Women's History*, vol. 26, no. 2, 2014, pp. 88–112.

[1278] Adams, Maurianne, *Teaching for Diversity and Social Justice* (Routledge, 1997)

18th century vocabulary for "black person" or "mixed race". [1279]

(Literature, 1977)

Open Letter

> *A self-important blog post written by someone whom nobody knows, about something which nobody cares.*

Letters for public view have a long history (such as St Paul's epistles) and the press often printed political overtures (such as *"Open letter to the English nation from Berlin."*, 1878[1280], or *"J'Accuse...!"* in 1898[1281]) and readers' complaints.

However, the vomit-inducing modern trend with its sanctimonious underbelly of people wanting to impose themselves as important neo-historical figures seems to be pervasive in regards to personal attention gained on *Twitter*. It would appear to tally with the practice of *"Scriptotherapy"* as detailed in *"Scriptotherapy: Therapeutic Writing as a Counseling Adjunct"* (Richard Rioradan, 1996 *American Counseling Association*)[1282].

(Journalism, 1878)

Open Relationship/Marriage

> *Swingers.*

[1279] Edwards, Bryan, *An Historical Survey of the French Colony in the Island of St. Domingo* (John Stockdale, 1797)

[1280] Walters, H. L., *An Open Letter Addressed to the English Nation From Berlin [on the Berlin Congress of 1878]* (1878)

[1281] Zola, Émile, 'J'Accuse...!', *L'Aurore*, 13 January 1898

[1282] Riordan, Richard J., 'Scriptotherapy: Therapeutic Writing as a Counseling Adjunct', *Journal of Counseling & Development*, 74.3 (January–February 1996), 263–69

The concept is a staggeringly nonsensical: a relationship is predicated on its exclusivity. The origin of the term is undoubtedly *New York Times* bestseller *"Open Marriage: A New Life Style for Couples"* by anthropologists George and Nena O'Neill in 1972[1283], who didn't exactly intend for it to be used as a justification for swingers' parties, but didn't help themselves either (*"Sexual fidelity is the false god of closed marriage"*).

(1972, Literature)

Oppression

> *A word people who want to sound intellectual™ use to irrationally and grossly inflate their sense of resentment. From their $1000 smartphone.*

Get your philosophy right: unjust exercise of authority.

Optics

> *A word people who want to sound intellectual™ use for "appearance".*

Optics are the scientific study of light and vision[1284]. In French, *optique* means perception or point of view (how *sophisticated!*)[1285]. That was, until President Jimmy Carter's special counsel on inflation, Robert Strauss, misused the term in 1978[1286].

However, the contemporary abuse of this doublespeak found its legs

---

[1283] O'Neill, Nena, and George O'Neill, *Open Marriage* (M. Evans, 1972)

[1284] Born, Max, and Emil Wolf, *Principles of Optics* (Cambridge Press, 1999)

[1285] Larousse, 'Optique', *Dictionnaire de Français*

[1286] 'Strauss Suggests Business Leaders' Visit to White House as "Nice Optical Step"', *The Wall Street Journal*, 31 May 1978

during the Libya crisis of Barack Obama's reign in 2011, as the media needed a word which sounded smarter[1287].

(Political Rhetoric, 2011)

(Sexual) Orientation

A Derrida-inspired perversion of the medical concept of "disorientation" into a geographic/pathfinding compass. Like a "spectrum".

You only need to orientate yourself if you *don't know* where you are. The original phrase appears to refer to general courtship around 1931[1288].

Radical gay rights groups began publicising the idea in the early seventies, but the term was popularised by John Money to replace *"sexual preference"* in his 1998 horror *"Gay, Straight, and In-Between: The Sexology of Erotic Orientation"*[1289].

The concept of *"deviant sexual orientation"*, far more appropriate to anything emerging from John Money's deeply disturbed brain, was set out by feminist psychologist Georgene Seward in her 1946 paper *"Sex and the Social Order"* which claimed:

> *Deviant sexual orientation in later life may originate in the child's inability to identify himself with his like-sexed parent*[1290].

(Psychiatry, 1946)

[1287] Lizza, Ryan, 'The Consequentialist', *The New Yorker*, 2 May 2011

[1288] Lichtenberger, James P., *Divorce* (McGraw-Hill, 1931)

[1289] Money, John, *Gay, Straight, and In-Between* (Oxford University Press, 1988)

[1290] Seward, Georgene H., *Sex and the Social Order* (McGraw-Hill, 1946)

(The) Other

> *Something which needs to be "neutralised" by "queering" a city with Pride parades.*

Very few other concepts owe so much to so many low-IQ usual suspects than "the other", *"otherness"*, or *"othering"*. The sheer amount of nonsense written on the subject is stupefying, with every idiot chipping in: Sartre, Derrida, Foucault, de Beauvoir, Lacan, and even Gramsci.

In 1807, *"The Phenomenology of Spirit"* by Georg Wilhelm Friedrich Hegel attempted to conceptualise a companion to *"The Self"*[1291]. Ever since then, every imposter with a pen has attempted to use it to give their bad ideas legitimacy.

(Philosophy, 1807)

Otherkin(d)

> *There's no snarky, cynical definition here which beats the actual one.*

According to the OED, *"otherkin"* is:

> *a person who identifies as non-human, typically as being wholly or partially an animal or mythical being.*[1292]

Where does one even begin?

According to pseudonymous historian *"Lupa"* from website *LiveJournal*, who describes xim/xer-self as a *"neopagan writer and psychologist"* and *"identifies"* as a wolf now instead of a *"therian"*, the term was created in

---

[1291] Hegel, Georg Wilhelm Friedrich, *The Phenomenology of Spirit* (1807)

[1292] 'Otherkin - Definition of Otherkin in English', *Oxford ED* (8 April 2017)

April 1990 by participants of the mailing list *"Elfinkind Digest"* (for *"elves and interested observers."*)[1293]. The first attempt at an academic paper was made by Daniel Kirby in 2008[1294].

The list of *"identities"* includes *"fictionkin"* (believing oneself to be a fictional character from *anime* of video games); *"weatherkin"* (clouds, etc); *"conceptkin"* (abstract concepts); *"spacekin"* (celestial bodies); *"musickin"*, *"timeperiodkin"*, and others[1295].

(Internet, 1990)

Over-represented

> *A state of demography which is deeply unfavourable to your victimhood storyline.*

Jews in *Nobel* prizes[1296], *Wall Street* firms[1297], legal professions, and *Hollywood*[1298]. Indians in *Silicon Valley* tech leadership positions[1299] and cricket[1300]. Filipinos as physicians and nurses[1301]. The English

---

[1293] Lupa, *A Field Guide to Otherkin* (Immanion Press, 2007)

[1294] Kirby, Danielle, 'Alternative Worlds: Metaphysical Questing and Virtual Community Amongst the Otherkin', in Frances Di Lauro (ed.), *Through a Glass Darkly: Collected Research* (Sydney University Press, 2006)

[1295] Beusman, Callie, '"I Look at a Cloud and I See It as Me": The People Who Identify as Objects', *Vice Media*, 3 August 2016

[1296] 'Jewish Nobel Prize Winners', *Encyclopaedia Judaica* (Gale, 2007)

[1297] Karp, Alan, 'Jews in American Business and Law', *Journal of American Jewish History*, 73.1 (1984), 25–38

[1298] Gabler, Neal, *An Empire of Their Own* (Crown Publishing, 1988)

[1299] Saxenian, AnnaLee, *The New Argonauts* (Harvard University Press, 2006)

[1300] Majumdar, Boria, *Twenty-Two Yards to Freedom* (Viking, 2004)

[1301] Lorenzo, Fely Marilyn E., et al., 'Nurse Migration from a Source Country Perspective: Philippine Country Case Study', *Health Services Research*, 42.3 (2007), 1406–18

producing fifty-one per cent of the world's inventions[1302]. Asians in IQ, and university achievement[1303]. Blacks in music[1304], violent crime[1305], and basketball[1306]. Mongolians in *Sumo*[1307].

(Newspapers, Mixed)

[1302] Mokyr, Joel, *The Enlightened Economy* (Yale University Press, 2009)

[1303] Zhou, Min, Jennifer Lee, *The Asian American Achievement Paradox* (Russell Sage, 2015)

[1304] Ramsey, Guthrie P., Jr., *Race Music* (University of California Press, 2003)

[1305] Hagan, John, and Ruth D. Peterson, eds., *Crime and Inequality* (Stanford Press, 1995)

[1306] Boyd, Todd, *Young, Black, Rich, and Famous* (University of Nebraska Press, 2003)

[1307] Brownell, Susan, *The Anthropology of Sport* (University of California Press, 2018)

P Q R

Pan

> *Entirely indiscriminate, amoral, promiscuous, undiscerning, indifferent.*

The Greek word *pan* means "all" or "every"[1308]. In *Pantheism*, "all things" are god; in *Panentheism*, god is in all things and outside it[1309]. The idea of *"pansexual"* behaviour is derived from Freud's theory of the sex instinct (*libido*) underlying all behaviour (*Journal of Abnormal Psychology*, 1910)[1310], which was universally... *panned*.

(Psychology, 1910)

[1308] Liddell, Henry George, and Robert Scott, *A Greek-English Lexicon*, revised and augmented by Henry Stuart Jones, 9th edn (Clarendon Press, 1940)

[1309] Flint, Robert, *The Philosophy of History in Europe* (William Blackwood and Sons, 1894),

[1310] Freud, Sigmund, *Three Essays on the Theory of Sexuality*, (Nervous and Mental Disease Publishing Co., 1910), pp. 23–57

Pansexual

> *Like Bi, but not. Willing to engage in sexual activity with anyone or anything.*

Despite it being a fashionably nonsensical new version of *"bisexual"*, the modern, post-Freudian use of the term can be traced back to the 1980 *Hudson Review*, which describes *"Mr. Maupin's people, mostly San Francisco homosexuals (of both sexes) or bisexuals or pansexuals"*[1311].

(Arts, 1980)

Paradigm (Shift)

> *A word people who want to sound intellectual™ use for "a way things are done".*

This loathsome idiom comes from the Greek verb *paradeiknynai*, which means "to show side by side". It was popularised c. 1962 by American philosopher Thomas Kuhn in his equally loathsome book, *"The Structure of Scientific Revolutions"*, which attempted to pervert the subject into something driven by psychology and sociology[1312].

(Philosophy, 1962)

[1311] *The Hudson Review*, Spring 1980, 33.1, p. 147

[1312] Kuhn, Thomas S., *The Structure of Scientific Revolutions* (U. of Chicago Press, 1962)

Patriarchy

> *Like The Illuminati, The Jews, and The Aliens, a sinister tyranny of rich, capitalist, cisgender white supremacist men aiming to generationally enslave women as broodmares for producing more white supremacist capitalist offspring. Something which has to be smashed so we can all live in huts again.*

Originally a term for "fatherhood" (paternity, patrimonial) or the church (as in Abraham being the *Patriarch of Nations* or the Pope as *Patriarch*), patriarchal structure has been debated back into the eighteenth century[1313]. The revealer of the scary conspiracy is generally considered to be lesbian feminist Kate Millett, in her 1970 rant *"Sexual Politics"*, where maleness is pretty much the cause of all suppression and rape[1314]. She didn't like her mother either, and suffered rather heavily from mental illness[1315].

Her sister, Mallory Millett, described her as the *"Mao Tse-tung of Women's Liberation"*[1316].

> *Kate was mentally ill for as long as I remember. She was five when I was born and our elder sister Sally says that once I arrived, Kate was hanging over my bassinet plotting my murder. We shared a bedroom from my birth. From my earliest memory I recall trembling from the vibrations of her insanity. She was the most disturbed, megalomaniacal, evil and dishonest person I have ever known. She tried to kill me so many times that it's now an enormous blur of traumatizing horrors. She was a sadist, a torturer, a deeply-engrained bully who took immense pleasure in hurting others.*

[1313] Sanderson, Stephen K., *Social Evolutionism* (Blackwell Publishers, 1990)

[1314] Millett, Kate, *Sexual Politics* (Doubleday, 1970)

[1315] Millett, Kate, *The Loony-Bin Trip* (Simon & Schuster, 1990)

[1316] Millett, Mallory, 'Marxist Feminism's Ruined Lives', *FrontPage Magazine*, 2 Sept 2014

Incorrigible and ruthless, she was expelled multiple times from every school she attended. I spent my childhood with heart hammering as I tiptoed through the house so as not to be noticed by the dreadful Kate. Our mother was helpless, paralyzed with terror in the face of Kate.[1317]

(Feminist Literature, 1970)

Peoplekind

Canada's most embarrassing moment.

Although it might have been attributed to the ridicule vomited on Woke high priest Justin Trudeau in 2018 as a *"gender-neutral alternative to mankind"*[1318], the neologism first emerged in popular culture around 1980 in a sarcastic *Rangelands* journal editorial[1319].

(Politics, 1980)

Performativity

Putting on make-up or wearing heels. Adopting a role or persona in a social situation to convince others of something about you, e.g. writing papers using the word "performativity" or "performant" instead of "performance" to appear intellectual™.

[1317] Millett, Mallory, 'My Sister Kate: The Destructive Feminist Legacy of Kate Millett', *FrontPage Magazine*, 5 Sept 2018

[1318] Cecco, Leyland, 'Justin Trudeau Tells Woman to Say "Peoplekind" Not "Mankind"', *The Guardian*, 7 February 2018

[1319] *Rangelands*, 2.4 (August 1980), p. 181

The French Philosopher's favourite idea of speech being an "act" was introduced by British philosopher John Austin around 1955 in his concept of the *"performative utterance"* as he delivered lectures at Harvard about the idea of making a promise to someone[1320]. To date, it's referred to as *"Speech Act Theory"*[1321] even though... it was never a formal theory, and it had nothing to do with speech being an act.

The concept was popularised by director Jonathan Miller during a 1971 TV debate on *The Dick Cavett Show* with British politician Enoch Powell[1322].

(Linguistics, 1955)

Personal Is Political

> *A banshee cry for Stepford wives to encourage them to initiate a constructive dialogue with the political enemies of 2nd wave feminism.*

From an essay of the same name in 1969 by *Women's Liberation* movement member and arch-TERF Carol Hanisch[1323]. Later echoed by Saul Alinsky in 1971 as *Rule #13* from extremist handbook *"Rules for Radicals"* ("Pick the target, freeze it, personalize it, and polarize it.")[1324].

(Feminist Literature, 1969)

[1320] Austin, J. L., *How to Do Things with Words*, (Harvard University Press, 1962)

[1321] Searle, John R., *Speech Acts* (Cambridge University Press, 1969)

[1322] The Dick Cavett Show, 'Jonathan Miller/Enoch Powell/Roger Moore', ABC Television Network, 14 May 1971.

[1323] Hanisch, Carol, 'The Personal Is Political', in *Notes from the Second Year: Women's Liberation*, ed. by Shulamith Firestone and Anne Koedt (Radical Feminism, 1970)

[1324] Alinsky, Saul D., *Rules for Radicals* (Random House, 1971)

Phile

> *A powerful suffix which can instantly legitimise anyone at all just by adding to any other word, making it sound like a legitimate medical condition only non-intellectual™ people wouldn't know. Also, a convenient way to rename extreme sexual depravity to sound like an eccentric hobby.*

Derived from *philia* (love), the renaming of sexual fetish practices to euphemistic *"paraphilias"* in the 1980 *DSM* psychiatric catalogue (*"The diagnostic status of homosexuality in DSM-III: A reformulation of the issues"*, American Journal of Psychiatry, Robert Spitzer, 1981)[1325] was inspired by the work of psychologist John Money, later documented in his 1988 book *"Gay, Straight, and In-Between: The Sexology of Erotic Orientation"*[1326].

(Psychiatry, 1980)

Phobe

> *A powerful suffix which can instantly stigmatise anyone at all just by adding to any other word, making it sound like a legitimate medical condition only non-intellectual™ people wouldn't know.*

The usage of "phobia" to denote irrational dislike was introduced around 1969 as a *"descriptor for the intolerant"* by psychotherapist George Weinberg's guesswork in a gay pornographic magazine, *Screw*[1327].

Phobos (Greek) originally meant "flight" in the sense of "swiftly running"

[1325] Spitzer, Robert L., 'The Diagnostic Status of Homosexuality in DSM-III: A Reformulation of the Issues', *American Journal of Psychiatry*, 138.2 (1981), pp. 210–15

[1326] Money, John, *Gay, Straight, and In-Between* (Oxford University Press, 1988)

[1327] Weinberg, George, *Society and the Healthy Homosexual* (St. Martin's Press, 1972)

(from the Proto-Indo-European root meaning "to run"), the meaning that Homer intended when the word appeared in *The Iliad* and *The Odyssey*[1328]. Only thereafter did it become the common word for "fear" due to its association with "fleeing" in a panic or a fright, before it was added to social descriptors at the start of the eighteenth century.

Curiously, two years earlier, the *USSR* had begun mass political abuse of *"punitive psychiatry"*, which involved pathologising ideological enemies as suffering from *"philosophical intoxication"*[1329].

(Psychotherapy, 1969)

Polyamorous

Promiscuity or adultery without the stigma.

Polygamy and polygyny have been with humanity since the first inceptions of marriage[1330]. The morality and commitment-free *Star Trek* relationship version of it - as practiced by chimps and bonobos[1331] - was presented in a 1990 article titled *"A Bouquet of Lovers"* by pagan priestess Morning Glory Zell-Ravenheart in *Green Egg* magazine[1332]. Two years later in 1992, *alt.poly-amory* was established on *Usenet*[1333].

(Internet, 1990)

[1328] Liddell, Henry George, Robert Scott, *A Greek-English Lexicon*, (Clarendon Press, 1940)

[1329] Bloch, Sidney, and Peter Reddaway, *Psychiatric Terror* (Basic Books, 1977)

[1330] Goody, Jack, *Production and Reproduction* (Cambridge University Press, 1976)

[1331] de Waal, Frans B. M., *Bonobo* (University of California Press, 1997)

[1332] Zell-Ravenheart, Morning Glory, 'A Bouquet of Lovers', *Green Egg Magazine*, 25.2 (Spring 1990), pp. 12–15

[1333] Kollock, Peter, and Marc A. Smith, *Communities in Cyberspace* (Routledge, 1999)

Populism

> Popular. The process of Hitler-wannabes appealing to unenlightened people who aren't intellectual™, who you can't really get away with calling racist because there are too many of them.

Although it's a concept which has been around forever, the name itself is a moniker adopted by the United States' *People's Party*, which attempted to break the Democrat/GOP duopoly at the 1892 elections[1334]. Generally attributed in contemporary terms to the analysis given in John Allcock's *"Populism: A Brief Biography"* in *Sociology* (1971)[1335]. It's also a noticeably French idea[1336]. Recently, it's just wannabe-journalists who need a way to avoid being sued for labelling people "racist."

(Sociology, 1892)

Porn

> Art. The harmless relationship-enhancing activity of destroying one's ability to relate to others by watching empowered strangers engage in sexual behaviour for financial reward.

Derived from *porne* (prostitution, or sexual immorality) and *graphos* (to record), *"a written description or illustration of prostitutes or prostitution"* entered French vocabulary in 1857[1337]. Denmark first legalised the

---

[1334] Hicks, John D., *The Populist Revolt* (University of Minnesota Press, 1931)

[1335] Allcock, John B., 'Populism: A Brief Biography', *Sociology*, 5.3 (1971), pp. 371–87

[1336] Ionescu, Ghita, Ernest Gellner, *Populism* (Weidenfeld and Nicolson, 1969)

[1337] Roberts, Mary Louise, *Disruptive Acts* (University of Chicago Press, 2002)

publication of obscenity in 1969[1338], it was defined as "art" during *Hustler Magazine v. Falwell* in 1988[1339], and it finally became universal to children of any age, anywhere, en masse, since the launch of *Youtube*-style sites in 2010 through one company in Quebec (*Mindgeek*)[1340].

(Literature, 1969)

Positionality

A word people who want to sound intellectual™ use for "position" or "perspective".

Related to idiotic *Standpoint Theory* (aka *"Feminist Standpoint Theory"*)[1341], the term is a less-qualified version of Nietzsche's concept of *Perspectivism*[1342]. It appeared in journal articles in the late-1960s, in articles like *"Social Participation and Social Structure"*[1343] and *"Social Distance Components in Integration Attitudes of Negro College Students"*[1344]. It was introduced to Women's Studies by "philosopher" Linda Alcoff in her 1988 horror *"Cultural Feminism versus Post-Structuralism: The Identity Crisis in Feminist Theory"*[1345].

(Sociology, 1966)

[1338] Stenvoll, Dagmar, 'Pornography and Censorship in Denmark: A Historical Overview', *Journal of Scandinavian Studies*, 35.2 (1999), pp. 205–21

[1339] *Hustler Magazine, Inc. v. Falwell*, 485 U.S. 46 (1988)

[1340] Nilsson, Patricia, "The Secretive World of MindGeek, the Montreal-Based Company Behind Pornhub and Redtube," *Financial Post* (21 January 2021)

[1341] Harding, Sandra, *The Science Question in Feminism* (Cornell University Press, 1986)

[1342] Nietzsche, Friedrich, *The Will to Power* (Random House, 1967)

[1343] Katz, Fred E., 'Social Participation and Social Structure', *Social Forces*, 44.3 (1966)

[1344] Hines, Ralph H., 'Social Distance Components in Integration Attitudes of Negro College Students', *The Journal of Negro Education*, 37.3 (1968), pp. 276–85

[1345] Alcoff, Linda, 'Cultural Feminism versus Post-Structuralism: The Identity Crisis in Feminist Theory', *Signs: Journal of Women in Culture and Society*, 13.3 (1988)

Post-

> Anti. Against. A handy placeholder term to put in front of any "ism" word you invented, indicating progress and edgy "discourse"; regardless if it has any merit or makes any sense. The most intellectual™ kind of "discourse".

Postmodernism (anti-modernism), *post-Structuralism* (anti-Structuralism), *post-Postmodernism* (anti-Postmodernism), *post-materialism* (anti-Materialism), *post-colonialism* (anti-Colonialism), *post-Genderism*, *post-humanism*, post-Contemporary, post-Hegemony, post-Theism, *post-*postmodernism, you name it.

The work widely recognised as marking the beginning of the postmodern era is James Joyce's *Ulysses* (1922)[1346], or perhaps Robert Venturi's *Complexity and Contradiction in Architecture* (1966)[1347].

Or as so beautifully put on *Urban Dictionary*:

> *Postmodernism is the ultimate lubricant invented by social sciences in order to f**k every concept and structure that humans ever came up with. At the same time it is used as a means for social sciences to penetrate one another.*[1348]

(Philosophy, 1955)

[1346] Joyce, James, *Ulysses* (Shakespeare and Company, 1922)

[1347] Venturi, Robert, *Complexity and Contradiction in Architecture* (Mus. of Modern Art, 1966)

[1348] tahabgd, 'Postmodernism', *Urban Dictionary*, 12 March 2010

Post-Truth

> *It doesn't matter if it's true or not. It's how i feel.*

A 1992 article by playwright Steve Tesich in *The Nation* claims *"we, as a free people, have freely decided that we want to live in some post-truth world"*[1349], possibly in reference to philosopher's Hannah Arendt's 1972 concept of *"defactualization"*[1350] or Baudrillard's *"hyperreality"*[1351].

The term *"post-truth politics"* was coined in a blog of the same name for *Grist* magazine by "climate and energy" writer David Roberts after Brexit and Trump's election victory in 2016[1352].

(Philosophy, 1992)

Praxis

> *A word people who want to sound intellectual™ use for "practice" (Latin).*

Get your philosophy right: exercise of a study or profession.

[1349] Tesich, Steve, 'A Government of Lies', *The Nation*, 6 January 1992

[1350] Arendt, Hannah, 'Lying in Politics: Reflections on The Pentagon Papers', *The New York Review of Books*, 17.8 (18 November 1971), pp. 30–39

[1351] Baudrillard, Jean, *Simulacra and Simulation* (University of Michigan Press, 1994)

[1352] Roberts, David, 'Post-Truth Politics', *Grist*, 1 April 2010

Preferred/Personal Pronoun

> *Your human right to be referred to in the third person, plural, or by words you have personally entered into the English language on a whim, which others must use under fear of prosecution, even if they sound like noises from a gurgling infant.*

Not a day goes by whereby the historical date strange pronouns were allegedly first used is conveniently moved back.

The etymology of the increasingly large collection is sporadic — to say the least — but inspired largely by sci-fi literacy. In 1970, "feminist writer" Mary Orovan created *"co/cos"* from usage observed in the *Twin Oaks* Virginia anarcho-communist camps[1353], and in 1996 Kate Bornstein introduced *"ze"* and *"hir"* in her terrible novel, *"Nearly Roadkill: An Infobahn Erotic Adventure"*[1354].

The *University of Vermont* appears to have led the trend of asking in students for their "pronoun" in 2015[1355]. It's been going on for 150 years. It's never panned out.

(Feminist Literature, 1970)

Prejudice Plus (Institutional) Power

> *A childlike Lacan-esque way to explain the hideous complexity of racism in formulaic terms.*

A classic example of *single-cause fallacy* (oversimplification). The inflammatory phrase was coined by Patricia Bidol in her 1970 book

---

[1353] Orovan, Mary, *Humanizing English* (1970)

[1354] Bornstein, Kate, and Caitlin Sullivan, *Nearly Roadkill* (High Risk Books, 1996)

[1355] 'UVM Introduces New Pronoun Policy', *The Vermont Cynic*, 15 Sept 2015

"Developing New Perspectives on Race: An Innovative Multi-media Social Studies Curriculum in Racism Awareness for the Secondary Level"[1356]. It was popularised eight years later in British "thought leader" Judith Katz's "White Awareness: Handbook for Anti-Racism Training"[1357].

(Education, 1970)

Privilege

> Like Marx's "Kapital", a clever method of intellectualising resentment towards Leninist/Maoist class enemies who are lucky or have advantages others don't. A form of secular Original Sin which can only be atoned for by public crawling.

Lenin's favourite idea. Rarely aimed at China's *Politbureau*, Castro, Islamic Mullahs, or anyone outside Western countries who share the same traits, the modern formulation of middle-class self-hatred is broadly attributed to feminist "scholar" Peggy McIntosh's 1988 paper, "White Privilege and Male Privilege: A Personal Account of Coming to See Correspondences Through Work in Women's Studies"[1358].

(Women's Studies, 1988)

[1356] Bidol, Patricia A., *Developing New Perspectives on Race: An Innovative Multi-Media Social Studies Curriculum in Racism Awareness for the Secondary Level* (New Perspectives on Race, 1972)

[1357] Katz, Judith H., *White Awareness* (University of Oklahoma Press, 2003)

[1358] McIntosh, Peggy, 'White Privilege and Male Privilege: A Personal Account of Coming to See Correspondences Through Work in Women's Studies', *Working Paper No. 189*, Wellesley College Center for Research on Women (1988)

Problematic

> *Everything, ever. A synonym people who want to sound intellectual™ use for "unwanted". Implies there might be some problems, but there is only ever one. For the same people.*

Get your science right: indefinite, in question, or unsettled.

Problematise

> *Whining.*

Marx had a fun, simple idea to ruin civilisation: criticise everything to death. In a letter written in September 1843 to Arnold Ruge, which was later published in the *Deutsch-Französische Jahrbücher* in 1844 as the essay *"Zur Kritik der Hegelschen Rechtsphilosophie. Einleitung."* ("For a Ruthless Criticism of Everything Existing")[1359].

In *"The History of Sexuality, Volume 2: The Use of Pleasure"*, Michel Foucault advocated a process by which certain phenomena which are not supposedly inherently problematic - such as paedophilia (which he should have been prosecuted for), in his own depraved mind - become "framed" as problems through *"societal discourse"* and *"power relations"*[1360].

(Sociology, 1985)

[1359] Marx, Karl, 'Zur Kritik der Hegelschen Rechtsphilosophie. Einleitung', *Deutsch-Französische Jahrbücher* (1844)

[1360] Foucault, Michel, *The History of Sexuality, Volume 2* (Vintage Books, 1985)

Profit Motive

> *The underlying pathology for the crime of capitalism.*

A detective attempts to uncover the motive of a criminal or villain. Ordinary people *without* bad intent respond to incentives as their *motivation*. The Marxist notion making a profit is a crime first emerged in an article about public utilities in the *Political Science Quarterly* a year before the *Russian Revolution*[1361]. It was later popularised by journalist Will Hutton in his 1996 book *"The State We're In"* as an individualistic "requirement" of capitalism[1362].

(Politics, 1916)

Progress

> *The distance between oneself and the edge of the moral cliff, determined by the extent to which one is increasingly free of moral constraints.*

Get your science right: movement towards an improved state.

Progressive-(ism)

> *When a cannibal uses a fork. Whether the thing you want to change has changed to your personal liking, e.g. the opinions of millions of people.*

[1361] Bauer, John, 'The Control of Return on Public Utility Investments', *Political Science Quarterly*, 31.2 (June 1916), pp. 260–88

[1362] Hutton, Will, *The State We're In*, (Vintage, 1996), p. 24

Progressivism is derived from *"progressism"*, both of which originated in the 1850s and relate to Kant's epoch of moving from barbarism to civilisation[1363]. Conveniently, a certain Karl Marx was influenced by Hegel's fascination with the idea society's progress related to its means' of production and annotated his highly flawed *"stages of history"*[1364] (which Engels called *"historical materialism"* in 1880[1365]). Progress, to Marx, was "evolving" from late capitalism to advanced communism, which is translated today as "moving forward" technologically.

(Political Science, 1850)

Pseud

An intellectually pretentious or affected person. Aka an "intellectual craze-monger" (Spectator).

In 1954, second editor of the British satirical magazine *"Private Eye"*, Richard Ingrams, wrote in *Salopian School Magazine*:

There is a tribe that in the world exists
Who might be called the pseudo-culturists...
He..Who quotes from Blake or from Professor Freud,
This man I label with the title 'Pseud'.[1366]

(Literature, 1954)

[1363] Nisbet, Robert A., *History of the Idea of Progress* (Transaction Publishers, 1980)

[1364] Marx, Karl, *A Contribution to the Critique of Political Economy*, (International Publishers, 1904)

[1365] Engels, Friedrich, *Socialism* (International Publishers, 1970)

[1366] Ingrams, Richard, *Salopian School Magazine* (1954)

Queer Theory

Foucault's sex dungeon legacy: a radically-politicised area of study of those who do not fit into traditional social definitions informed by science.

Science likes to study abnormalities; sociology likes to politicise them. Often attributed to lesbian Gayle Rubin[1367], star of documentary *"Blood-Sisters: Leather, Dykes and Sadomasochism"*[1368]. It's not capitalist and working class, it's *normal* vs *abnormal*.

This sociopathic "area of study" was coined by Foucault-loving Teresa de Lauretis, in a 1991 essay for *"Differences: A Journal of Feminist Cultural Studies"*, entitled *"Queer Theory: Lesbian and Gay Sexualities"*[1369][1370] Well documented in *"A Genealogy of Queer Theory"* (2000) by William Turner[1371].

"Queer theory" is infamous for its coded language supporting *"minor attracted persons"* (paedophiles) and child-adult sexual behaviour. It is variably referred to as *"alternate kinship"*[1372] or *"non-traditional family"*[1373].

[1367] Rubin, Gayle, 'Thinking Sex: Notes for a Radical Theory of the Politics of Sexuality', in *Pleasure and Danger: Exploring Female Sexuality*, ed. by Carole S. Vance (Routledge & Kegan Paul, 1984), pp. 267–319

[1368] Handelman, Michelle (dir.), *BloodSisters: Leather, Dykes and Sadomasochism* [documentary] (MM Anderson Productions, 1995)

[1369] de Lauretis, Teresa, 'Queer Theory: Lesbian and Gay Sexualities', *Differences: A Journal of Feminist Cultural Studies*, 3.2 (1991), iii–xviii

[1370] Wikipedia contributors, 'Teresa de Lauretis', *Wikipedia, The Free Encyclopedia* Professor of the *"History of Consciousness"* and *"feminist film theory"*.

[1371] Turner, William B., *A Genealogy of Queer Theory* (Temple University Press, 2000)

[1372] Butler, Judith, 'Is Kinship Always Already Heterosexual?', in *Out in Theory: The Emergence of Lesbian and Gay Anthropology*, ed. by Ellen Lewin (University of Illinois Press, 2002), pp. 14–30

[1373] Weston, Kath, *Families We Choose* (Columbia Uni. Press, 1991)

In one particularly disturbing paper, the grooming of children via *"drag"* (cross-dressing) shows[1374] has its purpose intimately outlined:

> *Drag Queen Story Hour provides a generative extension of queer pedagogy into the world of early childhood education. Drawing on the work of José Esteban Muñoz, the authors discuss five interrelated elements of DQSH that offer early childhood educators a way into a sense of queer imagination: play as praxis, aesthetic transformation, strategic defiance, destigmatization of shame, and embodied kinship.*
>
> *We offer that the kinship created by drag pedagogy might offer a way of thinking beyond both the cruel optimism (Berlant) and potential utopias of the horizon, to consider how alternate worlds are being made in the here and now.*[1375]

According to Kath Weston in 1991, *"embodied kinship"* means something like *"close, family-like connections with others, but in a way that goes beyond traditional family relationships"*. These "alternate worlds" and "potential utopias" appear to be ones where the statutory rape of children is possible and celebrated. One would not want to speculate what a "generative extension" is supposed to mean.

(Sociology, 1991)

[1374] Lindsay, James, 'Term of the Week: Drag Queen Story Hour', *New Discourses*, 27 February 2020

  Drag Queen Story Hour (DGSH) began in San Francisco, California, around 2015 with queer author Michelle Tea, who was at the time the outgoing Executive Director of the San Francisco literacy non-profit RADAR Productions. It was developed in conjunction with the incoming Executive Director Juli Delgado Lopera and Managing Director Virgie Tovar.

[1375] Keenan, Harper, and Lil Miss Hot Mess, 'Drag Pedagogy: The Playful Practice of Queer Imagination in Early Childhood', *Curriculum Inquiry*, 50.5 (2020), pp. 440–61

Quota

Magic Marxist bullet used to solve all problems of unequal distribution regardless of the context or outcome - which also conveniently makes politicians look like they are doing something.

Assigning portions or rations has been part of human history since the agricultural age[1376]. Quotas, conversely, are enforced in a planned/engineered system where a centralised authority is the sole owner of the means of production and mandates the minimum/maximum quantities of a producer's resources[1377].

The first large-scale experiment was the USSR's series of *Five-Year Plans*, starting in 1928[1378]. The first post-immigration racial quotas emerged after the 1964 *Civil Rights Act*[1379], and have flourished informally in US universities against Jews & Asians[1380]. Under a re-branding of "gender representation", they have been enforced within governance structures since 2003, but are illegal[1381].

(Political Science, 1928)

Racist

Anyone middle class and white, who you wish would stop talking.

At the turn of the twentieth century, the concept of dividing humans into

---

[1376] Fagan, Brian M., *The First Farmers* (Cambridge University Press, 2004)

[1377] Nove, Alec, *The Economics of Feasible Socialism Revisited* (HarperCollins, 1991)

[1378] Davies, R. W., *The Industrialisation of Soviet Russia* (Palgrave Macmillan, 1980)

[1379] Skrentny, John D., *The Ironies of Affirmative Action* (U. of Chicago Press, 1996)

[1380] Karabel, Jerome, *The Chosen* (Houghton Mifflin, 2005)

[1381] Krook, Mona Lena, *Quota Laws for Women in Politics* (Oxford Press, 2010)

sub-species - "races" - had taken hold in political circles as *"racialism"*[1382]. Richard Henry Pratt denounced "racism" in 1902, and it can be found in *La Libre Parole* around 1895 (Gaston Mery, *racisme*)[1383]. *"Germanists"* and *"racists"* had become a term for nationalist agitators in 1923[1384].

Despite the desperate attempts to unlink it from him, it was indeed arch-communist Leon Trotsky who popularised the parent word in his commentary of his ideological enemies, *"What is National Socialism?"* (*The Modern Thinker*, 1933)[1385].

Three years previously in *The Peculiarities of Russia's Development* of *The History of the Russian Revolution* (1930) he attacked *"Slavophilism"*, finishing with *"the old philosophy of the Slavophiles, but also the latest revelations of the "Racists [racistov]"*[1386]. After a surge in the Thirties, the terminology fell into comparative disuse until the sixties.

(*Political Rhetoric, 1895*)

Rape Culture

> *Rape being normal, accepted, and OK in our Western countries because women exist and we all hate them.*

Despite rape being generally punishable as a grave, morally repugnant criminal offence with an average twenty-year prison sentence (albeit with a dreadful two per cent conviction rate)[1387], and no evidence existing of a systemic belief or desire amongst half of the population to rape strangers

---

[1382] Banton, Michael, *Racial Theories* (Cambridge University Press, 1987)

[1383] Frederickson, George M., *Racism* (Princeton University Press, 2002)

[1384] Mosse, George L., *The Crisis of German Ideology* (Howard Fertig, 1999)

[1385] Trotsky, Leon, 'What Is National Socialism?', *The Modern Thinker* (1933)

[1386] Trotsky, Leon, 'The Peculiarities of Russia's Development', in *The History of the Russian Revolution* (1930)

[1387] RAINN, 'The Criminal Justice System: Statistics' (n.d.)

or relatives due to being born male, the idea originated Noreen Connell's *"Rape: The First Sourcebook for Women by New York Radical Feminists"* from the content of the 1971 *New York Radical Feminists' "Rape Conference"*[1388].

(Feminist Literature, 1974)

Reactionary

> *Someone who disagrees when an intellectual™ suggests what they think is a new idea, but is actually an old, bad idea.*

First used to describe an opponent of the *French Revolution* (*réactionnaire*)[1389], it became the Marxist slur for those opposed to communism from the name given to those who fought against the *Bolsheviks* in the 1917 *Russian Revolution*[1390]. In twentieth century politics, it became a term for anyone who opposed liberalism (communism, basically), from any side.

(Political Rhetoric, 1917)

Red Meat

> *The idea predation in nature leads to cancer in humans. Also, capitalism. White men.*

As far back as 1975, certain academic journals were attempting to prove consumption of animal products was linked to cancer. In 2015, the *International Agency for Research on Cancer* (IARC) - the cancer dept of the *World Health Organisation* (WHO) - reviewed eight hundred studies and

---

[1388] New York Radical Feminists, *Rape* (New York Radical Feminists, 1974)

[1389] Doyle, William, *The French Revolution* (Oxford Press, 2001)

[1390] Lenin, Vladimir I., *The State and Revolution* (International Publishers, 1964)

classified the consumption of red meat as *"Group 2A: probably carcinogenic to humans"*, specifically in relation to colon, pancreatic, and prostate cancer incidences[1391].

Four years later, researchers from *Dalhousie University* and *McMaster University* in Canada published a more detailed meta-analysis in the *Annal of Internal Medicine* which made it clear the conclusions were, in essence, completely politicised *nonsense*. Criticism focused on the staggeringly poor scholarship of practices such as tracking meat consumption in a large population without considering any other health factors (e.g. lifestyle), ignoring the lack of evidence in any of the studies, omitting studies of 1.6 million people dismissing any connection, and/or triggering cancer in sugar-fed rats without ascertaining any causal link - then simply blaming meat[1392].

(Medicine, 1975)

Redistribution

> *The idea an armed robber "redistributing" their "fair share" of other people's money from a bank vault is morally righteous if the bank has been keeping it for themselves as their property.*

Although it's largely an economic term (e.g. taxation) beginning with David Ricardo (*"On the Principles of Political Economy and Taxation"*, 1817)[1393] and John Stuart Mill's dad (John Mill), the concept is inexorably tied to Marx's design for socialism in *"Das Kapital"*[1394]. Even after the

---

[1391] International Agency for Research on Cancer, *Monographs on the Evaluation of Carcinogenic Risks to Humans: Volume 114* (World Health Organization, 2015)

[1392] Johnston, Bradley C., Zeraatkar, Dena, Han, Mehak A., Vernooij, Robin W., Valli, Claudio, El Dib, Regina, et al., 'Unprocessed Red Meat and Processed Meat Consumption' (2019)

[1393] Ricardo, David, *On the Principles of Political Economy and Taxation* (John Murray, 1817)

[1394] Marx, Karl, *Das Kapital: Critique of Political Economy* (1867)

mass murder of *dekulakisation*[1395], contemporary social scientists are still puzzled over why it doesn't work.

(Classical Economics, 1817)

Relationship

> *Any form of transaction with an animal, object, company, or brand. You don't own a phone; you are in a "relationship" with it like you are your pet and have an "experience" which conveys "intimacy".*

You're not a customer; you're part of the "family" in *"relationship marketing"*. Despite the enormous complexity of human relational structure and indicators, the idea of a company or corporation basing its marketing on long-term repetitive purchasing was broadly defined by Max Blackston's 1992 piece, *"Observations: Building Brand Equity by Managing the Brand's Relationships"* (Journal of Advertising Research)[1396].

(Business/Marketing, 1992)

Reparations

> *Free money for something you didn't suffer, from people who never wronged you. But not for anyone else.*

Historically speaking, reparations have almost always been used as punishment and humiliation, for example, towards Germany after the

---

[1395] Conquest, Robert, *The Harvest of Sorrow* (Oxford University Press, 1986)

[1396] Blackston, Max, 'Observations: Building Brand Equity by Managing the Brand's Relationships', *Journal of Advertising Research*, 32.3 (1992), 79–83

Great War[1397][1398]. The modern political claim regarding American slavery is predominantly from a 2000 article in *Harper's Magazine*, which estimated the amount due to be:

> *$97 trillion, based on 222,505,049 hours of forced labor between 1619 and 1865, regardless the United States wasn't a recognized independent country until after the Revolutionary War in 1787, compounded at 6% interest.*[1399]

(Politics, 1993)

Representation

> *Emphasised with special consideration and prominent placement in the media.*

To "re-present" something, or be "made present", presumes one would not be there otherwise; usually when the consequences would be significant. One must materialise a thing so it can be *present* where it should be. Legislators represent constituents who are not in the chamber; lawyers represent clients who are not trained in legal procedure; someone with power-of-attorney decides for someone in a coma.

The evolution of political agitation around this idea can be traced to *"The Concept of Representation"* (1967) by *Berkeley* professor Hanna Fenichel Pitkin[1400], *"critical race theory"* proponent Patricia Williams' rant in *"Metro Broadcasting, Inc. v. FCC: Regrouping in Singular Times"*

[1397] Henig, Ruth, *Versailles and After: 1919–1933*, 2nd edn (Routledge, 1995)

[1398] Keynes, John Maynard, *The Economic Consequences of the Peace* (Macmillan, 1920)

[1399] Hirt, Jack, 'Making the Case for Racial Reparations', *Harper's Magazine*, 301.1805 (November 2000), 37–46

[1400] Pitkin, Hanna F., *The Concept of Representation* (University of California Press, 1967)

(1990)[1401], and the formation of the *Gay and Lesbian Anti-Defamation League* (now the *Gay & Lesbian Alliance Against Defamation*, GLAAD) in 1985[1402].

Two per of any population self-report as same-sex-attracted[1403]; equitable "representation" of this demographic in a cast of ten characters in a film would formally equate to 0.2 (i.e. zero). There are 4.7 million Chinese people in the US[1404]; in a cast of a hundred, equitable demographic representation of the US population (360 million) would be one (1.4%). In a Chinese film, it would be one hundred.

Something added where it should not otherwise be is the act of *adulterating* or *defiling* it[1405]. Anne Boleyn was not black, therefore one cannot "make present" what did not exist in the past.

(Politics, 1967)

Reproductive Rights

> *The ability to engage in reproductive behaviour without reproducing, and remain sterile.*

In February 1978, foeticide provider *Planned Parenthood* opened a new headquarters in Washington, D.C. Sarah Brown, the president of the board of directors, announced, *"We have not attained the goal of reproductive freedom. The battle for reproductive rights is not yet won."*[1406]. Where the

---

[1401] Williams, Patricia J., 'Metro Broadcasting, Inc. v. FCC: Regrouping in Singular Times', *Harvard Law Review*, 104.2 (December 1990), 525–46

[1402] Gross, Larry P., *Up From Invisibility* (Columbia University Press, 2001)

[1403] Bailey, J. Michael, et al., 'Sexual Orientation, Controversy, and Science', *Psychological Science in the Public Interest*, 17.2 (2016), 45–101

[1404] 'Chinese Americans: A Survey Data Snapshot', *Pew Research Center*, 6 August 2024

[1405] 'Adulterate', *Oxford English Dictionary* (Oxford University Press, 2024)

[1406] Sauvé, Frances, 'Planned Parenthood Opens New Downtown Offices', *The Washington Post*, 15 February 1978

"right" to kill one's own offspring originates is somewhat of a mystery: it cannot be a *Natural* right derived from God or Nature, nor can it be a *Negative* right as no-one can prohibit either of those, or the government, from interfering.

(Business, 1978)

Rest In Power

> *Receive veneration and sainthood for a prominent role in militant activism.*

Although it might seem to have originated in the movements of the sixties, this odd phrase emerged in an artwork post to the *alt.graffiti* newsgroup as a tribute to a Californian graffiti artist killed in an armed robbery in 2000[1407]. In Oakland, which birthed the *Black Panthers* and the *Black Power* movement[1408].

(Internet, 2000)

Restorative Justice

> *Voluntarily providing your rapist with round two.*

As opposed to *retribution* (punishment), or *distribution* (aka treatment), "restoration" is the therapy couch-style idea victim and offender talk it out to "reconcile". The originator of this idea (*"creative restitution"*), which couldn't possibly go wrong, was American professor Albert Eglash. Inspired by *Alcoholics Anonymous,* he wrote about it in 1957 as *"creative restitution"* in the *Journal of Criminal Law, Criminology, and*

[1407] *alt.graffiti* newsgroup, 'Archived Messages' (2000)

[1408] Bloom, Joshua, Waldo E. Martin Jr., *Black Against Empire* (U. of California, 2013)

Police Science[1409], after his involvement with the *Mayor's Rehabilitation Committee on Skid Row Problems* in Detroit, and *The Commission on Children and Youth*.

Unsurprisingly, it has shown little to no improvement in recidivism whatsoever[1410].

(Criminology, 1957)

Right Wing / Far Right

> Anyone who is doubtful the communist utopia can be achieved or thinks it would be better not to break Western civilisation right now.

Related to the *French Revolution* (again), the subjective/relative phrase "far" was first discussed in Methodist publications, which described the "extreme left" as radical socialists, and the "far right" as reactionary parties. Apparently, it's all due to sexual repression, according to Wilhelm Reich in *"The Mass Psychology of Fascism"* (1933)[1411].

(Political Science, 1906)

Russian Bot

> Malevolent, demonic and invisible force stopping less enlightened ordinary people from realising the holy truth of Marxist social justice.

According to hard-left media outlets, ordinary people across the West

---

[1409] Eglash, Albert, 'Creative Restitution: A Broader Meaning for an Old Term', *Journal of Criminal Law, Criminology, and Police Science*, 48 (1957), 619–22

[1410] Fulham, Lindsay, Julie Blais, and Elizabeth A. Schultheis, 'The Effectiveness of Restorative Justice Programs: A Meta-Analysis of Recidivism and Other Relevant Outcomes', *Criminology & Criminal Justice*, OnlineFirst (2023)

[1411] Reich, Wilhelm, *The Mass Psychology of Fascism* (Farrar, Straus and Giroux, 1933)

– in their tens and hundreds of millions, and being too stupid to think for themselves – have been mass-brainwashed by a coordinated, secret psychological warfare army deployed by Vladimir Putin on a mission to buy exaggerated adverts on *Facebook* and other Internet comment sections.

This apparently is the cause of them supporting populist notions like *Brexit* or Donald Trump, rather than groupthink liberalism. The reasons they repetitively give when their puritan middle-class betters attempt to ask, – such as a) being endlessly insulted as racist, ignorant, or propagandised; b) the moderate centre-left ceasing to exist; c) disapproval of a loss of national identity/integrity; d) intense dislike of collectivist identity politics; e) endemic political nepotism and corruption; f) totalitarian smear campaigns, and so on[1412] – are nothing to do with it, and merely a symptom of their unenlightened worldview. Which, in turn, is a result of fifty hackers in a Russian data centre posting edgy memes on *Twitter*.

(Internet, 2016)

[1412] Howard, Philip N., and Bence Kollanyi, 'Bots, #StrongerIn, and #Brexit: Computational Propaganda During the UK-EU Referendum', *SSRN Electronic Journal* (2016)

STU

Safe Space

> The adult form of an infant playpen.

Despite a parallel between the "sacred circle" of paganism/witchcraft[1413], activist Moira Kenney claims in her 2001 book *"Mapping Gay L.A.: The Intersection of Place and Politics"* the idea originated in gay and lesbian bars during the sixties to evade sodomy laws[1414]. The women's movement of the same time sought to *"distance from men and patriarchal thought"* in order to promote "consciousness raising", according to Kathy Sarachild, a founder of pageant-disrupting *wimmin's lib* group the *New York Radical Women*[1415].

(*Feminist Literature, 1966*)

[1413] Cunningham, Scott, *Wicca: A Guide* (Llewellyn Publications, 1999)

[1414] Kenney, Moira, *Mapping Gay L.A* (Temple University Press, 2001)

[1415] Sarachild, Kathie, 'Consciousness-Raising: A Radical Weapon', in *Dear Sisters: Dispatches from the Women's Liberation Movement*, ed. by Carol Baxandall and Linda Gordon (Basic Books, 1978), pp. 145–50

Safety / Stay Safe

> *The most important thing in the whole world ever which has to come before anything else. Usually to prevent a lawsuit.*

A favourite of soccer moms and frightened dads everywhere since the eighties, but it's impossible to track the origin of safetyism in any reliable way[1416].

In *"The Coddling of the American Mind: How Good Intentions and Bad Ideas Are Setting Up a Generation for Failure"* (2018)[1417], Greg Lukianoff and Jonathan Haidt highlight Australian psychologist Nick Haslam's notion of *"concept creep"*, where, since the eighties, key concepts in clinical and social psychology, including abuse, bullying, trauma and prejudice, have expanded both "downward" and "outward" to apply to less severe circumstances and to take in novel phenomena[1418].

The rise of *"Health & Safety"* (HSE) regulation can be attributed to the US *Occupational Safety and Health Act 1970*[1419] and the *UK Health and Safety at Work etc. Act 1974*[1420].

(Psychology, 1980s)

[1416] Campbell, Bradley, Jason Manning, *The Rise of Victimhood Culture:* (Palgrave Macmillan, 2018)

[1417] Lukianoff, Greg, Jonathan Haidt, *The Coddling of the American Mind* (Penguin, 2018)

[1418] Haslam, Nick, 'Concept Creep: Psychology's Expanding Concepts of Harm and Pathology', *Psychological Inquiry*, 27.1 (2016), 1–17

[1419] *Occupational Safety and Health Act of 1970*, Pub. L. No. 91-596 (1970)

[1420] *Health and Safety at Work etc. Act 1974*, c. 37

Save The Planet

> What happens when you feed a generation of bipedal apes superhero movies, i Phones, and Al Gore TED Talks.

No-one could have articulated the absurdity of human conceit more hilariously than comic George Carlin in his 1992 HBO Special *"Jammin In New York"*[1421] - indicating how long this kind of messianic rhetoric has been going on. Apocalyptic literature has existed for thousands of years and the apocalyptic film genre since the fifties, but the "religious" aspect can be traced to not only the *"Y2K bug"* but the (often secular) umbrella belief structure of *millenarianism*[1422].

Henri Desroche observed in *"Dieux d'hommes. Dictionnaire des messianismes et millénarismes de l'ère chrétienne"* (1969) adherents shared a tripartite ideology of increasing oppression, "resistance" to it, and a resulting Utopian finality of liberation[1423] - which we have all heard before.

This latest round was almost undoubtedly triggered by the UN *Intergovernmental Panel on Climate Change* (IPCC) claim in its 2018 report regarding the number of years we have left until the carbon budget is used up for 1.5°C of warming (approximately twelve)[1424]. Letters signed by "hundreds of scientists" turned out to be mostly... social scientists, such as psychotherapists and gender studies professors.

We were to be in dire famine by 1975 (*Salt Lake Tribune*, November 17, 1967), disappeared in a cloud of blue steam by 1989 (*New York Times*, August 10 1969), in an ice age by 2000 (*Boston Globe*, April 16, 1970), food

---

[1421] Carlin, George, *Jammin' in New York* [TV special], (HBO, 1992)

[1422] Cohn, Norman, *The Pursuit of the Millennium* (Oxford University Press, 1957)

[1423] Desroche, Henri, *Dieux d'Hommes* (Gallimard, 1969)

[1424] IPCC, *Global Warming of 1.5°C: An IPCC Special Report on the Impacts of Global Warming of 1.5°C Above Pre-Industrial Levels* (2018)

rationing by 1980 (*Redlands Daily Facts*, October 6, 1970), yet another ice age (*Washington Post,* July 9, 1971, *NOAA*, October 2015, *Guardian*, January 29, 1974, *TIME,* June 24, 1974), all life was in peril (*NASA*), endless cooling (*New York Times Book Review,* July 18, 1976), days over 90F (1988), 30ft underwater in 2008 (*Agence France Press*, September 26, 1988), obliterated by rising seas by 2000 (*Associated Press,* June 30, 1989), famine again in 2010 (*The Independent,* March 20, 2000), Siberian climate by 2020 (*Guardian,* February 21, 2004), ice-free arctic by 2013 and 2018 (Al Gore, *Associated Press,* June 24, 2008), had only 8 years to save the world (Prince Charles, 2009), were 50 days from death (*Independent*: October 20, 2009), were 500 days before 'climate chaos' (French Foreign Minister, 2014), and in 1970 *"Earth Day"* issue of *The Progressive* magazine, four billion people would perish in the *"Great Die-Off"*[1425].

By far the most spectacular however, was Al Gore's infamous prediction Earth *"would reach a point of no return within 10 years"* - in 2006[1426].

(*Political Rhetoric, 1970*)

(The) Science

> *A Gnostic religious orthodoxy one must maintain faith in and political allegiance to. Something followed unquestionably by politicians, written down as scripture in journals, and decided by majority political opinion.*

Science isn't something to "follow", or what leaders are there to do. Nor is a faith system you "believe" in[1427]. Nor is it decided by consensus,

---

[1425] Bennett, Christine, 'Doomsday Addiction: Celebrating 50 Years of Failed Climate Predictions', *Farm Journal (AgWeb)*, 5 May 2023

[1426] Gore, Al, *An Inconvenient Truth* (Rodale Books, 2006)

[1427] Sagan, Carl, *The Demon-Haunted World* (Random House, 1996)

majority, political dogma etc (*Lysenkoism*)[1428]. The notion science should be our worldview, or we should follow scientists as priests, is *scientism* (F. A. Hayek)[1429].

The use of the word "follow" is used in philosophy and social "science", not the actual sciences. Although it's impossible to extract the first usage of this lamentable slogan, it appears to have hugely increased in UK political circles around 2004, specifically around the debate over *"climate change"*.

(*Political Rhetoric, 2004*)

Scientific Racism

A convenient slur for inconvenient facts.

When the humanities get upset, they get *very* upset indeed. Science, and its production of facts, is something which upsets them immeasurably. This absurd phrase is used, unironically, by people whose entire lives have been dedicated to misusing *"social science"* for political gain (and lacked the aptitude for studying the natural sciences), to accuse scientists of misusing science to justify racism and eugenics[1430][1431]. Typically, in reference to relativistic arguments promoting *"multiculturalism."*

They usually claim "science" supports them, citing the opinions of humanities' professors (anthropologists, mainly) in social science

---

[1428] Medvedev, Zhores A., *The Rise and Fall of T. D. Lysenko* (Columbia Press, 1969)

[1429] Hayek, Friedrich A., *The Counter-Revolution of Science* (Free Press, 1952)

[1430] Kenyon-Flatt, Brittany, 'How Race Was Made: The Origin of Scientific Taxonomy and Its Legacy', *Sapiens*, 19 March 2021

[1431] Saini, Angela, *Superior* (Beacon Press, 2019)

journals[1432][1433]. One 1994 book in particular, *"The Bell Curve: Intelligence and Class Structure in American Life"* by psychologist Richard J. Herrnstein and political scientist Charles Murray[1434], tends to receive more vitriol than others because of its unfortunate data correlating race with IQ.

At the turn of the twentieth century, there was a legitimate scientific debate over *Homo sapiens'* genealogical origins. *Monogenism* posited humans descended from a single line; *polygenism* posited our variations were evidence we emerged from different ones[1435]. After Darwin's discoveries, scientists were keen to understand if humankind could be divided into a taxonomy of heterogeneous sub-species[1436].

These ideas of *"biological essentialism"* were opposed by "blank slate" idealists such as communist Leon Trotsky[1437] (who termed it *"racistov"*) and anthropologist Frank Boaz (proponent of *"cultural relativism"*, with a strong interest as he was Jewish during the Interwar period)[1438]. They were also abused by the Nazis.

Racism is variously attributed to the idea of *polygenism* itself, French zoologist Georges Cuvier[1439], or the taxonomy system in biology created by Swedish physician Carl Linnaeus in his classic work *"Systema Naturae"*

[1432] Gould, Stephen Jay, *The Mismeasure of Man* (W. W. Norton and Co., 1981)
   Note: *Gould admitted using fraudulent data in his work to pursue political ends.*

[1433] Kurtz, Paul, 'Can the Sciences Help Us to Make Wise Ethical Judgments?', *Skeptical Inquirer*, September 2004

[1434] Herrnstein, Richard J., and Charles Murray, *The Bell Curve* (Free Press, 1994)

[1435] Livingstone, David N., 'The Preadamite Theory and the Marriage of Science and Religion', *Transactions of the American Philosophical Society*, 82.3 (1992), 1–81

[1436] Stocking, George W., 'The Turn-of-the-Century Concept of Race', *Modernism/Modernity*, 1.1 (1994)

[1437] Trotsky, Leon, 'What Is National Socialism?', *The Modern Thinker* (1933)

[1438] Moore, Jerry D., 'Franz Boas: Culture in Context', in *Visions of Culture: An Introduction to Anthropological Theories and Theorists* (Altamira, 2009)

[1439] Cuvier, Georges, *Le Règne Animal Distribué d'Après son Organisation, pour Servir de Base à l'Histoire Naturelle des Animaux et d'Introduction à l'Anatomie Comparée* (Deterville, 1817)

(1767)[1440]. The dispute is simply whether anthropology is scientific or not. *Spoiler: it's not.*

The actual term *"scientific racism"* was first used in Peter Viereck's 1941 book *"Metapolitics: From Wagner and the German Romantics to Hitler"*[1441] in regards to Weimar eugenicist Hans F.K Günther, but popped up again during the post-civil rights apartheid years in the American Quarterly[1442].

(Anthropology, 1919)

Self Care

Eating on the sofa in your pajamas.

Taking care of oneself is an important medical concept with a long historical precedent[1443]. However, its usage within the realm of "mental health" coincided with the broader inflation of "trauma" in self-help circles to describe sad things, such as *"Beyond Codependency: And Getting Better All the Time"* by Melody Beattie[1444], and *"Compassion Fatigue: Coping with Secondary Traumatic Stress Disorder in Those Who Treat the Traumatized"* by Charles Figley[1445]. The downward spiral into fragility was documented in in Frank Furedi's 2004 book *"Therapy Culture: Cultivating Vulnerability in an Uncertain Age."*[1446]

(Psychology, 1989)

[1440] Linnaeus, Carl, *Systema Naturae*, 12th edn (Laurentii Salvii, 1767)

[1441] Viereck, Peter, *Metapolitics* (1941),

[1442] Karcher, Carolyn L., 'Melville's "The 'Gees": A Forgotten Satire on Scientific Racism', *American Quarterly*, 27.4 (October 1975), 421–442

[1443] Orem, Dorothea E., *Nursing: Concepts of Practice* (McGraw-Hill, 1980)

[1444] Beattie, Melody, *Beyond Codependency* (Harper & Row, 1989)

[1445] Figley, Charles R., *Compassion Fatigue* (Brunner/Mazel, 1995)

[1446] Furedi, Frank, *Therapy Culture* (Routledge, 2004)

Self Esteem

> The notion of admiring yourself for the perfect little thing you are. What children should be made of.

In the mid-sixties, social psychologist Morris Rosenberg attempted to describe the idea of *"conceiving the self"*; naming it *"'self-esteem"* (self-admiration) through his book *"Society And The Adolescent Self-image"*. He developed the *Rosenberg Self-Esteem Scale* to "measure" it[1447].

To *esteem* is to *"to regard highly or favourably; regard with respect or admiration"*. In 1996, Roy Baumeister demonstrated psychopaths are group who are most prevalent in this area of self-perception[1448].

(Psychology, 1965)

Sensitivity Reader

> Unmarried forty-something victim-for-hire with large social science degree debt, no husband to restrain them, and no career prospects, employed by cowards as a Maoist censor.

In 1818, English physician Thomas Bowdler expurgated Shakespeare's plays with his sister Henrietta, so they were "suitable" for women and children, and published them as *"The Family Shakespeare"*[1449]. In 2015, a row broke out about the "lack of diversity" in *Young Adult Fiction* ("YA") sub-genre of the female-dominated publishing industry via the

---

[1447] Rosenberg, Morris, *Society and the Adolescent Self-Image* (Princeton Press, 1965)

[1448] Baumeister, R. F., Smart, L., & Boden, J. M., 'Relation of threatened egotism to violence and aggression: The dark side of high self-esteem', *Psychological Review*, 103.1 (1996), 5-33

[1449] Wheeler, Kip, 'Censorship and Bowdlerization', Carson-Newman University

completely organic *"We Need Diverse Books"* movement[1450] and the *#OwnVoices* hashtag[1451] started by disability activist author Corinne Duyvis.

Arguably the first victim of this absurd cancellation-insurance/protection scheme was Keira Drake's novel, *"The Continent",* prompting her publisher, *Harlequin Teen,* to apologise and delay the release while they hired two censors to review the copy for "harmful stereotypes" of "reddish-brown skin" and "painted faces"[1452].

As author Larry Correia, self-described *"Writer, Merchant of Death (retired), Firearms Instructor, Accountant.,"* and awesome potential drinking buddy, puts it:

> *A Sensitivity Reader is usually some expert on Intersectional Feminism or Cismale Gendernormative Fascism or some other made up goofiness who a publisher brings in to look for anything "problematic" in a manuscript. And since basically everything is problematic to somebody they won't be happy until they suck all the joy out of the universe. It is basically a new con-job racket some worthless scumbags have come up with to extort money from gullible writers, because there aren't a lot of good ways to make a living with a Gender Studies degree.*[1453]

(Publishing, 2015)

[1450] We Need Diverse Books, 'About Us', *We Need Diverse Books*

[1451] Duyvis, Corinne, '#OwnVoices Hashtag', Twitter, 2015

[1452] Harlequin Teen, 'Publisher Apologizes, Delays Keira Drake's *The Continent*', 2016

[1453] Correia, Larry, '"Sensitivity Readers" Are Bullshit, and You Are a Sucker If You Believe Them', *Monster Hunter Nation*, 1 March 2019

Sex Work(er)

Definitely not a prostitute. A word an intellectual™ uses to describe an entrepreneur sole trader running their own business of charging money in exchange for sex, or working to obtain cash through sex in person or videotape.

Author of *"Unrepentant Whore"* (2004), activist Carol Leigh[1454] suggested at the 1979 *Women Against Violence in Pornography and Media Conference* we all just call it the *"Sex Use Industry"*[1455], before her Marxian call *"Sex Workers Unite!"* (*"a vindication of the rights of whores"*) in 1984[1456].

By 1987, it was *"Sex Work: Writings By Women In The Sex Industry"* by Frederique Delacoste and Priscilla Alexander[1457].

(Women's Studies, 1979)

Sexism

Marxism for women. A way to get some of that civil rights movement limelight being stolen by black people demanding suffrage.

First a normal semi-scientific term exemplified as *"belonging to a particular sex"*, this buzzword became a new fashionable-to-hate kind of racism through *Director of Special Programs* at *Franklin and Marshall College*, Pauline Leet, around 1965 at a Student-Faculty forum[1458]. The *Morning Herald* reported Hollywood compared the idea to communism, during

---

[1454] Leigh, Carol, *Unrepentant Whore* (Last Gasp, 2004)

[1455] Dworkin, Andrea, *Pornography* (Perigee Books, 1981)

[1456] Pheterson, Gail, *A Vindication of the Rights of Whores* (Seal Press, 1989)

[1457] Delacoste, Frederique, and Priscilla Alexander, eds., *Sex Work* (Cleis Press, 1987)

[1458] Bird, Caroline, *The Case Against College* (David McKay Company, 1975)

the Civil Rights era when other people were getting all the attention.

It was repeated around 1968 in a speech by feminist author Caroline Bird to the *Anglican Church*[1459].

(*Women's Studies, 1965*)

Sexual Liberation

> *Unlimited freedom to imitate bonobos and chimpanzees without the crushing oppression of morality.*

The father of the *Sexual Revolution* is undoubtedly Freud and his theories of female sexual repression[1460]. Two other factors are highly prominent: Kinsey's fraudulent research in the forties[1461], and the invention of the contraceptive pill in 1960[1462]. Marcuse also linked libido to capitalism in *"Eros & Civilisation"*[1463].

Germaine Greer's 1970 polemic *"The Female Eunuch,"* argued the nuclear family represses women sexually and turns them into "eunuchs"[1464]. She later went on to reverse a lot of her stance by claiming rape wasn't as bad as murder[1465] and was banned by her own proteges for denouncing "transgender" religion[1466].

(*Feminist Literature, 1970*)

[1459] Bird, Caroline, *Born Female* (David McKay Company, 1968

[1460] Freud, Sigmund, *Three Essays on the Theory of Sexuality* (c.1905)

[1461] Kinsey, Alfred C., Wardell B. Pomeroy, Clyde E. Martin, *Sexual Behavior in the Human Male* (W. B. Saunders, 1948)

[1462] Marks, Lara V., *Sexual Chemistry* (Yale University Press, 2010)

[1463] Marcuse, Herbert, *Eros and Civilization* (Beacon Press, 1955)

[1464] Greer, Germaine, *The Female Eunuch* (MacGibbon & Kee, 1970)

[1465] Greer, Germaine, *On Rape* (Melbourne University Press, 2015)

[1466] *BBC News*, 'Calls to Ban Germaine Greer Lecture Over Trans Comments', *BBC News*, 23 October 2015

Shaming

A lost art. The suffix which can be added to any word in order to immediately stigmatise the person stigmatising you.

Shaming, or public humiliation, probably goes back to neanderthal times; for example, the barbaric twelfth century practice of *Tarring & Feathering* continued even into the *First World War*[1467]. It was extensively used during "struggle sessions" in Mao's communist utopia[1468].

The continually lengthening list of things being shamed - *body, fat, mom, slut, age, pill, thin/skinny* - almost certainly have their root in "victim-shaming", which in turn is derived from the politicised concept of *"victim-blaming"* from the same-titled 1971 book by psychologist William Ryan[1469].

However, in 1947, the language was in full bloom by a usual suspect, *Frankfurt School* critical theory sociologist Theodor Adorno, who described *"blaming the victim"* as a "fascist" characteristic in *"The Authoritarian Personality"* (1950)[1470]. The most comprehensive account to date is arguably Jon Ronson's 2015 book *"So You've Been Publicly Shamed"*[1471].

(Sociology, 1947)

[1467] Spear, Jennifer, 'The History of Tarring and Feathering', *Journal of Historical Research*, 45.1 (2018)

[1468] Schoenhals, Michael, *Doing Things with Words in Chinese Politics* (University of California Press, 1992)

[1469] Ryan, William, *Blaming the Victim* (Pantheon Books, 1971)

[1470] Adorno, Theodor W., Else Frenkel-Brunswik, Daniel Levinson, and Nevitt Sanford, *The Authoritarian Personality* (Harper & Brothers, 1950)

[1471] Ronson, Jon, *So You've Been Publicly Shamed* (Riverhead Books, 2015)

Sharing Economy

> Rentals.

In 1978, Marcus Felson and Joe L. Spaeth discussed the *"economy of sharing"* in their paper *"Community Structure and Collaborative Consumption"*[1472]. In 2004, Yochai Benkler authored a paper in the *Yale Law Review* about *"commons-based peer production"* titled *"Sharing Nicely: On Shareable Goods and the Emergence of Sharing as a Modality of Economic Production"*. Both of which are something to do with renaming the notion of "renting" as "sharing"[1473], which has absolutely nothing to do with, ahem, something Karl Marx advocated a century earlier or *kommunalkas* (communal living spaces) in the USSR[1474].

(Behavioural Science, 1978)

Shill

> What ordinary people - who don't agree with your extremist ideology - do for your enemies.

Get your history right: a swindler's accomplice.

(Sport, 1916)

[1472] Felson, Marcus, and Joe L. Spaeth, 'Community Structure and Collaborative Consumption: A Routine Activity Approach', *American Behavioral Scientist*, 21.4 (1978), 614–24

[1473] Benkler, Yochai, 'Sharing Nicely: On Shareable Goods and the Emergence of Sharing as a Modality of Economic Production', *Yale Law Journal*, 114.2 (2004), 273–358

[1474] Boym, Svetlana, *Common Places* (Harvard University Press, 1994)

Snowflake

Pussy.

Derived from self-esteem talk of being a *"special unique snowflake"* from a line in the excellent 1999 movie *"Fight Club"*[1475], but widely popularised as a pejorative term for *"Generation Snowflake"* millennials in ABC's sitcom *"Last Man Standing"*[1476].

In Clare Fox's 2017 book *"I Find That Offensive"* she blames:

> *official multiculturalism's relativistic conflation of tolerance with positive "recognition," narcissistic identity politics, and finally therapeutic educational interventions such as anti-bullying campaigns.*[1477]

(Film, 1999)

Social Anxiety

Shyness.

In 1968, the *DSM-II (Diagnostic and Statistical Manual of Mental Disorders, 2nd Edition)* briefly mentioned the state of *"phobic neurosis"*[1478]. In 1980,

---

[1475] Fincher, David (dir.), *Fight Club* [Film] (20th Century Fox, 1999)

[1476] ABC, *Last Man Standing* [Television series] (ABC Studios, 2016)

[1477] Fox, Claire, *I Find That Offensive!* (Biteback Publishing, 2016)

[1478] American Psychiatric Association, *Diagnostic and Statistical Manual of Mental Disorders* (2nd edn) (Washington, DC: American Psychiatric Association, 1968)

the *DSM-III* introduced *"social phobia"* as a formal diagnosis[1479]. In 1994, the *DSM-IV* renamed *"social phobia"* to *"Social Anxiety Disorder"* (SAD)[1480]. Treatment: lots of medications manufactured by *Big Pharma* which cost a lot of money.

(Psychiatry, 1980)

Social Construct

> *Something society made up all by itself which can be changed and engineered by re-programming bad people to think "correctly".*

Everything is a "construct" now, apparently. Otherwise known as nurture or conditioning, but neither of those sound intellectual™ for things deriving from Freud and Piaget, like *"social constructivism"*[1481]. Borrowed from the economics term "fictional entities", the discredited field of *"phenomenology"*, and *"personal construct theory"* (psychoanalysis)[1482], sociologists Peter Berger and Thomas Luckmann attempted a disastrous response to the theory of *"signs"* in a 1966 book *"The Social Construction of Reality"*[1483]. By 1982, Evelyn Kallen had translated it into law with *"Ethnicity and human rights in Canada"*[1484].

(Sociology, 1966)

[1479] American Psychiatric Association, *Diagnostic and Statistical Manual of Mental Disorders*, 3rd edn (Washington, DC: American Psychiatric Association, 1980)

[1480] American Psychiatric Association. (1994). *Diagnostic and Statistical Manual of Mental Disorders (4th ed.)*. Washington, DC: APA.

[1481] Gergen, Kenneth J., 'The Social Constructionist Movement in Modern Psychology', *American Psychologist*, 40.3 (1985), 266–75

[1482] Kelly, George A., *The Psychology of Personal Constructs* (W. W. Norton, 1955)

[1483] Berger, Peter, Thomas Luckmann, *The Social Construction of Reality* (Anchor Books, 1966)

[1484] Kallen, Evelyn, *Ethnicity and Human Rights in Canada* (Butterworths, 1982)

Social Contract

> *An invisible piece of paper you didn't sign, which you will be imprisoned for violating.*

In classical terms, the "social contract" is a left-wing *Enlightenment* idea individuals surrender rights and freedoms to the government in exchange for protection and order from the anarchic *State of Nature* (*"solitary, poor, nasty, brutish, and short."*)[1485]. It was posited in 1762 by the *"Father of the French Revolution"*, Jean-Jacques Rousseau, in his book *"Du "Contrat social ou Principes du droit politique"* (*"On the Social Contract; or, Principles of Political Right"*), as a response to Thomas Hobbes[1486]. The most vocal opponent of his tyrannical ideas was his friend David Hume, who opposed the *Whigs* proposing the same notion, and argued government should rest on the *consent of the governed*, not an imaginary hypothetical "contract"[1487].

(Philosophy, 1762)

Social Emotional Learning

> *A program to ensure children are entirely incapable of functioning in a world where communism has not yet been realised.*

In 1966, Dr Albert J. Solnit, *"a pediatrician, a psychoanalyst, and a social*

[1485] Hobbes, Thomas, *Leviathan or The Matter, Forme and Power of a Common-Wealth Ecclesiasticall and Civil* (Andrew Crooke, 1651)

[1486] Rousseau, Jean-Jacques, *Du Contrat Social ou Principes du Droit Politique (On the Social Contract; or, Principles of Political Right)* (Marc Michel Rey, 1762)

[1487] Hume, David, *Essays, Moral, Political, and Literary* (London: A. Millar, 1748)

activist" was hired to run the *Child Study Center* at *Yale Medical School*[1488]. Two years later, Dr James Comer created the *Comer Development School* with programs to intervene in broken schools with bad students, which provided excellent results[1489]. These achievements were entirely soiled via the paper *"Transformative Social and Emotional Learning (SEL): Toward SEL in Service of Educational Equity and Excellence"* finally published in 2019[1490], by the *Collaborative for Academic, Social, and Emotional Learning* (CASEL) after they were encased in law via the *Every Student Succeeds Act* (ESSA) of 2015[1491].

Bizarrely, *CASEL* emerged from the *Fetzer Institute*, which was set up by radio magnate John Fetzer[1492] to pursue his own obsession with the occultist teachings of lunatic theosophist Alice Bailey and her mind-bending ideas on *New Age* education[1493][1494].

(Education, 2019)

Social Media Consultant

Quarter-aged millennial female paid to sit on Facebook all day.

In the epic battle to come up with the most meaningless job role, social media is a heavyweight gorilla with a seemingly endless energy for ever-

---

[1488] Solnit, Albert J., 'Reflections on the Yale Child Study Center', *Journal of the American Academy of Child Psychiatry*, 25.3 (1986), 344–49

[1489] Comer, James P., 'Educating Poor Minority Children', *Scientific American*, 259.5 (1988)

[1490] Jagers, Robert J., Deborah Rivas-Drake, and Briana Williams, 'Transformative Social and Emotional Learning (SEL): Toward SEL in Service of Educational Equity and Excellence', *Educational Psychologist*, 54.3 (2019), 162–84

[1491] *Every Student Succeeds Act*, Pub. L. No. 114-95, 129 Stat. 1802 (2015)

[1492] Fetzer, James E., *The Search for the Soul* (Fetzer Institute, 1988)

[1493] Prophecy, Claude, *The Esoteric Philosophy of Alice A. Bailey* (Lucis Trust, 1986)

[1494] Bailey, Alice A., *Education in the New Age* (Lucis Publishing Company, 1954)

uglier word salad. Few media sectors have ever made so much money by actually telling people they are so full of it. As described effectively in *"Social Media Is Bullshit"* by social media expert Brandon J. Mendelson[1495] or *"No Bullshit Social Media"* by social media "star" Jason Falls[1496].

(Internet, 2007)

Sexual Orientation, Gender Identity, and Expression (SOGIE)

How your magic gender-soul woo-woos your bits.

A bit too long-winded to take off, and a little too close to "soggy", this LGBTQIA+ upgrade term for the sexually disturbed was actually *lengthened* to the absurd *"Sexual Orientation, Gender Identity and Expression, and Sex Characteristics"* (SOGIESC) by the *European Union*. Ultimately, this insanity traces back to the 2006 *Yogyakarta Principles on the Application of International Human Rights Law in Relation to Sexual Orientation and Gender Identity* legal framework[1497].

By 2010, it was widely adopted by the *United Nations Development Programme* (UNDP), *United Nations High Commissioner for Refugees* (UNHCR), and the *Association of Southeast Asian Nations* (ASEAN). In 2022, the Philippines' *14th Congress* passed the *SOGIE Equality Bill*[1498].

(Law, 2006)

[1495] Mendelson, Brian J., *Social Media Is Bullshit* (St. Martin's Press, 2012)

[1496] Falls, Jason, and Erik Deckers, *No Bullshit Social Media* (Que Publishing, 2011)

[1497] International Commission of Jurists and International Service for Human Rights, *Yogyakarta Principles: Principles on the Application of International Human Rights Law in Relation to Sexual Orientation and Gender Identity* (International Commission of Jurists, 2007)

[1498] *Senate Bill No. 11*, 'An Act Prohibiting Discrimination on the Basis of Sexual Orientation and Gender Identity and Providing Penalties Therefor (Anti-Gender Discrimination Act)', Republic of the Philippines, 30 June 2007

Solidarity

> *Socialist jargon people who want to sound intellectual™ use for "all us oppressed people".*

The concept was introduced into French Law at the turn of the nineteenth century[1499]. Since then, it has adopted multiple meanings (most notably a synonym for "emotional support"), but is traditionally a coded dog whistle for extreme trade unionists to assemble in preparation for *The Revolution*.

(Law, 1804)

Soul Tie

> *Lingering nostalgia for the ex-boyfriend you cheated on.*

Often touted by dodgy charismatic Christian churches (particularly the *Deliverance Ministries movement*) based on the "one-flesh" doctrine and *1 Samuel 18:1* (*"the soul of Jonathan was knit with the soul of David"*), the anti-biblical origin of this pagan idea is in two books from the crazy eighties. The first, *"Soul Ties"*, by Frank Hammond in 1988[1500], and the second, *"The Bondage Breaker"*, by Neil T. Anderson in 1990[1501].

See: sacred bonds (paganism), karmic bonds (Buddhism), etc.

(Self-help, 1988)

[1499] Elster, Jon, *The Cement of Society* (Cambridge University Press, 1989)

[1500] Hammond, Frank, *Soul Ties* (Impact Christian Books, Inc., 1988)

[1501] Anderson, Neil T., *The Bondage Breaker* (Harvest House Publishers, 1990)

Speak To

> A phrase people who want to sound intellectual™ use for "address".

I will speak to that later. This event *speaks to* the need for clarity. Can you *speak to that?* This odious, sermonising, and idiomatic phrasing has a four-hundred-year-old history from Parliament and the pulpit, but took on ubiquity in the early 2000s. It only has one purpose: to elevate the speaker in the eyes of the listener.

Spectrum

> Fashionable way to describe something which has variations similar to a colour chart despite there being no objective evidence it exists. Makes you sound "scientific" and intellectual™ if you just want to say "continuum", "range", or "scale".

The electromagnetic spectrum quantitatively measures frequencies of light, radio/audio, and other phenomena[1502]. Kinsey's research into sexual behaviour in 1948[1503] led to sociologists misappropriating *"spectrums"* of human sexuality (1980, Michael Storm *"EROS scale"*[1504]) and *"gender identity"*[1505].

(Psychology, 1948)

[1502] Halliday, David, Robert Resnick, Jearl Walker, *Fundamentals of Physics* (Wiley, 2013)

[1503] Kinsey, Alfred C., Wardell B. Pomeroy, and Clyde E. Martin, *Sexual Behavior in the Human Male* (W. B. Saunders, 1948)

[1504] Storm, Michael, 'The Development of the EROS Scale: A Measure of Erotic Orientation', *Journal of Homosexuality*, 5.1–2 (1980), 165–76

[1505] Fausto-Sterling, Anne, *Sex/Gender* (Routledge, 2012)

Spirit Murder

> Two women-of-a-certain-age's adventures into exotic animist mysticism.

Predominantly conceived by two Shamanic "professors" - lawyer Patricia Williams (author of *"Diary of a Mad Law Professor"*)[1506] and exam abolitionist Bettina Love - this preposterous animism was somehow published as an article (*"Spirit-Murdering the Messenger: The Discourse of Fingerpointing as the Law's Response to Racism"*, 1987) in the *University of Miami Law Review*[1507] and later in Love's risible *"We Want to Do More Than Survive"* (2020)[1508].

(Law, 1987)

Spiritual, Not Religious

> Vacuous, pretentious narcissist who sometimes feels a bit woo-woo. AKA, a Gnostic.

So achingly fashionable it has its own acronyms (SBNR, SBNA, or *"Spiritual but not affiliated"*)[1509]. The idea is so broad is impossible to attribute to one book or paper, but is more in line with the *New Age* (of *Aquarius*) Movement[1510] which emerged after the Beatles' popularisation

---

[1506] Williams, Patricia J., *The Alchemy of Race and Rights* (Harvard University Press, 1997)

[1507] Williams, Patricia J., 'Spirit-Murdering the Messenger: The Discourse of Fingerpointing as the Law's Response to Racism', *University of Miami Law Review*, 42.1 (1987), 127–57

[1508] Love, Bettina L., *We Want to Do More Than Survive* (Beacon Press, 2019)

[1509] Fuller, Robert C., *Spiritual, but Not Religious* (Oxford University Press, 2001)

[1510] Melton, J. Gordon, *New Age Encyclopedia* (Gale Research, 1992)

of Hinduism around the time of *Woodstock* and the creation of the *Esalen Institute* in 1962 to promote the *"Human Potential Movement"*[1511]. Most recently canonised by Sven Erlandson's 2000 book of the same name[1512].

(*Unknown, 1969*)

Stakeholder

What a CEO is until a Communist politburo decides they're not.

The nomenclature of a "stakeholder" emerged at the *Stanford Research Institute* in 1963 (*"The Strategic Plan", LRPS report no. 168*)[1513]. The modern usage of the term refers to Klaus Schwab's 1971 non-seller *"Modern Enterprise Management in Mechanical Engineering"*[1514] which ultimately became his unreadable 2021 disaster *"Stakeholder Capitalism"*[1515].

His former *WEF Young Global Leaders* pupil, so-called *"Third Way"* socialist British Prime Minister Tony Blair[1516], began evangelising for a *public-private partnership* (PPP) *"stakeholder economy"* in 1995[1517].

(*Academia, 1963*)

[1511] Kripal, Jeffrey J., *Esalen* (University of Chicago Press, 2007)

[1512] Erlandson, Stephen, *Spiritual, but Not Religious* (Bonzai Press, 2000)

[1513] Freeman, R. Edward, *Strategic Management* (Cambridge University Press, 1984)

[1514] Schwab, Klaus, *Moderne Unternehmensführung im Maschinenbau (Modern Enterprise Management in Mechanical Engineering)* (Verlag Moderne Industrie, 1971)

[1515] Schwab, Klaus, *Stakeholder Capitalism* (Wiley, 2021)

[1516] Schwab, Klaus, *The Global Competitiveness Report* (World Economic Forum, 2009)

[1517] Blair, Tony, *New Britain* (Basic Books, 1996)

Stereotype

> *Group reputation.*

A stereotype is a duplicated printing plate which is used instead of the original[1518]. The term was misappropriated by columnist Walter Lippman in his 1922 book *"Public Opinion"* before he came up with *"Cold War"*[1519].

(Literature, 1992)

Stigma

> *Label applied to people doing something stupid or disgusting which hurts their feelings.*

Get your theology and science right: a nail mark of disgrace on Christ's body (plural: *stigmata*), or the part of a flower pistil that receives pollen.

Stochastic Terrorism

> *A phrase people who want to sound intellectual™ use for "indirect incitement" when their husband was looking at the waitress. "You knew what you were doing."*

From the Greek *stochastikos*, meaning *"proceeding by guesswork"* and *"skillful in aiming"*, this invisible violence - which can only be detected by the female intuition of far-left academics and cannot be defined or

---

[1518] Barnhart, Robert K., *Barnhart Concise Dictionary of Etymology* (HarperCollins, 1995)

[1519] Lippmann, Walter, *Public Opinion* (Harcourt, Brace and Company, 1922)

prosecuted under any legal standard -, was popularised in 2008 by digital outlet *The Daily Kos*[1520] as *Fox News*' way of encouraging *"statistically predictable but individually unpredictable"* acts by "lone wolves".

(Internet Blog, 2011)

Stolen My Future

Primal cry of fragile, narcissistic brats who don't want to have to travel to a voting booth. What their professors felt in 1989 in Berlin.

In 1996, Al Gore wrote a foreword for a book (*"Our Stolen Future: Are We Threatening Our Fertility, Intelligence, and Survival? A Scientific Detective Story"*)[1521] which kick-started a list of *EPA* hearings[1522]. Although the phrase might well have some base in internet-era identity theft and dystopic Hollywood sci-fi, the extremist rhetoric was promoted most audibly as a slogan for teenagers and students the aftermath of the 2016 *Brexit Referendum* by the organisers of the so-called *"People's Vote"* campaign (created by extremist/socialist front groups *"Open Britain"*, *"the European Movement UK"*, *"Our Future Our Choice"*, *"For Our Future's Sake"*) and its press supporters[1523].

Two years later in 2018, extremist activists *"Extinction Rebellion"* emerged from the *"Rising Up!"* (from *"Earth First!"*, *"Occupy"*, *"Plan Stupid"*, *"Radical Think Tank"*, and *"Reclaim the Power"*) and *"climate mobilization"* communist front groups[1524].

In 2019, a Swedish fifteen-year-old teenage activist radicalised by activist group *"Fossil Free Dalsland"* (parent group *"Europe Rising!"*, parent

---

[1520] King, James, 'Stochastic Terrorism: Triggering the Shooters', *Daily Kos*, 3 June 2008

[1521] Colborn, Theo, Dianne Dumanoski, John P. Myers, *Our Stolen Future* (Dutton, 1996)

[1522] U.S. Environmental Protection Agency, 'Public Hearings and Meetings' (n.d.)

[1523] Shipman, Tim, *All Out War* (HarperCollins, 2019)

[1524] Henn, Cathy, *Extinction Rebellion and the New Climate Politics* (Zed Books, 2020)

group *350.org*), autistic Swede Greta Thunberg, performed an emotional rant at the United Nations screaming about "mass extinction" and politicians' having *"stolen my dreams and my childhood"*[1525].

(Politics, 2016)

Stop Asian Hate

An unsuccessful attempt to transfer the guilt for an epidemic of recorded violence towards wealthy, academic Chinese immigrants by black people onto anyone else.

A three-word-name united front formed at *San Francisco University* in January 2020 by the *Asian Pacific Policy and Planning Council* (A3PCON), *Chinese for Affirmative Action* (CAA), and the *Asian American Studies Department* (AAS)[1526]. Strangely around the time videos of racially motivated anti-Asian attacks flooded social media, ten years after *San Francisco PD* revealed eight-five per cent of attacks were perpetrated by the same demographic group[1527], and two years after the *US Justice Department* released statistics showing one demographic group attacked them more than any other[1528].

(University Activism, 2020)

[1525] Thunberg, Greta, 'United Nations Climate Action Summit', 23 Sept 2019

[1526] A3PCON, *Stop AAPI Hate: Responding to Discrimination* (2020)

[1527] San Francisco Police Department, *Hate Crime Report* (2021)

[1528] U.S. Department of Justice, *Hate Crime Statistics* (2021)

Straight White Male

> Like a Great White Shark, but much worse. The common enemy of Marxists everywhere.

There's no doubt this particular slur is descended from WASP (*"White Anglo-Saxon Protestant"*)[1529] which was popularised by Andrew Hacker in his 1957 article *"Liberal Democracy and Social Control"* published in *American Political Science Review*[1530]. Also related to the concept of the *"angry white male"* courted electorally in the nineties[1531]. It's impossible to say when and where the conjunction first arrived, but Crenshaw's *"intersectionality"*[1532] and McIntosh's *"white privilege"*[1533] are almost certainly the driving engine.

(Political Science, 1996)

Stress(ful)

> If you are predisposed to something, stress and bad life experiences will make you develop a disorder.

If might sound "medical"-ish. It's not. In 1962, psychologist Paul Meehl

---

[1529] Baltzell, E. Digby, *The Protestant Establishment* (Yale University Press, 1964)

[1530] Hacker, Andrew, 'Liberal Democracy and Social Control', *The American Political Science Review*, 51.4 (1957), 1009–26

[1531] Faludi, Susan, *Stiffed* (William Morrow, 1999)

[1532] Crenshaw, Kimberlé, 'Demarginalizing the Intersection of Race and Sex: A Black Feminist Critique of Antidiscrimination Doctrine, Feminist Theory, and Antiracist Politics', *University of Chicago Legal Forum*, 1989.1 (1989), 139–67

[1533] McIntosh, Peggy, 'White Privilege and Male Privilege: A Personal Account of Coming to See Correspondences Through Work in Women's Studies', *Working Paper No. 189*, Wellesley College Center for Research on Women (1988)

tried to explain schizophrenia. The resulting trend became referred to as the *Diathesis–Stress Model*, where the theory was the "equilibrium" of a person being disturbed would bring out a pre-existing condition[1534].

(Psychology, 1962)

Strong Female Character

> *The tokenistic casting of a New Soviet Woman with transparently implausible traits and interests into a story which invariably causes its complete rejection by the audience.*

2012, Hollywood's *"Year of Women"* was a real let-down in comparison to the 2017 *#MeToo* scandal collection. It continued a long, tedious historical trend of "scholars" writing about non-academic things no-one asked for or cares about, which bad filmmakers often implement to make films the public universally hate.

Although the term were popularised in a 2011 *New York Times* article by Carina Chocano (*"Tough, Cold, Terse, Taciturn and Prone to Not Saying Goodbye When They Hang Up the Phone'*)[1535], the cliche largely emerged from 1997's *"Buffy the Vampire Slayer"* and its "feminist" creator, Joss Whedon[1536] - who was later accused of infidelity, abuse, and unprofessional behaviour[1537].

(Film, Mid-90s)

[1534] Meehl, Paul, 'Schizotaxia, Schizotypy, Schizophrenia', *American Psychologist* (1962)

[1535] Chocano, Carina, 'Tough, Cold, Terse, Taciturn and Prone to Not Saying Goodbye When They Hang Up the Phone', *The New York Times*, 1 April 2011

[1536] Whedon, Joss (creator), *Buffy the Vampire Slayer* [TV series] (Mutant Enemy Productions, 1997–2003)

[1537] Miller, Julie, 'The Rise and Fall of Joss Whedon: From Hollywood Darling to Scandal', *Vanity Fair*, 2021

Sustainable-(ity)

> *A name for socialism people won't associate with mass starvation.*

Marx's failed theses were based on the premise the capitalist mode of production's internal contradictions would be its fatal flaw, prompting violent revolution by the working class to usher in socialism as the next stage of history. Capitalism wasn't *sustainable*.

His infamous pronouncement *"from each according to his ability, to each according to his needs"* was made in *"Critique of the Gotha Programme"* (1875)[1538].

In 1983, the *United Nations' Commission on Environment and Development* published *"Our Common Future"* (the *Brundtland Report*)[1539] under the guide of environmental husbandry, with all the telltale smuggling: a new "path" being required, "progress" into the future, according to our "needs".

(Politics, 1983)

Systemic

> *Existing as an invisible, omnipresent spiritual force within all things, and only detectable by specially attuned ideologues possessing magical skills.*

Everything in sociology is systemic: the entire disreputable subject is about magical, invisible *"social systems"* regardless of the measurability or observability of their existence.

[1538] Marx, Karl, *Critique of the Gotha Programme*, (Cambridge University Press, 1985)

[1539] World Commission on Environment and Development, *Our Common Future* (Oxford University Press, 1987)

-tive

> *A suffix people who want to sound intellectual™ add to other words to make them sound more sophisticated. Turning adjectives into nouns is extremely impressive.*

Get your English right: Latin "-tivus" = tending to.

TERF

> *Sensible Englishwoman.*

The slur *"Trans-Exclusionary Radical Feminist"* was coined by lunatic feminist blogger Viv Smythe, to describe the nature of *"RadFem"* journalists in the British press who were strongly against "penis-owners" from being allowed in "birthing persons' spaces"[1540]. Typically included in ladylike sentences such as *"TERFs must die"*, *"Kill all TERFs"*, and *"TERF scum"*.

(Internet, 2008)

Theory

> *A word charlatan frauds who want to sound intellectual™ - but don't want to subject their ideas to scrutiny - tend to wrongly use for their inane "hypothesis".*

Get your science right: a proposed *factual* explanation of the natural world, based on a substantial body of *evidence* which has been repeatedly tested and confirmed through observation and experimentation,

---

[1540] Smythe, Viv, 'Trans-Exclusionary Radical Feminists (TERFs)', (2008)

allowing for predictions about future occurrences.

They/Them

> Referring to oneself in the Royal Plural[1541].

In medicine:

> *Dissociative Identity Disorder (DID) is a complex psychological condition characterised by the presence of two or more distinct identities or personality states within a single individual. These identities may have unique names, histories, characteristics, and behaviors, and they often take control of the person's behavior at different times. The condition is frequently associated with severe trauma experienced during early childhood, often involving extreme, repetitive physical, sexual, or emotional abuse.*[1542]

In theology:

> *Then Jesus asked him, "What is your name?"*
> *"My name is Legion," he replied, "for we are many."*
> *And he begged Jesus again and again not to send them out of the area.*[1543]

[1541] Fowler, H. W., and F. G. Fowler, *The King's English* (Oxford Press, 1991)

[1542] Ross, Colin A., *Dissociative Identity Disorder* (Wiley, 1997)

[1543] *The Holy Bible*, Mark 5:1–20, Matthew 8:28–34, Luke 8:26–39 (NIV)

Tone Deaf

Violating the speech code prescribed by a little tyrant.

Amusia is a neurological condition which affects the ability to perceive pitch (the frequency of sound waves) accurately in the cochlea of the inner ear. It is linked to structural anomalies in the *arcuate fasciculus*, a bundle of nerve fibres connecting the auditory cortex to the frontal lobe[1544]. Its usage as an idiom for "lack of awareness" exploded around 1993, after the *New York Times* published *"The Tone-Deaf Corporation."*[1545]

(Newspapers, 1993)

Totality

A word people who want to sound intellectual™ use for "sum" or "whole".

Get your science right: an aggregate amount, forming completion.

Toxic

The comparison of a human being's behaviour to poison gas or fungi.

The traditional medical meaning of *toxin* (a poisonous substance produced by living cells or organisms), *toxic* (the property of being poisonous)

[1544] Peretz, Isabelle, Anne-Sophie Champod, and Krista Hyde, 'Varieties of Musical Disorders', *Annals of the New York Academy of Sciences*, 930.1 (2002), 58–70

[1545] *The New York Times*, 'The Tone-Deaf Corporation', 31 January 1993

and *toxicity* (the degree to which a substance can cause harm)[1546] were misappropriated into the social sciences at the beginning of the 1970s. The root of the psychology "relationship" genre (e.g. the idea of "mind games") was almost certainly Eric Berne's 1964 *"Games People Play"*[1547], and by 1972, the term *"toxic relationship"* had appeared in *"Voices"*, the journal of the *American Academy of Psychotherapists*[1548].

(Psychology, 1964)

Toxic Masculinity

> *The parts of men which aren't typically female, can be upsetting, and act similarly in nature to chemicals which poison workers in factories not wearing protective suits.*

Derived from a Marxist idea of *"hegemonic masculinity"* in Australian sociologist Raewyn Connell's *"Gender Order Theory"*. Although referenced in 1982, it was her silly 1995 book *"Masculinities"* which popularised the concept[1549], after the term was directly used around 1990 for a *New Republic* article by Daniel Gross titled *"The Gender Rap: 'Toxic Masculinity'"* (unavailable now, but discussed by *Sculos*)[1550]. Unsurprisingly, Cornell claims to be a *"trans-woman"*, and somehow was a professor at *Sydney*.

(Sociology, 1995)

[1546] *Stedman's Medical Dictionary*, 28th edn (Lippincott Williams & Wilkins, 2006)

[1547] Berne, Eric, *Games People Play* (Grove Press, 1964)

[1548] American Academy of Psychotherapists, *Voices*, 8.1 (1972)

[1549] Connell, R. W., *Masculinities* (University of California Press, 1995)

[1550] Gross, Daniel, 'The Gender Rap: "Toxic Masculinity"', *The New Republic*, 19 Nov 1990

Transgender

> The imaginary ability to change one form of human into another merely with social engineering. Advanced and intellectual™ because it seems impossible.

In 1965, psychiatrist John Oliven published *"Sexual Hygiene and Pathology"* in the *American Journal of the Medical Sciences*, which included a definition of *"transsexualism"*[1551]. Four years later, in 1969, the founder of cross-dressing magazine *Transvestia*, activist Virginia Prince, had begun to popularise the term with articles such as *"The Expression of Femininity in the Male"*[1552].

The Frankenstein experiments of lunatic paedophile John Money began the next year[1553]. Two years after that, Robert Stoller from the *Gender Identity Clinic* at *UCLA* was writing about a *"gender identity"* in *"Sex and Gender: On the Development of Masculinity and Femininity"*[1554].

By 1984, the term was being regularly used in *Female Mimics International*[1555].

(Psychiatry, 1965)

Transgender Suicide Epidemic

> The idea we can save gender-dysphoric people from killing themselves in record numbers by making up genders, pumping kids with

---

[1551] Oliven, Joseph, *Sexual Hygiene and Pathology* (Lippincott, 1965)

[1552] Stryker, Susan, *Transgender History* (Seal Press, 2008)

[1553] Colapinto, John, *As Nature Made Him* (HarperCollins, 2000)

[1554] Stoller, Robert J., *Sex and Gender* (Science House, 1968).

[1555] Prince, Virginia, *Female Mimics International*, various articles (1984)

hormones, dating them, funding surgeries, and letting them use a different toilet.

A wilful error of *correlation vs causation* to support a moral claim.

The *World Health Organisation* provides data on suicide rates. The most popularised study of transgender suicide cites a figure of forty-one per cent for *self*-reported *ideation* or "attempts" claimed by the *National Center for Transgender Equality* against a national average of four per cent[1556].

The data was preceded by *"Suicide risk among transgender individuals"* (2009) in *Psychology & Sexuality*[1557], *"Mental Health Disorders, Psychological Distress, and Suicidality in a Diverse Sample of Lesbian, Gay, Bisexual, and Transgender Youths"* (2010)[1558], the *"Transgender Mental Health Study 2012"*[1559], and it just keeps getting suspiciously higher.

There is no suicide data for LGBT people because there is *no data on LGBT people to begin with*[1560]. All of the studies are so flawed they are essentially useless — particularly because they ignore the co-morbidity of gender dysphoria with other serious mental illness (pointed out in

---

[1556] James, S. E., J. L. Herman, S. Rankin, M. Keisling, L. Mottet, M. Anafi, *Report of the 2015 U.S. Transgender Survey* (National Center for Transgender Equality, 2016)

[1557] Clements-Nolle, Kristen, Rani Marx, and Mitchell Katz, 'Attempted Suicide Among Transgender Persons: The Influence of Gender-Based Discrimination and Victimization', *Psychology & Sexuality*, 1.1 (2009), 41–54

[1558] Mustanski, Brian, Robert Garofalo, and Emilie Emerson, 'Mental Health Disorders, Psychological Distress, and Suicidality in a Diverse Sample of Lesbian, Gay, Bisexual, and Transgender Youths', *American Journal of Public Health*, 100.12 (2010), 2426–32

[1559] Bauer, Greta R., Ayden I. Scheim, Jessica Pyne, Robb Travers, and Rebecca Hammond, 'Intervenable Factors Associated with Suicide Risk in Transgender Persons: A Respondent-Driven Sampling Study in Ontario, Canada', *BMC Public Health*, 15.525 (2015)

[1560] Meyer, Ilan H., 'Prejudice, Social Stress, and Mental Health in Lesbian, Gay, and Bisexual Populations: Conceptual Issues and Research Evidence', *Psychology of Sexual Orientation and Gender Diversity*, 1.S (2013), 3–26

1997[1561]), which makes a causative diagnosis entirely impossible.

(Psychology, 2009)

Transphobia

Anything which undermines the reality-defying idea males can be females and females can be males, or that gender is linked to biology.

The first recorded usage was in the *New Woman Conference*'s *"Rites of Passage"* newsletter around 1993[1562]. The first usage in the popular press is in the same year, published in an article by the *DC U.S. News and World Report*[1563].

(Feminist Literature, 1993)

Trans Men Are Women

A pathologically-psychotic slogan repeated by online mobs of cross-dressing men, who aim to intimidate women into not publicly contesting their unfettered sexual access to women and children.

Get your science right: male = makes sperm; female = makes eggs.

[1561] Pfäfflin, Friedemann, and Astrid Junge, *Sex Reassignment: Thirty Years of International Follow-Up Studies After Sex Reassignment Surgery: A Comprehensive Review, 1961–1991*, International Journal of Transgenderism (1998)

[1562] Whittle, Stephen, *Respect and Equality* (Routledge, 2002)

[1563] *U.S. News & World Report*, 'Coverage of the Term "Transphobia"', 1993

Trauma

> The paralysing grief experienced from being exposed to anything outside one's pre-existing worldview or what the university campus declared virtuous.

In pathology, trauma has simply meant a physical wound since the seventeenth century[1564]. The idea of *"psychic"* trauma goes back to Freud's psychoanalytical theories speculating sexual traumas were the cause of hysteria, which he presented in *"The Aetiology of Hysteria" (1896)* as part of his wacky *"Seduction Theory"* at the Society for Psychiatry and Neurology in Vienna[1565].

(Psychology, 1894)

Trauma Bond

> Lacking the character to leave.

Popularised by Patrick Carnes in his book on addiction and abuse, *"The Betrayal Bond: Breaking Free of Exploitive Relationships"* (1997)[1566], this immeasurable, invisible, quasi-religious pablum, lacking any empirical research, was superseded by Evan Stark's concept of *"coercive control"* in 2007[1567].

(Psychology, 1997)

[1564] 'Trauma', in *Stedman's Medical Dictionary* (2022)

[1565] Freud, Sigmund, 'The Aetiology of Hysteria', reprinted in *The Standard Edition of the Complete Psychological Works of Sigmund Freud*, vol. 3, 1893–1899

[1566] Carnes, Patrick J., *The Betrayal Bond* (Health Communications, 1997)

[1567] Stark, Evan, *Coercive Control* (Oxford University Press, 2007)

Trigger (Warning)

> Anything which might upset a fragile, infantilised, or sheltered person who has never been to war.

In medical science, individuals who had been through extraordinarily shocking circumstances (e.g. war) and had been diagnosed with trauma often re-experience the same symptoms on a conditioned *Pavlovian* basis[1568]. The post-Vietnam concept of *Post-Traumatic Stress Disorder* (PTSD, or *"Shell Shock"*) was entered into the *DSM-III* in 1980 through activism by Chaim Shatan, Robert Lifton, and their psychiatric colleagues[1569].

The contemporary usage of a *"trigger warning"*, according to Andi Zeisler, co-founder of feminist publication *Bitch*, originated on the community forum of *Ms. Magazine*'s website in the late-nineties. By 2002, it had spread to *LiveJournal* amongst teenage girls posting *"pro-ana"* blog articles[1570].

(Psychiatry, 1988)

Troll

> Useful slur when being deliberately aggravated with information discrediting your extremist ideology. The only reason an intellectual™ would ever face opposition.

[1568] Van der Kolk, Bessel, *The Body Keeps the Score: Brain, Mind, and Body in the Healing of Trauma* (Viking, 2014)

[1569] American Psychiatric Association, *Diagnostic and Statistical Manual of Mental Disorders*, 3rd edn (APA, 1980)

[1570] Zeisler, Andi, *We Were Feminists Once* (PublicAffairs, 2016)

Otherwise known as winding people up and/or asking deliberately stupid and inflammatory questions, trolling has been around since computing and the internet began — and even since 1972 in the *US Air Force*. Although nerds say it was prevalent during the late-eighties, the earliest documented uses are on *Usenet (alt.folklore.urban)*[1571]. In 1997, Steven Johnson described the behaviour in *"Interface Culture: How New Technology Transforms the Way We Create and Communicate"*[1572].

(Internet, 1992)

(My/Your) Truth

> *The limited subjective experience and opinion of teenage girls falsely represented as a form of objective truth and profound worldly wisdom. Useful to an intellectual™ who could easily be proven wrong objectively.*

Objective truth is either true /false, can be wrong, and is about *things*. *Subjective* truth (opinion) is neither true or false, can't be wrong, and is about *perception*. The concept of there only being "interpretations" is the moral philosophy of the unrepentant criminal.

Revisiting what scientific philosopher Larry Laudan wrote in 1990:

> *The displacement of the idea that facts and evidence matter by the idea that everything boils down to subjective interests and perspectives is — second only to American political campaigns — the most prominent and pernicious manifestation of anti-intellectualism in our time.*[1573]

[1571] Dibbell, Julian, 'A Rape in Cyberspace', *The Village Voice*, 23 December 1993

[1572] Johnson, Steven, *Interface Culture* (HarperEdge, 1997)

[1573] Laudan, Larry, *Science and Relativism* (University of Chicago Press, 1990)

Trust & Safety

> *Dangerous promotion of fragility by censors who can't be trusted.*

The terms devised for "censor" never stop evolving to cover their unpopular true meaning. Facebook established the first *"Trust & Safety** team around 2011, when the *Federal Trade Commission* settled with the company for violating federal law and announced they had *"deceived consumers by telling them they could keep their information on Facebook private."*[1574] The company employs fifteen thousand censors[1575].

It was followed in 2016 by Twitter's now-dissolved *"Trust & Safety Council."* (the word "soviet" means "council")[1576] The *Trust & Safety Professional Association* now claims to have one hundred thousand professional members[1577].

During the *Reign of Terror* part of the *French Revolution*, fifteen thousand people were executed by the *Committee of Public Safety*[1578]. In the *Soviet Union*, political officers known as *Politruks* (political commissars) and *PartOrgs* (Party Organisers) were responsible for maintaining *Communist Party* loyalty and discipline within the military and civilian sectors[1579].

(Technology, 2011)

[1574] Federal Trade Commission, 'Facebook Settles FTC Charges That It Deceived Consumers by Failing to Keep Privacy Promises', 29 November 2011

[1575] *BBC News*, 'The Job of Moderating the Internet's Most Horrific Content', 24 Jan 2022

[1576] Twitter, Inc., 'Announcing the Twitter Trust & Safety Council', 9 February 2016

[1577] Trust & Safety Professional Association, 'About TSPA' (n.d.)

[1578] Hanson, Paul, *The French Revolution* (Oxford University Press, 2004)

[1579] Conquest, Robert, *The Great Terror* (Oxford Press, 1991)

Two-Spirit

A magical Canadian who is neither male nor female.

Although typically referred to as "evidence" of primitive human societies embracing a "third gender", the roots of this phrase lie in the 1990 attempt made at the *Third Annual Inter-tribal Native American, First Nations, Gay and Lesbian American Conference* in Winnipeg, Canada to replace the slur *"berdache"* describing cross-dressers (*"passive partner in sodomy, boy prostitute"*) in Native Indian culture for something nicer. It is a translation of the *Anishinaabemowin* phrase *"niizh manidoowag,"* meaning *"two spirits"*[1580].

Off Our Backs! Magazine documented the statement made *"on behalf of Janet Spotted Eagle and Two Spirited Thunder People, a group of Native American lesbians."*[1581] Like *"latinx"*, Native Indians hate it, and refuse to use it[1582].

(Activism, 1990)

Unconscious (Implicit) Bias

The intent you didn't know you had, but you actually did have. Like when you looked at that waiter/waitress. Even though you didn't. But you were thinking it.

The *Holy Grail* — a test for prejudice, SCIENCE! — was created by psychologists Mahzarin Banaji and Anthony Greenwald in 1995. They

---

[1580] Roscoe, Will, *Changing Ones* (St. Martin's Press, 1998)

[1581] *Off our backs!*, June 1991, 21.6

[1582] Driskill, Qwo-Li, 'Doubleweaving Two-Spirit Critiques: Building Alliances Between Native and Queer Studies', *GLQ: A Journal of Lesbian and Gay Studies*, 16.1–2 (2010),

called it the *"implicit association test"* (IAT)[1583]. It "measured" your magical, invisible mind.

Twenty years later, they disowned it, publicly stated it doesn't predict biased behaviour, and urged it not be used for anything[1584]. Whoops.

(Psychology, 1995)

Under-represented (Groups)

The precondition necessary for receiving a large check.

The explosion in the usage of this term is down to the 2002 survey by the *New York Times* shaming their competitors about minorities on magazine covers between 1998 and 2002. It included thirty-one prominent publications, spanning genres like news, fashion, entertainment, and lifestyle (*Time*, *Vogue*, *People*, and *Sports Illustrated*, etc.). They conveniently found, unlike themselves, only thirteen per cent of individuals featured by their competitors were from *"minority backgrounds"*.[1585]

(Newspapers, 2002)

(The) Undocumented

Illegal. Not possessing legal documentation granted by a required legal process.

Although it appeared earlier, the term was employed in the 1976 *Domestic*

[1583] Greenwald, Anthony G., and Mahzarin R. Banaji, 'Implicit Social Cognition: Attitudes, Self-Esteem, and Stereotypes', *Psychological Review*, 102.1 (1995)

[1584] Singal, Jesse, 'Psychologists Are Admitting the Implicit Association Test Can't Predict Individual Behavior', *New York Magazine*, 4 December 2017

[1585] Feminist Majority Foundation, 'Minorities Still Under-Represented on Magazine Covers', 15 November 2002

Council Committee Report on Illegal Aliens under Gerald Ford in regards to his *Executive Order 11935*[1586], and the *New Yorker*'s citation of it in 1977[1587]. The current term arises from a 2013 suggestion by the *Hispanic Leadership Network* to US Republicans they use the term and drop *"anchor baby"*[1588].

(Politics, 1976)

(The) Unhoused

Zombie-like herd denied their inherent right to socialist housing.

Adam Aleksic, a *Harvard* linguistics graduate who started the *Etymology Nerd* blog, notes the apparent first appearance of this Orwellian horror on *Twitter* occurred in October 2008[1589].

In May 2020, as everyone became homeless during the *Covid* crisis, *Regime* mouthpiece the *Associated Press* updated its stylebook to focus on magical *"person-first"* language; not to use *"the homeless,"* (a *"dehumanising"* term), but instead to use terms like *"homeless people"* or *"people without housing."* These people were *"experiencing homelessness."*[1590]

(Internet, 2008)

[1586] Ford, Gerald R., *11935: Citizenship Requirements for Federal Employment*, 2 Sept 1976

[1587] *The New Yorker*, "On the List Were, Among Other Things, ... Undocumented Workers (Illegal Aliens)," 23 May 1977, 112/3.

[1588] Hispanic Leadership Network, 'Suggested Terminology on Immigration Reform' (2013)

[1589] BlogNetNews, 'Glass City Jungle: Mayor Blames Cherry Street Mission for Increase in Unhoused...', X (formerly Twitter), 23 October 2008 https://x.com/ohioBNN/status/973201898.

[1590] Associated Press, 'AP Stylebook Updates Entry on Homelessness to Avoid Stigmatizing Language', *AP News*, 15 May 2020

(The) Universe

A way of saying "God" without appearing religious.

Buddhist cosmology, basically. Pantheism. A fashionable *Gnostic* term for the *Demiurge*. Or arch-charlatan Deepak Chopra — whomever you want to blame for possibly the stupidest idea imaginable. According to our current scientific understanding, the universe is 71.4% dark energy, 24% cold dark matter, and 4.6% atoms[1591].

Unrealistic Beauty Standards

Women selling products to other women by exploiting their insecurity and envy.

The concept of *"beauty standards"* is attributable to its popularisation in 1990 through Naomi Wolf's book *"The Beauty Myth: How Images of Beauty Are Used Against Women"*, which kick-started third-wave feminism[1592].

Unfortunately, Wolf had her next book (*"Outrages"*) recalled, because she didn't bother to research the laws (about sexual crimes against children) she was condemning as a form of gay persecution[1593].

(Literature, 1990)

[1591] Planck Collaboration, 'Planck 2018 Results. VI. Cosmological Parameters', *Astronomy & Astrophysics*, 641 (2018), A6

[1592] Wolf, Naomi, *The Beauty Myth* (HarperCollins, 1990)

[1593] Flood, Alison, 'Naomi Wolf's *Outrages* Pulled After Accuracy Concerns', *The Guardian*, 20 June 2019

(The) Unvaccinated

> *A feral underclass of ignorant, selfish grandma-murderers who refuse to comfort menopausal hypochondriacs by undergoing medical procedures and wearing signs of their compliance, and subsequently deserve gestures of their tolerant compassion. Such as being thrown in camps, cut off from society, and forcibly medicated.*

As a medical category, those who have not undergone vaccination have been discussed since 1813 in journals (e.g. *Edinburgh Medical and Surgical Journal*)[1594]. As a political class of refuseniks worthy of stigma and ostracism, *"The Unvaccinated"* refuseniks emerged as unwanted *Kulaks* in July 2021, spurred by an article in the *Los Angeles Times*[1595]

(*Newspapers, 2021*)

Use Your Platform

> *Abuse your position of impartiality for political gain.*

Since the twenties, extremist activists have been using the concept of a wooden crate in a public square in front of a noisy rabble as a metaphor for one's position in public life.

The howl to "use" it has invariably been to abandon impartiality and politicise it for political gain, but since the introduction of social media "platforms" via *Silicon Valley*'s abstract language, it has become more virulent.

[1594] *Edinburgh Medical and Surgical Journal*, 'Cases Illustrating the Effects of Vaccination and Revaccination', *Edinburgh Medical and Surgical Journal*, 54.146 (1840)

[1595] Garcia, Marissa, and Soumya Karlamangla, 'California's COVID-19 Crisis Is Increasingly Among the Unvaccinated, with Case Rates Rising Fast', *Los Angeles Times*, 27 July 2021

The political weaponisation of denying opponents a *"platform"* (after *"antifascist"* counter-protests of the *British Union of Fascists* during the thirties) was undoubtedly popularised via the *International Marxist Group* (IMG) of the *National Union of Students* (NUS) in the UK around 1972, as a flood of Ugandan refugees entered the country[1596].

(Student Activism, 1972)

[1596] National Union of Students, *NUS Conference Minutes* (1972)

V W

Vaccine

> A magical potion created under the Social Contract by the divine State to save the world.

The term *vaccination* was coined by surgeon Richard Dunning in his text *"Some observations on vaccination"* (1800) which discussed Edward Jenner's use of material from cowpox pustules to provide protection against smallpox in 1791, specifying the introduction of dead of a weakened foreign organism into the body to prevent disease (*"An Inquiry into the Causes and Effects of the Variolae Vacciniae"*, 1798)[1597].

Twenty-six thousand people have had life-threatening complications from it (fifty-two people per one million vaccinated), and two per million die[1598]. If sixty per cent of the US population were forcibly vaccinated, five hundred would die[1599].

In machinations which would make Comrade Lysenko proud, the

[1597] Jenner, Edward, *An Inquiry into the Causes and Effects of the Variolae Vaccinae, a Disease Discovered in Some of the Western Counties of England, Particularly Gloucestershire, and Known by the Name of Cow Pox* (Sampson Low, 1798)

[1598] Virginia Department of Health, 'Smallpox Vaccine' (n.d.)

[1599] Bozzette, Samuel A., et al., 'A Model for a Smallpox-Vaccination Policy', *New England Journal of Medicine*, 348.5 (2003)

definition was changed in 2015 from "prevention", to introducing a vaccine (circular reference) to "produce immunity", and by 2021 it had "evolved" as a "matter of semantics" to producing "protection"[1600][1601].

A vaccine introduces a *foreign* pathogen (possessing an antigen) which invokes an immunogenic response[1602]. Being injected with an artificial molecule which causes your own body to attack itself is an *autoimmune* response[1603].

(Medicine, 1800)

Vaccines Cause Autism

> *Vaccines are an unsafe experiment by the state and Big Pharma which makes kids autistic. Or something.*

Interestingly, the idea vaccines are suspicious can be traced back to a storyline in *"The X-Files"* where the *"Deep State"* (the *"Syndicate"*) uses bees to carry smallpox virus in preparation for extraterrestrial colonisation[1604].

In 1998, *The Lancet* published a study of twelve autistic children (*"Ileal-lymphoid-nodular hyperplasia, non-specific colitis, and pervasive developmental disorder in children"*) in which Dr Andrew Wakefield and

---

[1600] CDC, 'Immunization Basics: What Is a Vaccine?' (2021)

[1601] Science Feedback, 'Fact-Check: Did Merriam-Webster Change the Definition of "Vaccine" to Accommodate the Limitations of COVID-19 Vaccines?', 4 Nov 2021

[1602] Janeway, Charles A., Paul Travers, Mark Walport, and Mark J. Shlomchik, *Immunobiology* (Garland Science, 2001)

[1603] Rose, Noel R., and Ian R. Mackay, *The Autoimmune Diseases* (Elsevier Press, 2006)

[1604] Carter, Chris (producer), *The X-Files* (20th Century Fox Television, 1998)
   The storyline about bees carrying smallpox for the *Syndicate*'s colonisation plans is central to several episodes in Season 4 and 5, including *"Zero Sum"* (Season 4, Episode 21) and the 1998 movie *"The X-Files: Fight the Future"*.

eleven other co-authors suggested a link to the MMR vaccine[1605]. It became known as the Lancet MMR Autism Fraud, was retracted in 2010[1606], and Wakefield was struck off the medical register for serious professional misconduct.

(Medicine, 1997)

Vegan(ism)

A trendy, religious, planet-saving Hollywood slimming diet which also lets you protest against capitalist mass-production of meat and sacrifice yourself to prove plants are all we need to climb Mount Everest.

Although humans have been biologically omnivorous for millennia, the epidemic of obesity from processed sugar and corn syrup from an unregulated, genetically altered capitalist food supply chain has prompted celebrities like Paltrow to promote eating *"clean"*[1607]. Mostly with good reason.

From the sixties counter-culture emerged Frances Moore Lappe's 1971 book *"Diet for a Small Planet"*[1608], which was supplanted by climate change-linked *"Diet for a New America"* by John Robbins in 1987[1609] and the hidden camera documentary *"Earthlings"* in 2005[1610].

Vegetarianism (the *"vegetable regimen diet"*) emerged in England in

---

[1605] Wakefield, Andrew J., et al., 'Ileal-Lymphoid-Nodular Hyperplasia, Non-Specific Colitis, and Pervasive Developmental Disorder in Children', *The Lancet*, 351.9103 (1998), 637–41 [Retracted]

[1606] *The Lancet*, 'Retraction—"Ileal-Lymphoid-Nodular Hyperplasia, Non-Specific Colitis, and Pervasive Developmental Disorder in Children"', *The Lancet*, 375.9713 (2010), 445

[1607] Paltrow, Gwyneth, Julia Borgenicht, *It's All Good* (Grand Central Life & Style, 2013)

[1608] Lappé, Frances Moore, *Diet for a Small Planet* (Ballantine Books, 1971)

[1609] Robbins, John, *Diet for a New America* (Stillpoint Publishing, 1987)

[1610] Monson, Shaun (director), *Earthlings* [Documentary] (Nation Earth, 2005)

1838 via *Alcott House* school's publication of *The Healthian*[1611] and the *Vegetarian Society* in Manchester in 1847[1612]. However, the English animal activist founder of the *Vegan Society* who coined the term was Donald Watson, in 1944, in the first edition of *Vegan News*[1613].

(Literature, 1944)

Wellness

> *Not increasing your American employer's healthcare costs. A more fashionable name for homoeopathy.*

Credited to Halbert Dunn, chief of the *US National Office of Vital Statistics* and father of the alternative medicine *"Wellness Movement"*, in his 1961 book *"High-Level Wellness"*, which was derived from a series of twenty-nine lectures at a *Unitarian* Church in Virginia[1614]. John Travis bought a copy in 1972 and founded the *Wellness Resource Center* in California as an *"alternative"* medicine clinic[1615].

(Literature, 1961)

Whiteness

> *An invisible, omnipresent, magical demonic spirit living in all Western people which must undergo public exorcism; lest it cause them to make other people revise for exams and turn up on time.*

[1611] Alcott House School, *The Healthian* (1838)

[1612] Vegetarian Society, *The Vegetarian Messenger* (Vegetarian Society, 1847)

[1613] Watson, Donald, 'Editorial', *Vegan News*, 1 (November 1944)

[1614] Dunn, Halbert L., *High-Level Wellness* (R.W. Beatty Company, 1961)

[1615] Travis, John W., and Regina S. Ryan, *Wellness Workbook* (Ten Speed Press, 1981)

The silly pseudo-subject of *"whiteness studies"* is generally considered having begun with Albert Murray's 1983 book *"Omni-Americans: Some Alternatives to the Folklore of White Supremacy"*[1616], although conceptual mention was made by sociologist W. E. B. Du Bois in *"Darkwater"* (1920)[1617].

The contemporary tomes recognised as canonical are Barbara Applebaum's 2010 *"Being White, Being Good: White Complicity, White Moral Responsibility, and Social Justice Pedagogy"*[1618] and Robin DiAngelo's risible *"White Fragility: Why It's So Hard for White People to Talk About Racism"* (2018)[1619].

(Sociology, 1983)

White Fragility

> *One racist woman's total surprise that people don't react too well to being slandered as racist on account of the melanin levels of their skin, compiled from her own diary of blatant racism.*

A new buzz phrase-on-rotation featured heavily from the paper of the same name published by Robin DiAngelo in the *International Journal of Critical Pedagogy* in 2011[1620], and later in her 2018 book *"White Fragility: Why It's So Hard for White People to Talk About Racism"*[1621]. A professor who charges $15,000 per appointment[1622].

[1616] Murray, Albert, *The Omni-Americans* (Outerbridge & Dienstfrey, 1970)

[1617] Du Bois, W. E. B., *Darkwater* (Harcourt, Brace and Howe, 1920)

[1618] Applebaum, Barbara, *Being White, Being Good* (Lexington Books, 2010)

[1619] DiAngelo, Robin, *White Fragility* (Beacon Press, 2018)

[1620] DiAngelo, Robin, 'White Fragility', *International Journal of Critical Pedagogy*, (2011)

[1621] DiAngelo, R. (2018). *White Fragility* (Beacon Press, 2018)

[1622] Fraser, John, 'How Much Do Robin DiAngelo and Other Anti-Racism Advocates Charge for Their Speeches?', *The New York Post*, 15 July 2019

(Sociology, 2011)

White Supremacy

> *The notion the level of melanin present in a person's skin is inversely proportional to their psychological belief they should be the dominant race who rule over the earth.*

Exemplified as a historical attitude for hundreds of years before the 60s through publications such as Darwin's *"On the Origin of Species by Means of Natural Selection, or the Preservation of Favoured Races in the Struggle for Life)"*[1623].

The contemporary notion is first attributed to *"critical race theory"* activist and author of *"Confessions of an Identity Politician"*, Frances Lee Ashley, who published *"Stirring the Ashes: Race, Class and the Future of Civil Rights Scholarship"* in 1989[1624].

The concept was pre-dated by white "independent scholar" communist Theodore Allen, who distributed pamphlets about *"white skin privilege"* in 1965 before his magnum opus *"Class Struggle and the Origin of Racial Slavery: The Invention of the White Race"* ten years later[1625].

(Law, 1989)

[1623] Darwin, Charles, *On the Origin of Species by Means of Natural Selection, or the Preservation of Favoured Races in the Struggle for Life* (John Murray, 1859)

[1624] Ansley, Frances L., 'Stirring the Ashes: Race, Class and the Future of Civil Rights Scholarship', *Cornell Law Review*, 74.6 (1989), 993–1077

[1625] Allen, Theodore, *The Invention of the White Race*, (Verso, 1994)

Woke

> *Painfully cool perversion of the English language which bankrupts corporations. Being radicalised to see Marxist injustice everywhere, all the time.*

As far back as 1962, the *New York Times* had an article by novelist William Melvin Kelley entitled *"If You're Woke, You Dig It"*[1626].

In 2008, soul singer Erykah Badu released her terrible album *"New Amerykah Part One (4th World War)"* containing the song *"Master Teacher"*[1627].

In 2014, Michael Brown was shot by police in Ferguson, Missouri, and the term *"woke"* became synonymous with the *"Black Lives Matter"* movement which emerged after the shooting of Trayvon Martin in 2013[1628].

In sociological terms, it refers to possessing a *"critical consciousness"*[1629] after being brainwashed by the theological sophistry of *"critical constructivism"* (the fusion of American sociology and French postmodern philosophy taught on US university campuses).

(Newspapers, 1962)

[1626] Kelley, William M., 'If You're Woke, You Dig It', *The New York Times*, 20 May 1962

[1627] Badu, Erykah, *New Amerykah Part One (4th World War)* [Album] (Motown, 2008)

[1628] TTaylor, Keeanga-Yamahtta, *From #BlackLivesMatter to Black Liberation* (Haymarket Books, 2016)

[1629] Freire, Paulo, *Pedagogy of the Oppressed* (Herder and Herder, 1970)

Woman

> *Completely unknowable condition anyone may claim to have, on a whim, according to how they feel inside, on the day.*

The harebrained sentiment biological sex is merely a linguistic *"construct"* (i.e. a word) unrelated to biology emerged from Simone de Beauvoir's *"Second Sex"* (1949) with its infamous quotation *"one is not born, but rather becomes a woman"*[1630]. This idiocy, and the resulting barbarism of John Money[1631] a few years later, became merged with the *"social constructivism"* of the sixties[1632] and Michel Foucault's madness, before landing in Judith Butler's 1991 disaster, *"Gender Trouble"*[1633].

(Feminist Literature, 1949)

Women Defined By Men

> *Humanity is male, and women are reproductive slaves who are relative to men. And children should have sex.*

From the 1949 rant of a thirty-eight-year-old, unmarried, childless, and promiscuous bisexual French Marxist — *to be fair, an interesting kind of person* — complaining about the *"Other"* in her book *"The Second Sex"*[1634], the ignominious Simone de Beauvoir.

[1630] de Beauvoir, Simone, *The Second Sex* (Alfred A. Knopf, 1949)

[1631] Colapinto, John, *As Nature Made Him* (HarperCollins, 2000)

[1632] Berger, Peter, Thomas Luckmann, *The Social Construction of Reality* (Anchor Books, 1966)

[1633] Butler, Judith, *Gender Trouble* (Routledge, 1990)

[1634] de Beauvoir, Simone, *The Second Sex* (Alfred A. Knopf, 1949)

As feminist journal *Hipatia* notes[1635]:

> *In 1977 she signed, together with other authors including Foucault, a manifest publicly defending three men who had been condemned of sexually abusing minors, claiming that they did not deserve such condemnation given that their relationships with the minors were "consented".... Prior to that, it was also known that in 1938 she exploited her profession as a teacher to seduce female pupils (Seymour-Jones, 2008[1636]). In 1943, Beauvoir was suspended from teaching after being accused of sexually abusing her 17- year-old student in 1939[1637].*

(Feminist literature, 1949)

Women Are Sexually Repressed

> *Being a wife and mother strips you of your sexiness.*

Freud studied fifty frustrated aristocratic women in Austria he deemed *"men without penises"* who *"internalised"* everything into their *"unconscious"*[1638]. In 1970, seven years after Friedan's *"The Feminine Mystique"*, Australian legend Germaine Greer published *"The Female Eunuch"* in which she openly states *"I don't like women"*[1639].

(Feminist Literature, 1970)

[1635] Valls-Carol, Roser, Lídia Puigvert-Mallart, Alba Vidu, and Gemma López de Aguileta, 'Presenting Beauvoir as a Feminist: Neglecting Her Defense and Accusations of Pedophilia', *Social and Education History*, 11.2 (2022), 106–28

[1636] Seymour-Jones, Carole, *A Dangerous Liaison* (Overlook Press, 2008)

[1637] Rowley, Hazel, *Tête-à-Tête* (HarperCollins, 2005)

[1638] Freud, Sigmund, *The Interpretation of Dreams* (Macmillan, 1900)

[1639] Greer, Germaine, *The Female Eunuch* (HarperCollins, 1970)

Words/Thoughts Change Reality

> *Think about receiving lots of something enough and it will magically appear.*

Currently toted by *"Word of Faith"* prosperity gospel preachers like Joel Osteen and Benny Hinn[1640], the idea thoughts can affect the material world goes all the way back to Phileas Quimby's[1641] origination of the *"New Thought"* movement[1642] and the Mesmerism-inspired[1643] tenets of *"Mental Science"*[1644]. Among them were Emma Curtis Hopkins, Prentice Mulford, and Mary Baker Eddy (of *"Christian Science"* fame)[1645]. Mulford's 1886 essay *"Your Forces and How to Use Them"*[1646] is regarded as its seminal publication.

Believing words have magical powers to alter reality has an older definition: the practice in witchcraft of *casting a spell*.

(Literature, 1886)

[1640] Bowler, Kate, *Blessed* (Oxford University Press, 2013)

[1641] Gordon, Charlotte A., *Phineas Parkhurst Quimby* (Adventures Unlimited, 2003)

[1642] Braden, Charles S., *Spirits in Rebellion* (Southern Methodist University, 1963)

[1643] Crabtree, Adam, *From Mesmer to Freud* (Yale University Press, 1993)

[1644] Horowitz, Mitch, *The Power of the Mind to Heal* (HarperOne, 2009)

[1645] Eddy, Mary Baker, *Science and Health with Key to the Scriptures* (Christian Science Publishing Society, 1875)

[1646] Mulford, Prentice, *Your Forces and How to Use Them* (F.J. Needham, 1886)

X Y Z

Xenophobia

> *Irrational, unreasonable and outdated biological survival instinct derived from the wariness of infectious diseases, carried by strangers, easily spread to other populations without immunity. A racist social construct.*

Contrasted with *"xenomania"* and *"xenophilia"* in the *London Daily News* around 1880[1647] — before it was a synonym for "racist" — the term was first used to describe a fear of "foreigners" or "the Other", similar to agoraphobia, in 1903 repetitively in *The Nation*[1648]. It has no basis in science or medicine.

(Politics, 1880)

[1647] Ware, James Redding, *Passing English of the Victorian Era* (G. Routledge & Sons, 1909), quoting *Daily News*, 12 April

[1648] *The Nation*, 20 December 1919, 800/1

XYZ

Yoga

> *Exercise for people who are a bit too precious to make themselves undergo any strenuous effort. Also, profound.*

Yoga (from the Sanskrit root *"yuj,"* which means "to unite" or "to join" with the divine or higher consciousness) is Hindu pantheism[1649]; not exercise.

Although it found its way into the US in the 1890s via the transcendentalists (Swami Vivekananda's tours, along with Emerson and Blavatsky)[1650], it was the English translation of 1954 *"Le Yoga: Immortalite et Liberte"* (*"Yoga: Immortality and Freedom"*) by Romanian Mircea Eliade[1651] which was stuffed onto the bookshelves of musicians and artists in the lead-up to the counter-culture.

(Literature, 1958)

Zionism

> *Something suspicious and nationalistic both sets of extremists believe The Jews™ are up to. Favourite cause of intellectual™ people, because, Palestine.*

The term "semite" originated in the 18th century and was derived from "Shem," one of the sons of Noah in the Bible[1652]. The term "antisemitism" was coined by German journalist Wilhelm Marr in 1879 to describe

---

[1649] Feuerstein, Georg, *The Yoga Tradition* (Hohm Press, 2001)

[1650] Goldberg, Philip, *American Veda* (Harmony Books, 2010)

[1651] Eliade, Mircea, *Yoga: Immortality and Freedom* (*Le Yoga: Immortalité et Liberté*, 1954)

[1652] Hitti, Philip K., *History of the Arabs* (Macmillan, 1970)

hostility or prejudice specifically against Jews[1653].

"Zion" is a Hebrew translation for Jerusalem[1654]. The first use of the term is attributed to the Austrian Nathan Birnbaum, founder of the *Kadimah* nationalist Jewish students' movement; he used the term in 1890 in his journal *"Selbstemanzipation!"*[1655].

"New" anti-Semitism rose in 1967 after the *Six-Day War*[1656] when the USSR allied with Arab states[1657]. In 1969, Yuri Ivanov, the *Soviet Union*'s leading *"zionologist"* described the pathology *"zionology"* as a "world threat"[1658].

The Right hates *TheJews*™ because they control the financial system (or something), but the Left hates "them" because "they" apparently are a bunch of capitalist nationalists ruining the multicultural dream. The anti-Semitism problem on the has been out of control since Marx's days[1659].

(Political rhetoric, 1890)

[1653] Lindemann, Albert S., *Esau's Tears* (Cambridge University Press, 1997)

[1654] Ben-Arieh, Yehoshua, *Jerusalem in the 19th Century* (St. Martin's Press, 1986)

[1655] Vital, David, *Zionism* (Oxford University Press, 1982)

[1656] Wistrich, Robert S., *Antisemitism* (Pantheon Books, 1991)

[1657] Behbehani, Hashim S. H., *The Soviet Union and Arab Nationalism* (Routledge, 1986)

[1658] Hunter, Robert, ed., *Caution: Zionism!* (Association of Arab-American University Graduates, 1969)

[1659] Trachtenberg, Joshua, *The Devil and the Jews* (Yale University Press, 1943)

III

The Basics of Broken Thinking

Never attribute to malice what can adequately be explained by stupidity or ignorance. Our thinking is crowded with biases, fallacies, emotions, wishes, and bad data. We must learn the discipline of thinking and reasoning clearly. This section attempts to navigate through the most common ways ideas can be wrong, deceitful, or incoherent.

How Do You Know What Is True?

Truth *corresponds* to reality[1660].

It is described in the form of a *claim*. Interrogating one in an adversarial way to discern the truth about it is a *dialectic*[1661].

Truth can be *subjective* (true in my perception), *universal* (true for everyone), *objective* (true regardless of perception) or *absolute* (true despite anything else)[1662].

Truth should pass five tests[1663].

1. *Logical Consistency*: does it make sense?
2. *Empirical Adequacy:* Is there sufficiently valid evidence for it?
3. *Experiential Relevance*: does it exist or work in real life?
4. *Existential Deniability:* can it be denied without proving itself in the process?
5. *Rational Falsifiability*: can it be proved true or false?

Claim: the moon is made of cheese.

1. No, it does not make sense.
2. There is no evidence for it.

[1660] Aristotle, *Metaphysics*, Book II, Part 1, trans. by W. D. Ross (circa 350 BCE)

[1661] Toulmin, Stephen E., *The Uses of Argument* (Cambridge University Press, 1958)

[1662] Kirkham, Richard L., *Theories of Truth: A Critical Introduction* (MIT Press, 1995)

[1663] Popper, Karl R., *The Logic of Scientific Discovery* (Basic Books, 1934)

3. I have no personal experience with it.
4. It can denied without proving itself.
5. Yes. Rock from the moon can be tested for dairy content.

Its test results should meet a defined *Burden of Proof*[1664]:

1. *Reasonable indications*
2. *Reasonable suspicion*
3. *Reasonable to believe*
4. *Probable cause*
5. *Some credible evidence*
6. *Preponderance of the evidence*
7. *Clear and convincing evidence*
8. *Balance of probabilities*
9. *Beyond reasonable doubt*

You have no obligation whatsoever to believe or accept any truth claim[1665].

[1664] Stein, Alex, *Foundations of Evidence Law* (Oxford University Press, 2005)

[1665] Paul, Richard, and Linda Elder, *The Thinker's Guide to Critical and Creative Thinking* (Foundation for Critical Thinking, 2006)

How Do We Know What We Know?

Two fundamental approaches to knowledge and understanding emerged prominently during the *Enlightenment* period[1666]. Where does it come from?

Empiricism, championed by philosophers like John Locke[1667] and David Hume[1668], says knowledge comes primarily from sensory experience; we learn about the world through observation and experimentation. Empiricists trust sensory data and *posteriori* knowledge (knowledge gained *after* experience). Many of the major empiricists were British - John Locke, David Hume, George Berkeley, and later John Stuart Mill[1669].

For example, an empiricist would argue that a child learns that fire is hot not through innate knowledge, but by *experiencing* heat or seeing its effects. Empiricists emphasise the importance of *evidence* gathered through the *senses* and tend to be skeptical of claims that can't be verified through direct observation or experience.

Empiricism gave birth to *Logical Positivism* (only statements verifiable through empirical observation or logical proof are meaningful)[1670], *Prag-*

[1666] "Rationalism vs. Empiricism: The Foundations of Modern Western Philosophy." *Philosophy Institute*, 2022.

[1667] Locke, John. *An Essay Concerning Human Understanding.* Thomas Bassett; 1690

[1668] Hume, David. *An Enquiry Concerning Human Understanding.* Millar; 1748.

[1669] Berkeley G. *A Treatise Concerning the Principles of Human Knowledge.* 1710.

[1670] Ayer AJ. *Language, Truth, and Logic.* Gollancz; 1936.

matism (practical consequences and experience as the test of truth)[1671], and *Phenomenalism* (physical objects are actually just collections of sensory experience)[1672].

Rationalism, advanced by thinkers like René Descartes[1673] and Gottfried Leibniz[1674], contends certain fundamental truths can be known through *reason* alone, independent of sensory experience. Rationalists believe in innate ideas and the power of deductive reasoning. They emphasise *a priori* knowledge (knowledge independent of experience) and the power of reason to discover truth. Major rationalists like Descartes (French), Leibniz (German), and Spinoza (Dutch) were from continental Europe[1675].

A rationalist would argue we know 2+2=4 not through experience, but through a rational understanding of mathematics.

Rationalism gave birth to *German Idealism* (Kant, Hegel, the role of reason in structuring our experience and understanding of reality)[1676], and *Phenomenology* (Husserl, consciousness through rational reflection)[1677].

Imagine you're trying to learn how to make the perfect cup of coffee.

An empiricist would say the only way to learn is through experience and observation - trying different temperatures, amounts of coffee, brewing times, and tasting the results. They'd say you need to actually experiment and use your senses to figure out what works. You can read all the coffee guides you want, but until you actually make and taste coffee yourself, you don't really know anything about making it.

A rationalist would say that you can figure out a lot about making good coffee just by thinking logically about it. They'd say you can use

---

[1671] Dewey J. *Experience and Nature*. Open Court; 1925.

[1672] Mill JS. *A System of Logic*. John W. Parker; 1843.

[1673] Descartes, Rene. *Meditations on First Philosophy*. Cambridge University Press; 1641

[1674] Leibniz, Gottfried, W. *New Essays on Human Understanding*. Cambridge Press; 1704.

[1675] Spinoza B. *Ethics*. Penguin Classics; 1996.

[1676] Kant I. *Critique of Pure Reason*. Macmillan; 1781

[1677] Husserl E. *Logical Investigations*. Routledge; 1900

reason to understand that since water boils at 212°F (100°C), and you don't want to burn the coffee, you should use water that's a bit cooler than boiling. You can deduce principles about coffee-making through careful thinking, even before you make your first cup.

Or, a more complex example: how do babies learn language?

An empiricist would say babies learn entirely from hearing others speak and associating words with things they see and experience[1678].

A rationalist would say humans must be born with some built-in capacity for language - some basic "rules" about how language works which exist in our minds from birth[1679].

Utilitarianism, especially as developed by Jeremy Bentham[1680] and John Stuart Mill (the *Father of Free Speech*)[1681], has strong empiricist foundations and often combines both. Utilitarians believe in ways of measuring and quantifying happiness. They want to base moral decisions on observable outcomes rather than purely rational deduction from first principles. They are interested in developing ways to measure and compare different pleasures and pains.

The core utilitarian principle - that we should maximise happiness/wellbeing and minimise suffering - is based on the observable, measurable consequences of actions rather than abstract moral rules. When Mill argues we can determine what's good by observing what people actually desire and value, he's being an empiricist.

The idea we can derive a universal principle of morality (maximise utility) through reasoning, and then deduce correct actions from this principle, has a rationalist flavour. When Peter Singer argues we should extend our moral circle based on logical consistency[1682], he's using rationalist-style argumentation.

[1678] Skinner BF. *Verbal Behavior.* Appleton-Century-Crofts; 1957

[1679] Chomsky, Noam. *Aspects of the Theory of Syntax.* MIT Press; 1965

[1680] Bentham J. *An Introduction to the Principles of Morals and Legislation.* T. Payne;

[1681] Mill JS. *Utilitarianism.* Parker, Son, and Bourn; 1863

[1682] Singer P. *Practical Ethics.* Cambridge University Press; 1979

What Is Liberty?

In his 1958 essay *"Two Concepts of Liberty,"* which was originally delivered as his inaugural lecture at *Oxford University*, Russian-British philosopher Isaiah Berlin noted there are two types of freedom which can sometimes come into tension and conflict with each other. Claiming to maximise freedom, in general, overlooks these crucial distinctions. For instance, ensuring universal education might require limiting the freedom to avoid paying taxes. His commentary emerged from his direct observation of totalitarian regimes and their rhetoric of *"liberation."*

> *The essence of the notion of liberty, both in the 'positive' and the 'negative' senses, is the holding off of something or someone—of others, who trespass on my field or assert their authority over me, or of obsessions, fears, neuroses, irrational forces—intruders and despots of one kind and another.*[1683]

Positive Liberty (self-mastery or self-realisation) refers to having the actual capacity and resources to fulfil one's potential and achieve one's goals. It's about having the means, opportunities, and capabilities to act and make meaningful choices. This could include:

- Access to education that allows you to develop your abilities

---

[1683] Berlin, Isaiah, 'Two Concepts of Liberty', in Four Essays on Liberty (Oxford University Press, 1969)

- Possessing the economic means to pursue your chosen career
- Having the health and wellbeing needed to participate fully in society
- Access to public resources and infrastructure that enable personal development.

Negative Liberty (the absence of obstacles to individual choice), on the other hand, refers to freedom from external constraints or interference by others, especially by the government or other institutions. It's about the absence of obstacles or barriers that prevent you from doing what you want. Examples might include:

- Freedom from arbitrary arrest or detention
- Being able to practice your religion without interference
- Freedom to express your opinions without censorship
- Using your property as you see fit, without external control.[1684]

Berlin argued *Positive Liberty* could be dangerous when coupled with the belief there is one true path to human fulfilment or one rational way of life. He worried leaders or movements could claim to know what people "really" want better than they themselves do, and use this to justify coercing people *"for their own good."* It was not just theoretical - he saw this pattern in both fascist and communist regimes of his time.[1685]

He argued *Negative Liberty* should take priority because it is more clearly defined and less susceptible to manipulation.

[1684] Taylor, Charles, 'What's Wrong with Negative Liberty', in The Idea of Freedom: Essays in Honour of Isaiah Berlin, ed. by Alan Ryan (Oxford University Press, 1979),

[1685] MacCallum, Gerald C., 'Negative and Positive Freedom', The Philosophical Review, 76.3 (1967), 312-334

What Are Rights?

Rights are not nebulous ideas you can claim on a whim for whatever you please. They are explicit and specifically defined. They are legal, moral, or social permissions to do something, or entitlements to be treated in a certain way. They are meaningless if they can't be enforced[1686].

Rights *originate* from something as the basis of their authority.

They come from God or *Nature* ("natural rights" or "God-given rights"), existing independently of any government or human law. They are inherent, universal, and cannot be legitimately taken away - governments can only protect or violate these pre-existing rights, not create or destroy them. This is generally the traditional Anglo view which incorporates constitutional documents like the *Magna Carta* (1215) and the English *Bill of Rights* (1689)[1687].

This approach created the two most powerful[1688] and prosperous[1689] empires in history, the abolition of slavery, and man landing on the moon.

In 1765, Sir William Blackstone outlined their basis in English *Common Law*:

> *Rights are those liberties which God and nature have established,*

[1686] Hohfeld, Wesley N., 'Some Fundamental Legal Conceptions as Applied in Judicial Reasoning', *The Yale Law Journal*, 23.1 (1913), 16–59

[1687] British Parliament, *The Bill of Rights 1689*

[1688] Ferguson, Niall, *Empire* (Penguin, 2004)

[1689] McPherson, James M., *This Mighty Scourge* (Oxford University Press, 2003)

WHAT ARE RIGHTS?

and are therefore called natural rights, such as life and liberty, which no human legislature has power to abridge.[1690]

Most crucially, English case law from 1977 makes it crystal clear a "right" is not something equivalent to a preference or a whimsical claim of what one may think they "should" be able to do:

A legal right is one which is recognised and enforced by law... It is not a mere moral right.[1691]

Or they are purely human "fictions" which come from law and government ("legal positivism"), only existing because humans create and enforce them through laws and institutions[1692]. This is generally the European, Latin American, and East Asian view.

This approach led to two world wars[1693], and genocides in Poland, Ukraine, Russia, China, and Cambodia[1694].

In 1789, the French National Assembly its belief in the *Declaration of the Rights of Man and of the Citizen "* which led to the French *Civil Code*[1695] defining rights as *"the legal capacity to exercise rights and obligations in civil society."*

English definitions tend to emphasise common law traditions and practical enforcement, whereas. European definitions focus more on law philosophy and universal principles. The American revolution mixed both: the Founders wrote down the English tradition, but employed the political rhetoric of the French revolution[1696].

[1690] Blackstone, William, *Commentaries on the Laws of England*, (Clarendon, 1765)

[1691] *Gouriet v Union of Post Office Workers*, [1977] QB 729 (CA)

[1692] Hart, H. L. A., *The Concept of Law* (Oxford University Press, 1961)

[1693] Snyder, Timothy, *Bloodlands* (Basic Books, 2010)

[1694] Kiernan, Ben, *Blood and Soil* (Yale University Press, 2007)

[1695] Code civil [Civil Code], Article 7-8 (Fr.)

[1696] Wood, Gordon S., *The Radicalism of the American Revolution* (Vintage Books, 1992)

Black's Law Dictionary (American), originated in 1891 by Henry Campbell-Black, defines them as:

> *A power, privilege, demand, or claim possessed by a particular person by virtue of law.*[1697]

American jurisprudence published in 1951 clarified them as:

> *A legally enforceable claim of one person against another, that the other shall do a given act or shall not do a given act.*[1698]

The most recent definition is found in the *Stanford Encyclopedia of Philosophy*:

> *Rights are entitlements (not) to perform certain actions, or (not) to be in certain states; or entitlements that others (not) perform certain actions or (not) be in certain states.*[1699]

Natural rights are considered inherent to being human - they exist regardless of what any government or law says.

The classic examples come from John Locke[1700]:

- life, liberty, and property
- freedom of thought
- self-defence
- freedom of movement.

One has these rights simply by virtue of being human, whether in ancient

---

[1697] Garner, Bryan A., ed., *Black's Law Dictionary*, (Thomson Reuters, 2019)

[1698] 'Rights', §1, in *American Jurisprudence*, Vol. 77 (Thomson Reuters, 2015)

[1699] Wenar, Leif, 'Rights', in Edward N. Zalta (ed.), *Stanford Encyclopedia of Philosophy*

[1700] Locke, John, *Two Treatises of Government* (Awnsham Churchill, 1689)

WHAT ARE RIGHTS?

Rome, modern Japan, or a deserted island. They are "inalienable" or "God-given."

Legal rights, in contrast, are created and enforced by governments and legal systems[1701].

They can vary dramatically between countries and can change over time. Examples might be:

- voting
- social security benefits
- patent protection
- parental leave.

These rights only exist because society has decided to create and protect them through laws. The right to a jury trial isn't inherent to being human - it's a legal right granted by certain governments. Similarly, one's right to drive a car on public roads isn't natural - it's a legal privilege that can be granted or taken away by the state.

These rights can be further divided by what they permit or restrict.

Negative rights are freedoms FROM interference or actions by others (especially the government). What others *cannot* do to you[1702]. Classic examples include:

- freedom from arbitrary arrest
- freedom from torture
- freedom from censorship.

The key feature is that to honour these rights, others mainly need to *leave you alone* - they don't have to actively do anything.

Positive rights are entitlements TO something - they require active provision or assistance from others (usually the government) and typi-

---

[1701] Austin, John, *The Province of Jurisprudence Determined* (J. Murray, 1832)

[1702] Berlin, Isaiah, *Four Essays on Liberty* (Oxford University Press, 1969)

cally cost money to fulfil and require active government programs[1703]. Examples include:

- education (requires schools and teachers)
- healthcare (requires hospitals and medical staff)
- housing
- legal representation.

The tension between individual rights and state power lies at the heart of political and legal philosophy.

In the Anglo tradition based on common law, the *individual* is seen as primary - possessing natural rights that pre-exist government, with the state's role being to protect these pre-existing rights while being constrained by them[1704]. State power is seen as inherently suspect and potentially tyrannical, requiring strict limits and constant vigilance[1705].

The European tradition, influenced by Rousseau[1706] and Hegel[1707], tends to see the *state* as the essential guarantor and source of rights, viewing individual liberty not as pre-political but as something that can only meaningfully exist within an organised state that actively creates and protects rights. Collective welfare and social harmony are equally or more important than individual liberty, and views state power more positively as a tool for achieving social goals.

California's legal system represents a unique American-European hybrid[1708] that sets it apart from other U.S. states. It embraced significant European legal concepts from its earliest days, starting with its *1872 Civil*

[1703] Shue, Henry, *Basic Rights* (Princeton University Press, 1980)

[1704] Mill, John Stuart, *On Liberty* (John W. Parker and Son, 1859)

[1705] Dicey, Albert, *Introduction to the Study of the Law of the Constitution* (Macmillan, 1885)

[1706] Rousseau, Jean-Jacques, *The Social Contract* (Marc-Michel Rey, 1762)

[1707] Hegel, G. W. F., *Elements of the Philosophy of Right* (Nicolaische Buchhandlung, 1821)

[1708] Rabin, Robert L., *Law and the Administrative Process* (Foundation Press, 1980)

Code[1709] which drew heavily from European civil law traditions through the *New York Field Code*[1710]. This influence continues in California's emphasis on *positive* rights[1711].

After the Holocaust of the Second World War, a new class of "rights" was established to prevent it from happening again. The UN's approach to human rights, codified in the 1948 *Universal Declaration of Human Rights* (UDHR) was a hybrid of these traditions, and relies on *voluntary* state compliance[1712].

The UDHR and subsequent UN conventions combined Anglo-American civil and political rights (free speech, fair trial) with European social and economic rights (education, healthcare, housing), reflecting both its French primary drafter (René Cassin)[1713] and the Soviet Union's influence in negotiations[1714].

Two years later, definitions became even murkier.

The European "human rights" system, centered on the *European Convention on Human Rights* (ECHR, 1950) took a different path[1715]. While influenced by the UDHR, it initially focused more on classic civil and political rights, reflecting its origins as a Cold War Western European project[1716]. However, through the *European Social Charter* and *EU Charter of Fundamental Rights*, it has evolved to embrace positive social rights while maintaining stronger enforcement mechanisms than the UN system.

At the heart of it is a genuine supranational judiciary, the *European*

[1709] The Civil Code of the State of California, Mar 21, 1872 (Springer, 1872)

[1710] New York State, *The Field Code* (Weed, Parsons & Co., 1872)

[1711] Scheiber, Harry N., 'American Federalism and the Diffusion of Power: Historical and Contemporary Perspectives', *Harvard Law Review*, 96.3 (1982), 151–88

[1712] United Nations, *Universal Declaration of Human Rights* (1948)

[1713] Cassin, René, *Draft of the Universal Declaration of Human Rights* (United Nations, 1948)

[1714] Glendon, Mary Ann, *A World Made New* (Random House, 2001)

[1715] Council of Europe, *European Convention on Human Rights* (1950)

[1716] Bates, Ed, *Evolution of the European Convention on Human Rights* (Oxford Press, 2010)

Court of Human Rights in Strasbourg, which can issue binding decisions on EU member states. The incorporation of the ECHR into UK domestic law through the *Human Rights Act 1998*[1717] introduced contradictory chaos into British legal tradition which was made worse by the creation of a "supreme court" in 2003 which violated the constitutional principle of parliamentary sovereignty[1718].

International "human rights" are legal obligations which states voluntarily accept toward individuals, defined through treaties and enforced through international institutions.

They exist between states and individuals (not between individuals); they're indivisible (you can't pick and choose which to respect);, and they're enforced through international monitoring and peer pressure rather than direct judicial power. They are best described as *international standards of state behaviour,* rather the laws.

In essence, similar to postmodern art and philosophy, "human rights" rest on nothing, and are essentially meaningless.

Which, of course, makes them suffer mindless *inflation*. By declaring everything desirable a "human right," we diminish the moral and legal force of fundamental rights like freedom from torture or arbitrary detention. This has transformed "human rights" from vital protections into a "wishlist of social goods", making them harder to enforce and easier to dismiss.

Edmund Burke set out the distinction between rights and moral licence hundreds of years ago when comparing the Anglo and French approaches:

> *Government is not made in virtue of natural rights, which may and do exist in total independence of it... but their abstract perfection is their practical defect. By having a right to everything they want*

[1717] Her Majesty's Stationery Office, *Human Rights Act 1998* (HMSO, 1998)

[1718] Bogdanor, Vernon, *The New British Constitution* (Hart Publishing, 2005)

WHAT ARE RIGHTS?

everything.[1719]

More recently, Mary Ann Glendon argued the proliferation of "rights" claims has led to an impoverished public discourse where every preference gets reframed as a "right."

> *The strident rights rhetoric that currently dominates American political discourse poorly serves democratic values... [it] promotes unrealistic expectations, heightens social conflict, and inhibits dialogue that might lead toward consensus, accommodation, or at least the discovery of common ground.*[1720]

Among the more ridiculous proposals have been, so far:

- The right to leisure and tourism[1721]
- The right to Internet access[1722]
- The right to sleep[1723]
- The right to sports participation[1724]
- The right to *"hedonic happiness"*[1725]
- The right to *"love and be loved"*[1726]

[1719] Burke, Edmund, *Reflections on the Revolution in France* (J. Dodsley, 1790)

[1720] Glendon, Mary, *Rights Talk: The Impoverishment of Political Discourse* (Free Press, 1991)

[1721] *Manila Declaration on World Tourism* (UNWTO, 1980)

[1722] *The Promotion, Protection, and Enjoyment of Human Rights on the Internet* (A/HRC/32/L.20) (UNHRC, 2016)

[1723] Caitlyn Tabor, JD, MBE, and Katherine R. Peeler, MD, MA, "Sleep Is a Human Right, and Its Deprivation Is Torture," *AMA Journal of Ethics* (October 2024)

[1724] *International Charter of Physical Education, Physical Activity and Sport* (UNESCO, 1978)

[1725] United Nations, *World Happiness Report* (UN SDSN, 2012)

[1726] Donnelly, Jack, *Universal Human Rights in Theory and Practice* (Cornell Press, 2003)

- The right to air conditioning[1727]
- The right to football/soccer (proposed)[1728]
- The right to *"pleasant working conditions"*[1729]
- The right to *"cultural enrichment"*[1730]

[1727] Rose M. Mutiso, Morgan D. Bazilian, Jacob Kincer, and Brooke Bowser, edited by Sophie Bushwick, "Air-Conditioning Should Be a Human Right in the Climate Crisis," *Scientific American* (May 10, 2022).

[1728] Lev, Daniel S., 'The Right to Sports: Latin America's Path to Social Inclusion', *Latin American Perspectives*, 19.4 (1992)

[1729] International Labour Organization, *Declaration of Philadelphia* (ILO, 1944)

[1730] *Universal Declaration on Cultural Diversity* (UNESCO, 2001)

What Are Fallacies?

A fallacy is faulty, broken thinking. There are hundreds of different types[1731].

An *Argument* has three components of its *Logic* which appear as two *Forms*[1732]:

Affirming the Consequent

1. Humans are mortal.
2. I am a human.
3. *Therefore, I am mortal.*

Denying the Antecedent

1. Humans are mortal.
2. My cat is not a human.
3. *Therefore, my cat is not mortal.*

Often an argument given by someone can sound reasonable, but actually fall apart under questioning because its internal logic is not *Valid*[1733].

[1731] Copi, I. M., Carl Cohen, Kenneth McMahon, *Introduction to Logic* (Routl., 2016)

[1732] Hurley, Patrick J., *A Concise Introduction to Logic*, (Cengage Learning, 2015)

[1733] Walton, Douglas N., *Informal Logic* (Cambridge University Press, 2008)

An *Appeal* asking you to believe is *not* an *Argument*[1734].

Emotional Appeals

Emotions are powerful tools that can override our rational thinking processes, leading us to make decisions based on feelings rather than facts. These fallacies exploit our emotional vulnerabilities, using fear, pity, pride, or other strong feelings to persuade us while bypassing logical reasoning[1735].

- *Appeal to Fear (Ad Baculum)*: Using threats to force agreement
- *Appeal to Pity (Ad Misericordiam)*: Exploiting sympathy for support
- *Appeal to Flattery*: Using praise to manipulate
- *Appeal to Spite*: Rejecting something because of hatred
- *Appeal to Shame*: Using embarrassment to force compliance
- *Wishful Thinking*: Believing something because you want it to be true
- *Appeal to Anger*: Using rage to justify a position
- *Emotional Manipulation*: Using any emotion to override logic
- *Playing to Pride*: Exploiting ego for agreement
- *Appeal to Desperation*: Using urgency to bypass reasoning

Authority and Popularity

We often rely on experts and popular opinion as mental shortcuts for determining truth, but this tendency can lead us astray. These fallacies exploit our natural inclination to trust authority figures and follow the crowd, even when the authority might be irrelevant or the majority might be wrong[1736].

[1734] Groarke, Leo, Christopher W. Tindale, *Good Reasoning Matters!* (Oxford Press, 2013)

[1735] Walton, Douglas, *Informal Logic* (Cambridge University Press, 2008)

[1736] Cialdini, Robert B., *Influence* (Harper Business, 2021)

- *Appeal to Authority (Ad Verecundiam)*: Trusting expert claims blindly
- *Appeal to Popularity (Ad Populum)*: "Everyone does it"
- *Bandwagon Effect*: Following the crowd
- *Appeal to Tradition*: "It's always been done this way"
- *Appeal to Novelty*: "It's new, so it's better"
- *False Authority*: Expert in one field speaking about another
- *Celebrity Endorsement*: Famous person equals truth
- *Anonymous Authority*: "They say that…"
- *Appeal to Accomplishment*: Success in one area equals expertise in all
- *Genetic Fallacy*: Dismissing something based on its origin

Causal

Understanding cause and effect is fundamental to human reasoning, but our eagerness to find explanations can lead us to see causation where none exists. These fallacies represent the various ways we misunderstand or oversimplify cause-and-effect relationships in our world[1737].

- *Post Hoc Ergo Propter Hoc*: After this, therefore because of this
- *Correlation vs. Causation*: Connection doesn't equal causation
- *False Cause*: Assuming wrong cause for an effect
- *Complex Cause*: Oversimplifying multiple causes
- *Reverse Causation*: Mixing up cause and effect
- *Single Cause*: Ignoring multiple factors
- *Circular Cause*: A causes B causes A
- *Butterfly Effect Fallacy*: Overestimating minor causes
- *Prevention Paradox*: Assuming prevention didn't work because nothing happened
- *Causal Reductionism*: Oversimplifying complex causal chains

---

[1737] Pearl, Judea, *The Book of Why* (Basic Books, 2018)

Logical Structure

The architecture of an argument can contain hidden flaws that undermine its validity, even when individual components seem reasonable. These fallacies represent structural problems in reasoning that can make arguments appear stronger than they actually are[1738].

- *False Dichotomy*: Only two options exist
- *Hasty Generalization*: Jumping to conclusions
- *Slippery Slope*: If A happens, Z will inevitably follow
- *Composition/Division*: What's true of parts is true of whole
- *Begging the Question*: Circular reasoning
- *No True Scotsman*: Moving the goalposts
- *Special Pleading*: Making exceptions without justification
- *Fallacy of the Single Cause*: Complex event has one cause
- *Moving the Goalposts*: Changing criteria after they're met
- *False Equivalence*: Treating different things as identical

Language and Ambiguity

Language is inherently ambiguous, and this ambiguity can be either accidentally or deliberately exploited to create false arguments. These fallacies arise from the imprecise nature of language and the ways we can manipulate meaning through word choice and context[1739].

- *Equivocation*: Using multiple meanings of a word
- *Ambiguity*: Unclear language leading to confusion
- *Loaded Question*: Question contains assumption
- *Quoting Out of Context*: Misrepresenting by selective quotation
- *No True Definition*: Arguing about definitions

[1738] Copi, Irving M., and Carl Cohen, *Introduction to Logic* (Routledge, 2014)

[1739] van Eemeren, Frans H., Rob Grootendorst, *Argumentation Theory* (Springer, 2016)

- *Accent*: Changing meaning through emphasis
- *Category Error*: Applying properties to wrong category
- *Amphiboly*: Grammatical ambiguity
- *Fallacy of Composition*: Assuming what's true of parts is true of whole
- *Fallacy of Division*: Assuming what's true of whole is true of parts

Statistical and Probability

Our intuitive understanding of probability often conflicts with mathematical reality, leading to systematic errors in judgment. These fallacies represent the common ways we misunderstand, misuse, or misinterpret statistical information and probability[1740].

- *Gambler's Fallacy*: Past events affect independent probability
- *Base Rate Fallacy*: Ignoring background probability
- *Texas Sharpshooter*: Finding patterns in randomness
- *Regression Fallacy*: Not understanding return to mean
- *Sample Size Fallacy*: Small sample represents whole
- *Cherry Picking*: Selecting favorable data
- *Survivorship Bias*: Focus on survivors only
- *Statistical Manipulation*: Misusing statistics
- *Observation Selection*: Noticing only confirming cases
- *Extrapolation Error*: Extending trends inappropriately

Relevance

Not every seemingly related point actually bears on the truth of an argument, and irrelevant information can distract from the core issues at hand. These fallacies occur when arguments rely on information or attacks that may seem pertinent but actually have no logical connection

---

[1740] Kahneman, Daniel, *Thinking, Fast and Slow* (Farrar, Straus and Giroux, 2011)

to the conclusion[1741].

- *Red Herring*: Distracting from main issue
- *Straw Man*: Misrepresenting an opponent's argument
- *Ad Hominem*: Attacking person not argument
- *Genetic Fallacy*: Dismissing source not content
- *Tu Quoque*: "You too" fallacy
- *Guilt by Association*: Dismissing due to connections
- *Appeal to Hypocrisy*: Pointing out contradiction
- *Circumstantial Ad Hominem*: Attacking circumstances
- *Poisoning the Well*: Prejudicing audience
- *Two Wrongs Make a Right*: Justifying wrong with wrong

Presumption

Arguments often rest on unstated assumptions that may not be valid, leading to flawed conclusions even when the reasoning seems sound. These fallacies involve making inappropriate assumptions or shifting the burden of proof unfairly in an argument[1742].

- *Burden of Proof*: Shifting responsibility to prove
- *False Premise*: Starting with incorrect assumption
- *Begging the Question*: Assuming conclusion in premise
- *Complex Question*: Multiple questions as one
- *Accident*: Misapplying general rule
- *Converse Accident*: Generalizing from exception
- *False Analogy*: Comparing unlike things
- *Hasty Conclusion*: Insufficient evidence
- *Appeal to Ignorance*: No proof against equals true
- *Naturalistic Fallacy*: "Is" implies "ought"

[1741] Hamblin, Charles L., *Fallacies* (Methuen, 1970)

[1742] Walton, Douglas, *Presumption in Argumentation* (University of Alabama, 2008)

WHAT ARE FALLACIES?

Moral and Ethical

Moral reasoning requires careful navigation between facts and values, and many common errors arise from conflating what is with what ought to be. These fallacies represent various ways we can make illogical jumps in moral reasoning or misuse ethical principles[1743].

- *Appeal to Nature*: Natural equals good
- *Moralistic Fallacy*: Ought implies is
- *Is-Ought Fallacy*: Facts determine values
- *Appeal to Consequences*: Results determine truth
- *Might Makes Right*: Power equals correctness
- *Appeal to Perfect Solution*: Reject good for perfect
- *Moral Equivalence*: False comparison of moral issues
- *Two Wrongs Make a Right*: Evil justified by evil
- *Appeal to Common Practice*: Everyone does it
- *Noble Cause Corruption*: End justifies means

Perceptual and Memory

Our brains are not perfect recording devices, and our memories and perceptions are subject to various systematic distortions. These fallacies arise from the natural limitations and biases in how we perceive, remember, and process information about the world around us[1744].

Primary source:

- *Confirmation Bias*: Seeing what confirms beliefs
- *Anchoring Bias*: Over-relying on first information
- *Availability Heuristic*: Easy to recall seems common
- *Hindsight Bias*: Past seems predictable

[1743] Singer, Peter, *Practical Ethics* (Cambridge University Press, 2011)

[1744] Schacter, Daniel L., *The Seven Sins of Memory* (Houghton Mifflin, 2001)

- *Recency Bias*: Recent events seem more important
- *Duration Neglect*: Misremembering time periods
- *Peak-End Rule*: Judging by extremes and endings
- *Representativeness Bias*: Stereotyping
- *False Memory*: Creating incorrect memories
- *Change Blindness*: Missing gradual changes

What Are Sophistry & Casuistry?

In the second half of the fifth century BC, Athens had a class of intellectuals who abandoned excellence (*"arete"*) in their subjects, for simply using clever language. They stopped being correct and merely succeeded in being persuasive. A *"Sophos"* (*"wise man"*) taught the wisdom (*"sophia"*, the special insight of poets and prophets) of their profession to influential young people[1745].

Sophistry is the art of misleading.

A *Sophist* is a person who reasons with clever but fallacious and deceptive arguments; someone who makes an impressive-sounding case from broken logic, with the intent of deliberately deceiving the listener using rhetoric[1746].

An infamous example of sophistry is from Gorgias:

> *Nothing exists; even if something exists, nothing can be known about it; and even if something can be known about it, knowledge about it can't be communicated to others.*[1747]

It sounds persuasive and impressively deep. However, the statement undercuts its own premise. If "nothing can be known," then even this assertion itself can't be known or communicated, making the entire

---

[1745] Guthrie, W. K. C., *The Sophists* (Cambridge University Press, 1971)

[1746] Jowett, Benjamin, *The Dialogues of Plato*, Vol. 1 (Oxford University Press, 1871)

[1747] Gorgias, *On the Non-Existent* (1994; c. 380 BCE)

premise self-defeating.

Ten centuries later, French mathematician Blaise Pascal attacked Jesuit priests in his *"Provincial Letters"* (1656–57) about the reasoning they used for attracting donors. He complained "remorseful" aristocrats could confess a sin one day, re-commit it the next, then generously donate to the church and return to re-confess their sin, confident that they were being assigned a penance in name only[1748].

Casuistry is the art of falsely justifying.

The Latin word "casus" ("case" or "occurrence") forming the root of the word denotes a process of applying general moral principles or norms to specific cases. It refers to specious or overly subtle reasoning, intended to rationalise or excuse unethical behaviour; a means of justifying dubious or immoral actions by drawing spurious or "elastic" parallels to ethically acceptable cases[1749].

An infamous example from the *Counter-Reformation* Jesuits might concern a merchant considering whether to deceive his customers about the quality of a product. He recalls the moral teaching *"Do not lie."* To justify his decision, he reasons:

> *There was a case where a person lied to save someone's life, and that was deemed morally acceptable because it was for a greater good. In my situation, if I deceive my customers, I will earn more profit. This profit will enable me to provide better for my family, give more to charity, and help more people. Therefore, deceiving in this instance serves a greater good, just as lying to save a life does.*

This stretches the comparison between two very different cases to justify deception[1750]. While the original case of lying was to directly save a life, the merchant's situation involves personal gain, making the two cases not

---

[1748] Pascal, Blaise, *The Provincial Letters* (William Whyte and Co., 1847; c. 1656–1657)

[1749] Mahoney, John, *The Making of Moral Theology* (Oxford University Press, 1987)

[1750] Beauchamp, T, James, Childress, *Principles of Biomedical Ethics*, (Oxford Press, 2019)

genuinely analogous. By using such tenuous connections, the merchant appears to be engaging in self-serving justification rather than sincere moral reasoning.

What Is Reification?

Reification is wrongly referring to something imaginary as if it were physically real. To *reify* an idea is to treat or misplace it as concrete, when it is, in fact, abstract or ephemeral[1751].

Commonly reified ideas are the *"mind"*, *"fate"*, *"science"*, and *"Mother Nature"*. To say *"the ocean is calling me"* or *"science says..."* is erroneous as neither science nor the ocean is a conscious entity which can speak[1752].

Imagine a perfume advertisement that claims their fragrance captures *"love in a bottle."* Love, being an abstract emotion, cannot literally be contained within a bottle.

Statements such as *"the economy is taking a rest"* or *"the economy feels uncertain"* reify the economy. The economy doesn't have feelings or intentions; it's an abstract concept representing a system of trade and production.

Phrases like *"nature wants to find a way"* or *"nature intended for species to evolve in certain ways"* assign intentions and desires to nature. Nature doesn't have intentions or desires in the same way humans do.

In discussions about the internet or networks, one might hear, *"the information doesn't want to be confined; it wants to be free."* This ascribes desires and intentions to "information," which is an abstract concept[1753].

Saying *"the algorithm learned its behaviour from the data"* or *"the algorithm*

[1751] Copi, Irving, Carl Cohen, Kenneth McMahon, *Introduction to Logic* (Routledge, 2016)

[1752] Strawson, P. F., *Individuals* (Methuen, 1959)

[1753] Floridi, Luciano, *Information* (Oxford Press, 2010)

WHAT IS REIFICATION?

decided to show you this ad." Algorithms don't learn or decide in the conscious way humans do. They operate based on predefined instructions and computations.

If someone were to say, *"justice turned a blind eye to that incident,"* it reifies the concept of justice. Justice, being an abstract principle, doesn't have eyes or the capability to "see" events.

When a concept is reified in common everyday language, it can become an *Axiom*, or something which is generally accepted to be true[1754].

The entire canon of humanities literature is predicated on fallaciously reifying concepts and *"theories"* (which are actually hypotheses). Almost all of the material produced by the social sciences is *fashionable nonsense* which is *indistinguishable from fiction*.

[1754] Lakoff, George, and Mark Johnson, *Philosophy in the Flesh* (Basic Books, 1999)

What Is Magical Thinking?

Magical thinking is mistakenly attributing existence, or coincidence, to supernatural causes. It is primarily correlated with superstition, and is the belief one's ideas, thoughts, actions, words, or use of symbols can influence the course of events in the material world[1755].

Magical thinking is believed to be a form of anxiety relief as its occurrence peaks at times of uncertainty, danger, or distress, generally in children, or those with a greater desire for control[1756]. When one or more events is temporally contiguous, they are falsely inferred to have a causal relationship.

- *Observing superstitious rituals*
- *Predetermination, fate, or synchronicity*
- *Suspending disbelief watching a movie*
- *Divining the past or future from objects or phenomena*
- *Relaying Old Wives' Tales*
- *Gamblers believing they have lucky numbers*
- *Tribespeople seeing a smartphone*
- *Seeing patterns and pictures in objects*
- *Associating bad outcomes to unrelated events*
- *Believing thoughts can engineer prosperity*

[1755] Vyse, Stuart A., *Believing in Magic* (Oxford University Press, 2014)

[1756] Keinan, Giora, 'The Effects of Stress and Desire for Control on Superstitious Behavior', *Personality and Social Psychology Bulletin*, 28.1 (2002), 102–10

- *Being cured by placebo medication*

Believing in *"fate"* is an example of magical thinking. As is belief in divination, such as astrology or numerology[1757].

When attempts are made to represent magical superstition or imaginary notions into the academic realm, they are known as p*ara-ologies* or p*seudoscience*[1758].

Believing language can alter material reality is an example from the *"theory"* of *"social constructionism"* and has an alternative name: a *spell*.

[1757] Nagel, Thomas, *Mortal Questions* (Cambridge University Press, 1979)

[1758] Pigliucci, Massimo, Maarten Boudry, *Philosophy of Pseudoscience* (U. of Chicago, 2013)

What Are In/Out-Groups?

It's not what you know, it's *who* you know. We trust things we know which are familiar to us, and distrust those which aren't and feel strange. We trust people who look like us, and distrust those who don't. Scientific evidence shows humans, like other social animals, for better or worse, typically favour and cooperate with their own perceived group. Humans evolved living in small groups and developed mechanisms to quickly categorise "similar" vs. "different."

"In-group–out-group bias" refers to a tendency where people favour members of groups they recognise (*"in-groups"*) and show bias against those perceived as different (*"out-groups"*).

Gordon Allport's seminal work *"'The Nature of Prejudice"* (1954) established much of the foundational research on this phenomenon. He found people naturally categorise themselves and others into groups based on characteristics like ethnicity, religion, nationality, or even shared interests[1759]. *"In-group preference"* often develops even in minimal group situations where group assignments are completely arbitrary. Infants as young as six months show preferences for speakers of their native language over foreign language speakers[1760]. Various studies show

---

[1759] Pettigrew, Thomas F., and Hammann, Kerstin, 'Gordon Willard Allport: The Nature of Prejudice', in S. Salzborn (ed.), *Klassiker der Sozialwissenschaften* [Classics of Social Science] (Wiesbaden: Springer, 2016), pp. 174–78

[1760] Kinzler, Katherine D., Dupoux, Emmanuel, and Spelke, Elizabeth S., 'Native Language of Social Cognition', *Proceedings of the National Academy of Sciences*, 104.30 (2007), 12577–80

humans can categorise faces as in-group/out-group within *milliseconds*, suggesting deep evolutionary optimisation for this ability.

This makes obvious evolutionary sense.

Evolutionary biology helps explain observed patterns in human group behaviour: rapid categorisation of in-group/out-group; strong group loyalty mechanisms; inter-group competition; territory defence; resource competition; and genetic fitness strategies.

British biologist William Hamilton's theory of *"inclusive fitness"* (1964, *an organism's evolutionary success is not just measured by its own offspring, but also by the reproductive success of its genetic relatives*) demonstrated mathematically how favouring genetically related individuals increases the likelihood of one's genes being passed on to future generations.

Studies of hunter-gatherer societies show groups sharing food and resources among trusted members had better survival rates during periods of scarcity. Primatological studies show groups which maintain strong internal bonds are more effective at defending against threats. Groups that were better at recognising and responding to out-group threats were more likely to survive and pass on their genes.

Group living enables shared childcare, which increases offspring survival rates. Research in immunology suggests groups which stay relatively isolated develop shared immune responses to local pathogens. Historical evidence suggests groups that maintained boundaries often had better survival rates during epidemics.

Henri Tajfel's research in the 1970s further developed this concept through *"social identity theory"*. His studies demonstrated merely categorising people into groups, even based on trivial criteria, could trigger in-group favouritism[1761].

What is more interesting, arguably, is the inverse phenomena. Why would one prefer an *"out-group"*?

In 1993, philosopher Roger Scruton coined the term *"oikophobia"* (Greek "oikos" for "home"; "phobos" or "fear") to describe what he saw as

---

[1761] Tajfel, Henri, *Human Groups and Social Categories* (Cambridge University Press, 1981)

an intellectual tendency to reject one's own cultural traditions in favour of foreign or international elements.

An infamous study in 1947 involved 253 black children aged between three and seven. The researchers presented each child with four dolls, identical except for skin colour (two white, two brown). Children were asked a series of questions like identifying which doll they preferred to play with, which looked "nice," which looked "bad," and which doll "looks like you."

67% of children preferred to play with the white doll; 59% identified the white doll as the "nice" one; 59% identified the brown doll as the "bad" one; when asked to identify which doll looked like them, some children became emotionally distressed or left the testing room.

Betraying an in-group has evolutionary advantages. It could entail individual access to superior resources which outweigh the benefits of in-group cooperation; genetic advantages through mating opportunities and better survival chances by allying with a more powerful or resourceful group. If betraying the in-group leads to significantly better survival and reproduction outcomes, those behavioural tendencies could be selected for and passed on.

In primate studies and archaeological evidence, successful defection from one's group follows clear patterns. When the original group becomes severely weakened or faces existential threats, individuals are more likely to seek security elsewhere. This makes sense with basic survival instincts - there's little benefit in maintaining loyalty to a failing group.

The target group for defection needs to be significantly more powerful than the original group. This ensures better survival chances and access to resources. Archaeological evidence shows smaller groups were often absorbed into larger, more successful ones during periods of conflict or resource scarcity.

For defection to be successful, there must be a clear pathway to acceptance by the new group. This often involves having valuable skills, knowledge, or resources to offer. Historical evidence shows individuals with technical knowledge, military intelligence, or access to resources were more likely to be accepted by rival groups.

The risk of defection is substantially reduced when multiple individuals defect together. This creates a small support network within the new group and makes retaliation from the original group more difficult. It also suggests to the receiving group that there are serious problems with the original group, making the defectors more credible.

Game theory models demonstrate how power differentials between groups create opportunities for successful defection. When one group has significantly more resources, better territory, or stronger military capability, the benefits of switching allegiance increase dramatically. Population pressures and environmental threats can also shift the cost-benefit ratio - during famines, droughts, or similar crises, the advantages of joining a more resourceful group may outweigh the risks of leaving one's original group.

What Is Falsification?

A *zero-sum game fallacy* is a belief where, for one player to win, the other most lose. A fixed-pie of resources exists, and one individual's gain is another's loss[1762].

Falsifiability is whether a claim can actually be proved true or false. To establish the truth, and distinguish scientific theories from non-scientific ones, it is necessary to be able to ascertain if something is *untrue*[1763]. This idea was proposed by scientific philosopher Karl Popper, who also wrote *"The Open Society and its Enemies"*[1764], often known as the bible of modern liberalism[1765].

When denying an accusation, or the nature of a denial, is considered evidence of your guilt, such circular reasoning is known as a *"Kafka Trap"*[1766]. Similar to a witch sinking or floating in a medieval *Trial by Ordeal*.

Defaming someone as a racist, for example, is an unfalsifiable claim, because no means exists for the victim to prove it to be false. The defamer wins at the victim's expense.

[1762] von Neumann, John, and Oskar Morgenstern, *Theory of Games and Economic Behavior* (Princeton University Press, 1944)

[1763] Lakatos, Imre, 'Criticism and the Methodology of Scientific Research Programmes', in I. Lakatos and A. Musgrave (eds.), *Criticism and the Growth of Knowledge* (Cambridge University Press, 1970)

[1764] Popper, Karl R., *The Open Society and Its Enemies* (Routledge, 1945)

[1765] Popper, Karl R., *The Logic of Scientific Discovery* (Basic Books, 1934)

[1766] Kafka, Franz, *The Trial*, (Berlin: Verlag Die Schmiede, 1925; c. 1914–1915)

For example, the statement *"all swans are white"* is supported by every observation of a white swan. However, just one observation of a black swan immediately refutes it. Popper argued that no number of positive outcomes at the empirical level can confirm a scientific theory for good, but a single counterexample can refute it.

Instead of trying to prove a theory right, scientists should aim to prove it wrong. If a theory resists all attempts at falsification, it is strengthened (but not confirmed in an absolute sense).

If there is no way to prove a hypothesis or claim to be true or false, then it is not scientific; nor should it be subscribed to.

What Is Paralogic?

Para and *pseudo* both mean false or mistaken - *alongside* the truth[1767].

A *paralogism* is a false belief or misconception arising from incorrect or invalid reasoning, such as a fallacious argument[1768]. *Paralogic* thinking is often found in schizophrenic patients who are preoccupied with their own subjective thoughts and fantasies[1769].

Infamous examples of paralogisms include:

> *If it rains, then the ground will be wet. The ground is wet. Therefore, it rained.*
>
> *All roses are flowers. Some flowers fade quickly. Therefore, some roses fade quickly.*
>
> *All unicorns are white. Therefore, some unicorns are white.*

Someone might have watered the plants or there might have been a burst pipe; the premise doesn't state that all flowers fade quickly; unicorns don't exist.

A *paramorality* is a false perversion of morality, emphasising a sensual or hedonistic performance of apparently moral behaviour. *Paramoral* thinking is most often found in totalitarian dictatorships and psycho-

---

[1767] Copi, Irving, Carl Cohen, Kenneth McMahon, *Introduction to Logic* (Routledge, 2016)

[1768] Kant, Immanuel, *Critique of Pure Reason* (1781, Macmillan, 1929)

[1769] Frith, Christopher D., *The Cognitive Neuropsychology of Schizophrenia* (Lawrence Erlbaum Associates, 1992)

pathic criminals as a means of justifying harm; using moral-like language or concepts to defend or advocate for immoral behaviours[1770].

Infamous examples of paramorality include:

> *The Ends Justify the Means.*
> *Deus Vult ("God wills it").*
> *Different cultures have different moral codes, anything goes.*
> *It's for the Greater Good.*

An ideological *pseudo-reality* is a false conception of reality, or an apparent reality which is in fact, a delusion.

Using a paralogic and paramorality, a psychopathologically-compromised[1771] group manipulates or "engineers" a false vision of the world and what is real, designed to serve their needs in a totalitarian fashion.

[1770] Arendt, Hannah, *Eichmann in Jerusalem* (Viking Press, 1963)

[1771] Hare, Robert D., *Manual for the Revised Psychopathy Checklist* (U. of Toronto, 1991)

What Are Cognitive Biases?

No human being is free of bias. However, it does not mean we cannot arrive at objective truth or our biases are not useful or beneficial as "mental shortcuts" (aka *heuristics*) in many circumstances[1772].

Cognitive biases are patterns of deviation from norm or rationality in judgment. These biases can lead to perceptual distortion, inaccurate judgment, illogical interpretation, or what is broadly called *irrationality*. They are often a result of our brain's attempt to simplify information processing, and they can be caused by various factors, including short-cutting, social pressures, and emotional/moral motivations[1773].

There are believed to be ~200 identified so far[1774].

Memory

Memory biases affect how we store, recall, and use information from our experiences. They can lead to distortions in our memories, influencing how we remember events and make decisions based on past information[1775].

[1772] Gigerenzer, Gerd, 'Why Heuristics Work', *Perspectives on Psychological Science*, 3.1 (2008), 20–29

[1773] Kahneman, Daniel, and Amos Tversky, 'On the Reality of Cognitive Illusions', *Psychological Review*, 103.3 (1996), 582–91

[1774] Benson, Buster, 'Cognitive Bias Cheat Sheet', *Better Humans*, 2016

[1775] Schacter, Daniel L., 'The Seven Sins of Memory: Insights from Psychology and Cognitive Neuroscience', *American Psychologist*, 54.3 (1999), 182–203

- Bizarreness Effect: Remembering weird things better than ordinary ones.
- *Cryptomnesia*: Mistaking old memories for new thoughts.
- *False Memory*: Remembering something that didn't actually happen.
- *Google Effect*: Forgetting information that can be easily found online.
- *Levels of Processing Effect*: Remembering things better when you engage with them more deeply.
- *Misinformation Effect*: Recalling false information mixed with true memories.
- *Peak-End Rule*: Judging an experience mainly by its most intense point and its end.
- *Primacy Effect*: Remembering the first items in a list better than the middle ones.
- *Recency Effect*: Remembering the last items in a list better than the middle ones.

Social

Social biases influence how we perceive, interact with, and make judgments about other people and social situations. They can affect our relationships, group behaviour, and societal interactions[1776].

- *Actor-Observer Bias*: Explaining your own actions with circumstances, but others' actions with personality.
- *Bandwagon Effect*: Doing or believing things because others do.
- *Cheerleader Effect*: Thinking individuals are more attractive when they're in a group.
- *False Consensus Effect*: Overestimating how many people agree with you.
- *Fundamental Attribution Error*: Blaming others' personality for their

---

[1776] Ross, Lee, and Richard E. Nisbett, *The Person and the Situation* (Pinter & Martin Publishers, 2011)

actions, but circumstances for your own.
- *Groupthink*: Going along with bad ideas to avoid conflict in a group.
- *In-Group Bias*: Favouring people who are similar to you.
- *Just-World Hypothesis*: Believing people always get what they deserve.
- *Spotlight Effect*: Thinking others notice you more than they actually do.

Decision-Making

Decision-making biases impact how we evaluate options, make choices, and judge the outcomes of our decisions. They can lead to bad decisions in various aspects of life, from personal choices to business strategies[1777].

- *Anchoring Bias*: Relying too much on the first information you get.
- *Availability Heuristic*: Thinking easily remembered things are more important.
- *Confirmation Bias*: Only noticing things that support what you already believe.
- *Dunning-Kruger Effect*: Beginners overestimating their skills.
- *Framing Effect*: Changing your mind based on how information is presented.
- *Hyperbolic Discounting*: Preferring smaller, sooner rewards over larger, later ones.
- *Outcome Bias*: Judging a decision based on its outcome rather than the decision-making process.
- *Sunk Cost Fallacy*: Continuing something bad because you've already spent time or money on it.
- *Zero-Risk Bias*: Preferring to reduce small risks to zero instead of making a bigger risk reduction.

[1777] Kahneman, Daniel, *Thinking, Fast and Slow* (Farrar, Straus and Giroux, 2011)

WHAT ARE COGNITIVE BIASES?

Probability and Belief

These biases affect how we understand chances and form beliefs. They can make us misjudge how likely things are to happen and believe things that aren't true[1778].

- *Base Rate Fallacy*: Ignoring general information in favour of specific cases.
- *Clustering Illusion*: Seeing patterns in random events.
- *Gambler's Fallacy*: Thinking past events change the likelihood of future random events.
- *Conjunction Fallacy*: Thinking specific conditions are more probable than general ones.
- *Neglect of Probability*: Disregarding the likelihood of outcomes when making decisions.
- *Optimism Bias*: Believing good things are more likely to happen to you.
- *Pessimism Bias*: Believing bad things are more likely to happen to you.
- *Survivorship Bias*: Only paying attention to successful examples and ignoring failures.

Perception and Attention

Perception and attention biases influence how we focus on, interpret, and remember sensory information from our environment. They can affect what we notice, how we process information, and what we recall about our experiences[1779].

[1778] Tversky, Amos, and Daniel Kahneman, 'Judgment Under Uncertainty: Heuristics and Biases', *Science*, 185.4157 (1974), 1124–31

[1779] Chabris, Christopher F., and Daniel J. Simons, *The Invisible Gorilla* (Crown, 2010)

- *Attentional Bias*: Paying more attention to some things while ignoring others.
- *Frequency Illusion (Baader-Meinhof Phenomenon)*: Noticing something more often after learning about it.
- *Illusion of Transparency*: Overestimating how well others can read your emotional state.
- *Inattentional Blindness*: Failing to notice something obvious because you're focusing on something else.
- *Pareidolia*: Seeing patterns or meanings in random stimuli (like faces in clouds).

Self-Perception

Self-perception biases affect how we view ourselves, our abilities, and our role in events. They can influence our self-esteem, decision-making, and interactions with others[1780].

- *Bias Blind Spot*: Thinking you're less biased than others.
- *Illusion of Control*: Overestimating your influence over external events.
- *Naïve Realism*: Believing you see the world objectively and others are biased.
- *Overconfidence Effect*: Being too sure about your own abilities.
- *Self-Serving Bias*: Taking credit for good things, blaming others for bad things.

Emotional and Motivational

Emotional and motivational biases influence how our feelings and desires affect our thinking and behaviour. They can impact our judgment,

---

[1780] Pronin, Emily, Daniel Y. Lin, and Lee Ross, 'The Bias Blind Spot: Perceptions of Bias in Self Versus Others', *Personality and Social Psychology Bulletin*, 28.3 (2002), 369–81

decision-making, and interpersonal relationships[1781].

- *Empathy Gap*: Underestimating the influence of emotions on behaviour.
- *Impact Bias*: Overestimating the length or intensity of future emotional states.
- *Negativity Bias*: Remembering bad things more than good things.
- *Reactance*: Doing the opposite of what you're told, just to resist.
- *Status Quo Bias*: Preferring things to stay the same.

Economic and Marketing

These biases influence how we spend money and react to advertising. They can affect what we buy, how much we're willing to pay, and how we perceive the value of things[1782].

- *Decoy Effect*: Changing your choice when given a third, less attractive option.
- *Denomination Effect*: Spending more money when it's in smaller denominations.
- *Endowment Effect*: Valuing things more once you own them.
- *IKEA Effect*: Valuing things more if you made them yourself.
- *Money Illusion*: Focusing on the nominal value of money rather than its real value.

Processing

Cognitive processing biases influence how we think about and solve problems, process information, and apply our knowledge. They can

---

[1781] Loewenstein, George, 'Emotions in Economic Theory and Economic Behavior', *American Economic Review*, 90.2 (2000), 426–32

[1782] Thaler, Richard H., *Misbehaving* (W. W. Norton & Company, 2015)

affect our ability to learn, adapt to new situations, and think critically[1783].

- *Curse of Knowledge*: Finding it hard to imagine not knowing something you know.
- *Functional Fixedness*: Struggling to use objects in new ways.
- *Law of the Instrument*: Over-relying on a familiar tool or method.
- *Planning Fallacy*: Underestimating the time needed to complete a task.
- *Cognitive Dissonance*: Feeling uncomfortable when your beliefs don't match your actions.

Miscellaneous

Some biases that don't fit neatly into the other categories but still significantly impact our thinking and behaviour. They can affect diverse areas of our lives, from technology use to social interactions[1784].

- *Automation Bias*: Trusting automated systems more than human judgment.
- *Dunbar's Number*: Struggling to maintain more than about 150 stable social relationships.
- *Not Invented Here Syndrome*: Preferring in-house solutions over external ones.
- *Placebo Effect*: Feeling better just because you think a treatment will work.

[1783] Sternberg, Robert J., Karin Sternberg, *Cognitive Psychology* (Cengage Learning, 2012)

[1784] Bless, Herbert, Klaus Fiedler, Fritz Strack, *Social Cognition* (Psychology Press, 2004)

What Is Superstimulus?

As complex biological lifeforms, humans are a "supersystem-of-systems" regulated by hormones and neurotransmitters[1785]. The size of our brains is due to our need to process visual information through our eyes[1786].

Cortisol regulates metabolism, blood sugar, and inflammation; *insulin* allows cells to absorb glucose; *Triiodothyronine* (T3) and *Thyroxine* (T4) regulate metabolism, energy levels, and growth; *Epinephrine* increases heart rate, blood flow to muscles, and glucose release. *Oestrogen* and *Testosterone* are responsible for reproductive functions and secondary sexual characteristics[1787].

Dopamine is involved in reward, motivation, and motor control; *serotonin* regulates mood, sleep, appetite, and digestion; *Norepinephrine* (also a hormone) mediates attention, arousal, and the body's stress response; *Gamma-Amino-butyric Acid* (GABA) reduces neuronal excitability, promoting relaxation and reducing anxiety; *Glutamate* is essential for learning, memory, and brain development; *Acetylcholine* moderates learning, memory, and muscle contraction[1788].

Most of the phenomena, social behaviour or naturalised distribution

---

[1785] McEwen, B. S., 'Physiology and Neurobiology of Stress and Adaptation: Central Role of the Brain', *Physiological Reviews*, 87.3 (2007), 873–904

[1786] Barton, R. A., 'Visual Specialization and Brain Evolution in Primates', *Proceedings of the Royal Society of London. Series B: Biological Sciences*, 265.1409 (1998), 1933–37

[1787] Hadley, M. E., and J. E. Levine, *Endocrinology* (Pearson Prentice Hall, 2007)

[1788] Kandel, Eric R., James H. Schwartz, Thomas M. Jessell, Steven A. Siegelbaum, and A. J. Hudspeth, *Principles of Neural Science*, 5th edn (McGraw-Hill, 2013)

patterns "studied" by the humanities are explainable through simple natural science.

"Superstimulus" is a concept developed by Nobel Prize-winning ethologist Nikolaas Tinbergen in 1951. It refers to exaggerated or artificial stimuli that elicit a stronger-than-natural response in an organism. He first studied this in animals, observing how artificial enhancements could trigger stronger reactions than those triggered by natural objects. He demonstrated that birds would often choose to incubate large, artificial eggs over their real eggs, simply because the oversized eggs were more visually stimulating than the natural ones.

> *A supernormal stimulus... is an exaggerated version of the natural stimulus. By exploiting the animal's innate releasing mechanisms, it is more attractive than the real thing, leading the animal to prefer it over normal stimuli*[1789].

A strawberry is a natural stimulus for sweetness. A candy with artificial strawberry flavour and added sugar is a *super*stimulus - it's sweeter and more intense than what's found in nature[1790].

Real-life stories are natural stimuli for our brains. Movies and video games, with their heightened drama and non-stop action, act as superstimuli for them.

Face-to-face interaction is a natural stimulus for social connection. Social media, with its constant notifications and likes, acts as a superstimulus for social approval[1791].

Proposed examples include:

- *Processed foods:* high in sugar, salt, and fat, often more appealing than natural foods

---

[1789] Tinbergen, Niko, *The Study of Instinct* (Clarendon Press, 1951)

[1790] Dawkins, Richard, *The Extended Phenotype* (Oxford University Press, 1982)

[1791] Barrett, Deirdre, *Supernormal Stimuli:* (W. W. Norton & Company, 2010)

- *Pornography:* exaggerated and readily available sexual content
- *Social media:* constant social validation and information flow
- *Video games:* rapid, intense rewards and stimulation
- *Slot machines:* intermittent like natural risk-taking
- *Reality TV shows:* heightened drama and conflict compared to everyday life
- *Fast-paced action movies:* intense and frequent thrills than real-life excitement
- *Alcohol and drugs:* stronger rewards than natural pleasures
- *Highly caffeinated energy drinks:* more stimulating than natural sources of caffeine
- *Artificial sweeteners:* sweeter than natural sugars
- *Excessive shopping/materialism:* more than necessary for survival
- *Photoshopped images:* idealised versions of human appearance
- *Virtual reality experiences:* more immersive than real-world experiences
- *Refined carbohydrates:* quicker, more intense energy hit than complex carbs
- *Sensationalised 24/7 news:* more dramatic and attention-grabbing than typical events
- *Hyper-realistic video game graphics:* more visually striking than real-world scenes
- *Intensely flavoured snacks:* stronger taste than natural foods
- *Endless streaming content:* more engrossing than traditional storytelling
- *Extreme sports or thrill rides:* stronger adrenaline rushes than natural dangers

The most blatant exploitation of these powerful evolved mechanisms can be found in casinos, which go to extraordinary efforts to manipulate them for commercial purposes.

Clocks and windows are removed, with artificial "eternal afternoon" lighting to disrupt time awareness[1792]; floor layouts are confusing to make exits harder to find[1793]; "Sydney effect" sounds of winning are combined with music in C major and pleasant smells[1794]; oxygen and temperature levels are adjusted for player alertness[1795].

Variable rewards (unpredictable wins and losses) reinforce addictive habituation[1796]; near-misses are programmed to occur more frequently than chance, with small frequent wins to mask overall losses[1797].

Early wins are encouraged to increase risk-taking[1798]; sunk-cost fallacy is mitigated by loyalty programs[1799]; alcohol is distributed for free to impair judgment[1800]; complementary food and lodging is used to induce feelings of reciprocity and obligation[1801].

[1792] Zimbardo, Philip G., and John N. Boyd, 'Putting Time in Perspective: A Valid, Reliable Individual-Differences Metric', *Journal of Personality and Social Psychology*, 77.6 (1999), 1271–88

[1793] Finlay, K., H. H. C. Marmurek, V. Kanetkar, and J. Londerville, 'Casino Décor Effects on Gambling Emotions and Intentions', *Environment and Behavior*, 42.4 (2010)

[1794] Hirsch, Alan R., 'Effects of Ambient Odors on Slot-Machine Usage in a Las Vegas Casino', *Psychology & Marketing*, 12.7 (1995), 585–94

[1795] Griffiths, Mark D., and Jonathan Parke, 'The Environmental Psychology of Gambling', in G. Reith (ed.), *Gambling: Who Wins? Who Loses?* (Prometheus Books, 2003), pp. 277–92

[1796] Skinner, B. F., *Science and Human Behavior* (Simon and Schuster, 1953)

[1797] Clark, Luke, A. J. Lawrence, F. Astley-Jones, and N. Gray, 'Gambling Near-Misses Enhance Motivation to Gamble and Recruit Win-Related Brain Circuitry', *Neuron*, 61.3 (2009)

[1798] Thaler, Richard H., and Eric J. Johnson, 'Gambling with the House Money and Trying to Break Even: The Effects of Prior Outcomes on Risky Choice', *Management Science*, 36.6 (1990), 643–60

[1799] Narayanan, S., and P. Manchanda, 'An Empirical Analysis of Individual-Level Casino Gambling Behavior', *Quantitative Marketing and Economics*, 10.1 (2012)

[1800] Kyngdon, Andrew, and Mark Dickerson, 'An Experimental Study of the Effect of Prior Alcohol Consumption on a Simulated Gambling Activity', *Addiction*, 94.5 (1999), 697–707

[1801] Lucas, Anthony F., and John T. Bowen, 'Measuring the Effectiveness of Casino Promotions', *International Journal of Hospitality Management*, 21.2 (2002), 189–202

Is It Caused, Or Correlated?

If one thing comes after another, it does not mean the first *caused* the second, or vice versa (*post hoc ergo proptor hoc*)[1802]. Confusing these two ideas has led to deadly consequences. Cause is *linear*, and correlation is *parallel*; the former is one thing after another, and the latter is both at the same time.

Causation, or *"cause and effect"*, is a *philosophical* term where one event is the result of the occurrence of the other event. There is a *causal* relationship between the two. It implies that a change in one variable is responsible for a change in another.

Correlation is a *statistical* term for a measure (expressed as a number) describing the size and direction of a relationship between two or more things. It means that two variables change together[1803].

Examples might include:

> *During the summer months, ice cream sales increase. Similarly, the number of drowning incidents at beaches and pools also increases during this time.*
>
> *People with higher levels of education tend to earn higher incomes.*
> *Over the past few centuries, the global population of pirates has*

[1802] Summers, J. S., 'Post Hoc Ergo Propter Hoc: Some Benefits of Rationalization', *Philosophical Explorations*, 20.sup1 (2017), 21–36

[1803] Holland, P. W., 'Statistics and Causal Inference', *Journal of the American Statistical Association*, 81.396 (1986), 945–60

decreased, while global temperatures have increased[1804].

Causation fallacy would infer consuming more ice cream causes an increase in drownings. However, the rise in temperature in summer months leads to more people buying ice cream and more people swimming. The increase in swimmers, especially those who might not take adequate precautions, leads to more drowning incidents.

More education equips individuals with skills and knowledge that can increase their earning potential in the job market. But a decrease in the number of pirates clearly does not cause global warming.

It has been reported teenagers suffering gender dysphoria have a suicide rate of over forty per cent[1805]. Gender dysphoria is *comorbid* with depression and suicidal, indicating co-existence and a psychopathological *correlation*[1806]. Gender dysphoria is also *correlated* with puberty discomfort[1807] and autism[1808]. It does not mean gender dysphoria *causes* suicidality or autism.

In the same way, the distribution of men and women in different fields is not *caused* by social conditions, it is *correlated* with their differing interests[1809]. Criminality is *correlated* with relative education and poverty

---

[1804] Vigen, Tyler, *Spurious Correlations* (Hachette Books, 2015)

[1805] Haas, Ann P., Philip L. Rodgers, and Jody L. Herman, *Suicide Attempts Among Transgender and Gender Non-Conforming Adults: Findings of the National Transgender Discrimination Survey* (American Foundation for Suicide Prevention & The Williams Institute, 2014)

[1806] Dhejne, Cecilia, et al., 'Long-Term Follow-Up of Transsexual Persons Undergoing Sex Reassignment Surgery: Cohort Study in Sweden', *PLoS ONE*, 6.2 (2011), e16885

[1807] de Vries, Annelou L. C., et al., 'Puberty Suppression in Adolescents with Gender Identity Disorder: A Prospective Follow-Up Study', *Journal of Sexual Medicine*, 8.8 (2014), 2276–83

[1808] Van der Miesen, Airin I., Hayley Hurley, and Annelou L. de Vries, 'Gender Dysphoria and Autism Spectrum Disorder: A Narrative Review', *International Review of Psychiatry*, 28.1 (2016), 70–80

[1809] Pinker, Steven, *The Blank Slate* (Viking, 2002)

levels[1810]. It does not mean poverty or lack of education *causes* crime.

Correlation is often misused by political groups promoting a remedy for which they need to devise a cause[1811].

[1810] Hsieh, Ching-Chi, and M. D. Pugh, 'Poverty, Income Inequality, and Violent Crime: A Meta-Analysis of Recent Aggregate Data Studies', *Criminal Justice Review*, 18.2 (1993), 182–202

[1811] Best, Joel, *Damned Lies and Statistics* (University of California Press, 2005)

What Is Hegelian Dialectic?

No-one under forty should read Hegel, said his arch nemesis Arthur Schopenhauer, as the danger of intellectual corruption was too great[1812].

How does the world develop, and how do ideas evolve to drive its progress? It is that deceptively simple question which German alchemist Georg Wilhelm Friedrich Hegel, aka the *"father of modern historicism and totalitarianism"* (according to Karl Popper[1813]), set out to answer.

Along with Jean-Jacques Rousseau, Hegel possesses god-like divine status in humanities' faculty lounges across the Western world[1814].

He theorised history, ideas, and even reality itself, evolve through a continual process of *challenge* and *resolution*[1815]. This *"end of history"* thinking has intoxicated and captured ideologues for centuries, including all the worst dictators and tyrants.

It can be summarised as:

Thesis (Status Quo) + Antithesis (Opposition) = Synthesis (Resolution)[1816]

[1812] Schopenhauer, Arthur, *The World as Will and Representation*, (Dover Publications, 2010; orig. 1818)

[1813] Popper, Karl R., *The Open Society and Its Enemies* (Princeton Press, 1966)

[1814] Taylor, Charles, *Hegel* (Cambridge University Press, 1975)

[1815] Hegel, G. W. F., *The Science of Logic*, (c. 1812)

[1816] Hegel, G. W. F., *Phenomenology of Spirit*, c. 1807)

Or perhaps as:

Problem + Reaction = Solution

A *thesis* is the initial idea or starting point. It represents a current situation or state of things. Its *antithesis* is the opposite of or contradiction of it. It challenges or negates the initial idea.

A *Synthesis* emerges as a resolution to the conflict between the thesis and antithesis. It reconciles the differences between the two and creates a new understanding or situation. After this, the synthesis can become a new thesis, and the process can start again.

Simple analogies might be:

> *A chef follows the recipe to the letter (Thesis). The dish doesn't taste as expected or is missing something (Antithesis). The chef tweaks the recipe based on personal intuition or experiences, creating a new and improved version (Synthesis).*
>
> *Traditional acoustic music is widely accepted (Thesis). Electronic music emerges and gains popularity (Antithesis). Acoustic-electronic fusion genres arise, blending elements from both worlds (Synthesis).*
>
> *Capitalism + Communism = Socialism / Social Democracy*

Infamous Hegelians include Johann Gottlieb Fichte, Friedrich Wilhelm Joseph Schelling, Ludwig Feuerbach, Bruno Baue, Karl Marx[1817], Alexandre Kojève, György Lukács, and Theodor W. Adorno. Many of these names should be recognisable from former genocides and bloodthirsty campaigns.

While Marx is often seen as a *"Young Hegelian,"* he famously inverted Hegel's idealist dialectic to create historical materialism, emphasising material conditions over ideas[1818].

[1817] Marx, Karl, *Economic and Philosophic Manuscripts of 1844*, (c.1844)

[1818] Marx, Karl, and Friedrich Engels, *The German Ideology*, (c. 1845–46)

In his *"Philosophy of Right"*, Hegel provides his notion of the relationship between the individual and the state. Popper right condemns it as "bombastic and hysterical Platonism."[1819]

> *The State is the Divine Idea as it exists on earth ... We must therefore worship the State as the manifestation of the Divine on earth ... The State is the march of God through the world ... The State must be comprehended as an organism ... To the complete State belongs, essentially, consciousness and thought. The State knows what it wills ... The State ... exists for its own sake ... The State is the actually existing, realized moral life.*[1820]

For Hegel, the state is not a mere human institution or a necessary evil. Instead, it's a manifestation of the *World Spirit* (*Weltgeist*) or the rational structure of the universe as it plays out in human history .The state is the highest form of ethical life (*Sittlichkeit*). While morality (*Moralität*) is based on individual conscience and subjective intentions, ethical life is the external realisation of freedom in objective institutions, of which the state is paramount.

In essence, Hegel's philosophy of the state offers a vision where individual freedom and the authority of the state are not in opposition. Instead, the state, in its ideal form, is the embodiment and guarantor of true freedom.

Modern thinkers or influential figures we could class as "Hegelian" include:

- *Alexandre Kojève* (universal recognition)
- *Francis Fukuyama* (liberal democracy at the end point)
- *Marshall McLuhan* (the *"global village"*)
- *Pierre Teilhard de Chardin* (the *"Omega Point"*)

[1819] Popper, Karl R., *The Open Society and Its Enemies* (Princeton Press, 1966)

[1820] Hegel, G. W. F., *Philosophy of Right*, (c. 1820)

- *Jürgen Habermas* (rational dialogue, universal understanding)
- *Slavoj Žižek* (Lacanian psychoanalysis)
- *Ray Kurzweil* (technological singularity theory)
- *Nick Land* (accelerationism)

Do Fish Understand Water?

The post-Auschwitz liberal Western social democracies responsible for international institutions such as the *United Nations*, West Germany, the *EU*, or what we collectively refer to as the "liberal world order" (that is to say the victors: Britain, America, France) operate on a set of implicit assumptions, or axioms. These beliefs of *liberalism*, or perhaps better described as *neoliberalism*[1821], *"Boomer Truth"*, or even *modernism*, underpin how we live, how things should be, and what we believe is possible. The hard-left flavour of it is often known as *progressivism*.

Authors traditionally associated with this school of thought include David Hume[1822], John Locke[1823], John Stuart Mill[1824], John Maynard Keynes[1825], Isaiah Berlin[1826], Frederick Hayek[1827], Karl Popper[1828], John Rawls[1829], and Martin Luther King Jr.

Fish swim in water, but they have no concept of what water *is*. They

---

[1821] Harvey, David, *A Brief History of Neoliberalism* (Oxford University Press, 2005)

[1822] Hume, David, *An Enquiry Concerning Human Understanding* (A. Millar, 1748)

[1823] Locke, John, *An Essay Concerning Human Understanding* (Thomas Bassett, 1690)

[1824] Mill, John Stuart, *Utilitarianism* (Parker, Son, and Bourn, 1863)

[1825] Keynes, John Maynard, *The General Theory of Employment, Interest, and Money* (Palgrave Macmillan, 1936)

[1826] Berlin, Isaiah, *Four Essays on Liberty* (Oxford University Press, 1969)

[1827] Hayek, Friedrich A., *The Road to Serfdom* (University of Chicago Press, 1944)

[1828] Popper, Karl R., *The Open Society and Its Enemies* (Routledge, 2013; orig. 1945)

[1829] Rawls, John, *A Theory of Justice* (Harvard University Press, 1971)

don't know they are swimming in it, or even they are swimming at all. They have no concept of land, or mammals, or trees, or volcanoes; the entire rest of their world, in fact.

We are born fish in a certain type of water, and it can be difficult to conceive of it. Fish born in the *Democratic Republic of North Korea* swim in the waters of socialist tyranny, with a set of axioms which include the inaccessibility of food. Fish in the *Islamic Republic of Iran* swim in the waters of *Morality Police* and *Sharia*.

For the most part, liberalism, characterised generally by a belief in personal liberty, has been broadly responsible for an extraordinary boom of prosperity unparalleled in history, which has reduced poverty faster than any other period whilst the world's population quadrupled[1830].

This ascendancy of Western liberal democracy, which peaked around the turn of the millennium in the form of the *EU*, was referred to in dual terms. It was the conqueror at the *"end of history"*, according to Hegelian political scientist Francis Fukuyama in his controversial book *"The End of History and the Last Man"* (1992):

> *not just... the passing of a particular period of post-war history, but the end of history as such: That is, the end-point of mankind's ideological evolution and the universalization of Western liberal democracy as the final form of human government.*[1831]

Whereas in *"Democracy: The God That Failed"* (2001), German-American economist Hans-Hermann Hoppe attributes its failures - rising unemployment rates, expanding public debt, and insolvent social security systems - to the failure of politicians to deal with pressure groups seeking increased government expenditures, regulations and taxation.

> *Egalitarianism, in every form and shape, is incompatible with the*

[1830] Mirowski, Philip, Dieter Plehwe, *The Road from Mont Pèlerin* (Harvard Press, 2009)

[1831] Fukuyama, Francis, *The End of History and the Last Man* (Free Press, 1992)

idea of private property... If the right to vote were expanded to seven year olds ... its policies would most definitely reflect the 'legitimate concerns' of children to have 'adequate' and 'equal' access to 'free' french fries, lemonade and videos.[1832]

Despite its success, liberalism is also arguably responsible for the derangement of the sexual revolution; the cruelty of multiple economic collapses; the staggeringly vacuous postmodern European philosophies; an entirely decimated education system, medicated children, and repugnant art. For all its prosperity, liberalism has produced horrors which include the surgical butchery of children. Are these a feature, or a bug?

Among our axioms, we might say our leaders and institutions are captured by a social democracy managerial doctrine which can be outlined, perhaps, as the following:

1. *Human beings are born as a blank slate, a Universal Man to whom all the same things apply. Evil behaviour is attributable to insufficient childhood nurturing or a lack of education.*
2. *Inequality of distribution can be resolved through manual intervention by the state or other institutions.*
3. *The optimal way of organising society is a free market private sector which is highly taxed to pay for nationalised public services and welfare programs.*
4. *The pinnacle of Western achievement is the establishment of "human rights" which allow people to behave and live as they wish, without interference.*
5. *Progress is measured in moral permissiveness. The more morally and socially permissive a culture is, the more progress it is making.*
6. *The source of all war and conflict is the categorisation and maintenance of our human separateness and distinctions, such as borders and biological characteristics. They must be dissolved for wholeness and peace.*

[1832] Hoppe, Hans-Hermann, *Democracy: The God That Failed* (Transaction, 2001)

7. *Religious belief is an outdated form of mythology, which helps promote social cohesion.*
8. *The West's unsustainable population owes a debt to others to pay for its prosperity, such as the natural world for industrialisation and the Third World for historical mistreatment.*

Almost all of these assertions can true-*ish* in a limited context, but in extremis, or at scale, become categorically and provably *false*. Each one has run so far it has become entirely destructive.

They work insofar as social appetites and behaviours remain moderate, but collapse under the pressure of extremism.

Even if they do not personally believe this doctrine, our politicians *act* as if they do: the god of democracy, the divine law of equality, and the scripture of international charters.

"Live and let live" only works as a conflict management system as long as a significant proportion of your society does not start living in a way which is injurious to others, refusing to reciprocate the tolerance they are extended[1833].

Some people want to be recognised as the opposite sex. Others want the *"human right"* to kill their offspring in the third term of pregnancy. Their demands are entirely irreconcilable with the greater society they live in, yet they are predicated on Liberalism's core tenet of *live and let live* and its sole moral basis of the *Harm principle*[1834].

The question we must ask is what comes next, if the moral and social disasters we have experienced are the inevitable fulfilment of liberalism itself?

[1833] Mill, John Stuart, *On Liberty* (John W. Parker and Son, 1859)

[1834] Berlin, Isaiah, *The Crooked Timber of Humanity* (Alfred A. Knopf, 1990)

IV

Dark Arts & Dirty Tricks

Academic predators may not have the physiognomy of a biological threat, but they have their own weaponry and camouflage. Within the faculty lounge, bad faith actors spend their time on malicious activity. This section reveals many of the intellectual games played by people out to subvert our everyday life.

What Is A Black Legend?

A *"Black Legend"*, noted by Julián Juderías in 1914 in *"La Leyenda negra y la verdad histórica"*, in opposition to a *Golden Legend*, is the deliberate historical defamation and vilification of a country and its people[1835].

It refers to a negative, often distorted and exaggerated portrayal of a person, nation, or culture, usually spread by its rivals or enemies. This negative propaganda is intended to shape perceptions and can persist for centuries, influencing how history is taught and understood.

The root of the word "defamation" relates to the act of destroying the reputation of and bringing disgrace to a person through rumour, which would cause their family to disown them[1836].

Civilisations which have suffered the propagation of a *black legend* include Rome[1837], Russia[1838], Spain, Britain[1839], and the United States[1840]. The characteristics include describing the country and/or culture as:

- *Being in a state of permanent, degenerative material decadence or greed*

[1835] Juderías, Julián, *La Leyenda Negra y la Verdad Histórica: España en Europa* (Tipografía de la "Revista de Archivos, Bibliotecas y Museos", 1914)

[1836] Paul Mitchell, *The Making of the Modern Law of Defamation* (Hart Publishing, 2005).

[1837] Griffin, Miriam, *Roman Legacies and the Black Legend of Imperial Rome* (Routl., 2008)

[1838] Martin Malia, *Russia Under Western Eyes* (Harvard University Press, 1999)

[1839] Wilson, Jon, 'The Empire Strikes Back: Reassessing Britain's Black Legend in the Context of Colonialism', *Journal of Colonialism and Colonial History*, 13.1 (2012)

[1840] Pagden, Anthony, *Lords of All the World* (Yale University Press, 1998)

- *Lacking intellectual refinement or independence*
- *Entertaining sexual depravity or repressing sexuality*
- *Existing as a degenerative form of a predecessor*
- *Complicity in torture or unjustified violence*
- *Succeeding due to accident, malevolence, or opportunity*
- *Needing to be forced to act on moral necessity rather than self-interest*
- *Possessing an irredeemable inferiority which cannot be overcome or improved*

The most famous example of a "black legend" is the aforementioned *Spanish* variant. It specifically refers to the image of cruelty and intolerance attributed to the Spanish Empire, emphasising its colonisation of the Americas, the Inquisition, and its treatment of indigenous peoples.

This exaggerated portrayal was created and spread by rival European powers, especially the English and the Dutch, to undermine Spanish influence and justify their own imperial ambitions[1841].

The propaganda purpose of a "black legend" is to *demoralise* an enemy, so they become *resigned* to their fate, and to decrease their allies' *sympathy*.

Black legends were mostly found in revolutionary communist takeovers during the 20th century, but are now the backbone of every rights movement of the last sixty years. Modern examples include *"A People's History of the United States"* (1980) by Howard Zinn[1842], and the *"1619 Project"* by the *New York Times*[1843].

The contemporary "dark legend" as promulgated by radical academics since the *Civil Rights* era has been the Soviet-inspired notion the United States was the worst beneficiary of the transatlantic slave trade, denying its success on account it was *"built on slavery"*. This is accompanied by an updated *Noble Savage* mythology[1844] of its victims: Africans portrayed

---

[1841] Kamen, Henry, *Empire* (HarperCollins, 2003)

[1842] Zinn, Howard, *A People's History of the United States* (Harper & Row, 1980)

[1843] Hannah-Jones, Nikole, *The 1619 Project* (The New York Times, 2019)

[1844] Ellingson, Ter, *The Myth of the Noble Savage* (University of California Press, 2001)

WHAT IS A BLACK LEGEND?

as morally and technologically sophisticated rural folk.

Only 3.5% (305,000) of African slaves went to the US. 95% (5.8 million) were taken to South America and the Caribbean, mainly by the Portuguese to Brazil[1845]. Vermont banned slavery in 1777, before England did[1846].

The first legal slave owner in the US was black[1847]. The official U.S. Census of 1830 showed that 3,375 free blacks owned 12,740 black slaves[1848]. The U. S. Census of 1860 showed fewer than 385,000 (1.4% of 27 million white people) reported owning slaves[1849].

The infrastructure of slavery in Africa was created by Arabs in the eighth century, who traded seventeen million people, most of whom they castrated..The people in the slave markets were enemy prisoners of war sold by other Africans for profit[1850].

During the *Haitian revolution* of 1794 - 1804, the country's entire white population was eradicated[1851]. During the three centuries of the *Barbary Slave Trade*, corsairs captured and enslaved approximately 1-1.25 million Europeans[1852]. 2.5 million Eastern Europeans (*"slavs"*) were enslaved by the *Ottoman Empire*[1853]. 900,000 French were expelled from Algeria in 1962[1854]; 250,000 from Rhodesia by 2000[1855]; 500,000 Portuguese from

---

[1845] Eltis, David, David Richardson, *Atlas of the Transatlantic Slave Trade* (Yale Press, 2010)

[1846] Zilversmit, Arthur, *The First Emancipation* (University of Chicago Press, 1967)

[1847] Morgan, Edmund S., *American Slavery, American Freedom* (W. W. Norton & Co., 1975)

[1848] Berlin, Ira, *Slaves Without Masters* (Oxford University Press, 1974)

[1849] U.S. Census Bureau, *Population Schedules of the Eighth Census of the United States, 1860* (Government Printing Office, 1860).

[1850] Lewis, Bernard, *Race and Slavery in the Middle East* (Oxford University Press, 1990)

[1851] Dubois, Laurent, *Avengers of the New World* (Harvard University Press, 2004)

[1852] Davis, Robert C., *Christian Slaves, Muslim Masters* (Palgrave Macmillan, 2003)

[1853] Kolodziejczyk, Dariusz, 'Slavery and the Slave Trade in the Eastern Mediterranean, 15th–18th Centuries', *International Journal of Turkish Studies*, 12.1 (2006), 1–22

[1854] Horne, Alistair, *A Savage War of Peace* (Viking Press, 1977)

[1855] Mlambo, Alois S., *A History of Zimbabwe* (Cambridge University Press, 2014)

Angola and Mozambique in 1975[1856]; 100,000 Belgians from Congo in 1960[1857].

Saudi Arabia only abolished slavery in 1962[1858], Mauritania in 1981[1859]. The 2017 auction price for an African on sale in a Libyan slave market was $400[1860].

[1856] Pimenta, Fernando Taveira, 'Causas do Êxodo das Minorias Brancas da África Portuguesa: Angola e Moçambique (1974/1975)', *Revista de História das Ideias*, 31 (2010), 353–77

[1857] Hochschild, Adam, *King Leopold's Ghost* (Houghton Mifflin Harcourt, 1998)

[1858] William Gervase Clarence-Smith, *Islam and the Abolition of Slavery* (Oxford University Press, 2006).

[1859] Klein, Martin A., *Slavery and Colonial Rule in French West Africa* (Cambridge University Press, 1998)

[1860] Elbagir, Nima, Raja Razek, Alex Platt, and Bryony Jones, 'People for Sale: Where Lives Are Auctioned for $400', *CNN*, 14 November 2017

What Are Luxury Beliefs?

Making unrealistic beliefs fashionable is a time-honoured way for social elites to distinguish themselves from the aspirational middle classes. Just as peacock feathers signal biological fitness through their impracticality, "luxury beliefs" signal social status through their removal from practical concerns[1861].

Writer Rob Henderson observed this phenomenon during his journey from foster care to *Yale University* - noticing how wealthy peers promoted lifestyle choices they didn't follow themselves. He explained it in his 2024 book *"Troubled: A Memoir of Foster Care, Family, and Social Class"*[1862].

He defined it succinctly in an article for Quillette:

> *Luxury beliefs are ideas and opinions that confer status on the upper class while often inflicting costs on the lower classes.*[1863]

Where previous generations of elites displayed their status through expensive material goods, today's upper classes increasingly signal their position through *moral claims and social views*.

The more impractical or contrary to common sense a belief is, the better it serves as proof that one can afford to hold it. The ultimate luxury is being able to advocate for policies while being personally immune to

---

[1861] Veblen, Thorstein, *The Theory of the Leisure Class* (Macmillan, 1899)

[1862] Henderson, Rob, *Troubled* (Gallery Books, 2024), Preface

[1863] Henderson, Rob, 'Luxury Beliefs', *Quillette*, 13 November 2019

their consequences.

Examples include:

- *"College isn't necessary for success"* (said by those with elite degrees)
- *"Grades don't matter"* (while carefully curating their children's academic records)
- *"Marriage is just a piece of paper"* (while being married themselves)
- *"Monogamy is unnatural"* (while practicing it themselves)
- *"Work-life balance matters more than income"* (with high-paying jobs)
- *"We need to abolish the police"* (living in safe, well-policed neighbourhoods)
- *"Drugs should be legalised"* (while living in drug-free environments)
- *"Let children make their own choices"* (while heavily directing their own kids)
- *"Traditional discipline is harmful"* (while maintaining strict household rules)
- *"Status doesn't matter"* (while carefully maintaining social position)

What Are Hermeticism & Gnosticism?

In the vernacular, Gnosticism is claiming you are "spiritual, but not religious". It is when you possess special knowledge ("Gnosis") which makes you enlightened over ordinary people; or put more simply, *mysticism*[1864].

Academics who gave up going to church twenty years ago, who claim to be atheist and suffer from an obsession with knowledge, mostly fail to recognise the religion they have adopted to replace it.

There have been forms of it over the centuries, but contemporary versions include Madame Blavatsky's *"Theosophy"*[1865], Aleister Crowley's *"Thelema"*[1866], Hubbard's *"Scientology"*[1867], Carl Jung[1868], Kabbalah[1869], the secret Dead Sea "gospels" of Thomas and Judas[1870], most of the *"New Age"* & *"Human Potential"* movements, and most recently, "gender" ideology.

Gnosticism shares a common root with an older religion, *Hermeti-*

[1864] Jonas, Hans, *The Gnostic Religion* (3rd edn, Beacon Press, 2001)

[1865] Blavatsky, Helena Petrovna, *Isis Unveiled* (J. W. Bouton, 1877)

[1866] Crowley, Aleister, *The Book of the Law (Liber AL vel Legis)* (1904)

[1867] Hubbard, L. Ron, *Dianetics* (Hermitage House, 1950)

[1868] Jung, Carl Gustav, *The Collected Works of C. G. Jung, Vol. 9 (Part 1)*, trans. by R. F. C. Hull (Princeton University Press, 1959)

[1869] *The Zohar*, trans. by Daniel C. Matt (Stanford University Press, 2003)

[1870] *The Nag Hammadi Library*, ed. by James M. Robinson (Harper & Row, 1977)

cism[1871]. Both are based on the deification or rebirth of mortals through the knowledge (gnosis) of the one transcendent God, the world, and humankind.

The Egyptian god, *Thoth*, was also known by Greeks as *Hermes Trismegistos* (*"Hermes the Thrice-Greatest"*) and believed to be the inventor of writing[1872]. In first century Alexandria, scholars followed unified elements of Jewish and Christian mysticism with Hellenistic philosophy and Egyptian occult beliefs, contained in seventeen texts collected as the *Corpus Hermeticum*, or the *Hermetica*[1873].

Hermeticism teaches God is an unknowable essence from which everything emanates. The divine mind (*"Nous"*) is the first emanation, and from it arises the soul of the world, which shapes matter. Everything in the cosmos is interconnected; the soul can achieve salvation through knowledge (gnosis) and spiritual rebirth; and the world is infused with a divine essence or spirit (the source of life and intelligence) called *"pneuma."* The practices of astrology, alchemy, and theurgy (ritual magic) are there to align with these cosmic forces.

The classically understood movement of Gnosticism developed around the same time in the first century in the formative years of early Christianity[1874]. It emerged in the Hellenistic world, and blended Greek, Egyptian, Babylonian, and Persian beliefs. Early Christian gnostic groups had alternative interpretations of the *New Testament* and believed Jesus imparted esoteric hidden knowledge to a select few; a divine being in human form, attempting to lead humanity back to recognition of its own divine nature. Their texts deal not in concepts of sin and repentance, but with illusion and enlightenment.

Many of the so-called gnostic groups are characterised by a mythology that distinguishes between a dual pair combination of an inferior false

---

[1871] Copenhaver, Brian P., *Hermetica* (Cambridge University Press, 1992)

[1872] Fowden, Garth, *The Egyptian Hermes* (Princeton University Press, 1986)

[1873] Copenhaver, Brian P., *Hermetica* (Cambridge University Press, 1992)

[1874] Pagels, Elaine, *The Gnostic Gospels* (Vintage Books, 1979)

creator of the world (a *"Demiurge"*) who is ignorant of his status, and a more transcendent god[1875]. Another frequently encountered theme is that there is a special class or race of humans descended from the transcendent realm, - an enlightened priesthood - who are destined to achieve salvation and return to their spiritual origins. That salvation is usually a spiritual revelation, which reawakens knowledge (gnosis) of their divine identity.

The spiritual realm is pure and divine, while the material world is often seen as flawed, corrupt, or even malevolent. Humans are generally believed to possess a divine spark or spirit, a fragment of the divine essence that's trapped in the material body. Gnostic salvation involves awakening and liberating this spark, allowing it to return to the divine realm. The material world, and often the body itself, is seen as a prison or trap for the divine spark within humans[1876].

Gnosticism is what happens when you spend too much time in the sociology faculty lounge and the creative functions of your brain invisibly transform your academic ideas into religious precepts.

The works of Hegel, Marx, Freud, and others all bear the unmistakable hallmarks of Gnostic mystical thought[1877]. As do the endless papers submitted to social science journals, which function as scripture for political fundamentalists.

[1875] Turner, John Douglas, *Sethian Gnosticism* (Presses Université Laval, 2001)

[1876] Rudolph, Kurt, *Gnosis: The Nature and History of Gnosticism* (Harper & Row, 1987)

[1877] Voegelin, Eric, *The New Science of Politics* (University of Chicago Press, 1952)

What Is Millenarianism?

Millenarianism is a religious or social belief in a coming fundamental transformation of society, after which there will be a long period of peace, harmony, and human perfection. These beliefs often involve apocalyptic elements and expectations of significant social, political, or spiritual change[1878].

The term originates from Christian theology, specifically the belief in a thousand-year reign of Christ on Earth, as mentioned in the *Book of Revelation*. However, millenarian movements exist across many cultures and religions[1879].

Key characteristics of millenarian movements typically include:

- Belief in an imminent, dramatic transformation of society
- A sense that current social order is corrupt or fundamentally flawed
- Expectation of divine or supernatural intervention
- Often involves preparation for a specific predicted date or event
- Usually includes a charismatic leader or central prophetic figure

"Climate Change" movements exhibit millenarian characteristics in their predictions of imminent catastrophe and call for radical societal transformation[1880].

[1878] Wessinger, Catherine, *Millennialism, Persecution, and Violence* (Syracuse, 2000)

[1879] Cohn, Norman, *The Pursuit of the Millennium* (Oxford University Press, 1970)

[1880] Hulme, Mike, *Why We Disagree About Climate Change* (Cambridge Press, 2009)

WHAT IS MILLENARIANISM?

The *New Age 2012 Movement* believed the end of a Mayan calendar cycle in 2012 would bring about a global transformation of consciousness[1881].

Figures like futurist Ray Kurzweil and organisations like the MIRI (*Machine Intelligence Research Institute*) believe artificial intelligence will reach a point of recursive self-improvement, leading to an exponential explosion in technological capability. This moment - the transhuman *"singularity"* - is seen as a transformative event that will fundamentally reshape human civilisation[1882].

The 2015 *"QAnon"* hoax portrayed an impending *"Great Awakening"*, or *"Storm"*, which would expose a supposed cabal of corrupt elites, featuring prophecies of dramatic social transformation and punishment of evildoers[1883].

Klaus Schwab, founder and executive chairman of the *World Economic Forum* (WEF), has promoted the concept of the *"Fourth Industrial Revolution"* (4IR) which exhibits technocratic millenarian characteristics in its vision of technological and social transformation. Its *"Great Reset"* initiative, launched in 2020, builds on these *4IR* concepts and proposes a fundamental restructuring of global economic and social systems[1884].

[1881] Sitler, Robert, 'The 2012 Phenomenon: New Age Appropriation of an Ancient Mayan Calendar', *Nova Religio*, 9.3 (2006), 24–38

[1882] Kurzweil, Ray, *The Singularity Is Near* (Viking, 2005)

[1883] Bloom, Mia, *Pastels and Pedophiles* (Stanford University Press, 2021)

[1884] Schwab, Klaus, Thierry Malleret, *COVID-19: The Great Reset* (Forum, 2020)

What Is Scientism?

Scientism is the view empirical science is the *only* valid source of knowledge that scientific methods are the *only* reliable way to understand reality. It extends scientific authority beyond its appropriate domain, attempting to apply scientific methods to questions that may require other forms of inquiry or understanding.

August Comte's *positivism*, for example, argued human society would eventually abandon religious and metaphysical thinking in favour of purely scientific understanding[1885].

The term emerged in the 1870s in a French context through Philosopher Ernest Renan as *"scientisme."* The English term *"scientism"* started appearing in the early twentieth century[1886].

Friedrich Hayek helped popularise the criticism of scientism in his 1952 book *"The Counter-Revolution of Science,"* where he specifically mocked the application of natural science methods to the "social sciences"[1887].

A sufferer of scientism might claim that poetry or literature have no real truth value because their claims cannot be empirically verified, ignoring how these art forms can provide deep insights into human nature and

---

[1885] Comte, Auguste, *The Positive Philosophy of Auguste Comte*, trans. by Harriet Martineau (John Chapman, 1853)

[1886] Gregory, Andrew, *Scientism* (Continuum, 2008)

[1887] Hayek, Friedrich A., *The Counter-Revolution of Science* (Free Press, 1952)

experience[1888].

While neuroscience provides valuable insights into brain function, a fanatical adherent, such as Sam Harris, for example, might claim consciousness can be fully explained through only brain chemistry and physics, without considering phenomenological experience or philosophical questions about the nature of consciousness[1889][1890].

They might also believe technological and scientific advancement alone will solve issues like poverty, conflict, or meaning in life, while dismissing the role of social, political, and moral considerations[1891]. Faith in scientism itself becomes a dogma, accepting scientific claims without understanding the underlying evidence or methods[1892].

Scientific institutions function like their religious counterparts, with high priests (prestigious scientists), orthodox views that can't be questioned, heretics who challenge consensus, and excommunication of those who deviate from accepted theories or methods[1893].

The *Big Bang* theory, or evolution, are presented not as scientific theories supported by evidence, but as creation myths and complete explanations for existence itself, moving from scientific theory into metaphysical claims[1894].

The belief that science and technology alone will save humanity from all its problems, creating a kind of technological eschatology, is a form of *soteriology* (salvific doctrine)[1895].

[1888] Midgley, Mary, *Science as Salvation* (Routledge, 1992)

[1889] Harris, Sam, *The Moral Landscape* (Free Press, 2010)

[1890] Harris, Sam, *Waking Up* (Simon & Schuster, 2014) (*Harris has spoken extensively on how his experiences on MDMA have informed his beliefs about neuroscience.*)

[1891] Tallis, Raymond, *Aping Mankind* (Acumen, 2011)

[1892] Sorell, Tom, *Scientism* (Routledge, 1991)

[1893] Fuller, Steve, *Science vs. Religion?* (Polity, 2007)

[1894] Sorell, Tom, *Scientism* (Routledge, 1991)

[1895] Tallis, Raymond. *Aping Mankind* (Acumen, 2011)

Did It Originate In The Soviet Bloc?

The USSR had a propaganda machine like no other[1896] because Lenin valued it as a means of spreading socialist ideology[1897]. Its main aim was to sell itself to gullible US radicals as "the alternative society" or Hegelian *"antithesis"* of the US capitalist world operating as a force for world peace, as opposed to US military interventions[1898].

It portrayed itself as free from racial and/or gender discrimination (contrasting this with American segregation and racial tensions)[1899]; with guaranteed employment[1900], workers' rights, and the supposed absence of exploitation[1901]; a patron of the arts, free from market commercialisation[1902]; and as a supporter of anti-colonial movements

---

[1896] Central Committee of the Communist Party of the Soviet Union, *Directives on Agitation and Propaganda for the 24th Party Congress*, in *Collected Party Documents*, Vol. 12 (Progress Publishers, 1971)

[1897] Lenin, Vladimir Ilyich, 'The Tasks of the Youth Leagues', in *Lenin's Collected Works*, Vol. 31 (Moscow: Progress Publishers, 1920), pp. 288–96

[1898] Khrushchev, Nikita, 'On Peaceful Coexistence', speech presented at the 21st Congress of the Communist Party of the Soviet Union, 1959

[1899] Tereshkova, Valentina, *Women's Role in Soviet Society: Speech at the International Women's Congress* (International Women's Federation, 1963)

[1900] Stalin, Joseph Vissarionovich, *The New Soviet Constitution*, in *Works of Joseph Stalin*, Vol. 14 (Foreign Languages Publishing House, 1936)

[1901] Central Council of Trade Unions, *Labour in the Soviet Union* (Progress, 1955)

[1902] Zhdanov, Andrei, *Speech at the Conference of Soviet Writers*, in *Soviet Writers' Congress 1934: The Debate on Socialist Realism and Modernism* (Foreign Lang. House, 1935)

worldwide[1903][1904], appealing to those critical of US foreign policy[1905].

Carefully managed visits by American intellectuals, artists, and activists were used to create idealised impressions of Soviet life[1906]. The USSR provided moral and material support to various leftist organisations in the US[1907], and programs like international youth festivals were used to attract young radicals[1908].

Free education and healthcare were promoted as advantages of the socialist system[1909]. Soviet media (e.g. *Soviet Life* magazine) constantly highlighted economic inequalities and social problems in the US[1910]. The KGB actively worked to influence and recruit sympathetic individuals in radical circles (*"active measures"*)[1911].

The radical cohort of the *Baby Boomers* lapped this tale of ideological paradise up; *hook, line, and sinker*. They're in power, now, today, and many of their ideas aren't their own. Marx wrote in 1846, *"the first battle ground is to rewrite history to be unburdened by what was."*[1912]

The Soviet *black legend* of the US, which was brainwashed into the US

[1903] Khrushchev, Nikita Sergeyevich, *Speech at the 22nd Congress of the Communist Party of the Soviet Union* (Novosti Press Agency Publishing House, 1961)

[1904] Khrushchev, Nikita, *Speech to the United Nations General Assembly*, 1960, in *Documents of the 15th UN General Assembly* (Novosti Press, 1961)

[1905] Central Intelligence Agency, 'Soviet Accusations Against U.S. and French Actions in Chad', *CIA Reading Room*

[1906] Robeson, Paul, *Here I Stand* (Beacon Press, 1958)

[1907] Soviet Peace Committee, *The Struggle for Peace and Support for Progressive Movements in the Capitalist World* (Progress Publishers, 1953)

[1908] World Federation of Democratic Youth, *6th World Festival of Youth and Students: A Report* (International Publishers, 1957)

[1909] Ministry of Health of the USSR, *Achievements in Public Health in the USSR* (Progress Publishers, 1961)

[1910] *Soviet Life*, 'Equality and Opportunity for All: The Soviet Way', Vol. 12, Issue 5 (1963)

[1911] Mitrokhin, Vasili, Andrew, Christopher, *The Sword and the Shield* (Basic Books, 1999)

[1912] Marx, Karl, and Engels, Friedrich, 'The German Ideology', in C. J. Arthur (ed.), *The German Ideology* (New York: International Publishers, 1846), pp. 64–65

university radicals, had core common themes which resonated with their own social grievances:

- An aggressive "imperialist" empire seeking global domination[1913]
- *NATO* as an instrument of US control[1914]
- Capitalism as inherently exploitative, and US workers suffering cruel conditions[1915]
- *Wall Street* controlling US politics and society[1916]
- Wealth inequality and poverty amid abundance[1917]
- Segregation, racism, and discrimination, with violence against minorities[1918]
- The civil rights movement as evidence of systemic problems[1919]

These themes were incorporated into key literature distributed in academic and cultural circles.

Frankfurt School émigré "scholars" such as Herbert Marcuse became influential in sixties' radical movements[1920]. Howard Zinn's *"A People's History of the United States"* portrayed American history as primarily a struggle between oppressive elites and working people[1921]. William Appleman Williams and the *"Wisconsin School"* emphasised American economic imperialism[1922]. Gabriel Kolko argued progressive reforms

---

[1913] Urban, Joan Barth, *Moscow and the American Left* (Cornell University Press, 1986)

[1914] *Ibid.*

[1915] Heilbrunn, Jacob, *They Knew They Were Right* (Doubleday, 1994)

[1916] Lasch, Christopher, *The True and Only Heaven* (Norton, 1991)

[1917] Fitzpatrick, Sheila, *Everyday Stalinism* (Oxford University Press, 2000)

[1918] Dudziak, Mary L., *Cold War Civil Rights* (Princeton University Press, 2000)

[1919] Borstelmann, Thomas, *The Cold War and the Color Line* (Harvard Press, 2001)

[1920] Jay, Martin, *The Dialectical Imagination* (University of California Press, 1973)

[1921] Zinn, Howard, *A People's History of the United States* (New York: Harper & Row, 1980)

[1922] Williams, William Appleman, *The Tragedy of American Diplomacy* (Norton, 1959)

were tools of corporate control[1923].

Old Ideas With Western Packaging

There are dozens of ideas the West has to thank their *useful idiots*[1924] for importing from the old Soviet Bloc and repackaging as their own:

- Property as theft (1849)[1925]
- Mandated equality of outcome, aka "equity" (*uravnilovka*, 1917)[1926]
- Politicisation of intelligence services (1917)[1927]
- Human resources (*Orgburo*, 1917)[1928]
- Female suffrage (1917)[1929]
- State land planning (1917)[1930]
- Institutions publicly stating known lies (*vranyo*, 1917)[1931]
- An eight-hour work day (1918)[1932]
- Price controls (administered state pricing, 1918)[1933]
- Unlimited no-fault divorce (1918)[1934]

[1923] Kolko, Gabriel, *The Triumph of Conservatism* (Free Press, 1963)

[1924] Hollander, Paul, *Political Pilgrims* (Oxford University Press, 1981)

[1925] Proudhon, Pierre-Joseph, *Qu'est-ce que la propriété?* (Paris: Garnier, 1849)

[1926] Lenin, Vladimir Ilyich, *The Immediate Tasks of the Soviet Government*, in *Collected Works*, Vol. 27 (Progress Publishers, 1918)

[1927] Dzerzhinsky, Felix Edmundovich, *Tasks of the Cheka*, in *Collected Works* (State Publishing House, 1918)

[1928] Fainsod, Merle, *How Russia is Ruled* (Harvard University Press, 1953)

[1929] Smith, Stephen Anthony, *Revolution and the People in Russia and China* (Cambridge University Press, 2002)

[1930] Lenin, Vladimir Ilyich, *The Decree on Land*, in *Collected Works*, Vol. 26 (Progress Publishers, 1917)

[1931] Ledeneva, Alena V., *How Russia Really Works* (Cornell University Press, 2006)

[1932] Fitzpatrick, Sheila, *Everyday Stalinism* (Oxford University Press, 1999)

[1933] Nove, Alec, *The Soviet Economy* (Frederick A. Praeger, 1961)

[1934] Goldman, Wendy Z., *Women, the State and Revolution* (Cambridge Press, 1993)

- Equal pay for men and women (1918)[1935]
- Abolition of inheritance (1918)[1936]
- Universal basic income, maximum salaries, and a "living wage" (1918)[1937]
- Worldwide revolution leading to a global communist society (1919)[1938]
- Women's liberation (1919)[1939]
- Sex education for children (1919)[1940]
- Planning permission (1920)[1941]
- *"Partymindedness"* (*partiinost*) or *"correctness"* (1920)[1942]
- Unlimited abortion on-demand (1920)[1943]
- State-provided childcare (1920)[1944]
- Rejection of "backwards" religious belief in favour of atheism (1921)[1945]
- Dissolution of the idea of nation (1920)[1946]

[1935] Fitzpatrick, Sheila, *Everyday Stalinism* (Oxford University Press, 1999)

[1936] Lenin, Vladimir Ilyich, *The Immediate Tasks of the Soviet Government*, in *Collected Works*, Vol. 27 (Progress Publishers, 1918)

[1937] Lenin, Vladimir Ilyich, 'Six Theses on the Immediate Tasks of the Soviet Government', in *Collected Works*, Vol. 27 (Progress Publishers, 1918)

[1938] McDermott, Kevin, and Agnew, Jeremy, *The Comintern: A History of International Communism from Lenin to Stalin* (Macmillan, 1996)

[1939] Kollontai, Alexandra, *The Workers' Opposition*, in *Selected Writings of Alexandra Kollontai* (Greenwood Press, 1920)

[1940] Kadarkay, Arpad, *Georg Lukács* (Blackwell, 1991)

[1941] Harris, Steven E., *Communism on Tomorrow Street* (Johns Hopkins Press, 2013)

[1942] Medvedev, Roy, *Let History Judge* (Columbia University Press, 1971)

[1943] Stites, Richard, *The Women's Liberation Movement in Russia* (Princeton Press, 1990)

[1944] Goldman, Wendy Z., *Women, the State and Revolution* (Cambridge Press, 1993)

[1945] Froese, Paul, *The Plot to Kill God* (University of California Press, 2008)

[1946] Lenin, Vladimir Ilyich, *The Right of Nations to Self-Determination*, in *Collected Works*, Vol. 22 (Progress Publishers, 1920)

DID IT ORIGINATE IN THE SOVIET BLOC?

- Social welfare insurance for women (1920)[1947]
- Legalised homosexuality (1922)[1948]
- Multiculturalism (*korenizatsiya*, 1922)
- Political enforcement officers (*kommissars*) in the workplace (1922)[1949]
- Forced sharing of living spaces (*kommnalka*, 1923)[1950]
- Positive discrimination quotas for ethnic minorities (*Kvotirovanie*, 1924)[1951]
- *"Racist"* as a political slur (*Racistov*, 1929)
- Demonisation of landlords and the middle class (1929)[1952]
- Dissolution of ethnic national identity (1930)[1953]
- Elimination of homelessness through state housing (1930)[1954]
- A new type of engineered man (1930)[1955]
- *"Unpersoning"* and record erasure (1930)[1956]
- Communism as the only way to prevent an emergence of fascism (1931)[1957]
- Planting of communist messages in the key scenes of Hollywood movies[1958] by screenwriters sympathetic to socialism (1933)[1959].
- Enforcement of ideology through science "experts" and mandated

---

[1947] Goldman, Wendy Z., *Women, the State and Revolution:* (Cambridge Press, 1993)

[1948] Healey, Dan, *Homosexual Desire in Revolutionary Russia* (U. of Chicago Press, 2001)

[1949] Tucker, Robert C., *Stalin in Power* (Norton, 1990)

[1950] Buchli, Victor, *An Archaeology of Socialism* (Berg, 1999)

[1951] Martin, Terry, *The Affirmative Action Empire* (Cornell University Press, 2001)

[1952] Conquest, Robert, *The Harvest of Sorrow* (Oxford University Press, 1986)

[1953] Bichurin, Nikita, *Ethnic Minorities in the Soviet Union* (Progress Publishers, 1987)

[1954] Fitzpatrick, Sheila, *Everyday Stalinism* (Oxford University Press, 1999)

[1955] *Ibid.*

[1956] Conquest, Robert, *The Great Terror* (Oxford University Press, 1990)

[1957] Philby, Kim, *My Silent War* (Grove Press, 1968)

[1958] Weinstein, Allen, Vassiliev, Alexander, *The Haunted Wood* (Random House, 1999)

[1959] Schumacher, David, *When Hollywood Was Right* (U. Press of Kentucky, 2013)

science policy (1934)[1960]
- *"Disinformation"* (*dezinformatsiya*) as a military tactic (1940)[1961]
- *"Hate speech"* (1945)[1962]
- *"Anti-fascism"* (1945)[1963]
- Women in STEM (1950)[1964]
- *"Whataboutism"* as a propaganda technique (1953)[1965]
- Assistance to China in developing nuclear weapons (1957)[1966]
- Pathologising political enemies with psychiatric conditions (1960)[1967]
- *"Anti-imperialism"* (1961)[1968]
- Men performing housework to please women (1961)[1969]
- *"Anti-colonialism"* (1963)[1970][1971]
- *"Misinformation"* (1966)[1972]
- *"Human rights"* and protection of minorities as the purpose of "true

---

[1960] Graham, Loren R., *Science in Russia and the Soviet Union* (Cambridge Press, 1993)

[1961] Andrew, Christopher, Mitrokhin, Vasili, *The Sword and the Shield* (Basic Books, 1999)

[1962] Mchangama, Jacob, *Free Speech* (Basic Books, 2022)

[1963] Edele, Mark, *Soviet Veterans of World War II* (Oxford University Press, 2011)

[1964] Lebedeva, Natalya, 'Women and Science in the USSR', in *Gender Roles and Sex Equality in the Soviet Union*, ed. by Richard Stites (Macmillan, 1994)

[1965] Laqueur, Walter, *The Uses and Abuses of Sovietology* (Transaction Publishers, 1994)

[1966] Hershberg, James G., 'The Sino-Soviet Alliance and the Cold War in Asia, 1954–1962', *Cold War International History Project Bulletin*, 1.4 (1993), 22–31

[1967] Bloch, Sidney, Reddaway, Peter, *Russia's Political Hospitals* (Victor Gollancz, 1977)

[1968] Khrushchev, Nikita Sergeyevich, *Speech at the 22nd Congress of the Communist Party of the Soviet Union* (Novosti Press Agency Publishing House, 1961)

[1969] Heitlinger, Alena, *Women and State Socialism* (Macmillan, 1976)

[1970] Brezhnev, Leonid Ilyich, *Speech at the Conference of Non-Aligned Nations in Algiers* (Novosti Press Agency, 1973)

[1971] Gromyko, Andrei Andreyevich, 'Statement at the United Nations General Assembly on Decolonization' (United Nations, 1960)

[1972] Sakharov, Andrei Dmitrievich, *My Country and the World* (Vintage Books, 1974)

socialist democracy" as opposed to rule by majority (1970)[1973]

The Soviets supported communist movements in the name of "anti-imperialism" and "anti-colonialism" in China (1923, *CCP*), Spain (1936, Republicans), North Korea (1948, establishment), Vietnam (1954, *Viet Minh*), Afghanistan (1955, government), Algeria (1956, *National Liberation Front*), Cuba (1959, *Castro*), Guinea-Bissau (1963, *PAIGC*), South Africa (1961, *ANC*), Mozambique (1964, *FRELIMO*), Laos (1965, *Pathet Lao*), Yemen (1967, government), Chile (1970, *Allende*), Ethiopia (1974, *Derg* regime), Angola (1975, *MPLA*), Cambodia (1979, PRK), Nicaragua (1979, *Sandinista*), and Rhodesia (1972, *ZANU*).[1974]

They were the first to legalise no-fault divorce, abortion on-demand, homosexuality, female suffrage, equal pay, state childcare, maternity leave, and the eight-hour work day. And goodness do we thank them for what a blessing those things have been.

Self-Help From The State

They weren't only unpersoning dissenters; they were attempting to re-engineer men, women, children, and work with fashionable socialist ideology.

The concept of the *"New Soviet Man"* (*Novyy sovetskiy chelovek*) was a cornerstone of Soviet ideology, aiming to create the perfect communist citizen. This idealised individual was envisioned as selfless, highly educated, physically fit, and fervently devoted to the cause of communism. He was expected to prioritise *collective* interests over personal desires, embodying the virtues of industriousness, athleticism, and political awareness. Crucially, this model citizen was to be free from religious beliefs and bourgeois morality, focusing entirely on advancing the greater

---

[1973] Glendon, Mary Ann, *Rights Talk* (Free Press, 1991)

[1974] Westad, Odd Arne, *The Global Cold War* (Cambridge University Press, 2007)

good of socialist society[1975].

Complementing this was the idea of the *"New Soviet Woman,"* which sought to redefine gender under communism. The ideal Soviet woman was portrayed as fully equal to men in both capabilities and social standing. She was expected to balance the roles of worker, political activist, and mother. Soviet propaganda encouraged women to enter traditionally male-dominated fields, depicting them as strong, capable, and forward-looking. A key aspect of this concept was the notion that women would be liberated from domestic drudgery through communal services, allowing them to fully participate in building the communist society alongside men[1976].

György Lukács, the Hungarian Marxist philosopher and Deputy Commissar for Culture in Hungary's brief 1919 communist government, believed that traditional Christian morality and family structures were fundamental obstacles to communist revolution[1977], and that by reshaping sexual norms through education, these traditional social structures could be systematically dismantled[1978].

His strategy focused particularly on *sex education* as a tool for weakening family bonds and traditional values, especially among youth. He viewed this educational intervention as part of what he termed *"cultural terrorism,"* a broader revolutionary strategy aimed at transforming society's fundamental values[1979].

Humans As Resources

In 1935, Stalin famously declared, as part of the *Second Five-Year Plan* and *Stakhanovite Movement,*

[1975] Fitzpatrick, Sheila, *Everyday Stalinism* (Oxford University Press, 2000)

[1976] Stites, Richard, *The Women's Liberation Movement in Russia* (Princeton Press, 1978)

[1977] Eberstadt, Mary, *How the West Really Lost God* (Templeton Press, 2013)

[1978] Kadarkay, Arpad, *Georg Lukács* (Blackwell, 1991)

[1979] Heitlinger, Alena, *Women and State Socialism* (Macmillan, 1976)

DID IT ORIGINATE IN THE SOVIET BLOC?

"Human resources (Cadres [Personnel]) solve everything".[1980]

When the Bolsheviks took power in 1917, they were entirely led by the vanguard of Lenin and his friends. They were organised as the *Central Committee* and the *Central Body*[1981].

The *Organizational Bureau (Orgburo)* was authorised to make key decisions about organisational work. It supervised the work of local party committees and was empowered to select and place Communist cadres. The functions of the *Orgburo* and the *Politburo* were often intertwined, but the *Politburo* reserved the right to make final decisions. While the *Politburo* was mostly preoccupied with strategic planning and general monitoring, the *Orgburo* helped elaborate tactics by the proper distribution of party forces[1982].

During the ongoing civil war in the years after the revolution, *Komissars* were deployed to all Red Army units to keep comrades in line with the communists. They had the same rank as unit commanders and had authority to overrule them. Their job was to enforce compliance with communist orthodoxy[1983].

Two years later, in 1919, *Politruks*, or political leaders, were assigned into larger military units. In 1933, the *Central Committee of the Communist Party of the Soviet Union* started deploying "party organizers" (each being a *PartOrg* or *Partkom* ("party committee" secretary) into important infrastructure organisations: chemical plants, construction zones, collectivised farms, and other areas involving the means and mode of national production.

Members of the *Apparat* - desk bureaucrats with any political responsibility - were known as *Apparatchiks* ("agent of the apparatus"). They

---

[1980] Stalin, Joseph Vissarionovich, 'Speech at the First All-Union Conference of Stakhanovites', in *Collected Works* (Progress Publishers, 1935)

[1981] Ulam, Adam Bruno, *The Bolsheviks* (Macmillan, 1965)

[1982] Fainsod, Merle, *How Russia is Ruled* (Harvard University Press, 1953)

[1983] Reese, Roger R., *Red Commanders* (University Press of Kansas, 1996)

worked for senior people, *Nomenklatura*, and all of them for *Partmaximum*, or a "maximum wage"[1984].

These are known today in China's PLA Red Army as *zhengwei* (commissars), *jiaodaoyuan* (directors), and *zhidaoyuan* (instructors)[1985][1986].

More Than Entertainment

Hollywood had an infamous core adage coined by Samuel Goldwyn in regards to political messaging in films: *"From Western Union you get messages. From me you get pictures."*[1987]

Stalin saw Hollywood as a powerful medium for shaping public opinion, especially given the global reach of American cinema[1988][1989]. Soviet officials encouraged communist sympathisers within the American film industry (typically within the *Hollywood Anti-Nazi League* and the *Screen Writers Guild*) to incorporate class struggle themes, critiques of capitalism, and anti-fascist messages, particularly during the 1930s and 1940s[1990].

In one Comintern directive, it was noted :

> *American films... could be used to turn the public's sympathy toward the proletariat and against the exploitative ruling classes*[1991].

[1984] Shapiro, Leonard, *The Communist Party of the Soviet Union* (Eyre & S'woode, 1970)

[1985] Shambaugh, David, *Modernizing China's Military* (U. of California Press, 2002)

[1986] Saunders, Phillip C., Scobell, Andrew, and Kamphausen, Roy (eds.), *Chairman Xi Remakes the PLA: Assessing Chinese Military Reforms* (National Defense University Press, 2019)

[1987] Wetstein, Aleen, 'One Girl Chorus: If Goldwyn Has a Message He'll Keep It On a Telegram', *The Pittsburgh Press*, 27 July 1940

[1988] Epstein, Edward Jay, *The Big Picture* (Random House, 1995)

[1989] Clark, Katerina, *Moscow, the Fourth Rome* (Harvard University Press, 2011)

[1990] Whitfield, Stephen J., *The Culture of the Cold War* (Baltimore: Johns Hopkins University Press, 1991)

[1991] Klehr, Harvey, and Haynes, John Earl, *The American Communist Movement* (Twayne Publishers, 1992)

A Soviet cultural attaché in the 1930s is quoted as saying:

> *Hollywood wields enormous power over American workers; a well-placed story or film could influence millions... the cinema is not merely entertainment; it is a vehicle for political instruction.*[1992]

Vladimir Posner, a Soviet journalist who later became a Soviet spokesperson to the West, remarked in an interview about the potential impact of Western cinema:

> *In the realm of ideas, films are the strongest battleground. We believed that winning over the minds of workers, even in America, could be achieved through careful manipulation of this art form.*[1993]

Hate Speech Is Not Free Speech

At the start of the *Cold War* In 1948, the non-binding *Universal Declaration of Human Rights* suffered an ideological battle between the British and Soviet delegates of the drafting committee over *Article 19 (freedom of opinion and expression)*. The British aimed to allow the State to only limit speech advocating the use of violence[1994].

The communists (*"antifascists"* as they called themselves), however, who, at that time, had imprisoned 2.2 million in the Gulag system, wished to include an amendment proposing speech and assembly should,

> *"not be used for the purposes of propagating fascism, aggression and for provoking hatred as between nations"* or allow any organisation of *"fascist or antidemocratic nature".*

[1992] Taylor, Richard, *Film Propaganda* (I.B. Tauris, 1998)

[1993] Posner, Vladimir, *Parting with Illusions* (Atlantic Monthly Press, 1990)

[1994] Simpson, Alfred William Brian, *Human Rights and the End of Empire* (Oxford University Press, 2001)

The Western nations explicitly rejected the politicised amendment as they rightly realised the Soviets were unable to define "fascism" and were intending to codify their right to suppress the expression of the political and ideological enemies of communism[1995].

Two decades later, in 1966, during the drafting of the binding *International Covenant on Civil and Political Rights*, they tried again, proposing speech be restrained if it were an *"incitement to hatred"*. The communist bloc won the vote, as it did for the *International Convention for the Elimination of all Racial Discrimination* in 1969[1996] where the signatories were required to:

> declare an offence punishable by law all dissemination of ideas based on racial superiority or hatred, incitement to racial discrimination.[1997]

Under the noble guise of prohibiting unfair racial discrimination, as *"Repressive Tolerance"* was published[1998] and the *Black Panther Party* advocated racial communist ideology[1999], states became legally responsible for eliminating "intolerance" from "fascists" who objected, just as the Communist Bloc had originally envisioned.

Give Up Your Ultimate Deterrent

During *World War II*, the Soviet *NKVD* obtained US atomic blueprints from the Los Alamos *Manhattan Project* via espionage (Klaus Fuchs,

---

[1995] Mchangama, Jacob, *Free Speech* (Basic Books, 2022)

[1996] United Nations, *International Convention on the Elimination of All Forms of Racial Discrimination* (1969)

[1997] United Nations, *International Covenant on Civil and Political Rights* (1966)

[1998] Marcuse, Herbert, 'Repressive Tolerance', in *A Critique of Pure Tolerance* (Beacon Press, 1965), pp. 81–123

[1999] Bloom, Joshua, Martin, Waldo E., *Black Against Empire* (U. of California Press, 2013)

Theodore Hall, David Greenglass, Julius and Ethel Rosenberg, Harry Gold, Morris and Lona Cohen, George Koval) which they later provided to China[2000].

However, the USSR publicly supported nuclear disarmament groups, promoting the idea unilateral disarmament in the West would reduce tensions and lead to a more peaceful world while its own arms remained untouched[2001]. This position became the primary aim of the *Campaign for Nuclear Disarmament* (CND) and *"Ban the Bomb"* movement, which were heavily monitored by MI5[2002] because of how they were praised by Moscow[2003].

> *The Soviet Union has mounted a massive propaganda effort to sway public opinion in the West... They support so-called peace movements which, whether they know it or not, promote objectives favorable to the Soviet Union*[2004].

Political Pathological Isms And Phobias

The modern day practice of politically tarnishing one's ideological opponents by diagnosing dissidents with fabricated or exaggerated mental illnesses has its roots in the Soviet abuse of psychiatry[2005]. Three thousand people a year were committed to psychiatric hospitals for

---

[2000] Rhodes, Richard, *The Making of the Atomic Bomb* (Simon & Schuster, 1986)

[2001] Hackett, John, *The Third World War: August 1985* (Sidgwick & Jackson, 1978)

[2002] MI5, *Declassified Files on Soviet Influence*, The National Archives, KV 2/3335 (1985)

[2003] United States Information Agency (USIA), 'Soviet Active Measures in Western Europe', 1981
   "The Soviet press repeatedly praises the activities of the British Campaign for Nuclear Disarmament... As a mouthpiece, it seeks to amplify these voices while omitting or countering any suggestion of the Soviet Union's own arms."

[2004] Thatcher, M, 'Speech to the House of Commons on the Defence Debate', Mar 1983

[2005] Bloch, Sidney, and Reddaway, Peter, *Psychiatric Terror* (Basic Books, 1977)

political reasons[2006] and received antipsychotic drugs in large doses[2007].

> *The main symptoms of sluggish schizophrenia... included 'reformist delusions,' 'struggle for the truth,' and 'perseverance.' These symptoms were interpreted as evidence of a pathological mental state when they manifested in criticism of the Soviet system*[2008].

From The River To The Sea

The modern Left's obsession with "anti-Zionism" is directly traceable to Soviet propaganda after the *Six-Day War*, when the USSR allied with Arab states[2009]. In 1969, Yuri Ivanov, the Soviet Union's leading "Zionologist" described the pathology "Zionology" as a "world threat":

> *Modern Zionism is the ideology, a ramified system of organisations and the practical politics of the wealthy Jewish bourgeoisie which has closely allied itself with monopoly circles in the USA and other imperialist countries. The main content of Zionism is bellicose chauvinism and anti-communism*[2010]

On 1 April 1983, *Pravda* ran a full front-page article titled *From the Soviet Leadership*:

> *By its nature, Zionism concentrates ultra-nationalism, chauvinism and racial intolerance, excuse for territorial occupation and*

[2006] Reddaway, Peter, and Gluzman, Semyon, *Psychiatric Abuse in the Soviet Union* (International Association on the Political Use of Psychiatry, 1990)

[2007] Bukovsky, Vladimir, *To Build a Castle* (Viking Press, 1978)

[2008] Podrabinek, Alexander, *Punitive Medicine* (Karoma Publishers, 1979)

[2009] Behbehani, Hashim S. H., *The Soviet Union and Arab Nationalism* (1986)

[2010] Hunter, Robert, ed., *Caution: Zionism!* (Association of Arab-American University Graduates, 1969)

annexation, military opportunism, cult of political promiscuousness and irresponsibility, demagogy and ideological diversion, dirty tactics and perfidy... Absurd are attempts of Zionist ideologists to present criticizing them, or condemning the aggressive politics of the Israel's ruling circles, as antisemitic... We call on all Soviet citizens: workers, peasants, representatives of intelligentsia: take active part in exposing Zionism, strongly rebuke its endeavors; social scientists: activate scientific research to criticize reactionary core of that ideology and aggressive character of its political practice; writers, artists, journalists: fuller expose anti-populace and anti-humane diversionary character of propaganda and politics of Zionism.[2011]

Removing US Allies In Africa

The USSR was a central player in organising opposition to *Apartheid* ("apartness" or "separateness." in Afrikaans) within South Africa, which it saw as a Western-backed state with close ties to the US and NATO[2012]. It portrayed itself as a champion of oppressed peoples in Africa, and assisted Marxist student leaders in former European colonies to aid *"decolonisation"*.

It provided financial, military, and ideological support to the *African National Congress* (ANC) and the *South African Communist Party* (SACP). Training included guerrilla warfare, political theory, and Marxist-Leninist ideology[2013]. It provided weapons, funding, and training to support the ANC's armed wing, *Umkhonto we Sizwe* (MK), to oppose the government[2014].

Its extensive media networks spread anti-apartheid propaganda and

---

[2011] "From the Soviet Leadership", *Pravda*, 1 April 1983

[2012] Shubin, Vladimir, *The Hot 'Cold War'* (Pluto Press, 2008)

[2013] Ellis, Stephen, Sechaba, Tsepo, *Comrades Against Apartheid* (James Currey, 1992)

[2014] Thomson, Alex, *U.S. Foreign Policy Towards Apartheid South Africa, 1948–1994* (Springer, 2016)

agitated about human rights abuses, and held conferences via the *World Peace Council* and *Afro-Asian People's Solidarity Organization*[2015].

In 1982, the Soviet foreign ministry decried the *"imperialist"* and *"colonialist"* state:

> *Apartheid is not only a violation of the principles of human rights but also a threat to world peace. By maintaining ties with Pretoria, certain Western countries continue to fuel a system of racial oppression... the Soviet Union stands with the oppressed*[2016].

As it condemned apartheid as a *"crime against humanity"*, the USSR herself was guilty of imprisonment and silencing of dissidents, widespread censorship, and the brutal suppression of ethnic and national identities within its borders[2017].

[2015] Prashad, Vijay, *The Darker Nations* (The New Press, 2007)

[2016] Soviet Foreign Ministry, 'Apartheid', *Soviet Union Government*, 1982

[2017] Solzhenitsyn, Aleksandr Isayevich, *The Gulag Archipelago* (Harper & Row, 1974)

What Is Third Way Eurocommunism?

By the 1920s, it had become clear Marx's "scientific" predictions about the "inevitable" uprising of the working class were deeply flawed, even if his diagnosis was insightful. Marxian schools of thought branched and diverged into different flavours[2018].

The *Fabian Society* (whose insignia is a wolf in sheep's clothing) was founded in 1884, was named after Hannibal's General Fabius' war of attrition against the Carthaginian army. It advocated for a "gradual" or incremental democratic transformation of British society to socialism and evolved into the modern *Labour* parties across the old empire[2019].

> *The Fabian Society embodies the general notion that Socialism does not involve social catastrophe or sweeping expropriation, but must be brought about gradually by the democratic education of society to a cooperative commonwealth.*

Syndicalism (from the French *"syndicat,"* or trade union) emerged in France, Spain, and Italy around the turn of the century. In 1909, long-term socialist Benito Mussolini had taken up the cause of revolutionary *national syndicalism*. It laid the conditions for his *fascist* party[2020].

[2018] Kolakowski, Leszek, *Main Currents of Marxism* (Oxford University Press, 1978)

[2019] Pease, Edward R., *The History of the Fabian Society* (A. C. Fifield, 1916)

[2020] Gregor, Anthony James, *Young Mussolini and the Intellectual Origins of Fascism* (University of California Press, 1979)

Syndicalism was the school of life for the Italian proletariat; Fascism has been its university.[2021]

In Switzerland, Vilfredo Pareto, the *"Father of Statistics"* (or the *"theoretician of totalitarianism"*, according to Popper), had observed in 1896 eighty per cent of society's wealth was controlled by twenty per cent of its population[2022]. This phenomenon of a *power-law probability distribution* was found even in the size of meteorites. It was a natural law[2023].

> *The law of income distribution is independent of any economic or social system. The socialists think it arises from the capitalist system, but it can be seen in many societies that were never capitalist.*
>
> *Men are moved by sentiments, while they seek to justify their actions with reason. This is true for both the rulers and the ruled, and it is a fundamental error in Marx's belief that economic factors alone drive social change.*[2024]

Elsewhere in Switzerland, Vladimir Lenin, radicalised by the execution of his brother Alexander Ulyanov in 1887[2025], had decided the working class needed to organise as a vanguard political party. They became known as the *Bolsheviks* ('majority').

> *The fulfillment of this task, the destruction of the most powerful bulwark, not only of European but also (it may now be said) of Asiatic reaction, would make the Russian proletariat the vanguard*

[2021] De Grand, Alexander, *Italian Fascism* (University of Nebraska Press, 1995)

[2022] Pareto, Vilfredo, *Manual of Political Economy*, trans. by Ann S. Schwier, Alfred N. Page (Macmillan, 1971)

[2023] Newman, Mark E. J., 'Power Laws, Pareto Distributions and Zipf's Law', *Contemporary Physics*, 46.5 (2005), 323–51

[2024] Pareto, Vilfredo, *Manual of Political Economy* (Augustus M. Kelley, 1971)

[2025] Pipes, Richard, *A Concise History of the Russian Revolution* (Vintage, 1996)

WHAT IS THIRD WAY EUROCOMMUNISM?

of the international revolutionary proletariat. ... The role of the vanguard fighter can be fulfilled only by a party that is guided by the most advanced theory.[2026]

In Hungary, radical communist literary critic Georg Lukács blamed Christianity and the church, seeing "sex education" as a means of breaking its influence on future generations as part of a larger program he termed "cultural terrorism".

Christian ethics offer a path of individual repentance and salvation, but it denies the collective struggle that alone can bring about real change in this world.[2027]

In *Weimar* Germany, contrary to the *German Workers' Party*, Carl Grünberg had founded the *Institute of Socialist Research* at *Goethe University Frankfurt* (the *"Frankfurt School"*) with the aim of introducing Marxism into academia as it broke with the USSR. It attracted sociologists Max Horkheimer, Theodor W. Adorno, Erich Fromm, and Herbert Marcuse, who developed *Critical Theory*[2028]. It became known as *Neo-Marxism*[2029]. Marcuse revealed its true purpose as a think tank was devising new means of the communist revolution, for which it used coded language:

Our goal was never merely academic; it was to find the pathways to social transformation, to understand how human liberation could be realized in concrete, historical terms.[2030]

In Italy, journalist Antonio Gramsci, co-founder of *Partito Comunista*

[2026] Lenin, Vladimir Ilyich, *What Is to Be Done? Burning Questions of Our Movement* (1902)

[2027] Lukács, Georg, *History and Class Consciousness* (MIT Press, 1971)

[2028] Jay, Martin, *The Dialectical Imagination* (University of California Press, 1973)

[2029] Kellner, Douglas, *Critical Theory, Marxism and Modernity* (Johns Hopkins Press, 1989)

[2030] Marcuse, Herbert, *One-Dimensional Man* (Beacon Press, 1964)

Italiano, was imprisoned by Mussolini in 1926. Behind bars, he also broke away from Marx's economic thinking and developed a sophisticated theory detailing the need to infiltrate the worldview of the dominant ruling class (the *bourgeoisie*) to establish socialism, as it generally determines accepted status quo cultural norms, and shapes society. It became known as *"cultural hegemony"*.

> *One of the most important characteristics of any group that is developing towards dominance is its struggle to assimilate and to conquer 'ideologically' the traditional intellectuals.*[2031]

The poor rural working class didn't show up for the revolution, as Marx invited them to. They took the side of the German anti-communist *Völkisch* nationalists (the epithet *"nazi"* means "a foolish person, clumsy or awkward person"), the fin de siècle Italian *Fascio Rivoluzionario d'Azione Internazionalista*, and the nationalist *Bando sublevado* in Spain. They didn't want to overthrow the aristocrats and seize the means of production. They hated the socialist intelligentsia and wanted to become the bourgeois themselves[2032].

The despair associated with the *Holocaust*, the atomic bomb, and the utter collapse of the Marxist utopia into Soviet horror ultimately became the era of *Postmodernism*[2033]. Many of the key figures who survived fled to the US and integrated into her university system.

During the American boom of the Cold War and the contraceptive pill, Herbert Marcuse (*"Father of the New Left"*), attempted to marry the theories of Marx and Freud[2034], positing the comfortable hedonism of middle-class comfort fostered a repressive *"one-dimensional"* human

---

[2031] Gramsci, Antonio, *Selections from the Prison Notebooks* (International Publishers, 1971)

[2032] Payne, Stanley G., *A History of Fascism, 1914–1945* (U. of Wisconsin Press, 1995)

[2033] Lyotard, Jean-François, *The Postmodern Condition* (U. of Minnesota Press, 1984)

[2034] Marcuse, Herbert, *Eros and Civilization* (Beacon Press, 1955)

WHAT IS THIRD WAY EUROCOMMUNISM?

condition[2035]. His idea to protect against the inevitable re-emergence of fascism was simple: the working class needed to be replaced by a new revolutionary proletariat with a driving *libidinal* need to overthrow the system. But whom?

> *This new consciousness and the instinctual rebellion isolate such opposition from the masses and from the majority of organized labor, the integrated majority, and make for the concentration of radical politics in active minorities, mainly among the young middle-class intelligentsia, and among the ghetto populations. Here, prior to all political strategy and organization, liberation becomes a vital, "biological" need.*[2036]

At the same time in Italy, Spain, and France, communist parties had begun to break away from the brutality of the Soviet Bloc utopia after the 1968 invasion of Czechoslovakia[2037], and moved towards Gramsci's ideas. Their rejection of Soviet culture in favour of a softer European model of socialism became known as *Neocommunism* or *Eurocommunism*.

Their ideology was Marcuse's: abandon class struggle, embrace the middle class, and take up the cause of fashionable social movements to win culturally hegemonic political support. Their founding tract, "*Eurocomunismo y Estado*" was written in 1977 by the leader of the *Partido Comunista de España* (Communist Party of Spain), Santiago Carrillo.

> *Our conception of socialism includes the ideas of freedom and democracy...We reject the idea of the one-party state as an inherent part of socialism. Socialism must include pluralism in politics and ideas.*[2038]

[2035] Marcuse, Herbert, *One-Dimensional Man* (Beacon Press, 1964)

[2036] Marcuse, Herbert, *An Essay on Liberation* (Beacon Press, 1969)

[2037] Williams, Kieran, *The Prague Spring and Its Aftermath* (Cambridge Press, 1997)

[2038] Carrillo, Santiago, *Eurocomunismo y Estado* (Editorial Siglo XXI, 1977)

The communist parties sought to distance themselves from Moscow's influence and develop their own path to socialism. Like the *Fabian Society*, they believed it could be achieved through democratic means rather than revolution.

Their ideas for a European model of "social democracy" involved:

- Acceptance of parliamentary democracy and pluralism
- Rejection of the dictatorship of the proletariat
- Support for civil liberties and individual rights
- Criticism of Soviet authoritarianism
- Commitment to working within existing democratic institutions
- Support for gradual, democratic transition to socialism.

In a scathing critique of his former Trotskyist friends, journalist Peter Hitchens describes in broad terms the shift after the *Prague Spring*[2039]:

> *How was it done? Clever Marxists had begun to see Soviet communism as an albatross in the 1920s. They knew it would never work in advanced western countries.*
>
> *Out of this understanding came Eurocommunism, through which the continent's communists sidled back into the democratic and anti-Stalinist left, just as Soviet power vanished from the earth. It was and remains amazing just how little this new trend cares about once huge issues such as nationalisation and state control. It is, as David Aaronovitch's old comrade pointed out all those years ago, much more interested in sex, in more ways than one. It will cheerfully see the railways privatised, as long as childhood is nationalised, lifelong marriage is made obsolete, Christianity and patriotism are disempowered and defeated, borders are flung wide, and education becomes a mechanism for enforcing egalitarianism.*[2040]

[2039] Hitchens, Peter, *The Abolition of Britain* (Quartet Books, 1999)

[2040] Hitchens, Peter, 'What Happened to Communism?', *The Spectator*, 16 June 2018

He goes on to detail the antics of communist operatives in Britain, which included, among other things, *"carrier bags stuffed with tenners left for collection by KGB men at Barons Court tube station, and stored in the roof of a bungalow in Golders Green",* organised *"in the Labour Party by the journal 'Marxism Today'."*

Eurocommunism's emphasis on democratic institutions and rejection of Soviet-style economics laid crucial groundwork for *"Third Way"* thinking in the nineties. This is most clearly seen in Italy, where the *Italian Communist Party*'s (PCI) gradual transformation first into the *Democratic Left* (PDS), and later the *Democratic Party* (PD) providing a template for modernising leftist parties in other countries[2041].

Similar patterns emerged across Europe, as former Eurocommunist principles of accepting market mechanisms while maintaining social protections.

> *And so the real revolution in the Labour party, which most of Fleet Street has never understood, was inflicted not by Trotskyists, but by the legions of the dull — Eurocommunists who realised Bolshevism was obsolete, quietly captured think tanks and policy committees, and used the apolitical figure of Tony Blair as the front for a Gramscian cultural, constitutional, educational and sexual revolution, whose greatest triumph was to capture the Tory party as well as the Labour party.*[2042]

The creation of the *European Union* was influenced by various Eurocommunist parties and leaders, particularly in Southern Europe, who saw European integration as a pathway to democratic socialism and a safeguard against both Soviet influence and domestic authoritarianism.

The *Italian Communist Party* under Berlinguer, along with its French and Spanish counterparts, shifted from opposing to supporting European

---

[2041] Gundle, Stephen, *Between Hollywood and Moscow* (Duke University Press, 1995)

[2042] Hitchens, Peter, 'It's Not the Trots You Need to Worry About', *Spectator*, 20 Aug 2016

integration, helping shape EU social policies and trade unions[2043]. A notable figure in this convergence was Altiero Spinelli, who moved from communism to become a key EU founding father, authoring the influential *Ventotene Manifesto* and championing European federalism.

> *Europe must build a federal state. Only in a Europe freed from the limitations imposed by its own national sovereignties can we secure peace and a truly democratic order*[2044].

The *"Third Way"*, which emerged in the 1990s under leaders like Tony Blair and Bill Clinton, represented a different kind of Hegelian synthesis.

While Eurocommunists tried to democratise communist ideology, *"Third Way"* proponents sought to reconcile *social democracy* principles with market economics and globalisation (i.e. China's ascension to the WTO). They accepted the basic framework of capitalism while advocating for moderate market regulation and social welfare programs.

Their ideas for a European model of "social democracy" involved:

- Market capitalism but with active state management
- "Social investment" instead of traditional welfare
- Social benefits tied to civic obligations and workforce participation
- Social mobility through merit rather than structural redistribution
- Government as enabler rather than provider using public-private partnerships and and "third sector" organisations
- Embrace of "inevitable" globalisation

Its intellectual foundations were primarily laid by sociologist Anthony Giddens, director of the *London School of Economics*. His books *"Beyond*

[2043] Sassoon, Donald, *One Hundred Years of Socialism* (The New Press, 1996)

[2044] Spinelli, Altiero, and Rossi, Ernesto, *The Ventotene Manifesto*, trans. by David Gibbons (Altiero Spinelli Institute for Federalist Studies, 1988)

Left and Right" (1994)[2045], and *"The Third Way: The Renewal of Social Democracy"* (1997)[2046], were developed through close dialogue with Tony Blair and other *New Labour* figures about the effects of globalisation.

In the United States, the *Democratic Leadership Council* (DLC) had been developing similar ideas since the mid-1980s. Bill Clinton, as head of the DLC, helped articulate them through his *"New Democrat"* platform, drawing on policy work from think tanks like the *Progressive Policy Institute*[2047].

At a 1999 meeting in Florence, they produced the Blair-Schröder paper *"Europe: The Third Way/Die Neue Mitte"*, attempting to create a coherent international framework for *"Third Way"* social democracy politics which started with practical governance challenges and worked backward to create a theoretical framework[2048].

Both movements can be seen as attempts to adapt leftist politics to contemporary realities, but Eurocommunism remained more radical in its critique of capitalism and its ultimate objectives.

As Eurocommunism declined in the 1980s after the Cold War, many of its insights about democratic participation and gradual change influenced the development of *"Third Way"* thinking. However, where Eurocommunists sought to humanise socialism, *"Third Way"* advocates accepted the triumph of market economics and tried to humanise neoliberal *capitalism* instead.

[2045] Giddens, Anthony, *Beyond Left and Right* (Stanford University Press, 1994)

[2046] Giddens, Anthony, *The Third Way* (Polity Press, 1998)

[2047] From, Al, *Reinventing Democrats* (University Press of Kansas, 1995)

[2048] Blair, Tony, and Schröder, Gerhard, *Europe: The Third Way/Die Neue Mitte* (1999)

What Is The Paradox Of Tolerance?

In 1945, philosopher Karl Popper noted in *"The Open Society and Its Enemies"* if a society is endlessly tolerant, it would allow its most intolerant groups to seize control. Therefore, paradoxically, to maintain its own existence as a tolerant society, it would need to be *intolerant of intolerance.*

> *Unlimited tolerance must lead to the disappearance of tolerance. If we extend unlimited tolerance even to those who are intolerant, if we are not prepared to defend a tolerant society against the onslaught of the intolerant, then the tolerant will be destroyed, and tolerance with them.*[2049]

In 1965, Marxist sociologist Herbert Marcuse published his response *"Repressive Tolerance"*, in which he taught his followers to weaponise this concept. It forms much of political behaviour, and policy, in the modern day.

> *Liberating tolerance, then, would mean intolerance against movements from the Right and toleration of movements from the Left. As to the scope of this tolerance and intolerance: ... it would extend to the stage of action as well as of discussion and propaganda, of deed as well as of word. The traditional criterion of clear and present*

[2049] Popper, Karl, *The Open Society and Its Enemies*, (Routledge, 1945) *danger seems no longer adequate to a stage where the whole society is in the situation of the theater audience when somebody cries: 'fire'. It is a situation in which the total catastrophe could be triggered off any moment, not only by a technical error, but also by a rational miscalculation of risks, or by a rash speech of one of the leaders. In past and different circumstances, the speeches of the Fascist and Nazi leaders were the immediate prologue to the massacre. The distance between the propaganda and the action, between the organization and its release on the people had become too short. But the spreading of the word could have been stopped before it was too late: if democratic tolerance had been withdrawn when the future leaders started their campaign, mankind would have had a chance of avoiding Auschwitz and a World War.*

The whole post-fascist period is one of clear and present danger. Consequently, true pacification requires the withdrawal of tolerance before the deed, at the stage of communication in word, print, and picture. Such extreme suspension of the right of free speech and free assembly is indeed justified only if the whole of society is in extreme danger. I maintain that our society is in such an emergency situation, and that it has become the normal state of affairs.[2050]

It is crucial to understand this essay on the simple basis of how influential it is in the minds of today's activists and politicians. This, along with Lenin's 1920 notion of "partymindedness" (p*artiinost*, or ideological "correctness")[2051] forms the basis of what we pejoratively call *"political correctness"*.

Author Michael William lays the blame squarely on Marcuse's doorstep in his 2016 book, *"The Genesis of Political Correctness: The Basis of a False Morality"*:

[2050] Marcuse, Herbert, 'Repressive Tolerance', in *A Critique of Pure Tolerance* (Beacon Press, 1965)

[2051] Medvedev, Roy, *Let History Judge* (Columbia University Press, 1971)

> In the West, political correctness is the ascendant ideology since the rise of the so-called New Left in the 1960s. It has infiltrated the public sector and its devotees have gained access to legislative powers of enforcement and, importantly, public monies. Dissent is not tolerated. Dissenters, even children, are persecuted. Minorities are deemed victims and as being oppressed, while the majority are deemed the oppressors. A hatred of the West is aggressively promoted. Terrorism is excused. Free Speech is not allowed. Only politically correct views are tolerated. The media present propaganda instead of the truth. Human Rights are corrupted into being a vehicle for political correctness with lots of fees for its advocates. Sex attacks on women and even children by immigrants are covered up, if not tolerated. Democracy is undermined as bureaucrats and international organizations highjack the powers of the nation state. The interests and opinions of ordinary people are ignored. Economies are plundered. High taxes are imposed. In Europe, the interests of the EU take priority over national prosperity. The 'chauvinism of prosperity' is condemned. [2052]

In Marcuse's "work", there's a consistent pattern: whether he's writing about tolerance, sexuality, or social structures, his arguments, crafted to appeal to liberal intellectuals while advocating for illiberal outcomes, lead to positions that would weaken social cohesion and stability. While presenting these ideas as "liberating" or "progressive", they frequently point toward dismantling the stabilising institutions and norms that make gradual reform possible[2053].

This is no coincidence for a man like Marcuse. In *"Eros and Civilization"* (1955)[2054], his advocacy for *"free love"* and *"sexual liberation"* runs directly counter to the empirical findings of Joseph Unwin in his historical

---

[2052] William, Michael, *The Genesis of Political Correctness* (2016)

[2053] Ellis, John M., *Literature Lost* (Yale University Press, 1997)

[2054] Marcuse, Herbert, *Eros and Civilization* (Beacon Press, 1955).

masterpiece *"Sex and Culture."* Unwin's extensive anthropological research thirty years previously demonstrated societies with stricter sexual norms tended to develop more complex cultural, technological, and social achievements (which Marcuse would have been aware of). His data suggested that channelling sexual energy into social structures and institutions was a key factor in societal development and stability. Marcuse effectively prescribed the *inverse* of what Unwin's research showed builds strong societies, and sexual norms which reliably precede or accompany societal decline[2055].

His argument we should dismantle all the psychological and social structures which channel "libidinal" energy into work and productivity essentially hypothesised we should remove all the walls and support beams of the building because they're "oppressively" holding up the roof. The fact that the house would collapse without them is, presumably, just evidence of how thoroughly we've been brainwashed by architectural capitalism.

In *"One-Dimensional Man"* (1964)[2056], he argues we should dismantle technological society and rational thought because they're tools of control which have eliminated our ability to think critically or recognise our own oppression. Which is like saying the house is too comfortable, so we need to tear out all the utilities and modern conveniences because they're preventing us from realising we live in a house at all.

What he argued about "tolerance" was simple, yet wicked: the threat of a fascist uprising like Nazi Germany is always around the corner, and society is too fragile to wait until the danger has become obvious. We are in a permanent emergency; a crowded theatre where anyone could yell 'fire' at any moment. One wrong move, one inflammatory speech from a leader, and we could have a catastrophe. Speech and ideas must be shut down early, before any harm happens. We need a new kind of "tolerance" where we refuse to tolerate right-wing speech and activities,

---

[2055] Unwin, Joseph, *Sex and Culture* (Oxford University Press, 1934).

[2056] Marcuse, Herbert, *One-Dimensional Man* (Beacon Press, 1964).

and left-wing ideology is given infinite acceptance, even if it is extreme.

He presents it as a "defence" of democracy, but the practical effect would be to legitimise political suppression and likely trigger exactly the kind of social conflict that could lead to revolution. He suggests we should *burn down the house to protect it from burglars.*

The core weakness in Marcuse's argument lies in its inherent contradiction: *advocating for the destruction of democratic principles in order to save them*[2057].

The first flaw is practical: the argument assumes a clear, definable line between right and left-wing movements. In reality, political ideologies exist on a complex continuum and transform over time. The question of who would wield the power to make these distinctions is never adequately addressed.

The historical basis of the argument - drawing primarily from the rise of Nazi Germany - ignores numerous counter-examples where robust democratic discourse successfully contained extremist movements. This selective use of history overlooks how driving ideologies underground can actually *increase* their appeal and danger.

He ignored how parliamentary democracy was specifically designed as an adversarial system to contain and channel extremism through institutional means. When it works (which isn't always, but often), it turns potentially violent political conflicts into procedural ones. His "solution" would break the very mechanism - institutionalised opposition and debate - which has historically helped societies manage political extremes without resorting to outright suppression.

Perhaps most critically, the proposal created a framework of suppression which could easily be turned against any political movement. The mechanisms of censorship, once established, rarely remain limited to their original targets. By legitimising political suppression as a tool, Marcuse's approach created precisely the kind of authoritarian structure

---

[2057] Howes, Dustin, 'Marcuse's Repressive Tolerance Revisited', *Political Theory*, 36.6 (2008), 744–772.

it claimed it sought to prevent.[2058]

The argument also fails to address root causes. The rise of extremist movements typically stems from underlying social, economic, and political conditions. Merely suppressing their expression does nothing to resolve the fundamental issues that make such ideologies appealing in the first place.

[2058] Rosen, Stanley, *Hermeneutics as Politics* (Oxford University Press, 1987)

How Do Cults Recruit And Control?

Cults and political organisations often have much in common, despite the former being more associated with religious fervour.

Most worryingly, the modern university and the religious cult seem indistinguishable.

Based on research and theory on brainwashing in Maoist China, as well as *"cognitive dissonance theory"* by Leon Festinger[2059], Steven Hassan developed the *"BITE Model"* to describe the specific methods which cults use to recruit and maintain control. "BITE" stands for *"Behavior, Information, Thought, and Emotional"* control[2060].

Behaviour control refers to the ways in which cults regulate the behaviours of their members, which may include things like prescribing what they can wear, eat, or with whom they can associate. For example, *The Times* reported in 2023 Scottish universities were exposing students to *"nakedly ideological"* mandatory bias through investment in *"equality, diversity, and inclusion"* measures which suppress speech and dissent[2061].

Information control refers to the way cults often manipulate the information available to their members, discouraging them from accessing outside sources, and spoon-feeding them only the stories the cult wants them to believe. For example, during the 2023 Israel-Palestine conflict,

---

[2059] Festinger, Leon, *A Theory of Cognitive Dissonance* (Stanford University Press, 1957)

[2060] Hassan, Steven, *Combating Cult Mind Control* (Park Street Press, 1990)

[2061] Mark McLaughlin, 'Universities Are Pushing Nakedly Ideological Sex and Race Theory', *The Times*, 13 September 2023

Columbia University suspended recognition of its pro-Palestinian student groups, *Students for Justice in Palestine* (SJP) and *Jewish Voice for Peace*[2062].

Thought control relates to how cults influence and direct the thoughts of their members. This might involve black and white thinking, instilled phobias about the outside world, or a redefinition of terms to fit the cult's storyline. In *"The Coddling of the American Mind"* (2018), Greg Lukianoff and Jonathan Haidt describe how "safetyism" on campuses leads to black-and-white thinking, the instalment of phobias about the outside world and an *"us versus them"* mentality.[2063]

Finally, *emotional* control describes how manipulating emotions is a powerful tool for many cults. This could be in the form of shaming, inducing guilt, or even love bombing. In 2024, *The Times* further reported the encouragement and spread of peer-ostracisation over perceived offenses at *Oxford University* had led to widespread personal distress among students who reported feeling "terrified"[2064].

In their 1993 paper, John and Mimi Curtis observed certain circumstances and personality traits which increase susceptibility to cult recruitment[2065].

- *generalised ego-weakness and emotional vulnerability*
- *propensities toward dissociative states*
- *tenuous, deteriorated, or nonexistent family relations and support systems*
- *inadequate means of dealing with exigencies of survival*
- *history of severe child abuse or neglect*
- *exposure to idiosyncratic or eccentric family patterns*
- *proclivities toward or abuse of controlled substances*

[2062] Sarah Huddleston, 'Columbia Suspends SJP and JVP Following "Unauthorized" Thursday Walkout', *Columbia Daily Spectator*, 10 November 2023

[2063] Greg Lukianoff Jonathan Haidt, *The Coddling of the American Mind* (Penguin, 2018).

[2064] Alice Thomson, 'Cancel Culture on Campus: "Most of Us Are Terrified"', *The Times*, 27 November 2024

[2065] Curtis, James, and Curtis, Margaret, 'Factors Related to Susceptibility and Recruitment by Cults', *Psychological Reports*, 73.2 (1993), 451–60

- *unmanageable and debilitating situational stress and crises*
- *intolerable socioeconomic conditions*

Cult recruitment is a process by which such primed or predisposed individuals are introduced, indoctrinated, and eventually integrated into groups. The methods used to recruit and retain members can vary widely depending on the group, but there are common stages that many cults follow during the recruitment process[2066].

The process begins when an individual first comes into *contact* with the cult or its members. This could be through a friend, family member, online platform, seminar, workshop, or even a chance meeting.

Once contact is established, new recruits often experience overwhelming attention, affection, and approval from cult members, referring to as *love-bombing*. This can create a sense of belonging, especially if the individual is going through a vulnerable phase in their life.

Cults will often then *assess* a potential recruit's strengths, weaknesses, and vulnerabilities to determine how they can best be integrated and manipulated. They may use personal information shared in confidence against the person later.

The cult gradually *isolates* the recruit from their regular support system, including friends, family, and outside information sources. This makes the individual more dependent on the cult for their social needs, perspective, and information.

The next stage involves the systematic reprogramming of the recruit's beliefs or their *indoctrination*. This could involve long sessions of teachings, meditation, chanting, or even sleep deprivation. The goal is to replace the individual's previous beliefs with the cult's ideology.

Members might be encouraged or forced to *confess* past sins or wrongdoings, which the cult can later use as blackmail or leverage to ensure loyalty and silence.

[2066] Langone, Michael D., 'Cults, Psychological Manipulation, and Society', *ISKCON Communications Journal*, 7 (1999)

At this point, the cult will have ensured significant *dependency* of most aspects of the member's life, including finances, living situation, social connections, and more. Members are made to feel that they cannot survive or find happiness outside the confines of the group.

Rules, norms, and the cult's way of life are strictly *enforced*. Any deviation or questioning can result in punishment, shaming, or even expulsion.

Members are taught to monitor their thoughts and actions constantly, *self-policing* their whole existence. They might also be encouraged to report on others, fostering an environment of mistrust and ensuring conformity.

Once fully integrated, efforts shift towards *maintaining* the member's loyalty and commitment. This might involve regular meetings, rituals, or continued education sessions.

In 1976, US church membership dipped to seventy-six per cent. Four decades later, the figure was forty-eight per cent. In England, it was thirty-eight per cent.[2067]

Simultaneously, publications as politically widespread from *Jacobin* magazine to *The Spectator* have become increasingly alarmed at the mysterious emergence of religious imagery and behaviour in the political landscape[2068].

[2067] Stark, Rodney, and Iannaccone, Laurence R., 'A Supply-Side Reinterpretation of the "Secularization" of Europe', *Journal for the Scientific Study of Religion*, 33.3 (1994)

[2068] Douthat, Ross, *The Decadent Society* (Simon & Schuster, 2020)

What Is The Behavioural Sink?

Something exceedingly strange happens to animals when they live in environments which become overcrowded.

In the 1940s, ethologist John B. Calhoun began studying Norway rats in outdoor enclosures. His early work focused on what he called a "rat city" in an outdoor pen near Baltimore, where he first observed how social hierarchies and behaviours changed under different population densities. He called these cities *"universes"*[2069].

Edmund Ramsden wrote:

> *Calhoun's work became a scientific touchstone for the discussion of crowding and its effects... his rodent laboratories became templates for human society.*[2070]

The *Universe* experiments (numbered 1 - 25) evolved from these initial studies. They were conducted within the *Laboratory of Psychology* at the *National Institute of Mental Health* in Rockville, Maryland, where Calhoun had established his laboratory. Each *"universe"* was more sophisticated than the last, with *"Universe 25"* representing the culmination of his

---

[2069] Calhoun, John B., *The Ecology and Sociology of the Norway Rat* (U.S. Department of Health, Education, and Welfare, Public Health Service, 1963)

[2070] Ramsden, Edmund, and Jon Adams. 'Escaping the Laboratory: The Rodent Experiments of John B. Calhoun and Their Cultural Influence', *Journal of Social History*, 42.3 (2009), 761–92.

experimental design[2071].

What made these experiments particularly fascinating was their historical context. They were conducted during a *Cold War* period of rapid urbanisation and growing concerns about human overpopulation[2072]. The 1960s and early 1970s saw the publication of influential books like *"The Population Bomb"* and increasing public anxiety about humanity's future in increasingly crowded cities[2073].

Calhoun's experimental design was meticulous. The mouse habitat was a 101-square-inch metallic enclosure that rose 54 inches high. It was divided into four interconnected "quadrants" with ramps and corridors between them. Each quadrant contained food hoppers and water dispensers sufficient for over 9,500 mice - *far* more than would ever live there. The temperature was kept at a constant 70°F, and the enclosure was cleaned every four to eight weeks.

The mice used in *"Universe 25"*, his most famous experiment, were specifically chosen. They were the grandchildren of mice who had already proven their ability to thrive in previous experimental settings, theoretically giving them the *best* possible chance of success. He created an enclosed mouse *"utopia"* with *unlimited* food, water, and nesting material. The space could theoretically house 3,840 mice comfortably, but the population never reached that number.

The mice initially bred normally, and the population grew exponentially. However, as density increased, mice began exhibiting unusual social behaviours. Males became aggressive or withdrew completely from social interaction. Females abandoned their young or became aggressive themselves. Calhoun observed what he called *"beautiful ones"* - mice that did nothing but eat, sleep, and groom themselves, showing no

---

[2071] Calhoun, John B., 'Population Density and Social Pathology', *Scientific American*, 206.2 (1962), 139–48.

[2072] Wolfe, Audra J., 'The Cold War Context of John B. Calhoun's Behavioral Research', *Endeavour*, 36.2 (2012), 69–75

[2073] Ehrlich, Paul R., *The Population Bomb* (Ballantine Books, 1968).

interest in mating or social interaction.

They emerged in what Calhoun called *"Phase D"* or the *"death phase"* of the experiment. These mice would spend hours meticulously grooming their fur until it was immaculate. They would eat alone, sleep alone, and avoid all social contact. Despite their perfect physical appearance, they showed no interest in mating, fighting, or any form of social interaction - they had essentially checked out of mouse society entirely.

What made them particularly striking was their complete departure from normal mouse behaviour. Mice are typically social creatures with complex hierarchies and relationships. The *"beautiful ones"* represented a total rejection of these natural instincts. They wouldn't defend territory, attempt to mate, or even engage in normal aggressive behaviours with other males.

The name *"beautiful ones"* came from their pristine appearance - their fur was perfect, they were well-fed, and they showed no signs of the scars or marks typical of socially active mice. But this physical perfection masked what Calhoun saw as a complete psychological withdrawal. He viewed them as an embodiment of the death of social identity and purpose, even while the physical body remained healthy.

The emergence of the *"beautiful ones"* seemed to act like a contagion which acted to accelerate the colony's decline. As more males withdrew into this state, fewer mice engaged in normal social and reproductive behaviours, contributing to the eventual extinction of the population.

> *They were magnificent specimens physically, their coats were well groomed, they avoided conflict, they never fought, they never engaged in sexual approaches, and they never engaged in reproductive behaviour.*

The female mice exhibited disturbing behavioural changes in response to both the *"beautiful ones"* and the overall social collapse. Their maternal behaviours became severely disrupted.

Many females became aggressive and hyperactive. Unlike their normal protective maternal instincts, they would often abandon their pups before weaning them. In some cases, they became violent towards their own offspring, either killing them directly or neglecting them to death.

There was also a breakdown in nesting behaviour. Females would often move their pups from one nest to another, seemingly at random, sometimes injuring or dropping them in the process. Some females stopped building proper nests altogether.

In the later stages of the experiment, many females became incapable of carrying pregnancies to term. Those which did give birth often failed to care for their young. This combination of pregnancy failures, infant mortality, and maternal abandonment contributed significantly to the population's eventual extinction. Interestingly, some females also began exhibiting aggressive male-like behaviours, particularly towards other females and pups.[2074]

The term *"behavioral sink"* was coined by Calhoun to describe this collapse of social behaviour under crowded conditions.

> *Among the males the behavior disturbances ranged from sexual deviation to cannibalism and from frenetic overactivity to a pathological withdrawal from which individuals would emerge to eat, drink and move about only when other members of the community were asleep. The social organization of the animals showed equal disruption.*
>
> *The common source of these disturbances became most dramatically apparent in the populations of our first series of three experiments, in which we observed the development of what we called a behavioral sink. The animals would crowd together in greatest number in one of the four interconnecting pens in which the colony was maintained. As many as 60 of the 80 rats in each experimental population would assemble in one pen during periods of feeding. Individual rats would rarely eat except in the company of*

[2074] Calhoun, John B., 'Death Squared: The Explosive Growth and Demise of a Mouse Population', *Proceedings of the Royal Society of Medicine*, 66.1 (1973), 80–88.

> *other rats. As a result extreme population densities developed in the pen adopted for eating, leaving the others with sparse populations.*
>
> *In the experiments in which the behavioral sink developed, infant mortality ran as high as 96 percent among the most disoriented groups in the population.*[2075][2076]

Despite having all physical needs met, the mouse society essentially self-destructed through:

- Increased aggression
- Withdrawal from social roles
- Abandonment of reproductive behaviour
- Cannibalism
- Complete breakdown of normal social structures[2077]

The population peaked at 2,200 mice and then began declining, eventually going extinct despite abundant resources. The last birth occurred on day 600, and the population died out completely around day 1780[2078].

[2075] Calhoun, John B., 'Population Density and Social Pathology', *Scientific American*, 206.2 (1962), 139–48.

[2076] Calhoun, John B., 'Death Squared: The Explosive Growth and Demise of a Mouse Population', *Proceedings of the Royal Society of Medicine*, 66.1 (1973), 80–88.

[2077] Kirk, Robert G. W., 'Care in the Cage: John B. Calhoun's "Moral Equivalent of War"', *Journal of the History of Biology*, 47.4 (2014), 585–611

[2078] Dror, Otniel E., 'The Affect of Experiment: The Turn to Emotions in Anglo-American Physiology, 1900–1940', *Isis*, 90.2 (1999), 205–237

Are Women The Fairer Sex?

We are higher apes; a species of bipedal primate believed to be two hundred thousand years old[2079]. Broadly-speaking, male and female human primates are more similar than we are different[2080]. On almost every graph, males and females typically overlap more than they deviate[2081]. In IQ, for example, females cluster more narrowly towards the median average, whereas males extend outward in a wide range (both lower and higher)[2082].

One of the major differences in human primates, other than twenty per cent in size and anatomical structure, is *female sexual selectivity*[2083]. As opposed to other primates who are promiscuous[2084], human females display *assortative* patterns and distinct *mate choice bias* (often referred to as

---

[2079] Rob DeSalle and Ian Tattersall, *Human Origins* (Texas A&M Press, 2008)

[2080] Halpern, Diane F., Jonathan Wai, 'Sex Differences in Intelligence', in *The Cambridge Handbook of Intelligence*, ed. by Robert J. Sternberg (Cambridge Press, 2020)

[2081] Hyde, Janet Shibley, 'The Gender Similarities Hypothesis', *American Psychologist*, 60 (2005), 581–92.

[2082] Diane F. Halpern and Jonathan Wai, 'Sex Differences in Intelligence', in *The Cambridge Handbook of Intelligence*, ed. by Robert J. Sternberg (Cambridge University Press, 2020), pp. 317–345.

[2083] Buss, David. M. (1989) 'Sex Differences in Human Mate Selection: Evolutionary Hypotheses Tested in 37 Cultures', *Behavioral and Brain Sciences*, 12(1), pp. 1–49

[2084] Dixon, Alan F. *Primate Sexuality*, (Oxford University Press, 2017)

"hypergamy") for evolutionary fitness and resource provisioning[2085][2086]. This process is one of the reasons humans are so believed to be so evolved by comparison[2087].

However, there are a suite of behaviours which are engaged in by female human primates at such a one-sided frequency and prevalence they are statistically null in males by comparison. They may not be exclusive to females, or have a sex-specific biological cause related to female sex, but they are so rarely engaged in by men, if at all, they are differentiated as sex-characteristic. For all practical intents and purposes, we can define them as "female-specific" behaviours in the absence of counter-indicatory evidence.

These unflattering behaviours are rarely discussed or researched, and when they are, they are subject to extreme politicisation, or junk abstract psychobabble about *"society."* *"Social science"* types typically resort to citing exceptions, claiming they invalidate the rule. This is *exception fallacy,* or *"hasty generalisation from counterexample"*; a form of faulty generalisation where the mention of an extreme outlier or rare exception is cited as an attempt to invalidate a statistical trend or general pattern.

In simple terms, a sunny day in winter does not mean winter is not cold. In biological terms, a male exhibiting behaviour overly-predominant in females does not "equalise" it or make it a behaviour prevalent in both sexes[2088].

[2085] Conroy-Beam, Daniel, et al. (2015) 'Assortative Mating and the Evolution of Desirability' *Evolution and Human Behavior* 36.2: 119–128

[2086] Buss, David M. (1989) 'Sex Differences in Human Mate Selection: Evolutionary Hypotheses Tested in 37 Cultures' *Behavioral and Brain Sciences* 12.1: 1–49

[2087] Buss, David. M., and Schmitt, David. P., 'Sexual Strategies Theory: An Evolutionary Perspective on Human Mating', *Psychological Review,* 100 (1993), 204–32.

[2088] Walton, Douglas N. (1989) *Informal Logic,* Cambridge University Press

de Clérambault's Syndrome (RLO)

Delusional erotomania (*"romantic love obsession"*, or RLO) also known as *Erotomanic Delusional Disorder*, where a person believes an unobtainable older man, often of higher social status or a celebrity (alive or dead), is in love with them. This obsession can lead to persistent, intrusive, and sometimes harassing behaviour towards the perceived love interest[2089].

The number of studies is relatively limited due to its rarity, but almost all known cases are female with a history of psychiatric illness, often including stalking[2090].

Cult Recruitment

In 2014, *The Telegraph* questioned why seventy per cent of cult members worldwide are women[2091]. Former *FBI* officer Joe Navarro published fifty traits he found to be true in all infamous male cult leaders. All were, or are, pathologically narcissistic, and devalue cult members[2092].

A proportion of female cult members actively participate in recruiting other women and girls for victimisation. Many of these gender-specific tactics have been documented extensively[2093].

In *"Terror, Love and Brainwashing: Attachment in Cults and Totalitarian Systems"* (2017), Alexandra Stein studied women's roles in multiple cults, including the *Unification Church*, and documented how female recruiters

---

[2089] Hollender, M H, Callahan, A S, 'Erotomania or de Clérambault syndrome' (1975) 32(12) *Archives of General Psychiatry* 1574

[2090] Segal, J H, 'Erotomania revisited: From Kraepelin to DSM-III-R' (1989) 146(10) *The American Journal of Psychiatry*

[2091] Thackray, Jemima, 'Why are women more likely to join religious cults?' (2014) *The Telegraph*, 9 January

[2092] Navarro, Joe, 'What makes a pathological cult leader?' (2012) *Psychology Today*, 25 August

[2093] Whitsett, Doni and Stephen A. Kent, "Cults and Families", Families in Society: The Journal of Contemporary Social Services, 84.4 (2003), 491-502

exploited *"love bombing"* techniques[2094].

Janja Lalich's research, including *"Bounded Choice: True Believers and Charismatic Cults"* (2004), provides detailed case studies of women in leadership positions in *"Heaven's Gate"*. She identified female recruiters often rose to power by demonstrating exceptional loyalty through the successful recruitment of other women[2095].

Margaret Singer's research on the *"Children of God"* cult documented how female recruiters were specifically trained to use *"flirty fishing"* - a practice of using romantic/sexual attraction for recruitment, including towards other women[2096][2097].

The female *"Dominus Obsequious Sororium"* (*"Master Over Slave Women"*) subgroup of the *NXIVM* sex cult was run by Manhattanite female *"first-line masters"* who required *"collateral"* (blackmail material, usually a solo sex tape) before obliging other women to recruit their own "slaves" under the guise of an NLP *"empowerment"* group. They endured a ritual which required them to strip naked, then sit blindfolded in a circle, before having the male leaders' initials burned onto their skin by their female *"masters"* with a cauterising pen[2098].

Domestic Violence

Almost half of all women (48.4%) and men (48.8%) in the US have experienced aggression through an intimate partner in their lifetime[2099]. 528,000 in the UK men have been a victim of stalking in their lifetime by

---

[2094] Stein, Alexandra, Terror, Love and Brainwashing: (Routledge, 2017)

[2095] Lalich, Janja, Bounded Choice (University of California Press, 2004)

[2096] Singer, Margaret T., Cults in Our Midst (Jossey-Bass, 1995)

[2097] Raine, Susan. "Flirty Fishing in the Children of God: The Sexual Body as a Site of Proselytization and Salvation." *Marburg Journal of Religion*, vol. 12, no. 1, 2007

[2098] Berman, Sarah, Don't Call it a Cult (Viking, 2021).

[2099] Black MC, Basile KC, Breiding MJ, Smith SG, Walters ML, Merrick MT, et al. *The National Intimate Partner and Sexual Violence Survey (NISVS): 2010 Summary Report.* National Center for Injury Prevention and Control, CDC; 2011.

a current or ex-partner; 878,000 have been a victim of cyber stalking[2100].

According to the CDC, one in seven men age 18+ in the U.S. has reported *severe* physical violence by an intimate partner in his lifetime, and one in 10 men has reported rape, physical violence, and/or stalking by an intimate partner[2101]. In England and Wales, data from the *Crime Survey for England and Wales* (CSEW) indicates that 26.5% of *reported* domestic abuse victims in 2022 were male[2102].

Reciprocal (bidirectional) violence occurs in half of violent relationships. Women initiate violence *as* often, or *more* often, than men[2103]. Men tend to perpetrate violence *less* frequently than women in terms of minor incidents, but they more perpetrate more severe violence[2104]. Women are *more* likely to perpetrate minor acts of physical violence, such as slapping, pushing, or throwing objects[2105]. Female-perpetrated violence is often described as repeated acts of less severe physical aggression over time, while male-perpetrated violence is typically less frequent but more severe[2106]. Male victims consistently under-report female violence[2107].

Domestic violence in female-female (lesbian) relationships is *exception-*

[2100] Office for National Statistics. "Stalking:year ending March 2023"

[2101] Centers for Disease Control and Prevention. *The National Intimate Partner and Sexual Violence Survey (NISVS): 2010 Summary Report.* National Center for Injury Prevention and Control, Centers for Disease Control and Prevention; 2011

[2102] Office for National Statistics. "Domestic abuse prevalence and trends, England and Wales: year ending March 2023."

[2103] Whitaker DJ, Haileyesus T, Swahn M, Saltzman LS. "Differences in frequency of violence between reciprocal and nonreciprocal intimate partner violence." *American Journal of Public Health.* 2007;97(5):941–7

[2104] Archer, J. "Sex differences in aggression between heterosexual partners: A meta-analytic review." *Psychological Bulletin.* 2000;126(5):651–80

[2105] Straus MA, Gelles RJ, Steinmetz SK. *Behind Closed Doors* (Anchor Books; 1980)

[2106] Hines DA, Douglas EM. "Intimate terrorism by women towards men." *Partner Abuse.* 2010;1(3):286–313

[2107] Tsui V. "Male victims of intimate partner abuse: Use and helpfulness of services." *Social Work.* 2014;59(2):121–30

ally higher than in any other demographic group[2108]. 17-45% of lesbians report having been the victim of a least one act of physical violence, 50% have experienced sexual abuse, and up to 90% report psychological abuse[2109].

Eating Disorders (Dysmorphia)

Roughly 4.9% of women and 2.3% of men will experience one type of eating disorder in their lifetime[2110]. Dysfunctional patterns of nutrition overwhelmingly affect young women (85-90%), with most having an average onset between the age of 15 and 25[2111]. *Anorexia Nervosa* (90-95% women, 10:1 ratio) has a mortality rate of 4-11% (20% from suicide), which is twelve times more than the ordinary population[2112]; *Bulimia Nervosa* (87-90% women, 8:1 ratio) has a lower morality rate of around 4%[2113]. *Binge Eating Disorder* is more evenly distributed (65-70% women,

---

[2108] Walters ML, Chen J, Breiding MJ. *The National Intimate Partner and Sexual Violence Survey (NISVS): 2010 Findings on Victimization by Sexual Orientation.* Centers for Disease Control and Prevention; 2013

[2109] Rose, Suzana, "Lesbian partner violence fact sheet." *National Violence Against Women Prevention Research Center.* University of Missouri at St. Louis

[2110] Vankar, Preeti. "Number of U.S. female deaths due to eating disorders, 2018-2019, by age and condition." Statista, 29 Nov. 2023

[2111] Rohde, P, Stice, E, Marti, C N, 'Development and Predictive Effects of Eating Disorder Risk Factors during Adolescence: Implications for Prevention Efforts' (2014) 48(2) International Journal of Eating Disorders 187

[2112] Auger, N, Potter, B J, Ukah, U V, Low, N, Israël, M, Steiger, H, Healy-Profitós, J, Paradis, G, 'Anorexia nervosa and the long-term risk of mortality in women' (2021) 20(3) World Psychiatry 448,

[2113] Crow, S J, Peterson, C B, Swanson, S A, Raymond, N C, Specker, S, Eckert, E D, Mitchell, J E, 'Increased mortality in bulimia nervosa and other eating disorders' (2009) 166(12) The American Journal of Psychiatry 1342

2:1 ratio), and a later onset and lower mortality rate[2114].

Other less-known eating problems such as *Purging Disorder*[2115], *Avoidant Restrictive Food Intake Disorder* (ARFID)[2116], and *Rumination Disorder*[2117] are also overwhelmingly prevalent in girls.

Neurobiological factors identified in research include altered serotonin and dopamine function (particularly in reward pathways)[2118], differences in hypothalamic regulation of hunger/satiety[2119], disrupted gut-brain axis signalling[2120], and 50-80% genetic heritability in twin studies[2121].

Epidemic Hysteria

Studies on this unflattering topic have been noticeably "disappearing" over the years, or they are being moved/renamed, or they are being fraudulently conflated with general incidents of panic in men, moral panics, and others.

[2114] Castellini, G, Caini, S, Cassioli, E, Rossi, E, Marchesoni, G, Rotella, F, De Bonfioli Cavalcabo', N, Fontana, M, Mezzani, B, Alterini, B, Lucarelli, S, Ricca, V, 'Mortality and care of eating disorders' (2022) 147(2) Acta Psychiatr Scand 122

[2115] Smith, K E, Crowther, J H, Lavender, J M, 'A review of purging disorder through meta-analysis' (2017) 126(5) Journal of Abnormal Psychology 565

[2116] Bourne, L, [et al.], 'Avoidant/restrictive food intake disorder: A systematic scoping review of the current literature' (2020) 288 Psychiatry Research 112961

[2117] Mayes, S D, [et al.], 'Rumination disorder: differential diagnosis' (1988) 27(3) Journal of the American Academy of Child & Adolescent Psychiatry 300

[2118] Kaye, Walter H., et al., 'Neurobiology of Anorexia Nervosa: Clinical Implications of Alterations of the Function of Serotonin and Other Neuronal Systems', International Journal of Eating Disorders, 51.3 (2013), 248-259

[2119] Monteleone, Palmiero and Mario Maj, 'Dysfunctions of Leptin, Ghrelin, BDNF and Endocannabinoids in Eating Disorders: Beyond the Homeostatic Control of Food Intake', Nature Reviews Endocrinology, 9.11 (2013), 640-648

[2120] Herpertz-Dahlmann, Beate, et al., 'The Role of the Gut-Brain Axis in Psychiatric Disorders', Frontiers in Psychiatry, 8.43 (2017), 1-11

[2121] Bulik, Cynthia M., et al., 'Twin Studies of Eating Disorders: A Review', International Journal of Eating Disorders, 43.2 (2010), 113-120

Also known as *"mass hysteria"*, *"mass psychogenic illness"*, *"psychogenic epidemic"*, or *"conversion disorder"*, and not be confused with generalised *"hysteria"*, this condition, a social contagion, has a lengthy precedent in human history going back to 1374[2122]. An entire episode *"House M.D."* was dedicated to it[2123].

In the Middle Ages, groups of people across Europe began to dance spontaneously, without stopping, until they dropped from exhaustion[2124].

In 1842, Berlin women followed Franz Liszt down the street and picked up his old cigarette stubs, made bracelets from his broken piano strings, tried to rush him en masse, and pull out or cut locks of his hair[2125]. In the late 1800s, students in a number of girls' schools across Europe experienced tremors, shaking, convulsions, uncontrollable laughter, and even amnesia[2126].

In 1963, thousands of fanatical adolescent college girls screamed and feinted with delirium trying to storm stages during *"Beatlemania"*[2127]. In 1998, 800 children in Jordan were hospitalised with non-existent side effects of a tetanus-diphtheria vaccination they'd received at school[2128].

In 2011, high school girls in Leroy, New York, began to experience inexplicable muscle twitches, facial tics, and altered speech[2129]. In 2020 and 2021, girls and women around the world began to show vocal and

---

[2122] Sirois F. "Epidemic hysteria." *Acta Psychiatrica Scandinavica*. 1974;50(1):36–42

[2123] "Airborne." *House, M.D.* Season 3, Episode 18, directed by Elodie Keene, written by David Hoselton and David Shore, Fox, originally aired 27 March 2007

[2124] Waller J. *A Time to Dance, A Time to Die* (Icon Books; 2008)

[2125] Watson D. *Lisztomania*, (Faber & Faber; 2012)

[2126] Bartholomew R, Rickard B. *Mass Hysteria in Schools* (McFarland & Company; 2014)

[2127] Bartholomew RE, Goode E. *The Beatles, "Beatlemania," and the Sociology of Popular Culture*. (Routledge; 1997)

[2128] ProMED-mail. "Mass psychogenic illness in Jordan – Tetanus-diphtheria vaccine." *International Society for Infectious Diseases*. 1998

[2129] Meckler L. "Twitching and Tourette's: What happened at a New York school?" *The Washington Post*. 2012

motor tic-like behaviours after watching *TikTok* videos of people living with tic and movement disorders[2130].

Research indicates that adolescent girls, especially those nearing puberty, are affected by mass hysteria, particularly in school environments[2131]. Attack rates in girls are approximately 2.43 times higher than in boys, if the latter are affected at all[2132]. Outbreaks have been observed among women engaged in repetitive and monotonous tasks[2133]. Multiple attempts have been made to conflate the condition with "hysteria" and doctor evidence so boys appear to be affected at a rate of 10-20%[2134], but the historical evidence is clear: near 100% of all incidents demonstrate it is a phenomenon exclusive to women.

Family Breakdown

Across countries and cultures, research consistently shows women instigate 60-70% of divorces[2135]. Women in same-sex marriages divorce *each other* at even higher rates than they divorce men or gay men divorce at all[2136]; in some cases 29% higher for female-female marriages than

---

[2130] Heyman I, Liang H, Hedderly T. "COVID-19 related increase in tic disorders in children and adolescents: A case series." *BMJ Paediatrics Open.* 2021;5(1):e000847

[2131] Lahmeyer HW, Bagadia VN, Channabasavanna SM. "Epidemic hysteria in a rural secondary school in India." *Journal of the Indian Medical Association.* 1975;64(3):53–7

[2132] Small GW. "Mass hysteria: An analysis of 30 outbreaks." *American Journal of Psychiatry.* 1996;153(9):1233–6

[2133] Colligan MJ, Pennebaker JW, Murphy LR. "Mass psychogenic illness: A social psychological analysis." *American Psychologist.* 1982;37(4):382–92

[2134] Bartholomew RE, Wessely S. "Protean nature of mass sociogenic illness: From possessed nuns to chemical and biological terrorism fears." *The British Journal of Psychiatry.* 2002;180(4):300–6

[2135] Rosenfeld, Michael, "Who wants the breakup? Gender and breakup in heterosexual couples." *Journal of Marriage and Family.* Data based on the How Couples Meet and Stay Together survey, 2009–2015

[2136] Office for National Statistics. "Divorces in England and Wales: 2019." ONS. 2020

female-male marriages[2137].

Married female couples in the UK were approximately 2.5 times more likely to divorce than male couples[2138]; divorce risk for same-sex female couples compared to male couples in Norway and Sweden was 10% higher[2139]; the divorce rate for lesbian couples in the Netherlands was 14%, double the 7% rate for gay male couples[2140]; and in Denmark, female couples account for about 70% of same-sex divorces[2141].

In the UK, divorce was extremely uncommon before 1914, with just one divorce in every 450 marriages. A century later, after the liberalisation of divorce laws favouring women, more than 100,000 couples in the UK get divorced every year, and in the US, around half of marriages end in divorce[2142]. 64% of men typically remarry, compared to 52% of women[2143].

A *National Bureau of Economic Research* (NBER) study which reviewed around 500,000 lottery winners in Sweden found husbands statistically stand by their wives following a lottery win of SEK1 million (US$89,200) or more. A wife winning any *"sudden injection of money"* significantly increased the short or long-term chances of divorce[2144].

[2137] Zahl-Olsen, Rune, and Thuen, Frode. "Same-sex Marriage Over 26 Years: Marriage and Divorce Trends in Rural and Urban Norway." *Journal of Family History*, April 2023; 48(2): 200–212.

[2138] Office for National Statistics (ONS), *Divorces in England and Wales: 2016* (ONS, 2017)

[2139] Gunnar Andersson et al., 'The Demographics of Same-Sex Marriages in Norway and Sweden', *Demography*, 43.1 (2006)

[2140] Netherlands Statistics, *Marriage and Divorce in the Netherlands, 2006–2011* (CBS, 2012)

[2141] Danish National Centre for Social Research, *Trends in Same-Sex Marriage and Divorce* (SFI, 2022)

[2142] BBC. "Why women file for divorce more than men." *BBC Worklife*. 2022 May 11

[2143] Pew Research Center. "Chapter 2: The demographics of remarriage." *Pew Research Center: Social & Demographic Trends*. 2014 Nov 14

[2144] Cesarini D, Lindqvist E, Notowidigdo MJ, Östling R. "The effect of wealth on individual and household behavior: Evidence from Swedish lottery winners." *National Bureau of Economic Research (NBER)*. Working Paper No. 22304. 2016

Foeticide

The *World Health Organization* (WHO) estimates that there are around *73 million* induced abortions each year, which is 200,000 children killed per day[2145]. In the United States, nearly 20% of all pregnancies end by killing. Approximately 600-900,000 fetuses are killed in the US per year, 53% through medication they administer to themselves at home before thirteen weeks' gestation[2146].

In the UK, 10.2 million children have been killed since the *Abortion Act* received *Royal Assent* in 1967; one every two and a half minutes; or 26 lives every hour[2147].

In the US, there are 3,550 abortion providers and 22,001 clinicians willing to conduct the procedure: ob/gyns (72%), family physicians (9%), advanced practice registered nurses (8%), and nurse midwives (3%)[2148].

A 2011 study among practicing obstetrician–gynaecologists in *Obstetrics & Gynecology* found young female physicians were the most likely to provide killing[2149]. According to a later study in 2019, 25.9% of providers were women, while 74.1% were men[2150].

The reasons most frequently cited for killing are a) a child would interfere with education, work, or ability to care for dependents (74%); b) unable to afford a baby (73%); c) unwilling to be a single mother or

---

[2145] World Health Organization. "Abortion." *WHO Fact Sheets*

[2146] Pew Research Center. "What the data says about abortion in the U.S." *Pew Research Short Reads.* 2024 Mar 25.

[2147] Right to Life UK. "56 years of abortion in the UK." *Right to Life UK.*

[2148] Millard, Elizabeth, "Does the US have enough abortion providers?" *Medscape Medical News.* 2022 Mar 23

[2149] Stulberg DB, Dude AM, Dahlquist I, Curlin FA. "Abortion provision among practicing obstetrician–gynecologists." *Obstetrics & Gynecology.* 2011;118(3):609–14

[2150] Studnicki J, Longbons T, Fisher JW, Harrison DJ, Skop I, MacKinnon SJ. "Doctors who perform abortions: Their characteristics and patterns of holding and using hospital privileges." *Health Services Research and Managerial Epidemiology.* 2019;6:2333392819841211

relationship problems (48%). Less than 1% of abortions are sought for reasons of rape, and less than 0.5% are sought for reasons of incest[2151].

Before the UK *Abortion Act* was passed, data analysed by *CARE* suggests there were only 25-50 illegal backstreet abortions per year[2152]. In his 1993 book, Francis Beckwith notes the *U.S. Bureau of Vital Statistics,* in 1972, recorded 39 in the US[2153][2154].

Hybristophilia

Also known as *"Bonnie and Clyde Syndrome"*, a psychological phenomenon defined by sexologist Dr John Money (1986) where an individual is *"sexuoerotically turned on only by a partner who has a predatory history of outrages perpetrated on others"* [2155], or romantically and sexually attracted to someone who has committed a serious or violent crime, such as murder, rape, or terrorism[2156]. This attraction often persists even after the perpetrator's conviction and incarceration[2157].

Approximately 90-95% are women; around 60-70% of women are single or have been previously married; and 50-60% are university educated. Many exhibit a strong interest in true crime stories, serial

---

[2151] Finer, Lawrence, Frohwirth Lori, Dauphinee Lindsay, Singh Susheela, Moore Ann. "Reasons U.S. women have abortions: Quantitative and qualitative perspectives." *Perspectives on Sexual and Reproductive Health.* 2005;37(3):110–8

[2152] CARE. "Examining the arguments: What about backstreet abortions?" *CARE.*

[2153] Beckwith, Francis. *Politically Correct Death,* (Baker Book House; 1990).

[2154] VandenBerg M. "Abortion and women's health: A closer look at 'back-alley' abortions." *Center for Bioethics.* Spring 2007. Cedarville University

[2155] Money, John., *Lovemaps* (Irvington Publishers, 1986)

[2156] 'Romancing the Monster: What Is Hybristophilia?', MagellanTV, 2022

[2157] Matuszak, M., 'Hybristophilia: A White Paper', Center for Homicide Research, 2023

killers, or violent offenders[2158][2159].

At least 50-100 women have married serial killers in the United States since the 1970s[2160]. Up to 500-700 women have formed romantic relationships with serial killers, with a subset of these leading to marriage[2161]. At least 5 women proposed to or expressed interest in marrying Ted Bundy while he was on death row[2162].

Munchausen Syndrome by Proxy

Also known as *Factitious Disorder Imposed on Another* (FDIA), MSbP was described by British paediatrician Roy Meadow in 1977 as a form of child abuse in which a caregiver, usually a parent or guardian, fabricates or induces illnesses in a child to gain attention, sympathy, and emotional gratification for themselves[2163].

The exact ratio is difficult to quantify due to the rarity of the condition and variability in reporting, but a 2004 study in the *British Journal of Psychiatry* analysed 117 cases and found 93% of perpetrators were mothers, 5% were fathers, with an average age of 32.4[2164]. A 2018 review reported a female-to-male perpetrator ratio of approximately 9:1 (90.2%

[2158] 'Fear to Love: Fear Could Explain Women's Attraction toward Male Serial Killers', Research Archive, 2022

[2159] Silverwood, A. R., 'Would You Offer Your Heart to the Wolf with the Red Roses? The Lived Experience of Women in Relationships with Violent and Incarcerated Men', *Antioch University Dissertation*, 2023

[2160] Sheila Isenberg, *Women Who Love Men Who Kill* (Simon & Schuster, 1991).

[2161] Katherine Ramsland, *The Serial Killer's Wife* (Rowman & Littlefield, 2014).

[2162] Rule, A., *The Stranger Beside Me* (Signet, 1980)

[2163] Abdurrachid, N., and Gama Marques, J., 'Munchausen Syndrome by Proxy (MSBP): A Review Regarding Perpetrators of Factitious Disorder Imposed on Another (FDIA)', *CNS Spectrums*, 27.1 (2022), 16–26

[2164] Christine Bartsch, Manfred Risse, Harald Schütz, Nikola Weigand, and Günter Weiler, 'Munchausen Syndrome by Proxy (MSBP): An Extreme Form of Child Abuse with a Special Forensic Challenge', *Forensic Science International*, 137.2-3 (2003)

female, 9.8% male) with an average maternal age of 29.4. 60-80% are married with multiple children, 50-70% have a university education, and have a 10-20% have a background in nursing or healthcare[2165].

The *American Academy of Pediatrics* (AAP) notes that, in reported cases, *"more than 95% of perpetrators are biological mothers."* [2166]

Personality Disorders

The *DSM-5* divides personality disorders into three clusters (A, B, and C), and three disorders within these clusters show a far higher prevalence in women than men. Approximately 9% of the general population is affected by at least one personality disorder[2167]. Women tend to seek help for medical conditions more than men, and sufferers refuse to recognise problems, which makes data somewhat unreliable.

Women have much higher prevalence rates of avoidant, dependent, and paranoid personality disorders than men[2168]. According to an older review of the *DSM-3*, they also historically make up the significant proportion of diagnoses in *Primary Degenerative Dementia*, *Cyclothymic Disorder* (emotional ups and downs), *Dysthymic Disorder* (chronic low-level depression), *Agoraphobia*, simple phobia, *Panic Disorder*, *Somatization Disorder* (physical symptoms disproportionate psychological distress), *Psychogenic Pain Disorder* (caused by factors other than physical injury or

---

[2165] Gregory Yates and Christopher Bass, 'The Perpetrators of Medical Child Abuse (Munchausen Syndrome by Proxy) – A Systematic Review of 796 Cases', *Child Abuse & Neglect*, 72 (2017), 45–53

[2166] Goodpasture, M., and Sinal, S. H., 'Münchausen Syndrome by Proxy: Medical Child Abuse', in *American Academy of Pediatrics Textbook of Pediatric Care*, ed. by T. K. McInerny and others (American Academy of Pediatrics, 2009)

[2167] National Institute of Mental Health, 'Personality Disorders'

[2168] Grant, B. F., Hasin, D. S., Stinson, F. S., Dawson, D. A., Chou, S. P., Ruan, W. J., and Huang, B., 'Prevalence, Correlates, and Disability of Personality Disorders in the United States: Results From the National Epidemiologic Survey on Alcohol and Related Conditions', *The Journal of Clinical Psychiatry*, 65.7 (2004), 948–958

illness), *Multiple Personality Disorder,* inhibited sexual desire, and inhibited orgasm[2169].

Women are 40% more likely to develop depression than men. White women, ages 18-29, who identify as liberal, have been given a mental health diagnosis from medical professionals at a rate of 56.3%[2170].

Women constitute approximately 75% of *Borderline Personality Disorder* diagnoses across all age groups and backgrounds, with symptoms of intense fear of abandonment, emotional instability, and impulsivity[2171]. Women incarcerated for major violence were four times more likely to be diagnosed with BPD compared to those who perpetrated minor violence[2172].

Most alarming in this category is a 1991 American study which indicated 53% of women bringing their sons to clinics for *"gender identity disphoria"* met the criteria for BPD (compared to 8% of a control group). The researchers noted they *"had child-rearing attitudes and practices that encouraged symbiosis and discouraged the development of autonomy."*[2173] This is an academic way of saying they were trying to make their sons like themselves and re-merge them back into the womb. A British study five years later suggested mothers with BPD displayed higher levels of "disoriented" behaviour which severely disrupted the development of

---

[2169] Kaplan, Marcie, 'A Women's View on DSM-III', *American Psychologist*, 38.7 (July 1983), pp. 786-792.

[2170] Farrell, Gwen, "Over 50% of liberal, white women under 30 have a mental health issue. Are we worried yet?" *Evie Magazine.* 2021 Apr 12.

[2171] Skodol, Andrew E., and Donna S. Bender, 'Why Are Women Diagnosed Borderline More Than Men?', *Psychiatric Clinics of North America*, 26.1 (2003), 17–48

[2172] Sansone, Randy A., and Lori A. Sansone, 'Borderline Personality and Criminality', *Psychiatry (Edgmont)*, 6.10 (October 2009), pp. 16–20

[2173] Marantz, Sonia, and Susan Coates, 'Mothers of Males with a Gender Identity Disorder: A Comparison of Matched Controls', *Journal of the American Academy of Child & Adolescent Psychiatry*, 30.2 (1991), 310–315

their infants[2174].

It is extremely difficult to find a number for women diagnosed with *Histrionic Personality Disorder* (excessive attention-seeking), because, alongside the lack of data, a noticeable amount of time and effort has clearly gone into deliberately obscuring and discrediting it within the literature. The prevalence is estimated to range from 0.4% - 1.8%, and women are diagnosed at a rate *"approximately 4 times higher than men"*. Which is to say, at least 75%, and probably 100%. A conservative estimate places it at 65%[2175].

Last, the same trouble exists with *Dependent Personality Disorder* (DPD), where the prevalence range is 0.49 -1.0% for both sexes, and women account for a *"disproportionate number of diagnoses"*. It can only be said, to date, its prevalence is 0.6% in women as opposed to 0.4% in men[2176].

Prison "Families"

Female inmates tend to form pseudo-family structures, with roles like "mother," "sister," or "daughter" offering emotional support and protection[2177]. Violence is more likely to be relational, stemming from personal disputes or conflicts within close-knit social groups[2178].

Opposite-sex staff and inmates in co-ed jails take advantage of

---

[2174] Hobson, R. Peter, Matthew P. H. Patrick, Jessica A. Hobson, Lisa Crandell, Elisa Bronfman, and Karlen Lyons-Ruth, 'How Mothers with Borderline Personality Disorder Relate to Their Year-Old Infants', *The British Journal of Psychiatry*, 195.4 (2009)

[2175] Suinn, Richard M., *Fundamentals of Abnormal Psychology*, updated edn (Nelson-Hall, 1984), pp. 335-336.

[2176] Reitz, Kendra, and Bornstein, Robert F., 'Dependent Personality Disorder', in *Practitioner's Guide to Evidence-Based Psychotherapy*, ed. by Jane E. Fisher and William T. O'Donohue (Springer, 2006), pp. 230–237

[2177] Greer, Krystal R. "The Changing Nature of Interpersonal Relationships in Women's Prisons." *Journal of Offender Rehabilitation*, vol. 28, no. 3-4, 1999

[2178] Pollock, Joycelyn M. *Prisons and Prison Life* (Oxford University Press, 2005)

each other at much higher rates[2179]. Males exploit the emotional vulnerabilities of females, while females manipulate males by using their emotions or perceived vulnerability to gain resources, protection, or other benefits[2180].

Female sexual behaviour becomes hyperactive, with prisoners engaging in sexual relationships with each other because of emotional need[2181][2182]. Mental health problems manifest as "internalising" behaviours such as self-harm, depression, or anxiety[2183][2184][2185].

Indications from studies suggest lesbians are more likely to be involved in physical aggression and crime compared to heterosexual females[2186][2187].

[2179] Lambert, Eric G., et al. "Gender Similarities and Differences in Correctional Staff Work Attitudes and Perceptions." *Western Criminology Review*, vol. 8, no. 1, 2007

[2180] Smykla, John O. "Coed Corrections in the United States: A Look at Theory, Operations, and Research Issues." The Prison Journal, vol. 59, no. 1, 1979

[2181] Hensley, Christopher, Tewksbury, Richard, and Wright, John. "Exploring the Dynamics of Sexual Behavior in Women's Prisons." *Journal of Offender Rehabilitation*, vol. 37, no. 2, 2003, pp. 77–94

[2182] Greer, Krystal. "The Changing Role of Sexual Relationships in Women's Prisons." *Women and Criminal Justice*, vol. 8, no. 3, 1997

[2183] Power, Kate, et al. "Self-Harm in Women Prisoners: A Risk-Taking Behaviour and Response to Trauma?" *Journal of Forensic Psychiatry & Psychology*, vol. 9, no. 1, 1998

[2184] Plugge, Emma, Douglas, Nicola, and Fitzpatrick, Ray. "The Health of Women in Prison: Study Findings." *Journal of Public Health*, vol. 28, no. 3, 2006

[2185] Bartlett, Annie, and Hollins, Sheila. "Challenges and Mental Health Needs of Women in Prison." *British Journal of Psychiatry*, vol. 190, no. 3, 2007, pp. 181–183

[2186] Ellis, Lee, and Walsh, Anthony. "Criminality and Sexual Orientation: Toward a Sociobiological Explanation." *Journal of Homosexuality*, vol. 19, no. 2, 1990

[2187] Pinhey, Thomas K., and Brown, Mary S. "Gender, Sexual Orientation, and Risk Factors for Violence." *Journal of Family Violence*, vol. 20, no. 6, 2005, pp. 369–373

Prostitution

Males participate in prostitution, both as providers and victims. For example, the *United Nations Office on Drugs and Crime* (UNODC) reported that, as of 2020, about 20% of detected trafficking victims were men, and 15% were boys[2188].

However, women and girls constitute the majority of the *"world's oldest profession."* According to the *International Labour Organization* (ILO), approximately 71% of human trafficking victims are female[2189]. Of the 5,975 arrests in Virginia between 2002-2013, 78% (4,661) were female[2190]; in Chicago during 2015, it was 88%[2191]. This pattern continues in almost every culture. In Sweden, which implemented the *"Nordic Model"*, it was 92% in 2019[2192].

Decriminalisation makes no difference at all; prostitution is legal and regulated in Germany, yet 93% of prostitutes are female[2193]. After legalisation, prostitution *doubled* in the state of Thuringia[2194], the country became a destination for human traffickers[2195], and the establishment of large-scale brothels exploded nationwide[2196].

70% of *OnlyFans* models are women[2197], earning approximately $151

[2188] United Nations Office on Drugs and Crime, *Global Report on Trafficking in Persons 2020*

[2189] International Labour Organization, *Profits and Poverty* (2014)

[2190] Dank, Meredith, et al., *Estimating the Size and Structure of the Underground Commercial Sex Economy in Eight Major US Cities*, Final Report (Urban Institute, 2014)

[2191] Cook County Sheriff's Office, *Annual Report on Prostitution Arrests in Chicago*, 2015.

[2192] Swedish National Council for Crime Prevention, *Human Trafficking and Prostitution in Sweden 2019* (Brå, 2019).

[2193] Tampep (European Network for HIV/STI Prevention and Health Promotion among Migrant Sex Workers), *Sex Work in Europe* (Tampep International Foundation, 2009),

[2194] Bild, *Sexarbeit in Thüringen* (2023)

[2195] CSE Institute, *From Sexual Liberation to Hell on Earth* (2023)

[2196] Trauma and Prostitution European Network, *The German Model* (2019)

[2197] Fanso.io, *OnlyFans Statistics: Male vs Female Creators* (2024)

per month, with the top 1% of creators accounting for 33% of the platform's total income[2198].

Between 45% and 75% of individuals in street-based prostitution report experiencing sexual assault at some point during their involvement. In a 1998 study, 82% of reported being physically assaulted, and 68% reported being raped[2199][2200]. Estimates suggest that between 65% and 90% of individuals involved in prostitution have histories of childhood sexual abuse, 73% who had experienced incest[2201][2202].

Relational Aggression

Aggression is often shown in relational behaviours such as social exclusion, rumour spreading, friendship withdrawal, ally-incitement, and manipulation (not to be confused with the non-confrontational "passive" kind)[2203]. While it appears in both sexes, girls start to show higher rates around ages 7-11 at the same time as testosterone surges in boys, and then peaks in adolescence[2204].

Bullying and intentional provocation of distress manifests in indirect rumour-spreading; formation of exclusive friendship cliques; manipu-

---

[2198] EarthWeb, *OnlyFans Statistics 2024: Insights* (2024)

[2199] Farley, M., Baral, I., Kiremire, M., and Sezgin, U., 'Prostitution in Five Countries: Violence and Post-Traumatic Stress Disorder', *Feminism & Psychology*, 8.4 (1998)

[2200] Lowman, J., and Atchison, C., 'Men Who Buy Sex: A Survey in the Greater Vancouver Regional District', *Canadian Review of Sociology*, 43.3 (2006)

[2201] Bagley, C., and Young, L., 'Juvenile Prostitution and Child Sexual Abuse: A Controlled Study', *Canadian Journal of Community Mental Health*, 6 (1987)

[2202] Council for Prostitution Alternatives, *Annual Report* (1991)

[2203] Björkqvist K, Lagerspetz KMJ, Kaukiainen A. "Do girls manipulate and boys fight? Developmental trends in regard to direct and indirect aggression." *Aggressive Behavior*. 1992;18(2):117–27

[2204] Crick NR, Grotpeter JK. "Relational aggression, gender, and social-psychological adjustment." *Child Development*. 1995;66(3):710–22

lation of shared secrets; and complex social network manipulation[2205]. Social media has increased opportunities for these behaviours[2206].

Research suggests relational aggression is employed when physical confrontation against stronger opponents is too costly or risky, or stealth is a superior strategy. Men typically default to physical strategies when those are available and effective, explaining why women engage in it more frequently and intensely[2207][2208].

These plausibly deniable behaviours are generally met with less formal punishment than physical aggression as they are less visible to authority figures, can be executed while maintaining a favourable public image, and they coincide with peak social competition for status, peer acceptance, and romantic entanglement. In short: lower immediate risk, potentially high social reward[2209].

Female survival historically depended heavily on securing stable resources and protection; as well as group acceptance, for access to food, protection, and the social bonds required for maintaining childcare support. The ability to influence social hierarchies without physical risk preserved reproductive capacity and social alliances helped secure better positions for offspring[2210].

[2205] Hess NH, Hagen EH. "Sex differences in indirect aggression: Psychological evidence from young adults." *Evolution and Human Behavior.* 2006;27(3):231–4

[2206] Coyne SM, Nelson DA, Underwood MK. "Aggression in the cyber world: Characteristics and prevention of cyberbullying." In: Brown BB, Prinstein MJ, editors. *Encyclopedia of Adolescence.* San Diego: Academic Press; 2011. p. 446–55

[2207] Archer J. "Sex differences in aggression between heterosexual partners: A meta-analytic review." *Psychological Bulletin.* 2000;126(5):651–80

[2208] Campbell A. "Staying alive: Evolution, culture, and women's intrasexual aggression." *Behavioral and Brain Sciences.* 1999;22(2):203–52

[2209] Campbell A. *A Mind of Her Own* (Oxford University Press; 2002)

[2210] Hrdy SB. *The Woman That Never Evolved,* (Harvard University Press; 1981)

Serial Killing

According to the US *Bureau of Justice Statistics*, women represented approximately ten per cent of individuals serving life sentences for murder[2211]. They are more likely to target people they know (such as spouses, partners, children, etc), and research consistently shows they are more likely to murder men[2212]. Serial killing in women is much rarer than in men[2213].

In her 1992 book, *"Women Serial and Mass Murderers: A Worldwide Reference, 1580 Through 1990"*, author Kerry Segrave profiled eighty-five female serial killers and found the average women mass murderer kills for the first time at age thirty-one, continues to kill for five years before she is apprehended, by which time she has killed approximately seventeen people. Most victims are selected from immediate or extended family and are very young or very old. Most show little or no remorse for their actions, and their underlying motive is hatred of men[2214].

In a 2024 study of 105 female mass-murderers in the *Journal of Forensic Science*, it was revealed women were significantly less likely to employ firearms, the prevalence of psychotic signs was more than double that among males, and the rate of nonpsychotic psychiatric or neurological conditions was also much greater. Over half took or attempted to take their own lives, and more than three-quarters involved at least one family member as a victim[2215].

[2211] Bureau of Justice Statistics. (2021). *Prisoners in 2021*

[2212] Mann C. L. *Female Homicide Offenders: Women Who Kill.* Criminal Justice Research Bulletin. 1996;12(2):1–5

[2213] Farrell AL, Keppel RD, Titterington VB. "Lethal ladies: Revisiting what we know about female serial murderers." Homicide Studies. 2011;15(3):228–52

[2214] Segrave K. *Women Serial and Mass Murderers,* (McFarland, 1992)

[2215] Girgis RR, Hoang D, Hesson H, Dishy G, Lee K, Pia T, et al. An analysis of 105 female-perpetrated mass murders. *Journal of Forensic Science.* 2024;69(6):2120–6

Should Quacks Make Up Pathologies?

The modern discipline of psychiatry, a medical specialty charged with the treatment of biologically based mental diseases and pathologies, emerged at the beginning of the nineteenth century due to several predominant conditions requiring it: the pathologies of *"hysteria"*, dementia, syphilis, and *"shell shock"*[2216]. In many of these cases, the biological pathogenesis of them proved elusive, and studies have drifted towards evolutionary behavioural neuroscience.

The modern forerunner of psychology - the *"social science"* pseudo-discipline of *"psychophysics"* - began around the same time, in Germany[2217]. The ever-broadening area branched into *"parapsychology"* towards the end of the century with fads such as hypnotism and *"psychicism"*[2218][2219]. Ever since, it has fought allegations it is as equally disreputable and unscientific as the politicised notion of *"sociology"*[2220][2221].

[2216] Shorter, Edward, *A History of Psychiatry* (John Wiley & Sons, 1997)

[2217] Fechner, Gustav Theodor, *Elemente der Psychophysik* [Elements of Psychophysics] (Leipzig: Breitkopf und Härtel, 1860)

[2218] Mauskopf, Seymour H., and McVaugh, Michael R., *The Elusive Science:* (Johns Hopkins University Press, 1980)

[2219] Sommer, Andreas, 'Crossing the Boundaries of Mind and Body: Psychical Research and the Origins of Modern Psychology', *History of the Human Sciences*, 26.1 (2013)

[2220] Boring, Edwin G., *A History of Experimental Psychology* (Appleton-Century-Crofts, 1950)

[2221] Slife, Brent D., Reber, Jeffrey S., and Richardson, Frank C., *Critical Thinking About Psychology* (American Psychological Association, 2005)

Since the codification of the nebulous term *"addiction"* (habituation) in the fifties[2222], psychology has been proclaiming ever more hyper-politicised, pseudo-medical pathologies with precisely zero scientific evidence to support them.

It is well established the field is female-dominated, and left-leaning. Women make up eighty per cent of psychology students[2223,2224], and seventy-seven per cent of psychology professionals[2225,2226]. Over *ninety per-cent* lean left-wing politically[2227,2228]. In the US, there is a 17:1 ratio of Democrats to Republicans among psychology professors at elite institutions, with nearly half of these departments lacking a *single* Republican faculty member[2229].

In 2018, the *American Psychological Association* (APA) released its first-ever *"Guidelines for Psychological Practice With Boys and Men."* The contents of *Guidelines 1 & 3* were staggering. The association had decided, and published, for reasons known only to itself, preposterous claims about masculinity being an *"ideology"* which is *"harmful."*[2230]

As Dr Debra Soh put it, as part of a colossal twelve-panel shakedown from psychologists themselves, in widespread opposition to these new headmistress rules:

[2222] Courtwright, David T., *Forces of Habit* (Harvard University Press, 2001)

[2223] The Gender Imbalance in Psychology', *GradPsych* (2011)

[2224] 'Tackling the Gender Imbalance in Psychology', *The Psychologist* (2017)

[2225] CareerExplorer, 'Psychologist Demographics'

[2226] 'An Uneven Playing Field: Women in Academic Psychology', *Observer* (2018)

[2227] Inbar, Yoel, and Joris Lammers, 'Political Diversity in Social and Personality Psychology', *Perspectives on Psychological Science*, 7.6 (2012)

[2228] 'Membership Survey Report', *Society for Personality and Social Psychology* (2018)

[2229] Duarte, José L., Jarret T. Crawford, Charlotta Stern, Jonathan Haidt, Lee Jussim, and Philip E. Tetlock, 'Political Diversity Will Improve Social Psychological Science', *Behavioral and Brain Sciences*, 38 (2015), e130

[2230] *Guidelines for Psychological Practice with Boys and Men* (American Psychological Association, August 2018)

> *Perhaps a good starting point would be the belief that masculinity is an "ideology," "socially constructed," and "learned during socialization," as opposed to biological and the result of hormonal influence. Secondly, the guidelines portray abusive behavior as a natural extension of being male-typical, as opposed to being due to anti-sociality and negative views about women.*
>
> *Progressive talking points, like calling gender a "non-binary construct" and openly advocating for "participation in social justice activities," have no place in a document detailing professional best practices.*[2231]

Moreover, extremely aggressive lobbying has seen the diagnostic manuals become so ideological they list *"video game addiction"* as a medical disorder.

- *"Homo/Trans/Bi-phobia"*
- *Orthorexia*
- *Gender/Sexuality "Spectrum(s)"*
- *Narcissism*
- *Sex/Internet Addiction*
- *Mood Disorder*
- *"Stockholm/Lima/Jerusalem Syndrome"*
- *"Hyper/Toxic Masculinity"*
- *Parental Alienation Disorder*
- *"Social Anxiety Disorder"*
- *Misophonia*
- *Et cetera, ad nauseam*

In his 1873 Ph.D. dissertation on aesthetics, German philosopher Robert Vischer coined the term *"einfühlung"* (*"in-feeling"* or *"feeling into"*) as

---

[2231] Quillette, *Psychologists Respond to the APA's Guidance* (4 Feb 2019)

"esthetic sympathy"[2232]. In 1903, German aesthetics philosopher Theodor Lipps incorporated it into *"psychologism"* as *"projecting oneself onto the object of perception"*[2233].

In 1909, English structuralism psychologist Edward Bradford Titchener translated *Einfühlung* into English as *"empathy"*[2234], which is used somewhat interchangeably for sympathy, compassion, pity, or emotional contagion.

"Empathy" is an entirely made-up analogy for *sympathy* which was derived from an obscure, manufactured German word about people seeing themselves in art; it has no basis in science whatsoever as a separate phenomenon. Yet, decades later, a *lack* of it - a thing of which there is no proof actually exists - is a *symptom* of various psychological conditions.

In 1945, American psychologist Isaac Madison Bentley arbitrarily redefined the concept of gender in his paper *"Sanity and Hazard in Childhood"* as the *"socialized obverse of sex"*. In other words, biological sex is as nature, but gender is as nurture.

> *In the grade-school years, too, gender (which is the socialized obverse of sex) is a fixed line of demarcation, the qualifying terms being 'feminine' and 'masculine'. Many matters in grouping, playing, exercising, reciting, and the like, separate the boys from the girls. That these are social matters of gender may be demonstrated by a reference across to the domestic animals, where there is sex but no gender, sex which has its occasional demonstrations and signals but exerts little other influence upon the cattle, the horses, the cats and the chickens.* [2235]

[2232] Vischer, Robert, 'On the Optical Sense of Form: A Contribution to Aesthetics', in *Empathy, Form, and Space: Problems in German Aesthetics* (1873)

[2233] Lipps, Theodor, *Grundlegung der Ästhetik* (Leopold Voss, 1903)

[2234] Titchener, Edward Bradford, *Experimental Psychology of the Thought-Processes* (Macmillan, 1909)

[2235] Bentley, Irving M., 'Sanity and Hazard in Childhood', *American Journal of Psychology*, 58.1 (1945)

"Gender" as a concept analogous to the *soul*, is entirely made-up. It has no basis in science whatsoever.

In 1965, American psychologist George Weinberg witnessed a female friend being dis-invited from a dinner party on account of her same-sex attraction. In 1969, he described an imaginary psychological condition he had invented due to that incident, which he named *"homophobia"*, in a gay pornographic magazine, *Screw*. In his 1972 book, *"Society and the Healthy Homosexual"*[2236], he claimed those who felt disgust towards homosexual behaviour suffered from a psychological fear they themselves wanted to do the same.

> *It was a fear of homosexuals which seemed to be associated with a fear of contagion, a fear of reducing the things one fought for — home and family. It was a religious fear, and it had led to great brutality, as fear always does.*

"Homophobia" is indistinguishable from the emotion of *disgust*[2237], which is related to hygiene and the fear of contagion. It is entirely made up. It has no basis in science whatsoever. Its "creator" nakedly explained why he manufactured it.

Disgust is a universal emotion that evolved to protect humans from potential harm, such as pathogens, toxic substances, or social and moral transgressions. It is not a *pathology*. It manifests in distinct physiological responses, like nausea and facial expressions, and is processed in the brain's *insula*. It can be categorised into types: *core* disgust (e.g., revulsion to bodily fluids), *pathogen* disgust (e.g., fear of disease), *sexual* disgust (e.g., avoidance of incest), *moral* disgust (e.g., reaction to ethical violations),

---

[2236] Weinberg, George, *Society and the Healthy Homosexual* (St. Martin's Press, 1972)

[2237] Rozin, Paul, Haidt, Jonathan, and McCauley, Clark R., 'Disgust', in Michael Lewis, Jeannette M. Haviland-Jones, and Lisa Feldman Barrett (eds.), *Handbook of Emotions* (3rd edn, New York: Guilford Press, 2008), pp. 757–76

and *aesthetic* disgust (e.g., unpleasant sensory stimuli).[2238]

Disgust sensitivity is also distinctly linked to smell and political orientation. A 2018 study of 750 participants by Dr Jonas Olofsson at *Stockholm University* hypothesised body odour might be a primitive chemo-signalling system for regulating interpersonal contact and disease avoidance. Right-wing authoritarianism appeared to correlate with repulsion towards urine, sweat, and other body odours[2239].

Almost forty years after the first SSRI antidepressant (*"Prozac"*) was launched in 1984, a wide-scale review in *Molecular Psychiatry* (*"The serotonin theory of depression: a systematic umbrella review of the evidence"*) announced:

> *no consistent evidence of there being an association between serotonin and depression or that depression is caused by lowered serotonin activity or concentrations.*[2240]

Antidepressants might *treat* depression - in some unknown, mysterious way to do with changing neurotransmitters -, but there is no scientific evidence depression is *caused* by neurotransmitter levels.

A staggering amount of what we consider being irrefutable, axiomatic "science" is demonstrable *nonsense*[2241].

[2238] Curtis, V. and Biran, A., 'Dirt, Disgust, and Disease: Is Hygiene in Our Genes?', *Perspectives in Biology and Medicine*, 44.1 (2001), 17–31.

[2239] Liuzza, Marco Tullio, Torun Lindholm, Caitlin B. Hawley, Marie Gustafsson Sendén, Ingrid Ekström, Mats J. Olsson, and Jonas K. Olofsson, 'Body Odour Disgust Sensitivity Predicts Authoritarian Attitudes', *Royal Society Open Science*, 5.2 (2018), 171091

[2240] Moncrieff, Joanna, Cooper, Rachel E., Stockmann, Tom, Amendola, Silvia, Hengartner, Michael P., and Horowitz, Mark A., 'The Serotonin Theory of Depression: A Systematic Umbrella Review of the Evidence', *Molecular Psychiatry*, 27.4 (2022), 1–13

[2241] Lilienfeld, Scott O., Lynn, Steven Jay, and Lohr, Jeffrey M., *Science and Pseudoscience in Clinical Psychology* (New York: Guilford Press, 2003)

What Is Brain Jamming?

When you're in the midst of an argument, often your opponent can throw an accusation at you, which sends you onto the defensive back foot. It can cause a sense of *"brain freeze"* analogous to intellectual quicksand. You lose your train of thought trying to counter their spontaneous slur or charge. Your mind is being *"jammed"*, so to speak.

These terms are designed to end a discussion and shut down any further conversation or thought. Examples might be:

- *That's racist.*
- *That's homophobic.*
- *You're a fascist!*
- *They're entitled to their own opinion.*
- *It's all good.*
- *Here we go again.*
- *So, what?*
- *Whatever.*
- *Let's agree to disagree.*
- *Stop thinking so much.*
- *Educate yourself!*
- *According to you.*
- *Support our troops!*
- *Stay in your lane.*
- *Why do you care?*
- *Check your privilege!*

WHAT IS BRAIN JAMMING?

- *Believe all women!*
- *Just let it go.*
- *It is what it is.*
- *OK, Boomer.*
- *Trans women are women!*

The contemporary name for these "thought-stopper" terms, *"thought-terminating clichés"*, was popularised by Robert Jay Lifton in his 1961 book *"Thought Reform and the Psychology of Totalism"* about the structure of language used by the *Chinese Communist Party*.

They are usually brief, easily memorised phrases that trick people into believing they are insightful or an answer to their hard question, and are used to end an argument or quell cognitive dissonance.

> *The language of the totalist environment is characterized by the thought-terminating cliché. The most far-reaching and complex of human problems are compressed into brief, highly reductive, definitive-sounding phrases, easily memorized, and easily expressed. They become the start and finish of any ideological analysis.*[2242]

The modern march of sloganeering traces its origins to Lenin and his short pamphlet *"On Slogans"* from 1917[2243]. Russian historian Mikhail Heller explains within *"Cogs in the Wheel: The Formation of Soviet Man"* (1988):

> *Lenin developed a special way of writing that made it possible to establish the 'formula-slogan' in the mind of the reader or listener . . . Then, as the most important compositional element, there is the use of repetition, by means of which a rectangle is formed which concentrates the attention, narrows the field of possibilities, and*

[2242] Lifton, Robert, *Thought Reform and the Psychology of Totalism* (N. Carolina Press, 1961)

[2243] Lenin, Vladimir Ilyich, *On Slogans* (1917)

squeezes thought into a tight ring from which there is only one exit . . .

Soviet speech is always a monologue because there is no other party to talk to. On the other side is the enemy. In the Soviet language there are no neutral words – every word carries an ideological burden . . . That is why in Soviet language the same words are repeated over and over again, until they become a signal that acts without any effort of thought. The effect of set phrases and slogans is also assured by their always being repeated in absolutely the same form . . .[2244]

Slogans *stop* or *shut down* thought or conversation, as terminating clichés do. Both are tightly coupled with the tactic of enforcing speech codes, a notion summarised in the USSR as *"It might be factually correct, comrade. But it is not politically correct."* There is one party; one ideology; one prescription of orthodoxy; and it must be followed *correctly*. What we call "political correctness", the Soviets called "partymindedness" (*partiinost*).

In *"Our Culture, What's Left Of It",* English prison physician and psychiatrist Theodore Dalrymple astutely observes:

Political correctness is communist propaganda writ small. In my study of communist societies, I came to the conclusion that the purpose of communist propaganda was not to persuade or convince, nor to inform, but to humiliate; and therefore, the less it corresponded to reality the better.

When people are forced to remain silent when they are being told the most obvious lies, or even worse when they are forced to repeat the lies themselves, they lose once and for all their sense of probity. To assent to obvious lies is to co-operate with evil, and in some small way to become evil oneself. One's standing to resist anything is thus eroded, and even destroyed. A society of emasculated liars is easy to

---

[2244] Heller, Mikhail, *Cogs in the Wheel* (Alfred Knopf, 1988)

> *control. I think if you examine political correctness, it has the same effect and is intended to.*[2245]

Speech correlates in direct ways to raw political power. Not only in the persuasive strength of speeches delivering political rhetoric, but in the state's ability to control what its people say to one another.

The fortunate, if not ironic, quality of the thought-terminating cliché is they are joint weapons of attack *and* defence. The most powerful response to one is simply to answer with another.

That's racist! *According to you, comrade.*

[2245] Dalrymple, Theodore, *Our Culture, What's Left of It* (Ivan R. Dee, 2005)

What Is Malicious Conflation?

A strange tactic in modern political times is a cunning, lightweight sleight of linguistic hand where one thing is confused or twisted with another. It can be so subtle it ties a listener or opponent into knots without them even realising what is happening.

It is most tellingly used by lawyers in courtrooms, but it seems partisan media outlets are increasingly resorting to it in order to defend their political allies.

> Conflation, n.
> *the act or process of erroneously merging two or more separate sets of information, texts, ideas etc into one whole.*

Conflation leads to a form of intellectual chaos, and in many cases, it is entirely deliberate as a *Hegelian*[2246] or *Leninist*[2247][2248] strategy to "accelerate the contradictions." In simple terms, it means talking about one thing, when you mean the other.

Time flies like an arrow; fruit flies like a banana. All bats are animals. Some wooden objects are bats. Therefore, some wooden objects are animals.

An example in point might be immigration. In one corner, there is

---

[2246] Hegel, Georg Wilhelm Friedrich, *The Phenomenology of Spirit* (1807)

[2247] Lenin, Vladimir Ilyich, *Left-Wing Communism* (1920)

[2248] Hill, Christopher, ed., *The Lenin Reader* (Humanity Books, 2014)

the thorny issue of legal foreign residents, visa caps, and refugees legally seeking asylum. In the opposite corner, the issue of asylum abuse, people trafficking, and illegal migrants. Suspicious or cynical actors will talk of the latter in terms of the former: *only racists would disagree with quota caps on a path-to-citizenship for undocumented migrants.*

These dual, or perhaps, binary pairs - such as asylum and illegal immigration - are almost endless:

- *Equality and equity*
- *Morality and ethics*
- *Elections and democracy*
- *Free markets and capitalism*
- *Patriotism and nationalism*
- *Diversity and tokenism*
- *Europe and the EU*
- *Rights and moral license*
- *Money and credit*
- *Price and value*
- *Israel and Zionism*
- *Income and wealth*
- *Et cetera, ad nauseam*

Often, this intentional conflation is used in parallel with obscurantism to disguise or hide the true nature of an issue, program, or even as a defensive reaction to criticism.

"Critical race theory" ("CRT"), for example, which substitutes the notion of *class* in Karl Marx's *"Communist Manifesto"*[2249] for *race*, is more appropriately named *"communist race theory"*[2250].

The word *"critical"* is a cleverly substituted term for "communist" in all books written by authors who were, *quelle surprise*, dyed-in-the-wool

---

[2249] Marx, Karl, and Engels, Friedrich, *The Communist Manifesto* (1848)

[2250] Delgado, Richard, Stefancic, Jean, *Critical Race Theory* (New York Press, 2017)

communists attempting to overlay Marx's ideas on every subject or group found in the university.

Two ingenious conflations are employed to disguise this unpopular truth. The first, that Communist Race Theory is "just" an updated version of 60s Civil Rights movement philosophy (which it explicitly rejects). Second, that the educational practice of it in schools is not provided as timetabled lessons, making complaints about it an unfair demonisation.

These deliberate conflations aiming to score political points have grown in severity over time[2251]: legal-but-mean speech is hate speech; speech is violence; authority is fascism; skin colour is ethnic culture, free healthcare means healthcare doesn't cost anything; statues are real people, and so on.

It is important, if one wishes to win a game, to perceive which game is being played, and the grounds upon which it is being fought.

[2251] Edelman, Murray, *The Language of Politics* (Academic Press, 1977)

What Is Loaded Language?

Academics have a lot of time on their hands. Not merely a few hours here and there; days upon days of empty, dead time to dream up word games. Special interest lobby groups, such as partisan "watchdogs", deliberately employ wordsmiths to "spin" stories with political terminology, which is impossible to refute or oppose.

When picking a name for your cause, it's crucial to pick one your ideological enemies will find almost difficult to challenge. Within the abortion debate, both sides are *pro* something - "life" or "choice" - so they can charge their enemy as being *for* its antonym, such as being pro-death or anti-choice.

The childish formula is quite simple: divide the world into a binary black-and-white false dilemma between heroes and villains fighting over a moral cause; then frame oneself as the hero, your enemy as the antagonist.

Loaded language refers to words and phrases that induce a strong emotional response and carry a positive or negative connotation beyond their literal meaning[2252].

Examples of loaded political language are so numerous they would fill multiple books, but include:

- *Assault rifle*
- *Common sense gun control*

[2252] Bolinger, Dwight, *Language—The Loaded Weapon* (Longman, 1980)

- *Equity*
- *Family values*
- *Gender-affirming care*
- *Job creator*
- *Partial-birth abortion*
- *Sexual orientation*
- *Tax relief*
- *Undocumented immigrant*

The creation and usage of these "framed" phrases[2253] which function as "talking points" can be traced back to two men: pollster Frank Luntz, and cognitive linguist George Lakoff.

Luntz worked with Pat Buchanan, Ross Perot, Rudolph Giuliani, and Rush Limbaugh, and published an annual playbook *"The New American Lexicon"*.

> *Luntz suggested replacing "drilling for oil" with "exploring for energy;" "undocumented workers" with "illegal aliens;" and "estate tax" with "death tax." The substitutions often work — an April Ipsos/NPR poll found that support for abolishing the estate tax jumps to 76% from 65% when you call it the death tax.*[2254]

Lakoff is best known for his thesis in *"Metaphors We Live By"* (1980) that people's lives are significantly influenced by the conceptual metaphors they use to explain (*"frame"*) complex phenomena[2255]. In his 1996 book *"Moral Politics"*, Lakoff described conservative voters as being influenced by the *"strict father model"*, and liberal/progressive voters as being influenced by the "nurturant parent model".

[2253] Tversky, Amos, and Kahneman, Daniel, 'The Framing of Decisions and the Psychology of Choice', *Science*, 211.4481 (1981)

[2254] Luntz, Frank I., *Words That Work* (Hyperion, 2007)

[2255] Lakoff, George, and Johnson, Mark, *Metaphors We Live By* (U.of Chicago Press, 1980)

> *When you argue against the other side using their language, and quoting them, then you're helping them. The ball is in their court, you're playing on their field, and you're trapped.*[2256]

Loading politically charged language with presumptions and "framing" takes a malicious turn when it is used to obscure, inverse, or reverse the meaning of a word or phase[2257].

As literary critic George Orwell put it, nonsense terms *"construct your thoughts for you"* and *"perform the important service of partially concealing your meaning even from yourself."*

In *"Nineteen Eighty-Four"*, he described the formulation of *Doublethink*:

> *To know and not to know, to be conscious of complete truthfulness while telling carefully constructed lies, to hold simultaneously two opinions which cancelled out, knowing them to be contradictory and believing in both of them, to use logic against logic, to repudiate morality while laying claim to it, to believe that democracy was impossible and that the Party was the guardian of democracy, to forget whatever it was necessary to forget, then to draw it back into memory again at the moment when it was needed, and then promptly to forget it again, and above all, to apply the same process to the process itself—that was the ultimate subtlety: consciously to induce unconsciousness, and then, once again, to become unconscious of the act of hypnosis you had just performed. Even to understand the word—doublethink—involved the use of doublethink.*[2258]

Doublethink has a specific purpose: it enables the Party to alter historical records and pass off these distorted accounts as authentic. The brainwashed populace no longer recognises contradictions, and

---

[2256] Lakoff, George, *Moral Politics* (University of Chicago Press, 1996)

[2257] Jamieson, Kathleen Hall, Cappella, Joseph N., *Echo Chamber* (Oxford Press, 2008)

[2258] Orwell, George, *Nineteen Eighty-Four* (Secker & Warburg, 1949)

instead accepts the *Party*'s version of the past as accurate, even though that representation may change from minute to minute.

A specific case in point is the neologism *"gender-affirming care"*[2259].

This grotesque euphemism is deliberately constructed, not only to be impossible to oppose, but to invert the meaning of what it describes. So-called *"sex reassignment surgery"* (another euphemism) consists of chemical castration with *Lupron*[2260], and a century-old process of amputating sexual organs from pre-WWII *Weimar Germany*[2261].

Jargon, loaded terms, euphemisms, and doublethink are designed to conceal reality, bury the truth under vocabulary, and deceive the listener.

[2259] Turban, Jack L., and Ehrensaft, Diane, 'Gender Identity and Gender-Affirming Care', in David K. Lerner and Christine I. Stein (eds.), *Routledge Handbook of Youth Mental Health* (Routledge, 2018), pp. 299–311

[2260] Laidlaw, Michael K., 'The Gender Identity Phantom', *Journal of American Physicians and Surgeons*, 24.1 (2019), 9–14

[2261] Mancini, Elena, *Magnus Hirschfeld and the Quest for Sexual Freedom* (Palgrave Macmillan, 2010)

What Is Semantic Overloading?

There are few faster shortcuts to being perceived as an intellectual than using long, impressive-sounding words. It rarely matters if you have done the work or know what you are talking about, so long as your audience *believes* you do.

The purpose of language is to communicate a message. The clearer and more effective the communication of the message, the more able the other party is to comprehend its meaning. *Yes* and *No* are complete sentences. Brevity is something upon which air traffic control relies on as a matter of life and death.

The opposite of clear communication, where an author deliberately obscures its meaning under jargon, is called *obscurantism*. This abstruse, long-winded word salad packaging is there to limit understanding, and hides its (lack of) content.

This tactic confuses and disorientates the reader by *semantically overloading* them with words or phrases having more than one meaning (i.e. *polysemy*), used in ways that convey meaning based on their divergent constituent concepts[2262].

Truth is short, sharp.

In 1998, the *Philosophy and Literature Bad Writing Contest* named its

---

[2262] Workman, Michael, 'Cognitive Load Research and Semantic Apprehension of Graphical Linguistics', in Andreas Holzinger (ed.), *HCI and Usability for Medicine and Health Care* (Berlin: Springer, 2007), pp. 415–24

winner and runner-up[2263]. All of the entries, quite predictably, were from the social sciences.

Judith Butler, a *Guggenheim Fellowship*-winning professor of rhetoric and comparative literature at the *University of California at Berkeley*, admired as perhaps "one of the ten smartest people on the planet," as the author of *"Gender Trouble"*[2264], wrote the sentence that captured the contest's first prize.

> *The move from a structuralist account in which capital is understood to structure social relations in relatively homologous ways to a view of hegemony in which power relations are subject to repetition, convergence, and rearticulation brought the question of temporality into the thinking of structure, and marked a shift from a form of Althusserian theory that takes structural totalities as theoretical objects to one in which the insights into the contingent possibility of structure inaugurate a renewed conception of hegemony as bound up with the contingent sites and strategies of the rearticulation of power.*[2265]

A simpler translation of this might read:

> "We used to see money as a stable force in how people relate, but now we understand that power shifts and changes over time. This highlights how important time is, and gives us a new way to look at how power changes."

Homi K. Bhabha, a leading voice in the fashionable academic field of

---

[2263] Dutton, Denis, 'Bad Writing Contest Winners Announced', *Philosophy and Literature*, 22.2 (1998), 231–36

[2264] Butler, Judith, *Gender Trouble* (Routledge, 1990)

[2265] Butler, Judith, 'Further Reflections on the Conversations of Our Time', *Diacritics*, 27.1 (1997), 13–15

Postcolonial Studies, and a professor of English (!!!) at the *University of Chicago*, produced the second-prize winner.

> *If, for a while, the ruse of desire is calculable for the uses of discipline soon the repetition of guilt, justification, pseudo-scientific theories, superstition, spurious authorities, and classifications can be seen as the desperate effort to "normalize" formally the disturbance of a discourse of splitting that violates the rational, enlightened claims of its enunciatory modality.*[2266]

A simpler translation of this might read:

> "Attempts to use guilt, fake science, and false authorities to "normalize" and make sense of conflicting ideas only highlight the struggle to reconcile with rational and enlightened thinking."

This technique can also be a tool of great humour. Alan Sokal's 1996 literary hoax of the journal *Social Text* ("Transgressing the Boundaries: Towards a Transformative Hermeneutics of Quantum Gravity"[2267]) employed obscurantism extensively to deceive the editors into publishing a paper which suggested quantum gravity was a social convention. He intent was to expose their inability to discern sense from nonsense.

Its sequel, the 2017 "Grievance Studies Affair" of twenty absurd hoax papers, started by taking this deliberate obfuscation to a different level with *"The Conceptual Penis As A Social Construct"* published in the journal *Cogent Social Sciences*.

Its abstract reads like a genre-defining literary masterpiece:

> *Anatomical penises may exist, but as pre-operative transgendered*

[2266] Bhabha, Homi K., *The Location of Culture* (Routledge, 1994)

[2267] Sokal, Alan, 'Transgressing the Boundaries: Towards a Transformative Hermeneutics of Quantum Gravity', *Social Text*, 46/47 (1996), 217–52

women also have anatomical penises, the penis vis-à-vis maleness is an incoherent construct. We argue that the conceptual penis is better understood not as an anatomical organ but as a social construct isomorphic to performative toxic masculinity. Through detailed poststructuralist discursive criticism and the example of climate change, this paper will challenge the prevailing and damaging social trope that penises are best understood as the male sexual organ and reassign it a more fitting role as a type of masculine performance.[2268]

What this wall of jargon hides is the paper's wonderfully incoherent thesis,

> "Penises are an imaginary social custom responsible for climate change."

Put simply, if someone is using quadruple-syllable words in sentences which never end, be suspicious, and ask what they are attempting to hide.

[2268] Pluckrose, Helen, Lindsay, James A., and Boghossian, Peter, 'The Conceptual Penis as a Social Construct', *Cogent Social Sciences*, 3.1 (2017), 1330439

What Is The Science Of Homosexuality?

The sordid history of research around the understudied area of human sexual behaviour is so fraught with activism, motivated reasoning, and outright fraud, there is little way of extracting useful objective data from it.

When one considers the empirical evidence available from the natural sciences in regards to same-sex behaviours, the picture is markedly different. So different, in fact, one cannot help but shocked at the staggering level of dishonesty and fictional "storytelling" around the subject within the humanities, much of which has been increasingly engaged in by those apparently working in scientific institutions.

The field suffers from limited high-quality longitudinal studies; uselessly small sample sizes; heavy reliance on self-reported data; difficulty isolating variables; political and social coercion; a complete lack of clear biological markers; on top of inconsistent definitions and measurement methods.

The core issue around this area of research is authors falsely inflating the prevalence of same-sex activity by misrepresenting animal behaviours, whilst attempting to discredit previous studies which do not favour their worldview. They are not driven by evidence, but misinterpreting the natural world to support their own conclusion. They confuse - probably wilfully and deliberately - the idea of *means* and *ends*. They are unable to distinguish *function* from *dysfunction*; or *adaptation* from *maladaptation*.

Mating Is Always Procreative

There are around 5,400 mammal species[2269], and only 30–50 have solid natural science documentation supporting sexual behaviour *potentially* linked to pleasure[2270]. "Pleasure" is inferred by the presence of genital nerve endings (e.g. the clitoris in dolphins[2271] and primates[2272]); dopamine and oxytocin spikes during mating[2273]; activity outside of oestrus cycles or reproduction[2274]; and hypotheses about bonding and group cohesion[2275].

There is no evidence for pleasure-based mating in invertebrates; no direct evidence in reptiles, amphibians, or fish; and fewer than five species of birds have weak but observable cases (e.g., swans and albatrosses)[2276].

Bats show some evidence of oral-genital stimulation to prolong mating duration[2277]. Observations of lions suggest repeated copulations without

---

[2269] *The IUCN Red List of Threatened Species: Version 2022-2* (IUCN, 2022)

[2270] J. Pfaus, 'FRANK A. BEACH AWARD Homologies of Animal and Human Sexual Behaviors', *Hormones and Behavior*, 30.3 (1996), 187–200

[2271] Romano, G., et al., 'The Clitoris of the Dolphin (Delphinus delphis)', Anatomical Record, 290.11 (2007), 1315–1319

[2272] Cold, C. J., & McGrath, K. A. (1999). "Anatomy and histology of the penile and clitoral prepuce in primates." In *Male and Female Circumcision*, Springer

[2273] Czekala, N. M., et al., 'Opoid Receptor Activity in the Reproductive Cycle of the Female Pigtail Macaque (Macaca nemestrina)', *Journal of Reproduction and Fertility*, 93.2 (1991), 579–587

[2274] de Waal, Frans B.M. "Bonobo sex and society." *Scientific American*, vol. 272

[2275] J. Pfaus, T. Kippin, and G. A. Coria-Avila, 'What Can Animal Models Tell Us about Human Sexual Response?', *Annual Review of Sex Research*, 14 (2003), 1–63

[2276] Brook Vinnedge and P. Verrell, 'Variance in Male Mating Success and Female Choice for Persuasive Courtship Displays', *Animal Behaviour*, 56.2 (1998)

[2277] Gareth D. Jones and Jian-Xiang Duan, 'Fellatio by Fruit Bats Prolongs Copulation Time', *PLoS ONE*, 4.10 (2009), e7595

reproductive outcomes[2278]. Some behavioural studies of whales indicate sexual interactions beyond reproduction[2279]. Elephants have been observed to masturbate and engage in non-reproductive sexual interactions[2280]. Chimpanzees and orangutans have documented evidence of non-reproductive sexual behaviours[2281].

The most extensively documented variation of sexual behaviours has been found in dolphins (masturbation, aggressive pleasure-seeking, etc.)[2282], and bonobos (frequent and diverse sexual behaviours unrelated to reproduction). The latter of whom live in matriarchies where females engage in a form of male "enslavement."[2283]

Sexual Behaviour Is Rarely Related To Pleasure

Nature knows no concept of "consent" when it comes to mating. Moreover, mating in many species is violent, deadly, and painful. Mallards (*Anatidae*) engage in chasing, pinning, and biting the female which results in severe physical injury[2284]. Male cats (*Felis catus*) have barbed penises, which scrape the walls of the female's vagina during withdrawal and induce ovulation[2285]. Male honeybee (*Apis mellifera*) drones' genitalia explode during mating with the queen, resulting in

---

[2278] Paul L. Vasey, 'Same-Sex Sexual Partnering in Animals: Behavioural Diversity and Evolved Functions', *Trends in Ecology & Evolution*, 14.11 (1999), 464–468

[2279] Stack, Stephanie H., et al., 'An Observation of Sexual Behavior Between Two Male Humpback Whales (*Megaptera novaeangliae*)', *Marine Mammal Science*, 40.2 (2024)

[2280] Poole, Joyce H., 'Mate Guarding, Reproductive Success and Female Choice in African Elephants', *Animal Behaviour*, 37.5 (1989), 842–849.

[2281] Frans B. M. de Waal, *Chimpanzee Politics* (Johns Hopkins University Press, 2007)

[2282] M. M. Connor, R. S. Wells, and J. Mann, 'Sexual Behaviour in Bottlenose Dolphins', *Ethology*, 102.10 (1996), 892–907

[2283] Frans B. M. de Waal, 'Bonobo Sex and Society', *Scientific American*, 272.3 (1995)

[2284] McKinney, Frank, et al., 'Forced Copulation in Waterfowl', *Behaviour*, 86.3–4 (1983)

[2285] Wildt, David E., 'Fertilization in Cats', in *A Comparative Overview of Mammalian Fertilization*, ed. by Bonnie T. Dunbar and Minoru O'Rand (pringer, 1991)

their immediate death[2286]. Female octopuses (*Hapalochlaena spp.* and others) eat the male after or during mating[2287], as do praying mantises (*Mantodea*).

Male anglerfish (*Ceratiidae*) fuse with the female permanently, becoming a parasitic appendage[2288]. Female hyenas (*Crocuta crocuta*) have a pseudo-penis (elongated clitoris) through which mating and birth occur[2289]. Dominant male elephant seals (*Mirounga spp.*) aggressively control harems and forcefully mate with females[2290]. Male koalas (*Phascolarctos cinereus*) violently bite and grapple females[2291]. Male frogs (*Anura*) "overswarm" females, leading to physical injury or death due to drowning during *amplexus*[2292].

Misidentified Behaviour Is Linked To Male/Female Mating

There is little, if no, evidence from the natural sciences any mammals engage in same-sex behaviour as any form of mating. The hypotheses for these atypical behaviours involve correlation with evolved social

---

[2286] Koeniger, Gudrun, et al., 'Mating Biology of Honey Bees (*Apis mellifera*)', *Apidologie*, 16.1 (1985), 17–30

[2287] Hanlon, Roger T., et al., 'Behavior, Body Patterning, and Reproductive Biology of the Blue-Ringed Octopus (*Hapalochlaena lunulata*) in the Wild', *Journal of Experimental Marine Biology and Ecology*, 249.1 (2000), 29–49

[2288] Pietsch, Theodore W., 'Dimorphism, Parasitism, and Sex: Reproductive Strategies among Deep-Sea Ceratioid Anglerfishes', *Copeia*, 2005.4 (2005), 781–793

[2289] Glickman, Stephen E., et al., 'Androgens and Masculinization of Genitalia in Female Spotted Hyenas (*Crocuta crocuta*) 2: Effects of Prenatal Anti-Androgens', *Journal of Reproduction and Fertility*, 113.1 (1998), 117–127

[2290] Le Boeuf, Burney J., and Richard M. Laws, *Elephant Seals: Population Ecology, Behavior, and Physiology* (University of California Press, 1994)

[2291] Ellis, William A. H., et al., 'The Social and Reproductive Biology of the Koala (*Phascolarctos cinereus*) on Kangaroo Island, South Australia', *Australian Mammalogy*, 24.2 (2002), 207–217

[2292] McAllister, Natalie M., et al., 'Overcrowding and Mating Behavior in the Green and Golden Bell Frog (*Litoria aurea*)', *Herpetological Review*, 36.3 (2005)

behaviours which *serve* ordinary mating:

1. cohesion (reducing aggression)[2293]
2. hierarchy (reinforcing dominance for access to mates)[2294]
3. cooperation (territorial defence alliances)[2295]
4. practice/learning (younger or inexperienced individuals rehearsing courtship)[2296].

The male Amazon River Dolphin (*Inia geoffrensis*) and Bottlenose Dolphin (*Tursiops truncatus*) have been observed performing genital stimulation and penetration in the presence of females as a *competitive* display[2297][2298].

6–8% of male rams (*Ovis aries*) consistently mount other males even when fertile females are available, due to *hormonal* triggers like testosterone and oestrogen[2299].

Japanese Macaques (*Macaca fuscata*) show mounting and pelvic thrust-

---

[2293] Frans B. M. de Waal, 'Bonobo Sex and Society', Scientific American, 272.3 (1995)

[2294] J. M. Silverberg and J. P. Gray, 'Female Dominance in Bonobos (*Pan paniscus*): The Influence of Same-Sex Bonding on Social Hierarchy', American Journal of Primatology, 24.2 (1991), 83–98

[2295] R. G. Kirkpatrick, 'The Evolutionary Implications of Homosexual Behaviour in Nonhuman Animals', Current Anthropology, 41.3 (2000), 385–413

[2296] Paul L. Vasey, 'Same-Sex Partnering in Animals: Behavioural Diversity and Evolved Functions', Trends in Ecology & Evolution, 14.11 (1999), 464–468

[2297] Sylvestre, J.-P., 'Some Observations on the Behavior of Two Orinoco Dolphins (*Inia geoffrensis humboldtiana*) in Captivity at Duisburg Zoo', Aquatic Mammals, 11 (1985), 58–65

[2298] Mann, Janet, 'Establishing Trust: Socio-Sexual Behaviour and the Development of Male-Male Bonds among Indian Ocean Bottlenose Dolphins', in The Bottlenose Dolphin, ed. by Stephen Leatherwood and Randall R. Reeves (Academic Press, 1990)

[2299] Roselli, Charles E., et al., 'The Development of Male-Oriented Behavior in Rams', Physiology & Behavior, 105.3 (2012), 579–586

ing during the mating season for the same *hormonal* reason[2300].

Male lions in coalitions frequently engage in mounting behaviours with one another during territorial or pride-takeover events, as a precursor to mating *dominance*[2301].

The evidence we have suggests hormonal triggers direct mating behaviours; the *hypothalamus* in mammals does not always distinguish between male and female partners[2302]; and interactions may arise from "practice" or mimicking[2303].

Every single instance in the animal kingdom of same-sex sexual activity is a prelude, or in some way "orientated", to ordinary mating. There is no scientifically valid concept of a *"sexual orientation"* in the natural world whatsoever.

Anthropomorphic Research Driven By Motivated Reasoning

Starting with your own conclusion and finding evidence for it is not science. It is *motivated reasoning*. Projecting human behaviour onto animals is *anthropomorphism*.

There is a staggering amount of sophistry, wishful thinking, and outright lying which appear in print about the supposed "prevalence" of homosexuality in the animal kingdom, which always concludes as a fallacious *Appeal from Nature* demand to support a political cause.

Much of the confusion about human sexual behaviour can be traced back to primatologist Frans de Waal's work on *Bonobo* chimps in

---

[2300] Vasey, Paul L., 'Mounting Interactions between Female Japanese Macaques: Testing the Influence of Dominance and Age', *American Journal of Physical Anthropology*, 110.4 (1999), 487–497

[2301] Schaller, George B., *The Serengeti Lion* (University of Chicago Press, 1972

[2302] Roselli, Charles E., et al., 'The Volume of the Ovine Sexually Dimorphic Nucleus of the Preoptic Area Is Independent of Adult Testosterone Concentrations', *Brain Research*, 1127.1 (2007), 27–34

[2303] Monk, Julia D., et al., 'An Alternative Hypothesis for the Evolution of Same-Sex Sexual Behaviour in Animals', *Nature Ecology & Evolution*, 3 (2019), 1622–1631

zoos[2304][2305]. In his book *"Our Inner Ape"* (2005), de Waal explores their matriarchal cooperative tendencies, contrasting them with the more competitive and hierarchical nature of chimpanzees. He argued these traits explain the origin of human morality, and emphasised the role of sexual interactions beyond reproduction in bonobo societies as a tool for conflict resolution, bonding, and maintaining social harmony (*"make love, not war"*)[2306].

These ideas of chimps as sixties feminists, which were of course misused for political purposes, did not survive scrutiny. Among many others, Bernard Chapais pointed out human societies are more akin to chimpanzee structures than bonobos[2307]; Richard Wrangham explained male coalitional aggression and intergroup violence have been central to human evolutionary success[2308]; Craig Stanford asserted bonobos diverged from chimpanzees relatively recently, and their traits are likely responses to environmental factors like abundant resources, not reflective of ancestral hominin behaviour[2309].

A 2019 opinion article in *Nature Ecology and Evolution*, *"An Alternative Hypothesis for the Evolution of Same-Sex Sexual Behaviour in Animals"*, claims 1,500 species exhibit homosexual behaviours as ancestral traits. The author (Julia Monk, *"Yale School of Forestry and Environmental Studies"*, an "interdisciplinary" humanities department) hilariously wonders aloud about a self-evident *"Darwinian paradox."* Why would evolution produce a sterile dead end? Why indeed!

Her thesis is a triumph of science. *Why not?*

> *We aim to redefine the null hypothesis in studies of [same-sex*

[2304] Frans de Waal, *Chimpanzee Politics* (Johns Hopkins University Press, 1982).

[2305] Frans de Waal and Frans Lanting, *Bonobo* (U. of California Press, 1997)

[2306] Frans de Waal, *Our Inner Ape* (Riverhead Books, 2005)

[2307] Bernard Chapais, *Primeval Kinship* (Harvard University Press, 2008)

[2308] Richard Wrangham and Dale Peterson, *Demonic Males* (Mariner Books, 1996)

[2309] Craig Stanford, *The Ape in the Tree* (Harvard University Press, 2002)

behaviour]—put simply, we are proposing a shift from asking 'Why engage in SSB?' to 'Why not?'

An example she gives is of the aforementioned Japanese Macaques:

Female snow macaques routinely pair off and form temporary but exclusive relationships with other females, during which they engage in same-sex mounting complete with pelvic thrusting. Females will compete with males for access to other females and will sometimes preferentially associate with other females rather than available males.[2310]

Monk copies a table from a different paper and cites four sources to triple the figures:

1. A study from 2000 in the *"Journal of Lesbian and Gay Studies"* about *"queer animals"*[2311][2312]
2. A 2004 book by a mad *Stanford* professor, Joan Roughgarden, about *"gender identity"* in nature, who believes Darwin's idea is "false" and the *"Christian religion"* needs to recognise the *Bible*'s many verses on *"diverse"* depictions of *"gender"*[2313]
3. A 2009 article which cites 450 species, links them to *"gay rights"*, and provides its "scientific" definitions as unfalsifiable jargon from sociology[2314]

[2310] Monk, J. D., Giglio, E., Kamath, A., et al., 'An Alternative Hypothesis for the Evolution of Same-Sex Sexual Behaviour in Animals', *Nature Ecology & Evolution*, 3 (2019), 1622–1631

[2311] Roughgarden, J., *Evolution's Rainbow*, University of California Press, 2004.

[2312] Terry, J., '"Unnatural Acts" in Nature: The Scientific Fascination with Queer Animals', *GLQ: A Journal of Lesbian and Gay Studies*, vol. 6, 2000

[2313] Roughgarden, J., *Evolution's Rainbow*, University of California Press, 2004.

[2314] Bailey, N. W. and Zuk, M., 'Same-sex Sexual Behavior and Evolution', *Trends in Ecology and Evolution*, vol. 24, 2009, pp. 439-446.

4. A 2013 article claiming 110 species of insects and arachnids engage in "mistaken identity" related to female pheromone release[2315].

On a first look, this sophistry seems convincing to the unscientific eye of a hungry journalist with nothing else to publish. Examples of it being laundered include *Deutsche Welle* Aug 2017: *"10 animal species that show how being gay is natural!"*[2316], and the *Independent* Nov 2019: *"Homosexuality and bisexuality commonplace in thousands of animal species and may play key role in evolution, research finds"*)[2317].

Unfortunately, Japanese Macaques (*Macaca fuscata*) do not have *"relationships"*; nor do they *"pair off"* as if they are in a nightclub; and this behaviour does not make them *"bisexual"*. It is related to hormonal dysregulation, specifically during the mating season[2318].

Journalists at the BBC wilfully copy-paste this nonsense (*"Can animals be gay?"*), word-for-word:

> *This is in contrast to Japanese macaques, another primate in which same-sex sexual behaviour is commonly observed. Females of this species will routinely pair off with other females, forming temporary but exclusive sexual relationships known as 'consortships',* [2319]

[2315] Scharf, I. and Martin, O. Y., 'Same-sex Sexual Behavior in Insects and Arachnids: Prevalence, Causes, and Consequences', *Behavioral Ecology and Sociobiology*, vol. 67, 2013, pp. 1719-1730

[2316] Brändlin, Anne-Sophie, '10 Animal Species That Show How Being Gay Is Natural', *Deutsche Welle (DW)*, 2 Aug. 2017

[2317] Cockburn, Harry, 'Gay, Bisexual, and Homosexual Behaviour Found in More Than 1,500 Species, Including Some That Are Close to Extinction, Yale Study Finds', *The Independent*, 19 November 2019

[2318] O'Neill, Ann C., Fedigan, Linda M., and Ziegler, Toni E., 'Ovarian Cycle Phase and Same-Sex Mating Behavior in Japanese Macaque Females', *American Journal of Primatology*, vol. 63, no. 1, May 2004, pp. 25-31

[2319] Williams, Leoma, 'Can Animals Be Gay? Homosexual Behaviour in Animals Examined', *Discover Wildlife, BBC*, 18 Oct. 2023

The pattern is repetitive. Another preposterous 2010 book, *"Animal Homosexuality"*, by evolutionary ecologist Aldo Poiani declares some sheep have an *"exclusive homosexual orientation"*:

> *"O. aries (ram) only the second mammal known, apart from humans, capable of displaying exclusive homosexuality."*[2320]

As opposed to what? The promiscuous ones who aren't in a loving, committed relationship and just want to get married?

Contemporary absurdity traces back to 1999, when homosexual Canadian biologist Bruce Bagemihl published *"Biological Exuberance: Animal Homosexuality and Natural Diversity"* which claimed to document over four hundred mammals, birds, reptiles, and *insects* who engage in *"lifelong same-sex courtship, pair-bonding, sex, and co-parenting."* It was cited by the *American Psychological Association* and other groups in their *amici curiae* brief to the United States Supreme Court in *Lawrence v. Texas*, which struck down sodomy laws in the US.[2321]

From anthropomorphising *"lesbian seagulls"* and *"gay penguins"*; claiming animals socially "bond" in the same way humans do; citing incidental, unverifiable "observations" by amateur naturalists from individually captive animals (rather than the wild within groups); single onetime events over patterns; conflating "mounting" dominance behaviour with mating; having no clear mechanistic explanation of "exuberance" as an alternative to natural selection; to downplaying the reproductive costs of alleged same-sex behaviour in wild populations[2322,2323].

Bagemihl's magnum opus is patently ridiculous. It even goes so far as to claim animals are *"transgender"* and *"nonreproductive."*[2324]

[2320] Poiani, Aldo, *Animal Homosexuality* (Cambridge University Press, 2010)

[2321] Bagemihl, Bruce, *Biological Exuberance* (St. Martin's Press, 1999)

[2322] Wilson, Edward O., *Sociobiology* (Harvard University Press, 2000)

[2323] Anonymous, 'Review of *Biological Exuberance*, by Bruce Bagemihl', *Science*, 284 (1999)

[2324] 'Homosexuality and the Animal Kingdom', *Focus on the Family* (1999)

A final example which demonstrates how deeply this anti-scientific rot has set in to academia is a 2023 article in *USA Today* (*"Same-sex relationships are common in the animal kingdom – in fact, it reduces conflict."*), which makes claims so extraordinary they cannot be taken seriously; again citing the spurious *"1,500 species"* line and quoting *"researchers not involved in the work"*:

> *A study by Spanish researchers suggests same-sex sexual behavior among mammals – especially primates – is not only common and adaptive but supports social relationships and reduces conflict.*
>
> *"Homosexuality is present, widespread and eternal," said Joan Roughgarden, an emeritus professor of evolutionary biology at Stanford University in California. "If you somehow managed to exterminate it from one species it would re-evolve because it's adaptive."*
>
> *"It is still common for people to argue against homosexual behavior (or the entire LGBTQ+ community) on the basis that heterosexual sex is the only approved and natural kind of sex," Frans de Waal, a primatologist and professor emeritus at Emory University in Atlanta, said via email. "This review tells us that this is utter nonsense. Humans are by no means exceptional in the animal kingdom."*[2325]

In comes our notorious professor from *Stanford* Joan Roughgarden, with her opinions on *"gender identity"* in nature, and arch-atheist de Waal, who studied bonobos.

Except it is *not* what the study suggests at all. What it actually demonstrates is the wilful misrepresentation of science in a newspaper to manufacture a storyline for propaganda purposes, in a classic modern-day example of *Lysenkoism*[2326].

[2325] Weise, Elizabeth and Ramirez, Marc, 'Same-sex Relationships Are Common in the Animal Kingdom – in Fact, It Reduces Conflict', *USA TODAY*, 3 October 2023

[2326] Valery N. Soyfer, *Lysenko and the Tragedy of Soviet Science* (Rutgers Press, 1994)

The 2023 phylogenetic study, in *Nature Communications* ("The evolution of same-sex sexual behaviour in mammals"), warns of "limitations in our database, and in our overall conclusions, caused by the lack of information on the sexual behaviour of many mammalian species and by the existence of incomplete data (false negatives)." It goes on in great detail, saying the hypothesis of "same-sex behaviour" (SSB):

- "... has been recorded in about 5% of [mammals]";
- "... is not an ancestral trait in [mammals], and may have evolved multiple times in several disparate lineages.";
- "ancestral nodes are significantly younger than those ancestral nodes where this behaviour was absent. [SSB] was absent in the ancestors of Cebidae, Atelidae or Hylobatidae, three mammal families that seem to have originated very recently.";
- "... prevalence... is associated with sociality."
- "...may be related to social bonds, but our study (like any other comparative or experimental study) does not conclude that this is the sole cause of the evolution of same-sex sexual behaviour,"
- "...also associated with adulticide, but only for males."
- "... appears to be more common in social nonhuman primates forming multi-male/multi-female groups than in monogamous and polygynous species."
- "... seems to facilitate reconciliation among group members in female bonobos (Pan paniscus)."
- "...other studies have not found any evidence supporting these adaptive explanations. Same-sex sexual behaviour seems to be caused by mistaken identity in feral cats or as a side effect of excitement in some primate and deer species."

The authors go out of their way to state the following unequivocally:

Same-sex sexual behaviour is operationally defined here as any temporary sexual contact between members of the same sex. This behaviour should be distinguished from homosexuality as a more permanent same sex preference, as found in humans. For this reason, our findings cannot be used to infer the evolution of sexual orientation, identity, and preference or the prevalence of homosexuality as categories of sexual beings.[2327]

In other words, these scientists explicitly rebuke the idea of their research being used for political purposes, and what they *actually* found, among other things, was same-sex behaviour may well be an evolutionarily associated with adults *killing* other adults of their species.

Exaggerated Revisionist History In Human Behaviour

The word "sodomy" emerged by the Middle Ages as a broad legal and moral category covering various sexual acts, including homosexuality and beastiality. It was derived from the biblical tale of fire and brimstone (sulphur) raining down upon *Sodom & Gomorrah*. In the biblical account, two angels (in disguise as men) visit *Lot*, a resident of *Sodom*. The men of the city demanded to "know" the visitors and threatened to rape them if they were refused. Lot refused and offered his own daughters instead[2328].

Two potential sites have been posited by archaeologists. Their finds are intriguing but inconclusive.

The first is *Tall el-Hammam* (Jordan), located northeast of the *Dead Sea*, which has been excavated extensively by archaeologist Steven Collins[2329]. Evidence suggests the city was destroyed around 1700 BC by a catastrophic event, possibly a meteorite explosion or airburst,

---

[2327] José M. Gómez, A. González-Megías, and M. Verdú, 'The Evolution of Same-Sex Sexual Behaviour in Mammals', *Nature Communications*, 14.1 (2023)

[2328] Augustine, *The City of God Against the Pagans* (Cambridge Press, 1998)

[2329] Steven Collins, Latayne C. Scott, *Discovering the City of Sodom* (Howard Books, 2013)

as described in *Scientific Reports* (2021)[2330]. Findings include charred materials, melted pottery, and high levels of heat damage, suggesting an intense fire or blast.

The second, *Bab edh-Dhra* and *Numeira,* are Early Bronze Age cities south of the *Dead Sea* abandoned after being destroyed by fire[2331]. Evidence suggests they were thriving urban centres with advanced irrigation, fortified walls, and communal burial practices[2332].

The specific prohibitions of homosexual behaviour and cross-dressing in *Leviticus* (*to'evah* or *"abomination"*) are believed to have been codified between c. 700–500 BC during or after the *Babylonian Exile*[2333].

In ancient Mesopotamia and surrounding regions, the priests and devotees of certain pagan deities, particularly *"Ishtar"* (or *"Inanna"*), engaged in rituals and practices that included wearing garments associated with the opposite gender. *"Ishtar",* the Mesopotamian goddess of love, war, and fertility, was associated with fluidity in gender and sexuality. Her worship included the involvement of priests and cultic figures such as the *gala* (or *kalû*), who were often eunuchs or men who adopted feminine roles and attire during rituals as a reflection of Ishtar's domain over both creation and destruction, and her ability to transgress boundaries[2334].

Canaanite religious practices, which the Israelites sought to distance themselves from, included the worship of *"Asherah"* and *"Baal".* These deities were also associated with fertility and sexual rites. Phoenician cults, particularly in Tyre and Sidon, also featured priests who might blur gender distinctions during ceremonies, reflecting their roles in fertility

---

[2330] Malcolm A. Lecompte et al., 'A Tunguska Sized Airburst Destroyed Tall el-Hammam a Middle Bronze Age City in the Jordan Valley Near the Dead Sea', *Scientific Reports*, 11.1 (2021), 18632

[2331] Graham Philip and Douglas Baird, 'Landscape Archaeology and the Reconstruction of Ancient Settlement Patterns in the Near East', *Antiquity*, 74.283 (2000), 825–835

[2332] Paul Lapp, 'Bab edh-Dhra: Excavations in the Cemetery Directed by Paul W. Lapp (1965–67)', *Bulletin of the American Schools of Oriental Research*, 209 (1973), 3–20

[2333] John Barton, *The Hebrew Bible* (Princeton Press, 2019)

[2334] Stephanie Lynn Budin, *The Ancient Greeks and the Near East* (Cambridge Press, 2009)

worship[2335].

The *Manusmriti*, a key legal and ethical text in Hinduism, was composed between c. 200 BC–200 AD and includes prohibitions[2336]. Early Buddhist texts, such as the *Vinaya Pitaka* (disciplinary rules), written around 300 BC, discuss sexual misconduct within monasteries but do not specifically mention homosexuality[2337].

Our only real source of reliable historical evidence for homosexual cultural tradition outside the biblical texts, which is not deceitfully referred to as "inferring", or "suggesting" it in otherwise innocent artifacts, is pottery.

The tomb of *Niankhkhnum and Khnumhotep* (c. 2400 BC, Saqqara Necropolis), royal manicurists, has been interpreted as intimate depictions of two men of unspecified age embracing nose-to-nose, a pose often reserved for married couples. While there are thousands of Egyptian tombs with traditional husband-wife poses, it is one of very few known examples showing two men in such intimate poses[2338].

The *Moche Erotic Pottery* (100–800 AD, Peru), a set of ceramic vessels (huacos eróticos) depicts explicit scenes of sexual acts of no specified age, including male-male sexual anal intercourse. Archaeologists have uncovered thousands of these vessels, showing various sexual acts, suggesting they were a normal part of *Moche* cultural expression. They appear in regular burial contexts and seem to have been common ceremonial or educational objects, not exotic curiosities[2339].

The *Warren Cup* (*Roman Empire*, 1st Century AD) discovered near Bittir (modern Israel) and housed in the *British Museum*, depicts explicit

---

[2335] Mark S. Smith, *The Early History of God* (Eerdmans, 2002)

[2336] Patrick Olivelle, *Manu's Code of Law* (Oxford University Press, 2005)

[2337] Bhikkhu Ñāṇamoli and Bhikkhu Bodhi, *The Middle Length Discourses of the Buddha* (Wisdom Publications, 1995)

[2338] Ahmed Moussa, *The Tomb of Niankhkhnum and Khnumhotep* (Cairo Press, 1979)

[2339] Christopher B. Donnan, *Moche Art and Iconography* (UCLA Fowler Museum of Cultural History, 1976)

scenes of homosexual paedophilia on one side, and the other depicts two older men in an intimate embrace. Similar scenes appear on other Roman artifacts, particularly in private contexts like villa decorations and personal items. The high quality suggests it was a luxury item for elite consumption rather than an underground or exotic piece[2340].

Greek *Red-Figure* pottery (Ancient Greece, c. 500 BC) depicts explicit *pederasty*[2341]. Pederastic relationships between adult men and adolescent males (usually aged 12-17) were socially sanctioned practices in several ancient Greek city-states, particularly during the Archaic and Classical periods (roughly 800-300 BC) in places like Sparta, Thebes, and Crete[2342]. Quantitative data about actual prevalence rates is unavailable due to the historical distance and limitations of archaeological evidence, but it was sufficiently common to be reflected extensively in art and architecture, and integrated into civic institutions. The practice declined during the Hellenistic and Roman periods[2343].

Pederasty was largely an aristocratic practice, tied to upper-class education and social networking. The *Sacred Band of Thebes*, an elite military unit, was famously organised around these pairs. The typical sexual practice was *intercrural* (between the thighs) rather than penetrative. Penetrative acts were generally seen as *degrading* to the younger partner in Athenian society. To put it bluntly, the pederasty of ancient Greece was not sodomy at all[2344].

The *erastes-eromenos* relationship in ancient Greece followed strict social protocols that were deeply embedded in upper-class society. The older partner (*erastes*) would pursue the younger through formal courtship, offering gifts and demonstrating their worth as a mentor. This wasn't simply a romantic pursuit - it carried serious social obligations.

[2340] John Pollini, *The Warren Cup* (Cambridge University Press, 1999)

[2341] Andrew Lear, Eva Cantarella, *Images of Ancient Greek Pederasty* (Routledge, 2008)

[2342] Thomas Hubbard, *Homosexuality in Greece and Rome* (U. of California Press, 2003)

[2343] Kenneth Dover, *Greek Homosexuality* (Duckworth, 1978)

[2344] Plato, *Symposium*, trans. Alexander Nehamas and Paul Woodruff (Hackett, 1989)

The *erastes* took responsibility for their young partner's education in everything from politics to warfare, essentially serving as a gateway to adult male society.

The younger partner (*eromenos*) operated under equally strict social expectations. They were expected to maintain dignity and restraint, never appearing too eager or accepting too many suitors, as this would damage their reputation. The physical aspects of these relationships were governed by complex social rules - while intimate contact was permitted, the *eromenos* were never supposed to appear to seek or enjoy it.

The physical relationship was expected to be one-sided, with the older partner being the active participant, while the younger partner was expected to remain relatively passive and not show physical desire[2345].

These relationships were temporary by design, ending when the youth reached maturity (indicated by a full beard) as continuing in an *eromenos* role would have brought social shame. The system perpetuated itself as former *eromenoi* often became *erastai* themselves. Rather than being hidden, these relationships were public and formal, typically beginning in social spaces like the gymnasium where youths trained. They formed an integral part of upper-class education and social networking in many Greek city-states, particularly Athens, where they were seen as a crucial step in a young man's path to full citizenship[2346].

These were reflected during Japan's brief *Edo* period (1603–1868), where *shudō* (the *"way of the youth"*) referred to same-sex relationships between *Samurai* and adolescent boys[2347]. Certain Melanesian tribes, including the *Sambia* of Papua New Guinea, ritualised older males mentoring younger males, often through sexual acts, as a way to "transfer masculinity" and prepare them for adulthood[2348].

These practices persist today. The abhorrent tradition of *"Bacha bazi"*

[2345] Thomas K. Hubbard, *Homosexuality in Greece and Rome:* (U. of California Press, 2003)

[2346] Andrew Lear and Eva Cantarella, *Images of Ancient Greek Pederasty* (Routledge, 2008)

[2347] Ihara Saikaku, *The Great Mirror of Male Love* (1687)

[2348] Gilbert Herdt, *Guardians of the Flutes* (1981).

in Afghanistan, where early-pubescent homeless *"dancing boys"* (*"bacha baz,"* or *"bachabozlik"*) are forced to dress in women's clothing and dance for the entertainment of older married men before they are sodomitically raped for days[2349], is defended by Western journalists[2350], and denied by regional intellectuals[2351].

Homosexual acts were explicitly condemned within Christianity by the Apostle Paul around 50–60 AD[2352], and by *Byzantine* Emperor Justinian I in the 6th century within the *Corpus Juris Civilis*[2353].

Passages in the *Qur'an* condemning the behaviour of the people of *Lut* (Lot) date to the 7th Century[2354]. These were elaborated upon in *Hadiths* compiled between c. 8th–10th centuries[2355]. Islamic jurisprudence (*Sharia*) formalised punishments in the 8th–9th centuries AD through the codification of the major *Sunni* and *Shia* legal schools[2356].

Socially Prohibited Across All Cultures

Anti-sodomy laws were introduced in Europe during the medieval period and later codified in colonial empires. European colonial powers, particularly the British Empire, exported these laws to their colonies

---

[2349] Elton, Athena, 'Afghanistan's Bacha Baazi Practice and the Normalization of Sexual Violence against Boys', in *Violence: Probing the Boundaries around the World*, (Brill, 2020), pp. 146–156

[2350] Constable, Pamela, 'How Afghanistan's Mixed Messages on Homosexuality Play into the Orlando Shooting Debate', *The Washington Post*, 15 June 2016

[2351] Abdi, Ali, 'The Afghan Bachah and Its Discontents: An Introductory History', *Iranian Studies*, 56.1 (2023), 161–180

[2352] N.T. Wright, *Paul: A Biography* (HarperOne, 2018)

[2353] Peter Brown, *The Body and Society* (Columbia University Press, 1988)

[2354] Muhammad Abdel Haleem, *The Qur'an* (Oxford University Press, 2004)

[2355] Jonathan A.C. Brown, *Hadith* (Oneworld Publications, 2009)

[2356] Wael B. Hallaq, *The Origins and Evolution of Islamic Law* (Cambridge Press, 2005)

(with the exception of France, which legalised it in 1791)[2357]. As a result, sodomy laws were widespread in the United States, Australia, Canada, and India (e.g., *Section 377* of the *Indian Penal Code, 1860,* "*carnal intercourse against the order of nature.*")[2358].

Many countries in South America had sodomy laws inherited from Spanish and Portuguese colonial codes[2359]. In Muslim-majority regions, *Sharia*-influenced laws criminalised sodomy, often with severe punishments[2360]. East Asian countries (e.g., China, Japan) historically lacked explicit sodomy laws, but cultural disapproval has always been widespread[2361].

Some Native American tribes are believed to have honoured roles as shamans, healers, and mediators who practiced same-sex sexual behaviour[2362]. In some pre-colonial African societies, such as the *Nzema* in Ghana, "male wives" were documented. The *Buganda Kingdom* of Uganda had historical accounts among royalty[2363]. In Samoa, *fa'afafine* are men who embody feminine traits and often engage in same-sex relationships[2364].

Before 1960, 90–95% of recognised countries had laws criminalising same-sex acts such as sodomy[2365]. The first to decriminalise them was the *Soviet Union* in 1922, but they were recriminalised in 1934 under

---

[2357] James A. Brundage, *Law, Sex, and Christian Society in Medieval Europe* (University of Chicago Press, 1987)

[2358] Thomas Babington Macaulay, *The Indian Penal Code* (The Superintendent of Government Printing, 1860)

[2359] Jorge Cañizares-Esguerra, *Puritan Conquistadors* (Stanford University Press, 2006)

[2360] Ahmad ibn Naqib al-Misri, *Reliance of the Traveller* (Amana Publications, 1997)

[2361] Bret Hinsch, *Passions of the Cut Sleeve* (U. of California Press, 1990)

[2362] Walter L. Williams, *The Spirit and the Flesh,* (1986)

[2363] Stephen O. Murray and Will Roscoe, *Boy-Wives and Female Husbands* (1998)

[2364] Niko Besnier, *Gossip and the Everyday Production of Politics* (2009)

[2365] Hugh McLean, *The Legacy of Colonialism in Anti-LGBTQ Laws,* Open Society Foundations (2014)

Article 121 of the Soviet criminal code by Stalin until President Boris Yeltsin removed it in 1993[2366].

Under the *1749 Articles of War* for the *British Royal Navy*, sodomy was a capital offense. *Section 29* declared,

> *If any person in the fleet shall commit the unnatural and detestable sin of buggery, he shall suffer death.*[2367]

Modern laws of war (e.g., the *Geneva Conventions*[2368]) and maritime law (e.g., the *United Nations Convention on the Law of the Sea*[2369]) do not include provisions addressing or prohibiting it.

As of 2024, sixty-four countries (32.9% of 195 total) uphold laws against homosexuality, with most located in the Middle East, Africa, and Asia. In twelve of these countries, the death penalty is imposed, or at least a possibility.

The list includes Afghanistan, Algeria, Antigua and Barbuda, Bangladesh, Barbados, Belize, Bhutan, Botswana, Brunei, Burundi, Cameroon, Chad, Comoros, Dominica, Egypt, Eritrea, Eswatini, Ethiopia, Gambia, Ghana, Grenada, Guinea, Guyana, India, Indonesia, Iran, Iraq, Jamaica, Kenya, Kiribati, Kuwait, Lebanon, Liberia, Libya, Malawi, Malaysia, Maldives, Mauritania, Mauritius, Morocco, Myanmar, Namibia, Nigeria, Oman, Pakistan, Papua New Guinea, Qatar, Saint Kitts and Nevis, Saint Lucia, Saint Vincent and the Grenadines, Samoa, Saudi Arabia, Senegal, Sierra Leone, Singapore, Solomon Islands, Somalia, South Sudan, Sri Lanka, Sudan, Syria, Tanzania, Togo, Tonga, Tunisia, Turkmenistan, Tuvalu, Uganda, United Arab Emirates, Uzbekistan,

---

[2366] Daniel Healey, *Homosexual Desire in Revolutionary Russia:* (U. of Chicago Press, 2001)

[2367] *Articles of War: Statutory Rules and Orders Relating to the Royal Navy* (1749)

[2368] Jean-Marie Henckaerts and Louise Doswald-Beck, *Customary International Humanitarian Law* (Cambridge University Press, 2005)

[2369] United Nations, *United Nations Convention on the Law of the Sea* (UN, 1982)

WHAT IS THE SCIENCE OF HOMOSEXUALITY?

Yemen, Zambia, Zimbabwe[2370][2371].

Attitudes towards homosexuality in the world's two largest countries, China (1.42 billion) and India (1.45 billion), are overwhelmingly hostile. *Navtej Singh Johar v. Union of India* declared *Section 377* unconstitutional in 2018[2372], but only 37% are tolerant of the behaviour[2373]. The *People's Republic of China* labelled it *"bourgeois decadence"* in 1949[2374], but decriminalised in 1997[2375]. Only 15% are tolerant[2376]. Neither allow same-sex marriage or civil unions for homosexuals[2377].

There are approximately 2.3 billion Christians in the world (31%), approximately 1.8 billion Muslims (24%), and about 16 million Jews (0.2%). They total 51% of the world's 8 billion population[2378]. All three have strict prohibitions towards homosexual behaviour (albeit not consistently followed or advocated).

If one combines the sixty-four countries where homosexuality is illegal (2.23 billion, including the *entire* African continent), China and India (2.8 billion), one arrives at 5.1 billion. In total, on their own, they comprise 62.8% of the world's 8 billion population.

Thirty-six countries (18.5%) legally perform and recognise same-sex marriages[2379]. At the most generous, optimistic estimate, there is

---

[2370] International Lesbian, Gay, Bisexual, Trans and Intersex Association (ILGA), *State-Sponsored Homophobia Report: Global Legislation Overview* (2023)

[2371] *Laws Criminalising Same-Sex Sexual Conduct* (Amnesty International, 2023)

[2372] Navtej Singh Johar v. Union of India, *Supreme Court of India Judgment*, Writ Petition (Criminal) No. 76 of 2016 (Supreme Court of India, 2018)

[2373] *The Global Divide on Homosexuality* (Pew Research Center, 2020)

[2374] Gregory M. Pflugfelder, *Cartographies of Desire* (U. of California Press, 1999)

[2375] National People's Congress, *Criminal Law of the People's Republic of China (1997 Amendment)* (Adopted 14 March 1997; effective 1 October 1997)

[2376] Pew Research Center, *Attitudes on Homosexuality in China* (Pew Research, 2020)

[2377] United Nations Development Programme (UNDP) and USAID, *Being LGBT in Asia: China and India Country Reports* (UNDP, 2014)

[2378] World Population Review, *Religion by Population 2024* (2024)

[2379] Human Rights Campaign, *Marriage Equality Around the World* (2024)

no numerical scenario where tolerance or acceptance of homosexual behaviour in the human species exceeds a minority viewpoint of thirty-five per cent.

The data is extremely clear, without resorting to *Argumentum ad Populum* fallacy. Homosexual behaviour has been condemned, religiously, legally, and socially, for all of humanity's history. The majority condemn it today. Moreover, again today, two-thirds of the world's population consider it so egregious, it is prescribed death, imprisonment, or social exclusion.

Exhibited In Less Than Five Per Cent Of Humans

To the best of our knowledge, through anthropological studies, historical records, and surveys, before the Internet age, two to five per cent (2-5%) of any given human population exhibited same-sex attraction or behaviour[2380][2381][2382]. A 2021 *Ipsos* survey across twenty-seven countries reported the figure as four per cent[2383].

A 2023 report by the *California Department of Justice* indicated its own state figure was 9.5%, or 2.8 million[2384]. Approximately 2–3% of *Baby Boomers* (1946–1964) claim to be homosexual, 3.3% of *Gen X* (1965–1980), and 11.2% of *Millennials* (1981–1996), as opposed to 15-20% of *Gen Z* (1997–2012)[2385]. Approximately 72% of the latter self-report being *"bisexual"*, a term not explicitly defined within the survey

---

[2380] Sell, R. L., Wells, J. A., & Wypij, D. (1995). "The Prevalence of Homosexual Behavior and Attraction in the United States, the United Kingdom and France: Results of National Population-Based Samples." *Archives of Sexual Behavior*, 24(3), 235–248.

[2381] Laumann, E. O., Gagnon, J. H., Michael, R. T., & Michaels, S. (1994). *The Social Organization of Sexuality,* University of Chicago Press

[2382] Johnson, A. M., Wadsworth, J., Wellings, K., & Field, J. (1994). *Sexual Attitudes and Lifestyles.* Blackwell Scientific Publications.

[2383] Ipsos, *LGBT+ Pride 2021 Global Survey* (2021)

[2384] California Department of Justice, *Pride Report 2024* (Attorney General, 2024)

[2385] Gallup, *LGBT Identification in the U.S. by Generation* (Gallup, 2023)

questions, allowing participants to interpret and apply the label as they wished. If this specious category is removed, the figure for *Gen Z* returns to a familiar four per cent[2386].

Those displaying homosexual behaviour are over-represented in crowded urban areas (San Francisco: 15.4%; Seattle: 12.9%, Atlanta: 12.8%)[2387]; crowded prisons (5–40% of incarcerated individuals)[2388]; within movies (18.6% of major studio characters)[2389], spies (e.g. the *"Cambridge Five"*)[2390]; the media (theatre, fashion, and the arts)[2391], and activist non-profit organisations (*"human rights"* and *"social justice"*)[2392].

What the data we have reliably indicates is at least 95% per cent of human beings do *not* exhibit same-sex behaviour, and those who do are highly concentrated in specific areas and professions.

Biological Correlations But No Biological Cause

There are no single biological markers *exclusively* correlated with homosexuality. Current scientific thinking is sexual behaviour is *polygenic* (i.e. influenced by multiple genes) and not determined by any single genetic marker. Research to date has identified limited genetic, hormonal, and neurobiological factors that *may* be associated with these behaviours.

A large 2019 genome-wide association study (GWAS) involving nearly half a million participants found no single genetic marker exclusively associated with sexual behaviour but noted multiple genes, if found,

---

[2386] Melissa Dunne, 'Ipsos Pride Survey 2024: Gen Zers Most Likely to Identify as LGBT+', *Ipsos Global Advisor* (27 May 2024)

[2387] Gary Gates, *LGBT Demographics in the United States* (The Williams Institute, 2017)

[2388] Christopher Hensley, *Prison Sex: Practice and Policy* (Lynne Rienner Publishers, 2002)

[2389] GLAAD, *Where We Are on TV: 2023 Report* (GLAAD, 2023)

[2390] Andrew Lownie, *Stalin's Englishman* (Hodder & Stoughton)

[2391] Alan Sinfield, *Out on Stage* (Yale University Press, 1999)

[2392] Ruth Milkman, *A New Labor Movement for the 21st Century* (Routledge, 2020)

might contribute modestly[2393].

Concordance rates for homosexuality are higher in identical (*monozygotic*, or MZ) twins (7.7% for males, 5.3% for females) compared to fraternal (*dizygotic*, or DZ) twins (6.8% for male, 5.4% for female), however non-shared environmental influences in a study of 7,600 twins (male and female) present at 45–50%[2394].

Across studies, monozygotic twins consistently show higher concordance rates compared to dizygotic twins, suggesting a genetic contribution. Concordance rates below 100% indicate environmental and non-shared factors play a much more significant role[2395].

Exposure to androgens (male sex hormones) during critical periods of prenatal development may influence brain development and sexual attraction (indicated by the ratio between the second index and fourth ring digits)[2396].

Men with older brothers are statistically more likely to be homosexual, potentially because of maternal immune responses to male-specific antigens affecting brain development in subsequent male foetuses (*"Maternal Immune Hypothesis"*)[2397].

Some researchers suggest genes linked to homosexuality may enhance reproductive success in female relatives, balancing the reduced direct reproduction of homosexual males (*"Kin Selection Hypothesis"*). Others suggest female maternal relatives of homosexual men tend to have higher

---

[2393] Andrea Ganna et al., 'Large-Scale GWAS Reveals Insights into the Genetic Architecture of Same-Sex Sexual Behavior', *Science*, 365.6456 (2019), eaat7693

[2394] Richard C. Pillard and J. Michael Bailey, 'Human Sexual Orientation Has a Heritable Component', *Archives of General Psychiatry*, 55.5 (1998), 373–379

[2395] E. Eckert, T. Bouchard, Joseph Bohlen, and L. Heston, 'Homosexuality in Monozygotic Twins Reared Apart', *The British Journal of Psychiatry*, 148.4 (1986)

[2396] V. Headings, 'Etiology of Homosexuality', *Journal of Sex Research*, 16.3 (1980), 207–217

[2397] A. Camperio-Ciani, Francesca Corna, and C. Capiluppi, 'Evidence for Maternally Inherited Factors Favoring Male Homosexuality and Promoting Female Fecundity', *Proceedings of the Royal Society B: Biological Sciences*, 271.1554 (2004)

reproductive rates (*"Maternal Fecundity Hypothesis"*)[2398].

Homosexual individuals exhibit distinct patterns of response to pheromone-like substances (e.g., AND and EST, associated with male and female odours) compared to heterosexual individuals[2399].

The *Xq28* region, located at the tip of the X chromosome, is associated with male homosexuality in some studies, but results are mixed. They also suggest male homosexuality tends to cluster in maternal lineages (e.g., maternal uncles or cousins)[2400]. There are differences in the size of the INAH3 nucleus of the hypothalamus between heterosexual and homosexual men. Functional imaging studies show differences in amygdala connectivity and activation[2401].

Homosexual men and heterosexual women show similar patterns of brain hemisphere symmetry (a characteristic more often seen in female brains), while heterosexual men and homosexual women exhibit greater right-hemisphere asymmetry (a pattern traditionally associated with male brains)[2402].

[2398] Camperio-Ciani et al., 'Evidence for Maternally Inherited Factors Favoring Male Homosexuality and Promoting Female Fecundity', *Proceedings of the Royal Society B: Biological Sciences*, 271.1554 (2004)

[2399] Margie P. Vito, 'Factors Influencing Homosexuality in Men: A Term Paper', *International Journal of English Literature and Social Sciences* (2020)

[2400] Dean H. Hamer, Stella Hu, Victoria L. Magnuson, Nan Hu, and Angela M.L. Pattatucci, 'A Linkage between DNA Markers on the X Chromosome and Male Sexual Orientation', *Science*, 261.5119 (1993), 321–327

[2401] A. Ciani, Francesca Iemmola, and S. Blecher, 'Genetic Factors Increase Fecundity in Female Maternal Relatives of Bisexual Men as in Homosexuals', *Journal of Sexual Medicine*, 6.1 (2009), 449–455

[2402] Ivanka Savic and Per Lindström, 'PET and MRI Show Differences in Cerebral Asymmetry and Functional Connectivity between Homo- and Heterosexual Subjects', *Proceedings of the National Academy of Sciences of the United States of America*, 105.27 (2008), 9403–9408

Correlated With Childhood Sexual Trauma

Research consistently indicates individuals exhibiting homosexual behaviours self-report higher rates of *childhood sexual abuse* (or "CSA") compared to heterosexual individuals. There is a positive association between childhood maltreatment and same-sex sexuality in adulthood, with lesbians and gay men reporting 1.6 to 4 times greater prevalence of sexual and physical abuse than heterosexuals[2403]. Some studies have reported it at 3 to 8 times greater[2404].

The age when first abuse consistently falls is during early to mid-childhood (8–12), often slightly earlier for girls (7-10)[2405].

In gay men, a higher proportion of the abuse is same sex (40-50%) compared to the general population[2406]. It is overwhelming perpetrated by older males in positions of authority (95%), of whom 30–50% are family members (e.g., fathers, uncles, step-parents); 30–40% are trusted adults (e.g., teachers, coaches, neighbours, clergy), and 10-15% are strangers[2407][2408].

A 2015 meta-analysis revealed 39–47% of gay men reported CSA

[2403] Heather L. Corliss, Susan D. Cochran, and Vickie M. Mays, 'Reports of Parental Maltreatment During Childhood in a United States Population-Based Survey of Homosexual, Bisexual, and Heterosexual Adults', *Child Abuse & Neglect*, 26.11 (2002), 1165–1178

[2404] Clayton E. Cramer, 'An Open Secret: Child Sexual Abuse as One Possible Cause of Homosexuality', *Social Science Research Network*, 10 July 2015

[2405] Louise N. Silberberg, *The Condition of the Abused Child* (Springer, 2014)

[2406] Monique J. Brown et al., 'Childhood Sexual Abuse and Compulsive Sexual Behavior Among Men Who Have Sex with Men Newly Diagnosed with HIV', *AIDS and Behavior*, 24.4 (2024), 1–12

[2407] Gregory Phillips et al., 'Experiences of Community and Parental Violence Among HIV-Positive Young Racial/Ethnic Minority Men Who Have Sex with Men', *AIDS Care*, 26.2 (2014), 1–12

[2408] J. Briere, *Child Abuse Trauma* (Sage Publications, 1992)

experiences, compared to 22–25% of heterosexual men[2409]. The disparity is similarly evident in studies focusing on specific populations. For example, 57% of homosexual men newly diagnosed with HIV reported CSA[2410].

Studies examining broader populations show consistent findings. A 2021 literature review found CSA rates of 30–40%, far exceeding rates reported by heterosexual men[2411]. In Sweden, 33% of homosexual adolescents reported CSA, compared to just 18% of heterosexual males[2412]. This pattern holds across cultures, with studies reporting conservative rates of 34–47% in homosexual populations compared to 20–25% in heterosexual counterparts[2413].

Lesbians report higher rates of CSA compared to heterosexual women (30–40% vs 20–25%), but the disparity is not as pronounced as in gay men versus heterosexual men[2414]. The highest (40–50%) is reported in women who self-report as *"bisexual"*[2415]. As in male populations, most perpetrators are male (85–90%)[2416]. Unlike gay men, female victims

---

[2409] Yin Xu and Yong Zheng, 'Prevalence of Childhood Sexual Abuse Among Lesbian, Gay, and Bisexual People: A Meta-Analysis', *Journal of Child Sexual Abuse*, 24.3 (2015)

[2410] Monique J. Brown et al., 'Childhood Sexual Abuse and Compulsive Sexual Behavior Among Men Who Have Sex with Men Newly Diagnosed with HIV', *AIDS and Behavior*, 24.4 (2024), 1–12

[2411] A. D. Ménard and H. Macintosh, 'Childhood Sexual Abuse and Adult Sexual Risk Behavior: A Review and Critique', *Journal of Child Sexual Abuse*, 29.2 (2021)

[2412] G. Priebe and C. Svedin, 'Prevalence, Characteristics, and Associations of Sexual Abuse with Sociodemographics and Consensual Sex in a Population-Based Sample of Swedish Adolescents', *Journal of Child Sexual Abuse*, 18.1 (2009)

[2413] Á. Castro et al., 'Childhood Sexual Abuse, Sexual Behavior, and Revictimization in Adolescence and Youth: A Mini Review', *Frontiers in Psychology*, 10 (2019), 2018

[2414] Yin Xu and Yong Zheng, 'Prevalence of Childhood Sexual Abuse Among Lesbian, Gay, and Bisexual People: A Meta-Analysis', *Journal of Child Sexual Abuse*, 24.3 (2015)

[2415] Priebe and C. Svedin, 'Prevalence, Characteristics, and Associations of Sexual Abuse with Sociodemographics and Consensual Sex in a Population-Based Sample of Swedish Adolescents', *Journal of Child Sexual Abuse*, 18.1 (2009)

[2416] David Finkelhor, *Child Sexual Abuse* (The Free Press, 1984).

rarely report *same*-sex abuse. Male perpetrators are most commonly cited[2417]. In women, it is less frequently associated with compulsive or high-risk sexual behaviours[2418].

In one study of Latin American men around New York City, 45% reported experiencing CSA, which was strongly associated with high-risk sexual behaviours[2419]. Adolescent men with CSA histories were also shown to engage in elevated levels of same-sex sexual behaviours, often accompanied by other risky or compulsive tendencies[2420].

Correlated With Severely Negative Behaviours

There is considerably higher comorbidity of substance abuse and mental health disorders among homosexual men across the board. The specific issues include alcohol abuse (55.4%), depression (44.1%), anxiety (43.8%), suicidal ideation (39.4%), self-harm (24.5%), and eating disorders (16.1%)[2421]. 15-20% self-report using methamphetamine in the past year, including 23.1% of men with HIV[2422].

14.5% of gay men in an Australian study reported experiencing forced penetration; 10.3% in a UK national survey reported non-consensual

---

[2417] Susan Roth and Walter D. Friedman, 'Childhood Sexual Trauma and Adult Coping', *Journal of Consulting and Clinical Psychology*, 55.1 (1987)

[2418] Louise N. Silberberg, *The Condition of the Abused Child* (Springer, 2014).

[2419] Luis E. Nieves-Rosa, A. Carballo-Diéguez, and C. Dolezal, 'Domestic Abuse and HIV-Risk Behavior in Latin American Men Who Have Sex with Men in New York City', *Journal of Gay & Lesbian Social Services*, 11.1 (2000), 59–78

[2420] E. Leroux et al., 'The Association of Childhood Sexual Abuse With Non-Paraphilic and Paraphilic Sexual Behaviors Among Adolescents Who Have Sexually Offended', *Journal of Sex Research*, 57.2 (2020), 250–263

[2421] L. Ortiz-Hernández and María Isabel Gómez Torres, 'Efectos de la violencia y la discriminación en la salud mental de bisexuales, lesbianas y homosexuales de la Ciudad de México', *Cadernos de Saúde Pública*, 21.3 (2005), 913–925

[2422] Victoria Novak, *Disparities in Substance Abuse in Lesbian, Gay, Bisexual, and Transgender Individuals* (Master Essay, University of Pittsburgh, 2013)

sex (including attempted forced penetration)[2423]; and a 2014 *National Intimate Partner and Sexual Violence Survey* (NISVS) study found 16.2% of gay men experienced other forms of sexual violence[2424].

The figures were similar for women: 44.6% of lesbians had experienced partner violence[2425]. 14.2% reported they had been raped and 50% had been emotionally abused[2426][2427]. Lesbians divorced each other at a *much* higher rate than women divorce men or gay men divorce each other[2428], and only 51% of same-sex couples were interested in marriage; even less (15%) were interested in children[2429][2430].

The incarceration rate of self-identified homosexuals in 2011 was

---

[2423] Amy L. Hequembourg, Kathleen A. Parks, R. Lorraine Collins, and Tonda L. Hughes, 'Sexual Assault Risks Among Gay and Bisexual Men', *Journal of Sex Research*, 52.3 (2014), 282–295

[2424] Matthew J. Breiding, Sharon G. Smith, Kathleen C. Basile, Mikel L. Walters, Jieru Chen, and Melissa T. Merrick, *Prevalence and Characteristics of Sexual Violence, Stalking, and Intimate Partner Violence Victimization: National Intimate Partner and Sexual Violence Survey 2010 Findings* (National Center for Injury Prevention and Control, Centers for Disease Control and Prevention, 2014)

[2425] Claire Renzetti, 'Violence in Lesbian Relationships', *Journal of Interpersonal Violence*, 3.4 (1988), 381–399

[2426] Robin J. Lewis et al., 'Empirical Investigation of a Model of Sexual Minority Specific and General Risk Factors for Intimate Partner Violence Among Lesbian Women', *Psychology of Violence* (2016),

[2427] M. Descamps et al., 'Mental Health Impact of Child Sexual Abuse, Rape, Intimate Partner Violence, and Hate Crimes in the National Lesbian Health Care Survey', *Journal of Gay & Lesbian Social Services*, 11.1 (2000), 27–41

[2428] Office for National Statistics (ONS), *Divorces in England and Wales: 2019* (2020)

[2429] Pew Research Center, *Chapter 4: Marriage and Parenting, A Survey of LGBT Americans: Attitudes, Experiences and Values in Changing Times* (Pew Research Center, 2013)

[2430] US Census Bureau, *Fifteen Percent of Same-Sex Couples Have Children in Their Household* (2020)

more than three times that of the general US adult population[2431]. In 2023, 786,000 individuals were listed on sex offender registries across the U.S[2432], and at least 20% claimed to be "LGBTQ"[2433] despite "LGBT" being only 5.6% of the prison population as a whole[2434].

A disputed 1996 study found homosexual paedophiles represent a larger (11:1) proportion relative to their prevalence in the general population than heterosexual counterparts, and the proportion of "true paedophiles" (i.e., those with a primary sexual interest in children) is higher among individuals with a homosexual predisposition[2435].

The most virulent claims of a link between homosexual and paedophilic crime were published as an article, *"Homosexuality and Child Sexual Abuse"*, by the *Family Research Council*[2436].

An additional set of disputed studies by Paul Cameron reported a third of reported child molestations involved homosexual acts, with perpetrators estimated to be at least twelve times more likely to engage in such acts compared to heterosexuals[2437]. 34% of foster parent abuse cases in Illinois were alleged to involve homosexual perpetrators, with same-sex perpetrators accounting for 53% of abuse incidents against

---

[2431] Ilan H. Meyer, Andrew R. Flores, Lara Stemple, Adam P. Romero, Bianca D. M. Wilson, and Jody L. Herman, 'Incarceration Rates and Traits of Sexual Minorities in the United States: National Inmate Survey, 2011–2012', *American Journal of Public Health*, 107.2 (2017), 267–273

[2432] US Department of Justice, *National Sex Offender Public Website: Statistics* (2023)

[2433] Jody L. Herman, Taylor N.T. Brown, and Bianca D.M. Wilson, *LGBTQ Criminal Justice Interactions: Experiences on Sex Offender Registries*, The Williams Institute, UCLA School of Law (2022)

[2434] Bureau of Justice Statistics, *Correctional Populations in the United States*, 2023

[2435] Ray Blanchard, Howard E. Barbaree, Anthony F. Bogaert, R. Blanchard, and S. Hucker, 'Fraternal Birth Order and Sexual Orientation in Pedophiles', *Archives of Sexual Behavior*, 25.6 (1996), 555–574

[2436] Timothy J. Dailey, *Homosexuality and Child Sexual Abuse*, Issue No. 247 (Family Research Council, n.d.)

[2437] Cameron, Paul, 'Homosexual Molestation of Children/Sexual Interaction of Teacher and Pupil', *Psychological Reports*, 57.3 (1985), 1227–1236

WHAT IS THE SCIENCE OF HOMOSEXUALITY?

boys[2438].

In both sexes, narcissistic personality disorder was much higher in homosexuals[2439], as were non-clinical narcissistic tendencies[2440] and *"Dark Triad"* (Machiavellianism, psychopathy, and narcissism) traits[2441]. Risk-taking behaviours, such as unprotected sex and reckless driving, were significantly higher[2442]. Borderline personality disorder diagnosis was almost double, vying with increased non-clinical anti-social tendencies and sensation-seeking behaviour[2443].

Eighty-one countries (and two-thirds of US states) have laws criminalising the transmission of HIV or failing to disclose one's HIV status to sexual partners. Over seven hundred people have been convicted for knowing transmitting the disease to others[2444]. In its most extreme form, the disturbing *"bareback"* homosexual subculture of *"bugchasing"* arose in 1997 and involves men deliberately seeking HIV infection as a form of quasi-religious fetish[2445].

[2438] Cameron, Paul, 'Child Molestations by Homosexual Foster Parents: Illinois, 1997–2002', *Psychological Reports*, 96.1 (2005), 227–230

[2439] Jon E. Grant, Meredith Flynn, Brian L. Odlaug, and Liana R.N. Schreiber, 'Personality Disorders in Gay, Lesbian, Bisexual, and Transgender Chemically Dependent Patients', *American Journal on Addictions*, 20.5 (2011)

[2440] G. Rubinstein, 'Narcissism and Self-Esteem Among Homosexual and Heterosexual Male Students', *Journal of Sex & Marital Therapy*, 36.1 (2010)

[2441] Peter K. Jonason and Severi Luoto, 'The Dark Side of the Rainbow: Homosexuals and Bisexuals Have Higher Dark Triad Traits Than Heterosexuals', *Personality and Individual Differences*, 181 (2021), 111040

[2442] Meshram, S., 'Psychiatric Morbidity Responsible for Predisposing Individual for HIV Infection', *Indian Journal of Applied Research*, 5.10 (2015), 121–129

[2443] University of Michigan, 'Diagnosis Bias of Borderline Personality Disorder High Among LGB Community', *Michigan News* (10 Sept2020)

[2444] NAM Aidsmap, 'HIV Criminalisation Continues: Over 270 Arrests Recorded in 39 Countries in the Last Three Years', *Aidsmap* (July 2022)

[2445] Gregory Freeman, 'Bug Chasers: The Men Who Long to Be HIV+', *Rolling Stone*, 6 Feb 2003

Vastly Increased Public Health Risks

The median number of partners for gay men globally ranges between 10–20; mean values are regionally higher (UK: 19; US: 44.4; Australia: 15)[2446]; at least twice the number for heterosexual men (US: 6.4, UK: 4.7)[2447]. A 1994 study found the mean number of sexual partners for gay men was 42, with a median of 10[2448].

Despite the endless, ongoing attempts to "debunk" unflattering historical data, the 2008-2018 U.S. *General Social Survey* (GSS) conducted by the *National Opinion Research Center at the University of Chicago* found 10% of gay men reported having over a hundred sexual partners in their lifetime: 3.8% had 101–200; 2.9% had 201–300; 1% had 301–400 partners; and 1.9% had 400 or more[2449]. This somewhat conflicts with a 1978 *Kinsey Institute* book series featuring data about homosexuals in San Francisco by Alan P. Bell and Martin S. Weinberg (*"Homosexualities"*), which ambitiously claimed 28% of gay men had more than a thousand sexual partners[2450].

Lesbians typically report an average of 4–6 female sexual partners over a lifetime[2451] and were more likely to report having more than one sexual partner in the past 12 months (32%) compared to heterosexual

---

[2446] van Niftrik, J., 'Patterns of Sexual Behaviour and AIDS: A New Perspective', *Journal of Public Health*, 17.2 (1995), 172–178

[2447] A. Bowring et al., 'Identifying Risk: A Comparison of Risk Between Heterosexual-Identifying Bisexual Men and Other Bisexual Men in Vientiane, Laos', *Archives of AIDS Prevention*, 26.2 (2014)

[2448] Laumann, Edward O., John H. Gagnon, Robert T. Michael, and Stuart Michaels, *The Social Organization of Sexuality: Sexual Practices in the United States* (University of Chicago Press, 1994)

[2449] NORC at the University of Chicago, *General Social Survey, 2008–2018: Sexual Partner Statistics Among Gay Men*, GSS Data Explorer

[2450] Alan P. Bell and Martin S. Weinberg, *Homosexualities* (Simon and Schuster, 1978).

[2451] Julia N. Bailey, Clare Farquhar, Charlie Owen, Dawn Whittaker, 'Sexual Behaviour of Lesbians and Bisexual Women', *Sexually Transmitted Infections*, 79.2 (2003)

women (7%)[2452], and 77.3% reported one or more lifetime *male* sexual partners[2453]. They tend to engage in fewer and longer-term relationships compared to gay men, but are less likely to be sexually monogamous[2454].

The AIDS epidemic affected 35-40 million people with a fatality rate of 60%, more than half of whom were homosexual[2455]. By contrast, Covid-19 affected 7.9 billion, with a fatality rate of 0.1%[2456].

Sodomy and tribadism (female genital rubbing) have extraordinary medical implications as behaviours. Both the rectum and vagina have mucous membranes that can absorb viruses and bacteria, but vaginal tissue evolved specific protective features like beneficial bacteria and multiple epithelial layers, which provide additional barriers against infection[2457].

The *anal mucosa* is thinner, lacks natural lubrication, and is more prone to micro-tearing compared to the *vaginal mucosa*, allowing pathogens to enter the bloodstream more easily[2458]. Additionally, the rectum's absorption-optimised surface area and high concentration of immune cells (which can be targeted by viruses like HIV) contribute to increased

---

[2452] Matthews, S., L. Beardsworth, S. McLellan, and A. Taylor, 'Differences in Relationship Patterns Between Lesbian and Heterosexual Women', *Journal of Sexual Health*, 54.2 (2002), 117–123

[2453] A. Diamant, M. Schuster, K. McGuigan, J. Lever, 'Lesbians' Sexual History with Men: Implications for Taking a Sexual History', *Archives of Internal Medicine*, 159.22 (1999)

[2454] E. Rothblum, 'Lesbianism: Affirming Non-Traditional Roles', *Journal of Marriage and Family Counseling*, 11.2 (1985), 149–156.

[2455] Joint United Nations Programme on HIV/AIDS (UNAIDS), *Global AIDS Update 2023*

[2456] *COVID-19 Mortality Analysis* (John Hopkins University, 2023

[2457] Mingke Yu and M. Vajdy, 'Mucosal HIV Transmission and Vaccination Strategies Through Oral Compared with Vaginal and Rectal Routes', *Expert Review of Vaccines*, 9.8 (2010), 821–835

[2458] J. L. Anderson, 'Anorectal Mucosa and Its Vulnerability to Infection', *Journal of Clinical Gastroenterology*, 40.5 (2006), 386–392

transmission risk[2459].

The anus is close to the gastrointestinal (GI) tract, which can facilitate the transmission of *enteric* pathogens (e.g., bacteria, viruses, and parasites)[2460] and *blood-borne* pathogens (e.g., *HIV, Hepatitis*)[2461].

Sodomy transmits bacterial diseases staggeringly more prevalent in male homosexuals (*Gonorrhoea*: 30%[2462], *Chlamydia*: 20%[2463], *Shigella* (*Dysentery*): 90%[2464], *Escherichia Coli*[2465], *Monkeypox*: 90%[2466]). It transmits viral diseases (HIV: 70%[2467], *Herpes Simplex/Papillomavirus*: 43%[2468], *Hepatitis A/B/C*: < 5%[2469]). It also transmits parasitic infections (*Amoebiasis, Giardiasis*)[2470].

In lesbian sexual behaviour, the most common diseases are *Bacterial*

[2459] Mariia Patyka et al., 'Periluminal Distribution of HIV-Binding Target Cells and Gp340 in the Oral, Cervical and Sigmoid/Rectal Mucosae: A Mapping Study', *PLoS ONE*, 10.7 (2015), e0132942

[2460] S. Brody and R. Potterat, 'Epidemiology of Sexually Transmitted Infections and Anal Intercourse', *Archives of Sexual Behavior*, 42.7 (2013), 1131–1141

[2461] G. Rebbapragada and R. Kaul, 'The Role of Mucosal Barrier Integrity in HIV Transmission', *Current HIV/AIDS Reports*, 4.1 (2007), 20–26

[2462] CDC, *Sexually Transmitted Disease Surveillance 2022*

[2463] P. T. Chow et al., 'High Rates of Asymptomatic Chlamydia in Gay and Bisexual Men', *Sexually Transmitted Infections*, 91.5 (2015), 365–370

[2464] K. Mook et al., 'Shigella Outbreaks Among Gay Men: A Growing Concern', *Clinical Infectious Diseases*, 73.1 (2021), e15–e19

[2465] A. Clements et al., 'Sexually Transmitted E. Coli in Gay Men', *Journal of Infectious Diseases*, 218.2 (2018), 285–293

[2466] WHO, *Monkeypox Multi-Country Outbreak 2022*

[2467] UNAIDS, *HIV and Gay Men 2023 Update*

[2468] D. T. Bernstein et al., 'Genital HSV-2 and HPV Prevalence in Sexual Networks', *PLoS ONE*, 10.3 (2019), e0220034

[2469] A. L. Jin et al., 'Hepatitis Vaccination and Infection Rates in Gay and Bisexual Men', *Hepatology International*, 14.1 (2021), 5–10

[2470] J. C. Stark et al., 'Intestinal Parasites in Gay Men: A Comprehensive Review', *Journal of Gastroenterology*, 48.3 (2014), 423–430

Vaginosis (BV: 33-45%)[2471]; *Vulvovaginal Candidiasis* (VVC: 15-23%)[2472]; *Human Papillomavirus* (12-16%)[2473]; and *Herpes Simplex* (HSV-1: 26-30%, HSV-2: 21-25%)[2474].

Sexually transmitted infection is disproportionately more prevalent among homosexuals due to multiple sexual partners[2475] and lower contraceptive use[2476]. Gay men account for approximately 70% of new HIV infections[2477] and nearly 50% of primary and secondary *Syphilis* cases[2478]. Lesbians have a lower risk for many STIs compared to gay men but show higher rates of *Bacterial Vaginosis* and *Herpes Simplex* virus[2479].

High Probability Of Irreversibility

One subject vexes activists more than any other: the "fluidity" or immutability of the homosexual condition, or its apparent permanence. Few studies have been conducted in this area, which is telling in and of itself.

The data is extremely thin and muddy. A notable proportion of individuals who claim to be exclusively gay or lesbian have engaged

---

[2471] C. Skinner et al., 'A Case-Controlled Study of the Sexual Health Needs of Lesbians', *Sexually Transmitted Infections*, 72.4 (1996), 277–280

[2472] B. Wathne et al., 'Vaginal Discharge: Comparison of Clinical, Laboratory, and Microbiological Findings', *Acta Obstetricia et Gynecologica Scandinavica*, 73.3 (1994)

[2473] D. Ferris et al., 'A Neglected Lesbian Health Concern: Cervical Neoplasia', *Journal of Women's Health*, 5.3 (1996), 223–230

[2474] Hoyme, U. B., 'Urogenital Infections Caused by Sexually Transmitted Pathogens from the Gynecologic Viewpoint', *Der Urologe. Ausg. A*, 33.3 (1994), 217–223

[2475] G. Rebbapragada et al., 'Risk Behaviors and STIs in MSM', *Current HIV/AIDS Reports*, 11.2 (2014), 118–125

[2476] WHO, *HIV Prevention in Key Populations* (2021)

[2477] CDC, *HIV Surveillance Report, 2021* (2022)

[2478] CDC, *STD Surveillance Report, 2021* (2022)

[2479] C. Skinner et al., 'Bacterial Vaginosis and Sexual Behavior in Lesbians', *Sexually Transmitted Infections*, 72.4 (1996), 277–280

in heterosexual relationships at some point in their lives. A limited 2013 survey by the *Pew Research Center* found 2% of gay men and 1% of lesbians were in heterosexual relationships[2480], and 84% of individuals claiming to be "bisexual" were in opposite-sex relationships[2481].

Aversion therapies have been shown to reduce homosexual feelings and behaviour, but don't significantly change long-term outcomes[2482]. Among many others, the non-profit, interdenominational Christian organisation, *Exodus International*, founded in San Rafael, California around 1976 and closed in 2013, reported limited success in its attempts at intervention[2483].

Longitudinal research indicates while sexual behaviour remains stable for many individuals, other experience shifts[2484]. In *prospective* studies (following people over time rather than retrospective self-reports), rates of complete change to heterosexual behaviour/attraction are consistently under 2% among those who previously identified as exclusively homosexual in adulthood, and higher in women[2485][2486].

Studies of clinical attempts in religious settings to change behaviour have found similar or lower rates of change when using objective measures and long-term follow-up. Higher reported rates (3-5%)

[2480] Pew Research Center, 'A Survey of LGBT Americans: Attitudes, Experiences and Values in Changing Times', *Pew Research Center* (2013)

[2481] McNeill, T., 'Mixed-Orientation Relationships: Experiences of Individuals in Relationships with Gay or Bisexual Partners', *Archives of Sexual Behavior*, 44.1 (2015)

[2482] N. McConaghy, 'Is a Homosexual Orientation Irreversible?', *British Journal of Psychiatry*, 129 (1976), 556–63

[2483] Rogers, Sy, 'Perspectives on Exodus International's Ministry', *Christian Research Journal*, 17.4 (1994), 8–14

[2484] Savin-Williams, Ritch C., and Geoffrey L. Ream, 'Prevalence and Stability of Sexual Orientation Components During Adolescence and Young Adulthood', *Archives of Sexual Behavior*, 36.3 (2007), 385–94

[2485] Mock, Steven E., and Richard P. Eibach, 'Stability and Change in Sexual Orientation Identity Over a 10-Year Period in Adulthood', *Archives of Sexual Behavior*, 41.3 (2012)

[2486] Diamond, Lisa M., 'Female Bisexuality from Adolescence to Adulthood: Results from a 10-Year Longitudinal Study', *Developmental Psychology*, 44.1 (2008)

typically come from self-selected samples or rely solely on self-reported changes without behavioural verification[2487].

A Puzzle Attempted By Charlatans

The current evidence suggests a complex multi-factorial origin similar to left-handedness, personality traits, colour vision, or cognitive processing, involving:

- Some genetic components (~30-50% potential heritability in twin studies)
- Epigenetic factors (chemical modifications affecting gene expression)
- Developmental factors (hormonal exposure during key periods)
- Neurobiological differences (brain structure/function variations observed in studies)

The trait persists at modestly stable rates across populations and time periods, suggesting some underlying scientific mechanism we don't yet understand. The complete absence of viable explanatory models (evolutionary, genetic, developmental) is unusual. The combination of stability and resistance to change with no clear biological markers is scientifically puzzling. The inconsistency between twin study heritability data and the lack of direct genetic transmission creates an explanatory gap.

However, *none* of these things mean some animals are gay, people are born gay, the behaviour is historically widespread, or *any* of it is a social good which can be helped by encouraging more of it.

[2487] Jones, Stanton L., and Mark A. Yarhouse, 'A Longitudinal Study of Attempted Religiously Mediated Sexual Orientation Change', *Journal of Sex and Marital Therapy*, 33.5 (2007)

What Are Active Measures?

In 1944, the *Office of Strategic Services* - the forerunner to the CIA[2488] who employed chef Julia Child, sportsman Moe Berg, actor Sterling Hayden, and radical Herbert Marcuse[2489] - published a thirty-two-page *"Simple Sabotage Field Manual"*, which provided instructions to everyday people about how they could help the Allies weaken their country by reducing production in factories, offices, and transportation lines[2490].

For employees, it gave the following advice:

- *Work slowly.*
- *Contrive as many interruptions to your work as you can.*
- *Do your work poorly and blame it on bad tools, machinery, or equipment. Complain that these things are preventing you from doing your job right.*
- *Never pass on your skill and experience to a new or less skillful worker.*

To managers or those in any form of authority, it suggested:

- *In making work assignments, always sign out the unimportant jobs first. See that important jobs are assigned to inefficient workers.*
- *Insist on perfect work in relatively unimportant products; send back for refinishing those which have the least flaw.*

[2488] Troy, Thomas, *Donovan and the CIA* (University Publications of America, 1991)

[2489] Katz, Barry, *Herbert Marcuse and the Art of Liberation* (Verso, 1980)

[2490] Office of Strategic Services, *Simple Sabotage Field Manual* (1944)

WHAT ARE ACTIVE MEASURES?

- *To lower morale and with it, production, be pleasant to inefficient workers; give them undeserved promotions.*
- *Hold conferences when there is more critical work to be done.*
- *Multiply the procedures and clearances involved in issuing instructions, pay checks, and so on. See that three people have to approve everything where one would do.*

And finally, when it came to meetings, conferences, and other activities dependent on effective cooperation, it prescribed:

- *Insist on doing everything through "channels." Never permit short-cuts to be taken in order to expedite decisions.*
- *Make "speeches." Talk as frequently as possible and at great length. Illustrate your "points" by long anecdotes and accounts of personal experiences.*
- *When possible, refer all matters to committees, for "further study and consideration." Attempt to make the committee as large as possible — never less than five.*
- *Bring up irrelevant issues as frequently as possible.*
- *Haggle over precise wordings of communications, minutes, resolutions.*
- *Refer back to matters decided upon at the last meeting and attempt to re-open the question of the advisability of that decision.*
- *Advocate "caution." Be "reasonable" and urge your fellow-conferees to be "reasonable" and avoid haste which might result in embarrassments or difficulties later on.*

Many of these tactics can be observed in ordinary corporate offices as behaviours of lazy or cynical employees. However, they are also employed at scale within government departments and universities in order to frustrate national development.

Conversely, in 1969, a KGB agent named Yuri Alexandrovich Bezmenov defected to the United States[2491] and was rechristened Thomas Schuman by the CIA[2492] before being resettled in Canada. In 1984, he gave an interview to G. Edward Griffin in which he explained 85% of the old Enemy's work was:

> *a slow process which we call either ideological subversion, active measures, or psychological warfare.*[2493]

As part of his psychological warfare work for the KGB, he described the slow, multi-generational "demoralisation" process undertaken to ideologically transform a culture - such as India, where he had been stationed, or nearby Afghanistan - to the Marxist-Leninist orthodoxy which the Comintern's plans for global communism required[2494].

Regarding targets, he explained the KGB was interested in self-important academics:

> *You see, the useful idiots — the leftists who are idealistically believing in the beauty of Soviet socialist or communist or whatever system — when they get disillusioned, they become the worst enemies. That's why my KGB instructors specifically made the point: "Never bother with leftists. Forget about these political prostitutes. Aim higher." This was my instruction. Try to get into large circulation, established conservative media, reach filthy rich movie makers, intellectuals, so-called academic circles. Cynical, egocentric people who can look into your eyes with angelic expression and tell you a lie. These are the most recruitable people: people who lack moral principles, who*

[2491] Radosh, Ronald, 'The KGB and the World: Yuri Bezmenov's Revelations', *Commentary Magazine*, 78.5 (1984), 66–70

[2492] Bezmenov, Yuri, *Love Letter to America* (NATA, 1984)

[2493] Bezmenov, Yuri, *Soviet Subversion of the Free World Press: An Interview with Yuri Bezmenov (Tomas Schuman)*, G. Edward Griffin (1984)

[2494] Andrew, Christopher, Mitrokhin, Vasili, *The Sword and the Shield* (Basic Books, 1999)

are either too greedy or suffer from self-importance. They feel that they matter a lot. These are the people who KGB wanted very much to recruit.[2495]

But by far, the most sinister aggression was the formal "conversion" of a society to a new psychological paradigm *en masse*:

The other 85 percent is a slow process, which we call either ideological subversion or "active measures" — aktivnye meropriyatiya *in the language of the KGB*[2496] *— or psychological warfare. What it basically means is, to change the perception of reality of every [citizen] to such an extent that despite the abundance of information, no one is able to come to sensible conclusions in the interests of defending themselves, their families, their community, and their country. It's a great brainwashing process which goes very slow, and it's divided into four basic stages, the first one being demoralization. It takes from fifteen to twenty years to demoralize a nation. Why that many years? Because this is the minimum number of years required to educate one generation of students in the country of your enemy. Exposed to the ideology of the enemy. In other words, Marxism–Leninism ideology is being pumped into the soft heads of at least three generations of [target country] students without being challenged or counterbalanced by the basic values of [their nation], [national] patriotism. The result, the result you can see. Most of the people who graduated in the '60s, drop-outs or half-baked intellectuals, are now occupying the positions of power in the government, civil service, business, mass media, educational system. You are stuck with them. You cannot get rid of them. They are*

[2495] Bezmenov, Yuri, *Soviet Subversion of the Free World Press: An Interview with Yuri Bezmenov (Tomas Schuman)*, G. Edward Griffin (1984)

[2496] U.S. Congress, *Soviet Active Measures: Hearings Before the Permanent Select Committee on Intelligence, House of Representatives, Ninety-Seventh Congress, Second Session* (Government Printing Office, 1982)

contaminated. They are programmed to think and react to certain stimuli in a certain pattern. You cannot change their minds. Even if you expose them to authentic information, even if you prove that white is white and black is black, you still cannot change the basic perception and the logic of behavior. In other words, these people — the process of demoralization is complete and irreversible.[2497]

In essence, confuse people so much they accept any philosophy which fills the void and provides coherence. To do that, you need to poison the institutions which help them make sense of things.

There are only a few ways to win a war. One of the most powerful is to destroy the enemy's morale, so they lose the will to fight[2498]. An enemy within a fortress is far more devastating than the army besieging it from the outside[2499].

The "alternative society" of the Soviet Union sold to American radicals[2500] may have collapsed, but its ideas, methods, and apologist sycophants survived. Where did they go? Not only to Cuban beaches, fringe radical underground pickets, militant trade unions, non-profit front groups, and eco-terrorist units; many of them (e.g. Bill Ayers, Bernardine Dohrn, etc) were adsorbed into Western universities as professors[2501,2502,2503] - aka *Entryism*[2504] - where they went to work understanding how culture is reproduced through the education system.

[2497] Bezmenov, Yuri, *Soviet Subversion of the Free World Press: An Interview with Yuri Bezmenov (Tomas Schuman)*, G. Edward Griffin (1984)

[2498] Clausewitz, Carl von, *On War*, (c. 1832)

[2499] Machiavelli, Niccolò, *The Prince*, (Penguin Classics, 2003)

[2500] Barghoorn, Frederick C., *Soviet Foreign Propaganda* (Princeton University Press, 1964)

[2501] Horowitz, David, *Radical Son: A Generational Odyssey* (Simon & Schuster, 2006)

[2502] Powers, Richard Gid, *The War at Home* (Grossman Publishers, 1971)

[2503] Horowitz, David, *The Professors* (Regnery Publishing, 2007)

[2504] Trotsky, Leon, *The First Five Years of the Communist International*, (Pioneer, 1969)

What Is Evil?

One stubborn question which haunts theology, law enforcement, and most ordinary people is never addressed in any academic journal of the humanities. Which is entirely understandable, because it is utterly *fatal* to their worldview. It is also the root cause of the supposed *"postmodern condition."*[2505]

> How could the peak of humanity's "high society" and its associated technological achievements lead to the atrocities of the Holocaust?

In his 1983 book, *"People of the Lie: Toward a Psychology of Evil,"* psychiatrist Morgan Scott Peck describes different patients during his twenty-five-year career who were severely resistant to any form of treatment and shared common traits in their psychological profiles. In a disturbing chapter, he discusses the *"My Lai Massacre"* of 1968, the largest massacre of civilians by U.S. forces in the twentieth century[2506]. The incident, graphic and seemingly inexplicable, was notarised in military textbooks.

> The unit met no resistance in My Lai, which had about 700 inhabitants. Indeed, they saw no males of fighting age. They only found villagers eating breakfast. Nevertheless, over the next three

---

[2505] Hicks, Stephen R. C., *Explaining Postmodernism* (Oxford University Press, 2004)
[2506] Peck, M. Scott, *People of the Lie* (Simon & Schuster, 1983)

hours they killed as many as 504 Vietnamese civilians. Some were lined up in a drainage ditch before being shot. The dead civilians included fifty age 3 or younger, 69 between 4 and 7, and 27 in their 70s or 80s.

In addition, Vietnamese women were raped; other civilians were clubbed and stabbed. Some victims were mutilated with the signature "C Company" carved into the chest. One soldier would testify later, "I cut their throats, cut off their hands, cut out their tongues, scalped them. I did it. A lot of people were doing it and I just followed. I lost all sense of direction." [2507]

Why did Countess Elizabeth Báthory of Hungary, and four of her female servants, imprison, mutilate, and brutally murder over six hundred young peasant girls from 1590 to 1610?[2508]

Why did Japan's *Manchu Detachment 731* dissect living babies and pregnant mothers without anaesthesia after torturing them with biological and chemical weapons?[2509]

Why did David Parker Ray soundproof his *"Toy Box"* semi-trailer in New Mexico to rape, torture, and murder five drugged women a year between 1957 and 1999 with his pet dogs and friends for three months at a time?[2510]

Why did officers of the Khmer Rouge attach speakers to a *"Magic Tree"* outside Phnom Penh, where they smashed the skulls of infant babies to pieces as they cried?[2511]

Why did South Africa's *Project Coast*, headed up by the president's personal physician, seek to develop a "vaccine" to covertly sterilise black

---

[2507] Mintz, S., and McNeil, S., 'The My Lai Massacre', *Digital History*, 2021

[2508] Thorne, Tony, *Countess Dracula*, (Bloomsbury, 1997)

[2509] Harris, Sheldon H., *Factories of Death*, (Routledge, 2002)

[2510] Glatt, John, *Cries in the Desert* (St. Martin's True Crime, 2010)

[2511] Hinton, Alexander Laban. *Why Did They Kill?* (University of California Press, 2004)

WHAT IS EVIL?

Africans en masse?[2512]

Why did Jeffrey Lionel Dahmer murder seventeen men and boys between 1978 and 1991, then eat and sodomise their corpses, despite being found sane at his trial?[2513]

Why did soldiers in Darfur mass-rape female children on camera, then carve wounds in their thighs with machetes in 2003?[2514]

On 12 February 1993, two 10-year-old boys seen shoplifting in the area, Robert Thompson and Jon Venables, led a *two-year-old boy*, James Patrick Bulger away from the *New Strand Shopping Centre* in Bootle, after his mother had taken her eyes off him momentarily. They kicked him; stamped on him; threw bricks and stones at him; wrenched his foreskin back; sodomised him with a battery; and dropped a 22lb railway fishplate on his tiny head. They laid his body across the railway tracks and weighted his head down with rubble, hoping a train would hit him and the death would be ruled an accident. His body was found cut in half by a train two days later.

After being convicted as England's youngest murderers, it was revealed one confessed they had planned to abduct a child and push him into traffic. Venables was arrested and imprisoned repetitively in the subsequent years for child pornography offences.[2515]

In Dec 2024, William and Zachary Zulock, a homosexual couple from Georgia, were sentenced to a hundred years in prison each, without parole, after bragging about sodomising their "adopted" sons and pimping out the pornography from it to friends. National media covered the horrific crimes in vomit-inducing detail:

> *According to the report, the boys were adopted in November 2018 when the couple went through a now-shut down Christian adoption*

[2512] Burger, Marlene, Gould, Chandré, *Secrets and Lies*, (Zebra Press, 2002)

[2513] Davis, Don, *The Jeffrey Dahmer Story*, (St. Martin's Press, 1991)

[2514] Prunier, Gérard. *Darfur* (Cornell University Press, 2005)

[2515] Smith, David James, *The Sleep of Reason* (Faber & Faber, 2018).

agency focusing on special-needs children in Watkinsville, Georgia, called All God's Children, Inc.

After an investigation and interview with the suspect, police found that there was a secondary suspect who "was producing homemade child sexual abuse material with at least one adopted child who lived in the home with the perpetrator." Another affidavit states that Zachary Zulock filmed his husband, William Zulock, performing acts of sexual abuse on the child. Zachary allegedly told police in a recorded interview that the "routine" sexual abuse of their children was sent to "less than a dozen people."

Hunter Clay Lawless, 27, and Luis Armando Vizcarro-Sanchez, 25, were both part of the prostitution ring. Lawless told police that he received "numerous" Snapchat messages from Zachary which allegedly said "f—king [his] son tonight," telling him to "be prepared" to get images and "video documentation" of the sexual abuse, court documents state, adding that the men met on the gay hookup app Grindr. [2516]

Around the time they were sentenced, a Canadian woman, Irene Lima, was denied bail on four charges of beastiality for operating a members-only website (*"Goddess May Barefoot Premium Crush"*) which sold five-minute-long videos of her crushing vulnerable animals, including kittens and cats, to death with her bare feet for *"extreme satisfaction even to the point of orgasm without being touched."* During a search, officers found child pornography and text messages, which included plans to torture a child.

Police allege [the accused] created "an exclusive underground black-market network" for the animal torture content. Prospective members had to submit their own video to gain entry, and both

---

[2516] Sabes, Adam, 'Georgia couple accused of sexually abusing adopted boys, husband bragged about molesting son: report', *Fox News*, January 20 2023

WHAT IS EVIL?

accused profited financially from it, according to police.[2517]

Humanities "scholars" attempt to rationalise these malefic patterns with a bewildering array of amoral post-hoc vacuity: a breakdown in social institutions and community structures; *"systemic inequalities"* and institutional arrangements; culturally relative *"constructions"* which justify *"power structures"*; *"dehumanisation"* from in-group/out-group biases; situational forces and role expectations.; maintaining self-image to reduce cognitive dissonance; or, of course, just following orders.

They claim this behaviour is *"learned"* through social interaction and exposure to criminal values and techniques, or results from the gap between societal goals and available legitimate means to achieve them. Others mount evolutionary theories or game theory self-interest defences. These clowns do a bizarre equivocation dance, either asserting it is *"situational"*; something to do with *"systems"*; or a result of unspecified *"childhood trauma."* A transient nuisance which can be "educated" out of a people as de-Nazification programs in West Germany supposedly proved. All so painful reality snugly conforms to their *"blank slate"* beliefs.

Evil is *transcendent*. It manifests across history as a fundamental force with an ontological status independent of human behaviour or interpretation. You know it when you see it. You feel sense it. It is alien; foreign; other-worldly and shocking to the spirit, not merely the mind.

[2517] Gowriluk, Caitlyn, 'Woman accused of crushing animals to death with feet for dark web videos denied bail', *CBC*, December 20 2024

V

Deprogramming Alternative Theology

A foundation study program for teachers, parents, and students detailing the structural roots, historical events, intellectual theory, and activist tactics behind extreme left-wing radicalism.

Anti-Corruption & Counter-Extremism (ACCE)

Everyone wants to be important. In a world where any of the seven billion humans can contact one another instantly, everyone wants to be significant. Because when everyone is, no-one is. We all want to be a hero.

For young female college graduates disappearing from the male gaze behind Instagram glamour models, it's marching around city squares, pretending to be sixties'-era bra-burners fighting for the men the music industry sexually fetishises to them.

For young men, it's ever-present, always-available hardcore online pornography.

Two generations have been deliberately indoctrinated with an alternative worldview which is incoherent at best, and insane at worst. They have been taught to believe in the "progress of history" which only they are enlightened enough to perceive, and they are to be on the "right side" of:

- *White people are born with original sin due to their skin colour and heritage;*
- *Western societies were created through African slavery;*
- *The world is a system of invisible "oppressive" structures designed by a conspiracy of rich white men for their own benefit, which must be overthrown to liberate its victim captives;*

- *Oppression can be banished through socially stigmatising oppressors and disruptively "inverting" traditions;*
- *A Utopia of true democracy can be achieved by engineering outcomes through quotas and favouritism;*
- *Consumerism and liberal democracy are hoaxes which con ordinary people into a "false consciousness" of stability;*
- *Reality itself is "created" through the words we use;*
- *The world itself is continually under threat from "fascists" who want to eradicate minorities and institute totalitarianism;*
- *They have an "unconscious mind" they are not in any control of, and a "gender" spirit inhabiting their physical body;*
- *Carbon emissions from the Industrial Revolution have brought on the end of the planet via climate change;*
- *etc, etc.*

There is one simple story to explain it all. Social science tales with extraordinary exploratory power which are revelatory, like scripture is.

It also replaces the religiosity they've lost through their pursuit of fashionable secularism. Sociological theories which attempt to explain everything give them an alternative substitute theology for:

- God (self);
- Original Sin (slavery, racism, colonialism, privilege);
- The Fall (capitalism);
- The Devil (hate);
- The Soul (unconscious mind, neo-genders);
- Sin (oppression);
- Scripture (social science);
- Blasphemy (offence, hate speech);
- Heresy (incorrectness);
- Magic spells (creating reality through language);
- Kingdom of Heaven (advanced communism);
- Demons (fascists);

- Confession (struggle sessions);
- Salvation (revolution, liberation);
- Sanctification (doing *The Work*);
- Enlightenment (progress);
- Justice (redistribution);
- Child saints (Greta Thunberg, et al.);
- Martyrs (George Floyd);
- Theodicy (social justice);
- Dogma (codes of conduct);
- Theosis (empowerment);
- Morality (ethics);
- Parishes (campuses);
- Rebirth ("woke");
- Fasting (veganism);
- Priesthood (professors);
- Eschatology (re-emergence of fascism, climate change);
- Evangelism (activism);
- Vestments (cross-dressing);
- Excommunication (cancellation);
- etc, etc;

What is required is an *Anti-Corruption & Counter-Extremism (ACCE)* syllabus for deprogramming indoctrinated students.

Module 1: Destroying Traditions

The development of left-wing ideology, from its origins in Franco-Germanic idealism to the murderous fanatics of Communism.

A. European Idealist Theology

The roots of Leftism are in the French and German ideas of engineering, the perfect human existence; of man glorifying himself. Those trace back to *Hermetic Gnosticism*. Human achievement replaces God as the centre of life.

1. *Gnosticism*: concept & history[2518]
2. Jean-Jacques Rousseau & the *French Revolution*[2519]
3. Robert Malthus & scarcity[2520]
4. G.W.F Hegel & the *Dialectic*[2521]
5. Heidegger: our place in time and history[2522]

[2518] Jonas, Hans, *The Gnostic Religion* (Beacon Press, 2001)

[2519] Talmon, Jacob Leib, *The Origins of Totalitarian Democracy* (Secker & Warburg, 1952)

[2520] Sen, Amartya, *Poverty and Famines* (Oxford University Press, 1981)

[2521] Popper, Karl R., *The Open Society and Its Enemies* (Princeton University Press, 1966)

[2522] Farias, Victor, *Heidegger and Nazism* (Temple University Press, 1989)

MODULE 1: DESTROYING TRADITIONS

6. Alternative thinking: *Vegetarianism, Mesmerism, Theosophy*[2523][2524]

B. Revolutionary Theory

The key to drawing people into overthrowing everything they know is a strong story, and it must have heroes and villains. The *"arc of history"* (epoch) is a narration of human events which we are to be actively part of.

1. Historical materialism & the *"Eye of History"*[2525]
2. Karl Marx & the *Communist Manifesto*[2526][2527]
3. The *Fabian Society* & the *Labour* movement[2528]
4. Dark smear legends & national mythology[2529]

C. Vanguard Aggression

When the majority doesn't go along, or the fraud is uncovered, it requires a turn to the use of force. People don't know what's good for them, and a small group of highly motivated zealots can change the world if, instead of wholesale conquest, they form a small arrowhead group to infiltrate influential institutions ("entryism").

[2523] Kurlander, Eric, "Hitler's Monsters: The Occult Roots of Nazism and the Emergence of the Nazi 'Supernatural Imaginary'," *German History*, Volume 30, Issue 4, December 2012, Pages 528–549

[2524] Washington, Peter, *Madame Blavatsky's Baboon* (Secker & Warburg, 1993)

[2525] Popper, Karl R., *The Poverty of Historicism* (Routledge, 1966)

[2526] Hayek, Friedrich A., *The Road to Serfdom* (University of Chicago Press, 1944)

[2527] Mises, Ludwig von, *Socialism* (Yale Press, 1922)

[2528] Brett, Judith, *The Rise of the Labour Party, 1880–1945* (Macmillan, 1979)

[2529] Smith, Anthony D., *National Identity* (University of Nevada Press, 1991)

THE DEVILS' GLOSSARY

1. Lenin's *Red Terror* & the *Bolshevik* takeover[2530]
2. György Lukács & sex education[2531]
3. The *Weimar Republic* & the *Institutes of Sexuality*[2532]
4. The *Frankfurt School* and *Critical Theory*[2533]
5. Antonio Gramsci: march of the socialist religion[2534]

[2530] Conquest, Robert, *The Great Terror* (Oxford University Press, 1990)

[2531] Scruton, Roger, *Sexual Desire* (Free Press, 1985)

[2532] Gordon, Mel, *Voluptuous Panic*, (Feral House, 2008)

[2533] Douglas Kellner, *The Frankfurt School and Its Critics* (PoliPointPress, 2005)

[2534] Scruton, Roger, *Fools, Frauds and Firebrands* (Bloomsbury, 2014)

Module 2: Social Engineering

The infiltration and perversion of academia during the world wars, and its use as an intellectual justification in *Cold War* dystopias.

D. Misuse Of Psychology

Religion can be replaced by unfalsifiable social science theories which explain almost anything you throw them at. Humans' own internal wiring needs its storytelling software upgraded.

1. The *Frankfurt School*[2535]
2. Sigmund Freud & Popper's *Falsifiability*[2536]
3. Industrial propaganda & conditioning[2537]
4. Chinese/Korean *"brainwashing"* techniques[2538]

E. Sexual Derangement

The fastest way to disconnect people from their morality and encourage total breakdown is to sever their ties with religiosity in favour of animal passions and mental dysfunction.

[2535] Jay, Martin, *Marxism and Totality* (University of California Press, 1984)

[2536] Crews, Frederick, *Unauthorized Freud* (Viking, 1998)

[2537] Ellul, Jacques, *Propaganda* (Vintage Books, 1973)

[2538] Schein, Edgar H., *Coercive Persuasion* (W. W. Norton & Co. 1961)

1. Alfred Kinsey & homosexuality spectrum[2539]
2. John Money & *"gender"* theory[2540]

F. The Alternative Society

The first experiments in building the *Utopia* - the USSR, China, Cuba - all suffered failures ending in murderous totalitarianism which was covered up by a chorus of idealistic apologists.

1. The *New Soviet Man* & *New Soviet Woman*[2541]
2. *Dekulakization*, the *Holodomor* & the *Gulag*[2542]
3. Trofim Lysenko & the politicisation of science[2543]
4. Mao's murderous disasters[2544]
5. Cuba & the lionisation of Fidel and Che[2545]

[2539] Reisman, Judith, *Kinsey, Sex and Fraud* (Lochinvar-Huntington House, 1990)

[2540] Colapinto, John, *As Nature Made Him* (Harper Perennial, 2000)

[2541] Fitzpatrick, Sheila, *Everyday Stalinism* (Oxford University Press, 1999)

[2542] Conquest, Robert, *The Harvest of Sorrow* (Oxford University Press, 1986)

[2543] Soyfer, Valery N., *Lysenko and the Tragedy of Soviet Science* (Rutgers Press, 1994)

[2544] Dikötter, Frank, *Mao's Great Famine* (Walker & Company, 2010)

[2545] Fontova, Humberto, *Fidel* (Regnery Publishing, 2005)

Module 3: Ideological Subversion

The switch from political and military conflict to cultural subversion, via the radicalisation of demographic groups and word games.

G. Civil Rights As Weapons

Liberal democracy suffers from a *"tolerance paradox,"* and can be easily corrupted by leveraging minority groups and conflating moral license with state-based positive *"human rights"*.

1. The *Civil Rights Act* & Title VII *"Disparate Impact"*[2546]
2. Herbert Marcuse[2547] & identity-based neo-Marxism[2548]
3. Conflation/inflation of rights as moral licence[2549]

H. Student Militia Radicalisation

Idealistic young wannabe-heroes who want to change the world, and have been indoctrinated with new mythology, can be motivated by stoking their passions and resentments. The older they get, the less they want to change.

[2546] Epstein, Richard A., *Forbidden Grounds* (Harvard University Press, 1992)

[2547] Thompson, Kenneth, *Herbert Marcuse* (Martin Robertson, 1977)

[2548] Gottfried, Paul Edward, *The Strange Death of Marxism* (U. of Missouri Press, 2013)

[2549] Kekes, John, *The Morality of Pluralism* (Princeton University Press, 1993)

1. Feminist sexual revolution[2550]
2. Fashionable pagan hedonism[2551]
3. Cultural revolution & Mao's *"Red Guard"*[2552]
4. The *Gay Liberation Front*[2553]
5. The *Weather Underground*[2554]
6. Black nationalism[2555]

I. Postmodern Language Derangement

Language is a large key to how we find and communicate meaning. By destabilising it through euphemisms and self-refutation, human thought processes can potentially be blocked from maintaining previous traditions.

1. *"Social constructionism"*[2556]
2. Jacques Derrida & *"deconstruction"*[2557]
3. Michel Foucault[2558]
4. Lyotard, Lacan, Baudrillard[2559]

[2550] Sommers, Christina Hoff, *Who Stole Feminism?* (Simon & Schuster, 1994)

[2551] Himmelfarb, Gertrude, *The De-Moralization of Society* (Vintage, 1999)

[2552] MacFarquhar, Roderick, and Schoenhals, Michael, *Mao's Last Revolution* (Belknap Press of Harvard University Press, 2006)

[2553] Plummer, Ken, *Telling Sexual Stories* (Routl., 1995)

[2554] Jacobs, Ron, *The Way the Wind Blew* (Verso, 1997)

[2555] McCartney, John T., *Black Power Ideologies* (Temple University Press, 1992)

[2556] Sokal, Alan, and Bricmont, Jean, *Fashionable Nonsense* (Picador, 1998)

[2557] Ellis, John M., *Against Deconstruction* (Princeton University Press, 1989)

[2558] Eribon, Didier, *Michel Foucault* (Harvard University Press, 1991)

[2559] Eagleton, Terry, *The Illusions of Postmodernism* (Blackwell, 1996)

Module 4: Franco-American Scripture

The capture of the education system in an era of decadent *neoliberal* absurdity, as the first communist state collapsed.

J. Californian Gnosticism

California's wealth arose from speculation and counter-cultural imagination. so is intimately tied to its Utopian ideals. Its universities worship French intellectuals and its politicians venerate mixed economy Denmark.

1. The *"New Age"* & *"Human Potential"* movement[2560]
2. Self-help & *"safetyism"*[2561]
3. Hubbard's *"scientology"*[2562]
4. Eastern mysticism & *theosophy*[2563][2564]
5. Broecker's *"global warming"* & environmentalism[2565]

[2560] Lasch, Christopher, *The Culture of Narcissism* (W. W. Norton & Co., 1979)

[2561] Haidt, Jonathan, Lukianoff, Greg, *The Coddling of the American Mind* (Penguin, 2018)

[2562] Atack, Jon, *A Piece of Blue Sky* (Carol Publishing Group, 1990)

[2563] Washington, Peter, *Madame Blavatsky's Baboon* (Secker & Warburg, 1993)

[2564] Caldwell, Diana, *The Guru Papers* (North Atlantic Books, 2000)

[2565] Lomborg, Bjørn, *The Skeptical Environmentalist* (Cambridge Press, 2001)

K. Immigration & Belonging As A Weapon

Social integration between groups is a stabilising force which dissolves the inter-group antagonism needed for revolutionary action. New immigrants are open-minded, meaning the population can be organised into a proletariat.

1. Derrick Bell & *"critical legal studies"*[2566]
2. Delgado & *"critical race theory"*[2567]
3. Said, Fanon, & *"decolonisation"*[2568][2569]

L. Female Sexual Derangement

Women have unique vulnerabilities which can be easily exploited if they are separated from the love and protection of their family, predominantly around the notion of "performing" socially.

1. *"Womens' studies"* & *"white privilege"*[2570]
2. *"Queer studies"* & paedophilia[2571]
3. *"Fat studies"* & *"disability studies"*[2572]
4. Crenshaw & *"intersectionality"*[2573]

[2566] Farber, Daniel, and Sherry, Suzanna, *Beyond All Reason* (Oxford Press, 1997)

[2567] McWhorter, John, *Woke Racism* (Portfolio, 2021)

[2568] Windschuttle, Keith, *The Killing of History* (Encounter Books, 1996)

[2569] Lewis, Bernard, 'The Question of Orientalism', *New York Review of Books*, 1982

[2570] McWhorter, John, *Winning the Race* (Gotham Books, 2005)

[2571] Pluckrose, Helen, Lindsay, James, *Cynical Theories* (Pitchstone Publishing, 2020)

[2572] *Ibid.*

[2573] Hughes, Geoffrey, *The Case Against Intersectionality* (Oxford University Press, 2020)

MODULE 4: FRANCO-AMERICAN SCRIPTURE

M. Indoctrinating The Teachers

Students can be indoctrinated by simply corrupting the "meta" level of education, such as the people they look up to who choose their reading lists. Teachers aren't subject to democratic accountability as the curriculum is.

1. Paolo Friere & *"critical pedagogy"*[2574]
2. Henry Giroux & America's replacement education system[2575]
3. Howard Zinn's alternative dark legend of America's past[2576]
4. Science vs humanities academic wars[2577][2578]

[2574] Hirsch, E. D., *Cultural Literacy* (Vintage, 1987)

[2575] Bloom, Allan, *The Closing of the American Mind* (Simon & Schuster, 1987)

[2576] Schweikart, Larry, Allen, Michael, *A Patriot's History of the US* (Sentinel, 2004)

[2577] Snow, Charles Percy, *The Two Cultures* (Cambridge University Press, 1963)

[2578] Gross, Paul R., and Levitt, Norman, *Higher Superstition* (Johns Hopkins Press, 1994)

Module 5: The Communist Dragon

The struggle for public-private power through control of information in a globalised world, by weaponising renamed ideology within institutions.

N. China's Malign Influence

China has a specific plan to return from its "century of humiliation" by the British Empire. It intends to usurp the US as the global hegemon through raw economic and military power, and 5th generation warfare.

1. The *"Confucius Institute"*[2579]
2. Predatory investment & *"wolf warrior diplomacy"*[2580]
3. *"Great Firewall"* censorship[2581]
4. The *"Great Propaganda Plan"*[2582]
5. The *"Thousand Talents Program"*[2583]
6. Social credit scoring systems & high-tech surveillance[2584]

[2579] Brady, Anne-Marie, *China's Foreign Propaganda Machine* (Routledge, 2015)

[2580] Hamilton, Clive, Ohlberg, Mareike, *Hidden Hand* (Oneworld Publications, 2020)

[2581] King, Gary, Pan, Jennifer, and Roberts, Margaret E., 'How Censorship in China Allows Government Criticism but Silences Collective Expression', *American Political Science Review*, 107.2 (2013), 326–43

[2582] Brady, Anne-Marie, *Marketing Dictatorship* (Rowman & Littlefield, 2008)

[2583] Hamilton, Clive, and Joske, Alex, *The Chinese Communist Party's Coercive Recruitment Methods* (Australian Strategic Policy Institute, 2018)

[2584] Strittmatter, Kai, *We Have Been Harmonized* (Custom House, 2020)

O. Social Media As A Weapon

Governments and tech companies have realised social media is an even more powerful method of manipulating public opinion than television. The abuse of new media is just as deep and broad.

1. *"Astroturfing"* with *"sockpuppets"*[2585]
2. Perception management & consensus manufacturing[2586]
3. *"Brigading"* & harassment[2587]
4. Malignant addictive product design[2588]
5. Teenage bodily and sexual derangement[2589]

P. Corruption Of Governance

China's effectiveness has encouraged many international bad actors to pursue methods of maintaining centralised planning control. Most of these schemes are ways of circumventing democratic processes involving merit or consensus.

1. The *World Economic Forum* & its contempt for democracy[2590]
2. *Occupy Wall Street* & "Woke" corporations[2591][2592]
3. *"Diversity, equity, inclusion, justice"* & HR policymaking[2593]

[2585] Benkler, Yochai, Faris, Robert, Roberts, Hal, *Network Propaganda* (Oxford Press, 2018)

[2586] Lippmann, Walter, *Public Opinion* (New York: Harcourt, Brace and Company, 1922)

[2587] Marwick, Alice, and Lewis, Rebecca, *Media Manipulation and Disinformation Online* (Data & Society Research Institute, 2017)

[2588] Alter, Adam, *Irresistible* (Penguin Press, 2017)

[2589] Dines, Gail, *Pornland* (Beacon Press, 2010)

[2590] Bello, Walden, *The Future in the Balance* (Food First Books, 2001)

[2591] Gitlin, Todd, *Occupy Nation* (HarperCollins, 2012)

[2592] Kauffman, L. A., *Direct Action* (Verso, 2017)

[2593] Sowell, Thomas, *Affirmative Action Around the World* (Yale University Press, 2004)

Module 6: Deprogramming

Political de-radicalisation as renouncing membership in a ideo-religious cult, rather than a cognitively based worldview.

Q. Recognising Personal Vulnerabilities

Bad actors exploit specific weaknesses they identify via the social sciences, which typically are inherited yearnings and intellectual fallacies. Combined with personality traits, they can be accurate recruitment tools.

1. Human religiosity[2594]
2. Susceptibility to authoritarian traits[2595]
3. Utopianism & *"virtue signalling"*[2596]
4. Disgust sensitivity[2597]
5. Infantilism & delayed adulthood[2598]
6. Disconnection from family[2599]
7. Personal trauma & *"Stockholm syndrome"*[2600]

[2594] Stark, Rodney, and Finke, Roger, *Acts of Faith* (U. of California Press, 2000)

[2595] Altemeyer, Bob, *The Authoritarian Specter* (Harvard University Press, 1996)

[2596] Scruton, Roger, *Where We Are* (Bloomsbury, 2017)

[2597] Curtis, Valerie, *Don't Look, Don't Touch* (Oxford University Press, 2013)

[2598] Lasch, Christopher, *The Culture of Narcissism* (W. W. Norton & Co., 1979)

[2599] Putnam, Robert D., *Bowling Alone* (Simon & Schuster, 2000)

[2600] Young, Allan, *The Harmony of Illusions* (Princeton University Press, 1995)

MODULE 6: DEPROGRAMMING

R. Confronting Manipulative Tactics

Once a hostage has been captured in a group via storytelling and sentimentality, their membership must be policed using social reward/punishment, such as stigma, exclusion, and so on, to ensure they adhere to orthodoxy.

1. Religious behaviour in politics[2601][2602]
2. Groupthink & relational aggression[2603][2604]
3. Cult recruitment tactics[2605]
4. Sexual grooming behaviours[2606]
5. Domestic abuse behaviours[2607]
6. Language manipulation[2608]

S. Reconnecting With A Lost World

Recovering from identity membership in a cult leaves a huge void of purpose, meaning, belonging, and understanding. A counterfeit family which is lost must be replaced by the gain of authentic human relationships.

1. Diagnosing, understanding, forgiving, healing
2. Rebuilding family connections

[2601] Stark, Rodney, and Bainbridge, William Sims, *A Theory of Religion* (Rutgers University Press, 1996)

[2602] Berger, Peter L., *The Desecularization of the World* (Eerdmans, 1999)

[2603] Janis, Irving L., *Victims of Groupthink* (Houghton Mifflin, 1972)

[2604] Buss, David M., *Evolutionary Psychology* (Allyn & Bacon, 1999)

[2605] Singer, Margaret T., Lalich, Janja, *Cults in Our Midst* (Jossey-Bass, 1995)

[2606] Salter, Anna C., *Predators* (Basic Books, 2003)

[2607] Dutton, Donald G., *The Abusive Personality* (Guilford Press, 2007)

[2608] Lakoff, George, *Women, Fire, and Dangerous Things* (U. of Chicago Press, 1987)

3. Replacing social support networks
4. Rediscovering literature and academic texts
5. Understanding core concepts: *Free Will, democracy, consensus*

Reloaded Language

Abortion...*Foeticide*
Accountability...*Mob Justice*
Activism...*Harassment*
Activist..*Provocateur*
Addiction...*Habitation*
Affirm...*Advocate*
Align...*Concede*
Ally..*Collaborator*
Allyship..*Compliance*
Antifascist..*Communist*
Antiracist...*Neoracist*
Antiracism..*Race Communism*
Assault Rifle..*Defence Weapon*
Assault Weapon..*Self-Defence Weapon*
Assigned At Birth..*Observed At Birth*
Autonomy..*Supremacy*
Body Positivity...*Obesity Acceptance*
Born This Way..*Raised That Way*
Call Out..*Defame*
Cancellation...*Heckler's Veto*
Challenge Norms..*Defile*
Civil Partnership...*Pre-Marital*
Climate Change..*Planetary Heating*
Climate Crisis...*Climate Socialism*
Close-Minded..*Resolved*
Collusion..*Cooperation*

THE DEVILS' GLOSSARY

Colonisation	*Mercantilism*
Come Out	*Announce*
Community Guidelines	*Moral Standards*
Consciousness	*Radical Extremism*
Consequences	*Retaliation*
Compassion	*Naivety*
Conspiracy Theory	*Mythologist*
Critical	*Communist*
Cultural Appropriation	*Adoption*
Deadname	*Death Name*
Decentre	*Replace*
Decolonise	*Debase*
Deconstruct	*Defile*
Democratic Socialist	*Pre-communist*
Democratic Socialism	*Voluntary Socialism*
Denier	*Skeptic*
Deny	*Reject*
Deplatform	*Sabotage*
Direct Action	*Direct Violence*
Discourse	*Dialogue*
Discrimination	*Unfair Discrimination*
Dismantle	*Destroy*
Disparate	*Disproportionate*
Diverse	*Varied*
Diversity	*Unity*
DEI	*Unity, Opportunity, Qualification*
Division	*Partiality*
Dog Whistle	*Imaginary Signal*
Educate	*Indoctrinate*
Empathy	*Sympathy*
Empowerment	*Aptitude*
Energy	*Disposition*
Equality	*Opportunity*

Equity	*Unearned*
Erase	*Ignore*
Ethics	*Morality*
Far-Right	*Anti-Establishment*
Feminist	*Female Supremacist*
Fluid	*Unstable*
Fragility	*Provocation*
Framework	*Dogma*
Gender	*Tertiary Sex Characteristics*
Gender-Affirming	*Gender-Removing*
Gender Roles	*Gender Distinctions*
Glass Ceiling	*Imaginary Barrier*
Group Identity	*Tribal identity*
Gun Control	*Gun Confiscation*
Harm	*Distress*
Harmful	*Challenging*
Hate	*Disgust*
Hate Speech	*Provocative Speech*
Homophobic	*Disgusted*
Homosexual	*Sodomy*
Human Rights	*Artificial Rights*
Identity	*Magic Gender-Soul*
Identify As	*Claims To Be*
Impact	*Effect*
Implicit	*Automatic*
Incel	*Nerd*
Inclusion	*Favouritism*
Inclusive	*Unqualified*
Injustice	*Injury*
Institutional	*Corporate*
Internalised	*Involuntary*
Intersection	*Collision*
Intersectional	*Confrontational*

Invalidate	Reject
Islamophobia	Anti-Jihad
Lens	Bias
Lesbian	Tribadism
Liberate	Debase
Liberation	Abolition
Lived Experience	Opinion
Manifest	Imagine
Marginalise	Minimise
Marginalised	Discredited
Microaggression	Sleight
Misinformation	Mistake
Misogynist	Chauvinist
Misogyny	Misanthropy
Moderator	Censor
Movement	Fad
Multicultural	Plural
Narrative	Narration
Nonbinary	Unidentified
Normalise	Accept
Normative	Typical
Offensive	Upsetting
Oppression	Pressure
Oppressive	Burdensome
Pervert	Distort
Policy	Dogma
Pan	Indiscriminate
Patriarchy	Father-Led
Pay Gap	Motherhood Gap
Political Correctness	Speech Code
Polyamorous	Adulterous
Pride	Narcissism
Privilege	Advantage

Pro-Choice	*Pro-Killing*
Problematic	*Difficult*
Profit Motive	*Market Reward*
Progressive	*Degenerative*
Racist	*Post-Racial*
Reparations	*Reparations*
Representation	*Special Presentation*
Respectful	*Deferent*
Rights	*Duty*
Safety	*Immunity*
Safe Space	*Anxiety Area*
Same-Sex Marriage	*Counterfeit Marriage*
Scientific Racism	*Darwinian*
Self-Care	*Self-Indulgence*
Self-Esteem	*Self-Involvement*
Sensitivity Reader	*Censor*
Sexual Orientation	*Appetite*
Sex Reassignment	*Genital Removal*
Sex Work	*Prostitution*
Shaming	*Condemnation*
Social Construct	*Social Custom*
Social Justice	*Revenge*
Socialism	*Pre-Communism*
Solidarity	*Allegiance*
Spectrum	*Range*
Stakeholder	*Investor*
Stereotype	*Reputation*
Stigma	*Rejection*
Structural	*Statistical*
Subvert	*Corrupt*
Supremacy	*Ascendancy*
Supremacist	*Majoritarian*
Sustainable	*Unprofitable*

Systemic..*Intrinsic*
Systemic Racism..*Historic Racism*
Theory...*Hypothesis*
Tolerant..*Permissive*
Toxic...*Disruptive*
Training...*Programming*
Transgender...*Gender-Confused*
Transphobe..*Trans-Skeptic*
Transphobic...*Sex-Affirming*
Trigger Warning..*Sensitivity Warning*
Trust & Safety...*Censorship*
Unconscious Bias..*Invisible Bias*
Under-Represented..*Ignored*
Undocumented..*Unauthorised*
Unhoused...*Unhousable*
Use Your Platform..*Abuse Your Position*
Woke..*Gay Race Communist*

Anger, Bad Faith, Treachery

- *Asperity, n.* harshness of tone or manner.
- *Bilious, adj.* caused by too much bile, that can cause vomiting.
- *Calumny, n.* false and defamatory statements to damage a person's reputation.
- *Captious, adj.* expressing criticisms about matters that are not important.
- *Choleric, adj.* very angry or easily annoyed.
- *Colubrine*, adj. relating to or resembling a snake.
- *Envenoming, v.* put poison on or into; make poisonous.
- *Iracund, adj.* easily provoked to anger; irascible.
- *Infelicitious, adj.* not appropriate or well-timed.
- *Furibund, adj.* a propensity to be furious; choleric, irate.
- *Lochetic, adj.* lying in wait for prey.
- *Murine, adj.* relating to or affecting mice or related rodents.
- *Ophidian, adj.* relating to or denoting snakes.
- *Oppugnant, adj.* hostile, opposing, antagonistic.
- *Perfidious, adj.* unable to be trusted, or showing no loyalty.
- *Pettish, adj.* childishly bad-tempered and petulant.
- *Rebarbative, adj.* causing annoyance, irritation, or aversion; repellent.
- *Recreant, adj.* unfaithful or disloyal to a belief, duty, or cause.
- *Retortion, adj.* A turning, bending, or twisting back.
- *Splenetic, adj.* marked by bad temper, malevolence, or spite.
- *Stercoration, n.* the act of dressing with manure.
- *Sulfurous, adj.* pertaining to the fires of hell; hellish or satanic.
- *Talionic, adj.* punishment in kind.

THE DEVILS' GLOSSARY

- *Telarian, adj.* spinning a web, as a spider.
- *Unbidden, adj.* not invited or wanted.
- *Verbicide, n.* willful distortion or depreciation of a word.
- *Vesuvian, adj.* marked by sudden or violent outbursts.
- *Vesicant, adj.* tending to cause blistering.
- *Vespine, adj.* relating to, or resembling wasps.
- *Vituperative, adj.* given to censure; containing or characterized by verbal abuse.
- *Waspish, adj.* readily expressing anger or irritation.

Condemn, Accuse, Rebuke

- *Abjure, v.* withdraw one's word or professed belief.
- *Abnegate, v.* refuse or deny oneself.
- *Abrade, v.* scrape or wear away by friction or erosion.
- *Anathematize, v.* pronounce an anathema against; denounce; curse.
- *Approbate, v.* give official sanction, consent or authorization to.
- *Asperse, v.* attack or criticize the reputation or integrity of.
- *Asservate, v.* affirm or declare positively or earnestly.
- *Calumniate, v.* make false and defamatory statements about.
- *Confute, v.* prove to be false, invalid, or defective
- *Contemn, v.* treat or regard with contempt.
- *Discountenance, v.* refuse approval or support to; discourage.
- *Disprize, v.* regard as of low value; not prize.
- *Expostulate, v.* express strong disapproval or disagreement.
- *Homologate, v.* approve; confirm or ratify.
- *Imprecate, v.* deliver a curse or verbally attack someone.
- *Importune, v.* make repeated, forceful requests for something.
- *Impugn, v.* oppose or attack as false or lacking integrity.
- *Famicide, n.* one who destroys another s reputation; slanderer.
- *Fustigate, v.* hit someone with a club.
- *Hector, v.* harass by efforts to break down.
- *Keelhaul, v.* haul under the keel of a ship as punishment.
- *Immolate, v.* kill or destroy especially by fire.
- *Lancinate, v.* stab, pierce, or tear.
- *Malefactor, n.* person who violates the law; criminal.
- *Inculpate, v.* to charge with fault; blame; accuse.

- *Objurgate, v.* reproach or denounce vehemently.
- *Obloquy, n.* strong public criticism or verbal abuse.
- *Oppugn, v.* call into question the truth or validity of.
- *Parvanimity, adj.* a little or ignoble mind; pettiness; meanness.
- *Ruction, n.* uproar; noisy or quarrelsome disturbance.
- *Scarify, v.* express strong disapproval of someone in a cruel way.
- *Repine, adj.* fretfully discontented.
- *Traduce, v.* speak maliciously and falsely of; slander.
- *Umbrageous, adj.* Irritable, easily upset.
- *Villipend, v.* hold or treat as of little worth or account.
- *Vitiate, v.* make imperfect, faulty, or impure; spoil; corrupt.

Disgust, Revulsion, Ugliness

- *Abhorrent, adj.* causing or deserving strong dislike or hatred.
- *Abominable, adj.* repugnantly hateful; detestable; loathsome.
- *Acescent, adj.* slightly sour or turning sour.
- *Acidulous, adj.* sour or sharp in taste.
- *Acrid, adj.* sharp, bitter, stinging, or irritating to the taste or smell.
- *Anaphrodisiac, n.* tending to diminish sexual desire.
- *Beldam, n.* old woman, especially an ugly one.
- *Brackish, adj.* somewhat salty or briny.
- *Cankered, adj.* evil, unhealthy, or decayed.
- *Contumelious, adj.* insolently abusive and humiliating.
- *Disrelish, adj.* find unpalatable or distasteful.
- *Emesis, n.* an act or instance of vomiting.
- *Erose, adj.* Irregular or uneven as if eaten or worn away.
- *Execrable, adj.* utterly detestable; abominable; abhorrent.
- *Fetid, adj.* smelling extremely bad and stale.
- *Fetor, n.* a strong offensive smell.
- *Florid, adj.* elaborately or excessively ornamented.
- *Fustigation, n.* cudgel; beat; punish severely.
- *Impudicity, adj.* lacking in decisiveness; without strength or character.
- *Incondite, adj.* poorly constructed or composed.
- *Insalubrious, adj.* unpleasant, dirty, or likely to cause disease.
- *Maculate, adj.* morally blemished; stained or impure.
- *Mephitic, adj.* noxious vapor or exhalation.
- *Misopedia, n.* Hatred of, or contempt for, children.

- *Misprision, n.* neglect or wrong performance of official duty.
- *Morbific, adj.* causing or leading to disease.
- *Mordant, adj.* biting and caustic in thought, manner, or style.
- *Nolsome, adj.* offensive to the point of arousing disgust; foul.
- *Opprobrious, adj.* outrageously disgraceful or shameful.
- *Orgulous, adj.* proud; haughty; disdainful.
- *Pavonine, adj.* relating to, or resembling the peacock.
- *Pestiferous, adj.* spreading or bearing disease.
- *Pestilential, adj.* Infectious, plague-causing, and disease-bearing.
- *Purulant, adj.* containing, consisting of, or being pus.
- *Scabrous, adj.* covered with scales or scab.
- *Streptious, adj.* characterized by much noise : clamorous, noisy, boisterous.
- *Suppurate, v.* form or discharge pus.
- *Ugsome, adj.* ugly; horrible; disgusting.
- *Verrucous, adj.* wart-like, resembling a verruca.
- *Virago, n.* woman who demonstrates abundant masculine traits.

Depravity, Degeneracy, Rotten

- *Acarpous, adj.* producing no fruit; sterile.
- *Avulsion, n.* forcible tearing or surgical separation.
- *Carious, adj.* affected with cavities or decay.
- *Cadaverous,* adj. resembling a corpse in being very pale, thin, or bony.
- *Contumelious, adj.* Rudeness or contempt arising from arrogance; insolence.
- *Coprolalla, n.* involuntary swearing or utterance of obscene words.
- *Copropraxia, n.* irrepressible use of inappropriate and rude gestures.
- *Cupidity, n.* greedy desire for money and possessions.
- *Declension, n.* bending, sloping, or moving downward.
- *Edacious, adj.* very eager for something, especially a lot of food.
- *Excrescent, adj.* abnormal, excessive, or useless outgrowth.
- *Fescennine, adj.* scurrilous or obscene.
- *Harmartiology, n.* the study of sin.
- *Helotism, n.* class, minority, nation, etc held in a state of subjection.
- *Impecunious, adj.* very little or no money, usually habitually.
- *Imprecate, v.* swear, curse, or blaspheme.
- *Indocile, adj.* not willing to receive teaching, training, or discipline.
- *Ingravescent, adj.* increasing in severity.
- *Labefaction, n.* weakening, ruining, etc.; downfall; deterioration.
- *Lickerish, adj.* lecherous; lustful; lewd.
- *Lubricious, adj.* inappropriately or offensively sexual.
- *Nacreous, adj.* exhibiting lustrous or rainbow-like colors.
- *Ostrobogulous, adj.* slightly risqué or indecent.
- *Paraphiliac, n.* unusual or bizarre fantasies for sexual excitement.

- *Penurious, adj.* excessively unwilling to spend.
- *Plutolatry, n.* excessive devotion to wealth.
- *Prurient, adj.* arousing an immoderate or unwholesome interest or desire.
- *Roister, v.* revel noisily or without restraint.
- *Saprogenic, adj.* producing putrefaction or decay, as certain bacteria.
- *Scrofulous, adj.* relating to, resembling, or having scrofula.
- *Stygian, adj.* extremely and unpleasantly dark.
- *Sybaritic, adj.* loving or involving expensive things and pleasure.
- *Valetudinarian, adj.* weak or sickly constitution.

Evil, Malicious, Wicked

- *Algolagnia, n.* abnormal sexual pleasure derived from inflicting or suffering pain.
- *Anthropophagous, adj.* eating of human flesh; cannibalism.
- *Aphotic, adj.* growing in the absence of light.
- *Baleful, adj.* threatening or foreshadowing evil or tragic developments.
- *Bellicose, adj.* warlike or hostile in manner or temperament.
- *Caliginious, adj.* dark, misty, and gloomy.
- *Crocodillian, adj.* of, relating to, or resembling a crocodile.
- *Deuced, adj.* devilishly; damnably.
- *Diablerie, adj.* diabolic magic or art; sorcery; witchcraft.
- *Ectothermic, adj.* cold-blooded animal.
- *Extirpate, v.* remove or destroy totally; do away with; exterminate.
- *Facinorous, adj.* extremely wicked.
- *Fell, adj.* evil, cruel, wicked, deadly, fierce.
- *Flagitious, adj.* marked by scandalous crime or vice; villainous.
- *Lethiferous, adj.* deadly; bringing death or destruction.
- *Liverish, adj.* having a sour disposition; peevish; cross.
- *Infandous, adj.* too odious to be expressed or mentioned.
- *Iniquitous, adj.* absence of all signs of justice or fairness.
- *Invidious, adj.* unpleasant and likely to cause bad feelings in other people.
- *Irremissible, adj.* not to be remitted or forgiven.
- *Lupine, adj.* sharing some of the characteristics of a wolf.

- *Malefic, adj.* doing mischief; producing disaster or evil; inauspicious.
- *Mendacious, adj.* given to deception or falsehood; lying.
- *Minacious, adj.* of a menacing or threatening character.
- *Minatory, adj.* expressing a warning or a threat.
- *Ophiolatry, n.* worship of snakes.
- *Saturnine, adj.* sluggish in temperament; gloomy; taciturn.
- *Suilline, adj.* of or relating to a pig or the pig family.
- *Tenebrous, adj.* gloomy, shadowy, or dark.
- *Termagent, n.* violent, turbulant or brawling woman.
- *Thanatoid, adj.* resembling death; apparently dead.
- *Viperine, adj.* of, relating to, or resembling a viper.

Frauds, Charlatans, Phoneys

- *Blackguard, n.* thoroughly unprincipled person; a scoundrel.
- *Bathetic, adj.* overly sentimental, gushy, and insincere.
- *Chantage, n.* use of threats to extort money; blackmail.
- *Charlatan, n.* a person falsely claiming to have a special knowledge or skill.
- *Chiromancy, n.* the art of reading palms to tell someone's future.
- *Coquette, n.* courting the admiration of men without sincere intent.
- *Defalcate, v.* secretly taking money that is in your care.
- *Euphuistic, adj.* excessive refinement and elegance of language.
- *Fabulist, n.* someone who invents or tells fables.
- *Factitious, adj.* not spontaneous or natural; artificial; contrived.
- *Fastuous, adj.* proud; haughty; disdainful.
- *Frippery, adj.* silly or unnecessary, only done or worn for pleasure.
- *Fulsome, adj.* offensively, excessively flattering.
- *Imposture, n.* pretending to be someone else in order to deceive others.
- *Jacobinal, adj.* extremely radical.
- *Kakistocracy, n.* government by the worst, least qualified, or most unscrupulous.
- *Knavery, adj.* unprincipled, untrustworthy, or dishonest dealing; trickery.
- *Lusus, n.* freak, mutant, or monster.
- *Mendicant, n.* begging; practicing begging; living on alms.
- *Milksop, n.* a weak or cowardly man.
- *Misologist, n.* hatred of argument, reasoning, or enlightenment.

THE DEVILS' GLOSSARY

- *Monomania, n.* inordinate or obsessive zeal for or interest in a single thing.
- *Mopery, n.* dawdling, vagrancy.
- *Mountebank, n.* a person who sells quack medicines.
- *Mulct, v.* penalize by fining or demanding forfeiture.
- *Nescient, adj.* uneducated in general; lacking knowledge or sophistication.
- *Odalisque, n.* female slave or concubine in a harem.
- *Pasquinade, n.* a satire or lampoon, esp. one posted in a public place.
- *Peculate, v.* steal or take dishonestly.
- *Philodox, n.* someone in love with their own opinions.
- *Piquant, adj.* agreeably pungent or sharp in taste or flavor.
- *Poltroon, n.* ignoble or total coward; a dastard; a mean-spirited wretch.
- *Postiche, adj.* inappropriately applied; sham. false or artificial.
- *Pseud, n.* an intellectually pretentious or affected person.
- *Scapegrace, n.* complete rogue or rascal; a habitually unscrupulous person.
- *Sciolism, n.* pretentious attitude of scholarship; superficial knowledge.
- *Slattern, n.* untidy slovenly woman.
- *Supposititious, adj.* lacking in decisiveness; without strength or character.
- *Tartuffe, n.* hypocrite who pretends to religious piety.
- *Ultrafidian, adj.* def

Incompetence, Boring, Laziness

- *Acedia, n.* spiritual or mental sloth; apathy.
- *Ambisinister, adj.* clumsy or unskillful with both hands.
- *Anfractuous, adj.* having a lot of bends or curves.
- *Cataleptic, adj.* trancelike state marked by loss of voluntary motion.
- *Edacious, adj.* very eager for something, especially a lot of food.
- *Incogitant, adj.* thoughtless; inconsiderate. · not having the faculty of thought.
- *Dyslogistic, adj.* disapproving; opprobrious
- *Dysthymic, adj.* extreme anxiety and depression accompanied by obsession.
- *Enervate, v.* to make someone feel weak and without energy.
- *Excursive, adj.* moving away from the usual.
- *Frowzy, adj.* not attractive, new, or fashionable.
- *Imposture, n.* pretending to be someone else in order to deceive others.
- *Impulsant, adj.* lacking physical strength or vigour.
- *Inaniloquent, adj.* Tending to speak profusely; loquacious; garrulous.
- *Obnubilate, v.* darken, dim, or cover with or as if with a cloud.
- *Occlude, v.* hide or obscure from prominence or view.
- *Otiose, adj.* serving no practical purpose or result.
- *Rhadamanthine, adj.* showing stern and inflexible judgment.
- *Ridder, v.* cause (someone) to be free from something; relieve or disencumber.
- *Periphrasis, n.* use of a longer phrasing in place of a possible shorter form.

- *Plangent, adj.* loud, reverberating, and often melancholy.
- *Pleonasm, n.* the use of more words than are necessary to convey meaning.
- *Pseudology, n.* the study of lying; the art or science of lying.
- *Pusillanimous, adj.* showing a lack of courage or determination; timid.
- *Raddled, adj.* showing signs of age or fatigue.
- *Subreption, adj.* a concealment of the pertinent facts in a petition.
- *Sclerotic, adj.* becoming rigid and unresponsive; losing the ability to adapt.
- *Temulent, adj.* drunken or intoxicated.
- *Tortile, adj.* coiled, twisted, sinuous.
- *Verbigeration, n.* constant or obsessive repetition of meaningless words.
- *Vermiculate, adj.* infested with or damaged (as if eaten) by worms.

Nonsense, Absurd, Worthless

- *Addlepated, adj.* confused or stupid; befuddled.
- *Adumbrate, v.* produce a faint image or resemblance of.
- *Alogism, n.* a statement that is nonsensical or illogical.
- *Amphigory, n.* a message that seems to convey no meaning.
- *Befog, v.* cover with or envelop in fog; make foggy.
- *Blandiose, adj.* simultaneously dull and overblown.
- *Bovarism, n.* glamorized estimate of oneself; conceit.
- *Cankered, adj.* destroyed by the feeding of a cankerworm
- *Cachexia, n.* continuous decline in skeletal muscle mass..
- *Chimerical, adj.* unchecked imagination; fantastically visionary or improbable.
- *Coprology, n.* preoccupation with excrement.
- *Coprophagous, adj.* consumption of faeces.
- *Edulcorate, v.* free from soluble impurities by washing.
- *Effluvium, n.* unpleasant or harmful odor, secretion, or discharge.
- *Egesta, n.* waste material from the body; excrement.
- *Embrangle, v.* make more complicated or confused through entanglements.
- *Eristic, adj.* argumentative as well as logically invalid.
- *Excrementious, adj.* of or like excrement.
- *Fabulation, n.* the act of inventing or relating false or fantastic tales.
- *Feculent, adj.* of or containing dirt, sediment, or waste matter.
- *Flocuent, adj.* fluffy or woolly appearance.
- *Folderol, n.* mere nonsense; foolish talk or ideas.
- *Flummery, n.* praise or behaviour that is not sincere and does not

mean anything.
- *Garbology, n.* scientific study of trash and the way it reflects upon a group.
- *Gelastic, adj.* characterized by inappropriate, uncontrolled laughter.
- *Hysterogenic, adj.* inducing hysteria.
- *Kalopsia, n.* The delusion of things being more beautiful than they are.
- *Laliation, n.* baby-talk or gibberish.
- *Iatrogenic, adj.* induced unintentionally by a physician.
- *Malversation, n.* improper or corrupt behaviour in office.
- *Marasmus, n.* chronic undernourishment.
- *Marginalia, n.* notes in the margin of a document
- *Mawkish, adj.* sweet, weak, sickening taste; insipid or nauseating.
- *Meretricious, adj.* alluring by a show of flashy or vulgar attractions; tawdry.
- *Miasma, n.* noxious exhalations from putrescent organic matter.
- *Midden, n.* dunghill or refuse heap.
- *Mythomania, n.* excessive or abnormal propensity for lying and exaggerating.
- *Nugatory, adj.* being without worth or significance.
- *Operatic, adj.* extravagantly theatrical; overly dramatic.
- *Ordure, n.* solid waste from the bowels of people or animals.
- *Pablum, n.* overly bland or simplistic.
- *Paracosm, n.* a prolonged fantasy world invented by children.
- *Paralogical, adj.* characterized by incorrect reasoning; illogical.
- *Pedagese, n.* jargon used by teachers.
- *Psuedodoxy, n.* an erroneous belief.
- *Risible, adj.* deserving of being laughed at.
- *Scatophagous, adj.* feeding on dung or excrement.
- *Solecism, n.* breach of good manners or etiquette.
- *Sophomania, n.* delusion of having superior intelligence.
- *Spilth, n.* spilt, or freely poured out; slop; effusion.
- *Superbity, n.* haughtiness, arrogance; thinking oneself superb.

- *Superrogatory, adj.* going way beyond what's required.
- *Stercoraceous, adj.* of, relating to, or consisting of dung or excrement.
- *Strabismic, adj.* cross-eyed; broken perception.
- *Sibylline, adj.* exorbitantly expensive; oracle-like predicting powers, clairvoyant.
- *Tabescent, adj.* progressively emaciating ; wasting away.
- *Tetched, adj.* mildly deranged, somewhat mentally dysfunctional.

Partisan, Favouritism, Partiality

- *Craven, adj.* lacking even the rudiments of courage; abjectly fearful.
- *Credenda, n.* doctrines to be believed ; matters of faith.
- *Diffident, adj.* hesitant in acting or speaking through lack of self-confidence.
- *Fustian, adj.* overblown, pretentious speech or writing.
- *Gnathonic, adj.* deceitfully flattering ; sycophantic.
- *Grandiloquence, n.* lofty, high-flown style of talking lacking substance.
- *Hagiographic, adj.* writing with excessive or undue admiration.
- *Homogamy, n.* interbreeding of individuals with like characteristics.
- *Improbity, n.* lack of honesty or moral scruples.
- *Obsecration, n.* begging for something or supplicating.
- *Parious, adj.* dangerously shrewd or cunning.
- *Refractory, adj.* not affected by a treatment, change, or process.
- *Retrocede, v.* give back; return.
- *Sequacious, adj.* highly impressionable or unquestioning.
- *Subaltern, n.* low ranking in a social, political, or other hierarchy.
- *Tendentious, adj.* a tendency in favour of a particular point of view.
- *Tricoteuse, n.* woman who sits and knits at executions.
- *Uxorious, adj.* excessive or submissive fondness for one's wife.
- *Vagarious, adj.* characterized or caused by vagaries; irregular or erratic.
- *Votary, n. a* person bound by solemn religious vows.

Stupidity, Foolishness, Self-Love

- *Abulia, n.* lack of will, drive, or initiative for action, speech and thought.
- *Akrasia, n.* lack of self-control or acting against one's better judgment.
- *Apolaustic, adj.* devoted to seeking enjoyment; self-indulgent.
- *Asthenic, adj.* a slight build or slender body structure.
- *Bacchic, adj.* stupefied or excited by a chemical substance, e.g. alcohol.
- *Bovine, adj.* of, relating to, or resembling cattle.
- *Duncical, adj.* blockheaded, boneheaded, duncish, fatheaded.
- *Exanimate, adj.* deprived of life; no longer living.
- *Excerebrose, adj.* having no brains.
- *Farrow, n.* production of a litter of pigs.
- *Fatuous, adj.* obnoxiously stupid; vacantly silly; content in one's foolishness.
- *Hebetude, n.* mental dullness or lethargy.
- *Hidebound, adj.* painfully old-fashioned, with chauvinistic, inflexible ideas.
- *Icarian, adj.* characteristic of Icarus; being excessively ambitious.
- *Incogitant, adj.* thoughtless; inconsiderate.
- *Indurate, v.* make insensitive or callous; deaden feelings or morals.
- *Inurbane, adj.* not urbane; lacking in courtesy, refinement.
- *Inutile, adj.* lacking in utility or serviceability; not useful.
- *Insipience, n.* Lack of sapience or wisdom; folly.
- *Narcosis, n.* state of stupor or drowsiness.
- *Oligophrenia, n.* less than normal mental development.

- *Otiose, adj.* serving no practical purpose or result.
- *Paedomorphic, adj.* retention of juvenile characteristics by an adult.
- *Parapraxis, n.* minor error in speech or action.
- *Parvanimity, adj.* a little or ignoble mind; pettiness; meanness.
- *Pervicaceous, adj.* very obstinate; stubborn; wilfully contrary or refractory.
- *Porcine, adj.* of, relating to, or suggesting swine : piggish.
- *Puerile, adj.* childishly silly and trivial.
- *Purblind, adj.* slow or unable to understand; dimwitted.
- *Selcouth, n.* foolish or thoughtless young person.
- *Simian, adj.* relating to, resembling, or affecting apes or monkeys.
- *Thrasonical, adj.* a braggart; boastful; vainglorious.
- *Torpid, adj.* sluggish in functioning or acting.
- *Unasinous, adj.* having the same amount of stupidity.
- *Voluptuary, adj.* devoted to luxury and sensual pleasure.

Further Reading List

- Hayek, Friedrich, *The Road to Serfdom* (Chicago: University of Chicago Press, 1944).
- Orwell, George, 'Politics and the English Language' (1946).
- — *Nineteen Eighty-Four* (London: Secker & Warburg, 1949).
- Snow, C. P., *The Two Cultures and the Scientific Revolution* (Cambridge: Cambridge University Press, 1959).
- Lifton, Robert Jay, *Thought Reform and the Psychology of Totalism: A Study of "Brainwashing" in China* (Chapel Hill: University of North Carolina Press, 1961).
- Lasch, Christopher, *The Culture of Narcissism: American Life in an Age of Diminishing Expectations* (New York: W.W. Norton, 1979).
- Postman, Neil, *Amusing Ourselves to Death: Public Discourse in the Age of Show Business* (New York: Penguin Books, 1985).
- Conquest, Robert, *The Harvest of Sorrow: Soviet Collectivization and the Terror-Famine* (Oxford: Oxford University Press, 1986).
- Bloom, Allan, *The Closing of the American Mind: How Higher Education Has Failed Democracy and Impoverished the Souls of Today's Students* (New York: Simon & Schuster, 1987).
- Johnson, Paul, *Intellectuals* (London: Weidenfeld and Nicolson, 1988).
- Soyfer, Valery N., *Lysenko and the Tragedy of Soviet Science* (New Brunswick: Rutgers University Press, 1989).
- Kirk, Marshall, and Hunter Madsen, *After the Ball: How America Will Conquer Its Fear and Hatred of Gays in the '90s* (New York: Doubleday, 1989).
- Kimball, Roger, *Tenured Radicals: How Politics Has Corrupted Our*

Higher Education (New York: Harper & Row, 1990).
- Reisman, Judith, *Kinsey: Crimes & Consequences* (Crestwood, KY: Institute for Media Education, 1990).
- Chang, Jung, *Wild Swans: Three Daughters of China* (London: HarperCollins, 1991).
- Gross, Paul R., and Norman Levitt, *Higher Superstition: The Academic Left and Its Quarrels with Science* (Baltimore: Johns Hopkins University Press, 1994).
- Sowell, Thomas, *The Vision of the Anointed: Self-Congratulation as a Basis for Social Policy* (New York: Basic Books, 1995).
- Hogan, Kevin, *The Psychology of Persuasion: How to Persuade Others to Your Way of Thinking* (Gretna, LA: Pelican Publishing, 1996).
- Courtois, Stéphane, et al., *The Black Book of Communism: Crimes, Terror, Repression* (Cambridge, MA: Harvard University Press, 1997).
- Sokal, Alan, and Jean Bricmont, *Intellectual Impostures* (London: Profile Books, 1998).
- Hitchens, Peter, *The Abolition of Britain: From Winston Churchill to Princess Diana* (London: Quartet Books, 1999).
- Colapinto, John, *As Nature Made Him: The Boy Who Was Raised as a Girl* (New York: Harper Perennial, 2000).
- Kimball, Roger, *The Long March: How the Cultural Revolution of the 1960s Changed America* (San Francisco: Encounter Books, 2000).
- Gordon, Mel, *Voluptuous Panic: The Erotic World of Weimar Berlin* (Los Angeles: Feral House, 2000).
- Buchanan, Patrick J., *The Death of the West: How Dying Populations and Immigrant Invasions Imperil Our Country and Civilization* (New York: Thomas Dunne Books, 2001).
- Pinker, Steven, *The Blank Slate: The Modern Denial of Human Nature* (New York: Viking, 2002).
- Hicks, Stephen R.C., *Explaining Postmodernism: Skepticism and Socialism from Rousseau to Foucault* (Tempe, AZ: Scholargy Publishing, 2004).
- Wheen, Francis, *How Mumbo-Jumbo Conquered the World: A Short*

History of Modern Delusions (London: Harper Perennial, 2005).
- Thaler, Richard H., and Cass R. Sunstein, *Nudge: Improving Decisions About Health, Wealth, and Happiness* (New Haven: Yale University Press, 2008).
- Schüll, Natasha Dow, *Addiction by Design: Machine Gambling in Las Vegas* (Princeton: Princeton University Press, 2012).
- Haidt, Jonathan, *The Righteous Mind: Why Good People Are Divided by Politics and Religion* (New York: Pantheon Books, 2012).
- Murray, Charles, *Coming Apart: The State of White America, 1960–2010* (New York: Crown Forum, 2012).
- Critchlow, Donald T., *When Hollywood Was Right: How Movie Stars, Studio Moguls, and Big Business Remade American Politics* (New York: Cambridge University Press, 2013).
- William, Michael, *The Genesis of Political Correctness: The Basis of a False Morality* (Guildford: Moon Rock Books, 2016).
- Gottesman, Isaac, *The Critical Turn in Education: From Marxist Critique to Poststructuralist Feminism to Critical Theories of Race* (New York: Routledge, 2016).
- Crews, Frederick, *Freud: The Making of an Illusion* (New York: Metropolitan Books, 2017).
- Gilley, Bruce, *The Case for Colonialism* (Singapore: Palgrave Macmillan, 2017).
- Walsh, Michael, *The Devil's Pleasure Palace: The Cult of Critical Theory and the Subversion of the West* (New York: Encounter Books, 2017).
- Murray, Douglas, *The Strange Death of Europe: Immigration, Identity, Islam* (London: Bloomsbury Continuum, 2017).
- Lukianoff, Greg, and Jonathan Haidt, *The Coddling of the American Mind: How Good Intentions and Bad Ideas Are Setting Up a Generation for Failure* (New York: Penguin Press, 2018).
- Rectenwald, Michael, *Springtime for Snowflakes: "Social Justice" and Its Postmodern Parentage* (Nashville: New English Review Press, 2018).
- Grabar, Mary, *Debunking Howard Zinn: Exposing the Fake History That Turned a Generation against America* (Washington, D.C.: Regnery

History, 2019).
- Murray, Douglas, *Madness of Crowds: Gender, Race and Identity* (London: Bloomsbury Continuum, 2019).
- Beckeld, Benedict, *Western Self-Contempt: Oikophobia in the Decline of Civilizations* (Lanham, MD: Lexington Books, 2020).
- Murray, Charles, *Human Diversity: The Biology of Gender, Race, and Class* (New York: Twelve, 2020).
- Shrier, Abigail, *Irreversible Damage: The Transgender Craze Seducing Our Daughters* (Washington, D.C.: Regnery Publishing, 2020).
- Shellenberger, Michael, *Apocalypse Never: Why Environmental Alarmism Hurts Us All* (New York: Harper, 2020).
- Pretsell, Douglas, *Magnus Hirschfeld, Racism, and the Making of Gay Rights: A Sexologist, His Student, and the Empire of Queer Love* (Cham, Switzerland: Palgrave Macmillan, 2020).
- Trueman, Carl R., *The Rise and Triumph of the Modern Self: Cultural Amnesia, Expressive Individualism, and the Road to Sexual Revolution* (Wheaton, IL: Crossway, 2020).
- Kengor, Paul, *The Devil and Karl Marx: Communism's Long March of Death, Deception, and Infiltration* (New York: TAN Books, 2020).
- Pluckrose, Helen, and James Lindsay, *Cynical Theories: How Activist Scholarship Made Everything about Race, Gender, and Identity—and Why This Harms Everybody* (Durham, NC: Pitchstone Publishing, 2020).
- Soh, Debra, *The End of Gender: Debunking the Myths about Sex and Identity in Our Society* (New York: Threshold Editions, 2020).
- McWhorter, John, *Woke Racism: How a New Religion Has Betrayed Black America* (New York: Portfolio, 2021).
- Parvini, Neema, *The Populist Delusion* (London: Rogue Scholar Press, 2021).
- Wilson, Rachel, *Occult Feminism: The Secret History of Women's Liberation* (London: Arktos Media Ltd., 2021).
- Mchangama, Jacob, *Free Speech: A History from Socrates to Social Media* (New York: Basic Books, 2022).
- Land, Nick, *The Dark Enlightenment* (London: Arktos Media Ltd.,

2022).
- Biggar, Nigel, *Colonialism: A Moral Reckoning* (New York: William Collins, 2022).
- Desmet, Mattias, *The Psychology of Totalitarianism* (Chelsea, MI: Chelsea Green Publishing, 2022).
- Perry, Louise, *Case Against the Sexual Revolution: A New Guide to Sex in the 21st Century* (Cambridge: Polity, 2022).
- Harrington, Mary, *Feminism Against Progress* (New York: Regnery Publishing, 2024).

www.ingramcontent.com/pod-product-compliance
Lightning Source LLC
Chambersburg PA
CBHW070603030426
42337CB00020B/3688